22.50

D1553678

**Speech and Language in the
Laboratory, School, and Clinic**

Proceedings of a conference entitled "The Implications of Basic Speech and Language Research for the School and Clinic" in a series entitled "Communicating by Language," sponsored by the National Institute of Child Health and Human Development, National Institutes of Health.

Other Books in the Communicating by Language Series:

The Speech Process (1964) U.S. Government Printing Office
The Genesis of Language (1966) The MIT Press
The Reading Process (1968) U.S. Government Printing Office
Language by Ear and by Eye (1972) The MIT Press
The Role of Speech in Language (1975) The MIT Press

**Speech and Language in the
Laboratory, School, and Clinic**

JAMES F. KAVANAGH
AND WINIFRED STRANGE, EDITORS

The MIT Press, Cambridge, Massachusetts, and London, England

This book was set in Monotype Baskerville and printed and bound by Halliday Litho Corp. in the United States of America.

Library of Congress Cataloging in Publication Data

Main entry under title:

Speech and language in the laboratory, school, and clinic.

  Proceedings of a conference in the Communicating by language series, sponsored by the National Institute of Child Health and Human Development, held May 23–26, 1976, at Belmont, Elkridge, Md.
  Proceedings of the 6th of a series of meetings; proceedings of the 5th are entered under the title: The Role of speech in language.
  Includes bibliographies and index.
  1. Speech disorders in children—Congresses.
2. Children—Language—Congresses. 3. Speech—Physiological aspects—Congresses. I. Kavanagh, James F. II. Strange, Winifred. III. United States. National Institute of Child Health and Human Development.
RJ496.S7S63   618.9′28′55   77–27289
ISBN   0–262–11065–2

Contents

Preface

This book reports the proceedings of a conference entitled "Implications of Basic Speech and Language Research for the School and Clinic," the sixth conference in the Communicating by Language series, sponsored by the Growth and Development Branch of the National Institute of Child Health and Human Development (NICHD), National Institutes of Health (NIH). The meeting was held from May 23 through May 26, 1976, at Belmont, the Smithsonian Institution's conference center at Elkridge, Maryland. Dr. James J. Jenkins of the University of Minnesota and Dr. James Kavanagh of the Growth and Development Branch were the cochairmen.

At the first conference in this series, convened in April 1964, we indicated that one of our purposes was to reveal existing and potential directions for fundamental research in the communicative processes, research that our then recently established NICHD could appropriately support. That interdisciplinary meeting of scientists concerned with the speech process did stimulate new and significant research. Each subsequent conference in the series had as its primary purpose the identification and stimulation of existing and potential directions for further fundamental research.

From the earliest days of the Institute to the present we have trained and supported scientists to conduct a large number of excellent fundamental research projects concerned with speech and language acquisition and development, the reading process and its disorders, and related areas of human learning and communication. Our mission has been and will continue to be the support of fundamental research on the mechanisms and processes of human communication.

At this sixth conference in our series we reflected on the fundamental information acquired by our grantees and others during the past dozen years and attempted to identify where this information might have implications and applications for therapy and for education. As Dr. Donald S. Fredrickson, Director of the National Institutes of Health, pointed out, "There is growing public interest in making sure that the fruits of research are applied promptly and universally as better measures for the diagnosis, treatment, or prevention of disorders. Society hopes and expects that information derived from [basic] research will indeed be transformed not only into knowledge but also into compassionate care and better health."

This is not to say that the National Institutes of Health is turning away from fundamental research nor does it indicate that we can or should support therapeutic or pedagogical procedures. But it is a fact that the NIH has been directed by the Congress to improve the dissemination of information from the research it supports. In its report to the U.S. House of Representatives concerning the 1977 fiscal year budget, the Committee of Appropriations indicated that the NIH has a responsibility for ensuring that usable research results are communicated to those who might use them. This requires us to examine the findings of our fundamental research for possible implications and then to communicate these findings in such a way as to maximize their use by clinical researchers and practitioners.

Although the NIH believe that communication among the members of the scientific community is reasonably effective, conversion of scientific information to knowledge useful to the health practitioner or into wisdom useful to the public is something we are unaccustomed to doing and, perhaps, do less well.

This conference and its resultant publication should offer reassurance to those who have asked for practical results of research and should allay the fears of those who believe that our research is for the researcher's sake, rather than for the ultimate good of this country's people. It should also answer the question we occasionally are asked that implies research findings—"cures" for important health problems—are gathering dust on a laboratory shelf somewhere because scientists have neglected to make them known. We know that all the motivations and mores of the research community assure the reporting of such findings, but we must be alert to the possibility that gaps in communication can exist and that the best and latest is in fact not universally practiced.

The conference participants were

Lois Bloom
Program in Developmental Psychology
Teachers College
Columbia University
New York, New York

John D. Bransford
Department of Psychology
Vanderbilt University
Nashville, Tennessee

Robin S. Chapman
Department of Communicative
    Disorders
University of Wisconsin
Madison, Wisconsin

Robert G. Crowder
Department of Psychology
Yale University
New Haven, Connecticut

James F. Curtis
Department of Speech Pathology and
    Audiology
University of Iowa
Iowa City, Iowa

James E. Cutting
Department of Psychology

Wesleyan University
Middletown, Connecticut
    and Haskins Laboratories
New Haven, Connecticut

Katherine S. Harris
Department of Speech and Hearing
    Sciences
Graduate School and University
    Center
City University of New York
New York, New York
    and Haskins Laboratories
New Haven, Connecticut

James J. Jenkins
Center for Research in Human
    Learning
University of Minnesota
Minneapolis, Minnesota

James F. Kavanagh
Human Learning and Behavior Branch
National Institute of Child Health and
    Human Development

William Labov
Department of Linguistics
University of Pennsylvania
Philadelphia, Pennsylvania

Margaret Lahey
Department of Communicative
  Sciences and Disorders
Monclair State College
Upper Montclair, New Jersey

Alvin M. Liberman
Haskins Laboratories
New Haven, Connecticut

Leija V. McReynolds
Hearing and Speech Department
Ralph L. Smith Mental Retardation
  Research Center
University of Kansas Medical Center
Kansas City, Kansas

George A. Miller
The Rockefeller University
New York, New York

Ronald Netsell
Department of Communicative
  Disorders
University of Wisconsin
Madison, Wisconsin

James M. Pickett
Sensory Communication Research
  Laboratory
Hearing and Speech Center
Gallaudet College
Washington, D.C.

Ralph L. Shelton
Department of Speech and
  Hearing Sciences
University of Arizona
Tucson, Arizona

Carl E. Sherrick
Department of Psychology
Princeton University
Princeton, New Jersey

Kenneth N. Stevens
Department of Electrical Engineering
  and Computer Science
and Research Laboratory of Electronics
Massachusetts Institute of Technology
Cambridge, Massachusetts

Winifred Strange
Center for Research in Human
  Learning
University of Minnesota
Minneapolis, Minnesota

Gerald A. Studebaker
Department of Speech and Hearing
  Sciences
Graduate School and University
  Center
City University of New York
New York, New York

Paula Tallal
Johns Hopkins Medical Institutions
John F. Kennedy Institute
Baltimore, Maryland

Grace H. Yeni-Komshian
Human Learning and Behavior Branch
National Institute of Child Health and
  Human Development

Edgar B. Zurif
Aphasia Research Center
Boston University School of Medicine
and Boston VA Hospital
Boston, Massachusetts

Portions of Lois Bloom's chapter were taken from *Language Development and Disorders*, a manuscript currently in progress with Margaret Lahey. Dr. Bloom expresses her gratitude to John Wiley and Sons, the publishers, for their permission to use this material. She also thanks Karin Lifter for her careful help in the preparation of the chapter.

John Bransford and Kathleen Nitsch are grateful to Jeff Franks, Jon Doner, and Sharon Doner for their insightful comments on earlier drafts of the manuscript and to Sue Bright for help in preparing the chapter. However, John and Kathleen indicate that none of these people should be held responsible for mistakes or faulty arguments contained therein. The authors are also grateful to the National Institute of Education for the grant (NE-6-00-3-0026) that helped support their theoretical and experimental work.

Support for the preparation of Robin Chapman's chapter was provided in part by a grant from the Graduate School of the University of Wisconsin, project no. 160450. Jon F. Miller, Roberta E. Dihoff, Larry L. Kohn, and Joe Reichle are thanked for the discussions of the issues and the manuscript.

Preparation of Robert Crowder's manuscript and some of the research contained in it was supported by USPHS Grant 1 R01 MH 26623–01.

Katherine Harris's work was supported in part by a grant from the National Institute of Dental Research. She also benefited from comments by Fredericka Bell-Berti, Gloria Borden, and Thomas Gay.

James J. Jenkins gratefully acknowledges the support of the Center for Research in Human Learning at the University of Minnesota and the Institute for the Study of Intellectual Behavior at the University of Colorado.

William Labov is indebted to Osamu Fujimura, Max Matthews, and Marian Macchie for their assistance and for making the Bell Laboratories facilities available.

Many of the ideas expressed in Margaret Lahey's paper were developed in conjunction with Lois Bloom. Portions of Dr. Lahey's paper were taken from *Language Development and Language Disorders*, coauthored by Lois Bloom and Margaret Lahey, to be published by John Wiley and Sons. Permission of John Wiley and Sons to use this material is acknowledged. Dr. Lahey also thanks Kathy Fliess for her help in the preparation of her paper.

Leija McReynolds acknowledges support for her research from the National Institute of Neurological and Communicative Disorders and Stroke (NS 010468–01) and from the National Institute of Child Health and Human Development (HD 00870–10) to the Bureau of Child Research, Ralph L. Smith Mental Retardation Center, University of Kansas.

Ronald Netsell expresses his appreciation to James Abbs and Raymond Kent of the University of Wisconsin for help with his presentation. Support for preparation of his manuscript was provided in part by research grant NS 09627 from the National Institutes of Health.

George Miller's paper was supported in part by grant no. GM 21796 from the National Institutes of Health, PHS, to the Rockefeller University.

Ralph Shelton wishes to thank Mrs. Anita Johnson and R. Richard Curlee for assistance in the preparation of his paper. Certain information reported in Ralph Shelton's paper, including the data and figures, was obtained as part of a research project supported by a grant (No. DE 03350) from the National Institute of Dental Research, National Institutes of Health, U.S. Department of Health, Education and Welfare.

Carl Sherrick's report was prepared under grant no. NS 04755 from the National Institute of Neurological and Communicative Disorders and Stroke, NIH, DHEW, to Princeton University.

Preparation of Kenneth Steven's paper was supported in part by a grant (NS 04332) from the National Institutes of Health. Examples of speech from deaf children were prepared with support from an Office of Education contract (No. 300–76–0116) to Bolt, Beranek, and Newman.

Paula Tallal wishes to thank the American Association of University Women, Cecil and Ida Green, the Grant Foundation of New York, the Medical Research Council of Great Britain (grant no. G973/144/C), and the National Institutes of Health (NINCDS Contract No. 75–09) for their generous support of the research in her chapter. She would also like to thank Kathleen Nardini for her help in preparing the manuscript.

The research reported by Edgar Zurif and Alfonso Caramazza in their chapter was supported by NIH Grants No. 11408 and 06209 to Boston University School of Medicine. The following friends read and helped them with the manuscript: Harold Goodglass, Sheila Blumstein, Howard Gardner, Laird Cermak, and Errol Baker. They are also indebted to Michael Walsh, a therapist at the Aphasia Research Center, who provided them with counsel and reprints on aphasia therapy.

James Kavanagh expresses his sincere appreciation to Mary Cross for her as-sistancew ith this manuscript and to Daphene Cave for invaluable help in preparation for the conference and the subsequent publication of the conference proceedings.

Winifred Strange acknowledges the support of the Center for Research in Human Learning at the University of Minnesota in providing clerical assistance in the preparation of the manuscript. Special thanks go to Sharon Deering and Kathleen Casey. The center is supported by grants from NICHD and NSF and the Graduate School of the University of Minnesota. Dr. Strange also wishes to thank the staff of the Institute for the Study of Intellectual Behavior at the University of Colorado for its assistance in preparing parts of the manuscript. Special thanks go to Colleen Tovani.

James F. Kavanagh
Winifred Strange

International Phonetic Alphabet

VOWELS

Stressed
i	tree
u	blue
a	stop
I	sip
u	foot
ɔ	ball
ɛ	set
æ	cat
ʌ	hub
ʒ	turn

Unstressed
e	chaotic
o	obey
ə	better
ə	sofa

Diphthongs
eI	baby
ai	night
ɔI	boil
ou	show
au	how

CONSONANTS

Stops
p	pot
t	top
k	kite
b	bag
d	dime
g	game

Nasals
m	mouth
n	nose
ŋ	ring

Glides
l	live
r	run
j	(or y) yes
w	win

Fricatives
hw	whether (in some alalects)
f	fast
θ	think
s	sit
ʃ	(or š) shoe
h	hat
v	voice
ð	the
z	zoo
ʒ	(or z) vision

Affricates
tʃ	(or č) lunch
dʒ	(or ǰ) judge

Implications of Basic Research: Thoughts Behind the Conference

JAMES J. JENKINS

History

This conference, like the others in the series, owes its existence to the energy and enthusiasm of James F. Kavanagh and faith and confidence at the higher administrative levels of the National Institute of Child Health and Human Development (NICHD). Under Kavanagh's gentle guidance and with the support of NICHD a remarkable series of conferences has evolved over the last fifteen years. In retrospect each conference seems to contain the seeds of its successor. This conference is a mild exception in that it owes its origin to all of its predecessors rather than to a single one. It attempts to survey basic research across the whole area of speech and language as it relates to fields of ongoing and potential application.

In 1975 Kavanagh convened a meeting of Liberman, Curtis, and me and asked us whether the time was ripe for a conference on the applications of basic research on speech and language to the problems of the school and clinic. The previous conference reports were rich in such suggestions but the sustained effort to point out such implications had not been made. We all agreed that the time was propitious and the topic appropriate in terms of the growth of the series of conferences, the state of the research field, and the national atmosphere of concern regarding the usefulness of basic research.

In keeping with the tradition (largely because I had expressed concern about applications at the last conference), I was asked to be cochairman of the conference with Kavanagh. All four of us, however, worked on the design of the conference and the rationale for the structure of the papers. Several of the participants (Bloom, McReynolds, Harris, and Strange) joined us at a subsequent meeting and further refined the plans for the papers and their discussion.

Basic Research and Applications

The nature of the relation of basic research to problems as they are seen in various fields of application is a delicate one, of course. Minds more subtle than ours have struggled with the problem of specifying the complex relationships that exist (or are supposed to exist) between the "ivory tower" and the "firing line." Within a given area of research and application, however, it seems possible to make some reasonable observations and to point toward some plausible relationships. Most of us agree that basic research on the one hand and applications of knowledge on the other can be seen as end points on a continuum. Although they are very different endeavors, we see them as fundamentally interrelated by the nature of the subject matter. Most of us worry from time to time that there is too little communication between the poles, and we are concerned that knowledge from basic research may not be communicated to the practitioners in the field or that the researchers may fail to realize where practitioners urgently need more basic support.

The report of the President's Biomedical Research Panel is reassuring with respect to these concerns. The panel solicited two studies of the sequence by which a laboratory discovery moves to widespread clinical application. Both studies used retrospective examinations of the history of medical advances: the first, a study of advances in a specific field of medicine; the second, a study of twenty-five case histories of successful innovation in diverse areas. Their conclusions are of interest.

The two factors that seemed to expedite innovation were the availability of an adequate science base and the degree of interest shown by the research community, as indicated by the number of investigators working on the subject in parallel or in competition. . . . Generally, the two studies are corroborative and show that the research process is such that the rate of movement of research findings into practical use depends on scientific advances along a broad front. (DHEW 1976, p. 9)

The "broad front" description seems highly applicable to research in speech and language. Research in this area involves a very large number of investigators from many disciplines. All aspects of research seem to be moving forward vigorously, and researchers in a variety of fields find their interests intermingling in the study of speech production and perception, the development of speech and language skills in the child, the use of language in solving problems, its use in the communication of knowledge, and the abstract analysis of language as a vehicle for thought and expression. By the criteria of the president's panel, the prospect for speedy application of research findings in speech and language appears bright. The proceedings of the conference are relevant testimony in this regard.

The Need
Although it is not specifically discussed in this book, there is an enormous need in our society for basic knowledge concerning speech and language and the application of that knowledge to education and to remediation of disorders. Disabilities affecting speech and language often receive little recognition because they are not fatal, progressively destructive, or dramatically interesting. Their cost in quality of life, however, may be devastating indeed. When the vast number of sufferers is considered, the cost to our society is staggering. A few examples (see Swets 1974) may make clear the magnitude of the clinical and educational problems involved.
- There are six million handicapped school-aged children in the United States. Two million (one-third) of these children have organic or functional speech disorders that interfere with oral communication.
- More than a half million children have "learning disabilities." These disabilities are ordinarily defined as disorders in one or more of the basic psychological process involved in understanding and using spoken or written language. Thus, while the disabilities may be manifested in listening, thinking, speaking, writing, reading, spelling, or calculating, they are essentially speech and language deficits.
- More than three-hundred thousand children are deaf or hard of hearing.
- From 10 to 20 percent of children otherwise judged normal have difficulty learning to read.
- Two million adults are judged totally deaf as far as communication is concerned, and fourteen million suffer from impairments of hearing sufficient to disturb communication severely.
- Although no one knows the exact number, it is estimated that as many as ten

million adults suffer from speech and language disfluencies, ranging from stuttering to the complete loss of language as a result of stroke or accident. Probably an equal number of adults has some difficulty with written communication as a result of partial loss of vision.

In brief, there is no question that a pressing social need exists at all ages for alleviation of problems involving speech and language.

The Strategy of the Conference

The conference was designed around a theory (orginally implicit) that became more clearly articulated as the planning proceeded. The theory is that workers in the content area are distributed along a hypothetical dimension that runs from the "pure" researcher at one end to the "pure" clinician at the other. The points along the continuum are occupied by people who share, to varying extents, the values, interests, knowledge, and vocabularies of the two polar positions. Thus, even though clinicians and basic researchers might have trouble communicating with each other, it seemed that it should be possible to find persons in the middle of the continuum (clinic-oriented researchers and research-oriented clinicians) who spoke both languages and who were aware of the problems as seen from both poles.

As a result of this conception, we did not try to span the continuum in a single stride and bring together archetype researchers who had never been in an applied setting and archetype clinicians who had never been in a laboratory. We attempted, rather, to assemble basic researchers and clinical researchers with the idea of making a half step along the way. Our assumption was that the findings of basic research flow through clinical researchers and teachers of clinicians to the clinical setting. We realize that it puts a tremendous burden on the clinical researcher and teacher to be placed in the mediator's position, but we believe that the best of such researchers and teachers are willing to assume this burden.

There are difficulties and dangers in being satisfied with the separation of the ends of the continuum. The danger on the applied end is that clinical work can be uninformed and shallow, concentrated on the surface problems that demand the immediate attention of the clinician. In these circumstances one may fail to penetrate to the deeper underlying levels where the fundamental problems may lie. At the other end it is possible that basic research will exhaust itself "chasing its own tail," doing experiments about experiments, long after the phenomena have lost contact with problems in the real world. Fortunately, the conference participants belong to neither of these hypothetical classes. Indeed, many of the participants have held positions at several places along the continuum at one time or another in their careers.

Central in importance in planning the conference was the conviction that we could find knowledgeable basic researchers who could summarize the state of the art in each of the various segments of speech and language research we had designated. We asked each of these investigators to survey a particular segment of the field and to look forward to potential areas of application of this basic knowledge. At the same time we did not really suppose that they could easily span the full continuum. Accordingly, we turned to clinical researchers as discussants. We asked these experts, chosen from clinical and educational domains, to look at the state-of-the-art papers from their more real-world, problem-oriented points of view. They were asked to what extent they could see projections of basic research into the applied areas that they knew. We also asked them to appraise the coverage of basic research and report unmet clinical needs of which they were aware.

The order of procedure of the conference and the book is a logical series from the more "physical" problems of speech perception and production, through to the more "mental" problems of language meaning and memory. The discussants and their fields of application are, of course, matched to their appropriate basic research areas and move through a similar sequence. The final paper in the book reflects on selected themes of the conference and attempts to articulate what we have learned about the relation of basic research to areas of application.

If we have been correct in our assessment of the relation between basic research and applications of knowledge, and if we have been successful in our choice of participants, this volume should provide solid support to clinical researchers and teachers who are ready to take the second step. That step will move the knowledge from its abstract form in this book into applications in practice in the school and clinic. If the book is helpful toward reaching that end, it will have achieved its objective.

Speech and Language in the Laboratory, School, and Clinic

The Speech Signal

KENNETH N. STEVENS

The most direct manifestation of spoken language is in the sound that emerges from a speaker's lips, the speech signal. The papers in this volume will emphasize that the processes of producing an utterance by a speaker or understanding an utterance by a listener involve much more than the generation or the auditory processing of this signal. The speaker's or the listener's knowledge of the constraints imposed by the language and by the situational context in which an utterance occurs can have a significant influence on how sounds are generated or decoded. Nevertheless, for the listener the sound is an essential ingredient of the process of understanding speech, and for the speaker there is a requirement to produce at least some portions of the sound stream with appropriate characteristics that are related to the linguistic description underlying the utterance.

In this paper I shall attempt to provide a brief descriptive account of the sounds that emerge from a speaker's vocal tract when different linguistic units are intended—units ranging in size from phonetic features to sentences. I shall try to indicate how these different units are manifested in the acoustic signal. I shall, however, also attempt to show that the study of speech acoustics and of the generation and reception of sound leads to the specification of a set of constraints within which spoken language must operate—constraints relating to the inventory of units that underlie speech. Given the articulatory system's capabilities for generating sounds with particular properties and the auditory system's capabilities for extracting attributes or properties from an acoustic signal, it is possible to draw some conclusions about what sounds or sound attributes might be used for purposes of transmitting information by acoustic means between a talker and a listener. The sounds are those with stable acoustic characteristics that the speech production system can produce without imposing too severe a requirement on accuracy of manipulating the articulatory structures. They are also the sounds to which the auditory system responds distinctively such that they can be categorized unambiguously.

Sound Generation in the Vocal Tract

The basic mechanism of speech sound generation is the modulation of the flow of air through the upper respiratory passages. Pressure is built up in the lungs, air from the lungs is expelled through a constriction, and sound is generated in the vicinity of the constriction in the upper airways. The forces responsible for expelling air from the lungs, which are the result of finely controlled contraction of respiratory muscles superimposed on passive recoil forces of the respiratory mechanism, are such that a relatively constant lung pressure is maintained during an utterance in spite of rapid fluctuations in airflow (Hixon 1973). These fluctuations in airflow depend upon the kinds of constrictions formed in the airways as different types of sounds are generated. To place emphasis on a particular syllable or word of an utterance, a brief increase in lung pressure is generated (Lieberman 1967). It is recognized by many speech pathologists that improper control of lung pressure and of the expiratory airflow during speech production can lead to poor voice quality and to inappropriate speech intensity (Cooper 1971).

Modulation of the airflow produces sources of sound, either in the vicinity of the larynx or at some point in the airways above the larynx. These sources of sound can be of several types, but there are two principal kinds of sources: the quasi-periodic modulation of flow by the vibratory folds and the random acoustic noise that results from turbulent airflow, usually in the vicinity of an obstacle or a constriction (Stevens and Klatt 1974). Finer distinctions in the properties of the sound generated by this process are achieved by filtering the sound from these sources through appropriate adjustments of the shapes of the acoustic cavities that form the vocal tract (Fant 1960).

A variety of sounds can be produced at the larynx as a consequence of adjustment of the position and state of the vocal folds and the arytenoid cartilages to which they are attached. Normal vocal fold vibration for vowels is achieved by positioning the vocal folds close together and applying pressure from the lungs. The resulting in and out movements of the vocal folds cause periodic brief puffs of air to pass through the space between the vocal folds of the glottis, and these form the source of acoustic excitation for the supraglottal cavities. The frequency of vocal fold vibration can be adjusted by manipulating the stiffness or tension of the vocal fold surfaces through contraction of appropriate muscles. A space can be created between the arytenoid cartilages such that turbulence is produced in the rapid airflow in this region at the same time that the vocal folds are vibrating, resulting in a noise source combined with a periodic acoustic source. This laryngeal adjustment leads to a breathy voice. Vocal fold vibration can be inhibited in various ways: reducing the pressure difference across the glottis, stiffening the vocal folds, or tightly approximating the vocal folds or spreading them relatively widely apart. In the latter condition of a spread glottis turbulence noise is generated in the glottis without vocal fold vibration and thus the acoustic excitation of the vocal cavities is noise rather than periodic air pulses.

The other principal type of sound source is created by forming a constriction at some point along the length of the vocal tract, such that a rapid airflow is created at the constriction and turbulence results (Meyer-Eppler 1953; Stevens 1971a). The sound generated as a consequence of this turbulent airstream has a broad energy spectrum. This noise source has a greater amplitude if the airstream is directed against an obstacle, such as the upper incisors in the case of the /s/.

The sound radiated from the lips or nose is a consequence of filtering of the sound sources by the vocal cavities. In general, this filtering results in accentuation of spectral energy in certain rather narrow frequency regions, called formants, and reduction of spectral energy in other regions. The frequency positions of the formants are determined by the shapes of the vocal cavities, which can, of course, be manipulated by appropriate movements of the tongue, lips, and other structures. When the sound source is at the glottis, a number of formants (usually four or five for adult speakers or three or four for children) appear in the spectrum within the frequency range from 200 to 5000 Hertz(Hz). In the case where a noise source is in the vicinity of a constriction in the vocal tract above the glottis,

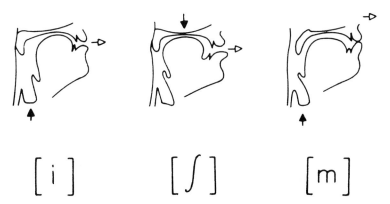

Figure 1. Sketches of articulatory configurations in the midsagittal plane for three speech sounds as indicated, together with source (solid arrows) and output (open arrows) locations. For the sounds [i] and [m] the source is at the glottis. (The symbol [ʃ] represents the initial consonant in the word *shoe*.)

the number of formants that can be observed in the sound is usually smaller and these are usually at frequencies above 2000 Hz.

Figure 1 schematizes the sound generation process for the two source types and different vocal tract shapes. For vowels the source is at the glottis, the vocal tract does not contain a major constriction, and sound radiation is from the mouth. Nasal consonants are also produced with a glottal source, but the oral cavity is closed, the velopharyngeal port is open, and sound is radiated from the nose. The source is at a constriction above the glottis in the case of a fricative consonant, as shown by the configuration in the middle of figure 1.

The acoustic properties of the sounds produced with various sources and vocal tract shapes are illustrated in the spectrogram of figure 2 (Koenig, Dunn, and

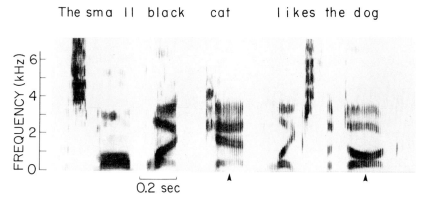

Figure 2. Sound spectrogram of the sentence indicated.

Lacy 1946). The utterance is *The small black cat likes the dog.* This two-dimensional frequency-time representation shows the regions of high intensity with well-defined formant structure during the vowel nuclei of the syllables. These regions of voicing (periodic excitation from the glottal source) are characterized by regularly spaced vertical lines on the spectrogram, one for each glottal pulse. The spacing between lines varies, of course, with the frequency of vocal fold vibration. The formant locations depend on the vowel, and during a diphthong (such as [ai] in the word *likes*) there are formant motions between the two vowel targets. For example, the arrows at the bottom of the spectrogram identify the midpoints of the vowels [æ] in *cat* and [ɔ] in *dog.* Measurements from the spectrogram show that the first three formant frequencies for [æ] are 640, 1650, and 2450 Hz, whereas for [ɔ] they are 590, 950, and 2600 Hz. The frequency of vocal fold vibration as determined from the distance between the regular vertical striations varies from 160 Hz in the word *small* to 90 Hz in the word *dog.* Other vowels are, of course characterized by different formant frequencies (Peterson and Barney 1952), and the range of fundamental frequency varies from one speaker to another. High-frequency noise is evident in the [s] sounds and the [k] in *cat* shows the acoustic consequence of noise generated at the glottis during this aspirated stop consonant. A stop consonant like [d] (in the final word *dog*) consists of an interval of silence (except for evidence of weak low-frequency energy due to vocal fold vibration) followed by a brief burst of noise energy, followed in turn by formant onsets that then undergo movements or transitions toward the following vowel.

This spectrographic representation indicates two different kinds of acoustic information that are carried by the speech signal. On the one hand there are portions of the signal in which the spectral characteristics change relatively slowly and smoothly, reflecting the continuous movements of the articulatory structures during time intervals in which the type of acoustic source remains fixed. These time intervals are usually in the range of 50 to 300 milliseconds (msec) and are best exemplified in figure 2 by the vowel regions, in which the source of vocal tract excitation is at the vibratory glottis, and by the regions in which the fricative consonant /s/ occurs. The other type of acoustic information is at points of relatively abrupt changes or discontinuities in the short-time spectrum, usually as a consequence of rapid changes in the source or in the vocal tract shape (Stevens, 1971b). Some of the properties of these transientlike sounds, in which relevant acoustic data are present over time intervals of a few tens of msec, are not well displayed on the spectrogram, although the auditory system appears to assign some importance to these brief sounds. Examples in figure 2 are the events at the onset and termination of the vowel in the word *dog* and the rapid spectral change that occurs at the release of the sound [m] in the word *small.* There is evidence that the manner of processing the transient sounds in the auditory system is somewhat different from the way in which the more slowly changing sounds are processed. This evidence comes from experiments on making patterns produced by steady and transient sounds (Leshowitz and Cudahy 1975) and from various results in speech perception suggesting that different processes are involved in the perception of vowels and consonants (Studdert-Kennedy 1976).

Factors Determining the Inventory of Phonetic Segments Used in Language and their Acoustic Manifestations

The discussion of the sound generation process in the vocal tract implies that a wide range of sounds can be generated by adjusting the parameters and locations of the sound sources in different ways and by manipulating the shape of the vocal cavities over a range of configurations. In fact, however, the sounds employed in language, and the vocal tract configurations used to produce these sounds, fall into discrete or quantal classes. Consequently there appears to be a closed set of sounds that are used in the languages of the world rather than a continuum of variation in the characteristics of the sounds.

The principles that govern the selection of sounds used in languages are not completely understood at present, but it is possible to comment on the nature of these principles.

STATIC ARTICULATORY TARGETS

One of the principles assumes that a string of phonetic segments underlies the speech process. A segment is defined in terms of a target configuration or state of the articulatory structures. Speech production is viewed, then, as a sequence of movements whose aim is to manipulate the articulatory structures from one set of configurations or states to another. This view regards the underlying segments as specified in terms of static states. Almost all of traditional phonetics, and particularly the description of an utterance in terms of a string of discrete phonetic symbols, is based on this view. (See, for example, Abercrombie 1967.)

Whereas such a static description is the basis for representing an utterance in terms of underlying segments, it is important to note that most of the time during an utterance the articulatory structures are in motion from one configuration to another. Thus much of the time the acoustic representation of speech tends to reflect the movements of the articulatory system rather than the static target states. This fact would suggest, then, that the acoustic manifestation of a particular target state of the articulatory structures is strongly dependent on the context (Liberman et al. 1967). Nevertheless, the auditory system seems to be capable of decoding this sequence of acoustic events into a string of segments. It seems to be able to pick out the aspects of the acoustic signal that are invariant for a particular phonetic segment or segment class and ignore the aspects that are context dependent. Possible mechanisms for extracting these attributes from the signal will be discussed later.

The fact that the process of speech production is a sequence of motions between articulatory target states suggests that the motor activity involved in producing speech consists of muscle contractions that are necessary to achieve these movements. Thus the motor commands that are necessary to move to configuration B from configuration A depend not only on the target configuration B that is to be produced next but also on the starting point, configuration A. That is, the motor commands needed to actualize a particular phonetic segment are highly context dependent. The generation of speech is oriented toward sequences of invariant goals or targets rather than toward sequences of invariant motor commands. This point of view implies that feedback—particularly orosensory feedback—may be involved in the production of speech and that the motor commands to the articulators are conditioned in part by the state of the system as established by patterns of sensory feedback (MacNeilage 1972; Folkins and Abbs 1975). The process of acquiring speech production skills presumably involves learning not only how to achieve the various articulatory target configurations but also how to embed these targets in context. Those who are concerned with speech therapy, particularly for the deaf, are well aware of this distinction.

THE QUANTAL NATURE OF ARTICULATORY-ACOUSTIC RELATIONS.

The inventory of articulatory states used in language is determined in part by the nature of the relations between articulatory configurations or states and the resulting sounds. There are certain configurations or states of the articulatory structures that lead to the generation of sounds with well-defined stable acoustic characteristics. That is, these characteristics are distinctively different from those produced by other articulatory configurations and are relatively uninfluenced by small perturbations in these configurations about some ideal target state. It is these articulatory configurations that are selected for use in language. Target configurations for which the properties of the resulting sound are sensitive to small perturbations in articulation are avoided (Stevens 1972). This situation is illustrated in figure 3, which shows a schematized relationship between a typical acoustic param-

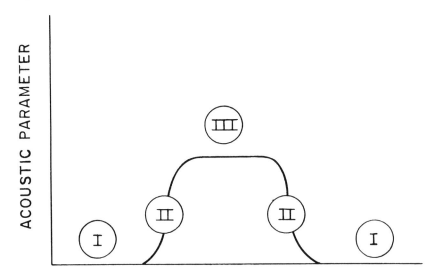

ARTICULATORY PARAMETER

Figure 3. Schematized relation between an acoustic parameter of speech and a parameter that describes some aspect of articulation. Regions I, II, and III are discussed in the text.

eter of the speech signal and an articulatory parameter. There is a region III in which the acoustic parameter is significantly different from its value in regions I and in which small perturbations in articulation give rise to negligible changes in the sound. Shifting the articulation through region II causes an abrupt change in the properties of the sound. It is assumed that the auditory system responds in a unique way to the sound with properties in region III.

Thus, for example, there is a clear acoustic distinction between sounds that are produced with a narrow vocal tract constriction and those produced with a relatively open vocal tract. The narrow opening results in the generation of noise but the open tract does not. In the case where complete closure is made in the vocal tract, the sound produced when this closure is released has an abrupt onset, in contrast to a more gradual onset that results from other configurations. For the class of sounds produced with a relatively open vocal tract with no noise generation, raising the tongue body gives rise to a sound with a maximally low first formant. Finally, a stop consonant that is produced by raising the tongue blade against the hard palate produces a sound at the consonantal release that has a distinctive acoustic spectrum at the onset, characterized by diffusely spread energy with a spectrum that slopes upward toward high frequencies. This sound is distinctly different from that produced when the constriction is formed at other places in the vocal tract.

These are just a few examples of the relations between articulatory configurations and sound that suggest that there are preferred articulatory states leading to distinctive properties of the sound (Klatt and Stevens 1969; Stevens 1973; Stevens 1975). These are presumably the states or configurations that are selected for use as phonetic units in language.

As one attempts to go systematically through the inventory of phonetic segments or articulatory target states used in language, one is struck by the fact that many of the target states seem to be characterized not only by distinctive acoustic endproducts but also by distinctive sensory consequences within the vocal tract. Thus, for example, there is a class of consonants formed with a narrow or complete closure in the vocal tract. The articulatory consequence is a pressure buildup behind the constriction, which is presumably sensed by pressure receptors on the vocal tract surface. Or the acoustic manifestation of a so-called low vowel is a distinctively high-frequency first formant. Examination of X-ray pictures of speech articulations suggests that the low tongue position for such vowels places the lateral edges of the tongue out of contact with the upper teeth and palatal surfaces (Stevens 1975). This tongue position, therefore, has a sensory consequence in the vocal tract that is distinctively different from that for other vowels. It is not unreasonable to suppose that such distinctive sensory representations of articulatory gestures, coupled with acoustic outputs with well-defined properties, are prerequisites for the development of an inventory of phonetic segments that are used in language. It has been observed in the past that the experience of an organism in performing movements and in observing the consequences of these movements helps to establish how stimuli of various kinds are organized. (See, for example, Held and Freeman 1963.)

If this view of the sensory consequences of speech gestures is correct, it could have implications with regard to the speech training of deaf children. These children could perhaps be made more aware of the "feeling" in their mouth when particular classes of phonetic segments such as obstruents or low vowels are produced.

DISTINCTIVE FEATURES

Examination of a number of articulatory-acoustic relations of the type illustrated in figure 3 shows that the sounds generated by the vocal tract can be organized into classes according to their articulatory attributes, their acoustic attributes, or both (Stevens 1971c). For example, raising the tongue body to an extremely high position while grooving the tongue surface to maintain a free flow of air through the point of maximum vocal tract constriction produces a vowel characterized by a maximally low first formant frequency. This acoustic characteristic occurs independent of whether the tongue body is positioned in a fronted or a backed location in the oral cavity. If the tongue surface is not grooved, maximal raising of the tongue body yields a consonant with unique acoustic characteristics

Table 1. Partial listing of distinctive features with a brief description of their articulatory and acoustic correlates.

Features	Correlates
Consonantal	Narrow constriction on midline of vocal tract; rapid change in spectrum at release of consonant.
Obstruent	Pressure buildup behind constriction in vocal tract; noise is present in sound.
High	Tongue body in maximally high position; low first formant frequency for vowels, spectral energy concentration in midfrequency range for consonants.
Low	Tongue body in low position, out of contact with hard palate; high first formant frequency.
Back	Tongue body in back position; low second formant frequency.
Coronal	Tongue blade raised, with contact between edges of tongue blade and hard palate; for obstruent consonants, spectrum at consonantal release diffuse, with predominant high-frequency energy.
Spread glottis	Arytenoid cartilages in larynx spread; noise generated at glottis.
Nasal	Velopharyngeal port open; acoustic spectrum characterized by additional resonances.
Continuant	Vocal tract constriction not completely closed; continuous sound generated during construction

relative to those for other places of articulation (a velar stop consonant) /g/ or /k/ or a velar nasal or fricative). Thus the target articulatory configuration produced by raising the tongue body gives rise to distinctive acoustic properties (presumably leading to distinctive responses of the auditory system) independent of the adjustment of other structures or components within the vocal tract. This particular target state of the tongue body identifies phonetic segments that are classified by the feature [+ high] (Chomsky and Halle 1968).

Another example of a class of phonetic segments is the group of sounds formed by creating a narrow vocal tract constriction giving rise to a pressure buildup within the vocal tract behind the constriction. This maneuver results in a sound characterized by turbulent noise generation independent of where the constriction is made within the vocal tract. Phonetic segments produced with a target state that yields such an intraoral pressure increase are identified by the feature [+ obstruent].

The total inventory of features that can be identified in this way is roughly twenty, not all of which play a role in any one language. The kinds of quantal articulatory-acoustic relations shown in figure 3 suggest that the features are two-valued or binary. A segment either has the acoustic property indicated by region III of the figure or it does not.

A partial inventory of distinctive features is given in table 1 together with a brief description of some of their articulatory and acoustic correlates (Jakobson, Fant, and Halle 1963; Chomsky and Halle 1968; Fant 1973). These features represent, in effect, the capabilities of the articulatory system for producing sounds with distinctive properties and the capabilities of the auditory system for processing these sounds. A phonetic segment can be regarded as a bundle of such features and any utterance can be represented as a matrix of such features, the columns indicating the successive segments and the rows the features. For example, a partial feature matrix for the word *black* is shown in table 2.

These distinctive features play a central role in specifying the constraints on the sequences of sounds that can occur in a given language. In fact, study of these phonological constraints provides strong evidence for the concept of the feature

Table 2. Partial matrix of distinctive features for the word *black*.

	b	l	æ	k
Consonantal	+	+	−	+
Obstruent	+	−	−	+
High	−	−	−	+
Low	−	−	+	−
Back	−	−	−	−
Coronal	−	+	−	−
Spread glottis	−	−	−	+
Continuant	−	−	+	−
Nasal	−	−	−	−

and helps to support the selection of a particular system of features. While certain of the features are well established and agreed upon by linguists, others are still a matter of controversy and debate. (See, for example, Ladefoged 1971.)

TIMING STRATEGIES FOR SEGMENTAL CUES

The process of speech production is, of course, more than the generation of movements of the articulatory structures from one configuration or state to another. These movements of different structures must be properly timed relative to one another so that the acoustic signal provides the cues necessary to identify the target configurations or features. In general, it is not appropriate to move all structures synchronously toward the appropriate target states for a particular phonetic segment.

For example, a laryngeal configuration that is used to produce a distinctive sound class in English is a spread glottis, which leads to the voiceless aspirated consonants [p], [t], and [k]. In order to make this spread glottal configuration evident in the signal in these stop consonants, it is necessary to maintain the glottal spreading until some time following the release of the consonant so that aspiration appears in the signal for a few tens of milliseconds and can be identified as such by a listener (Lisker and Abramson 1964). This temporal relation between onset of noise and onset of voicing can be seen in the initial consonant in the spectrogram of the word *cat* in figure 2. An alternative strategy, which is not used in English but is found in some languages, is to spread the glottis at the end of the vowel preceding the consonantal closure, leading to a preaspirated stop consonant. In the case of a syllable-final voiceless consonant in English, it is sometimes difficult to register the fact that the consonant is voiceless if it is not released into a vowel. Speakers often use the strategy of shortening the preceding vowel in order to provide the cue for voicelessness (House and Fairbanks 1953). In figure 2 the vowel in the word *likes* is shortened as a consequence of the final voiceless consonant.

Other examples of special timing strategies to provide segmental cues are the shortening of lax vowels in relation to tense vowels (the vowel in *bit* is shorter than in *beet* ([House 1961]), the shortening of voiced fricatives in relation to voiceless fricatives (/z/ in *razor* is shorter than /s/ in racer), and the delayed release of the tongue constriction in the affricate /tʃ/ (as in *cheer*). In the latter case, the sequence of gestures is complete closure, release of the tongue tip while maintaining a narrow constriction appropriate for a fricative consonant, and release of the constriction and onset of vocal fold vibration.

In the production of sequences of phonetic segments, movements toward the articulatory goal for one segment sometimes begin well in advance of the time the goal is to be achieved, particularly if the anticipatory movement does not substantially interfere with the achievement of appropriate target states for preceding segments. An example of this kind of anticipatory coarticulation occurs in the word *black*, in which the articulatory goal for the segment [l] is achieved before the initial consonant [b] is released. Other examples of coarticulation are the nasalization of a vowel preceding a nasal consonant, due to anticipatory lowering of the velum during the vowel, and the rounding that occurs in consonants preceding a rounded vowel, as in the word *stool*. Coarticulation rules represent important aspects of the speech production strategies that must be learned by a speaker of a language.

Thus there are subtleties in timing of the articulatory movements that are required to provide the listener with cues for the pattern of features for an utterance and to permit the speaker to achieve the sequence of articulatory states with minimal effort and with sufficient rapidity. These aspects of segmental speech timing should be important components of the speech training of a deaf child in both production and reception.

Acoustic Attributes of Sentences
The generation of speech is organized not only in terms of sequences of segments or sounds but also in terms of larger units consisting of words, phrases, and sentences. There are markers in the acoustic signal to indicate the boundaries of these units. In addition, when an utterance with a duration that is more than one syllable is produced, different amounts of prominence are assigned to various syllables, depending upon the lexical stress pattern on the words in the utterance and upon the semantic role of different words. Finally, when different amounts of prominence are put on the syllables, and when words are joined together to form sentences, the articulatory target configurations or states used to generate some of the sounds may be modified in systematic ways.

Thus, in addition to being able to produce the proper sequence of sounds with the articulatory system, speakers must possess two kinds of capabilities: they must be able to produce the articulatory gestures needed to mark phrase and sentence boundaries and to indicate various degrees of prominence on different syllables, and they must know a set of rules that govern where phrase boundaries should be placed, what degree of prominence should be assigned to each syllable, and what modifications should be made in sounds when they occur in different contexts, particularly when words are concatenated. Many deaf speakers lack both of these capabilities, and thus their speech is poorly timed and the words are not properly grouped together (See, for example, Nickerson 1975.)

In clinical applications such as speech training of the deaf, attention has been paid primarily to segmental aspects of speech production, while the prosodic aspects of the generation of a sentence-length utterance have been neglected. One reason for this neglect is that the acoustic manifestations of prosodic variables have not been adequately understood. Recent research, however, has helped to correct this deficiency (Lehiste 1970; Lea 1973b; Klatt 1976; O'Shaughnessy 1976).

Lack of progress in quantifying the prosodic aspects of speech is due in part to the many options in the way these prosodic parameters are imposed on a sentence and substantial individual differences in the way these aspects of an utterance are actualized. There may also have been a conviction in the past that the information in the speech signal is retrieved primarily by decoding the phonetic segments and that the prosodic information is secondary. This attitude is now changing, and it is recognized that, particularly in everyday speech reception situations, the segmental cues are often weak or are masked by noise and greater reliance must be placed on prosodic cues, which are usually more resistant to masking by noise. Furthermore, at least in the case of the speech of the deaf, the articulation of individual speech sounds may be sufficiently poor that improper manipulation of the prosodic aspects will render sentence material highly unintelligible, particularly for untrained listeners.

SEGMENT DURATIONS AND FUNDAMENTAL FREQUENCY VARIATIONS IN SENTENCES

A sentence-length unit is usually produced on one breath. When a sentence is too long to be produced on one expiration of air in the lungs, it is usually divided into major constituents that are separated by pauses during which inspiration of air occurs. Inspiration almost always occurs at a major syntactic break during read speech, whereas for spontaneous speech pauses for inspiration often are inserted at other locations (Goldman-Eisler 1968). The length of a breath group, or utterance that is produced on one breath, is, of course, limited by the duration of an expiration. Thus such a sentence type of utterance usually does not exceed 2 to 3 seconds (sec) in length, and there is a pause of 0.5 sec or more while an inspiration occurs prior to onset of the next breath group. The number of syllables produced on an expiration generally does not exceed ten to fifteen, although occasional longer expirations are possible.

As a consequence of this correspondence between a sentence (or breath group) and an expiration from the respiratory system, a sentence is often marked by certain acoustic attributes that are related to the expiratory cycle. For example, the position of the larynx seems to change as lung volume decreases because of its connection to the sternum, which undergoes downward displacement during an expiration (Maeda 1976). The result seems to be a gradual decrease in vocal fold tension and hence a gradual fall of the fundamental frequency (F_0), except in special situations (like certain questions), where this fall is prevented. This gradual fall in F_0, which seems to add naturalness to a sentence and to delineate a breath unit, does not occur if an improper breathing pattern and larynx posture are used in speech. Superimposed on this slow fall are various more rapid rises and falls due to semantic, syntactic, and segmental influences. Unless the sentence begins with a stressed vowel, the fundamental frequency at the beginning of the sentence shows an initial rise, presumably as the initially lowered larynx (which is at a resting position during inspiration) is being raised to a starting position appropriate for the first stressed vowel.

A further general characteristic of a sentence is that the final syllable is lengthened relative to its duration when embedded within the sentence (Klatt 1976; Lindblom and Rapp 1973). This lengthening is the clearest example of a general duration increase that always occurs at the end of a phrase, usually before a pause (Klatt 1975). The prepausal lengthening is superimposed on the intrinsic lengths of the segments in the syllable.

In addition to the sentential pattern, there are changes in F_0 characteristic of phrase-size units: an initial F_0 rise on the first stressed syllable of the phrase and a fall that occurs in the final stressed syllable and continues on any unstressed sylla-

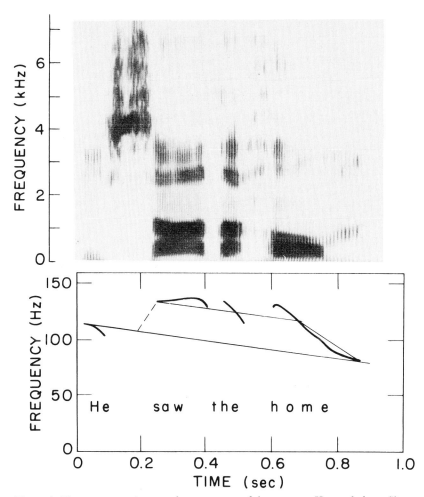

Figure 4. The upper part is a sound spectrogram of the sentence *He saw the home*. Shown below is the fundamental frequency (F₀) contour of the sentence (heavy lines). Super-imposed on the F₀ contour (light lines) is a schematization of the baseline fall of F₀ for the breath group, the rise and fall on the stressed syllables *saw* and *home*, and the intervening plateau in F₀. The dashed line indicates that the F₀ rise actually occurred before the onset of voicing in *saw*.

bles that may follow the stressed syllable. The fundamental frequency usually remains high on a plateaulike region between the initial rise and the final fall (Hart and Cohen 1973). The laryngeal gestures that produce this initial rise and final fall are different from the gestures that cause the gradual fall during an expiration and presumably consist of a stiffening and slackening of the vocal folds through manipulation of the cricothyroid and other muscles (Atkinson 1973; Maeda 1976). There has been speculation that this type of rise and fall that delineates a phrasal unit represents a quantal jump in F_0 by a fixed amount above the baseline F_0 (the amount of jump depending on the speaker), but this suggestion needs to be studied further (Maeda 1976).

A short sentence, with length 1 sec or less, is usually produced as one phrase with no further subdivision into smaller phrasal units. Thus a short sentence contains both the characteristics of a phrase and the overall pattern of the sentence. The spectrogram and F_0 contour in figure 4 show some of these attributes for a simple sentence. The lengthened final vowel can be observed together with the baseline fall in F_0 and the F_0 rise and fall that indicate the beginning and end of the phrase. The figure also illustrates the effects of prominence of a syllable on its duration. The two words *He* and *the* are less prominent than the other words and thus the vowels are of shorter duration. The fundamental frequency in *the* does not, however, show a significant fall but remains close to the plateau defined by the rise preceding *saw* and the fall on *home*.

The effect of putting extra prominence on a particular word is illustrated in figure 5 for the sentence *He might be home*, with emphasis on the word *might*. The high F_0 peak on this prominent word is evident, and this high F_0 peak causes a depressing of the F_0 contour in the surrounding syllables (O'Shaughnessy 1976).

When the sentence is longer than about 1 sec, the speaker usually divides it into two or more phrases. (Subdivision into more than one phrase can also occur for short sentences, since the duration of a phrase may be as short as 0.2 sec, and it may encompass just one word.) Each phrase is characterized by a rise in F_0 at the beginning, a fall in F_0 at the end, and usually a lengthening of the final syllable. The boundary between two phrases, where F_0 falls and then rises, is usually located at a major syntactic break in the sentence. There are no good data on the average length of a phrase, but informal observations suggest that it is about 0.8 sec, although the length can vary from as little as 0.2 sec to as long as 1.5 sec or more in rare situations. At normal speaking rates a duration of 0.8 sec would correspond to about four syllables.

A sentence that is divided into two phrases is illustrated in figure 6, which shows the spectrogram and the F_0 contour for the sentence *The dog likes the small black cat*. Superimposed on the measured F_0 contour are piecewise linear segments that indicate the baseline fall and the rises and falls that delimit the two phrases within the sentence. Large peaks in F_0, above the level of the plateau, can be observed for syllables that the speaker wishes to make more prominent, in this case in the words *dog* and *small*.

Data of the type shown in these figures, for a large number of sentences, are being used to formulate rules for segment durations (Klatt 1976) and for F_0 varia-

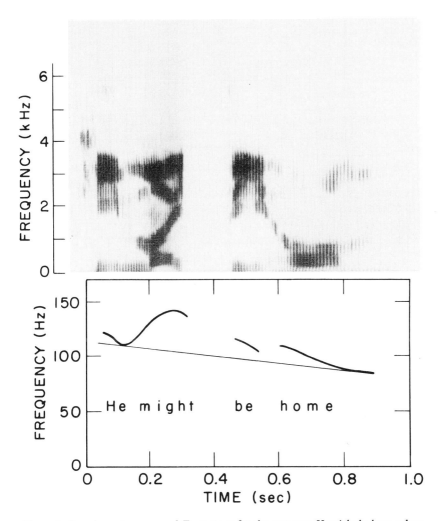

Figure 5. Sound spectrogram and F₀ contour for the sentence *He might be home*, where emphasis is placed on the word *might*. The baseline fall is shown by a light line.

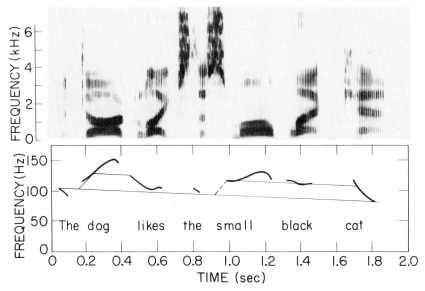

Figure 6. Sound spectrogram and F_0 contour for a sentence containing two phrasal units. The light lines represent a schematization of the F_0 contour in the manner shown in figure 4.

tions in English sentences (Mattingly 1966; Lea 1973a). Not all of the detailed rises and falls are perceptually important, and hence it is not necessary for a speaker to reproduce all of the fluctuations. Experiments suggest, however, that the rises and falls in the vicinity of stressed syllables that delimit phrase boundaries, corresponding to the straight-line approximations shown in the figures, are necessary if the sentence is to sound natural and that inappropriate locations for these rises and falls should be avoided (Maeda 1976). The additional rise-fall of F_0 on specific words adds emphasis to those words. One of the basic questions to be answered by current research is a determination of which words should receive prominence based on their semantic role in the sentence.

It might be speculated that the phrase forms a natural unit in terms of which sentences are decoded and represents the maximum length that must be placed in precategorical store so that the prosodic information can be scanned and interpreted. There is, in fact, evidence that a store with a miximum duration of about seven syllables plays a role in the auditory processing of prosodic information (Kozhevnikov and Chistovich 1965). The rules for encoding prosodic information within a phrase are probably largely independent of the prosodics in adjacent phrases. A duration of 0.8 sec is well within limits of the time span of the precategorical store. One might expect that *some* limits are imposed on the length of a phrase as a consequence of constraints on the articulatory apparatus, particularly the larynx, as well as constraints imposed by the listener. It might be speculated, for example, that production of a long string of syllables on an F_0 that is raised relative to the baseline may require undue "effort" and hence there must be occasional returns of F_0 to the baseline contour. The places where one phrase ends and the next one begins are determined, therefore, not only by the location of the major syntactic breaks in the sentence but also by timing factors, such that relatively long phrases are avoided.

PHONOLOGICAL RULES FOR PHONETIC SEGMENTS IN SENTENCES

The remarks concerning the acoustics of sentences up to this point have dealt with the variations in segment durations and fundamental frequency that occur as a consequence of the relations between words in the sentences. The other aspects of continuous speech generation that represent a deviation from a representation of speech in terms of a sequence of articulatory targets are the modifications that occur in these targets when some syllables are produced with reduced prominence and when words and morphemes are concatenated. These kinds of phonological variations can be observed in figure 7, which is a spectrogram of the utterance *Did you destroy John's shoe?* At the boundary between the first two words the sequence /d/ + /j/ becomes /dʒ/. The unstressed vowel in the word *destroy* is eliminated and the sequence /z/ + /ʃ/ at the boundary between the last two words becomes a single /ʃ/. These kinds of phonological changes are typical of the many changes that segments undergo in sentence contexts, particularly in the vicinity of unstressed vowels and at word boundaries. Current research is seeking to determine the inventory of such rules, many of which are optional, and to determine how these rules might be expressed in a compact and efficient way (Oshika et al. 1975; Cohen and Mercer 1975).

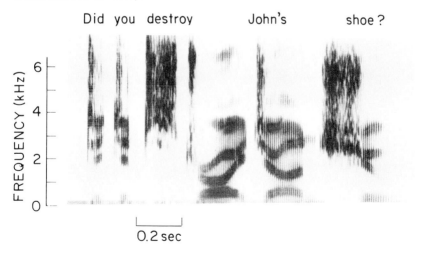

Figure 7. Sound spectrogram of a sentence illustrating the occurrence of several phonological rules that describe the modification of segments in a sentence context.

MY SISTER HAS A FISH

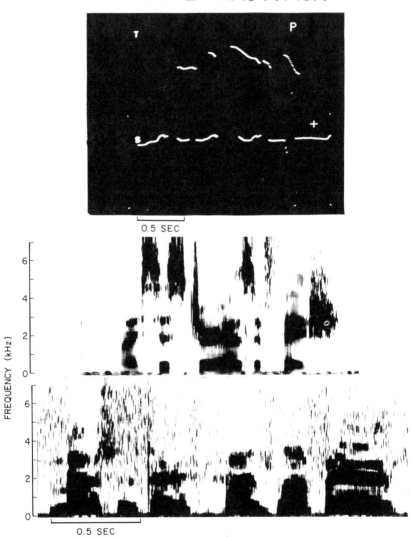

Figure 8. The lower two panels represent sound spectrograms of the sentence *My sister has a fish* produced by a normally hearing adult male speaker (upper) and by a deaf child (lower). The top panel shows fundamental frequency contours of the same two sentences as displayed on the oscilloscope of a system of speech training aids for the deaf.

These rules are of some significance to a deaf listener equipped with a speech analyzing aid to provide a tactile or visual display of certain aspects of speech. Such a listener must learn to account for these rules. For example, an aid that is intended to display the presence of an /s/ or /z/ might miss the /z/ in *John's* as a consequence of these phonological rules. Thus the training of a listener with such an aid should not consist only of training with individual words because there is some question as to whether this training can be generalized to words in sentences. The speech training of deaf children should emphasize that the production of sentences is not simply a matter of stringing a sequence of words together. As we learn more about the acoustics of sentences, it is hoped that this knowledge can be applied toward the development of more effective procedures for speech training of the deaf and other individuals with speech impairments and for the training of deaf listeners in the reception of sentences, particularly when they are equipped with nonauditory inputs, including lipreading.

Some Deviations in the Speech of Deaf Individuals

In our discussion of the normal speech production process we have observed that the production of speech involves three kinds of skills: the achievement of appropriate target positions or states for the articulators in order to produce different speech sounds; the actualization of proper timing in maintaining the articulators at their target positions and in effecting the movements from one target position to another; and grouping of words into phrasal units, assigning appropriate prominence to each syllable, and implementing rules for modifying segmental units in various contexts. It is well known that deaf children have difficulty in learning all of these different aspects of speech production.

A few examples will illustrate the kinds of speech problems observed in deaf children and familiar to their speech teachers. The lower part of figure 8 shows spectrograms of a normally-hearing adult speaker and a deaf child saying the sentence *My sister has a fish.* The upper picture is a contour of F_0 versus time for the normal-hearing speaker (upper trace) and the deaf child (lower trace). The acoustic analysis of the deaf child's utterance shows that each syllable is produced as a separate unit with about the same duration and the same fundamental frequency with no evidence of increased or decreased prominence on particular words. There is no baseline fall in F_0 throughout the sentence, suggesting that the breath group is not forming a unit for the child. Problems with the generation of particular sounds are evident; for example the /s/ sounds are poorly articulated and there is no attempt to produce the /s/ in the sequence /s/ + /t/.

Another example in which speech production for a deaf child appears to proceed on a syllable-by-syllable basis is shown in figure 9. In this figure the upper display represents the amplitude of the output of an accelerometer attached to the nose and indicates the amount of vibration of the nose surface and hence is a measure of the amount of nasalization. Among the articulation and timing problems that can be observed are inadvertant nasalization of certain vowels for example, the vowel in *you*), replacement of the consonant sequence /b/ + /k/ by /k/ (that is, elimination of the nasal), and substitution of /b/ for /m/ in the word *milk.*

YOU CAN DRINK YOUR MILK

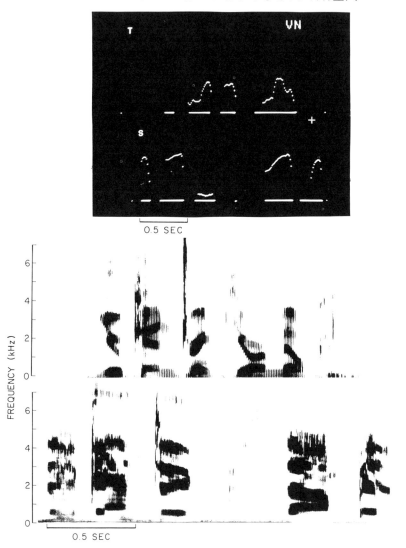

Figure 9. The lower two panels represent sound spectrograms of the sentence *You can drink your milk* produced by a normally hearing adult male speaker (upper) and by a deaf child (lower). The top panel shows time functions representing the amplitude of the output of a small accelerometer attached to the nose and provides a measure of nasalization as a function of time. The solid horizontal lines on the oscilloscope display represent intervals of voicing.

The fuzziness or irregularities in the lower spectrum indicate a harsh or breathy voice, suggesting that this student has an improper posture for the vocal folds during voiced sounds.

Implication for the Clinic and School

What are the implications of recent research on the speech process for the management of speech production and speech perception problems, particularly for deaf children? One obvious implication relates to technical advances that have been made in procedures for the extraction of acoustic and articulatory parameters from speech and for displaying these parameters. These displays can be used either for speech training or as aids for speech reception.

For example, devices have been developed in the laboratory for sensing the position of a point on the articulators (Jankelson et al. 1975) and for sensing the regions of contact between the tongue and hard palate (Fujimura, Tatsumi, and Kagaya 1973). Small accelerometers can be attached to the surface of the nose to provide a measure of acoustic coupling to the nasal cavity through the velopharyngeal port (Stevens, Kalikow, and Willemain 1975). When attached at a suitable point on the neck surface, the accelerometer gives a modified version of the pattern of glottal vibration. When coupled to appropriate visual or tactile displays, these devices can give a rather direct indication of certain articulatory activities. Thus the difficult problem of extracting this information from the acoustic signal is avoided. Examples of such displays are shown at the top of figures 8 and 9. They were obtained from the oscilloscope of a small computer system that has been developed to provide a variety of displays being used to assist speech training of deaf students at a school for the deaf (Nickerson, Kalikow, and Stevens 1976).

Advances have also been made in techniques for the extraction of parameters directly from the acoustic signal. Digital processing methods have permitted rapid manipulations of the signal, and these kinds of processing can now be done with small, lightweight components. Thus, for example, laboratory devices for displaying a running speech spectrogram of high quality are available, as are methods for detection of voicing, fundamental frequency, the occurrence of an /s/, and other acoustic attributes of the speech signal.

Techniques for manipulation of the speech signal so that it is better matched to the auditory capabilities of a hearing-impaired listener are being developed. Two such techniques are shifting high frequencies down to a lower frequency region where some listeners have better hearing acuity and compressing the amplitude range of speech (Ling 1969; Villchur 1973). These processing methods have the possibility of being implemented in small portable packages.

Another class of technical advances of potential help in the school and clinic consists of various kinds of transducers for presenting information to a subject through the ear, the eye, or the skin. These include improved hearing aid receivers, small lights that can be mounted in eyeglass lenses to indicate certain features of the sound (Upton 1968), and small vibrotactile and electrotactile transducers. (See, for example, Saunders 1973; Miller 1975.)

Perhaps of greater significance for the school and clinic are recent advances in our understanding of the acoustics of speech, particularly the prosodic aspects. While the importance of the prosodic aspects (especially the timing) in the speech training of deaf children has been emphasized since the time of A. G. Bell (see Hudgins and Number 1942), programs for working with these types of problems have been hampered by lack of knowledge concerning the prosodics. As noted earlier in this paper, we are now beginning to be able to quantify the principal rules for timing of phrases and sentences and for imposing F_0 contours on the sentences. As the important aspects of these rules become further understood, speech training procedures can be developed for mastering the gestures for producing the prosodic parameters and for implementing the rules. This improved knowledge of the speech signal should make it possible to develop nonauditory displays that will represent the salient aspects of these acoustic attributes as aids for the reception and training of speech.

Finally, as the relevant aspects of the speech signal and its relation to the underlying linguistic description become further specified, it should become possible to develop more effective procedures for evaluation of the communicative abilities of those with communication disorders. For example, tests of the speech production capabilities of an individual should be devised to assess not only articulatory skills in isolated words but also the ability to produce appropriate timing and intonation patterns and to concatenate words in a sentence context. Likewise, tests of speech reception should include not only evaluation of speech sound discrimination but also the capability for utilizing prosodic cues and for bringing to bear contextual information of various types in sentence comprehension tasks.

References
Abercrombie, D. A., 1967. *Elements of General Phonetics*. Edinburgh: Edinburgh University Press.
Atkinson, J. E., 1973. Aspects of intonation in speech: Implications from an experimental Study of fundamental frequency. Ph.D. Thesis, The University of Connecticut.

Chomsky, N., and M. Halle, 1968. *The Sound Pattern of English*. New York: Harper and Row.

Cohen, P., and R. Mercer, 1975. The phonological component of an automatic speech recognition system. In D. R. Reddy (ed.) *Speech Recognition*. New York: Academic Press, pp. 275–320.

Cooper, M., 1971. Modern techniques of vocal rehabilitation for functional and organic dysphonias. In L. E. Travis (ed.) *Handbook of Speech Pathology and Audiology*. New York: Appleton-Century-Crofts, pp. 585–616.

Fant, C. G. M., 1960. *Acoustic Theory of Speech Production*. The Hague: Mouton.

———, 1973. *Speech Sounds and Features*. Cambridge, Mass.: MIT Press.

Folkins, J., and J. H. Abbs, 1975. Lip and jaw motor control during speech: Responses to resistive loading of the jaw. *J. Speech and Hearing Res.* 18, 205–220.

Fujimura, O., I. F. Tatsumi, and R. Kagaya, 1973. Computational processing of palatographic patterns. *J. of Phonetics* 1, 47–54.

Goldman-Eisler, F., 1968. *Psycholinguistics: Experiments in Spontaneous Speech*. New York: Academic Press.

'tHart, J., and A. Cohen, 1973. Intonation by rule: A perceptual quest. *J. of Phonetics* 1, 309–327.

Held, R., and S. J. Freeman, 1963 Plasticity in human sensorimotor control. *Science* 142, 455–462.

Hixon, T. J., 1973. Respiratory function in speech. In F. D. Minifie, T. J. Hixon, and F. Williams (eds.) *Normal Aspects of Speech, Hearing and Language*. Englewood Cliffs, N. J.: Prentice-Hall, pp. 73–125.

House, A. S., 1961. On vowel duration in English. *J. Acoust. Soc. Am.* 33, 1174–1178.

House, A. S., and G. Fairbanks, 1953. The influence of consonantal environment upon the secondary acoustical characteristics of vowels. *J. Acoust. Soc. Am.* 25, 105–113.

Hudgins, C. V., and F. C. Numbers, 1942. An investigation of the intelligibility of the speech of the deaf. *Genetic Psychology Monographs* 25, 289–392.

Jakobson, R., C. G. M. Fant, and M. Halle, 1963. *Preliminaries to Speech Analysis*. Cambridge, Mass.: MIT Press.

Jankelson, B., C. W. Swain, P. F. Crane, and J. D. Radke, 1975. Kinesiometric instrumentation: New technology. *J. Amer. Dental Assoc.* 90, 834–840.

Klatt, D. H., 1975. Vowel lengthening is syntactically determined in a connected discourse. *J. of Phonetics* 3, 129–140.

———, 1976. The linguistic uses of segmental duration in English: Acoustic and perceptual evidence. *J. Acoust. Soc. Am.* 59, 1208–1221.

Klatt, D. H., and K. N. Stevens, 1969. Pharyngeal consonants. Quarterly Progress Report No. 93, Research Laboratory of Electronics, M.I.T., pp. 207–216.

Koenig, W., H. K. Dunn, and L. Y. Lacy, 1946. The sound spectrograph. *J. Acoust. Soc. Am.* 17, 19–49.

Kozhevnikov, V. A., and L. Chistovich, 1965. *Rech 'artikulyatsiya i Vospryatie*. Moscow-Leningrad: Nauka. (English transl. Speech: Articulation and Perception. Joint Publication Research Services, U. S. Dept. of Commerce, No. 30543).

Ladefoged, P., 1971. *Preliminaries to Linguistic Phonetics*. Chicago: University of Chicago Press.

Lea, W. A., 1973a. An approach to syntactic recognition without phonemics. *IEEE Trans. Audio and Electroacoustics* AU 21, 249–258.

———, 1973b. Segmental and suprasegmental influences on fundamental frequency contours. In L. J. Hyman (ed.) *Southern California Occasional Papers in Linguistics No. 1. Consonant Types and Tone*. Los Angeles: University of Southern California Press, pp. 15–70.

Lehiste, I., 1970. *Suprasegmentals*. Cambridge, Mass.: The MIT Press.

Leshowitz, B., and E. Cudahy, 1975. Masking patterns for continuous and gated sinusoids. *J. Acoust. Soc. Am.* 58, 235–242.

Liberman, A. M., F. S. Cooper, D. P. Shankweiler, and M. Studdert-Kennedy, 1967. Perception of the speech code. *Psych. Rev.* 74, 431–461.

Lieberman, P., 1967. *Intonation, Perception, and Language*. Cambridge, Mass.: The MIT Press.

Lindblom, B., and K. Rapp, 1973. Some temporal regularities of spoken Swedish. Publication No. 21, Institute of Linguistics, University of Stockholm.

Ling, D., 1969. Speech discrimination by profoundly deaf children using linear and coding amplifiers. *IEEE Trans. Audio and Electroacoustics* AU-17, 298–303.

Lisker, L., and A. Abramson, 1964. A cross-language study of voicing in initial stops: Acoustical measurements. *Word* 20, 384–422.

MacNeilage, P. F., 1972. Speech physiology. In J. H. Gilbert (ed.) *Speech and Cortical Functioning*. New York: Academic Press, pp. 1–72.

Maeda, S., 1976. A characterization of American English intonation. Unpublished Ph.D. thesis, Massachusetts Institute of Technology.

Mattingly, I. G., 1966. Synthesis by rule of prosodic features. *Language and Speech* 9, 1–13.

Meyer-Eppler, W., 1953. Zum Erzeugungsmechanismus der Gerauschlaute. *Z. Phonetik* 7, 196–212.

Miller, J. D., 1975. Preliminary research with a three-channel vibrotactile speech-reception aid for the deaf. In G. Fant (ed.) *Speech Communication*, Vol. 4. Stockholm: Almqvist and Wiksell, pp. 97–103.

Nickerson, R. S., 1975. Characteristics of the speech of deaf persons. *The Volta Review* 77, 342–362.

Nickerson, R. S., D. N. Kalikow, and K. N. Stevens, 1976. Computer-aided speech training for the deaf. *J. Speech and Hearing Disorders* 41, 120–132.

O'Shaughnessy, D., 1976. Modelling fundamental frequency, and its relationship to syntax, semantics, and phonetics. Ph.D. thesis, Massachusetts Institute of Technology.

Oshika, B. T., V. W. Zue, R. V. Weeks, H. Neu, and J. Aurbach, 1975. The role of phonological rules in speech understanding research. *IEEE Trans. Acoust. Speech and Signal Processing* ASSP-23, 104–112.

Peterson, G. B., and H. L. Barney, 1952. Control methods used in a study of the vowels. *J. Acoust. Soc. Am.* 24, 175–184.

Saunders, F. A., 1973. An electrotactile sound detector for the deaf. *IEEE Trans. Audio and Electroacoustics* AU-21, 285–287.

Stevens, K. N., 1971a. Airflow and turbulence noise for fricative and stop consonants. *J. Acoust. Soc. Am.* 50, 1180–1192.

————, 1971b. The role of rapid spectrum changes in the production and perception of speech. In L. L. Hammerich and R. Jakobson (eds.) *Form and Substance (Festschrift for Eli Fischer-Jorgensen)*. Copenhagen: Akademisk Forlag, pp. 95–101.

————, 1971c. Linguistic factors in communications engineering. In G. E. Perren and J. L. M. Trim (eds.) *Applications of Linguistics*. Cambridge: Cambridge University Press, pp. 101–112.

————, 1972. The quantal nature of speech. In E. E. David and P. B. Denes (eds.) *Human Communication: A Unified View*. New York: McGraw-Hill, pp. 51–66.

————, 1973. Further theoretical and experimental bases for quantal places of articulation for consonants. Quarterly Progress Report No. 108. Research Laboratory of Electronics, M.I.T., pp. 247–252.

————, 1975. Quantal configurations for vowels. *J. Acoust. Soc. Am.* 57, S70. (Abstract).

Stevens, K. N., and D. H. Klatt, 1974. Current models of sound sources for speech. In B. Wyke (ed.) *Ventilatory and Phonatory Control Systems*. London: Oxford University Press, pp. 279–292.

Stevens, K. N., D. N. Kalikow, and T. R. Willemain, 1975. A miniature accelerometer for detecting glottal waveforms and nasalization. *J. Speech and Hearing Research* 18, 594–599.

Studdert-Kennedy, M., 1976. Speech perception. In N. J. Lass (ed.) *Contemporary Issues in Experimental Phonetics*. New York: Academic Press, pp. 243–293.

Upton, H., 1968. Wearable eyeglass speech reading aid. *Amer. Ann. Deaf* 113, 222–229.

Villchur, E., 1973. Signal processing to improve speech intelligibility in perceptive deafness. *J. Acoust. Soc. Am.* 53, 1646–1657.

Some Applications of Basic Research on the Acoustics of the Speech Signal

A Discussion of Stevens's Paper

GERALD A. STUDEBAKER

The paper by Dr. Stevens has provided information that has a diversity of implications for the activities taking place today in our schools and clinics. To review briefly, some of the major topics covered were a description of basic data concerning the acoustics of speech, including such things as the mechanism of vocal cord vibration, the generation of turbulence noise by the speech mechanism, and the filtering of the sound by the vocal tract; work concerning the quantal nature of speech signal generation and perception; and information on the acoustic attributes of sentences. The paper also described some deviations from normal speech associated with deafness, and the author suggested a number of implications that basic research in these areas has and will have for those working with the speech-, language-, and hearing-impaired.

Reception Tests for the Hearing-Impaired

I was particularly pleased to see that Stevens's presentation included a discussion on the speech of the deaf. In this paper I will make some comments concerning speech reception tests for the severely hearing-impaired. Of course, we cannot approach the thoroughness with which the topic of communication by the hearing-impaired was covered by the workshop group sponsored by the Information Center for Hearing, Speech, and Disorders of Human Communications held in Baltimore in 1973, but I believe the area is so important that some further emphasis is justified.

When I was in charge of a clinical audiology operation several years ago, one of our principal activities was to evaluate children with moderate to severe hearing impairments. I can vividly recall the frustration of not having adequate tools to evaluate the speech reception capabilities of those children with severe hearing impairments of all ages. In our clinic there was a small oral training program. It was our observation that the children in this program varied greatly with regard to their ability to derive information from auditorily presented speech even when their pure tone audiograms were fairly similar. It seemed intuitively obvious to us that those children who could understand or derive some reasonable amount of information from auditory speech were more likely to succeed and were in fact succeeding better in this aural training program than those children with relatively low capabilities in this area. We had a great desire to measure this capability in the young hearing-impaired child so that some effort to predict success in aural training could be attempted. However, a search of the literature at that time revealed no satisfactory way of even attempting such an evaluation. All standardized tests were too difficult. Certain other procedures seemed inappropriate for various reasons. Therefore on the basis of what we knew about speech and speech signals we (and, I might add, several other clinics across the country) developed informal closed set response procedures based on the use of a small number of objects or pictures as response items. We used two or three alternative response procedures in which the test items varied in factors such as syllable number, phonemic content, and stress pattern that were selected on the basis of information from the basic research literature of the time. Gradually, the procedure was partially systematized but due to the complexities of the problem and the highly individual needs of each young client we never developed the procedure into a formal test. This was ten to twelve years ago. We depended entirely upon information developed by researchers in the previous fifteen years.

It may be suggested that progress has been made since that time and, indeed, in some areas it has. However, in a 1976 issue of *The Journal of Speech and Hearing Disorders* an article appeared that presents a scheme not greatly different from that used by us and by a large number of other clinics around the country before and since. I do not wish to criticize this work because it does provide clinical data not available in the past and it does formalize and publicize the multilevel of difficulty test. But the work is also instructive in that it is an indication of the current level of the application of basic research to clinical evaluation in this area. What the authors (Erber and Alencewicz 1976) present is a closed set of twelve words represented by pictures. The test words consist of three monosyllables, three trochaic, and three spondaic words that can be varied. The confusion matrices developed reveal both intra- and intercategorical confusions. While this work is a reasonable application of some of the information derived from basic research, its level of sophistication is, in relation to the research reported here today, not very high. It is a good start but more needs to be done. In fact the information upon which this test is based has been available for many, many years. Except for a certain systematization, clinical procedures for the evaluation of such children appear to have changed very little over the past thirty years.

There are two related aspects that I believe need attention in this area. The first is the development of speech tests based upon test signals other than the isolated word. A number of options appear to be available. One good example is the SPIN test developed by Kalikow and his collegues (1976). This test, based upon the sentence, has the advantages of a high degree of face validity, a one-word response, and provision for the control of the predictability of the key response word.

The second aspect, which is intimately related to the first, is to develop a set or sets of procedures that examine various levels of speech comprehension difficulty and tap the various ways in which significant information is encoded in the speech signal. At present there are a number of procedures that test word intelligibility in open or closed set formats that test sentence intelligibility or the ability to identify or discriminate among individual phonemes. However, there is a need for a coherent set of procedures designed to tap the variety of the fundamental performance capabilities of the young hearing-impaired child. For example, can children unable to understand isolated words understand words contained in a known sentence structure? If not, can they discriminate from among a closed set of phonemes? If so, which phoneme types or categories can they discriminate between or within and which can they not? Can they make use of speech rhythm or speech intonation as an aid in the communication process? Can they perceive and make use of the acoustic cues provided by the prosodics of the sentence as discussed by Professor Stevens? A further question is whether such basic skills can be arranged into some sort of hierarchy or profile and, if so, could such a profile be used successfully to predict the success of the individual hearing-impaired child in training programs with particular sets of goals and procedures. It should be emphasized that such studies must be carried out with the hearing-impaired child; the hierarchy or profile of significance for such children might be different from that derived from persons with normal hearing or who developed their hearing loss after language acquisition.

Several years ago we pursued such a goal. We started out in a very simple way by constructing a closed response set test consisting of sets with four response alternatives. The response items in a set were chosen so that they varied in only one phoneme position. The phonemes in the variable positions were selected on the basis of their place or manner of production. We initially attempted a multilevel error analysis such as mentioned earlier by combining voiced and voiceless pairs in a set. This aspect was subsequently dropped because most contrasts other than place of articulation seemed to be too easy to be of differential value. Given another six or eight years to consider it, I now think we may have simply been applying the test to the wrong subjects. We developed an eight alternative set vowel test as well and analyzed error substitutions based on formant frequency in relation to hearing loss configuration. It soon became evident that this procedure was not sufficiently difficult to provide meaningful information about the performance of the average adult hard-of-hearing listener. However, application of these procedures to a series of severely hearing-impaired children revealed that these tests correlated better with the children's achievement tests and evaluation of the children's performance by their teachers than did monosyllabic or spondaic word tests. But no relation was noted between vowel substitutions and hearing loss characteristics that were different from those seen with normals except for total number of errors. It became apparent to us in the course of these investigations that these tests were not sufficient. There were some children for whom this test as well as the standardized tests were inappropriately difficult. Tests of the more basic aspects of speech perception were needed.

The work of Erber (1972) suggests that even speech-modulated noise can convey significant information to the deaf individual in a lipreading situation. His work also suggests that utilization of such information is learned. Aside from the intrinsic interest of such a research finding, the practical implications of such data are very great. But one additional step is necessary before full utilization of information of this sort can be realized. This step is to determine what basic auditory system functions are associated with a reasonable likelihood of success of the individual hearing-impaired child in training programs with particular philosophical and procedural characteristics. For example, if a child can make use of rhythmic, pulselike information provided by amplified speech to assist in lipreading, as demonstrated by Erber, but cannot derive information of a more sophisticated nature from that signal what is the likelihood of success in a purely aural training program? O course, clinical questions can seldom be answered so simplistically. But questions concerning the educational placement of hearing-impaired children continue to arise every day. Clinicians need this kind of information, even if it is imperfect.

Progress in this area is dependent, I believe, upon a basic knowledge of the constituent parts of the speech communication process and upon the relative contributions of these aspects to the success or failure of the hearing-impaired child in learning to communicate aurally. What does this child need to succeed under any given set of circumstances? At what point along the continuum of skills or what profile of capabilities should cause the clinician or teacher to recommend this or that type of training activity? There are, of course, many factors other than hearing per se that may affect this decision. Nonetheless, speech hearing capability must be a basic determiner of success. The need for such objective information is so great, in my view, because the uncontrolled forces that now influence the selection of training programs for the individual hearing-impaired child continue to be more influential than the forces of logic and data.

Application of Speech Analysis and Synthesis Techniques

On a related topic, I would like to comment upon what I believe is one of the great and all too often overlooked tragedies of life for the young hearing-impaired person that might one day be partially overcome through applications of the findings of basic research, particularly in the areas of speech analysis and synthesis. The tragedy I refer to is the inability of aurally trained, moderately to severely hearing-impaired children to communicate effectively with their peer group. While it is difficult for these children to understand normal speech, it is virtually impossible for them to understand the speech of their hearing-impaired classmates. Such a failure in communication occurs to various degrees even in those cases where the child can understand normal speech moderately well. The implications for children of any system that would improve this communicative link are obvious. If machines can be produced to receive and translate normal speech, it must be presumed that such devices could also be developed to receive the speech of a hearing-impaired person and translate it into a more intelligible acoustic form for presentation to another hearing-impaired listener. Wearable translators must necessarily await the development of adequately miniaturized circuits, but that appears to be only a matter of time. The implications for moderately hearing-impaired children of any system that would improve their communications with their peer group are enormous. Basic research in the areas of analysis and synthesis of speech signals would, of course, be instrumental to the success of such an endeavor.

Another application of speech and language research techniques to clinical research and training relates more to instrumentation development than to basic research findings. However, it seems representative of the kind of implications that such research can have for clinicians and clinical researchers.

Our clinic serves a substantial number of laryngectomized patients. These patients represent a broad range of abilities both in general and with particular regard to the quality of the speech they produce. One aspect in which they differ substantially is in the amount of stoma noise they generate. It was hypothesized by John A. Irwin of our center many years ago that those individuals who produced a great deal of stoma noise and who seemed unable to control it even after extended periods of training might have a hearing loss that prevented them from hearing the noise. To investigate, records were kept on listener judgments of stoma noise and audiograms for about six hundred individuals over a period of twenty years and an apparently significant relationship was observed. However, it was not possible to determine precisely the relationship of stoma noise to hearing loss because the acoustic nature of the stoma noise was not known. A recently available device, the real-time spectrum analyzer (RTA), proved very well suited to the solution of this problem.

The investigation proceeded by recording the speech of laryngectomized patients both with and without stoma noise on audio recording tape. These tapes were subsequently spectrally analyzed using the RTA through the use of its transient capture capabilities. It was soon discovered that the stoma noise could be readily observed on the RTA and that it consisted of a band of noise about one octave wide and centered at about 2000 Hertz (Hz). Unfortunately it was hearing loss at 4000 Hz that appeared to have been related to the stoma noise. It has therefore proved necessary to reconsider the evidence. The project has not been concluded because of the illness of the clinician-researcher who was working with the patients.

A number of potential applications for the real-time spectrum analyzer in clinical training and clinical research suggest themselves. Full use of the potential applications of this device, which will soon be widely available to the clinical researcher, rests squarely upon the basic research in acoustic phonetics of the past thirty years. Investigations of the possible relationships between extraneous speech production noise and hearing loss is but one simple example of these potential applications. The quantitative evaluation of the acoustic nature of certain speech and voice defects is another. The device could possibly have some usefulness as an alternative or additional feedback channel in the retraining of individuals with certain kinds of deviant speech or voice.

The Use of Speech as a Test Signal
We are all familiar with the idea of testing a communications system using test words or syllables that are received and responded to by the normal hearing listener after having been processed by the communication system under investigation. Another widely known concept is that of the articulation index, in which basic research information is utilized to define an area on a signal-to-noise by frequency display. These applications of research findings have had significant utility in the engineering and communicative sciences but have not found great application in the study of aural communication by the hearing-impaired, principally because the effects of hearing loss cannot be described simply on a frequency by signal-to-noise ratio surface.

Kiang (1975) has used speech as a test signal to evaluate the neural coding in the auditory nervous system. His work has several implications, particularly in giving us some notion of the complexity of this coding mechanism. Further, he provides us with an appreciation of the fact that surgeons across the country who are implanting devices in people to stimulate the cochlea or eighth nerve directly are premature at best. We must agree with Kiang that a most important implication of his work is that the successful application of implants that stimulate the cochlea or central nervous system directly must await further basic research on the fundamental code used by the auditory nervous system at its several levels of organization. Interpretation of Kiang's work on the relationship between the characteristics of the speech input signal and the resulting central nervous system activity is highly dependent upon a firm foundation of basic research on the characteristics of the speech signal and the relationship of these characteristics to speech intelligibility and aural communication.

In the same sense that Kiang has used speech as a test signal for the auditory nervous system, it can be used to test the performance of electroacoustic devices such as hearing aids. Speech signals can be delivered to hearing aids, the output of which is then analyzed on a sound spectrograph. The results of such analyses are interesting but, because spectrographs do not display intensity in a manner that can be easily quantified, the results prove to be only minimally useful. However, another line of investigation has opened up new possibilities into use of speech as a test signal to evaluate electroacoustic instruments. To explain, let me first present the basics of a method we have developed that we call "the noise subtraction method." In this procedure, a broad-band thermal noise is presented to a hearing aid (which is simply an example of devices that can be tested); the signals are delivered by a loudspeaker. The noise passes through the hearing aid to an acoustic coupler and then to an RTA where a time-averaged spectral analysis of the hearing aid's output signal is produced. This representation of the intensity-by-frequency output of the hearing aid is then transferred to a digital adder/subtractor and stored there. A second microphone placed near the hearing aid microphone is subsequently used to pick up the noise signal being delivered to the hearing aid. This signal is delivered to the spectrum analyzer where a time-averaged spectral analysis similar to the first is produced. The result is a representation of the frequency response of the signal delivered to the hearing aid. This representation is then deducted from the previously obtained output from the hearing aid in the adder/subtractor. Because gain as a function of frequency, or frequency response, is equal to the difference between the input and output signals of the device under test, the result of the described procedure represents the frequency response of the hearing aid.

The beauty of this system is that the result is essentially independent of the input signal spectrum; thus nearly any signal can be used as the test signal provided only that an adequate signal-to-noise (or signal noise-to-background noise) ratio is maintained at all frequencies of interest and provided that the input signal can be exactly replicated, within reasonable limits, whenever desired. Speech signals can be used in a manner that fulfills these goals. For example, we have produced a sixteen-talker babble on tape and used this signal to test the frequency response of hearing aids just as with a thermal noise as described above. The result is essentially

identical to that obtained with noise with the exceptions that speech babble produces a somewhat less repeatable result that has a relatively poor signal-to-noise-
ratio at the high-frequency end. This latter problem can be largely corrected by
frequency weighting the speech babble that is delivered to the hearing aid in order
to emphasize the high-frequency end.

The face validity of testing a hearing aid with actual speech rather than with a
noise signal designed to simulate speech spectrally or pure tones is appealing but, as
it turns out, often unnecessary because speech babble, thermal noises, and pure
tones usually produce the same result. The "usually" in this case means, however,
only when the hearing aid is operating below saturation. The performance of some
hearing aids at or near saturation is quite different, depending upon whether thermal noise or pure tone test signals are used to test that performance. We are of the
opinion that thermal noise signals produce test results that more accurately reflect
the performance of hearing aids in real life situations than do pure tones. We are
currently testing this thesis by using speech babble as the test signal.

We also plan other more sophisticated uses of speech signals as test signals beyond using them simply as substitutes for thermal noise or as a means of verifying
results obtained with thermal noises or pure tones. These procedures are potentially more interesting and are based upon the subtractive technique described
earlier. In this procedure, individual phonemes are utilized as test signals. Reasonably steady-state phonemes with duration of 100 to 200 milliseconds (msec)
are introduced to the hearing aid by a loudspeaker. The spectrum of the input
signal to the hearing aid is deducted from the output signals spectrum as described
earlier or alternately input and output spectra are compared directly. In the case
of vowels the result is a line spectrum display that includes the effects of the gain
and frequency weighting introduced by the hearing aid plus all the harmonic and
intermodulation products introduced by the hearing aid and perhaps (depending
upon the noise level of the equipment used) some evidence concerning the signal-
to-noise ratio of the hearing aid as a function of frequency. Artificially generated
speech signals would prove very useful in such applications because of the ability
to control spectral content over time and the ability to control precisely the spectral composition of such signals.

The potential significance of such a procedure is unknown. However, it appears
to have potential as a means of providing a more complete understanding of hearing aid performance and of the nature of the modifications of the speech signal
introduced by hearing aids of various designs. Our preliminary results suggest a
considerable modification of formant relationships and a considerable smoothing
of the formant structure at least with those few hearing aids we have tried. Such a
procedure could possibly provide a means of evaluating the applicability of a
particular hearing aid to a particular type of hearing loss. A weighted evaluation
of performance could be provided in which the weighting was dependent upon the
relative importance of the distortions the hearing aid produces in selected acoustic
characteristics of the speech signals, which have, in turn, been weighted on the
basis of relative importance to the communicative process.

A necessary, though not sufficient, requirement for the success of such an application is basic research to determine what aspects of speech are most important to the intelligibility of speech by the hearing-impaired listener and what modifications in that signal most severely degrade its intelligibility for these persons. It is, of course, hardly news that speech intelligibility testing is a crude and inadequate method to determine whether a hearing aid is a good hearing aid or whether it is a good hearing aid for a particular individual. Although speech intelligibility must remain the final arbiter, more analytical and more reliable techniques are needed. It is evident that after twenty-five years of effort, those techniques are yet to be identified. However, I have confidence that they will be identified and that when they are, a basic understanding of the acoustics of the speech signal will have played an important role in their generation.

References

Erber, N. P. 1972. Speech-envelope cues as an aid to lipreading for profoundly deaf children. *J. Acoust. Soc. Amer.*, *51*, 1224–1227.

Erber, N. P., and Alencewicz, C. M. 1976. Audiologic evaluation of deaf children. *J. Speech Hear. Disord.*, *41*, 256–267.

Kalikow, D. N., Stevens, K. N., Gerstman, H. L., and Morrison, R. K. 1976. The Speech Perception In Noise Test: Description and clinical data. Unpublished manuscript. Bolt, Beranek, and Newman.

Kiang, N. Y. S. 1975. Stimulus representation in the discharge patterns of auditory neurons. In *The Nervous System*. Tower, D. B., ed. Vol. 3: *Human Communication and its Disorders*. New York: Raven Press, 81–96.

General Discussion of Papers by Stevens and Studebaker

The Invariance Problem

Much of the discussion of Stevens's paper centered around the problem of specifying acoustic invariants for phonemes. The discussants agreed that there might be many static dimensions of speech signals that could be found to be invariant with respect to phonetic segments. However, Harris and Liberman pointed out that an important question is whether these (static) invariants served as sufficient cues for phoneme identification. For instance, in the case of the consonant bursts, there are invariant articulatory target positions for initial consonants in different syllabic contexts that yield more or less constant acoustic starting points. But are these starting points sufficient cues for the identification of consonants? Sometimes they are; often they are not. Further, these static cues are certainly not the only cues for the phonemes. Dynamic variables such as formant transitions (that are not constant across vowel contexts) have been shown to provide important information about both consonants and vowels in syllable contexts. Harris stressed that the findings of the complex dynamic characteristics of the signal—for example, the timing relations in sentences reported by Stevens—argue for the importance of such dynamic invariants for perception at both the phonetic and prosodic levels.

Labov raised the additional problem of the variation in the acoustic instantiation of a phoneme produced by different speakers, even within the same dialect. For instance, for the vowel /u/, the second formant can range in frequency from 550 to Hertz 1900 (Hz). When different dialects are considered, the range is even greater. There is currently no satisfactory answer to the question of how a child (or an adult) is able to extract the invariant information for phonemes across contextual variation, speaker variation, and dialect variation.

Labov added that much of the research on acoustic invariants has concentrated on initial consonants before stressed vowels, which are actually a minority of the total occurrences. Studies of final consonant production show that in many dialects of English the final consonants do not include release bursts, so that cues such as the length of the preceding vowel and the formant transitions must provide information for their perception. There is even more variation in how the consonants are represented acoustically for consonant clusters.

Labov suggested that this variation in the acoustic representation of consonants in different syllabic contexts might be related to reading problems, which seem to be concentrated on consonants that come at the end of the syllable. He described a typical pattern in which the child gets the first consonant correct, attempts to identify the vowel, and then "dives into empty space." This could be because there is very little correlation between the alphabet and what the child has heard as final and intervocalic consonants. This is exacerbated by the emphasis on initial consonants in early stages of teaching reading and the neglect of consonants in other contexts where the problems of letter-sound correspondence seem greatest.

Liberman mentioned that the probability of making reading errors on vowels is equal regardless of syllabic position and errors on vowels are more frequent than errors on consonants. He suggested that these results could be interpreted in terms of linguistic awareness.

Prosodics in the Speech of the Deaf

The discussants agreed that one important application of basic research on the speech signal was the analysis and remediation of abnormalities in the speech of the deaf. Stevens reemphasized that the prosodic aspects of deaf speech were seriously deviant. Recent research on the acoustic specification of prosodic information in normal speech will help in developing procedures that incorporate variables such as pitch, timing, and rhythm into the speech training of the deaf. Stevens suggested that as far as possible speech should be trained in the frame of the phrase rather than the consonant-vowel syllable in order to include these important prosodic aspects of speech.

Shelton pointed out that the use of visual displays for teaching speech to the deaf might be effective for manipulating variables one at a time, but there may still be a problem when one tries to integrate them in an utterance. He suggested that such visual displays might be more effective for simpler problems such as training deaf laryngectomized patients to control stoma noise.

Somesthetic Monitoring of Articulatory States

On a related issue, Shelton wondered whether one could utilize Stevens's notion of target states in teaching speech to the deaf. He mentioned that an old method of training speech, called the moto-kinesthetic method, was based on this kind of idea, that is, teaching awareness of the somesthetic signals. He did not think it had been tested adequately and said it had been abandoned.

Perception by the Deaf

Harris pointed out that there is a need for more research on speech perception by the deaf at levels other than the isolated word. She asserted that it was dangerous to generalize from the isolated word level to the sentence level on the basis of studies with normal-hearing subjects. That is, the relationship of intelligibility at different levels may not be the same for deaf perceivers as it is for normal perceivers. Specific research with deaf subjects is needed to investigate the effects of context on perception, particularly the effects of complex timing relations on perception by the deaf.

An Information-Processing Approach to Speech Perception

JAMES E. CUTTING AND DAVID B. PISONI

For most of us perceiving speech is an effortless and overlooked task. When engaged in conservation one is primarily aware of tracking meaning; the sound pattern of what is heard is "linguistically transparent" (Polanyi 1964), that is, it goes largely unnoticed. The nature of this unnoticed but crucial half of language's dual structure is of particular interest to psychologists, linguists, and engineers—speech perception is the primary means of picking up linguistic information. The process of converting acoustic information into linguistic message, the underlying structure of that process, and its seemingly unusual design fascinate those who study speech perception. The process is also of particular interest to teachers and applied speech scientists; when it goes awry in the young child or adult, it is they who must try to bolster, realign, or circumvent the vocal/auditory system. The plan in this chapter is to take a small step toward mapping some emerging theoretical views of speech perception onto some of the findings in the school and clinic. The view presented, however, is not accepted dogma. It is the authors' own coalition of material from two separate subdisciplines within psychology: information processing and speech perception. Many of our colleagues may disagree with this description of speech perception processes.

In this discussion we will speak of a process in speech perception because speech perception is not instantaneous; it takes time. We will also speak of a series of stages in this process organized roughly in a hierarchical fashion. Information enters a particular stage, is transformed into something new, enters a new stage, is transformed again, and so forth until the linguistic message is understood. Between some of these stages are memory stores, temporary repositories for information that has flowed in. They help break up the dogged linearity of the auditory system. Finally, many of these stages and memory stores have limited capacity. That is, each can hold only so much information before it becomes saturated and information is lost. For those familiar with the *Zeitgeist* of cognitive psychology, these assumptions are easily recognized as hallmarks of the information-processing approach to perception (Broadbent 1965; Neisser 1967; Haber 1969), offspring of information theory and computer modeling within psychology.

First, the validity of these four assumptions will be established: (1) that speech perception is a process, (2) made up of stages, (3) involving memory stores, and (4) that the stages and memories are limited in their capacity. Second, the various stages of speech perception will be assembled into a flow diagram, both at a macrolevel including the entire speech/language system and at a microlevel including only those portions relevent to the lower levels of speech processing. Third, evidence supporting the layout and flow of information to and from each stage will be presented. Fourth, the nature of each phonetic level stage will be considered first in experimental terms and then in terms of ontogenetic development, comparative organization in animals, and possible neurological locus. Fifth, recurring issues within this information-processing approach will be broached, focusing on the phonetic level. The final step in this progression will be devoted to possible clinical applications.

Speech Perception as Information Processing

AS A PROCESS

People occasionally question the notion that pattern recognition in general, and speech perception in particular, is a process. Malcolm (1971, p. 386), for example, states that "when one recognizes a friend on the street there is usually no process of recognition. You see his face in the crowd; you smile at him and say 'Hi, John.' You do not think, 'Now where have I seen that face before?' "

Similarly, one might paraphrase and extend Malcolm's statement with regard to speech perception: You hear his voice in the crowd, speaking to you; you turn and smile and say "Hi, John." You do not think, "Now what did he say and where have I heard that voice before?"

There are three problems with this kind of refutation of cognitive processing as it is conceived here. First, recognition rarely, if ever, involves subvocal speech. Second, one need not be aware of a process for processing to occur. Third, and most important for this discussion, rapid recognition does not imply instantaneous recognition. If speech perception can be shown to take time, this will constitute strong evidence for a process. In fairness to Malcolm (1971) there is a kernel of argument underlying his statement that is the crux of current controversy in speech perception, but discussion of it—invariance—will be deferred until a later section.

Two kinds of evidence suggest that speech perception takes time. First there is an upper limit on how rapidly speech can be understood by the listener. For artificially compressed speech, comprehension can occur at rates of about 400 words per minute (Foulke and Sticht 1969; Orr, Friedman, and Williams 1965). At an average of about four phonemes per word, this rate translates conservatively into 30 to 40 milliseconds (msec) per phoneme. These high transmission rates are achieved only with considerable practice, only for brief periods of time, and even then with considerable errors. At faster rates speech melts into a patterned blur (Liberman et al. 1967). One twenty-fifth of a second per phoneme, albeit a very brief period of time, is not infinitesimally brief.

A second line of evidence, one more congruous with the information-processing approach, demonstrates that this time domain, roughly 30 to 40 msec per phoneme, is compatible with what is known about processing limitations from other research using different kinds of stimuli. If one presents a synthetic consonant-vowel (CV) syllable, say /ba/ as in *bottle*, to one ear and another syllable, /ga/, to the other ear and if the onset of /ba/ precedes the onset of /ga/ by about 50 msec, the listener will have considerable difficulty in identifying the first syllable as /ba/ (Studdert-Kennedy, Shankweiler, and Schulman 1970; Pisoni 1975a). This difficulty has been attributed to backward masking, a phenomenon in which the identification of a first-arriving item is interfered with by a later-arriving item. That is, the effect of a second stimulus masks backward in time the identity of the first by not allowing pattern recognition processes to operate on it. The domain of this masking effect seems to be about 50 to 150 msec.

MADE UP OF STAGES

To demonstrate that speech perception consists of a series of stages, one could note that the auditory system is made up of component parts: cochlea, cochlear nucleus, trapezoidal body, superior olivary complex, inferior colliculus, and certainly many cortical elements. Given our incomplete knowledge of functional neurophysiology, however, physiological and anatomical data will not be relied on for evidence of separate stages. Instead let us consider some logical requirements of the system.

First, those portions of the central nervous system responsible for speech perception can never be directly affected by an acoustic signal; they can only respond to neural events transmitted along the auditory pathway. Thus there must be at least one stage in the system that transforms acoustic signal into neural signal. Second, these portions of the processing system devoted to speech must share the auditory pathway with many other auditorily based systems, much as a single telephone user might share a party line with several other users. Thus at some level the neural signal must be general enough to be useful to systems that process not only speech but other sounds as well, such as music, environmental sounds, and infant cries. Subsequent to this level, it seems likely that the attributes of the neural signal peculiar to speech are transformed a second time, this time into a linguistic description of what has been said, then a third time into meaning (Licklider 1952).

These three transformations—acoustic signal to general neural code, general neural code to phonetic transcription, and phonetic transcription to meaning—may be only a few of those necessary in processing speech. Indeed, as it will be shown later, there are probably many more. Liberman, Mattingly, and Turvey (1972) have estimated that the transformation of a reasonably intelligible acoustic signal into a phonetic representation of speech—involving two of the transformations just mentioned—is equivalent to transforming a fourty-thousand bit-per-second signal into a forty-bit-per-second signal. This rapid thousandfold reduction of information results in a coded form of speech suitable for even further reduction by coding into meaningful linguistic units. Such magnitude of information reduction is requisite in speech perception. It is our opinion that such feats could only be accomplished by having the signal pass through and be transformed by several different processing stages.

The exact number of stages needed for the processing of speech is not known, although their general layout in a flow chart is commonly agreed on. A familiar convention used in information-processing models is to draw boxes and lines to represent stages and the flow of information between them. That enterprise will be repeated here. Drawing boxes and connecting them with lines is, as Roger Brown (1973, p. 4) says, "an odd interest, dependent, [we] suspect, on some rather kinky gene which, fortunately for our species, is not very widely distributed in the population." Nevertheless, fruitful insights and testable hypotheses arise from such ventures. In formulating these pencil-and-paper systems, however, one must be careful. The information-processing scientist must be selective but not overly economical in the number of stages postulated in that system. On the one hand, he or she must try to avoid such atrocities as Whorf's (1940) tongue-in-cheek fifteen-stage process for translating English into French; yet on the other hand, he or she cannot postulate too few stages, without regressing ultimately to Malcolm's (1971) one-stage direct-processing view of perception.

INVOLVING MEMORY STORES

Most of us have experienced the following embarrassing situation. Imagine yourself sitting across the table from a friend. Both of you are absorbed in different activities but intermittently you talk to one another. A period of silence goes by and suddenly your friend asks you a question. About the time she finishes you say, "Sorry, what did you say?" Distressingly, almost before you finish and certainly before she has a chance to repeat the question, you already know what it was. From where did the question reemerge? The answer must be that it had been stored unused in some kind of memory until the general speech processing system and consciousness gained access to it.

This kind of anecdote demonstrates that speech perception can use memosy. We, as well as Robert Crowder (this volume) hope to demonstrate that speech perception requires the use of memory. This discussion will be prefaced with a brief note on why more than one kind of memory is necessary in an information-processing approach to speech perception. Aside from the anticipated inclusion of echoic memory, short-term memory, lexical memory, and semantic memory within the general speech/language system, one must remember that speech perception is very fast yet is made up of several stages of processing. Add to this the fact that speech is a dynamic signal in which interrelations among spectral parts are constantly changing and changing at a constantly varying rate. Some portions of the signal may be very easy to process, while others are more difficult. These variations must be coped with and processed. According to an information-processing approach, the only plausible manner in which this can be done in "real time"—that is, without stepping outside the natural context and artificially slowing down the signal so that the more recalcitrant aspects of speech become amenable to analysis—is through the copious use of a series of memory stores or buffers whose contents are constantly updated and overwritten by subsequent information. Moreover, the contents of these stores must be accessible to a number of stages in the system. Just how these buffers and stages are interrelated will be developed in the next section.

LIMITED IN THEIR CAPACITY

Although the central nervous system is made up of billions of cells and quite possibly many millions of them are devoted almost exclusively to speech and language, the resources of this system are far from unlimited. Consider first the memories. Echoic memory, often thought of as a kind of an audio tapeloop that is constantly rerecorded, lasts about two seconds. Thus there is a temporal limit to the amount of information that can be stored in a fairly unanalyzed form. If the listener wishes to "play back" a speech sample just heard, it must be done quickly or its relatively unencoded form will be gone forever (Crowder 1971; Darwin and Baddeley 1974; Pisoni 1973).

Short-term memory (STM) is the conscious, largely verbal memory so well studied by psychologists. It is the memory that fails when one forgets a telephone number between directory look-up and dialing. It seems not to be limited so much by time as by amount and content; seven (Miller 1956) or, more likely, five (Broadbent 1975) unrelated items are about all this memory can hold and recycle for further analysis. The items themselves can be syllables, words, or even multiword units, but it seems that they cannot be sentences of any length and certainly not paragraphs. Thus if a linguistic message is to be understood, its gist must be quickly abstracted or it runs the risk of never being fully processed.

Echoic memory seems neurologically expensive, but short-term memory seems less so. If in fidelity echoic memory approaches the quality of tape recording, it would require something approximating the forty-thousand bit-per-second storage mentioned earlier (see also Norman 1972). While the early stages of auditory analysis could easily handle this load, one can see why man was not engineered to have an indefinitely long echoic memory: Billions of brain cells would be involved. Short-term memory, on the other hand, is likely to be of the forty bit-per-second variety and better adapted to hold the more highly coded linguistic message. It is limited in its capacity nonetheless, whether by neurological design or by evolutionary caprice. Only lexical memory (the dictionary-in-the-head) and semantic memory (that used for comprehension) are thought to be functionally unlimited in their capacity. Their lack of limits make them neurologically expensive and in a pneumatic fashion may force capacity constraints on other parts of the system.

The most important limitations, however, are not those placed on memories, but those placed on the entire system by attention. It appears that one can pay attention to, roughly, only one thing at a given time (Broadbent 1958, 1971). Thus from all inputs from all perceptual systems only one source of information can ride high within consciousness. That is, in an information-processing analysis of attention, only one source of input can survive attentional selection. The locus of this squeeze on inputs has been the source of controversy for twenty years, but it now appears that attentional selection occurs quite late in the system, after perceptual processing (see, for example, Shiffrin, Pisoni, and Castaneda-Mendez 1974). This fact is important in speech perception because, as noted in the introduction, one often is aware of attending to the meaning of a discourse without direct awareness of sound pattern. Attentional constraints appear to play a role in the "transparency" of sound. Moreover, if attention is subsequent to perception, the representation of speech in the what-did-you-say situation cited previously is likely to be in a more highly coded form than that of echoic memory. The message was processed and simply awaited attentional focus. Full awareness of the sound pattern of speech may be possible only when the listener has disengaged himself/herself from meaning as when one listens to a conversation spoken in a language that one does not understand or to the first babblings of a young child.

An Information-Processing Model of Speech Perception

PRODUCTION AND PERCEPTION TOGETHER

Before putting these assumptions together into a model of speech perception, it is necessary to establish a conceptual framework for it. De Cordemoy (1668) first postulated a connection between the perception and production of speech, but only since Lashley have psychologists taken this notion seriously. Lashley (1951, p. 120) appealed to parsimony: "The processes of comprehension and production of speech have too much in common to depend on wholly different mechanisms."

Some of the processes thought to be held in common between perception and production are shown schematically in figure 1. In producing speech, for example, one starts with some conceptual representation, coded in "mentalese" (Fodor, Bever, and Garrett 1974), and moves through a series of at least four other stages until the acoustic structure of speech is reached. Thus at the two ends of the process are meaning and sound. Between them are stages of deep structure, surface structure, and phonetic structure and a series of transformational processes—semantics, syntax, phonology, and speech. This system can easily be elaborated,

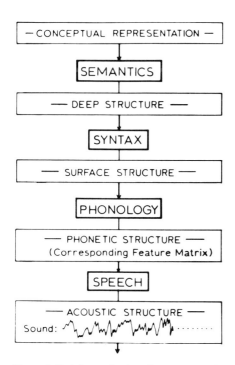

Figure 1. Serial organization of some stages of speech production. Arrows can be reversed for an approximation of the process in speech perception. (Adapted from Liberman 1970.)

either at the conceptual end (see Fodor, Bever, and Garrett 1974, p. 391) or at the speech end (see Cooper 1972, p. 34). The importance of this display, however, is that the arrows can be reversed in this representation of the speech production process to achieve a fairly accurate conceptualization of speech perception.

PARALLEL PROCESSES
What is missing in this conceptual display of speech production and perception are the multiple interrelations between and simultaneity of operations within these stages. While the stages are likely to be serial in some respects, they must also be parallel. This is not quite like having one's cake and eating it too. Decisions at one level can be made on the basis of preliminary information sent up or down the system from another level, rather than each stage waiting for ultimate decisions. Again, one needs not be aware that these intermediate decisions are being made; one needs only to be aware of the ultimate outcome. In such a dynamic system there must be careful executive monitoring of parallel processes so that each stage does not act on misinformation. Improper monitoring may result in occasional metatheses, or spoonerisms, in speech production (Fromkin 1971; MacKay 1970) and undetected errors of pronunciation in speech perception (Cole 1973; Marslen-Wilson 1975). In summary, the hierarchical representation of the stages of processing represented in figure 1 is probably not wrong, but it is misleading. Perhaps a better organization, at least from an information-processing point of view, is a more heterarchical one proposed elsewhere (Pisoni 1975b, forthcoming-b) and shown in figure 2.

This is a macrolevel model of speech perception that includes the entire speech/language system. It allows, in real-time operation, the simultaneous functioning of phonetic, phonological, lexical, syntactic, and semantic processes to derive a linguistic representation of a sentence. Its advantage is that it is fundamentally a dynamic approach to speech and language perception rather than a more tem-

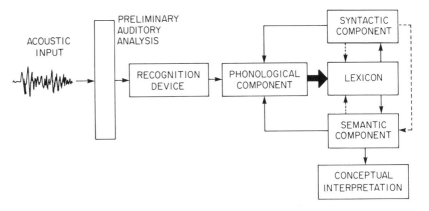

Figure 2. Functional organization of the components of the speech perception system.

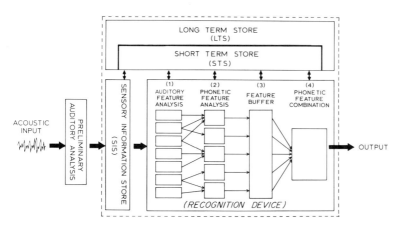

Figure 3. Functional organization of the phonetic recognition component of the speech perception system (from Pisoni and Sawusch 1975).

plate-matching, taxonomic one (Massaro 1975); it allows language to act as a "support system" for speech perception (Bransford and Nitsch, this volume).

Since the brunt of this paper is directed toward speech perception rather than language perception, the recognition device, shown in figure 2, will be further elaborated and described in a microlevel model. This device handles only the phonetic recognition process. It is shown as Pisoni and Sawusch (1975) first conceived of it in figure 3. According to this diagram, the acoustic input enters the system and undergoes a series of transformations. First it enters a stage called *preliminary auditory analysis*, where acoustic energy is transformed into neural energy, preserving to a large degree the time, frequency, and intensity relations among the components of the signal. (The term *acoustic* refers to the signal before it enters the ear; *auditory* refers to the signal after it is transformed by the ear into mechanical and neural impulses.) The information then enters a *sensory information store*. Many information-processing models call this stage preperceptual auditory storage (Massaro 1975; Massaro and Cohen 1975; see also Neisser 1967). This storage is thought to be very brief in nature, on the order of 50 to 250 msec, and is thought to account for, among many other phenomena, the backward masking results discussed earlier. The auditory system does not appear to be able to resolve separate information within a smaller time domain than 20 to 40 msec (Stevens and Klatt 1974; Hirsh 1974). This smearing or integration of the signal occurs in preliminary auditory analysis. Preperceptual auditory storage appears to reflect a "time window" or perceptual moment (Allport 1968) that travels along the acoustic signal. The window is not sharply defined; instead it has graded edges that may extend the integrating field to as much as 100 msec or more in some circumstances.

Information is then transmitted to the recognition device and undergoes a series of at least four stages of analysis. These stages, and the previous registration of the acoustic signal within the sensory information store, are mandatory and not under the conscious control of the listener.

Within the recognition device are stages of *auditory feature analysis* and *phonetic feature analysis*, a *phonetic feature buffer*, and a mixer in which the coded signal undergoes *phonetic feature recombination*. In stage one of the recognition device auditory features of the speech signal are recognized in parallel by a whole system of units whose sole job is to parse the incoming information, looking for prominent auditory features. Following Stevens (1975), some attributes that might be included are the presence or absence of rapid change in the spectrum—information that can aid in the recognition of consonants versus vowels; the direction, extent, and duration of change within a portion of the spectrum—information that can aid in distinguishing consonants from one another; other factors such as the frequency range, duration, and intensity of noise—information that can aid in the distinguishing of fricatives from one another (Hughes and Halle 1956; Gerstman 1957); and the relative onset of periodic and aperiodic portions of the signal (Lisker and Abramson 1964; Lisker 1975), The output of auditory feature analysis is some combination of the (possible) features present in the signal, which is then sent on to the next stage of processing (see Sawusch 1976).

Stage two concerns phonetic feature analysis, where a complex of decision rules maps the many auditory features onto phonetic features. It is within this stage that neural signal becomes language. It is presumed that this stage has knowledge of articulatory constraints of the vocal tract. The output of this many-to-one and one-to-many mapping is a set of abstract phonetic features sent on to the third stage.

Stage three, the feature buffer, is a form of memory not talked about previously. It is simply a holding bin that preserves the phonetic feature composition of the particular syllable being processed. A feature buffer is needed here because it cannot be assumed that all phonetic features are processed at the same rate. Moreover, some memory is needed to preserve and maintain phonetic feature information independently for subsequent linguistic processing, particularly for phonological processing, while prior stages begin to process later-arriving material. This holding bin is intimately related to short-term memory.

Stage four, the final stage within the recognition device, is a mixer for the recombination of phonetic features. It is at this stage that clusters of phonetic features are assembled into a phonetic string. This time-tagged distinctive feature matrix is sent on to higher levels of linguistic processing that modify and extend it through phonological, lexical, syntactic, and semantic analyses.

Before being sent to higher levels of analysis, information from any of these four stages and from the sensory information store can be placed in short-term memory, where the listener first has control over it and can selectively rehearse, encode, or make decisions about it. Long-term memory (LTM) is also assumed to be made accessible during the recognition process; and consistent with recent accounts of their relationship, short-term memory is thought to be simply that portion of long-term memory temporarily activated (Bjork 1975; Shiffrin 1975). Long-term memory includes episodic memory (Tulving 1972), which stores episodes of personal history according to spatial and temporal tags, and more important, semantic and lexical memory (Collins and Quillian 1969; Miller 1972, this volume), which are thought to be those portions of long-term memory "necessary for the use of language. [They are the] mental thesaurus, organized knowledge a person possesses about words and other verbal symbols, their meanings and referents, about relations among them, about rules, formulas, and algorithms for the manipulation of these symbols, concepts, and relations" (Tulving 1972, p. 386). Although not overtly marked in figure 3, STM and LTM must also be able to gain access to the higher levels of the speech/language system (the lexicon and syntactic rules) diagramed in figure 2.

The models in figures 2 and 3 are preliminary. A number of revisions will surely be needed. Nevertheless, their current form provides a convenient framework for many of the results of the past twenty-five years in speech perception. Moreover, these schemata suggest future research questions about speech perception in the normal population and perhaps experiments with listeners belonging to special populations. First, however, let us consider evidence that supports this general model.

Language Contributions to Speech Perception

Consider the macrolevel model presented in figure 2. Evidence from many sources demonstrates contributions of higher order components to speech perception. Perhaps the most direct proof comes from the many studies of the perception of speech under noise. Here "redundancy" of the speech pattern makes otherwise unintelligible sections of speech considerably more intelligible. Within the context of this information-processing approach, this redundancy gain can be attributed to contributions of higher levels of processing in the speech/language system. Bransford and Nitsch (this volume), for example, discuss the contribution of a conceptual component to the perception of speech under noise.

Syntactic and semantic aids to speech perception are shown in the results of Miller, Heise, and Lichten (1951) and Miller (1962). The intelligibility of isolated words at a signal-to-noise ratio of 0 decibels (db)—that is, when the signal and noise have the same amplitude—was only about 40 percent. Those same words, however, when they appeared in sentences under noise, were intelligible nearly 70 percent of the time. Thus when the speech signal is impoverished, the higher level components of the system help to distinguish the important features. How exactly this is done is not known, but many have suspected that linguistic context reduces the number of alternatives. A related effect can be seen in the results of Pollack and Pickett (1963, 1964) where the intelligibility of excerpts from conversation is shown to be directly related to the duration of these excerpts and to the number of words contained in them.

Syntactic and semantic contributions can be isolated, demonstrating separate effects. Again presenting speech in noise, Miller and Isard (1963) found that ungrammatical, largely meaningless strings of words were more difficult to repeat than equally meaningless grammatical strings. These sentences in turn were more difficult to repeat than meaningful grammatical strings. Thus syntax improves speech perception and the addition of an easy to interpret semantic component improves it even further.

Lexical memory, that part of LTM concerned specifically with meanings of words, also plays an important role in perceiving speech. Varying signal-to-noise ratios, Howes (1957) and Savin (1963) have shown that word recognition for common words is very different from that for rare words; common words are recognized and identified when presented in noise 20 db more intense than the corresponding threshold level for rare words. This phenomenon is attributed to the fact that common words are readily accessible in lexical memory. Rare words, on the other hand, subsist in musty, seldom-visited corners of the lexicon. The number of possible alternatives in an ambiguous situation demonstrates a similar effect. Miller, Heise, and Lichten (1951) varied the set size of words to be played under noisy conditions and found that at a signal-to-noise ratio of − 12 db words from a set size of 256 items were about 10 percent recognizable, those from a set size of 32 items were about 40 percent recognizable, and those from a set size of 4 items were about 70 percent recognizable. The frequency of a word and the number of possible alternatives in a situation of signal in noise clearly can play a vital role in speech perception.

Phonological cues are also a great aid. The phonological component provides information about the sound structure of a given language, and this information is imposed on the phonetic feature matrix to derive a phonological matrix. Some aspects of this component are universal and some are language specific. General syllabic form and information about intonation contour, or prosody, are also processed at this stage. (But see Crowder, this volume.)

Stress pattern, one aspect of prosody and a speech variable processed by the phonological component, can be a potent cue in word identification. Kozlowski (in press) has used this fact as a tool in the study of tip-of-the-tongue (TOT) phenomenon (Brown and McNeill 1966). The TOT state is a tantalizing mental condition: the individual searches for a word, knows it is there, but cannot obtain it from lexical memory. Certain attributes of the word, however, such as syllabic structure and initial and final letters, can be recalled. Kozlowski explored the nature of this lexical wraith. He presented his subjects with definitions of rare words thought likely to be in a college student's recognition vocabulary but not in their active vocabulary. When his subjects declared themselves to be in the TOT state, he presented them with an auditory cue. This cue was a severely distorted version of the target word in which low-pass filtering essentially removed from the speech signal everything except fundamental frequency, some gross aspects of intensity envelope, and general syllabic structure—hence only the stress pattern of the target word remained. The end result sounded as if an individual were talking through a pillow. Kozlowski found this cue potent enough that his listeners perceived the target word in 35 percent of all TOT states. False cues, filtered words that were not the correct answer, provided only 15 percent "recognition" of the TOT word, a rate that may reflect spontaneous remission of the TOT state. Phonological cues clearly are important to the perception of speech; having available the meaning of a word but not its precise phonological form, one can often obtain the word given only its stress and syllabic patterns.

Before turning to the phonetic level model of figure 3, we should add that one more extraphonetic component aids the perception of speech; it is the speaker's facial display (Erber 1969, 1975; O'Neill 1954; Sumby and Pollack 1954). This component, not shown in figure 2, is often overlooked by the basic speech research-er. Erber (1969), for example, notes that listeners with normal hearing who try to understand words spoken under intense noise (signal-to-noise ratios of -20 db) may not be able to identify any words. If the same words are given to these lis-teners under the same noise conditions but with the opportunity to observe the speaker, their identification improves to as much as 60 percent. Not surprisingly, much of this gain is attributable to visual access to cues of place of articulation (Binnie, Montgomery, and Jackson 1974), a feature that is often highly masked by a noisy context (Miller and Nicely 1955) but carries a wealth of linguistic impact. Erber (1975) notes that for the hearing-impaired individual most of speech perception is a task very similar to this latter experimental situation. (The fact that conference participants came to Belmont and gathered around a table rather than engaging in one large conference telephone call can be taken as evidence for the importance of visual cues on normal speech perception.)

Note that the particular layout of stages in figure 2 allows nearly maximum interaction between phonological, lexical, syntactic, and semantic components. This arrangement was chosen to stress the heterarchical structure of the speech/language system. The pieces are both semiindependent and intersupportive. This plan also allows for the hedging of bets. The role of the lexicon has been a con-troversial issue among both linguists (Fodor, Bever, and Garrett 1974) and psychologists (Miller, this volume). A major question concerns where individual isolated words fit into the general scheme of syntax and semantics in the process of generating and perceiving sentences. Since there appears to be no clear answer as yet, the lexicon has been placed near the middle of everything in this model. In linguistics, current views of transformational grammar take this approach as well (Bresnan 1976).[1]

[1]At this point the reader may wonder why aspects of language that overtly have nothing to do with speech perception—at least as that subdiscipline has come to be known—have been dealt with so extensively. Specifically, one may ask why the research with speech under noise has been considered. The response to the first point is twofold. First, an in-formation-processing account of a system as complex as speech perception demands thoroughness. The whole system must be considered; without a holistic approach, a proper phonemic description is not possible (Chomsky 1964). Second, language percep-tion is a dynamic, whirling process for which speech perception, in most listeners, is the linchpin. Speech and language are not easily divisible in a working system, just as a wheel and its hub are not easily divided in a moving vehicle. To consider speech without regard for the higher processes of language is, if not an empty pursuit, certainly one that will mislead both the basic and the applied researcher. Our response to the second point is similar in tenor. Speech perception under conditions involving background noise—be it patterned, white, or shaped—is speech perception as it is accomplished every day. Speech and noise are as natural in combination as speech and language.

Phonetic Perception and Information Processing
Now to speech perception, or, as it might properly be called, phonetic perception. Evidence that will be considered in terms of the information-processing model is fairly recent. Results from many experimental paradigms appear to converge on the likelihood of a model such as that shown in figure 3 (see, for example, Studdert-Kennedy, Shankweiler, and Pisoni 1972; Day and Wood 1972; Wood 1974, 1975; Wood, Goff, and Day 1971; Pisoni 1973, 1975a; Cutting 1974, 1976). In general these results point to the facts that speech is treated by the listener as a multidimensional display, some attributes of which are auditory with little bearing on language, and some which are phonetic and integral to the speech code; these auditory and phonetic attributes appear to be coded differently in memory and may be established in different parts of the central nervous system; and auditory processes are logically prior to phonetic processes, but in most situations the two go on in parallel.

EXPERIMENTAL EVIDENCE WITH NORMAL ADULTS
After preliminary auditory analysis, the signal is transmitted to a sensory information store. Some of this information is then shipped to echoic memory (Neisser 1967; Crowder and Morton 1969), which is viewed as a component of short-term memory. Placing this storage early in the system has the advantage that the listener can "postpone classification of some items momentarily, recheck his or her categorization of others, and, generally, transcend the strict pacing" imposed by the temporally linear aspect of audition (Crowder 1972, pp. 254–255). What resides within this memory store is an auditory code of the input particularly well suited to prosodic features and certain speech segments. All speech segments, however, are not equally suited for this code. Stop consonants, for example, appear to be considerably less amenable to such storage than vowels (Crowder 1971, this volume; Pisoni 1973). Moreover, the difference between the two phoneme classes does not appear to be related to phonetic coding but rather to the fact that rapidly moving transients such as those found in stop consonants cannot be laid down in echoic form as easily as the more steady-state attributes of vowels (Darwin and Baddeley 1974). While certain auditory properties of stop consonants can be obtained by short-term memory and consciousness (Barclay 1972), the more typical situation is one in which only the form of the vowels and perhaps the fricatives can be extracted from the sensory information store. Thus much of the unanalyzed signal may bypass the echoic portion of short-term memory and be transmitted directly from sensory information store to auditory feature analysis. This "bypassing" is a signal-dependent process. What can be stored in echoic memory is stored; what cannot be stored is not.

The next stage of processing is auditory feature analysis, which has recently assumed a larger role in accounts of speech perception (Stevens 1972, 1975). This stage may not be vital for vowels and other relatively easy to process segments. An auditory husk may be available for the taking in echoic memory for up to 2 sec before one needs to transform the signal into a more parsimonious phonetic feature code. In fact, steady-state vowels might possibly be directly coded into phonetic form from the echoic portion of STM. As it is conceived here, however, the usual course of events demanded by the speech signal, particularly by those portions that will be perceived as consonants, entails auditory feature analysis.

Perhaps the best experimental evidence supporting the existence of this auditory feature detection stage comes from a paradigm recently imported from vision research (Blakemore and Campbell 1969). It is called selective adaptation. Although its original purpose was to rally support for a direct phonetic feature detection model of speech perception (Eimas and Corbit 1973; Eimas, Cooper, and Corbit 1973), recent evidence using this paradigm supports an auditory feature detection view (Tartter and Eimas 1975; J. L. Miller 1975; J. L. Miller and Eimas 1976; Pisoni and Tash 1975; Cutting, Rosner, and Foard 1976; see Cooper 1975 for a review). In this experimental situation, the listener is presented with dozens, perhaps even hundreds, of tokens of the same utterance and then asked to identify members of an array of stimuli. Results show that previously ambiguous items in the array, those at the boundary between two categories of stimuli, are afterward identified as unambiguous examples of the stimulus category opposite to that which has been adapted. This result is important because it suggests how speech perception might be aided by opponent process binary devices relatively early in the information processing system. The phenomenon is complex, thus it behooves us to discuss first two other phenomena—categorical perception and chromatic afterimages.

Categorical perception is a peculiar, nonlinear mode of perceiving typically associated with stop consonants. For example, if an array of seven stimuli from /ba/to/da/, shown schematically in the top left of figure 4, is randomized and each token is presented many times, the listener usually identifies Stimuli 1 through 3 as /ba/ and Stimuli 5 through 7 as /da/. Stimulus 4 is identified as /ba/ about 40 percent of the time and /da/ about 60 percent of the time. When these items are presented for discrimination listeners/find it very difficult to tell the difference between Stimuli 1 and 3, for example, or between Stimuli 5 and 7, but they have no difficulty discriminating Stimulus 3 from Stimulus 5. This set of results is interesting because the seven stimuli in this /ba/to/da/ array differ from one another in equal acoustic increments in terms of the amount of difference in starting frequency of their second formant transitions. That is, Stimuli 3 and 5 are no more different than Stimuli 1 and 3 or Stimuli 5 and 7 by this acoustic criterion. Typical results of the identification and discrimination tasks are shown in the lower left panel of figure 4 (see Liberman et al 1957; Studdert-Kennedy et al. 1970; Pisoni 1973).

Now let us jump temporarily to the perception of color. A well-known phenomenon is the chromatic afterimage. A viewer who stares at a patch of blue for 15 to 30 sec and then stares at a blank white wall illuminated to the same degree will see a patch of yellow whose contour conforms to the original blue patch. Blue is at some level of analysis the opposite color from yellow; white is chromatically neutral. Staring at the blue patch fatigues the blue receptors in the retina and sets

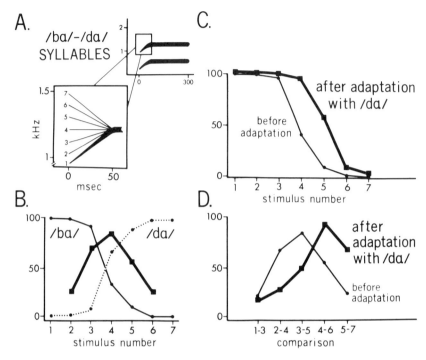

Figure 4 (a). Schematic spectrograms of an array of stimuli from /ba/ to /da/, (b) identification and discrimination functions for that array, (c) and (d) those functions before and
after adaptation with Stimulus 7, /da/.

up a temporary imbalance in the opponent processing system for color. Presented
with a neutral stimulus, a white wall, the viewer then sees a color that is unambiguously yellow.

In the speech domain, at some level of analysis /ba/ can be thought to be the
opposite from /da/ in that it contrasts in place of acticulation. The listener cannot
stare at or even listen to a normal speech syllable for any length of time. However,
if a syllable such as /da/ is presented over and over, thus replenishing the auditory
trace, both the identification and the discrimination functions for the set of stimuli
are temporarily shifted toward /da/, as shown in the right panels of figure 4. The
analogy between this effect and chromatic afterimage breaks down at this point.
The adaptation effect for speech syllables is not in the cochlea (the counterpart
to the retina) but farther along in the processing system and at least partly beyond
the point in the auditory pathway where the two ears converge (Eimas, Cooper,
and Corbit 1973).

Note that these /ba/to/da/ stimuli differ in what Whitfield (1965) has called
"auditory edge." Those stimuli identified as /ba/ have a rising second formant
transition; those identified as /da/ have a falling second formant transition. It is a

bit unusual that the boundary between two stop consonants in CV syllables falls at the level "nonramped" second formant onset, but this case is not unique and probably many other such boundaries can be seen as a variation on this theme. It would appear that in the adaptation situation where /da/ is the adapting stimulus, Stimulus 5 rather than Stimulus 4 is now "perceived" at Stage 1 of our model to have a zero-sloped transition. By this account, it is the auditory feature analysis stage of our model that has been temporarily affected. Arguments for this interpretation instead of a direct, phonetic feature detector interpretation are complex and the reader is referred to Cooper and Blumstein (1974), Pisoni and Tash (1975), Tartter and Eimas (1975), J. L. Miller (1975), Cutting (1977), and Cutting, Rosner, and Foard (1976).[2]

Auditory features from Stage 2 are mapped in a many-to-one and one-to-many fashion onto phonetic features in Stage 3 of the recognition device. This mapping appears to be accomplished partly with reference to invariant information in the signal and partly with regard to knowledge about articulation and its acoustic consequences. How such mapping is accomplished remains one of the recurring unknowns that will be discussed in the next section.

A many-to-one mapping is necessary because a phonetic feature value, such as the voicelessness of /p/ in English, can be cued acoustically in many different ways. In syllable-initial position, for example, this value can be cued by cutback in the first formant transition (Liberman, Delattre, and Cooper 1958) and by delay in voice onset time (VOT) (Lisker and Abramson 1967). This distinction can be cued in intervocalic position by the silent interval between the offset of the previous syllable and the onset of the target syllable (Liberman et al. 1961). In syllable-final position it can be cued by the duration of the previous vowel (Raphael 1972). A one-to-many relationship is also needed since, for example, a single burst can cue different stop consonants (Liberman, Delattre, and Cooper 1952; Schatz 1954). The phonological component further maps phonetic features onto phonemes in a second type of many-to-one and one-to-many fashion not shown in figures 2 and 3.

Support for the existence of a feature buffer (Stage 3 of the recognition device) and a store in which these features are recombined (Stage 4) comes from dichotic listening tasks. If /ba/ is presented to one ear and /ta/ is presented simultaneously to the other ear, the listener often reports hearing a syllable not presented, and most often that syllable is /da/ or /pa/ (Halwes 1969; Cutting 1976). For instance, for the response /da/, it appears that the voicing feature value for /ba/ is perceptually combined with the place of articulation feature value for /ta/, and /da/ results. This is an example of perceptual synthesis of a new syllable from the phonetic feature values of the stop consonants presented to opposite ears. This combination appears to be phonetic because variation in the carrier vowel of the syllables appears to have little effect on the frequency of such "blends" (Studdert-Ken-

[2]The assumption that adaptation effects were due to "fatigue" of phonetic feature detectors appears to have arisen from the assumed equivalence of the term *feature* as in phonetic features (regarding distinctive features of Jakobson, Fant, and Halle 1951) and as in feature detectors as the concept was borrowed from the vision literature.

nedy, Shankweiler, and Pisoni 1972); for instance, /bi/-/tu/ pairs appear to yield as many /d/ and /p/ fusion responses as /bi/-/ti/ pairs. These fusions, or phonetic feature value combinations, appear to occur in Stage 4 of figure 3. Stage 3, the feature buffer, would probably contain on a /bi/-/ti/ trial, for example, all phonetic feature values of the two stop consonants—voiced and voiceless manners of production, and labial and alveolar places of articulation. Since a stop consonant cannot simultaneously be voiced and voiceless, or labial and alveolar, only one feature value of each can be combined in a response.

EXPERIMENTAL EVIDENCE WITH YOUNG INFANTS
A one-month-old infant does not possess any lexical, syntactic, or semantic processes or phonological processes that correspond to any degree to those of adults. Thus the infant affords the opportunity to observe the workings of the model presented in figure 3 at some stage of development without the necessity of considering the whole system shown in figure 2. In earlier days many would have referred to the "prelinguistic" child (Kaplan and Kaplan 1971). In some sense, however, this turns out not to be true. The work of Eimas (1974, 1975, et al. 1971), Moffitt (1971), and Morse (1972) has shown that infants are quite sensitive to speech distinctions. They can discriminate phonetic distinctions such as those between /ba/-/pa/ and /ba/-/da/, but they cannot distinguish between members of the same phonemic category. These results are parallel to those for adults in categorical perception (see, for example, Mattingly et al. 1971). Moreover, young infants can distinguish between the initial liquid phonemes in /ra/ and /la/ (Eimas 1975) better than adults in cultures where this distinction is not phonemic (Miyawaki et al. 1975). It would appear then that young infants come equipped with a capacity to discriminate the relevant acoustic attributes that underlie many phonetic features.

The question remains, however, whether these infants are perceiving speech in a linguistic sense (Stevens and Klatt 1974). In terms of our information-processing model, where, for example, does such processing occur? A few years ago it was believed that such discriminations must be accounted for on the basis of phonetic feature analysis (see, for example, Cutting and Eimas 1975). Today that belief is in question. The brunt of the evidence supports the view that auditory feature analyzers determine the results. It was previously claimed that the experiments on selective adaptation appear to work at a stage prior to phonetic analysis. Given that position, it is suggested that the infant studies indicate perception at the same stage, that is, these results indicate not so much that young infants perceive speech as they indicate that they can perceive speech-relevant dimensions of an acoustic signal (Jusczyk et al., 1977) that they will later apply to the process of speech perception. As Roger Brown (1973, p. 37) noted, such perception in infants is "only linguistic by courtesy of its continuity with a system which in fully elaborated form is indeed . . ." speech perception.

An important aspect of infant research on speech perception that is missing at this point is the performance, by the infant, of many-to-one and one-to-many mapping of acoustic features onto phonetic features. Fodor, Garrett, and Brill

(1975) have taken a small step in this direction using older infants. They found that four and five-month-old infants, like adults, perceived the phonemic identity of consonants in the syllables /pi/ and /pu/ as different than in the syllable /ka/, yet in all three syllables the voiceless stop consonant is cued by similar acoustic information (Schatz 1954). Until such evidence for one-cue-to-many-phoneme mappings can be assembled more fully, along with corresponding many-to-one results, the infant data may be regarded as indicating speech-relevant perception rather than speech perception.

EXPERIMENTAL EVIDENCE WITH ANIMALS
Further support for the allocation of sophisticated analyses to auditory feature processing stems from some recent studies with rhesus monkeys and chinchillas. Their discriminations of synthetic speech syllables differing in place of articulation (Morse and Snowden 1975) and identifications along voice onset time (Kuhl and Miller 1975) look suspiciously like categorical perception, although the data are not complete. Although these results may be subject to range effects (see Parducci 1974; Waters and Wilson 1976) and some speech dimensions may not be perceived categorically by animals (Sinnott, et al. 1976), it is clear that the once firm base of empirical data thought to be indicative of phonetic perception may actually be a data base supporting the existence of a sophisticated auditory feature analysis stage of processing (see Cutting and Rosner 1974; Cutting Rosner, and Foard 1976; Cutting 1977; J. D. Miller, et al., 1976; Pisoni 1976). These animals, and perhaps the human infants as well, do not perceive speech as language but as a multidimensional complex of acoustic events.

Embedded in this view is the assumption that underlying categorical perceptions are auditorily based rather than phonetically based decision processes; that is, categorical perception may be accounted for at Stage 1 of the model rather than Stage 2, as assumed in the past. Are the outputs from the separate auditory feature detectors always discrete and categorical? At this point it is simply not known. It may be that more "continuous" perception, such as that found for steady-state vowels (Pisoni 1973), is distinguished from categorical perception solely in the interaction of the roles of echoic memory and of auditory feature analysis.

EXPERIMENTAL EVIDENCE FOR NEUROLOGICAL LOCUS
Mapping the stages of an information-processing model onto neurological structure is not an easy task. While the clinician in particular needs to know about such facts as can be compiled, it must be remembered that the fractionation of the speech/language system with regard to clinical populations can be a hindrance rather than an aid (Jenkins 1975).

In general, the great majority of linguistic processes appear to be associated with the left cerebral hemisphere of the human brain (Geschwind 1970). However, whereas lexical, semantic, and syntactic operations may be best performed by this hemisphere, the right hemisphere also appears to play an important role in the perception of phonological cues such as stress (Blumstein and Goodglass 1972) and intonation (Blumstein and Cooper 1974). Thus the dynamic role of both hemispheres in the language process should not be ruled out, especially in view of the therapeutic value of exercising right hemisphere functions on the recovery of language abilities after stroke (Albert, Sparks, and Helm 1973; Keith and Aronson 1975).

Phonetic-level processing may occur, in part, in the right hemisphere as well as in the left hemisphere. Considering the stages of the recognition device shown in figure 3, there is no reason to assume that preliminary auditory storage is not perfectly bilateral, with equipotential left and right ear components. Most aspects of acoustic feature analysis (Stage 1) may also be bilateral, but certain aspects, such as the analysis of rapid frequency changes (Halperin, Nachshon, and Carmon 1973; Cutting 1974) and the processing of rapid amplitude modulations in the acoustic signal (Blechner, in press). The remaining stages may reside entirely in the left hemisphere, but it is only the stage of phonetic feature combination (Stage 4) for which this seems a logical necessity. Since combination can be seen as a "blending" of phonetic features, be they from two dichotic inputs or one binaural input, a single mixing device is needed. While this mixing could be duplicated in both hemispheres, it seems unlikely given the nature of the auditory pathways to each hemisphere (Milner, Taylor, and Sperry 1968). If this device were in the right hemisphere, it would be removed from many of the other aspects of language. Economy of design, then, would warrant placing it within the left hemisphere. Data supporting this allocation stem from electrophysiological (Wood, Goff, and Day 1971; Wood, 1975) and dichotic listening analyses (Studdert-Kennedy, Shankweiler, and Pisoni 1972).

Short-term memory is certainly bilateral, but different forms of it may be hemispherically specialized. Verbal forms of STM information, for example, appear to occur in the left hemisphere and spatial imagery forms appear to occur in the right hemisphere (Seamon and Gazzaniga 1973). This is a reflection of what the separate hemispheres appear to do best (Kimura 1967).

Some Controversies in Speech Perception
The basic issues in speech perception today are nearly the same as they were twenty-five years ago—the apparent lack of invariance in the acoustic signal, the related problem of segmentation, and the question the appropriate units for analysis. As for the third issue, it can be pointed out that in the approach presented here all units, including auditory features, phonetic features, phonemes, phonological features, morphemes, words, clauses, sentences, and paragraphs are deemed appropriate. All are important in speech perception and all are used, and the great body of literature in experimental psycholinguistics bears out this view. Awareness, or reversing Polanyi's metaphor "linguistic opacity," of some of the speech units, however, appears to develop in the child only after language acquisition is well advanced (Liberman et al 1974; Mattingly 1972) and can delay onset of reading readiness. This topic is discussed further in the next section.

Lack of invariance and the problem of segmentation are less easily dealt with in this model. The acoustic representation of speech is a tour de force in parallel

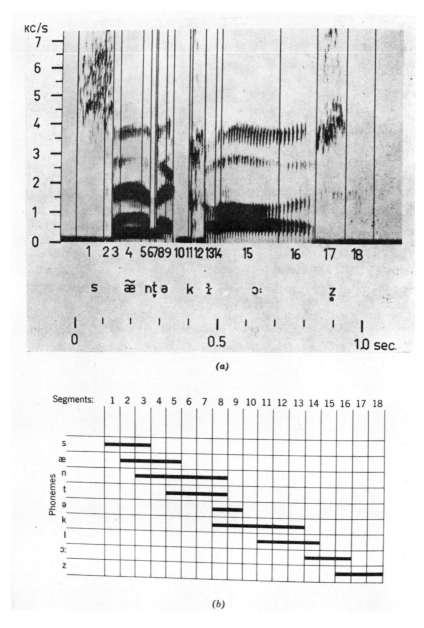

Figure 5. Perceptually, speech sounds seem to follow one another like a train of independent speech segments. Acoustically, however, there is considerable overlap. (a) A spectrogram of the words SANTA CLAUS, where vertical lines mark acoustically different segments, and (b) the assignment of phonemes to those segments. (Adapted with permission from Fant and Lindblom 1961.)

transmission of information, as shown in figure 5. Here the words SANTA CLAUS are spectrographically displayed and parsed roughly according to acoustic segments (a). These acoustic segments are then mapped onto phonemic segments (b), and the amount of parallel transmission can be seen. Segment 8, for example appears to carry information about four phonemes, /ntək/, in only 50 msec; the phone /n/ can be seen to be smeared across acoustic segments 3 through 8, a duration of roughly 200 msec. Thus the acoustic shapes of each phoneme are folded into one another to a very great degree, confounding the problem of invariance in the acoustic display.

Not only is the acoustic shape of one phoneme contingent on its immediate neighbors, but also on phonemes that may be three more phonemes away. For example, the /s/ in STREAK is different from the /s/ in STROKE because in anticipation of the different vowels /i/ and /o/ the lips are unrounded in the first example, creating a more high frequency noise, and rounded in the second, creating noise of slightly lower frequency. Such coarticulation can be so extreme that, as mentioned earlier, identical acoustic events can cue different phonemes in certain contexts and quite different events can cue the same phoneme in others (Liberman et al. 1967).

Some have viewed this position as overstated; and they have a point, especially in view of the time window perceptual moment hypothesis discussed previously. Burst cues of stop consonants, for example, are often only 5 to 10 msec in duration, well below the threshold of auditory resolution. These brief segments surely integrate into following acoustic segments to form a single auditory feature or set of features. Cole and Scott (1974a, 1974b) have claimed that such features are invariant cues that aid the process of speech perception.[3] We remain unconvinced, however, that such cues can account for the perception of all conditioned variation in speech (Liberman et al. 1967).

Without great amounts of invariance speech perception might seem to be an implausible endeavor. Although some aspects of the signal seem invariant—certain aspects of some stressed vowels, of fricatives, and of nasals—many simply are not. How then is speech perceived? Two allied views that suggest a way to cut through (if not unravel) this Gordian knot are the motor theory (Liberman et al. 1967; Studdert-Kennedy et al. 1970; Cooper 1972) and analysis by synthesis (Stevens 1960, 1972; Stevens and House 1972). Both are dynamic views of speech perception and both can be placed easily within the information-processing scheme of figures 2 and 3. In the motor theory the invariance problem is thought to be resolved at the neuromotor level; in analysis by synthesis it is resolved at the neuroacoustic level. Both accounts, when applied to our model, would add the assumption that many-to-one and one-to-many mappings of auditory features onto phonetic features are done with tacit knowledge of articulation (the motor theory) or of its acoustic consequences (analysis by synthesis). Kuhn (1975) has

[3]This is a position that Malcolm (1971), for one, would like. If true, it makes possible a simple, *direct* approach to speech perception without circuitous interconnections of stages and without the need for overt contributions of the human perceiver. In our opinion, however, direct perception of speech is not possible despite the attractiveness of this view.

suggested a way in which the latter might be done. A portion of the supralaryngeal vocal tract, the front cavity, may provide invariant information of a kind different from that suggested by Cole and Scott (1974a). The front cavity may allow straightforward computation of place of articulation through selective perception of the second formant or a weighted combination of the second and third formants. The only knowledge necessary for perception of place of articulation, then, is the general size of the vocal tract. The importance of the front cavity resonance to perception has yet to be explored fully, but it may bring us closer to understanding the transformation from auditory feature to phonetic feature and it is knowledge of this transformation that is crucial to understanding speech perception.

Segmentation, according to motor theory and analysis by synthesis views, is also accomplished with regard to articulation. One parses the incoming speech stream according to the way speech is produced. Thus all the stages within the recognition device would appear to have access to knowledge about speech gestures or their resultant effects on acoustic shape.

Implications for the School and Clinic

AUDITORY PROCESSES
In considering the possible implications of this model for school and clinic situations, the discussion will be limited to a consideration of phonetic perception; the macromodel is considered by other contributors to this volume. Whereas the micromodel that was presented is based on the normal speaker/listener, it should apply to certain special populations if the dynamic relationships within it are modified in appropriate ways. Before beginning, however, a few caveats are in order. First, it would be very surprising to find a single person whose language deficit could be attributed solely to the malfunction of a single stage in this model. The model itself would predict that under a long-lasting deficit anomalies would develop that run through the entire system. Second, this model must be discarded in its entirety when applied to the person who has been profoundly deaf since birth. If this individual substitutes sign language for speech, the phonetic aspect of the model may have no relevance. Recent developments in the linguistic analysis of American Sign Language (ASL) have shown it to be quite different from speech (Bellugi and Fischer 1972; Bellugi, Klima, and Siple 1974/1975; Bellugi and Klima 1975; Frishberg 1975; Friedman 1975; Lane, Boyes-Braem, and Bellugi 1976).

The first important stage to be considered is the initial registration of the signal or preliminary auditory analysis. Relevant here are considerations of certain aspects of hearing and deafness. As Danaher, Osberger, and Pickett (1973, p. 439) have noted, "Most persons with sensorineural hearing loss have some impairment of speech discrimination ability," and generally the discrimination of consonants is poorer than that of vowels. This difference could stem from several causes.

There are many kinds of sensorineural deafness. Persons can be classified as having "flat" fairly constant losses across the frequency spectrum or "sloping" losses that increase substantially for each octave above 500 Hertz (Hz) (Danaher,

Osberger, and Pickett 1973). Moreover, these pure tone audiograms are not related in any simple way to speech-sound discrimination (Danaher and Pickett 1975). Thus even at this first stage of analysis considerable complexity is found. Part of the resolution must be that the deficit is not restricted to a single stage of processing.

Danaher and Pickett (1975) note three types of masking that appear to reduce the discriminability of second formant transitions. The first is a simple upward spread of masking of peripheral origin. That is, low frequency components of the speech signal mask higher frequency components. These individuals improve their discriminations when the signal level of the first formant is reduced by 10 db or when the lower frequency components of the signal are presented to one ear and the upper frequency components to the other. However, presenting the first formant to one ear and the upper formants to the other, as Broadbent (1955) and others (Rand 1974; Cutting 1976) have done in nonclinical settings, does not alleviate upward spread of masking in all individuals. Dichotic split-formant presentation is of little help in this second group. A third type of masking, as Danaher and Pickett (1975) note, complicates the issue even further. It is a type of simple backward masking in which information in a steady-state portion of a vowel reduces the detectability of initial formant transitions.

Relating these three types of data to the model cannot be straightforward, especially since hard-of-hearing individuals differ in their clinical histories. Nevertheless it appears that whereas decrements due to preliminary auditory analysis probably occur in all three types of masking, differential decrements at other stages may also be involved. The difference between monaural and dichotic upward spread of masking may be attributable to differences in ability to perform auditory feature analysis. In the monaural case the decrement in performance may be attributable to preliminary auditory analysis; in the latter case the decrement may be attributable to that stage as well as to auditory feature analysis. If it is possible that the two groups of people differ in the duration of their hearing loss, the latter group's auditory feature analyzers may have become inoperative through longer-term disuse. (This is only speculation, but the dichotic situation is an unusual one, not experienced outside the laboratory. It may be that these auditory feature analyzers have not been stimulated for a long period of time and have "atrophied" [Eimas 1975], that is, become inoperative through lack of use.)

Speech discrimination loss attributable to backward masking would appear to be of a different kind. Backward masking is a temporal phenomenon, whereas upward spread of masking is one of frequency. Temporal phenomena implicate memories and integrating time windows; part of this loss of information may be attributable, therefore, to limitations on coding information in sensory information store, as well as auditory feature analysis.

This assumption appears to be supported by results of research on quite a different population. Tallal and Piercy (1973, 1974, 1975) have studied children diagnosed as developmental aphasics (see also Tallal, this volume). These children have normal audiograms but have extreme difficulty perceiving temporally patterned auditory signals. In a series of careful studies these researchers found that the developmental aphasic has much more difficulty discriminating consonants than vowels and that cue duration appears to be the primary cause. This result is interesting since normal listeners often report no difficulty in identifying target vowels of even shorter duration in a similar situation (Dorman, et al. 1976).

The results from studies of these children appear to implicate a deficit in sensory information store and perhaps auditory property analysis. As Tallal and Piercy point out, these children appear to have an auditory system whose early stages are more "sluggish" than the norm. Perhaps their integrating time windows are larger. Without remediation of this difficulty, deficits throughout the system, especially at the higher levels, are likely to persist and even spread, as Tallal (this volume) suggests.

The deficits discussed thus far can be considered deficits primarily in auditory analysis rather than deficits of speech perception per se. These deficits clearly have effects higher in the system, but those probably result from anomalies at this lower level rather than the converse.

PHONETIC PROCESSES

Evidence for phonetic impairment without auditory impairment is much more difficult to come by. In fact, given the importance recently attributed to the stage of auditory feature analysis, there may be no such evidence at the present time. Moreover, we are not particularly optimistic about possible applications to the school and clinic. Results from normal listeners that used to be taken as indicative of phonetic processing (see Wood 1975, p. 16) now appear to be indicative of auditory feature analysis (see Cutting, Rosner, and Foard 1976). Evidence found for Stage 2 may be contaminated by the operation of prior stages or even subsequent ones. Instead let us consider some of the problems of such contamination and the more general problems of applying experimental paradigms to field situations in the school and clinic. The research using a dichotic listening paradigm is a case in point.

The standard dichotic listening procedure used in the laboratory during the last fifteen years may not yield decisive information for professionals in the school and clinic. The reasons for this assessment stems from several sources. First, it is difficult, and sometimes unwise, to lump together persons with similar perceptual problems. Given the great complexity of the human organism, these individuals are likely to differ greatly even if they fit into the same diagnostic category, as suggested by the results of Danaher and Pickett (1975). Thus individual-oriented procedure would seem best. But this is precisely where the utility of the dichotic listening procedure and most other laboratory techniques is strained. In dichotic listening a right ear advantage may be attributable to a number of causes including those associated with almost every stage shown in figures 2 and 3. The existence of a right ear advantage would tell the applied researcher that some part of the speech/language system is running properly. Even by using nonsense syllables as stimuli, the applied researcher may gain no more information than that (Dorman and Geffner 1974; Dorman and Porter 1975). The lack of a right ear advantage *may* be indicative of malfunction in one stage, but even in the best of situations it does not necessarily tell the researcher which stage, and in the worst of situations it does not imply that any stage is malfunctioning. The existence of a right ear advantage even among the normal population is only a probabilistic occurrence, and the lack of an ear advantage should not be seen as an abnormality (Shankweiler and Studdert-Kennedy 1975). (We feel strongly about this, if only for the reason that one of us consistently yields no ear advantage in these tasks.) Moreover, left ear advantages for linguistic material are not uncommon and must be interpreted with caution even in the most extreme instances (see Fromkin et al. 1974).

Results from other paradigms may be more interpretable, but they may not indicate much about phonetic processing per se. The application of identification and discrimination paradigms associated with categorical perception, selective adaptation, and tasks requiring selective attention to different dimensions of the speech stimulus may be valuable in terms of knowledge about general auditory processing and may serve as verification (or falsification) of certain aspects of the model proposed here (although again, there is no cause for optimism, in our opinion). In spite of this skepticism, there are some recent results in speech perception combined with reading that may bode an important message for the school and clinic. These findings relate to one of the overriding issues in speech perception— units of analysis.

UNITS OF SPEECH ANALYSIS AND READING

Although all units of speech analysis are relevant to speech perception, not all of them are equally apparent, especially to the child. Conscious access to, or knowledge of, speech parsing routines is important in the acquisition of reading skill. In logographic writing, where words are the primary unit, as in Chinese and in the Japanese Kanji script, knowledge about words is imperative. In syllabaric writing, where syllables are the primary unit, such as in the Japanese use of Kana script (see Sasanuma 1975) and in the Cherokee script (Walker 1974) knowledge of syllables is imperative. In alphabetic writing, as in English, where the phoneme is the principal unit, knowledge of phonemes is imperative.

To the young child, syllables and phonemes are not equally amenable units of analysis. I. Liberman et al. (1974) examined the ability of nursery schoolers, kindergarteners, and first graders to tap out the number of syllables and phonemes in common words. Measured for each child was the number of trials needed to reach a criterion of six consecutive correctly tapped trials without demonstration by the experimenter. Ability to segment by syllable was shown by half of the four-year-olds but none of them could segment by phoneme. By age six, 90 percent of the children could segment by syllable but only 70 percent by phoneme. From these results, Liberman et al. suggested that one of the reasons that children under the age of five or six are not ready to learn to read is because they are not yet consciously aware of the units on which written English is based.

Another important aspect of reading readiness, as Conrad (1972) notes, is the ability to code verbally information into short-term memory. I. Liberman, et al.

(1976) applied this notion to good and poor beginning readers. They suspected that good beginning readers would be those who actively use their newly acquired skill of parsing language into phonemes and develop the appropriate coding in short-term memory based on phonemic structure. Poor readers, on the other hand, might still be baffled by phonemes and therefore be unable to use the parsimonious phoneme code. To these two groups of beginning readers, who had been equated for intelligence, they presented two types of consonant strings to view. One type of string consisted of consonants with rhyming names (B, C, D, G, P, T, V, Z) and the other had nonrhyming names (H, K, L, Q, R, S, W, Y). Subjects were then tested in conditions of immediate recall and delayed recall. In general, the good readers made fewer errors than the poor readers on both rhyming and nonrhyming consonants, although the rhyming consonants were more difficult for all. More importantly, the advantage shown by the good readers disappeared for the rhyming consonants in the delayed recall condition but did not disappear for the nonrhyming consonants. The implication is that the decrement in the delayed condition shown by the good readers, but not by the poor readers, is attributable to the use of phonetic codes in short-term memory by good readers and the possible use of some other code, perhaps a visual one (Conrad 1972), by the poor readers. (See Crowder, this volume, for a further discussion of this research.)

These results imply that for the beginning reader of English reading is in part a derivative of speech perception. Acquisition of reading skill depends on mastery of certain linguistic skills and on the youngster's awareness of the proper units of analysis. The availability of a phonetically organized short-term memory may not be enough to learn to read an alphabetically written language. In addition to memory the children must have phoneme parsing skills. Reading instruction and remediation programs might therefore take as an early goal the teaching of awareness of speech segments.

Summary

The goal of this chapter has been to present one point of view about the perceptual analysis of speech sounds. It is a process that takes time; consists of many stages; uses a number of memory stores; is limited in certain ways; and uses all levels of the speech/language system, including phonetic, phonological, lexical, syntactic, and semantic components. Evidence has been presented to support the speech perception model from research with adult and infant humans, as well as with animals. This evidence, of course, does not confirm this model and disprove alternative views; but the evidence, plus important logical considerations, make the view a plausible one. Speech perception and speech production appear to be inextricably intertwined, both on grounds of parsimony, as Lashley (1951) suggested, and on grounds that there is too complex a mapping from auditory features to phonetic features and from phonetic features to phonological features for any alternative method of speech perception to be feasible. Finally, the implications of some of the general views and findings of speech perception research have been applied to problems in the school and clinic. Certain experiments with aphasic and hard-of-hearing listeners may help support the proposed view of speech perception. Other findings of speech research, especially those connected with reading, may help the applied researcher in the school and clinic.

References

Albert, M. L., R. W. Sparks, and N. A. Helm. 1973. Melodic intonation therapy for aphasia. *Archives of Neurology, 29*, 130–131.

Allport, D. A. 1968. Phenomenal simultaneity and the perceptual moment hypothesis. *British Journal of Experimental Psychology, 59*, 395–406.

Barclay, J. R. 1972. Noncategorical perception of a voiced stop: A replication. *Perception and Psychophysics, 11*, 269–273.

Bellugi, U., and S. Fischer. 1972. A comparison of sign language and spoken language. *Cognition, 1*, 173–200.

Bellugi, U., and E. S. Klima. 1975. Aspects of sign language structure. In *The role of speech in language*, J. F. Kavanagh and J. E. Cutting (eds.) Cambridge, Mass.: MIT Press. 171–203.

Bellugi, U., E. S. Klima, and P. Siple. 1974/1975. Remembering the signs. *Cognition, 3*, 93–125.

Binnie, C. A., A. A. Montgomery, and P. L. Jackson. 1974. Auditory and visual contributions to the perception of selected English consonants. *Journal of Speech and Hearing Research, 17*, 619–630.

Bjork, R. A. 1975. Short-term storage: The ordered output of a central processor. In *Cognitive theory*, Vol. 1, F. Restle, R. M. Shiffrin, N. J. Castellan, H. Lindman, and D. B. Pisoni (eds.). Hillsdale, N.J.: Erlbaum Associates. 151–172.

Blakemore, C., and F. W. Campbell. 1969. On the existence of neurons in the human visual system selectively sensitive to the orientation and size of retinal images. *Journal of Physiology, 203*, 237–260.

Blechner, M. In press. Right-ear advantage for musical stimuli differing in rise time. *Perception and Psychophysics*.

Blumstein, S., and W. E. Cooper. 1974. Hemispheric processing of intonation contours. *Cortex, 10*, 146–158.

Blumstein, S., and H. Goodglass. 1972. The perception of stress as a semantic cue in aphasia. *Journal of Hearing and Speech Research, 15*, 800–806.

Bransford, J., and K. E. Nitsch. This volume. Coming to understand things we could not previously understand.

Bresnan, J. 1976. Toward a realistic model of transformational grammar. Paper presented at the conference on New Approaches to a Realistic Model of Language, MIT, Cambridge, Mass., March 9.

Broadbent, D. E. 1955. A note on binaural fusion. *Quarterly Journal of Experimental Psychology, 7*, 46–47.

———. 1958. *Perception and communication*. London: Pergamon Press.

————. 1965. Information processing in the nervous system. *Science*, *150*, 457–462.

————. 1971. *Decision and stress*. New York: Academic Press.

————. 1975. The magic number seven after fifteen years. In *Studies in long term memory*, A. Kennedy and A. Wilkes (eds.). London: Wiley, 3–18.

Brown, R. 1973. *A first language*. Cambridge, Mass.: Harvard University Press.

Brown, R., and D. McNeill. 1966. The "tip of the tongue" phenomenon. *Journal of Verbal Learning and Verbal Behavior*, *5*, 325–337.

Chomsky, N. 1964. Current issues in linguistic theory. In *The structure of language*, J.A. Fodor and J. J. Katz (eds.). Englewood Cliffs, N.J.: Prentice-Hall. 50–118.

Cole, R. A. 1973. Listening for mispronunciations: A measure of what we hear during speech. *Perception and Psychophysics*, *13*, 153–156.

Cole, R. A., and B. Scott. 1974a. The phantom in the phoneme: Invariant cues for stop consonants. *Perception and Psychophysics*, *15*, 101–107.

————. 1974b. Toward a theory of speech perception. *Psychological Review*, *81*, 348–374.

Collins, A. M., and M. R. Quillian. 1969. Retrieval time from semantic memory. *Journal of Verbal Learning and Verbal Behavior*, *8*, 240–248.

Conrad, R. 1972. Speech and reading. In *Language by ear and by eye*, J. F. Kavanagh and I. G. Mattingly (eds). Cambridge, Mass.: The MIT Press. 205–240.

Cooper, F. S. 1972. How is language conveyed by speech? In *Language by ear and by eye*, J. F. Kavanagh and I. G. Mattingly (eds.). Cambridge, Mass.: MIT Press. 25–46.

Cooper, W. E. 1975. Selective adaptation to speech. In *Cognitive theory*, Vol. 1, F. Restle, R. M. Shiffrin, N. J. Castellan, H. Lindman, and D. B. Pisoni (eds.). Hillsdale, N. J.: Erlbaum Associates. 23–54.

Cooper, W. E., and S. E. Blumstein. 1974. A "labial" feature anlayzer in speech perception. *Perception and Psychophysics*, *15*, 591–600.

de Cordemoy, G. 1668. *A Philosophical discourse concerning speech*. London: J. Martin.

Crowder, R. G. 1971. The sound of vowels and consonants in immediate memory. *Journal of Verbal Learning and Verbal Behavior*, *10*, 587–596.

————. 1972. Visual and auditory memory. In *Language by ear and by eye*, J. F. Kavanagh and I. G. Mattingly (eds.). Cambridge, Mass.: MIT Press. 251–276.

————. This volume. Language and memory.

Crowder, R. G., and J. Morton. 1969. Precategorical acoustic storage (PAS). *Perception and Psychophysics*, *5*, 365–373.

Cutting, J. E. 1974. Two left-hemisphere mechanisms in speech perception. *Perception and Psychophysics*, *16*, 601–612.

————. 1976. Auditory and linguistic processes in speech perception: Inferences from six fusions in dichotic listening. *Psychological Review*, *83*, 114–140.

————. 1977. The magical number two and the natural categories of speech and music. In *Tutorial essays in psychology*, N. S. Sutherland (ed.). Hillsdale, N. J.: Erlbaum Associates. 1–33.

Cutting, J. E., and P. D. Eimas. 1975. Phonetic feature analyzers and the processing of speech in infants. In *The role of speech in language*, J. F. Kavanagh and J. E. Cutting (eds.). Cambridge, Mass.: The MIT Press, 127–148.

Cutting, J. E., and B. S. Rosner. 1974. Categories and boundaries in speech and music. *Perception and Psychophysics, 16*, 564–570.

Cutting, J. E., B. S. Rosner, and C. F. Foard. 1976. Perceptual categories for musiclike sounds: Implications for theories of speech perception. *Quarterly Journal of Experimental Psychology, 28*, 361–378.

Danaher, E. M., and J. M. Pickett. 1975. Some masking effects produced by low-frequency vowel formants in persons with sensorineural loss. *Journal of Speech and Hearing Research, 18*, 261–271.

Danaher, E. M., M. J. Osberger, and J. M. Pickett. 1973. Discrimination of formant frequency transitions in synthetic vowels. *Journal of Speech and Hearing Research, 16*, 439–451.

Darwin, C. J., and A. D. Baddeley. 1974. Acoustic memory and the perception of speech. *Cognitive Psychology, 6*, 41–60.

Day, R. S., and C. C. Wood. 1972. Interactions between linguistic and nonlinguistic processing. *Journal of the Acoustical Society of America, 51*, 79(A).

Dorman, M. F., and Geffner, D. S. 1974. Hemispheric specialization for speech perception in six-year-old black and white children from low and middle socio-economic classes. *Cortex, 10*, 171–176.

Dorman, M. F., and R. J. Porter. 1975. Hemispheric lateralization for speech perception in stutterers. *Cortex, 11*, 181–185.

Dorman, M. F., D. Kewley-Port, S. Brady, and M. T. Turvey. In press. Vowel recogniton: Inferences from studies of forward and backward masking. *Quarterly Journal of Experimental Psychology*.

Eimas, P. D. 1974. Auditory and linguistic processing of cues for place of articulation by infants. *Perception and Psychophysics, 16*, 513–521.

———. 1975. Auditory and phonetic coding of the cues for speech: Discrimination of the [r–1] distinction by young infants. *Perception and Psychophysics, 18*, 341–347.

Eimas, P. D., and J. D. Corbit. 1973. Selective adaptation of linguistic feature detectors. *Cognitive Psychology, 4*, 99–109.

Eimas, P. D., W. E. Cooper, and J. D. Corbit. 1973. Some properties of linguistic feature detectors. *Perception and Psychophysics, 13*, 206–217.

Eimas, P. D., E. R. Siqueland, P. W. Jusczyk, and J. M. Vigorito. 1971. Speech perception in infants. *Science, 171*, 303–306.

Erber, N. P. 1969. Interaction of audition and vision in the recognition of oral speech stimuli. *Journal of Speech and Hearing Research, 12*, 423–425.

———. 1975. Auditory-visual perception of speech. *Journal of Speech and Hearing Disorders, 40*, 481–491.

Fant, G., and B. Lindblom. 1961. Studies of minimal speech and sound units. Speech Transmission Laboratory, Royal Institute of Technology, Stockholm, Sweden. *Quarterly Progress Report, 2*, 1–11.

Fodor, J. A., T. G. Bever, and M. F. Garrett. 1974. *The psychology of language*. New York: McGraw-Hill.

Foder, J. A., M. F. Garrett, and S. L. Brill. 1975. Pi ka pu: The perception of speech sounds by prelinguistic infants. *Perception and Psychophysics, 18,* 74–78.

Foulke, E., and T. G. Sticht. 1969. Review of research on the intelligibility and comprehension of accelerated speech. *Psychological Bulletin, 72,* 50–62.

Friedman, L. A. 1975. Space, time, and person reference in American sign language. *Language, 51,* 940–961.

Frishberg, N. 1975. Arbitrariness and iconicity: Historical change in American sign language, *51,* 696–719.

Fromkin, V. A. 1971. The non-anomalous nature of anomalous utterances. *Language, 47,* 27–52.

Fromkin, V. A., S. Krashen, S. Curtiss, D. Rigler, and M. Rigler. 1974. The development of language in Genie: A case of language acquisition beyond the "critical period." *Brain and Language, 1,* 81–107.

Gerstman, L. J. 1957. Perceptual dimensions for the friction portion of certain speech sounds. Ph.D. dissertation, New York University.

Geschwind, N. 1970. The organization of language and the brain. *Science, 170,* 940–944.

Haber, R. N. 1969. Introduction. In *Information-processing approaches to visual perception,* R. N. Haber (ed.). New York: Holt, Rinehart, Winston. 1–15.

Halperin, Y., I. Nachshon, and A. Carmon. 1973. Shift in ear superiority in dichotic listening to temporal pattern nonverbal stimuli. *Journal of the Acoustical Society of America,* 53, 46–50.

Halwes, T. G. 1969. Effects of dichotic fusion on the perception of speech. Ph.D. dissertation, University of Minnesota. *Dissertation Abstracts International,* 1970, 31, 1565b. (Univ. Microfilms No. 70–15, 736.)

Hirsh, I. J. 1974. Temporal order and auditory perception. In *Sensation and measurement: Papers in honor of S. S. Stevens,* H. R. Moskowitz, B. Sharf, and J. C. Stevens (eds.). Boston: D. Riedel. 251–258.

Howes, D. 1957. On the relation between the intelligibility and frequency of occurrence of English words. *Journal of the Acoustical Society of America 29,* 296–305.

Hughes, G. W., and M. Halle. 1956. Spectral properties of fricative consonants. *Journal of the Acoustical Society of America, 28,* 303–310.

Jakobson, R., G. Fant, and M. Halle. 1951. *Preliminaries to speech analysis.* Cambridge, Mass.: MIT Press (1963 ed.).

Jenkins, J. J., E. Jiménez-Pabón, R. E. Shaw, and J. W. Sefer. 1975. *Schuell's aphasia in adults.* New York: Harper and Row.

Jusczyk, P. W., B. S. Rosner, J. E. Cutting, C. F. Foard, and L. Smith. 1977. Categorical perception of nonlinguistic sounds in the two month old infant. *Perceptions and Psychophysics, 21,* 50–54.

Kaplan, E. L., and G. Kaplan. 1971. The prelinguistic child. In *Human development and cognitive processes,* J. Eliot (ed.). New York: Holt, Rinehart, and Winston. 358–381.

Keith, R. L., and A. E. Aronson. 1975. Singing as therapy for apraxia of speech and aphasia: Report of a case. *Brain and Language, 2,* 483–488.

Kimura, D. 1967. Dual functional asymmetry of brain in visual perception. *Neuropsychologia, 4,* 275–285.

Kozlowski, L. T. in press. Effects of distorted auditory and of rhyming cues on the retrieval of tip-of-the-tongue words by poets and nonpoets. *Memory and Cognition* 69–72.

Kuhn, G. M. 1975. On the front cavity resonance and its possible role in speech perception. *Journal of the Acoustical Society of America, 58,* 428–433.

Lane, H., P. Boyes-Braem, and U. Bellugi. 1976. Preliminaries to a distinctive feature analysis of handshapes in American Sign Language. *Cognitive Psychology, 8,* 263–289.

Lashley, K. 1951. The problem of serial order in behavior. In *Cerebral mechanisms in behavior,* L. Jeffress (ed.). New York: Wiley, 112–136.

Liberman, A. M. 1970. The grammars of speech and language. *Cognitive Psychology, 1,* 301–323.

Liberman, A. M., P. C. Delattre, and F. S. Cooper. 1952. The role of selected stimulus variables in the perception of the unvoiced stop consonants. *American Journal of Psychology, 65,* 497–516.

———. 1958. Some cues for the distinction between voiced and voiceless stops. *Language and Speech, 1,* 153–167.

Liberman, A. M., I. G. Mattingly, and M. T. Turvey. 1972. Language codes and memory codes. In *Coding processes in human memory,* A. W. Melton and E. Martin (eds.). New York: Winston. 307–334.

Liberman, A. M., F. S. Cooper, D. P. Shankweiler, and M. Studdert-Kennedy. 1967. Perception of the speech code. *Psychological Review, 74,* 431–461.

Liberman, A. M., K. S. Harris, H. S. Hoffman, and B. C. Griffith. 1957. The discrimination of speech sounds within and across phoneme boundaries. *Journal of Experimental Psychology, 54,* 358–368.

Liberman, A. M., K. S. Harris, P. D. Eimas, L. Lisker, and J. Bastian. 1961. An effect of learning speech perception: The discrimination of durations of silence with and without phonemic significance. *Language and Speech, 4,* 175–195.

Liberman, I. Y., D. P. Shankweiler, F. W. Fischer, and B. Carter. 1974. Reading and the awareness of linguistic segments. *Journal of Experimental Child Psychology, 18,* 201–212.

Liberman, I. Y., D. P. Shankweiler, A. M. Liberman, C. Fowler, and F. W. Fischer. Forthcoming. Phonetic segmentation and recording in the beginning reader. In *Towards a Psychology of Reading:* Proceedings of the CUNY Conference. A. S. Reber and D. Scarborough (eds.). Hillsdale, N.J.: Erlbaum Associates.

Licklider, J. C. R. 1952. On the process of speech perception. *Journal of the Acoustical Society of America, 24,* 590–594.

Lisker, L. 1975. Is it VOT or a first-formant transition detector? *Jorunal of the Acoustical Society of America, 57,* 1547–1551.

Lisker, L., and A. S. Abramson. 1964. A cross-language study of voicing in initial stops: Acoustical measurements. *Word, 20,* 384–422.

———. 1967. Some effects of context on voice onset time in English stops. *Language and Speech, 10,* 1–28.

MacKay, D. G. 1970. Spoonerisms: The anatomy of errors in the serial order of speech. *Neuropsychologia, 8,* 323–350.

Malcolm, N. 1971. The myth of cognitive processes and structures. In *Cognitive development and epistemology,* T. Mischel (ed.). New York: Academic Press. 385–392.

Marslen-Wilson, W. D. 1975. Sentence perception as an interactive parallel process. *Science, 189*, 226–228.

Massaro, D. W. 1975. Language and information processing. In *Understanding language*, D. W. Massaro (ed.). New York: Academic Press. 3–28.

Massaro, D. W., and M. M. Cohen. 1975. Preperceptual auditory storage in speech perception. In *Structure and process in speech perception*, A. Cohen and S. G. Nooteboom (eds.). Heidelberg: Springer Verlag. 226–243.

Mattingly, I. G. 1972. Reading, the linguistic process, and linguistic awareness. In *Language by ear and by eye*, J. F. Kavanagh and I. G. Mattingly (eds.). Cambridge, Mass.: MIT Press. 133–148.

Mattingly, I. G., A. M. Liberman, A. Syrdal, and T. Halwes. 1971. Discrimination in speech and nonspeech modes. *Cognitive Psychology, 2*, 131–157.

Miller, G. A. 1956. The magical number seven, plus or minus two: Some limits on our capacity for processing information. *Psychological Review, 63*, 81–96.

———. 1962. Decision units in the perception of speech. *IRE Transactions on Information Theory, IT-8*, 81–83.

———. 1972. English verbs of motion: A case study in semantics and lexical memory. In *Coding processes in human memory*, A. W. Melton and E. Martin (eds.). New York: Winston. 335–372.

———. This volume. Lexical meaning.

Miller, G. A., and S. Isard. 1963. Some perceptual consequences of linguistic rules. *Journal of Verbal Learning and Verbal Behavior, 2*, 217–228.

Miller, G. A., and P. Nicely. 1955. An analysis of some perceptual confusions among some English consonants. *Journal of the Acoustical Society of America, 27*, 338–352.

Miller, G. A., G. A. Heise, and W. Lichten. 1951. The intelligibility of speech as a function of the context of the test materials. *Journal of the Acoustical Society of America, 41*, 329–335.

Miller, J. D., C. C. Wier, R. E. Pastore, W. J. Kelly, and R. J. Dooling. 1976. Discrimination and labeling of noise-buzz sequences with varying noise-lead times: An example of categorical perception. *Journal of the Acoustical Society of America, 60*, 411–417.

Miller, J. L. 1975. Properties of feature detectors for speech: Evidence from the effects of selective adaptation in dichotic listening. *Perception and Psychophysics, 18*, 389–397.

Miller, J. L., and P. D. Eimas. 1976. Studies on the selective tuning of feature detectors for speech. *Journal of Phonetics, 4*, 119–127.

Milner, B., L. Taylor, and R. W. Sperry. 1968. Lateralized suppression of dichotically presented digits after commissural section in man. *Science, 161*, 184–185.

Miyawaki, K., W. Strange, R. Verbrugge, A. M. Liberman, J. J. Jenkins, and O. Fujimura. 1975. An effect of linguistic experience: The discrimination of [r] and [l] by native speakers of Japanese and English. *Perception and Psychophysics, 18*, 331–340.

Moffitt, A. R. 1971. Consonant cue perception by twenty- to twenty-four-week-old infants. *Child Development, 42*, 717–731.

Morse, P. A. 1972. The discrimination of speech and nonspeech stimuli in early infancy. *Journal of Experimental Child Psychology, 14*, 477–492.

Morse, P. A., and C. T. Snowden. 1975. An investigation of categorical speech discrimination by rhesus monkeys. *Perception and Psychophysics, 17*, 9–16.

Neisser, U. 1967. *Cognitive Psychology*. New York: Appleton-Century-Crofts.

Norman, D. A. 1972. The role of memory in understanding language. In *Language by ear and by eye*, J. F. Kavanagh and I. G. Mattingly (eds.). Cambridge, Mass.: MIT Press. 277–288.

O'Neill, J. J. 1954. Contribution to the visual components of oral symbols to speech comprehension. *Journal of Speech and Hearing Disorders*, *19*, 429–439.

Orr, D. B., H. L. Friedman, and J. C. Williams. 1965. Trainability of listening comprehension of speeded discourse. *Journal of Educational Psychology*, *56*, 148–156.

Parducci, A. 1974. Contextual effects: A range-frequency analysis. In *Handbook of perception*, Vol. 2, E. C. Carterette and M. P. Friedman (eds.). New York: Academic Press. 127–141.

Pisoni, D. B. 1973. Auditory and phonetic memory codes in the discrimination of consonants and vowels. *Perception and Psychophysics*, *13*, 253–260.

————. 1975a. Dichotic listening and processing phonetic features. In *Cognitive theory* Vol. 1, F. Restle, R. M. Shiffrin, N. J. Castellan, H. Lindman, and D. B. Pisoni (eds.). Hillsdale, N.J.: Erlbaum Associates. 79–102.

————. 1975b. Information processing and speech perception. In *Speech communication*, Vol. 3, G. Fant (ed.). New York: John Wiley and Sons. 331–337.

————. 1976. Identification and discrimination of relative onset time of two-component tones: Implications for voicing perception in stops. *Quarterly Progress Report*, Research Laboratory of Electronics, MIT, Cambridge, Mass., *118*, 212–229.

————. Forthcoming-a. Mechanisms of auditory discrimination and coding of linguistic information. In *Second auditory processing and learning disabilities symposium*, J. V. Irwin (ed.). Memphis, Tenn.: Memphis State University Press.

————. Forthcoming-b. Speech perception. In *Handbook of learning and cognitive processes*, Vol. 5, W. K. Estes (ed.). Hillsdale, N.J.: Erlbaum Associates.

Pisoni, D. B., and J. R. Sawusch. 1975. Some stages of processing in speech perception. In *Structure and process in speech perception*, A. Cohen and S. Nooteboom (eds.). Heidelberg: Springer-Verlag. 16–34.

Pisoni, D. B., and J. B. Tash. 1975. Auditory property detectors and processing place features in stop consonants. *Perception and Psychophysics*, *18*, 401–408.

Polanyi, M. 1964. *Personal knowledge*. New York: Harper and Row.

Pollack, I., and J. M. Pickett. 1963. The intelligibility of excerpts from conversation. *Language and Speech*, *6*, 165–171.

————. 1964. Intelligibility of excerpts from fluent speech: Auditory vs. structural context. *Journal of Verbal Learning and Verbal Behavior*, 3, 79–84.

Rand, T. C. 1974. Dichotic release from masking for speech. *Journal of the Acoustical Society of America*, *55*, 678–680.

Raphael, L. J. 1972. Preceding vowel duration as a cue to the perception of the voicing characteristic of word-final consonants in American English. *Journal of the Acoustical Society of America*, *51*, 1296–1303.

Sasanuma, S. 1975. Kana and Kanji processing in Japanese aphasics. *Brain and Language*, *2*, 369–383.

Savin, H. B. 1963. Word-frequency effect and errors in the perception of speech. *Journal of the Acoustical Society of America, 35,* 200–206.

Sawusch, J. R. 1976. The structure and flow of information in speech perception. Ph.D. dissertation, Indiana University.

Schatz, C. 1954. The role of context in the perception of stops. *Language, 30,* 47–56.

Seamon, J. G., and M. S. Gazzaniga. 1973. Coding strategies and cerebral laterality effects. *Cognitive Psychology, 5,* 249–256.

Shankweiler, D. P., and M. Studdert-Kennedy. 1975. A continuum of lateralization for speech perception. *Brain and Language, 2,* 212–225.

Shiffrin, R. M. 1975. Short-term store: The basis for a memory system. In *Cognitive theory,* Vol. l, F. Restle, R. M. Shiffrin, N. J. Castellan, H. Lindman, and D. B. Pisoni (eds.). Hillsdale, N.J.: Erlbaum Associates. 193–218.

Shiffrin, R. M., D. B. Pisoni, and K. Castaneda-Mendez. 1974. Is attention shared between the ears? *Cognitive Psychology, 6,* 190–215.

Sinnott, J. M., M. D. Beecher, D. B. Moody, and W. C. Stebbins. 1976. Speech sound discrimination by monkeys and humans. *Journal of the Acoustical Society of America, 60,* 687–695.

Stevens, K. N. 1960. Toward a model for speech perception. *Journal of the Acoustical Society of America, 32,* 47–55.

———. 1972. The quantal nature of speech: Evidence from articulatory data. In *Human communication: A unified view,* E. E. David and D. P. Denes (eds.). New York: McGraw-Hill. 51–66.

———. 1975. The potential role of property detectors in the perception of consonants. In *Auditory analysis and perception of speech,* G. Fant and M. A. A. Tatham (eds.). New York: Academic Press. 303–330.

Stevens, K. N., and A. House. 1972. Speech perception. In *Foundations of modern auditory theory,* Vol. 2, J. V. Tobias (ed.). New York: Academic Press. 1–62.

Stevens, K. N., and D. H. Klatt. 1974. Role of formant transitions in the voiced-voiceless distinction for stops. *Journal of the Acoustical Society of America, 55,* 653–659.

Studdert-Kennedy, M., D. P. Shankweiler, and D. B. Pisoni. 1972. Auditory and phonetic processes in speech perception: Evidence from a dichotic study. *Cognitive Psychology, 2,* 455–466.

Studdert-Kennedy, M., D. P. Shankweiler, and S. Schulman. 1970. Opposed effects of a delayed channel on perception of dichotically and monotically presented CV syllables. *Journal of the Acoustical Society of America, 48,* 579–594.

Studdert-Kennedy, M., A. M. Liberman, K. S. Harris, and F. S. Cooper. 1970. Motor theory of speech perception: A reply to Lane's critical review. *Psychological Review, 77,* 234–249.

Sumby, W. H., and I. Pollack. 1954. Visual contributions to speech intelligibility in noise. *Journal of the Acoustical Society of America, 34,* 58–60.

Tallal, P. This volume. Implications of speech perceptual research for clinical populations.

Tallal, P., and M. Piercy. 1973. Developmental aphasia: Impaired rate of nonverbal processing as a function of sensory modality. *Neuropsychologia, 11,* 389–398.

————. 1974. Developmental aphasia: Rate of auditory processing and selective impairment of consonant perception. *Neuropsychologia, 12*, 83–93.

————. 1975. Developmental aphasia: The perception of brief vowels and extended stop consonants. *Neuropsychologia, 13*, 69–74.

Tartter, V. C., and P. D. Eimas. 1975. The role of auditory feature detectors in the perception of speech. *Perception and Psychophysics, 18*, 293–298.

Tulving, E. 1972. Episodic and semantic memory. In *Organization of memory*, E. Tulving and W. Donaldson (eds.). New York: Academic Press. 381–403.

Walker, W. 1974. Cherokee. In *Studies of Southeastern Indian languages*, J. Crawford (ed.). Athens, Ga.: University of Georgia Press. 189–236.

Waters, R. S., and W. A. Wilson. 1976. Speech perception by rhesus monkeys: The voicing distinction in synthesized labial and velar stop consonants. *Perception and Psychophysics, 19*, 285–289.

Whitfield, I. C. 1965. "Edges" in auditory information processing. In *Proceedings of the XXIII International Congress of Physiological Sciences*, Tokyo, 245–247.

Whorf, B. L. 1940. Linguistics as an exact science. *Technology Review, 43*, 61–63, 80–83. In *Language, thought, and reality*, J. B. Carroll (ed.). Cambridge, Mass.: MIT Press, 1956, 220–232.

Wood, C. C. 1974. Parallel processing of auditory and phonetic information in speech discrimination. *Perception and Psychophysics, 15*, 501–508.

————. 1975. Auditory and phonetic levels of processing in speech perception: Neurophysiological and information-processing analyses. *Journal of Experimental Psychology: Human Perception and Performance, 1*, 3–20.

Wood, C. C., W. R. Goff, and R. S. Day 1971. Auditory evoked potentials during speech perception. *Science, 173*, 1248–1251.

Implications of Speech Perceptual Research for Clinical Populations

A Discussion of Cutting and Pisoni's Paper

PAULA TALLAL

Cutting and Pisoni have presented a model that provides a framework for discussion of research concerning the mechanisms underlying normal speech perception. The purpose of this paper will be to discuss how the research that led to the formulation of this model may be applicable to issues of interest in the clinic and the classroom. We are at a stage when great benefit may be obtained by focusing our experimental attention on those pathological conditions we wish in the long run to ameliorate. By using techniques with language-impaired patients similar to those used in the experimental study of normal speech perception, we are not only providing a more precise delineation of the various processes that are disturbed in these pathological conditions; such studies provide unique and valuable insights into the normal perceptual mechanisms as well. The discussion of such work will form the basis of this chapter. We shall also see that some recent results of experiments with language-impaired populations already offer the possibility of improving diagnosis and providing novel methods of remediation.

I will use the model of speech perception presented by Cutting and Pisoni as a basis and framework for discussing the recent research that has been done with patients with communicative disorders. As our understanding of, and experimental research in, abnormal processes is not as advanced as it is for normal processing, evidence pertaining to every stage in Cutting and Pisoni's microlevel model of speech perception is not yet available. Therefore, this discussion will in general be based on the macrolevel model of speech perception described in the previous paper. (See figure 2 in Cutting and Pisoni, this volume.) Where possible, however, evidence pertaining to the microlevel model will also be included. Of course, one should bear in mind that evidence derived from the study of impaired speech processing may change our concepts of the possible microlevel stages involved in normal speech perception as well.

Auditory Aspects of Speech Perception

There is no doubt among those actually working with patients with language disorders that these patients have difficulty with various aspects of higher linguistic processing. Evidence for syntactic, semantic, and conceptual deviations among patients with language disorders is not difficult to document. However, the results of studies that investigate higher level linguistic and cognitive abilities of patients with language impairments can be extremely difficult to interpret. In such patients deviations in linguistic performance may be attributable to difficulty with higher order concepts, phonological or syntactic rules. However, it is also possible that cognitive or linguistic deficits could result from a more primary perceptual problem, such as a difficulty in detecting signal change, in discriminating temporal or spectral features, or in integrating different aspects of complex signals over time.

Until we can effectively rule out any malfunctions in these more primary perceptual mechanisms, it will be extremely difficult to differentiate effectively between disorders that may arise in the different stages of language processing. If we are to understand eventually the precise etiology of language disorders, and hence to improve diagnosis and therapeutic techniques for dealing with them, it seems imperative to investigate in detail and in a systematic manner the underlying sensory and perceptual hierarchies involved in language before "placing the blame" on malfunctioning, higher order linguistic systems.

STAGE I: PRELIMINARY AUDITORY ANALYSIS (SENSORY REGISTRATION OF THE ACOUSTIC SIGNAL)

Hearing deficit does not prevent the understanding of speech, but it does prevent the acquisition of language. (Blesser 1974, p. 147)

There are great differences between the organization and functions of the developing brain and those of the adult brain. The mechanisms required to develop a function and those involved in maintaining that function once developed may not be identical. The differences between the hearing-impaired child and adult are an excellent example. An impairment at the preliminary auditory analysis stage (sensation) or within the stages involved in Cutting and Pisoni's "recognition device" will be much more devastating to the child who is developing language than it will be to the adult who has had, at one point, a well-developed language system. Even though the cause of the resulting language disability (elevated sensory threshold) may be the same for both, the effect of such a loss and the methods needed for remediation may be quite different. Whereas adequate reception of the acoustic aspects of the speech signal is important to the patient who has become hearing-impaired as an adult, it is not as critical as it is for the child first developing language. Broadbent (1974) has pointed out that the speech signal itself is so redundant that if the listener has some knowledge of what to expect and if even a small part of the signal is intact, its meaning can be derived adequately. However, without this knowledge, the adequate reception of the physical acoustic aspects of the speech signal must be critical for normal language development. One need only observe the immense difficulties experienced by congenitally deaf children attempting to learn language in the absence of normal acoustic input to begin to understand the magnitude of importance of the preliminary auditory analysis stage of speech perception. Blesser (1974) has suggested that the problem with deaf children is that their concept of the gross structure of language is not secure and thus their ability to benefit from redundancies and those aspects of the acoustic message available to them is not very great.

The precise sensory capabilities of hearing-impaired children have been well documented elsewhere (Stark 1974). Efforts are being made to relate specific patterns of sensory disability of hearing-impaired individuals to their patterns of impairment in speech perception (Danaher and Pickett 1975) and speech production (Stark 1972). These are areas of research that should eventually be useful in the clinic in designing and fitting hearing aids to meet the specific needs of individual patients. Although a great deal more research in this area is still needed, the result of such endeavors will provide an even better understanding of the critical role of the preliminary auditory analysis stage of speech perception and language functions.

It is thus obvious that dysfunction in the primary sensory registration of the auditory signal is sufficient to disrupt speech perception and give rise to a global language disorder. Is there experimental evidence for any other intervening sensory or perceptual mechanisms that could underlie communicative disorders?

STAGE II: RECOGNITION DEVICE (PERCEPTUAL ANALYSIS OF THE ACOUSTIC SIGNAL)

We should not look upon the aphasias as a unique disorder of language, but rather as an inevitable consequence of a primary perceptual deficit in temporal analysis, in placing a "time label" upon incoming data. (Efron 1963, p. 418).

The role of auditory perception in language disabilities has been an area of controversy for many years (see Rees 1973 for review). However there is mounting evidence that patients with language disabilities have specific auditory processing impairments that may underlie their language dysfunction. Knowing, as we do now, the devastating effects of impairment of auditory sensation on the subsequent language development of deaf children, it seems imperative that we take seriously the mounting evidence of auditory perceptual impairments in children and adults with language disabilities.

Temporal Perceptual Ability
Orton (1939) suggested as early as 1937 that children with developmental communicative disorders may be perceptually impaired, particularly in their ability to perceive temporal sequences of events. He concluded that it may be a deficit in auditory temporal processing that underlies developmental communicative disorders. Since Orton's time, clinical and experimental reports continue to stress the predominance of auditory temporal processing and memory disabilities in children and adults with communicative disorders (Monsees 1961; McGinnis 1963; Benton 1964; Hardy 1965; Eisenson 1972).

SEQUENCING EXPERIMENTS
I shall now discuss a number of sequencing experiments that, while giving important insights concerning temporal processing deficits, have nonetheless resulted in conflicting data that has clouded some basic issues.

Efron (1963) studied both auditory and visual temporal sequencing abilities of adult aphasics using a similar paradigm to that employed by Hirsh (1959) in his original auditory experiments with normal subjects. Subjects were required to indicate which of two different stimuli in a rapidly presented sequence occurred first. Analysis of results showed that aphasic patients required a significantly longer average interstimulus interval (ISI) to report which of two stimuli came first than that found by Hirsh (1959) to be required by normal subjects. On the basis of these results Efron hypothesized that the left temporal lobe plays a primary role in the analysis of temporal information. He suggested that it is the disruption of the ability to analyze information temporally that resulted in the language impairment of aphasic patients.

If this were indeed the case, one might expect the impairment of auditory temporal ordering ability, which Efron reported for aphasic subjects, to be directly and positively correlated with the degree of speech comprehension of these subjects. More specifically, it would be expected that receptive aphasic patients (those patients who are specifically impaired in speech comprehension) should prove to be more impaired than expressive aphasics (patients who are specifically impaired in speech production). However Efron's data showed that the opposite was the case. That is, expressive aphasics were more impaired than receptive aphasic subjects on these tests of auditory temporal order perception. This is an apparent contradiction of Efron's hypothesis, a fact he acknowledged in his discussion but failed to reconcile satisfactorily.

Since 1963 several other authors have investigated the sequencing abilities of aphasic patients in an attempt to understand further the exact nature of the sequencing disorder, and particularly its relationship to the language impairment of aphasics. These investigations have confirmed Efron's original findings in as much as these authors were also able to demonstrate a sequencing deficit in aphasic patients, but they have failed to further our understanding of this perceptual deficit and its exact role in language impairment. Swisher and Hirsh (1972) provide an excellent review of this literature pertaining to temporal sequencing abilities of adult aphasic patients.

We can conclude from these studies that a deficit in the performance of sequencing tasks certainly appears to be concomitant with adult aphasia. But whether a deficit in sequencing is a primary impairment in adult aphasia, is specific to the auditory modality, or is positively correlated with the degree of language impairment was still open to debate. Efron hypothesized in 1963 that when the speech rate exceeds the capacity of the aphasic to sequence properly, complete failure of communication on the receptive side might result.

However, both Holmes (1965) and Edwards and Auger (1965) have argued that many aphasics who require long intervals to determine auditory temporal order nevertheless show adequate language comprehension. Efron suggests that this is possibly due to reliance on contextual cues, redundancy in language, and other benefits of long and successful premorbid exposure to language. Such benefits from previously successful experience with language, however, are not available to the developmentally dysphasic child and indeed developmental dysphasic children have also been found to be severely impaired in their ability to make temporal order judgments. Lowe and Campbell (1965) studied children they classified as "aphasoid" using the same methods originally employed by Efron (1963) and found similar results.

Each of the many studies that have investigated temporal order in the auditory perception of patients with communicative disabilities has concluded that a sequencing disorder might underlie these patients speech impairment. But did these experiments, in fact, demonstrate a *primary* sequencing disorder? In order to sequence accurately a rapidly presented two-element stimulus pair, one must first perceive the two elements as separate rather than fused and then discriminate the two as different from each other and identify them. In the previous experiments with both normal and language-impaired subjects, investigators unfortunately failed to ensure that subjects could perform both of these more primary perceptual tasks as the ISI was reduced to establish the limit of "sequencing ability." In all the "sequencing impairments" reported, subjects were allowed to respond only as to which of two stimulus items presented sequentially occurred first. It is conceivable that subjects could respond correctly in this task by attending to the first signal only. If this were in fact the case, one cannot be assured that these subjects perceived the two elements of the sequence as separate rather than fused and that they were able to discriminate the two as different from each other. Thus, although it is clear that these language-impaired patients have some form of temporal processing difficulties, it is still unclear from these studies whether subjects' failure to respond correctly to signals presented rapidly in succession is indicative of an inability to discriminate between the stimulus items at rapid rates of presentation or an inability to perceive their temporal order. (In addition to this general methodological criticism of sequencing experiments, these studies have also been criticized on several theoretical grounds. See Rees 1973.)

More important, investigators have failed to establish a positive correlation between the perceptual sequencing disorders of language-impaired subjects and their degree of language comprehension impairment. (Efron 1963; Holmes 1965; Edwards and Auger 1965). Thus even if a basic perceptual difficulty can be isolated in language-impaired individuals, there is little evidence from these studies to indicate that these problems are directly related to the language disability.

My own previous work has been directed at solving some of these problems (Tallal 1973; Tallal and Piercy 1973 1974 1975). In order to understand the relationship between basic perceptual disorders and language disorders, it seemed necessary to move away from the previously used experimental paradigms. A new operant experimental method that enables subjects to report in detail exactly what they perceived in a nonverbal manner was devised.

Using these new experimental methods, several studies with computer-generated complex nonverbal signals have demonstrated that a well-defined group of children with specific language delay (developmental dysphasics) are impaired in their ability to report the temporal sequence of rapidly presented auditory signals (Tallal 1973). This finding confirmed the work of other investigators previously cited. However, unlike the results of previous investigators, and most important, these children also showed equally inferior discrimination of sound quality of these rapidly presented auditory stimuli, a dysfunction that must be more primary to their sequencing difficulty (Tallal and Piercy 1974). This deficit was demonstrated by systematically varying the demands made on auditory processing by altering the duration of the ISI between two complex nonverbal tones presented in sequence while holding the duration of the tones constant.

The same language-disordered subjects and controls were also tested for their ability to perceive additional binary sequences of nonverbal stimuli in the auditory modality and the visual modality using the same operant techniques (Tallal and Piercy 1973). Performance was studied in relation to the duration of stimulus elements, the interval between elements, and the number of elements in a sequence. No significant differences between groups were observed on any of the visual tests. However on the auditory tests the language-impaired subjects, but not the controls, were adversely affected by decreases in the duration of the stimulus elements, decreases in the interval between elements, and increases in the number of elements. The total duration of the stimulus patterns correlated significantly ($r_s = 0.89$) with the performance of these children. For example, these same children could adequately respond to two- and three-element sequences at slow rates of presentation (stimulus tones 250 milliseconds (msec) in duration) but were incapable of responding correctly to the same nonverbal stimuli presented at more rapid rates. These children with developmental language delay are thus incapable of responding correctly to acoustic information presented at a rapid rate and the possibility was considered that this auditory perceptual impairment might underlie their language impairment.

STUDIES WITH SYNTHETIC SPEECH
How could a defect in processing rapidly changing acoustic information affect the speech perception abilities of language-disordered patients? As Cutting and Pisoni described in their paper, recent basic research in speech synthesis and perception has demonstrated that vowels and certain consonants have different spectral features and are processed differently by normal subjects. These basic differences in phoneme perception have been attributed to the differential duration of the critical formant information of these two classes of speech sounds, as well as their differently shaped formants. For the stop consonants there appears to be a relatively complex relationship between the phoneme and its auditory representations. An essential acoustic cue is a rapidly changing spectrum provided by the formant transitions. Further, these transitional components are relatively short in duration (approximately 50 msec). On the other hand, the major cue for the synethetic vowels used in perceptual experiments is the steady-state frequencies of the first three formants, which have relatively long durations (approximately 250 msec) and remain constant over the entire length of the stimulus (Fry et al. 1962; Liberman et al. 1967).

The results of our previous experiments demonstrated that, unlike normal children, children with developmental language delay are incapable of processing nonverbal stimuli presented at rapid rates but can process the same stimuli at slower rates of presentation. On the hypothesis that impaired auditory processing of rapidly changing acoustic cues in speech is a primary disability of language-impaired children, it was predicted that these children would show no impairment in discriminating steady-state vowels (for example, / ɛ / and / æ/) that were the same duration (250 msec) as the nonverbal steady-state tones studied previously with which they have no difficulty, but they would show impaired discrimination of synthesized stop consonants (in consonant-vowel (CV) syllables like /ba/ and

/da/) that differed only in the initial 43 msec transition components (although the syllables had the same total duration of 250 msec as the steady-state vowels).

This hypothesis was examined using the same subjects and procedures as in the previous experiments but with substitution in one instance of synthesized vowels and in another of synthesized stop consonants for the previously studied complex nonverbal stimuli (Tallal and Piercy 1974).

The results of these experiments were striking. Discrimination of vowel stimuli by the language-impaired subjects did not differ significantly from controls or from their own discrimination of nonverbal auditory stimuli of the same duration on any of the perceptual or serial memory tasks studied. Performance by these children clearly does not deteriorate simply as a consequence of changing from nonverbal to verbal auditory stimuli when both are of a steady-state character. However, the results with synthesized stop consonants were entirely different. On all tasks studied, discrimination of consonant stimuli by the language-impaired subjects was significantly inferior both to their own discrimination of vowel and nonverbal stimuli and to that of their matched controls.

Further experiments showed that the limiting factor underlying the inferior performance of these language-disordered children on the consonant tasks was the duration of the rapidly changing initial portion of the acoustic spectrum. In these experiments the initial formant transitions of the same stop consonants (/ba/ and /da/) were extended (by use of a speech synthesizer) from 43 to 95 msec while maintaining the total length of the stop consonant at 250 msec. The ability of language-disordered children to discriminate between the different consonants, incorporating transitions of this longer duration, was now found to be unimpaired. It is important to note that normal children still perceived these "extended" consonants as /ba/ and /da/. The language-disordered children were able to perform as well as the controls on both the discrimination and sequencing of these same stop consonants once the formant transitions had been extended in time (Tallal and Piercy 1975). The potential therapeutic value of this specialized "stretching" technique, which allows these children to discriminate previously indiscriminable speech sounds, is an exciting area now under study.

In summary, these studies with language-impaired children demonstrate that it is the brief duration of acoustic information that results in their inability to identify and discriminate certain phonemes, such as stop consonants. These same children are, however, unimpaired in their ability to identify and discriminate phonemes that do not incorporate rapidly changing acoustic information, such as isolated steady-state vowels. Furthermore, the same previously indiscriminable stop consonants are discriminated by these language-impaired children when the duration over which the critical acoustic information occurred is extended by use of a speech synthesizer.

RELATION BETWEEN SPEECH PERCEPTION AND SPEECH PRODUCTION

If a primary cause of the observed gross speech disorder of these children is a failure to perceive certain speech sounds, then it might be supposed that these same speech sounds would be produced incorrectly or omitted in their speech. This hypothesis was also investigated (Stark, Tallal, and Curtiss 1975; Tallal, Stark, and Curtiss 1976).

Language-impaired and matched control children were tested for their ability to imitate the following sounds produced by the examiner: isolated steady-state vowels such as /æ/ and /ɛ/ (these are not the same as vowels in word context, as such vowels rarely reach the steady-state spectral pattern), stop consonants in consonant-vowel syllables (such as /bɛ/, /dɛ/), stop consonants in consonant-vowel-consonant nonsense syllables (such as bɛk, dɛg), and stop consonants in clusters (such as blɛ, prɛ). Second subjects were required to produce the names of objects that were pictured individually on cards. Single-syllable words comprising stop consonants in the initial and final positions (bed, cup), as well as words comprising primarily vowels (eye, ear), diphthongs, and nasals (knife, nose), were pictured. Subjects responses were recorded on magnetic tape and later transcribed phonetically by two independent listeners.

The results of this study showed that the control children were able to produce isolated vowels, nasals, stop consonants, and consonant clusters equally well. For the language-impaired subjects, production of isolated vowels was also within normal limits (just as their perception of these speech sounds has previsously been shown to be). However, their production of stop consonants, both singly and in clusters, was grossly impaired. The relationship between speech perceptual impairment and speech production impairment is even clearer when the errors of the individual language-impaired children are examined.

Of the group studied in the perceptual experiments, five of the twelve subjects were unimpaired in their discrimination of stop consonant-vowel syllables when they were presented one at a time. The remaining seven subjects were unable to discriminate these phonemes adequately. The perceptually impaired children were significantly poorer than the controls and perceptually unimpaired children on all four measures of speech production studied. Furthermore, their pattern of impairment matched what might be expected from their perceptual abilities, that is, the production of isolated vowels and nasals was significantly less impaired than that of stop consonants and particularly stops in clusters. In comparison, the unimpaired group performed as well as normal control subjects on the production of isolated vowels and stop consonants. They were also normal in their production of nasals, although the perception of nasals by language-impaired children has not as yet been investigated.

These findings suggest that the speech production impairment of language-impaired children mirrors their speech perceptual abilities. Those speech sounds incorporating rapid spectral changes that are critical for their perception are most difficult for these children to perceive and are also most often misproduced. The analysis of the patterns of confusions in the speech production errors of dysphasic children has led to several interesting observations that we are pursuing further with new lists of words. These studies should enable us to understand in more detail the interrelationship between perception and production impairments in language-impaired children.

Temporal Processing, Speech Perception, and Hemispheric Asymmetry
Previous findings strongly support the hypothesis that some developmental language disorders may result from a primary impairment in auditory temporal analysis. However, one of the major criticisms of the hypothesis that deficits in auditory perception are critically involved in some language disabilities has been the contention that nonverbal and verbal auditory processing occur in different hemispheres of the brain (Milner 1971). One of the most basic assumptions related to hemisphere asymmetry is that the left cerebral hemisphere is predominantly involved in language processing for most normal people and the right hemisphere is involved in nonverbal acoustic processing.

The dichotic stimulation technique has been used to show that when two different acoustic signals are presented simultaneously to a listener, one to each ear, most normal listeners are more accurate in perceiving the verbal stimuli presented to the right ear. Kimura suggested that the right ear advantage (REA) for dichotically presented verbal material indicates that this material is being processed in the left hemisphere (see Kimura 1967 for a discussion of this phenomenon).

New computerized techniques that allow for synthesizing speech while selectively controlling various acoustic variables have been used in an attempt to understand how speech is distinguished from nonspeech and why it is processed in the left hemisphere. It has been demonstrated that not all classes of speech sounds produce an equally strong REA when they are presented dichotically. Cutting (1974) demonstrated that the largest REA is produced when stop consonants (/b, d, g, p, t, k/) were presented in pairs dichotically; liquids (such as /l/ and /r/) produce a less strong REA and steady-state isolated vowels (such as /æ/ and /ɛ/) do not produce any REA.

The magnitude of the right ear advantage has been directly related to the degree of verbal encodedness, in other words, the degree to which speech sounds undergo context-dependent acoustic variation (Haggard 1971). Furthermore, the degree of encodedness of classes of speech sounds has also been shown to be related to the extent to which these sounds are perceived categorically, that is, the degree to which two acoustically different speech sounds identified as belonging to the same speech category can be discriminated (see Liberman et al. 1967 for review).

Interestingly, highly encoded phonemes are also characterized by very abrupt changes in frequency over time. Thus the magnitude of the REA Cutting described for stop consonants, liquids, and vowels, in addition to being correlated with the degree of encodedness of these classes of speech sounds, also correlates with the rapidity of frequency changes in these speech sounds. Fujisaki and Kawashima (1970) demonstrated in a series of elegant experiments that the degree to which vowels were perceived categorically depended on their duration. Relatively long-duration, isolated, steady-state vowels, used most often in speech perception experiments, were shown not to be perceived categorically; but the same vowels were perceived categorically if they were very brief in duration (about 20 msec) or presented in a fixed phonemic context. Halperin, Nackshon, and Carmon (1973) were able to demonstrate REA for nonverbal dichotically presented tone sequences containing abrupt changes in frequency or duration. These experiments indicate that the degree of speech lateralization may be related to the duration over which the critical acoustic aspects occur within certain sounds. Despite these few excellent studies, however, most evidence continues to favor the hypothesis that the REA indicates specific verbal material must be processed in the left hemisphere by phonetic feature analyzers and that this lateralization results from processing occurring beyond the level of acoustic analysis (see Liberman 1973).

Our recent finding that subjects with communicative disorders are unable to discriminate speech sounds that incorporate rapidly changing acoustic spectra but can discriminate these same speech sounds when the duration over which the critical acoustic information occurs is extended (Tallal and Piercy 1975) indicates that the processing of rapidly occurring acoustic information may be a critical feature of speech perception.

STUDIES WITH ADULT APHASICS
The hemisphere involved in such processing of rapidly occurring acoustic information could not be established from our studies since there was no history or other direct evidence of specific brain lesions in the children studied. Therefore, in collaboration with Freda Newcombe, these same perceptual abilities were investigated in adult patients who had sustained missile wounds of the brain. The purpose of this study was to investigate whether the very precise pattern of impairment in responding to rapidly presented acoustic information, previously demonstrated for children with developmental language disorders, was also characteristic of adults with acquired aphasia resulting from left hemisphere lesion and whether any impairment in responding to rapidly presented acoustic information was positively correlated with receptive language ability.

The experimental subjects we studied were twenty ex-servicemen who had sustained missile wounds of the brain during World War II or the Korean War. All subjects had a unilateral injury; ten had left hemisphere lesions and ten right hemisphere lesions. Six control subjects were also tested. None of the groups differed significantly in age, general intellectual ability, or hearing acuity.

The ten men with left hemisphere lesions were all considered to show residual dysphasia on detailed psychological testing, although in three cases the dysphasia was only slight. The ten men with right hemisphere lesions had never been diagnosed as dysphasic and showed little, if any, language dysfunction on a wide range of psychological tests. The same stimuli and test procedures used previously in our studies with language-impaired children were employed in this study. In addition, the Token Test of Language Comprehension was administered to all of the subjects.

The results of these studies demonstrated that the pattern of impairment in auditory processing for the left hemisphere lesion group of adult aphasics was similar to that previously demonstrated for children with developmental language disorders. In contrast, only one of the ten right hemisphere lesioned subjects demonstrated difficulty with these perceptual tasks and there was a very high positive correlation ($r_s = 0.83$) between the degree of language comprehension impairment of these adult aphasics and their ability to respond correctly to rapidly changing verbal and nonverbal acoustic stimuli. It is important to note that not all the left hemisphere lesion patients showed the same pattern of impairment. Those patients who had a marked expressive language impairment but did not have diffi-culty in receptive language were not impaired on our perceptual tests. Further-more, although the procedure of extending the duration of the formant transitions within the CV syllables studied (/ba/, /da/) was beneficial in improving the discrim-ination performance of some of these men, the most severely impaired subjects (in both perception and language comprehension) were not helped by this pro-cedure. The results of this study strongly suggest that impairment in responding to rapidly changing acoustic information is, in most cases, concomitant with recep-tive language impairment, both being most likely to result from selective left hemi-sphere lesions.

Other recent studies with adult aphasics also lend support to this conclusion. Lackner and Teuber (1973) report that performance on an elementary percep-tual task of two-click dichotic fusion was significantly impaired by left hemisphere but not by right hemisphere lesions. Impaired fusion thresholds in this study were characteristic of subjects who had left hemisphere lesions and were also dysphasic. Albert and Bear (1973) also reported impaired temporal fusion thresholds in a patient with a severe comprehension impairment and word deafness resulting from left hemisphere dysfunction. Their studies, using auditory evoked potentials, suggested although there was intact brain stem processing of rapid nonlinguistic two-click stimuli, there was a failure of the higher level binaural summation in the left temporal lobe. These authors concluded that damage to the left hemisphere impairs temporal resolution of acoustic nonverbal stimuli.

I would like to emphasize, however, that I am certainly not suggesting this is the only deficit that aphasic patients have or that all patients with language disabilities show this same pattern of impairment. For example, Blumstein et al. (1976) have very recently demonstrated that there may be several different subgroups of adult aphasic patients who are characterized by, among other things, their pattern of acoustic and phonetic processing disabilities. However, for patients who do demonstrate this pattern of auditory temporal processing impairment, Cutting and Pisoni's microlevel model of normal speech perception may be helpful in delineating the precise mechanisms underlying these patients' disorder, as well as in formulating future research questions.

FURTHER STUDIES OF TEMPORAL PROCESSING IMPAIRMENT
Our results seem to implicate malfunctioning of those processing levels prior to stage 2 (phonetic feature analysis) in the recognition device. That is, these subjects seem to have difficulty at the stage of auditory feature analysis and particularly with analysis of temporal properties. Whether all aspects of temporal analysis or only specific aspects of temporal analysis are affected remains to be determined, however. Some of the present studies that I am now doing in collaboration with Rachel Stark should help to clarify this issue. Language-impaired children are being examined for their ability to discriminate between various pairs of speech sounds that differ in specific temporal cues. For example, one such distinctive pair

differs only in their voice onset time (/da/ versus /ta/); another pair (/sa/ versus /sta/) differs only in the duration of the silent interval between the offset of frequency noise and the onset of vowel formants. Other stimulus contrasts we are now studying include steady-state vowels of various durations as well as stop consonant vowel syllables (/ba/ versus /da/) with various duration formant transitions.

Recent studies of patients with sensorineural deafness may also be helpful in interpreting our results. Daneher and Pickett (1975) described two types of masking that appear to reduce the discriminability of the second formant transitions in stop consonants. The first is upward spread of masking in which the low-frequency components of the first formant mask the higher frequency components of the second formant. This type of masking is of peripheral origin and is most probably due to elevated sensory thresholds (preliminary auditory analysis stage). In the second form, backward masking, which might be applicable to our own results, the steady-state portion of the vowel in CV syllables interferes with the detectability of the initial formant transitions. In our studies, language-disordered patients were impaired in their ability to discriminate between stop consonant stimuli that differed only in the direction and extent of the second formant transitions. However, when the duration over which this information occurred was extended, their performance improved. The total duration of the stimulus was not changed. Thus by extending the duration of the formant transitions, two aspects of the signal were actually altered: the duration of the formant transition was increased, allowing for additional time for coding information in sensory information store, and the duration of the steady-state vowel was decreased, reducing the possible negative effects of backward masking. Therefore we cannot at this time be certain exactly which stages of processing are impaired in this population. Further experiments are necessary to clarify these issues.

Summary and Conclusions

The results of many of the studies presented here support the hypothesis that some language disorders may result at least in part from an impairment at the auditory feature analysis stage of speech perception. More specifically, many language-impaired patients, both children and adults, seem to have particular difficulty analyzing rapidly changing acoustic information. These data further indicate that the degree and pattern of perceptual impairment demonstrated by such patients is highly correlated with their degree of language comprehension impairment and, for children, their pattern of speech production errors, too. Finally, these data demonstrate that the widely accepted hypothesis that nonverbal acoustic information is processed in the right hemisphere of the brain and verbal information in the left (or dominant) hemisphere is grossly oversimplified. The studies reported here suggest that the dominant hemisphere must play a primary role in the analysis of specific rapid temporal acoustic features, whether verbal or nonverbal, and that such analysis is critically involved in the development and maintenance of language.

Could a problem in the perception of rapid transitions, such as those incorporated in stop consonants, result in a global language disability? Liberman et al.

(1967) pointed out that two unique characteristics of speech perception are the rate at which it can be perceived and the accuracy with which temporal order information is preserved. It has been established that the rate at which speech can be comprehended (400 words per minuut or approximately 30 phonemes per second) without temporal order confusions (Orr, Friedman and Williams 1965) far surpasses the temporal resolving power for nonverbal stimuli (Hirsh 1959).

Recent studies by Dorman, Cutting, and Raphael (1975) demonstrate, at least in part, why the analysis of rapidly changing temporal acoustic features may play such an important role in speech perception. They found in a series of elegant studies that the temporal order perception of phoneme segments in running speech is much superior to the temporal order perception of concatenated speech sounds (that is, a vowel series with no transitions). They demonstrated that the more rapid rates of temporal order perception that are possible in running speech may be due largely to the presence of formant transitions. These authors concluded that whereas the first function of transitions is to carry phonetic information and the second is to carry it in such a manner that there is parallel transmission of the phonetic segments (see Liberman et al. 1967), a third function is to bind together phonetic segments so that at rapid transmission rates the temporal order of speech may be preserved (see also Cole and Scott 1973).

It is precisely in this third area, the analysis of rapidly changing formant transitions and the perception of temporal order, that many of the children and adults with language disorders that we have studied are most impaired. According to the recent findings by Dorman, Cutting, and Raphael, we can hypothesize that for these language-impaired patients the misperception of rapid transitions may give rise not only to the misperception of specific phonemes but also, and certainly more important, disturbance in the whole temporal sequencing and segmentation of the speech stream. Such a disability would grossly disrupt speech perception and result in a global language disability.

This hypothesis would predict that an effective therapy to employ with such language-impaired patients might be to slow down the rate of presentation of speech input. Our own studies indicate that the use of synthetic speech with formant transitions that are extended in duration significantly improves dysphasics' discrimination abilities (Tallal and Piercy 1975). Other studies have shown that slowing down the rate of speech input by inserting silent pauses between phonemes and syllables but not words within sentences all serve to improve the comprehension performance of aphasic patients (Sheehan, Aseltine, and Edwards 1973; Salvatore 1975). Although a great deal more research is needed along similar lines, this certainly seems to be an area that holds promise for improved diagnostic and therapeutic techniques for use in the clinic and classroom.

Cutting and Pisoni (this volume) suggested that considerations of speech without regard for thehigher processes of language is, if not an empty pursuit, certainly one which will mislead both the basic and applied researcher. The results of our studies with patients with language disabilities lead us to conclude that, conversely, to consider language without regard for the primary processes involved in speech perception may be equally misleading for both basic and applied researchers.

I would like to conclude by asking all concerned to keep in mind that going from basic to applied research is a process. Cutting and Pisoni (this volume) have argued that processes are not instantaneous; they take time, and occur in a series of stages. Some of the work that has been done in the initial stages of going from basic to applied research has been discussed in this paper. It is sincerely hoped that future research efforts in this area, together with that other essential ingredient—time—will bring us closer to the applications of our efforts that are so urgently needed in clinics and classrooms.

References

Albert, L. A., and Bear, D. 1973. Time to understand a case study of word deafness with reference to the role of time in auditory comprehension. *Brain, 97,* 373–384.

Benton, A. L. 1964. Developmental aphasia and brain damage. *Cortex, 1,* 40–52.

Blesser, B. 1974. Discussion: Perceptual and cognitive strategies. In R. E. Stark (Ed.) *Sensory Capabilities of Hearing-Impaired Children.* Baltimore: Universtiy Park Press, 129–153.

Blumstein, S. E., Cooper, W. E., Zurif, E., and Caramazza, A. 1975. Levels of speech perception dissociated in aphasia. Paper presented at the Academy of Aphasia.

Broadbent, D. E. 1974. Division of function and integration of behavior. In F. O. Schmitt and F. G. Worden (Eds.) *The Neurosciences: Third Study Program.* Cambridge, Mass.: The MIT Press. 31–41.

Cole, R. A., and Scott, B. 1973. Perception of temporal order in speech: The role of vowel transitions. *Canadian Journal of Psychology, 27,* 441–449.

Curtiss, B. C., Stark, R. E., and Tallal, P. 1975. Perception and production of stop consonants in developmental dysphasic children. *Journal of the American Speech and Hearing Association, 17,* 657. (Abstract).

Cutting, J. E. 1974. Two left-hemisphere mechanisms in speech perception. *Perception and Psychophysics, 16,* 601–612.

Cutting, J. E., and Pisoni, D. B. This volume. An information-processing approach to speech perception.

Danaher, E. M., and Pickett, J. M. 1975. Some masking effects produced by low frequency vowel formants in persons with sensorineural loss. *Journal of Speech and Hearing Research, 18,* 261–271.

Dorman, M. F., Cutting, J. E., and Raphael, L. J. 1975. Perception of temporal order in vowel sequences with and without formant transitions. *Journal of Experimental Psychology: Human Perception and Performance, 104,* 121–129.

Edwards, A. E., and Auger, R. 1965. The effect of aphasia on the perception of precedence. *Proceedings of the 73rd Annual Convention of the American Psychological Association,* 207–208.

Efron, R. 1963. Temporal perception, aphasia and deja vu. *Brain, 86,* 403–424.

Eisenson, J. 1972. *Aphasia in Children.* London: Harper and Row.

Fry, D. B., Abramson, A. S., Eimas, P. D., and Liberman, A. M. 1962. The identification and discrimination of synthetic vowels. *Language and Speech, 5,* 171–189.

Fugisaki, H., and Kawashima, T. 1970. Some experiments on speech perception and a model for the perceptual mechanism. *Annual Report of the Engineering Research Institute*, University of Tokyo, *29*, 207–214.

Haggard, M. P. 1971. Encoding and the REA for speech signals. *Quarterly Journal of Experimental Psychology*, *23*, 34–43.

Halperin, Y., Nackshon, S., and Carmon, A. 1973. Shift of ear superiority in dichotic listening to temporally patterned nonverbal stimuli. *Journal of the Acoustical Society of America*, *53*, 46–50.

Hardy, W. G. 1965. On language disorders in young children: A reorganization of thinking. *Journal of Speech and Hearing Disturbances*, *8*, 3–16.

Hirsh, I. J. 1959. Auditory perception of temporal order. *Journal of the Acoustical Society of America*, *31*, 759–767.

Holmes, H. L. 1965. Disordered perception of auditory sequences in aphasia. Unpublished thesis, Harvard University.

Kimura, D. 1967. Functional asymmetry of the brain in dichotic listening. *Cortex*, *3*, 157–178.

Lackner, J. R., and Teuber, H. L. 1973. Alterations in auditory fusion thresholds after cerebral injury in man. *Neuropsychologia*, *11*, 409–415.

Liberman, A. M. 1974. The specialization of the language hemisphere. In F. O. Schmitt and F. G. Worden (Eds.) *The Neurosciences: Third Study Program*. Cambridge, Mass.: The MIT Press, 43–56.

Liberman, A. M., Cooper, F. S., Shankweiler, D. P., and Studdert-Kennedy, M. 1967. Perception of the speech code. *Psychological Review*, *74*, 431–461.

Lowe, A. D., and Campbell, R. A. 1965. Temporal discrimination in aphasoid and normal children. *Journal of Speech and Hearing Research*, *8*, 313–314.

McGinnis, M. 1963. *Aphasic Children*. Washington, D.C.: A. G. Bell Association for the Deaf, Inc.

Milner, B. 1971. Interhemispheric differences in the localization of psychological processes in man *British Medical Bulletin*, *27*, 272–277.

Monsees, E. K. 1961. Aphasia in children. *Journal of Speech and Hearing Disorders*, *26*, 83–86.

Orr, D. B., Friedman, H. L., and Williams, J. C. 1965. Trainability of listening comprehension of speeded discourse. *Journal of Educational Psychology*, *56*, 148–156.

Rees, N. S. 1973. Auditory processing factors in language disorders: The view from Procrustes' bed. *Journal of Speech and Hearing Disorders*, *38*, 304–315.

Orton, S. T. 1937. *Reading, Writing and Speech Problems in Children*. New York: Norton.

Salvatore, A. P. 1975. The effects of pause duration on the sentence comprehension of aphasic individuals. *ASHA*, *17*, 629 (Abstract).

Sheehan, J. G., Aseltine, S., and Edwards, A. E. 1973. Aphasic comprehension of time spacing. *Journal of Speech and Hearing Research*, *16*, 650–657.

Stark, R. E. 1972. Some features of the vocalizations of young deaf children. In J. F. Bosma (ed.) *Third Symposium on Oral Sensation and Perception: The Mouth of the Infant*. Springfield, Ill: Charles C. Thomas, 431–443.

―――. 1974. *Sensory Capabilities of Hearing-Impaired Children*. Baltimore: University Park Press.

Stark, R. E., Tallal, P., and Curtiss, B. 1975. Speech perception and production errors in dysphasic children. *Journal of the Acoustical Society of America, 57*, 524 (Abstract).

Swisher, L., and Hirsh, I. J. 1972. Brain damage and the ordering of two temporally successive stimuli. *Neuropsychology, 10*, 137–151.

Tallal, P. 1973. Auditory perception in childhood developmental dysphsia. Unpublished Ph.D. dissertation, University of Cambridge, England.

Tallal, P., and Piercy, M. 1973. Developmental aphasia: Impaired rate of non-verbal processing as a function of sensory modality. *Neuropsychologia, 11*, 389–398.

―――. 1974. Developmental aphasia: Rate of auditory processing and selective impairment of consonant perception. *Neuropsychologia, 12*, 83–94.

―――. 1975. Developmental aphasia: The perception of brief vowels and extended stop consonants. *Neuropsychologia, 13*, 69–74.

Tallal, P., Stark, R., and Curtiss, B. 1976. Relation between speech perception and speech production impariment in children with developmental dysphasia. *Brain and Language, 3*, 305–317.

General Discussion of Papers by Cutting and Pisoni and Tallal

Information, Time, and Information Processing

The discussion of the paper by Cutting and Pisoni centered largely around the concepts of information and information processing. Jenkins distinguished between information processing in the broad sense and the narrow sense and expressed a concern that the latter had some problems in interpretation. Information processing in the broad sense involves the investigation of the kinds of stimulus energy that provide information for the perceiver, how that information is detected, how it is transformed, and so on. Students of speech and language are all interested in this endeavor. However, information processing (in the narrow sense) is often equated with the use of reaction time studies to ask questions about psychological processing. Jenkins gave an example of a study that demonstrates the danger of misinterpretation with such an approach. The investigator conducted a factorial study using a reaction time measure and then assigned average times to each factor. The experimenter interpreted his results in terms of a processing analysis that included a "stage" of processing labeled "sex differences." Jenkins cautioned that the results of studies on stages of processing are often specific to the experimental paradigm used and the particular laboratory setting. When one tries to replicate the results using converging operations, the stages change.

In discussing the relationship between information, time, and processing, Jenkins emphasized that the important information in speech is displayed over time. Early research on the speech stream tried to isolate invariants within single slices of time—that is, energy at some particular frequency region within some very narrow span of time— that served as "cues" for the phonemes. In this approach, perceptual and memorial processes are postulated to put the pieces back together to form the linguistic message (for example, phenomes from acoustic features). Jenkins asserted that this makes the mistake of Zeno's paradox, which considers the flight of an arrow. If time is sliced fine enough, the arrow stands still in the air; this creates the problem of how the arrow gets from the archer to the target. Psychologists are in the same predicament; they are trying to explain how things get back together that came apart only because they took them apart in their analysis.

Jenkins stressed the need for more research that looks for invariants of a very abstract sort specified over time rather than invariants at particular time slices and particular frequency regions. He pointed to the work of James Gibson in visual perception as an example of how abstract, higher order invariants (such as visual flow fields) can be specified very precisely such that a display can be synthesized in which viewers see themselves being propelled through space in the appropriate direction and so on (See Warren 1976). But the specification is not in any single snapshot; rather it involves changes over time that the viewer detects.

Liberman elaborated on the invariance problem and the question of what constitutes information in speech. He stated he once believed that context-conditioned variation (that is, lack of invariance at the segmental level) was merely a function of the physiological constraints of articulation and as such was "noise."

The job of the perceptual apparatus was to "hear through" this variation and arrive at the canonical forms of the phonemes. He now believes that this variation conveys information, that is, *allophonic variation conveys important information about phonetic structure*. Information provided by this variation is not just about what the segments are, but about in what order they come, what the stress is, and where the syllable boundaries are.

He used as an example the fricatives /s/ and /ʃ/. They are in one sense relatively invariant phones (in terms of the frequency range of aperiodic energy); it is possible to perceive synthetic tokens of /s/ and /ʃ/ on the basis of absolutely invariant information. Yet for naturally produced fricatives there is evidence for a great deal of context-conditioned variation in duration, and to some extent in spectral composition, as a function of phonemic context, stress, rate of speaking, and other variables. In other words, the information is not ordinarily invariant (in any simple sense) and the lack of invariance at the segmental level is important for perception of phonological structure in the linguistic message. This is one of the reasons for the difficulty in synthesis with the fricatives; important information has not been incorporated. More generally, Liberman asserted that the chief difficulty with speech that is synthesized by rule is that too many corners have been cut—too many of the cues are invariant—and this imposes a hardship on the listener, who is robbed of much important information.

Auditory and Phonetic Levels of Processing
The discussion turned to more specific comments about the experimental paradigms presented by Cutting and Pisoni. Many of the concerns centered around the interpretation of the evidence for auditory and phonetic levels of processing. Liberman agreed with Cutting that the research using the selective adaptation paradigm indicated that the phenomena reflected processing at the auditory level. But he added that the recent research of Ades (in press) and others suggests that the adaptation effect is voice specific. If these effects are to be attributed to some kind of (auditory) feature detectors, then every listener would have to possess separate sets of detectors for every speaker. Unless there is some reasonable limit placed on how many feature detectors are postulated, the concept becomes untenable and falls of its own weight. This suggests that there must be some simpler way to conceptualize the problem.

Liberman went on to discuss the explanation of categorical phenomena in terms of the auditory feature stage of processing. He cited the study by Cutting and Rosner (1974) in which a distinction between nonspeech stimuli—a "plucked" sound and a "bowed" sound—was perceived categorically. The distinction is cued acoustically by the duration from onset to full amplitude or rise-time of the singal. The same distinction in synthetic speech signals is sufficient to differentiate the fricative /ʃ/ and the affricate /tʃ/ as in "shop" and "chop"; these stimuli are also perceived categorically. Thus the categorical results for both nonspeech and speech distinctions could be accounted for by an auditory feature detector for rise-time.

However, it can be shown that whether one hears "shop" or "chop" depends on four or five different interdependent cues. The distinction can be influenced by the duration of the aperiodic energy (frication noise) or the rise time (as in the pluck-bow effect). Further, if the phrase "Now say shop" is recorded, the perception can be changed from the fricative /ʃ/ to the affricate /tʃ/ by introducing exactly the right silent interval between the "say" and the "shop." In other words, the duration of the silent interval preceding the consonant can determine its perception as a fricative or an affricate. An explanation of this result in terms of an auditory detector would have to include a process whereby the setting of the detector (that is, the acoustic parameter values to which it is optimally sensitive) is changed as a consequence of something that happened prior to the frication.

Liberman described a further level of complexity found in this experiment. Starting from the situation in which the "now say" and the "shop" are separated in time and the listener reports hearing "now say chop" if the "now say" is presented in one loudspeaker and the "shop" is presented in another speaker separated in space, the listener now hears "shop" for all temporal intervals. That is, if listeners have reason to believe they are listening to two vocal tracts and not one, the phenomenon breaks down and they hear "now say shop" all the time.

Liberman asserted that an interesting question was whether one would obtain the same sort of interdependent phenomena with the nonspeech signals. He suggested that while there may be auditory feature detectors that are used for speech as well as nonspeech distinctions, auditory processes will not be sufficient to explain phonetic perception—the way we perceive the difference between fricatives and affricates under all these conditions. Liberman and his colleagues are currently testing whether the acoustic variables for the fricative-affricate distinction are perceived categorically and whether the categorical boundary is moved predictably as a consequence of changes in any one of these factors. If it is, it would not be easy to say that in these instances categorical perception depends upon the auditory features alone. It would more likely be at the phonetic level.

Along similar lines, Labov pointed out that an explanation of categorical perception in terms of property detectors must take into account the lability of the phenomenon as a function of dialect differences. He has been conducting some studies that show differences in categorization and discrimination of vowel continua (/æ/ to /ɛ/ to /I/) between people with western dialects and those from New York and Philadelphia. Perception appears thus to be influenced by social experience. (See Labov, this volume, and also Strange and Jenkins, forthcoming, for a discussion of the role of linguistic experience in categorical perception.)

The Cutting-Pisoni Model

With respect to the specific model proposed by Cutting and Pisoni, Zurif pointed out that the model, at least as used by Tallal to describe results with clinical populations, implies a serial flow of information from auditory to phonetic to higher levels of language processing. Deficits at the phonetic level imply that higher level analyses are not possible. He cautioned that studies of comprehension that do not allow the subjects to use plausibility constraints provided by syntactic information are not fair tests of the notion of serial flow of information in understanding utterances. Would subjects that could not represent facts at the phonetic level necessarily show deficits at the syntactic level if given materials that were sufficiently rich to provide for this comparison?

Crowder commented that the Cutting-Pisoni (this volume) model as presented in figure 3 (microlevel model) seems to make the perception of stop consonants impossible. Cutting equates sensory information store with echoic memory, as studied by Crowder. Crowder has found that while this kind of memory system works well for vowels, it is very poor for stop consonants (see Crowder, this volume). Since in the Cutting-Pisoni model sensory information store is placed at a very early stage in the flow diagram, this would preclude the perception of stop consonants. Crowder and Cutting agreed that this was a problem with the model but offered no solution.

Applications of Reading Research

With respect to the work of I. Liberman and others reported by Cutting and Pisoni, Labov mentioned that some researchers (Gleitman and Rozin 1976; Rozin and Gleitman 1976) are currently attempting to apply the information on the relationship between phonology and orthography in developing a system of teaching reading. They have reached the stage where they are ready for commercial testing. When Labov had a chance to observe their system at work in an experimental kindergarten, he was impressed with the rapidity with which readers reached the stage of putting words together by bypassing the consonant-vowel distinction.

Developmental Trends in Temporal Processing

Tallal was asked to elaborate on possible developmental trends in temporal processing by dysphasic children. She presented data from a study (Tallal 1976) that compares the perception of binary sequences of nonverbal auditory stimuli by normal children age four-and-a-half to eight-and-a-half years, normal adults, and dysphasic children (average age eight-and-a-half years). Figure 1 presents errors in performance as a function of temporal interval between stimulus elements. As can be seen in the figure, the performance of the dysphasics does not mirror that of any other group of subjects studied. Errors made by the dysphasics on the short-interval pairs were significantly greater than error rates for even the youngest normal children. For longer interstimulus intervals the dysphasic children performed appropriately for their age group. That is, the dysphasic children are extremely poor, much worse than even the four-year-olds, for temporal intervals up to 150 msec, then they are immediately as good as adults. It is an all-or-none effect, unlike the developmental trends for the normal children. Individual differences in the dysphasic children also show no developmental trend. It is interesting to note, however, that some of these children "grow out" of their impairment.

Temporal Processing by Adult Aphasics

With respect to adult aphasics Tallal mentioned that there seems to be a relation between degree of language impairment and performance on the speech and

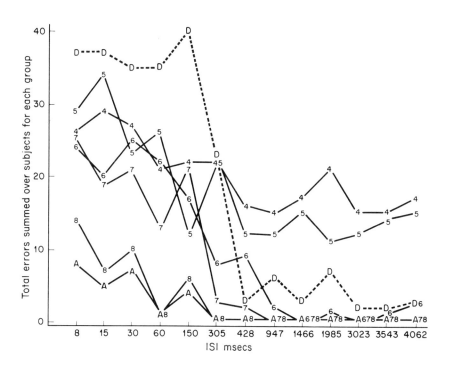

D Dysphasic children
A Normal adult
4 $4\frac{1}{2}$
5 $5\frac{1}{2}$
6 $6\frac{1}{2}$ Year age group
7 $7\frac{1}{2}$
8 $8\frac{1}{2}$

N = 12 subjects in each group

Figure 1. Errors in performance as a function of temporal interval between stimulus elements.

nonspeech temporal tasks. There appears to be a hierarchy; some patients are slightly impaired in a nonverbal domain but do not show impairment on tests of stop consonants. Some are impaired both nonverbally and for stop consonants with normal duration transitions but not for those with slowed transitions. Another group is so severely impaired that they are not helped by the slowed transitions; they are also the most severely impaired in the language comprehension test.

Adult aphasics with expressive language disabilities had no difficulties on the temporal processing tests, but those with receptive language difficulties did. Their degree of receptive language disability seemed to correlate with their degree of difficulty with both the nonverbal and verbal auditory processing tests.

Tallal emphasized that while the temporal disorder illustrated in her studies is certainly not the only difficulty that aphasics have, there is a very consistent pattern of impairment with certain types of patients. She urged that this kind of auditory processing problem for these patients be taken as seriously as is the difficulty in sensation for the deaf patient in investigations of language processing disabilities.

References

Ades, A. E. In press. Source assignment and feature extraction in speech. *Journal of Experimental Psychology: Human Perception and Performance.*

Crowder, R. G. This volume. Language and memory.

Cutting, J. E., and Pisoni, D. B. This volume. An information processing appoach to speech perception.

Cutting, J. E., and Rosner, B. S. 1974. Categories and boundaries in speech and music. *Perception and Psychophysics*, 16, 564–570.

Gleitman, L. R., and Rozin, P. 1976. Structure and acquisition of reading I: Relations between orthographies and the structure of language. In A. S. Reber and D. Scarborough (eds.) *Toward a Psychology of Reading: Proceedings of the CUNY Conference.* Hillsdale, N. J.: L. Erlbaum.

Labov, W. This volume. Gaining access to the dictionary.

Rozin, P., and Gleitman, L. R. 1976. Structure and acquisition II: The reading process and the alphabetic principle. In A. S. Reber and D. Scarborough (Eds.) *Toward a Psychology of Reading: Proceedings of the CUNY Conference.* Hillsdale, N. J.: L. Erlbaum.

Strange, W., and Jenkins, J. J. Forthcoming. The role of linguistic experience in the perception of speech. In H. L. Pick, Jr. and R. D. Walk (eds.) *Perception and Experience.* New York: Plenum Publishing Corp.

Tallal, P. 1976. Rapid auditory processing in normal and disoriented language development. *Journal of Speech and Hearing Research*, 19, 3, 561–571.

Warren, R. 1976. The perception of egomotion. *Journal of Experimental Psychology, Human Perception and Performance*, 3, 448–456.

Physiological Aspects of Speech Production

KATHERINE S. HARRIS

Why Study Speech Production?

Since the theme of this volume is the insight that might be provided by modern research in language to the clinician working in the clinic or school, I should begin with a consideration of what I believe about the characteristics of the clinician's population. I will confine my attention to speech pathology and hope that the problems faced by audiologists are adequately covered by others.

My own particular research interest is in the physiology of speech production, so the application of the research is presumably to the speech production problems of the clinician's population. A preoccupation with articulation and its disorders has recently become unfashionable among speech pathologists; interest has focused on the language- and learning-disabled child and students are more excited by courses in psycholinguistics and syntax than in physiology and phonetics. While this trend probably cannot be reversed, I think we can make a case for the clinical importance of a continuing research commitment to these traditional topics.

In a few clinical populations, particularly the cleft palate group, the profoundly deaf, and the severely dysarthric, the patient's speech is so unintelligible that communication with the world is seriously impaired and remediation of the symptom itself, by whatever means, is a problem of direct importance. While the size of these populations is substantial enough to bring the groups to the attention of makers of health policy, most clients in the case load of the average speech pathologist are far less seriously handicapped. Stamping out voice disorders is not high on anyone's list of national health priorities. However, there is considerable evidence that the importance of voice and articulation disorders may be not only in the symptoms themselves but also in their value as diagnostic signs for other disorders. Well-known examples are hoarseness as an early sign of laryngeal tumor and slurred speech as a symptom of stroke. Learning more about the physiology and neurophysiology of speech production would enable us to make better use of speech symptoms as tools for the diagnosis of structural and neurological damage, as well as to improve symptom treatment per se.

As a field of study, speech production has a curious double nature. On the one hand it is a complicated form of motor behavior, like walking, and can be studied by the same techniques of movement analysis. On the other hand it is the output of the communication system, so that the movements themselves generate acoustic consequences that must engage the perceptual capabilities of the listener to be effective.

Levels of Study of Speech Production

Given that the study of speech production is a topic of general interest, it is perhaps worthwhile to consider how it might be studied by considering an elementary description of the speech production process itself. The listener in hearing speech

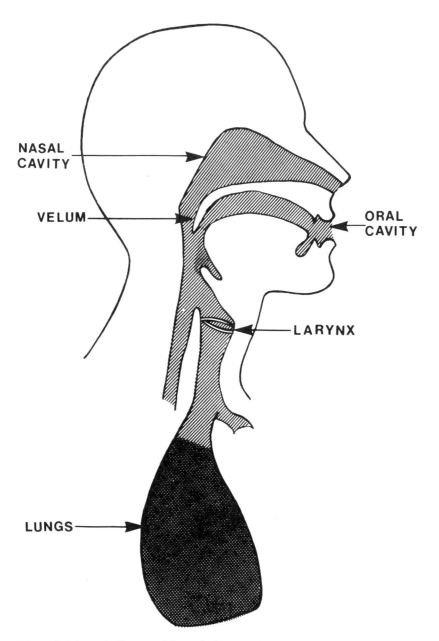

Figure 1. Schematic diagram of the articulatory system.

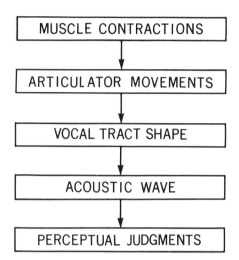

Figure 2. The last stages of the production side of the speech chain.

operates upon an acoustic signal that has been generated by an extremely complicated system. Figure 1 shows a schematic diagram of this system.

The system can be considered to be made up of three parts. The system is driven by energy supplied by the lungs during expiration. When inspiration takes place, the lungs, a pair of elastic, balloonlike structures, are filled with air. Since the walls of the lungs are elastic, they will tend to deflate to a neutral condition, and air can in addition be forced from them by the action of those muscles that control expiration. The larynx acts as a valve that can be moved into place over the expiratory airstream to convert the relatively steady expiratory airflow into puffs of air. The sequence of puffs of air (the volume velocity waveform) excites the upper vocal tract (the oral and nasal airspaces) lying above the larynx. When the velum is lowered, air flows out the nose and mouth; when it is elevated, the nasal airspace is closed off so that air flows out the mouth only. The upper vocal tract acts as a variable acoustic filter on the output of the larynx; its properties as a filter depend on its shape. The shape is controlled by the movements of the articulators. The velum is a muscle mass that acts to connect or shut off the nasal branches of the upper vocal tract from the airspace below. The nasal airspace has an almost constant shape. On the other hand, the oral airspace has a shape that varies considerably depending on the position of the various articulators, such as the tongue, jaw, and lips. The position of the articulators, in turn, is controlled chiefly by the complex interactions of a large number of muscles.

This whole system can be studied at a number of levels, as indicated in figure 2, which can be considered an enlargement of the lower segment of figure 1 in Cutting and Pisoni, this volume. While these levels are closely related to each other, the relations between them are complex. In order to simplify the material to be

discussed somewhat, I will not discuss aerodynamic factors or respiratory phenomena.

Speech disorders are probably most often studied by perceptual means (shown
at the bottom of figure 2)—that is, the observer or therapist listens to the speech
of the subject or client and makes some kind of judgment about the speech. The
most usual kind of judgment is about the phonetic string that the speaker has
conveyed; at a less analytical level, the listener could make a gross judgment that
the speech was normal or defective, either overall or on some kind of unit-by-unit
basis. I will comment on the problem of making judgments of abnormal production by perceptual means later in this paper. With respect to making judgments
about normal speech, I am discussing the characteristics of speech perception
generally, discussed in Cutting and Pisoni's paper in this volume.

Referring again to figure 2, the next level at which speech can be studied is the
level of the acoustic signal. The acoustic signal conveys a great deal of information
about the speech production process itself through recently developed analytic
techniques that are best summarized by Fant (1960). Briefly, the acoustic signal
can be considered the product of a source function and a filter function. The
source function can be directly related to the behavior of the vocal folds and the
filter function can be related to the shape of the upper vocal tract.

A number of authors have suggested the use of the acoustic analysis for the detection of laryngeal pathology. The technique is to use analysis procedures to reveal the source function uncontaminated by the acoustic filtering effects of the
upper vocal tract. The source function can then be used to infer the behavior of
the vocal folds. Variants of this procedure have been proposed by Lieberman
(1963), Rothenberg (1973), Koike and Markel (1975), and Davis (in preparation)
as a technique for early detection of laryngeal pathology; large-scale clinical trials
of these techniques still lie in the future.

Simpler types of acoustic analysis of abnormal voice production have been in
widespread use for some time. One is the analysis of such factors as the average
pitch of patients or clients of various types (for example, Canter's study [1963] of
the speech characteristics of patients with Parkinson's disease).

The filter function, or the positions of the resonant frequencies of the vocal tract,
are fairly well represented in a spectrographic display, although additional analysis procedures, such as linear predictive coding (Markel and Gray 1976) can be
used to estimate the resonant frequencies directly. The relationship between
vocal tract shape and resonant frequencies has been the subject of study since the
time of Helmholtz, but progress has been far more rapid since the Second World
War (see Fant 1960 and the references therein). There are two major limitations
on the use of acoustic techniques for estimating vocal tract shape. First, in spite of
great strides in relating shape to filter function, there are still some unknown factors preventing the verification of a complete model—such as acoustic losses due
to absorption in the tract walls. A more serious problem is that the relationship
between shape and acoustic output is inherently asymmetric—the shape determines
the output, but a given output may result from more than one shape (Stevens and
House 1955). Furthermore, a given shape may result from several equivalent artic-

ulatory postures (Lindblom and Sundberg 1971). Therefore even if the shape could be related unequivocally to the formant positions, an acoustic analysis is an inherently incomplete substitute for physiological observation.

Acoustic analysis has not been widely used as a technique for studying abnormal articulatory movement. There are two general and rather preliminary studies of the dysarthrias using spectrographic analysis (Lehiste 1965; Lindblom, Lubker, and Fritzell 1974). These studies show the usefulness of spectrographic analysis for inferring such articulatory faults as restricted range of articulatory movement as shown by vowel neutralization, abnormal rate of overall articulator movement, and abnormal control of the timing of the onset and offset of voicing. The same types of observations have been made from spectrographic analysis for the speech of deaf talkers. Angelocci, Kopp, and Holbrook (1964) have shown that the vowels of deaf talkers are severely neutralized. In addition, the timing of articulatory movement is grossly abnormal (Monsen 1974), as is transitional movement from consonant to vowel (Monsen 1976). Despite the limitations of the inferences that can be made, acoustic techniques probably deserve more exploration than they have received, particularly because of their totally noninvasive nature.

Referring again to figure 2, the movement of the articulators can be studied. This is difficult because, except for the lips and jaw, they are extraordinarily difficult to observe directly. Direct viewing of the vocal folds as a technique for the study of laryngeal pathology was pioneered by Moore (1938) and von Ledan, Moore, and Timke's (1960) study of high-speed movies. While this work has been useful, the use of the laryngeal mirror makes it impossible to study anything other than sustained phonation; and the task of analyzing any significant number of cases by the technique is laborious because of the necessity of measuring the fold movement on a frame-by-frame basis. Attempts have recently been made to automate the latter procedure.

The limitations on the use of the laryngoscope have been partly overcome by the development of the flexible fiber laryngoscope (Sawashima and Hirose 1968). While it allows the viewing of the larynx during running speech, it does not transmit enough light for examination of single cycles of laryngeal vibration. However, good use of the technique has been made by McCall, Skolnick, and Brewer (1971) in videofluoroscopic examination of the larynx in spasmodic dysphonia.

The flexible fiberscope can also be used to view the velopharyngeal port and has been so used for studying velar height during closure by Bell-Berti and Hirose (1975) and by Ushijima and Hirose (1974). Similar techniques probably will be useful as a substitute for X-ray movies now in common use for assessing the adequacy of cleft palate repair.

The tongue is probably the most important articulator and the most difficult to view directly. The only practical widely used method for viewing the shape of the upper vocal tract and the movement of the articulators is cinefluorography. In the technique, X-ray motion pictures are taken of a sagittal view of the head, usually with salient points marked with pellets. In later analysis, the movies are projected frame by frame and the movement of the articulatory structures tracked by the marking of the pellet positions in successive frames (Kent 1972; Houde 1967).

There are both obvious and not so obvious limitations of this technique. First, the analysis is extremely time consuming, although computer techniques can be used to simplify the measurement problems. Second, a given subject can only be used for a few minutes every six months because of the dangers of exposure to excessive radiation. This limitation precludes the use of a number of factors of experimental design, such as repeated use of the same subject. Because of these limitations there has been inadequate exploration of differences both from individual to individual and from condition to condition.

In spite of these limitations, the description of normal or abnormal articulatory movement taken from X-ray movies is probably the most widely used technique in speech production research today. Much of the development of the technique can be ascribed to the efforts of Moll and his coworkers. Cinefluorography has long been a standard way of assessing the adequacy of velopharyngeal function after cleft repair in clinical research (see, for example, Subtelny, Koepp-Baker, and Subtelny 1961; Moll 1960.) The same methods have been recently used in studying the dysarthrias (Netsell and Kent 1976; Kent and Netsell 1975; Kent, Netsell, and Bauer 1975). Using these techniques, this group has been able to observe the lack of gross disturbance of motor programming in ataxic and paroxysmal dysarthria.

Again referring to figure 2 we see that one can study not only the movement of the articulators but even the control signals that lie behind the movements by studying the electromyographic (EMG) signals to the muscles. Two slightly different approaches have been taken to the recording of EMG signals in speech research. The difference between the approaches can be better understood by discussing the relevant signal at slightly greater length.

The chief cause of articulator movements is the contraction of the attached muscles. Each muscle is made up of a number of fibers that contract by longitudinal sliding of their constituent myofibrils. When this shortening occurs, electrical changes occur in the muscle; these can be picked up by appropriate electrodes and amplifiers. Muscle fibers are grouped into motor units, each consisting of a neuron with its axon and the muscle fibers it supplies. The muscle fibers of a given motor unit contract almost simultaneously, and the recorded electrical changes will consist of a complicated series of positive and negative waves whose precise size and shape will depend on the physical relationship of the recording electrode and the firing fibers. The fibers of adjacent motor units overlap spatially, so that any electrode may record from one to several motor units. As the force of contraction increases, the interpulse intervals of a given motor unit action potential train decrease (DeLuca and Forrest 1973) and other motor units are recruited. Thus as the force of contraction increases, the spikes visible in a recording from an electrode typically become both larger and denser. The recording from several motor units is called an interference pattern. To deal with this pattern quantitatively it is customary to rectify and integrate it. An early study shows that the amplitude of integrated EMG is linearly related to muscle force in isometric contraction (Bigland and Lippold 1954), and the relationships between force and EMG measures under various other conditions has been a subject of continuing study (Bouisset 1973). The relations between muscles and movement for the speech musculature is so complicated that an analytic quantitative model for the relationship seems inherently unlikely. However, it has been shown that during selected speech tasks there is a monotonic relationship between EMG amplitude of the levator palatini muscle and palate height (Bell-Berti and Hirose 1975) and between amplitude of activity in the posterior cricoarytenoid (PCA) muscle (the PCA is an abductor of the vocal folds) and the size of laryngeal opening (Hirose 1975). Thus we might assume the relationship between EMG amplitude and articulator movement is some sort of increasing function, although the detailed shape of the relationship may be impossible to establish experimentally.

To return to the two types of approach to EMG signals, the approaches are different because the goals are different. On the one hand, one may be interested in the nervous control of individual muscle units in the speech musculature in normal or abnormal conditions. For example, MacNeilage and his associates (MacNeilage 1973; MacNeilage, Sussman, and Powers, forthcoming) have been interested in characterizing the various muscles of the orofacial area with respect to their action potential trains. For this purpose, single motor units must be recorded with an electrode with minimum field size. The corresponding clinical work is reflected in any standard text on clinical electromyography. There have been few studies of this general type with respect to the speech musculature except for a few studies of lip muscles (Netsell and Cleeland 1973; Netsell, Daniel, and Celesia 1975; Leanderson, Persson, and Öhman 1970). In general, the technique has been used to show generalized hypertonia or muscle weakness.

One may also be interested in electromyographic signals from a kinesiological point of view; that is, one may be interested in the forces acting on an articulator to cause a given movement for normal or abnormal cases. For work of this sort, one wishes to use a recording technique that will characterize the behavior of the whole muscle.

As indicated above, the relationship between EMG signals in any form and articulator movement is complicated. What is less commonly recognized is that it is as difficult to specify important muscles for a given movement from an observation of the movement as it is to move in the other direction. This difficulty is due in part to the lack of anatomical studies of the orofacial region and in part to the fact that what appears on anatomical grounds to be a possible mechanism for muscular control of a structure may not be so used. Furthermore, the speech structures are tied together in such a complex way that it is often impossible to distinguish active from passive movement by observation of structural movement alone.

Questions about the mode of closure of the velopharyngeal port to shut off the nasal airspace provide a good example of this point. The velopharyngeal valve is surrounded by muscles whose primary purpose is to block the opening between the oropharynx and the nasopharynx. The levator palatini, the major muscle of the velum, can close the port by moving the velum up and back. The muscle of the upper pharynx, the superior constrictor, could close the port by pulling the posterior pharyngeal wall forward. The two muscles of the faucal pillars, the palato-glossus and the palatopharyngeus, could contract to pull the velum down or could, on anatomical grounds, act with the other muscles to close off the port in a sphinc-ter fashion.

Electromyographic studies of the velopharyngeal mechanism have been under-taken by several investigators to determine which muscles are active in closing the port and which muscles are active in its opening for speech articulation. Fritzell (1969) concluded that the levator palatini is the most important muscle involved in closure in normal speech and superior constrictor activity is similar to that of the levator palantini; palatopharyngeus activity is different from individual to indi-vidual; and palatoglossus is active in lowering the velum for nasal articulations. Lubker, Fritzell and Lindqvist (1970) confirmed Fritzell's (1969) original report that for speech levator palatini activity is highly correlated with velopharyngeal closure and palatoglossus activity is highly correlated with velopharyngeal port opening. Bell-Berti (1976) has also confirmed Fritzell's finding that the levator palatini is the most important muscle involved in velopharyngeal closure in nor-mal speech. However, Bell-Berti's results do not conform to Fritzell's on the supe-rior constrictor and palatopharyngeus or to Fritzell or Lubker and Lindqvist on the palatoglossus. She reported no consistent pattern of EMG activity in the supe-rior pharyngeal constrictor but found palatopharyngeus activity to be very similar in pattern to levator palatini activity. Palatoglossus activity was related to tongue body and lateral pharyngeal wall movement rather than to velar lowering; velar lowering is thus assumed to result largely from relaxation of the muscles of velo-pharyngeal closure.

There is no evidence in Bell-Berti's results that the superior constrictor contri-butes in a substantial way to velopharyngeal closure in a sphincteric fashion, as suggested by Skolnick, McCall, and Barnos (1973). However, she examined only three subjects, and a larger sample may reveal significant individual differences in this regard. The point here is that a possible mechanism is not a necessary mechan-ism.

This summary is intended to show the interrelationships and overlap between various possible levels of study of the articulatory system. Ideally, any articulatory disorder should be discernible at every level, but a number of practical considera-tions stand in the way. In addition to the problems referred to above, most phy-siological techniques require a cooperative, or even a brave subject, which dimin-ishes the usefulness of such techniques for some patients and for small children. Acoustic techniques are totally noninvasive but may require equipment not avail-able in the clinic setting. Therefore, perceptual techniques have been widely used, in spite of their incompleteness. Before I return to the perceptual techniques gen-erally, however, I would like to discuss the argument that one or another of the other levels in the production process has some kind of primacy in terms of the goals of the production process. The argument is usually made with respect to either lack of contextual variability of the units at some level or retrainability. After considering these arguments, I will describe the perception techniques themselves and how they might be made more useful.

The Goals of Articulatory Organization

Another reference to figure 2 makes it clear that the primacy argument has arisen out of views of the nature of the speech perception processes that have gone under the label of "motor theories." These views have become noticeably more vague as time has passed. A comparison of two quotations will make this point clear. The first (Liberman et al. 1962) states that "Given the complex, highly encoded relation between phonemes and sound, and the more nearly one-to-one correspondence between phoneme and articulation, we have been led to assume that a reference articulation might well be a stage in the perceptual process. . . . Consideration of how the speech production system works . . . makes it clear why the acoustic signal should be rather complex and remote from the phoneme, and, further, why the simplest relation to the phoneme might be found in the motor commands that actuate the articulators" (p. 7). A recent formulation is given by Cutting and Pisoni (this volume) who quote Lashley (1951, p. 120) in saying "The processes (of perception and production) have too much in common to depend on wholly different mechanisms." While it is oversimplifying both points of view to let the quotations stand alone, the notable thing about the comparison is that while the view of the relation between perception and production remains quite similar in the two quotations, the statement about the locus of the interaction vanishes in the second. The further history of the hypothesis with respect to speech perception is summarized elsewhere (Liberman, 1975). We will consider only what might be called a motor theory of speech production.

Essential to the production component of the motor theory was the hypothesis that the motor inputs to the muscles involved in generating a phonetic segment are more nearly invariant than is either the articulatory or the acoustic target. The basis for the assumption was the spatial and temporal smear resulting from the recombination of adjacent elements. While some early EMG studies (Harris, Lysaught, and Schvey 1965; MacNeilage 1963) showed invariance of signal in varying environments, the notion of motor invariance at the muscle contraction level was strongly challenged by the combined EMG and cinefluorographic study of thirty-six consonant-vowel-consonant (CVC) monosyllables by MacNeilage and DeClerk (1969).

In many ways, their conclusions have been more influential than their observations. "In every possible case, some aspect of the motor control (that is electromyographic signal) of a later syllable component was influenced by the identity of a previous one. Except in a few cases, some aspect of the motor control of an earlier syllable component was influenced by the identity of the following one." This work lead MacNeilage (p. 1217) in a later paper (MacNeilage 1970, p. 184) to conclude, "Paradoxically, the main result of the attempt to demonstrate invariance at the electromyographic level has not been to find such invariance but to demonstrate the ubiquity of variability . . . the essence of the speech production process is not an inefficient response to invariant central signals, but an elegantly controlled variability of responses to the demand for a relatively constant end."

MacNeilage and DeClerk's work was done with surface electrodes (the technology of the period), so it is difficult to know what specific aspect of the muscle signals were being examined. But a careful examination of the EMG data shows that while some signals were influenced by the adjacent phone, some were not. Thus although the paper counters the argument that a motor command representation contains much less variability than an articulatory position representation, their data and that of others show variability with context at both levels and do not give a clear picture of when or to what degree context effects may be expected. Although the paper suggests an articulatory target formulation, it does not specify the rules governing failure to achieve that target.

An alternative to either invariant muscle control signals or invariant articulatory targets is a hypothesis that the speaker tries to reach acoustic targets. This point of view has been suggested by Ladefoged (1967), Ladefoged et al. (1972), Lieberman (1973), and Stevens (1973). Ladefoged's views are based on two studies of vowel production. In the first study he showed that speakers who believed they were producing equivalent articulations in the form of equivalent cardinal vowels were producing equivalent acoustic vowels. In the second study he showed that different speakers, when asked to produce the "same" vowel, will use widely different combinations of tongue and jaw displacement, thus getting the same tract shape for different articulatory maneuvers.

Lieberman (1973) and Stevens (1973) have pointed out that at some points in the vocal tract a small change in the position of the constriction will have a large effect on the acoustic output, while at other points it will have relatively little. The positions corresponding to the "point" vowels /i/, /a/, and /u/ are relatively stable. Thus their acoustic signals are likely to be stable even if the articulatory target is not quite reached, due either to sloppy articulation or coarticulation. Furthermore, at a dynamic level articulatory movement for a vowel might enter a quantal region sometime before—and remain there until sometime after—the articulatory target was reached. Although the articulators might be moving steadily, the acoustic vowel would thus be relatively stable.

Although these points of view have been much discussed, there is very little solid information, other than that already mentioned, about the relative amounts of coarticulation at acoustic, movement, and control signal levels. It seems worthwhile to review a few experimental studies together with a review of the implications of the studies for retraining.

COARTICULATION

Lindblom (1963), Stevens and House (1963), Öhman (1965), Stevens, House, and Paul (1966), Gay (1973), Bell-Berti and Harris (1975), and Ohde and Sharff (1975) have all reported coarticulatory interactions in speech signals at an acoustic level. It is possible for the latter two studies to compare the magnitude of anticipatory and carryover effects of consonants on an intermediate vowel; in general, carryover effects are more substantial.

At an articulatory level, interest has been concentrated on showing the number of segments over which coarticulatory effects spread and the effects of such markers as word boundaries on coarticulatory spread. The most often quoted results show that anticipatory coarticulation (Daniloff and Moll 1968; Benguerel and Cowan 1974) and carryover coarticulation (Dixit and MacNeilage 1972) may spread over as many as four segments, although the limitation of coarticulatory effects have not been carefully specified. This work is summarized and the theoretical implications discussed by Daniloff and Hammarberg (1973). One point has received perhaps less attention than it should have. As was pointed out above, the same acoustic result could in some instances be achieved by different articulations, yet there is little evidence that different articulators are used for a given acoustic effect when context changes. For example, a given degree of mouth opening might be generated by tongue or jaw, depending on context. There is no evidence that this happens that I know of.

Context effects, particularly carryover effects, are substantial at the level of muscle contractions, as MacNeilage and DeClerk (1969) noted. Part of the reason for this is the nature of the muscle signals that occur in speech. In general the magnitude of electromyographic signals is related to articulator movement. Therefore the signal will be related to the distance between articulator positions; for example, the activity of the muscles that raise the jaw will be greater for a given consonant after an open vowel than after a closed vowel. If the electromyographic signal for a given phone is different in two phonetic environments, then the position of the associated articulator was probably different for the preceding phone. If the electromyographic signal is the same, the position was probably the same (if rate of articulator movement did not change). Again, while analysis of the muscle signals could be used to establish that a different path is used to achieve the same vocal tract shape in different environments, there is no very convincing evidence of this type of reorganization.

Summing up, there seems to be no reason to choose one level of articulatory organization over another as showing less coarticulation. It can be shown to occur at all levels to which we have experimental access. There may be theoretical value to posit invariant signals at some level prior to the motor units, but such speculations are not open to experimental check.

RETRAINING
The specification of the goals of articulatory organization has both theoretical and practical significance. If the speaker stores some kind of internalized spatial or acoustic target as the representation of a phonetic unit, then interference with the articulation should be followed by rapid articulatory adjustment, whether the interference is in the sensory feedback that guides articulator placement or in the articulatory structures themselves.

With respect to the importance of acoustic feedback for retraining, the evidence is ambiguous. It is well known that profoundly deaf children are unlikely to develop normal speech, but the effects of later adventitious deafening do not seem as severe. People who have developed speech normally will continue to speak intelligibly, with rather modest effects on pitch and intensity, under high noise level conditions (Ringel and Steer 1963), although the noise levels that can safely be used may not mask all feedback. However, delayed auditory feedback has well-known devastating effects on articulation, although the nature of the articulatory failure is not well understood.

Many studies have aimed at showing the effects of interfering with tactile and kinesthetic feedback from the articulators. The largest group consists of the nerve block studies of Ringel and his associates (Ringel and Steer 1963; Scott and Ringel 1971a, 1971b; Putnam and Ringel 1972; Horii et al. 1973). In these studies dental anesthesia blocks, which were considered to interrupt the sensory feedback from the articulators and hence interfere with correct articulation, were administered. It has recently been shown that the nerve blocks used are likely to have interfered with motor as well as sensory innervation of the articulators (Borden, Harris, and Catena 1973; Abbs, Folkins, and Sivarajan 1976). The results of this technique are thus difficult to interpret, and further research along these lines seems unprofitable unless a different technique can be developed.

A more promising approach to both theoretical and applied problems is the direct investigation of the effects of articulatory interference. In an applied sense, these experiments provide evidence of speech adaptation after dental or surgical reconstruction. In spite of the obvious practical nature of this work, there is very little objective or quantitative information on speech adaptation (Hamlet 1973). Some investigators have offered essentially anecdotal observations of reorganization as proof of target theories of production. For example, MacNeilage (1970) has pointed out that pipe smokers can produce essentially normal articulations with a pipe clenched between the teeth, eliminating normal jaw movement. Nooteboom (1970) points out that many speakers can produce the acoustic equivalent of the vowel /u/, which is normally produced by rounding the lips, by lowering the larynx without lip rounding. The vocal tract is thus changed in the appropriate way by adding length to the larynx end instead of the lip end. He considers this as evidence for an acoustic, rather than an articulatory, target.

More formal experiments have been of two types. In one type an intermittent interference is applied during an articulatory movement. Smith and Lee (1972) and Folkins and Abbs (1975) have conducted preliminary experiments of this sort. In the latter experiment, loads were applied abruptly and without warning to the jaw during closure for the bilabial stops. Speakers had no difficulty making appropriate adjustments of lip activity so that appropriate closure was made. In the second type of experiment, a prosthesis of some type is put in the mouth and the course of adjustment is studied. For example, Amerman and Daniloff (1971) used listener judgments to evaluate speech produced while the speaker was wearing a prosthesis. The vowels were judged to be normalized within five minutes of insertion; however, careful acoustic measurements were not made.

A more thorough set of studies on speech adaptation has been made by Hamlet and Stone (1976). They collected phonetic, acoustic, and physiological measurements from subjects wearing alveolar-palatal dental prostheses. The nature of the compensations resulting from the prosthesis varied considerably among subjects. Compensatory patterns were evident within fifteen minutes of insertion, but defective speech was observed immediately after insertion of the prosthesis, after wearing it for a week, and fifteen minutes after removal. Consonant defects were easily observed; acoustic analysis revealed vowel formant shifts of which the subjects were unaware.

Summarizing the altered articulation experiments makes it clear that opinions differ substantially as to the speed with which a speaker is able to adjust to a structural change. One has the impression that the more carefully the motor behavior is studied, the longer are the estimates of adjustment time. There is not at present an experiment that provides unequivocal evidence of acoustic or articulatory loci as the goal of articulatory organization by a convincing demonstration of immediate adjustment to an alteration.

Speech Perception as a Technique for the Study of Speech Production

Returning to perceptual techniques as the way the clinician ordinarily studies speech production, I will now discuss some systems currently in use and suggest what kinds of research might make them more useful. Of course, one can argue that perceptual adequacy is the ultimate test of normal speech. However, clinicians sometimes feel that perceptual techniques are useful beyond this level, in classification of deviant speech or in therapy. Two rather different kinds of techniques deserve some special comment.

The first is the use of descriptors. A well-developed use of this technique is that of Darley, Aronson, and Brown (1969a, 1969b, 1975). In their studies the speech of groups of patients was ranked on a seven-point scale with respect to a large number of descriptors and the rankings were later factor analyzed. The disorders were then described by the highest ranking (most deviant) descriptors. For example, the four most deviant dimensions for patients with cerebellar lesions are imprecise consonants, excess and equal stress, irregular articulatory breakdown, and distorted vowels. If the descriptors are easy to apply, statistically reliable, and discriminate well among syndromes, they are clinically useful for the classification of new cases.

A limitation of the technique is that there is no tight temporal link between the descriptor and the acoustic signal that gave rise to it. For example, we don't know which vowels in the above example were perceived as defective. Furthermore, we don't know what characteristics of the signal caused any segment to be perceived as a defective vowel.

Phonetic transcription is a partial solution to this problem in that it links labels to short segments in the speech sequence. The traditional technique within the speech pathology literature was to describe sounds as being correct, substituted, omitted, or distorted (Templin 1957). The refinement of feature description has recently been introduced (McReynolds and Engmann 1975; Pollack and Rees 1972; Compton 1970; Cairns, Cairns, and Williams 1974). Most of these analyses have been loosely based on the Chomsky and Halle (1968) treatment of the phoneme as a bundle of features, although the analyses differ in whether they consider only the features of the target phoneme or those of both the target and substituted phoneme, the feature system used for the analysis, and the status of distorted phones in the analysis. While these differences are substantial and affect the results of the analysis in major ways, the analysis procedure itself is perceptual, like the descriptor procedure, whether the feature labels have a physiological re-referent (like "voiced") or whether they do not (like "distributed"). The characteristics of the speech perception mechanism itself are as much an issue in one of these descriptions as in another.

How good a guide to the underlying speech production is perceptual feature labeling? While there are sound theoretical reasons for believing in the interrelatedness of perception and production (as discussed above) and in the perceptual reality of at least some features at some level (Wickelgren 1966; Studdert-Kennedy and Shankweiler 1970), it can also be shown that listeners do not have a clear awareness of the basis for their judgments.

In a recent paper, Strange et al. (1976) have shown that the identification of natural vowels is far better if the vowels are produced in CVC context than if they are produced in isolation. Transitional information is apparently being used by the listener in making what appear as judgments of steady-state features or targets. It is not, as the target formulations suggest, that a target vowel can be extracted from the changing signal; rather, the listener makes some use of the transition portion of the vowel in making the identification.

Listeners can be badly deceived as to what is wrong with defective speech. A good example is provided by Calvert's 1961 study of deaf speech. He was examining the often reported observation that deaf speakers have a characteristic voice quality. He recorded deaf and normal speakers producing simple sustained vowels and dissyllables. Although the listeners were experienced in listening to deaf speech, they could not discriminate between deaf and normal speakers unless they heard dissyllables (what was perceived as a voice defect was in fact an articulatory disorder).

The object of this discussion is not to condemn perceptual analysis of speech production. A number of investigators, myself included, have made use of the types of analyses cited above (Shankweiler and Harris 1966). The problem is to make perceptual analyses yield better data about the speech production process. This is a two-stage problem. First, we need to find out more about the acoustic effects of movement disorders. Second, we need to find out more about what characteristics of the acoustic signal give rise to the perception of deviant speech.

Improving the Usefulness of Perceptual Analysis
The acoustic signal is probably the most underused level of description of speech production. One way of getting a better understanding of the acoustic effects of deviant production is to synthesize it. Modern computer techniques make it possible to manipulate acoustic variables and study the perceptual effects. This approach amounts to an examination of the psychophysics of feature and descriptor perception. One might feel that the whole history of the study of the cues for speech perception represents such an attempt—for example, the study of the second formant transition as a cue for the voiced stops (Liberman et al. 1954). However, an important limitation on these studies is that they were performed with total synthesis; that is, visual patterns that seemed on the basis of spectrogram

inspection to provide likely cues for some discrimination between phones were generated. Thus one cannot tell whether a particular acoustic pattern was a possible output of the human articulatory system. Neither does one know whether the cue manipulated in a given experiment is the one that a real speaker varies to generate the cue.

Another approach to the investigation of cues that has been tried in some laboratories is the manipulation of real speech. For example, a way of investigating intonation is to record and analyze real speech signals, change the fundamental frequency of the analyzed signal, and resynthesize it.

This same kind of analysis by synthesis approach could be used with deviant speech. For example, in Calvert's study the results appeared to show that deaf speakers were discriminated from normals because of deviant temporal patterns in their speech. This hypothesis could be checked experimentally by manipulating the durational characteristics of real samples. In the case of Darley's descriptors it would be possible to manipulate deviant speech to isolate the factors giving rise to the judgment of deviancy or to see what the "halo effect" of deviant articulation of one segment is on another. There are few examples of studies using this approach. Wendahl (1963, 1966) investigated perceived harshness by manipulating a synthesized glottal tone. This was, however, a total synthesis experiment and had the limitations described above.

I will conclude with a specific example, again from a study of deaf speech. It is well known that deaf speakers make a wide variety of errors and that the number of errors is highly correlated with the overall rated intelligibility of the speech. It can also be shown that the children's speech shows gross temporal distortion, both because the words themselves are produced slowly and because there are long pauses between words. Furthermore, formants for different vowels appear to be very similar and do not show the usual amount of movement in time. A student, Mary Joe Osberger, is experimenting on this speech to see if its intelligibility will be improved by temporal manipulation. If the speech is unintelligible because it is slowly produced, then manipulation of the vowel durations and elimination of the pauses between words should make it more intelligible. (While it is instrumentally more complicated, the formant tracts can also be manipulated systematically by resynthesis.)

What this approach amounts to is a kind of instrumental speech correction. The approach will, by inference, isolate the aspects of the acoustic signal judged to be deviant. Of course, this will still leave the problem that alternative articulatory mechanisms can generate the same acoustic effect, as we have discussed in an earlier section of this paper. The importance of a perceptually based strategy, on the one hand, is that it keeps the physiological researcher from mere botanizing; on the other hand, it defines for the clinician a class of physical variables that may be deviant.

References

Abbs, J. H., J. W. Folkins, and M. Stivarajan. 1976. Motor impairment following blockade of the infraorbital nerve: Implications for the use of anesthetization techniques in speech research. *J. Speech and Hearing Research*, 19, 19–35.

Amerman, J. D., and R. Daniloff. 1971. Articulation patterns resulting from modification of oral cavity size. *ASHA*, 13(9), S59(A).

Angelocci, A. S., G. A. Kopp, and A. Holbrook. 1964. The vowel formants of deaf and normal-hearing eleven-to fourteen-year-old boys. *J. Speech and Hearing Disorders*, 29, 156–170.

Bell-Berti, F. 1976. An electromyographic study of velopharyngeal function in speech. *J. Speech and Hearing Research*, 19, 225–240.

Bell-Berti, F., and K. S. Harris. 1975. Some acoustic measures of anticipatory and carryover coarticulation. *Haskins Laboratories Status Report on Speech Research*, SR-37/38, 73–78.

Bell-Berti, F., and H. Hirose. 1975. Short communication. Palatal activity in voicing distinctions: A simultaneous fiberoptic and electromyographic study. *J. Phonetics*, 3, 69–74.

Benguerel, A.-P., and H. A. Cowan. 1974. Coarticulation of upper lip protrusion in French. *Phonetica*, 30, 41–55.

Bigland, B., and O. C. J. Lippold. 1954. The relation between force, velocity, and integrated electrical activity in human muscles. *J. Physiology*, 123, 214–224.

Borden, G., K. S. Harris, and L. Catena. 1973. Oral feedback II. An electromyographic study of speech under nerve-block anesthesia. *J. Phonetics*, 1, 297–308.

Bouisset, S. 1973. EMG and muscle tone in normal motor activities. In *New Developments in Electromyography and Clinical Neurophysiology*, Vol. 1, J. E. Desmedt (ed.). Basel: Karger 547–583.

Cairns, H. S., C. E. Cairns, and F. Williams. 1974. Some theoretical considerations of articulation substitution phenomena. *Language and Speech*, 17, 160–173.

Calvert, D. R. 1961. Some acoustic characteristics of the speech of profoundly deaf individuals. Unpublished Ph.D. dissertation. Stanford University.

Canter, G. J. 1963. Speech characteristics of patients with Parkinson's disease: I. Intensity, pitch, and duration. *J. Speech and Hearing Disorders*, 28, 221–229.

Chomsky, N., and M. Halle. 1968. *The Sound Pattern of English*. New York: Harper and Row.

Compton, A. 1970. Generative studies of children's phonological disorders. *J. Speech and Hearing Disorders*, 35, 315–339.

Cutting, J. E., and D. B. Pisoni. This volume. An information-processing approach to speech perception.

Daniloff, R. G., and R. E. Hammarberg. 1973. On defining coarticulation. *J. Phonetics*, 1, 239–248.

Daniloff, R. G., and K. L. Moll. 1968. Coarticulation of lip-rounding. *J. Speech and Hearing Research*, 11, 707–721.

Darley, F. L., A. E. Aronson, and J. R. Brown. 1969a. Differential diagnostic patterns of dysarthria. *J. Speech and Hearing Research*, 12, 246–269.

———. 1969b. Clusters of deviant speech dimensions in the dysarthrias. *J. Speech and Hearing Research*, 12, 462–496.

———. 1975. *Motor Speech Disorders*. Philadelphia: Saunders.

Davis, S. B. In preparation. Computer evaluation of laryngeal pathology based on inverse filtering of speech. Ph.D. dissertation. University of California at Santa Barbara.

DeLuca, C. J., and W. J. Forrest. 1973. Probability distribution function of the interpulse intervals of single motor unit action potentials during isometric contractions. In *New Developments in Electromyography and Clinical Neurophysiology*, Vol. 1, J. E. Desmedt (ed.). Basel: Karger.

Dixit, R., and P. MacNeilage. 1972. Coarticulation of nasality: Evidence from Hindi. Paper presented at the eighty-third meeting of the Acoustical Society of America, 52, 131 (A).

Fant, G. M. 1960. *Acoustic Theory of Speech Production*. The Hague: Mouton.

Folkins, J. W., and J. H. Abbs. 1975. Lip and jaw motor control during speech. Responses to resistive loading of the jaw. *J. Speech and Hearing Research*, 18, 207–221.

Fritzell, B. 1969. The velopharyngeal muscles in speech: An electromyographic and cineradiographic study. *Acta Otolaryngologica*, Suppl. 250.

Gay, T. J. 1973. A cinefluorographic study of vowel production. *J. Phonetics*, 2, 255–266.

Hamlet, S. L. 1973. Speech adaptation to dental appliances: Theoretical considerations. *J. Baltimore College Dental Surgery*, 28, 52–63.

Hamlet, S. L., and M. Stone. 1976. Compensatory vowel characteristics resulting from the presence of different types of experimental dental prostheses. *J. Phonetics*, 4, 199–218.

———. Forthcoming. Reorganization of speech motor patterns following changes in oral morphology produced by dental appliance. In *Proceedings of Speech Communication Seminar, Stockholm, Sweden, 1–3 August 1974*. Uppsala: Almqvist and Wiksell.

Harris, K. S., G. F. Lysaught, and M. M. Schvey. 1965. Some aspects of the production of oral and nasal labial stops. *Language and Speech*, 8, 135–147.

Hirose, H. 1975. The posterior cricoarytenoid as a speech muscle. *Annual Bulletin of the Institute of Logopedics and Phoniatrics*, No. 9, 47–66.

Horii, Y., A. House, K.-P. Li, and R. Ringel. 1973. Acoustic characteristics of speech produced without oral sensation. *J. Speech and Hearing Research*, 16, 67–77.

Houde, R. A. 1967. A study of tongue body motion during selected speech sounds. *SCRL Monograph No. 2*. Santa Barbara: Speech Communications Research Laboratory.

Kent, R. D. 1972. Some considerations in the cinefluorographic analysis of tongue movements during speech. *Phonetica*, 26, 16–32.

Kent, R. D., and R. Netsell. 1975. A case study of an ataxic dysarthric: Cineradiographic and spectrographic observations. *J. Speech and Hearing Disorders*, 40, 52–71.

Kent, R. D., R. Netsell, and L. L. Bauer. 1975. Cineradiographic assessment of articulatory mobility in the dysarthrias. *J. Speech and Hearing Disorders*, 40, 467–480.

Koike, Y., and J. Markel. 1975. Application of inverse filtering for detecting lanyngeal pathology. *Ann. Otol., Rhinol., Laryngol.*, 84, 117–124.

Ladefoged, P. 1967. *Three Areas of Experimental Phonetics*. London: Oxford University Press.

Ladefoged, P., J. DeClerk, M. Lindau, and G. Papcun. 1972. An auditory-motor theory of speech production. *Working Papers in Phonetics* (Linguistics Department, University of California at Lot Angeles)22, 48–75.

Leanderson, R., A. Persson, and S. Öhman. 1970. Electromyographic studies of the facial muscles in dysarthria. *Acta Otolaryngologica*, 263, 89–94.

Lehiste, J. 1965. Some acoustic characteristics of dysarthric speech. *Bibliotecha Phonetica Fasc. 2*. Basel: Karger.

Liberman, A. M. 1975. How abstract must a motor theory of speech perception be? In *Proceedings of the Eighth International Congress of Speech*, Leeds, England, August 17-23. Also in *Haskins Laboratories' Status Report on Speech Research*, SR 44, 1975, 1-15.

Liberman, A. M., F. S. Cooper, K. S. Harris, and P. F. MacNeilage. A motor theory of speech perception. In *Proceedings of the Speech Communication Seminar, Stockholm, 1962*, Vol. 2. Stockholm: Royal Institute of Technology, paper no. D3 (available at Haskins Lab., New Haven, Conn.), 1-12.

Liberman, A. M., P. C. Delattre, F. S. Cooper, and L. J. Gerstman. 1954. The role of consonant-vowel transitions in the perception of the stop and nasal consonants. *Psychological Monographs*, 68, no. 379.

Lieberman, P. 1963. Some acoustic measures of the fundamental periodicity of normal and pathologic larynges. *J. Acoust. Soc. Amer.*, 35, 344-353.

———. 1973. On the evolution of language: A unified view. *Cognition*, 2, 59-94.

Lindblom, B. E. F. 1963. Spectrographic study of vowel reduction. *J. Acoust. Soc. Amer.*, 35, 1773-1781.

Lindblom, B., and J. E. F. Sundberg. 1971. Acoustical consequences of lip, tongue, jaw and larynx movement. *J. Acoust. Soc. Amer.*, 50, 1166-1179.

Lindblom, B., J. F. Lubker, and B. Fritzell. 1974. Experimentalfonetiska studier av dysartri. *Papers from the Institute of Linguistics, University of Stockholm*, no. 27.

Lisker, L. 1975. Of time and timing in speech. In *Current Trends in Linguistics*, Vol. XII, T. Sebeok (ed.) The Hague: Mouton, 2387-2418.

Lubker, J. F., B. Fritzell, and J. Lindqvist. 1970. Velopharyngeal function: An electromyographic study. *Quarterly Progress and Status Report* (Speech Transmission Laboratory, Royal Institute of Technology, Stockholm), STL-QPSR 4/1970, 9-20.

MacNeilage, P. F. 1963. Electromyographic and acoustic study of the production of certain clusters. *J. Acoust. Soc. Amer.*, 35, 461-463.

———. 1970. Motor control of serial ordering of speech. *Psychological Review*, 77, 182-195.

———. 1973. Preliminaries to the study of single motor unit activity in speech musculature. *J. Phonetics*, 1, 55-71.

MacNeilage, P. F., and J. DeClerk. 1969. On the motor control of coarticulation in CVC monosyllables. *J. Acoust. Soc. Amer.*, 45, 1217-1233.

MacNeilage, P. F., H. M. Sussman, and R. K. Powers. Forthcoming. Firing patterns of single motor units in speech musculature. *Proceedings of the 8th International Congress of Phonetic Sciences, Leeds, England, 17-23 August 1975*.

Markel, J. D., and A. H. Gray. 1976. *Linear Prediction of Speech*. Berlin: Springer Verlag.

McCall, G. N., M. L. Skolnick, and D. W. Brewer. 1971. A preliminary report of some atypical patterns in the tongue, palate, hypopharynx and larynx of patients with spasmodic dysphonia. *J. Speech and Hearing Disorders*, 36, 446-470.

McReynolds, L. V., and D. L. Engmann. 1975. *Distinctive Feature Analysis of Misarticulations*. Baltimore: University Park Press.

Moll, K. L. 1960. Cinefluorographic techniques in speech research. *J. Speech and Hearing Research*, 3, 227-241.

Monsen, R. B. 1974. Durational aspects of vowel production in the speech of deaf children. *J. Speech and Hearing Research,* 17, 386–398.

———. 1976. Second formant transitions of selected consonant-vowel combinations in the speech of deaf and normal-hearing children. *J. Speech and Hearing Disorders,* 19, 279–289.

Moore, P. 1938. Motion picture studies of the vocal folds and vocal attack. *J. Speech and Hearing Disorders,* 3, 235–238.

Netsell, R., and C. S. Cleeland. 1973. Modification of lip hypertonia in dysarthria using EMG feedback. *J. Speech and Hearing Disorders,* 38, 131–140.

Netsell, R., and R. D. Kent. 1976. Paroxysmal ataxic dysarthria. *J. Speech and Hearing Disorders,* 41, 93–109.

Netsell, R., B. Daniel, and G. G. Celesia. 1975. Acceleration and weakness in Parkinsonian dysarthria. *J. Speech and Hearing Disorders,* 40, 170–178.

Nooteboom, S. G. 1970. The target theory of speech production. *IPO Annual Progress Report* (Institute for Perception Research, Eindhoven, Holland), 5, 51–55.

Ohde, R. N., and D. J. Sharf. 1975. Coarticulatory effects of voiced stops on the reduction of acoustic vowel targets. *J. Acoust. Soc. Amer.,* 58, 923–927.

Öhman, S. E. G. 1965. Coarticulation in VCV utterances: Spectrographic measurements. *J. Acoust. Soc. Amer.,* 39, 151–168.

Pollack, E., and N. Rees. 1972. Disorders of articulation: Some clinical applications of distinctive feature theory. *J. Speech and Hearing Disorders,* 37, 451–462.

Putnam, A. H. B., and R. L. Ringel. 1972. Some observations of articulation during labial sensory deprivation. *J. Speech and Hearing Research,* 15, 529–542.

Ringel, R. L., and M. D. Steer. 1963. Some effects of tactile and auditory alterations on speech output. *J. Speech and Hearing Research,* 6, 369–378.

Rothenberg, M. 1973. A new inverse filtering technique for deriving the glottal air flow waveform during voicing. *J. Acoust. Soc. Amer.,* 53, 1632–1645.

Sawashima, M., and H. Hirose. 1968. New laryngoscopic technique by use of fiberoptics. *J. Acoust. Soc. Amer.,* 43, 168–169.

Scott, C. M., and R. L. Ringel. 1971a. Articulation without oral sensory control. *J. Speech and Hearing Research,* 14, 804–818.

———. 1971b. The effects of motor and sensory disruption on speech: A description of articulation. *J. Speech and Hearing Research,* 14, 819–828.

Shankweiler, D., and K. S. Harris. 1966. An experimental approach to the problem of articulation in aphasia. *Cortex,* 2, 277–292.

Skolnick, M. L., G. N. McCall, and M. Barnes. 1973. The sphincteric mechanism of velopharyngeal closure. *Cleft Palate J.,* 10, 286–305.

Smith, T., and C. Lee. 1972. Peripheral feedback mechanisms in speech production models. In *Proceedings of the 7th International Congress of Phonetic Sciences, Montreal, 1971,* A. Rigault and R. Charbonneau (eds.). The Hague: Mouton, 1199–1204.

Stevens, K. N. 1973. The quantal nature of speech: Evidence from articulatory-acoustic data. In *Human Communication: A Unified View,* E. E. David and P. B. Denes (eds.). New York: McGraw Hill. 51–66.

Stevens, K. N., and A. S. House. 1955. Development of a quantitative theory of vowel articulation. *J. Acoust. Soc. Amer.*, 27, 484–493.

———. 1963. Perturbations of vowel articulations by consonantal context: An acoustical study. *J. Speech and Hearing Research*, 6, 111–128.

Stevens, K. N., A. S. House, and A. P. Paul. 1966. Acoustic description of syllable nuclei: An interpretation in terms of a dynamic model of articulation. *J. Acoust. Soc. Amer.*, 40, 123–132.

Strange, W., R. R. Verbrugge, D. P. Shankweiler, and T. R. Edman. 1976. Consonant environment specifies vowel identity. *J. Acoust. Soc. Amer.* 60, 213–224.

Studdert-Kennedy, M., and D. P. Shankweiler. 1970. Hemispheric specialization for speech perception. *J. Acoust. Soc. Amer.*, 48, 579–594.

Subtelny, J. D., H. Koepp-Baker, and J. D. Subtelny. 1961. Palatal function and cleft palate speech. *J. Speech and Hearing Disorders*, 26, 213–224.

Templin, M. 1957. *Certain Language Skills of Children.* Minneapolis: University of Minnesota Press.

Ushijima, T., and H. Hirose, 1974. Electromyographic study of the velum during speech. *J. Phonetics*, 2, 315–326.

von Leden, H., P. Moore, and R. Timke. 1960. Laryngeal vibrations: Measurements of the glottic wave. Part III. The pathologic larynx. *Archives of Otolaryngology*, 71, 16–35.

Wendahl, R. W. 1963. Laryngeal analog synthesis of harsh voice quality. *Folia Phoniatrica*, 15, 241–250.

———. 1966. Laryngeal analog synthesis of jitter and shimmey, auditory parameter of harshness. *Folia Phoniatrica*, 18, 98–108.

Wickelgren, D. 1966. Distinctive features and short-term memory for English consonants. *J. Acoust. Soc. Amer.*, 39, 388–398.

Research on Normal and Abnormal Speech Production: A Two-Way Street
A Discussion of Harris's Paper

RONALD NETSELL

Many implications as well as direct statements in Harris's paper point out that the relationship between research on normal speech physiology and clinical research or rehabilitation is a two-way street. My remarks concerning this reciprocal relationship will be organized around two general topics. The first topic deals with the need for basic research in several areas of normal speech physiology. As these topics are mentioned, it should be apparent that the clinical worker would be in a much better position to understand certain speech disorders if these aspects of the normal mechanism were better understood. The second topic focuses upon some experimental observations of selected neuromotor speech disorders (certain forms of dysarthria) and how these observations must be accounted for in any complete model of the normal speech production process. To extend this point, the presentation will conclude with two clinical examples that have influenced my thinking about normal mechanisms.

Before taking up these topics, a comment concerning the relative importance of these matters in the larger context of human communication and its disorders seems in order. Some of my colleagues in language disorders and "applied linguistics" have made comments that have led me to believe they relegate speech production to the phonologic doldrums as rather straightforward, mechanistic phenomena, only the details of which remain to be worked out. I would agree this might be the case, indeed, if all the data were in. Unfortunately, the data are not all in. The speech machine is poorly understood, and it is probably far more complex than is hypothesized.

Neural Mechanisms for Speech Production
What is it we do not know about the neuroanatomic and neurophysiologic substrates of speech production? The shorter list by far would contain those items that were absolute knowns. In the following pages, the unknowns discussed are those that seem to have the greatest urgency in the sense that their solution might be immediately incorporated in the evaluation and treatment of individuals with a neuromotor speech disorder who currently appear in clinics throughout the country. Although the comments made here are restricted for the most part to neural mechanisms, there is a similar need for information about individual differences in muscle anatomy, muscle fiber typing, innervation ratios, and the developmental changes and associated biomechanics of the various structures used in speech production.

NEUROANATOMY
It will be convenient to discuss this area in terms of receptor morphology, the peripheral nervous system (PNS), and the central nervous system (CNS).

Even though there are numerous published reports concerning the morphology of receptors in the muscle, ligament, and joint of structures used for speech, the results are sufficiently contradictory to yield an ambiguous overall view. For example, there are conflicting conclusions regarding the presence or absence of muscle spindles in the tongue, although most evidence supports their presence. Assuming that higher spindle density relates to finer, more elegant muscle control, the distribution of spindles in the several tongue muscles, as well as throughout the speech musculature, would provide valuable predictions for the role the various muscles might play in speech movements. Several people have suggested that receptors other than spindles might provide continuous afferent information to the nervous system. For example, tactile receptors on and in the tongue conceivably could create a pressure mosaic that reflects the position and rate of change in the various muscle components of the tongue.

Even though receptor morphology information of this type would help us in predicting aspects of movement control, information regarding the nature of the afference and its possible uses in speech movement is far more critical. The question of what receptors are present and what their function is seems more immediate to those using such afferent-based therapy as the facilitation techniques of Margaret Rood (1956) and her students. In this procedure graded stimuli of temperature, touch, and pressure are applied to the skin for the purpose of differentially triggering underlying receptors. Impulses from these receptors are fed through nerves of differing diameter to different levels of the nervous system. According to the rationale of this therapy technique, these forms of afference facilitate various aspects of inhibition and excitation involved in the control of posture and movement. More complete and current information concerning the receptor morphology, nerve diameter, and central projections in the perioral and intraoral regions would certainly be helpful to those attempting to optimize these clinical procedures in the orofacial region.

In almost any neuroanatomy text the "wiring diagrams" of the peripheral nervous system are presented for the most part as rather straightforward knowns. For example, according to these accounts, input (afference) from the face to the brainstem is carried along three large branches of the fifth cranial nerve and motor output (efference) traverses a clearly drawn seventh cranial nerve, the facial. What is not presented in these textbook accounts is that such a portrayal of the facial nerve is only one of six possible patterns of distribution for this nerve and that the most predominant pattern is found in only about 20 percent of the population (Baumel 1974). In addition, there are multiple axonal interconnections (anastomoses) between branches of the seventh nerve and between branches of the seventh and fifth cranial nerves. Anatomically then, there is the potential for crosstalk at the most peripheral extensions of the neural communication lines.

This fact has some interesting implications for the nature of speech motor control, some of which will be discussed shortly. Traditional thinking about which nerves are motor, sensory, or both probably needs revision. For example, the maxillary branch of the trigeminal nerve has been regarded as a purely sensory nerve, but some recent evidence opens this to question as motor weakness in cer-

tain facial muscles was recorded following anesthetization of this "sensory" nerve
(Abbs, Folkins, and Sivaragan 1976). These are just a few examples of the anatomic uncertainty at the most peripheral and accessible parts of the nervous system
as it relates to speech. The unknowns multiply as we consider the complex organization of the cranial nerve nuclei and their interconnections in the brainstem
(Brodal 1969).

The anatomic picture gets even more confusing when the parts and interconnections of the central nervous system that might be involved in speech production
are considered. Whereas cortical and subcortical motor supply to the limbs is
fairly well delineated, its counterpart to most of the cranial nerve nuclei (innervat-
ing most of the speech muscles) is not nearly as well defined. Briefly, it is probably
the case that afferent projections from cranial nerve nuclei to higher centers go to
many different places but meet at least at various thalamic nuclei before moving
to the cortex. The possible afferent and efferent pathways that interconnect the
CNS nuclei and cortices are vast indeed. A simpler conception of the nature of
this complex system might be one showing parts that are not directly connected.

Knowledge of the neuroanatomy subserving speech movements is more than an
academic matter to the neurosurgeon and patient as they consider removal or
destruction of neural tissue. A clear specification of the critical neural parts and
their interconnections should result in fewer speech production problems secondary to the surgery as well as guide the surgeon in contemplating restorative surgery for speech improvement.

NEUROPHYSIOLOGY

Most of the notions regarding the neuromotor commands and controls for speech
have developed from studies of articulator movements, mainly through the use of
cineradiography. More recent studies have combined electromyographic (EMG)
and movement analyses in an attempt to strengthen the inferences as to the nature
of the neural inputs and controls. I am not aware of an EMG-movement paradigm
that has disambiguated the size or control of these neural commands and it is
difficult to imagine the particulars of such a paradigm. Nevertheless, these descriptive studies of kinematic or kinesiologic character are critical to understanding
the contraction and coordination of muscles in generating speech movements. In
turn, these normative data are requisite to a meaningful interpretation of the
muscle and movement control problems in the dysarthrias.

Two areas of study that may signal more traditional neurophysiologic approaches to the speech motor control problem have emerged recently in speech
research. These two approaches are presented here not because they are models
to follow but because they illustrate just how fundamental our need for information is with regard to the most basic neurophyisologic mechanisms operating
during speech production. The first area deals with the motor unit characteristics
of the speech muscles and the second is an attempt to use reflex modulation as an
index of the excitatory-inhibitory signals to these muscles.

MacNeilage (1973) and his colleagues have been conducting motor unit studies
that yield physiologic descriptions that can serve as a basis for inferences about

the size and function of the units in various speech muscles. The manner in which these units are recruited in developing muscle contractile force is now being addressed by these researchers and parallel studies with the neurologically impaired speaker may provide additional insights into their neuromotor speech problems.

The second study area deals with the use of reflexes in studying speech movement control (Netsell and Abbs 1975). A short latency reflex (10 to 15 msec) can be elicited electrically and recorded electromyographically as a single biphasic response from the upper lip (presumably *orbicularis oris superior*). Preliminary data with normal subjects indicates the reflex amplitude is increased during muscle contraction and decreased during antagonistic muscle actions when compared to its level when the muscle is at rest. It is possible that this paradigm could be refined to yield an essentially continuous waveform of reflex modulation where the amplitude at any point in time reflects the level of excitation or inhibition in this peripheral pathway during speech movements. The authors are currently planning to conduct similar studies with various dysarthric individuals. Based upon data from comparable studies of foot movement (Pierrot-Deseiligny and Lacert 1973) individuals with upper motor neuron lesions would be expected to have exaggerated reflex levels or possibly a lack of antagonistic muscle inhibition during voluntary movements. It may be that these same individuals could modify this reflex hypersensitivity if given appropriate biofeedback. Recent studies have shown that neurologically normal subjects can reduce reflex sensitivity in the arm with a concomitant decrease in muscle tone (Nielson and Lance 1976). It is exciting to contemplate an extension of this paradigm to the speech muscles and the dysarthric individual.

In concluding this part of the discussion, some comments regarding the possible roles that afferent mechanisms might play in the development and maintenance of normal speech movements are appropriate. Additional knowledge about afferent control in speech represents a potentially powerful tool for the clinician, yet we have little basic knowledge about such mechanisms. What afferent modalities do we use to control speech movements? Do we use any at all? If we do, what is the temporal-spatial character of this information and how is it disturbed by various neurologic disorders?

Hardy (1970) offered some suggestions that are relevant to this discussion. The auditory modality undoubtedly has a primary role as we learn to speak and becomes tightly coupled with movement afference to the extent that the adult can lose all hearing and maintain normal speech movements for a considerable time. Assuming for the moment that the adult speaker is relying in part upon movement afference for the control of speech movements, the clinical question becomes how speech movements are disrupted by abnormalities in this afference.

One of the first attempts to answer this question came from two studies that investigated the relation between oral form recognition ability and the degree of speech defectiveness in various forms of dysarthria as measured by listener ratings (Murphy 1972; Creech, Wertz, and Rosenbek 1973). The correlations were low and there was a temptation to conclude that there was little dependence of speech motor control upon afferent mechanisms in general. Unfortunately, oral form recognition ability may be several transformations away from the afference generated by speech movements, and Harris (this volume) has pointed to some of the hazards of inferring defects in speech movements from perceptual impressions of the speech acoustics.

A preferable observation level would include the speech movements themselves, associated EMG activity, and afferent information returning from the muscles to the brain stem. This is technologically difficult but perhaps not impossible. Recent work by Vallbo (1973) on human thumb movements has included the recording of muscle spindle afferents during the movements. This afferent activity corresponds directly to the velocity of movements and not the displacement. Vallbo hypothesizes a role for this afferent flow in the continuous "velocity smoothing" of the thumb movements. It may not be too futuristic to accomplish similar studies during speech. Given that the afferent information generated by the abnormal movements of dysarthric individuals is faulty, could they make use of this information in their attempts to normalize speech movements?

Assuming that rather elaborate afferent information is being generated at the periphery as a result of speech movements, the speaker either makes use of it or ignores it in some way. Not too long ago I favored the view that we used this afference in learning speech movements and, once learned, the CNS played out a "motor tape" of highly stereotypic neural commands that were not dependent upon feedback. Several rather recent observations are difficult to reconcile with this simple view of speech movement control.

In addition to the "motor equivalence" data reviewed by Harris (this volume), there is recent evidence that the same speaker will use various combinations of upper lip, lower lip, and jaw movement to effect essentially identical vertical openings between the lips in repeated utterances of a given sentence (Abbs and Netsell 1973; Abbs and Hughes 1976). With the presence of short latency reflexes between the tongue, lips, and jaw (see Bratzlavsky 1975), neural impulses of the "motor tape" would be differentially distributed at the periphery according to the instantaneous situation of the articulators as signaled by their afference. This peripheral reorganization could be effected in 5 to 15 msec. Recent experiments with monkeys show that fine coordination is noticeably disturbed by peripheral nerve deafferentation (Terzuolo, Soechting, and Ranish 1974). Evidence that saccadic eye movements (perhaps our quickest) are adjusted during head movements by afferent activity originating in the vestibular system (see Bizzi 1974) weakens the criticism that some speech movements are too "ballistic" to be influenced by peripheral feedback.

The above speculations regarding possible PNS roles do not rule out CNS involvement in the reorganization of ongoing speech movements. The cerebellum, thalamus, and many other CNS structures are massively interconnected with each other and the periphery such that they could quickly modify "initial motor commands" to meet the predicted or realized structural movements of the particular speech sequence. Of course, the character and locus of these initial motor commands has a long history of rather unproductive debate in the area of experimental phonetics (see Kent 1976 for review).

ONTOGENY

Although very little is known about the neural mechanisms that subserve adult speech production, even less is understood concerning neural maturation and aging. These matters seem important for at least two reasons. First, increased knowledge of maturation and aging effects on the control of speech movements may well provide additional insight into the neural control for speech of the adult system. For example, studies of the normal developmental course of infantile orofacial reflexes and the development of speech and nonspeech movements may result in testable hypotheses regarding the use of reflex control in speech production. At the other end of the continuum, electromyographic (EMG) and movement studies of the aging may reveal the robust or delicate nature of the neural controls for speech. The second way the ontogenic data would be valuable is in providing the clinical worker with better normative information about speech production mechanisms. Considerable data about phonetic development in children is available but little is known about parallels with respect to movement control of the speech apparatus and its neural and muscular components. These data would seem especially pertinent in working with the neurologically handicapped child. In the case of aging, a great deal of acoustic and perceptual data is accumulating regarding the changes associated with the older person; but, again, what about speech movement and its neural control? The speech physiology data from dysarthrias of advanced age can be interpreted more meaningfully against the knowledge of aging effects upon the neural and muscular components of their neurologically normal counterparts. For example, how much of the voice tremor, short duration, and small amplitude EMG signals and reduced voice loudness seen in a given Parkinsonian individual is attributable to normal aging processes? The answers to such questions await further basic research.

Neuromotor Speech Disorders
It should be clear from the preceding remarks that I know very little about the inner workings of the nervous system responsible for the generation of speech. Experimental neurologists, neurophysiologists, bioengineers, psychologists, and the like only recently have begun large scale study of the neural controls for normal and abnormal movements; and the movement systems being studied for the most part are the eyes, arms, hands, and legs. But the beginnings are there and some help from these disciplines in the study of speech movement control problems can be expected. In fact, one such interdisciplinary program is underway (Abbs 1975) and a second is starting.

It is very difficult to guess what is wrong with a dysfunctioning system if one does not already have some pretty good ideas as to how it works properly. Some try to fix malfunctioning automobile engines. Those who are willing to attempt a repair have some idea of how the engine is put together, what part is malfunctioning, and how to fix it. In the human nervous system it is not known how the speech engine works, it cannot be taken apart to find out, and what is wrong with it must be inferred from what is heard and seen. With some awareness of these problem areas, clinical researchers have begun to take a systematic look at and listen to some of these malfunctioning speech motors.

DAMAGE TO THE NEURAL CONTROLS FOR SPEECH

The traditional neurologic approach says that damage to different levels or aspects of the neuraxis results in different conditions that will adversely affect movement (for example, flaccidity, spasticity, and rigidity). Individuals who ostensibly have sustained damage to a specific aspect of the neuraxis will present a dysarthria with characteristics of speech and voice that have a unique perceptual identity (see Darley, Aronson, and Brown 1975). The need exists to study a number of dysarthric individuals at both the perceptual and sensorimotor levels in order to test and revise initial hypotheses concerning the underlying neural and muscular problems for the various forms of dysarthria.

In a physical sense, the various dysarthrias can be viewed as a set of movement disorders. These movement disorders result from muscle contraction problems of nervous system origin. Normal patterns of muscle contraction for speech movement depend upon proper levels of background tension (or tonus), strength or contractile force, and timing (the activation and deactivation of all the muscles at the proper time). Disturbances in the PNS or CNS control of these muscle actions are responsible for abnormalities in the range, velocity, and direction of speech movements. The crux of the research problem is to determine the exact nature of these PNS and CNS controls, and the joint study of neurologically normal and abnormal speakers represents one important and viable approach in this area. The crux of the clinical problem obviously is to improve or maintain current levels of speech intelligibility for the individual client, and the thesis proposed here is better treatment plans will be developed with greater knowledge of the precise character of the speech movement disorder and the underlying neural control problem.

Some observations from the dysarthrias underscore the two-way street previously mentioned and reinforce the physical or kinesiologic approach just mentioned. The observations presented here point up some characteristics seen only in the damaged nervous system; however, in my opinion they must be accounted for in any complete explanation of the neural controls of speech production. The two sets of observations presented here are discussed as problems with tone and tremor.

The condition of hypertonicity is seen in several neurological conditions where antagonistic muscles are involuntarily overcontracted. This condition can reduce or completely stop the motion that would be generated by the prime mover or agonist muscle. One form of this balanced hypertonicity is called rigidity. Various pharmacological, neurosurgical, and behavioral treatments have provided some relief. A common observation is that with the remission of this hypertonicity there is an increase in the range and velocity of movement. This raises the question of partially or totally independent controls for phasic and tonic muscle contractions, the former possibly being controlled by neural circuits for movement and the latter by circuits for posture or tone or both. Many current models of normal speech production do not address this issue of the mechanisms of tonicity at all.

The second set of observations deals with abnormal oscillatory phenomena called tremor. I have seen five cases in the past few years that present a very regular tremor (between 3 and 8 Hz) that can be specific to the vocal folds or spread to the pharynx, velopharynx, tongue, jaw, and lips. The rhythm of these patients' speech is jerky, and consonant misarticulations are irregular. Articulations or movements that are disrupted are those coincident with the highly regular beat of the tremor (the disturbing tremor is superimposed upon the particular muscle contractions used in the movement). That is, this very complex sounding and appearing dysarthria can be viewed as a problem with a tremor circuit. There are several unanswered questions regarding this problem. For example: Is the apparent superimposition of the tremor upon otherwise normal speech movements evidence of tremor circuitry that is independent of movement circuitry? Are these tremors exaggerations of normal tremors? Are they abnormal or additional oscillations that resulted from the neuropathology? Are neural oscillatory circuits used in any way in speech production?

IMPLICATIONS FOR SPEECH EVALUATION AND REMEDIATION

Many of the evaluation and remediation procedures used in our clinical studies of the dysarthrias were drawn directly from experimental procedures and instrumentation used in normal speech physiology. Our experiments with biofeedback in dysarthria have been provocative but will undoubtedly be strengthened as information is gained about the role of afference in normal speech production. It has been the thesis of this paper that the joint study of normal and abnormal mechanisms and the interactions between the laboratory and clinical settings are central to the optimal progress of anyone interested in the problems. The two-way nature of this interaction is emphasized by the helpful interpretations and challenging questions directed to the investigator of normal processes by the clinician. It has been my experience that even the most basic of researchers respond to such challenges.

References

Abbs, J. H., 1975. Neuromuscular mechanisms underlying speech production. Program Project NS 11780, National Institute of Neurological, Communicative Disorders and Stroke.

Abbs, J. H., and Hughes, O. M., in press. Labial-mandibular coordination in the production of speech: Implications for the operation of motor equivalence. *Phonetica*.

Abbs, J. H., and Netsell, R., 1973. Coordination of the jaw and lower lip during speech production. Paper presented at American Speech and Hearing Association, Detroit, Michigan.

Abbs, J. H., Folkins, J. W., and Sivaragan, M., 1976. Motor impairment following blockade of the infraorbital nerve: Implications for the use of anesthetization techniques in speech research. *J. Speech and Hearing Research*, 19, 19–35.

Baumel, J. J., 1974. Trigeminal-facial nerve communications: Their function in facial muscle innervation and reinnervation. *Arch. Otolaryngol.*, 99, 34–44.

Bizzi, E., 1974. Common problems confronting eye movement physiologists and investigators of somatic motor functions. *Brain Research*, 71, 191–194.

Bratzlavsky, M., 1975. Inhibitory interactions between group Ia masseter afferents and labial mechano-sensitive input in man. *Brain Research*, 96, 124–127.

Brodal, A., 1969. *Neurological Anatomy: In Relation to Clinical Medicine.* London: Oxford University Press.

Creech, R. J., Wertz, R. T., and Rosenbek, J. C., 1973. Oral sensation and perception in dysarthric adults. *Perceptual and Motor Skills*, 37, 167–172.

Darley, F. L., Aronson, A. E., and Brown, J. R., 1975. *Motor Speech Disorders.* Philadelphia: W. B. Saunders Co.

Hardy, J. C., 1970. Development of neuromuscular systems underlying speech production. ASHA Reports No. 5, 49–68.

Harris, K. S. this volume. Physiological aspects of speech production.

Kent, R. D., 1976. Models of speech production. In *Contemporary Issues in Experimental Phonetics*, N. Lass (ed.), Springfield, Ill.: C. C. Thomas.

MacNeilage, P. F., 1973. Preliminaries to the study of single motor unit activity in speech musculature. *J. Phonetics*, 1, 55–71.

Murphy, M. L., 1972. The relationship between oral stereognosis and speech defectiveness in athetoid and spastic quadraplegic cerebral palsy children. Unpublished M.A. thesis, University of Iowa.

Netsell, R., and Abbs, J. H., 1975. Modulation of perioral reflex sensitivity during speech movements. *J. Acoust. Soc. Amer.*, 58, S41 (Abstract).

Nielson, P. D., and Lance, J. W., 1976. Action tonic stretch reflexes; (i) Their voluntary suppression in man. Paper presented at Symposium on Human Reflexes and Motor Disorders, Brussels.

Pierrot-Deseilligny, E., and Lacert, P., 1973. Amplitude and variability of monosynaptic reflexes prior to various voluntary movements in normal and spastic man. In *New Developments in Electromyography and Clinical Neurophysiology*, J. E. Desmedt (ed.), Basel: Karger, 3, 418–427.

Rood, M. S., 1956. Neurophysiological mechanisms utilized in the treatment of neuromuscular dysfunction. *Amer. J. Occupational Therapy*, 10, 220–225.

Terzuolo, C. A., Soechting, J. F., and Ranish, N. A., 1974. Studies on the control of some simple motor tasks. V. Changes in motor output following dorsal root section in squirrel monkey. *Brain Research*, 70, 521–526.

Vallbo, A. B., 1973. Muscle spindle afferent discharge from resting and contracting muscles in normal human subject. In *New Developments in Electromyography and Clinical Neurophysiology*, Desmedt, J. E., (ed.), Basel: Karger, 3, 251–262.

General Discussion of Papers by Harris and Netsell

Limits of Plasticity

A general topic of discussion centered on the notion of alternative patterns of articulation (trade-off relations) and the degree to which these trade-offs were limited. Curtis suggested that more information was needed on the variables that condition these limits. For example, what is the range of individual differences and what is the relation of age and plasticity with respect to alternative articulation patterns? Netsell reiterated that recent research has shown there are a great many neural interconnections at the periphery between tongue, lips, and jaw that provide for the possibility of trade-offs at these very low levels. The research of Abbs and his colleagues (reported in Netsell's paper) demonstrates trade-offs of this kind. The simplistic notion of a highly preprogrammed set of motor activities controlled exclusively by the central nervous system is no longer viable.

Stevens commented that at one level the limits on trade-offs are determined by the fact that the speaker must achieve the same acoustic output and the same articulatory target position to the extent that the position determines that output. Thus, for instance, there can be jaw movement with compensatory tongue movement such that the tongue forms more or less the same area function, that is, the same shape of the vocal cavities. The trade-offs mentioned in the paper by Harris— different ways of closing off the velopharyngeal port—all have the same acoustic effect. But there may not be many other possibilities that result in a constant acoustic effect.

Harris agreed that there are many instances in which there are very few alternatives in articulation. For example, there are very few ways of lifting the tongue tip efficiently. There are other places where there is just one mechanism available in the articulatory system. For instance, there is no substitute for the functioning of the posterior cricoarytenoid. She suggested that a way to study trade-off possibilities is to look for individual differences across many subjects. Finding few differences among subjects would constitute evidence that few trade-offs are available. Harris added that in her opinion few good experimental studies have been done in this area.

Afferent Feedback in Articulatory Control

A related topic concerned the role of auditory and kinesthetic afference in motor control generally and specifically in control of alternative articulation patterns. Pickett reported that some results by Bishop, Ringel, and House (1973) on oral form discrimination by deaf speakers showed that while the subjects had normal two-point threshold discrimination on the tongue, their oral form discrimination was defective. In contrast, they did as well as normal subjects on manual form discrimination with the same forms. This implies that there is an auditory-motor link in oral form discrimination that is deficient in the deaf speakers. Bishop did not compare subjects according to their speaking ability, however. That would be a way to separate auditory components from moto-kinesthetic components.

Harris commented that while there have been a number of experimental failures to find a relationship between tactile-kinesthetic feedback and normal speech production (reported in Netsell, this volume), the conclusion of most researchers in this field is that the experimental techniques have not been sensitive enough to demonstrate the relationship. The interference studies with dental appliances have been done with incomplete auditory masking; they are badly in need of replication with good physiological monitors and good acoustic analyses. There is a practical problem in that noise levels needed to mask auditory feedback effectively are dangerously high. (There was a brief discussion about possible techniques for effectively masking auditory feedback.)

Further discussion was concerned with the possibility of the presence of receptors such as muscle spindles in the tongue that could provide a continuous flow of information about the velocity of movements of the articulators and information about where the tongue was in space. While there is no joint in the tongue that could provide kinesthetic feedback of the traditional kind, the complex structure of the muscles pulling in different directions could substitute for a joint structure in conveying such information. The discussants agreed that very little is known about the possible functioning of such structures. Auditory and kinesthetic feedback must be critically important in the development of articulatory patterns, but there is no firm knowledge about the extent to which this afferent information is utilized in the maintenance of normal articulation or in the control of alternative articulatory patterning.

Measurements of Velopharyngeal Closing

The discussion turned to methods of measuring velopharyngeal closing. Shelton reported on a new technique by Sprinson that uses a very thorough visual inspection of the closing mechanism. A nasal pharyngoscope throughout the nose monitors from above, while a scope in the mouth monitors what is happening from below. Videofluorographic observations are taken from saggital, frontal, and oblique views. Although Shelton thought information from this technique would yield much more complete information, he expressed concern for the radiation exposure levels entailed in this method. Harris suggested that there may be other effective techniques for measuring the velopharygeal closing mechanism that do not use fluorography and thus avoid the danger of overexposure.

Palatometers for Monitoring Deaf Speech

Pickett inquired of the group whether they knew of an effective device for measuring variations in airflow in the vocal tract. Shelton described a device being developed by Fletcher at the University of Alabama (Fletcher, McCutcheon, and Wolf 1976). It consists of a very thin plate of acrylic that carries about forty tiny electrodes and can be fitted to the maxilla. Information is fed into a computer and a real-time display of articulation in the front of the mouth is presented on a television screen. Shelton has been interested in this as a possible training device.

Harris reported that this device is very similar to the palotometer developed by Shibata (1968) in Tokyo. She added that these devices were too complex to be generally useful for gaining quick access to articulatory movements on many speakers. They require "Japanese skill in knot tying" in addition to complicated computer facilities.

References

Bishop, M. E., Ringel, R. L., and House, A. S. 1973. Orosensory perception, speech production, and deafness. *J. Speech and Hearing Research*, 16, 257–266.

Fletcher, S. G., McCutcheon, M. J., and Wolf, M. B. 1976. Dynamic palatometry. *J. Speech and Hearing Research*, 18, 812–819.

Shibata, S. 1968. A study of dynamic palatometry. *Annual Bulletin of the Research Institute of Logopedics and Phoniatrics*, 2, 28–36.

Behavioral and Linguistic Considerations in Children's Speech Production

LEIJA V. MCREYNOLDS

The behavioral and linguistic disciplines have had a strong influence on the form and content of treatment programs for communication disorders. At times the two disciplines appear to represent the end points on a continuum from a strictly environmental to a strictly nativisitic position; at other times the divergence is less obvious. To those working with speech disordered populations the difference in views need not necessarily be a hindrance or a problem. The diverse positions frequently give rise to different sets of questions about the same phonemenon, dictating methodologies suitable to the kinds of questions asked. This is an advantage, for the speech pathologist can profit from studying the methodologies employed by both disciplines and the information offered from their studies. In addition, if the questions differ, the information obtained may apply to different aspects of a disorder that must be considered in developing treatment programs. For example, linguists frequently explore the content of a behavior while the behaviorist explores events influencing its occurrence. Content and occurrence are not necessarily unrelated, but they may be. Information on both aspects of the behavior is relevant for developing treatment programs. Similarly, the methodologies used by linguists and behaviorists often appear suitable in assessment and treatment of communication problems. Speech pathologists certainly need to know what to train, but equally urgently they need to know how to train. In addition, the sequence in which content is to be trained is important. There can be a close relationship between behavioral and linguistic research and the development of treatment procedures for speech and language disorders.

Developmental studies have always contributed useful data for designing speech and language training programs. In recent years the developmental information on various aspects of language behavior seems to have become more sophisticated and detailed. This in turn leads to the possibility that developmental information can contribute ever more relevant data to designing treatment programs. Developmental data are frequently used in a descriptive or comparative manner, but predictive use is less frequent except in a somewhat broad sense. Perhaps the predictive value of developmental data will increase with the more detailed information on patterns, processes, and sequences in acquisition. Speech pathologists are provided with an opportunity to explore the importance of an increasing number of variables identified by linguists and behaviorists in their research.

In this paper I will present information from both behavioral and linguistic research regarding vocal behavior of children from infancy to about the time when their phonological systems match the adult system (anywhere from four to seven years). The purpose is not to enter into the issues of nativist versus environmentalist or learning theory versus linguistic theory except to recognize the existence of the issues and report data bearing on them. Rather, data from both disciplines are reported and discussed when possible. The data are explored in relation to disordered speech and to usefulness in assessment and treatment of some communication problems.

Relationship of Infant Vocalizations to Language Acquisition

It is generally accepted that infant vocalizations from birth to approximately one year of age can be divided into several stages (Lewis 1951; Simon 1957; Carroll 1961). The stages are not discrete and vocalizations overlap from one stage to another, but each stage is characterized by previously unobserved vocal behavior. Some observers have described more stages than others, but all generally agree on at least four stages.

In stage one, crying, coughs, and gurgles are present, with crying the most frequent vocalization. In this stage several patterns of crying have been identified. Stage two is marked by a greater variety of vocalizations and begins at about three weeks of age. Although crying continues, by the end of this second period the infant is producing several noncry vocalizations. Stage three, the babbling stage, has received considerable attention and has been discussed widely in the literature. The stage has sometimes been described as consisting of substages. Appearance of this stage has been identified anywhere from six weeks to sixteen weeks, but it usually is described as beginning somewhere around ten weeks of age. In this stage the infant's vocalizations begin to sound speechlike in that consonant and vowellike sounds appear. The infant also produces reduplicated syllables; intonation patterns similar to the adult's patterns appear at this stage. Stage four, which begins at about nine months and lasts until about twelve months, finds the child producing utterances that have been described as true speech or language because the first words appear and even nonword vocalizations generally adhere to the phonological constraints of the language. It has been suggested that there is a definite decrease in the number and variety of sounds produced by the child in this stage.

Theories to account for these periods of infant vocalizations have been proposed. Psychologists and linguists in particular are interested in the relationship between early vocal behavior and later phonological and language acquisition. Two primary theories of this relationship have emerged from infant investigations. Briefly, views concerning the importance of infant vocalizations to later language acquisition can be categorized into continuity versus discontinuity theories. Those with a linguistic viewpoint are usually associated with the discontinuity theory, but the restriction is probably artificial. Continuity theorists are frequently represented by psychologists or individuals in child development, but this limitation may also be somewhat arbitrary. The continuity theorists, however, are probably more behaviorally inclined than are individuals who hold to the discontinuity theory. The continuity theory is often referred to as learning theory. The two theories have been discussed and reported competently (Kagan 1971; Kaplan and Kaplan 1971, Hellmuth 1967). They will be outlined briefly in this paper so that contributions to the theories from recent studies in infant speech production can be examined and discussed in relation to disordered communication.

DISCONTINUITY THEORY

According to the discontinuity theory, there is no essential relationship from one stage of infant vocalization to the next (Lenneberg 1967; Jakobson 1968). If the first three stages are related to each other and to the fourth stage, the language acquisition stage, it is only in a superficial manner. Lenneberg (1964) describes this as a period of biological maturation. The content of the infant's productions are irrelevant to language acquisition in the fourth stage. The infant up to approximately nine months to a year can be considered to be a "prelinguistic child." Proponents of this theory suggest that the articulated sound segments in the first three stages are unpatterned and randomly produced. The sounds are not under voluntary control. Evidence for this is that the child in stage four has difficulty producing sounds previously produced without effort. The distinction is between production of a sound randomly and the systematic use of that sound later that is, vocalizations that adults do not and do understand. Inability to produce sounds at stage four cannot be related to any motor deficiency according to this theory because the earlier productions demonstrate this motoric ability. Support for the random nature of the productions is derived from the lack of a developmental progression during these first three stages. According to Jakobson (1968), for example, two universal principles must be considered in evaluating infant productions. One is the frequency principle. According to this principle, sounds found in all languages will appear early in development. Sounds not appearing in all languages will be acquired later. The second principle is that secondary components of languages are not found if primary components are not present, but primary components are found in the absence of secondary components. Primary components will also be acquired before secondary components. For instance, stop consonants are found in all languages, but fricatives are not. Thus stops are primary components and fricatives are secondary components. Not only will stops be acquired earlier than fricatives, but stops may be found without fricatives. However fricatives, being secondary components, may not be found without stops. These regularities, according to linguists, have not been shown to exist in infant vocalizations in the first three stages. Thus there are two stages in infant vocal behavior in a linguistic model. The first stage, being random and involuntary, is not related to later language acquisition; but the second stage, which follows an orderly progression of sound acquisition, is related to language acquisition.

A modified version of the discontinuity theory (or perhaps of the continuity theory) is offered by individuals who regard the babbling stage as a period of practice with the articulators (Fry 1966; Van Riper 1963; Winitz 1966; Berry and Eisenson 1956). These individuals regard babbling as an essential period in which the infant practices producing sounds to be used later in language production (Carroll 1961; Wood 1964) or in which a child induces knowledge about vocal tract geometry (Studdert-Kennedy, 1976). The emphasis is on exercising the articulatory mechanism not on the content of the infant's productions, that is, not on vocal parameters that show a continuous progression through all stages.

CONTINUITY THEORY
The learning or continuity theory position contends that vocalizations of the infant at each stage are related to language acquisition in the fourth stage (Skinner 1957; Osgood 1965); there is essential continuity from one stage to another. The

basis for this contention, as in the discontinuity theory, is derived from the babbling stage of infant vocalizations. Inference from the first two stages are seldom
made in either theory. The premise in continuity theory is that infants produce all
the sounds they will later produce in their language acquisition period. Through
a process of imitation and differential reinforcement, children differentiate sounds
that are relevant in their language from those that are not. They eliminate the
irrelevant sounds and progress to approximations of the adult forms during development. Evidence for developmental progression and systematization is provided
by accounts showing that infants start babbling with vowels. These are followed
by consonants and the syllable structures of the consonant-vowel (CV) and CVCV
patterns.

Behaviorists have studied infant vocalizations during the first three periods. The
dependent variable in these experimental studies has usually been vocalization rate
rather than vocalization content (Siegel 1969; Rees 1972). The principle of reinforcement provides the continuity prior to and during language acquisition. For
many who subscribe to this view, continuity is related to environmental events;
reinforcement and imitation function in all stages of child language development
and are responsible for changes in infant vocal behavior.

Mowrer's autism theory (1960) exemplifies to some extent the components of
continuity theory. Because it was a very popular theory in the sixties, it is rather
well known. Briefly, the theory is based on the principles of imitation and secondary reinforcement. The infant imitates the caretaker's productions and is reinforced by the caretaker for these imitations. Later, when alone, the infant produces
the imitated responses and is reinforced because they are similar to the caretaker's
productions. Experimental studies of this theory have had somewhat disappoint-
ing results (Siegel 1969), and the theory has been discussed less often in the 1970s.
Interest has shifted more to other principles of learning, although Skinner's (1953,
1957) ideas are undoubtedly influencing research in child development to a great
extent. Within this framework, language learning is not considered a unique behavior, different from other behaviors acquired by the child, at least not in terms
of the principles that influence language acquisition. Experimental studies conducted within the Skinnerian framework provide important information about
child language acquisition but not a great deal about the content and form of the
child's productions at any of the stages

SUMMARY OF THE TWO THEORIES

Studies unequivocally supporting one or the other theory are not numerous, or
perhaps it would be more correct to say they are not definitive. This is due partly
to problems inherent in the population studied; infants do not make easy subjects
for study. Partly, however, the problem may lie in our inability to define continuity
clearly. Many changes are taking place within the infant as well as in the environment, and it is difficult to evaluate or isolate the influence of all of them in a rapidly
shifting scene.

The two theoretical positions appear to dictate the factors to be studied. Continuity theorists are exploring events or external processes with only minor con-

cern for content while discontinuity theorists are exploring content with reference to processes only if they show up in relation to content. One group of investigators believes in applying scientific rigor in their investigations, which means experimental designs and reliability checks, while the other group places more reliance on personal observations ("rich" observations) with less concern about strict procedures. A common ground, however, is both group's agreement that longitudinal studies need to be conducted to arrive at some determination of continuity or discontinuity in vocal behavior from birth to one year. Recent studies of infant vocalizations present data bearing on this issue.

Recent Studies of Infant Vocalizations
Infant vocalizations during stages one and two have been studied, but few studies have attempted to delineate the parameters of the sounds produced by infants, except to differentiate forms of crying. Stark, Rose, and McLagen (1975), however, wished to compare and contrast features of crying, fussing (discomfort sounds), and vegetative activity in order to determine if features present in these primitive reflexive sounds later appear in the cooing and babbling of the same infants. They hoped to obtain information about the relationship of vocal behaviors in infants from one stage to another.

The vocal behavior of two normal infants was recorded in their homes when they were one to two weeks, three to four weeks, and eight weeks of age. Each recording was thirty minutes long, commencing during part of the feeding and ending after the feeding as the mother played with the infant before putting her to sleep. The experimenter provided a commentary on tape during the period the baby was silent.

Cry sounds were defined as a series of sounds produced in acute distress because of such things as hunger, pain, or temporary absence of parent. Discomfort sounds were defined as sounds produced in distress of a lesser degree than cry sounds. Vegetative sounds were defined as cough, burp, sneeze, hiccup, or sucking snort. Grunts made with effort or in the course of activity and sighing after the effort were included.

Features selected for describing the infant vocalizations were derived from listening to the utterances and examining sound spectrograms of those utterances. They included features of breath direction, voicing, pitch, and loudness; degree of constriction of the vocal tract above the glottis; features of open, vowellike sounds and features of closed, consonantlike sounds. Primary and secondary features were identified, secondary features being dependent on the presence of primary features (pitch dependent on presence of voicing).

Stark, Rose, and McLagen (1975) found that age level had no effect on the occurrence of either the primary or secondary features. However, the two infants they studied differed from each other with respect to the frequency of both primary and secondary features. These differences characterized the vocal output of each infant, making it possible to distinguish one from another. Results showed that the cry, discomfort, and vegetative sounds differed from one another in certain respects in both segmental and suprasegmental features. Vegetative sounds were brief consonantlike elements such as friction and clicks, somewhat faint because of lack of voicing or of voicing accompanied by breathiness. They were ingressive more often than the cry and discomfort sounds. Cry and discomfort sounds resembled one another in segmental features; they were mostly sonorants, liquids, and nasals. They were also typically voiced. Segmental features formed distinctive combinations in crying; harshness, breathiness, subharmonic breaks, and pharyngeal friction were combined in various ways. These combinations were not found in discomfort sounds. Discomfort and vegetative sounds resembled one another more closely in suprasegmental than in segmental features and were of shorter duration than cry segments.

Stark, Rose and McLagen (1975) noted that many of the features in the analysis were not features that could be used contrastively in English; they would not be expected to contribute to an infant's ability to learn English. On the other hand, features such as the stops, liquids, and voicing are used contrastively in English. As the infant learns speech production skills, these features must enter into new combinations with one another and with other features not yet present at eight weeks of age. Stark, Rose, and McLagen note that the earliest example of such new combinations may be found in the sounds of cooing, which are egressive, voiced, and resemble discomfort sounds in suprasegmental features. Vegetative vocal tract activity is still elicited at that time, but this activity may be a precursor to the nonsonorant consonantlike elements in cooing. Such sounds are not found in the early cry or discomfort sounds. According to Stark, Rose and McLagen, it is possible that what has appeared in the past to be a discontinuity in vocal development when cooing emerges may in reality be an early example of incorporation of one kind of activity of the vocal tract into another. From this incorporation may emerge a new combination of features, for example, the combination of voicing and egressive breath direction with nonsonorant consonantlike elements.

INTONATION PATTERNS IN INFANT VOCALIZATIONS

Intonation patterns have been observed in early infant vocalizations and imitation of intonation patterns is recognized by adults prior to imitation of phonetic stimuli (Nakazima 1965/1966; Murai 1963). Delack's (1974) investigations of the prosodic aspects of infant vocalizations within the first year support the view that there is differential use of intonation at an early age. Spectographic analysis and statistical evaluation of acoustic parameters of infant fundamental frequency contours were examined in relation to various contexts in which infants vocalized. Findings indicated that infants alter their intonation patterns according to contexts. For example, when infants are alone their vocalizations are shorter and have less elaborated fundamental frequency contours than when they are with a familiar adult. Delack raised the possibility that infants may use their intonation to express "semantic intent," interpreting the results as demonstrating the infant's ability to adapt to his environment in a differential manner. This ability, he contends, is present prior to maturation of the visual and auditory system and is later integrated into the infant's development of communication.

Nakazima found that infants begin to imitate adult intonation patterns long before they begin to imitate phonetic elements. Lieberman (1967) reports that infants of ten to thirteen months change their fundamental frequency in vocalizations as a function of stimulation by male and female voices. Further evidence is offered from a study by Webster, Steinhardt, and Senter (1972) in which seven-month-old infants were stimulated with recordings of selected vowel sounds spoken with either high or low pitch. The sounds /æ/, /a/, /i/, /ou/ and /u/ were used at two fundamental frequencies, high pitch (500 to 600 Hz) and low pitch (150 to 200 Hz). When the stimuli were presented, suppression of vocalization was obtained followed by an increase in the poststimulation period. The investigators obtained a significant change in fundamental frequency of infant vocalizations from baseline to high-pitch stimulus periods but no change from baseline to low-pitch stimulus periods. The authors suggest that their findings support Lieberman's results of changes in fundamental frequency in infants as a function of the input stimuli pitch. However, the change was in one direction only.

Following Webster, Steinhardt, and Senter's (1972) suggestion of a relationship between infant production suppression and pitch changes as a function of pitch of the input stimulus, Barrett-Goldfarb and Whitehurst (1973) studied the effect of stimulation on child production when stimulation was presented by either the mother or the father. A suppression effect was obtained, but the parent presenting the stimulation had no differential effect on the pitch of the infant's vocalization. The suppression effect was interpreted as an indication of the degree to which an infant chooses to listen to the vocalization presented to him. The lack of differential effects of male and female voices serving as reinforcers was substantiated in a study by Banikiotes, Montgomery, and Banikiotes (1972). The infants increased vocalization, but equally with input from both sexes. Measures of the infants' fundamental frequencies showed that no changes in fundamental frequency occurred during the course of the study with either the male of female adult presentation. However, the infants were only three months of age as compared to Lieberman's ten- to thirteen-month-old infants.

STUDIES OF BABBLING
According to discontinuity theory, infant babbling from the age of approximately two months to nine months represents a period of maturation of the articulatory mechanism (Lenneberg 1964). Infants may be described as playing with or exercising their articulators. If this period is a precursor to speech and language development, it is so only in the sense that it provides a period of practice; the content or structures do not relate to the content and structures produced when true speech begins.

Lenneberg, Rebelsky, and Nichols (1965) have produced evidence that this period is a period of maturation. They studied the vocalizations of six children born to deaf parents and ten children of normally hearing parents. One of the six children born to deaf parents was also deaf. Data were obtained on the children from approximately two weeks to three months of age. Although the stimulation in the environment was considerably different for the two populations of infants, the children did not differ significantly in their vocalizations. Even the congenitally deaf child's vocalizations were similar to the other infants' vocalizations. Since the infants' vocalizations were not different regardless of the auditory environment in which they lived, the authors concluded that early vocal development is related to physical and biological maturation, not environmental stimulation. Thus, contrary to the learning theory position, auditory experiences are of little relevance during the babbling stage.

Results of a recent study of hearing-impaired infants has raised questions about these conclusions. Marya Mavilja (1969) studied babbling of three hearing-impaired infants from three to four months of age through the sixth and seventh month. The infants' productions were compared to productions of normally developing infants as reported in the literature and one normally developing infant included in the study. Mavilja was interested in determining if hearing-impaired infants pass through a period of babbling in which phonological activity occurs.

She identified three kinds of activities: speechlike babbling in which identifiable vowels and consonants according to adult phonemic productions occurred; nonspeechlike vocalizations of sounds that could be classified as grunt, cry, chuckle, and whisper; and silence, defined as the absence of any vocal production. The infants were recorded for three thirty-minute periods once a week over a three-month period. The vocalizations were sampled within a half-hour after feeding in the morning, after lunch, and in mid-afternoon.

The hearing-impaired infants' babbling reached a peak at about twenty-three weeks, seventeen weeks, and twenty-five weeks for the individual infants after which babbling decreased and silence increased. Mavilja noted that normally hearing infants display a steady increase in babbling prior to the stage of imitation, while the hearing-impaired showed a marked decline.

The infants produced single vowels, single consonants, and vowel-consonant combinations in various patterns. The front vowels /ɛ, æ, e/ and the medial vowel /ʌ/ were produced most frequently. Other medial vowels remained underdeveloped while the back vowels increased slightly with maturity. In all cases vowel production was more frequent than consonant production. By the twenty-fourth week /g/, /k/, and /d/ were produced. The most frequently produced phoneme was /ɛ/. Developmental order in babbling conformed with that generally reported for normally developing infants.

In the total vocal behavior, babbling constituted the smallest portion of time and nonspeech vocalization one-third of the time. Silence constituted the greatest amount of time. A number of phonemes were produced in whimpering that were later heard in babbling, suggesting to the author that early phonemes may emerge in nonspeech vocalizations before they appear in babbling. The most characteristic aspect of the infant vocalizations was spontaneous repetition of sounds, that is, reduplication was observed. Phonemes that had emerged earlier in the infant vocalizations appeared later in babbling. Mavilja raised the possibility that the aimless vocal activity of early weeks may be an indispensable preliminary to the speech that comes later. A high-risk infant studied by the author in another study also produced sounds in early vocalizations that appeared later in babbling.

Some corroboration for Mavilja's findings is found in a study by Cairns, Karchmer, and Butterfield (1976). They obtained longitudinal records of two infants' vocalizations. One infant came from a home with normally hearing parents; the parents of the other infant were deaf. Thus the auditory environments for the two infants differed considerably. The infants' vocalizations were sampled on four separate days each week for a period of forty-seven weeks. The normal-environment infant was observed from one to twenty weeks of age and the infant with deaf parents was observed from age four to thirty-two weeks. Rather than a phonetic transcription, the infant vocalizations were divided into two classes: speech and nonspeech.

Results showed that both infants increased their rate of speech production. The infant of the deaf parents, however, showed a smaller increase than the infant with normally hearing parents. In comparing their data with the data from Mavilja's study, Cairns, Karchmer, and Butterfield noted that systematic changes in vocal behavior occurred as early as six weeks of age. Relating their findings to deaf infants, they speculated that the patterns of vocal activity of deaf infants may diverge from those of hearing infants far earlier than has previously been suggested.

Increase in infant vocalization rates in all stages of development are influenced by environmental stimuli. Numerous studies have been completed that provide evidence that some control is exerted by stimuli administered in the infant's presence either prior to or following vocalization. Many of the studies employ an operant paradigm in which vocalizations are measured prior to administration, during presentation, and after removal of the independent variable.

Effectiveness of a variety of stimuli has been explored as reinforcers for increasing the vocalization rate. Sheppard (1969) demonstrated that a gentle vibrator, flashing lights, and a recording of the mother's voice each functioned to increase vocalizations in an infant less than three months of age. Food, tactile stimulation, and adult vocal imitations resulted in increases in frequency of vocalizations in three-to six-month-old institutionalized infants (Haugan and McIntire 1972). Of the three reinforcers studied, adult vocal imitation was consistently the most effective. Some studies have attempted to determine if specific parameters of adults are important when serving as reinforcers (for example, the presence and absence of an adult figure during presentation of phrases such as "pretty baby," "hello baby," and "nice baby") (Todd and Palmer 1968). Although increases in frequency of occurrence have been obtained in both conditions, significantly more vocalizations are produced when an adult is present.

As previously mentioned, advocates of the discontinuity theory feel that babbling is not directly related to language and speech production, and some base their evidence on descriptions of babbling content. Infants are thought to produce all the sounds of their native language during babbling, sounds they later are unable to produce spontaneously when language appears. In addition, they are thought to produce sounds not in their native language or in any other language. Some recent evidence tends to argue against these assumptions, however.

Cruttenden (1970) examined a variety of sounds produced in babbling by his twin daughters from birth to fifteen months of age. Once a month he made tape recordings of about two hours duration of each twin and phonetically transcribed their utterances. He found that sounds of frequent occurrence in world languages were also frequent in the infants' productions, as Jakobson proposed. But contrary to expectations the infants did not produce many sounds that were dissimilar to sounds in the English language. Cruttenden concluded that the children produced neither all the sounds of English (they had a limited repertoire) nor a wide range of non-English sounds. His findings are supported by Weir (1966), who found that the repertoire of American and Chinese infants' sounds appeared to drift progressively in the direction of the language of their particular culture.

Cruttenden's findings were similar to the early normative findings by lrwin and his colleagues (lrwin 1941; Chen and lrwin 1946; McCurry and lrwin 1953; Winitz and lrwin 1958). Infants start with a limited sound system that grows gradually as new sounds are acquired. An ongoing study at the University of Oregon Medical School (Pierce 1974) presents similar data. Linguistic behavior of seven hundred and fifty children at various age levels has been observed, recorded, and transcribed. Pierce reports data for the period from birth through twelve months at three-month intervals, that is, three-month level, six-month level, nine-month level, and twelve-month level. Each level consists of twenty-six boys and twenty-five girls.

At three months the vowels produced by a child are restricted to the low front and mid-central area of the vowel chart. The number is small initially and gradually increases over levels until at twelve months most of the English vowels are produced. Like Cruttenden's children, the infants did not produce an infinite range of sounds during the period from three to twelve months. According to the Oregon data, only [ʔ], [h], and [w] were produced by the average three-month-old child, although individual children produced a greater variety. By the sixth month the children's consonant inventory had increased by four new consonants. Five new consonants were added by the ninth month and again by the twelveth month. A few sounds that could not have been learned from the environment were present in the children's repertoires, but the overwhelming majority were consonantlike sounds resembling sounds in common use. Pierce's conclusion that both the range and quality of sound types increases gradually from a small restricted set at three months to a large set by twelve months substantiate conclusions reached by lrwin and Cruttenden.

In conditioning studies, too, sounds in babbling can be affected differentially as a function of reinforcer presentation. In a study by Routh (1969) vocal responses of infants from two to seven months were followed by a smile, three "tsk" sounds, and a light touch by the experimenter. For two days the infants' vocalizations were counted but no consequent event was presented. Thereafter some infants were reinforced for vowel productions, some for consonant productions, and some for both vowel and consonant productions. On the last day the infants were returned to baseline conditions.

Routh defined consonants as vocalizations containing at least one sound in which the vocal tract was constricted in some way, exclusive of crying, fussing, protesting, sneezing, sighing, and so forth. Vowels were defined as vocalizations containing open voiced sounds. During conditioning the infants increased their productions of vocal responses. The experimental treatment produced significantly different effects for consonants and vowels in that the infants tended to increase production of the class of vocal responses receiving reinforcement. Thus Routh concluded that environmental events will influence the form as well as the amount of infant vocalization.

On the other hand, Webster (1969) demonstrated a suppression of vocalization during presentation of vocal stimuli. In this situation, of course, the vocal stimuli were not presented as reinforcers. It seemed possible, however, that following stimulation an infant may increase the frequency of producing the vowel or consonant type presented during stimulation. Webster's conjecture was tested by Dodd (1972). The stimuli in Dodd's study consisted of fourteen consonant phonemes presented in the context of three vowels and two nonspeech sounds. The CV sequences were babbled to the infant in reduplicated syllables for thirty seconds during one stimulation presentation in one of two conditions: in a playpen or seated on the experimenter's lap. In a third condition the subjects were played with and talked to, but the specific CV syllables were not presented. Only children receiving the social-vocal stimulation increased the number and length of utterances containing consonants; however, the range of different types of consonants and vowels showed no change from pre- to poststimulation conditions. Since the increase in vocalizations was nonspecific in terms of the CV syllables, only partial support for Mowrer's theory that infants are rewarded by hearing themselves produce sounds similar to the rewarding adult sounds can be found in the results. In fact, Dodd concluded that infants are unlikely to increase their range of phoneme types by such forms of speech stimulation, although they may increase the number and length of consonant utterances with frequent presentations.

If, as proposed in Mowrer's theory, imitation functions in shaping infant vocalizations to match adult models, to what parameters do children attend? Acoustically analyzing the speech of children whose productions are acceptable to adults and comparing them to children whose productions are unacceptable to adults offers one way to learn how children's speech gradually becomes more adultlike (Klein 1971). Klein had an adult model ten different syllables with /l, r, w, y/ and /h/ followed by /it/ and /ut/. Two-and-a-half to four-and-a-half-year-old children imitated the models, which the adults then judged for accuracy of productions. Spectograms were made of the adult and child productions. Interestingly, the children did not match adult utterances specifically, but they may have tried to match differences between two of their utterances to differences between two adult utterances. For instance, one of the features that distinguishes /w/ from /r/ in adult speech is that the origin of the second formant (F2) movement is lower for /w/ than it is for /r/. Although the children did not match the value of their F2 origin for /r/ to the adult value, they made it higher for /r/ than for their /w/ productions. What may be matched, according to Klein, is the contrast that exists in adult speech, not the absolute value for each sound. This occurrence would provide some indirect evidence for Mowrer's theory that children attempt to match adult speech. However, consideration of this possibility necessitates recognition that a child's vocal tract is quantitatively and qualitatively different from an adult's.

Infant vocalizations have been studied within a Piagetian framework by Nakazima, whose longitudinal study of several Japanese and American children is reported in a series of articles (1962, 1965/1966, 1970, 1972). At the beginning of the study the infants' ages ranged from twenty-eight days to seven months. They were recorded approximately once every two weeks until they were about twelve to seventeen months old. Six of the children were Japanese and four were American; but all lived in Japan and were exposed to the Japanese language.

Six stages in infant vocalization development from birth to one year were identified and interpreted within the six sensorimotor periods in Piaget's developmental theory. Other measures of cognition were not employed although observations were made of environmental events and interactions between the infants and their caretakers during the course of the study. The six stages, according to the author, describe the development of the infant's articulatory mechanism.

In the first period, the first month, the schema of using sounds to evoke reactions from other persons develops from the infant's crying. An increase in vocalizations occurs between one and two months, but the productions remain random and involuntary and are related to the infant's physical needs. In the second stage, beginning in the second month, the articulatory organs gain maturity and the infant uses them for play, thus making a distinction between using his articulators for functional and organic needs. These productions are made in quiet times, when physical needs have been cared for, and so the schema of producing noncrying utterances spontaneously by use of the vocal chords is developed. This is the schema of phonation.

It is during the third stage, from two to five months, that an increase in variety of sounds and pitch changes is noted. Although the infants respond to adult vocalizations, they do not imitate the utterances. Central and peripheral organs continue to mature and children exercise their articulators in numerous ways. Vocalizations are described as circular reactions in which infants repeat an action over and over again without consideration for using their productions in communicative situations. At the end of this period an early form of secondary circular reaction appears that fits Piaget's description of the third sensorimotor stage. Infants produce sounds and the sounds stimulate them to produce more sounds. A decrease in infant responses to stimulation from others during this period is attributed to the self-stimulation of the infant. In the first two months infants' responses to others provide them with practice in phonation and articulation. Once the phonation-articulation schemas have developed, infants respond more to themselves than to others.

In the fourth stage, from six to eight months, repetitive babbling consisting of combinations of vowellike or consonantlike sounds occurs. The babbling is not related to utterances in any meaningful form. That is, the babbling is unrelated to later language development. Nevertheless, Nakazima noted that the Japanese and American infants' vocalizations began to show the influence of their respective languages, much as Weir's infants; so that by the end of this period most of the phonemes of the infants' language are in their repertoires. They had also become aware of their relationship to the environment, sometimes attending to the verbalizations of others.

The decrease in babbling at about nine months is attributed partially to the almost complete maturation of the articulatory mechanism. Although infants are not yet ready to apply the articulations consciously to new situations, they are ready to apply intonations and intonation patterns. Evidence for this differential readiness is derived from observations that the infant still does not imitate segmental productions but does imitate intonation patterns. In addition, infants begin to understand others using specific noncrying utterances to express their physical needs. The change is from primary to secondary circular reactions in which vocalizations are directed toward producing results in the environment rather than directed toward the infant. Productions are used as a means of expression and representation. It is toward the end of this stage that the infant displays coordinated schemata. In the previous stages each schema emerged and developed, but in this stage they are coordinated in order to be used in communicative interaction. Thus the schema of phonation and articulation, the schema of responding to others' voices, the schema of evocation, and the schema of using production in expression are coordinated and applied to communication situations.

Study of infant vocalizations from a Piagetian viewpoint would suggest that each stage of development constitutes a prerequisite to emerging representational and symbolic behavior. Vocal behavior may be discontinuous in relation to language content, but the child learns an intent to communicate and in that sense the stages are related to language. Sinclair-de Zwart (1974) explains that the behaviors preceding language show functional continuity and thus are preparation stages for language. Babbling, according to her, serves to give the baby the idea of communication. She goes further than Nakazima, however, speculating that the oppositions of using grunts, whistles, shouts, and other vocalizations to express differential infant reactions could contribute to later development of the phonological system with its distinctive features. The way children construct their phonological rules has a parallel in their babbling in that they share some common structural features. These in turn have commonality with the general principles of cognitive development; for example, babbling is constructed of patterns of sound sequences as is later speech.

Infant vocalizations have been explored in relation to other developmental factors in another longitudinal study (Roe 1975). Three issues were studied: amount of vocalization as a function of age under naturalistic conditions, the amount of vocalization under stimulating conditions, and the relationship between infant vocalizations and other aspects of infant development.

A younger group of fourteen infants was observed from three to nine months and an older group of fourteen was followed from nine to fifteen months of age. Neutral talking was the primary measure but crying, fussing, and laughter were also recorded. Neutral talking included cooing and babbling sounds, expressive jargon, and all other sounds not covered in the other categories. Neutral talking did not change across ages while fussing and crying decreased as a function of age.

The original analysis of neutral talking revealed no relationship with other developmental variables; however, two peaks occurred in the amount of talking in patterns for individual subjects. A "talkogram developmental age" was developed on the basis of the patterns, revealing that the timing for peaks, that is, greater amount of neutral talking, was individually determined. It seemed that the more precocious infants, as measured by the Gesell Developmental Schedules, reached their peak of neutral talking earlier than the less precocious infants.

FIRST WORDS
The transition from babbling to words has been described as a more or less discrete step or hasn't been described at all. This may be due to a change in interest on the part of investigators once a child produces a sequence of sounds for which a referent is made clear to the adult or it may constitute evidence for the difficulty encountered in defining first words. Babbling does not end abruptly when meaningful speech increases rapidly. The child continues to babble while acquiring words, at least in terms of utterances adults can understand. Nevertheless, it is observed that babbling decreases markedly at this point, and according to many sources children lose their effortless production of sounds with the beginning of meaningful speech. At face value, then, the relationship between babbling and language seems discontinuous or elusive at best, but the evidence is weak enough not to deter continued efforts to define the nature of the relationship in some manner. Several conjectures have recently been offered concerning the levels at which continuity can be observed. One proposal is that babbling and language share the same function (Peters 1974). In an anecdotal account Peters explains that children's babbling productions at seven months function in the same way as their productions at seventeen months. Five functions are ascribed to the productions: communication sounds such as fuss, cry, and satisfaction; vocal play; verbal imitation; rudimentary dialogue with adults (practice in taking turns even though the productions are not recognizable); and comment or naming in which a verbal production is associated with an object or event. Because the vocalizations have continued to serve the same purpose through ten months, they represent a form of continuity from babbling to language.

A continuous relationship between babbling and language may be discovered if one examines the form of pattern preferences in babbling (Oller et al. 1976). Babbled utterances are not random vocalizations. Rather, they constitute systematic forms of expression in which the child shows phonetic preferences that are related to the child's later meaningful speech. The same preferences are revealed in later speech during pronunciation of adult words and are similar to certain phonological universals in adult language.

Data in the Oller et al. study were derived from thirty-minute recordings of children's vocal behavior from age four to thirteen months in which babbling was defined as vocalizations containing identifiable syllables. Predictions about the frequency of different babbled elements were derived from meaningful speech processes and were as follows: (1) It was predicted that single consonants would outnumber clusters in babbling. Over 90 percent of all positions in which consonants occurred were filled with single consonants in babbled speech. This process appears related to children's consonant cluster reduction in later meaningful speech. (2) Final consonant deletions were expected to be more numerous than initial consonant deletions. An analysis revealed that the ratio of initial to final consonants in babbling was two or more to one in each subject. Additional predictions of babbling patterns were made on the basis of substitution patterns found in true speech: It was predicted that more unaspirated than aspirated stops would be produced in babbling because children tend to avoid production of aspirated stops in early speech. The prediction was confirmed by finding only three aspirated plosives in the entire corpus. Children devoice final consonants in meaningful speech; therefore, a preference for final unvoiced consonants was predicted. As expected, of fifty final obstruents in the babbling data, only five were voiced. Children also substitute initial stops for fricatives and affricates in early language. In the babbling data initial stops outnumbered fricatives by ten to one. Furthermore, in early speech children prefer to substitute fricatives and affricates for stops in final position. Thus the babbling data were expected to indicate this preference. Asymmetry in production of stops and fricatives in initial and final positions was obvious in that final fricatives outnumbered stops by three to one. It was predicted that glides would outnumber liquids in babbling due to frequent substitution of /w/ and /i/ for prevocalic liquids /l/ and /r/ in child language. Indeed, fifty-two glides and only seven prevocalic liquids were found in the babbling productions. Finally, children prefer apical over dorsal place of artication, that is, alveolar and dental over palatal and velar-uvular consonants. In the babbling data, this preference held for the older infants, but an opposite preference was found for the younger infants.

Contrary to Jakobson and others, babbling appears to be governed by restrictions and preferences similar to those found in early linguistic stages of sound development. The most common substitutions and deletions in early sound acquisition could be predicted from the patterns identified in babbling. Continuity in patterns apparently exists between babbling and language.

A tendency to look for generalization and rules in child phonology may result in overlooking some important characteristics of productions in early stages of phonological acquisition. Ferguson and Farwell (1975) studied children from eleven months of age to the week in which the fiftieth word type was recorded. Study of early words is in contrast to many studies in which children's vocabularies number one hundred and fifty or more lexical items at the beginning of the study. Suprisingly, the children produced an unexpected number of correct forms in their first words. As a matter of fact, as learning progressed the children's accurate forms became less accurate. An example from Hildegard Leopold's vocabulary (Leopold 1939, 1947, 1949a, 1949b) was used to demonstrate the change. She produced "pretty" accurately at ten months, but it changed until at one year and nine months it was produced [pIti]. The implication is that children may be able to perceive and produce accurately phonetic aspects of speech earlier than suspected and these early productions are related to their phonological development. In the desire to look for rule-governed systems, these correct productions may have been missed. Thus it may not be entirely accurate to suggest, as Jakobson has, that children do not produce sounds correctly in first words that they had previously produced in babbling. Phonetically, the productions may be accurate and used appropriately. The transition from babbling to meaningful speech is not necessarily marked by one's need to relearn production of the sounds of one's language. The point in time when productions are examined may be the issue. As the authors point out, productions change progressively during acquisition; the changes seemingly occur as children acquire phonological rules and the utterances come under the control of these rules. A more accurate profile of the child's production and perception abilities, however, may be obtained if early utterances are included in the analysis.

SUMMARY
On the basis of both intuition and available data, it seems more reasonable to view vocalizations as a continuum in the first year of infancy. Data point to a relationship between the productions in the babbling stage and the first words uttered by the child, perhaps on the phonetic level or in the pattern or function of productions. The relationship between very early infant vocal behavior and babbling is not yet clear, but the possibility of feature continuity in some form is suggested. In any event, modifications in infant vocalizations can be obtained with appropriate manipulation of environmental events, although the degree to which specific parameters of vocal behavior can be changed has yet to be explored. Infants obviously can no longer be viewed as passive organisms wholly dependent on biological maturation for modification of vocal productions. They are rather active organisms in interaction with their environment, assumed to be aware at some levels of events in their surroundings. They are able to use their awareness to modify their utterances for communication purposes, or at least for what adults infer to be communication purposes. If irregularities can be identified on any of the levels in continuity, they could have diagnostic and intervention implications.

Phonological Development
The issue of continuity versus discontinuity does not apply as explicitly to variables operating in early stages of children's phonological development. However, linguists and behaviorists in their studies continue to emphasize and explore different variables in their investigations of early vocabulary acquisition.

BEHAVIORAL ASPECTS IN PHONOLOGICAL DEVELOPMENT
According to the behavioral position, once the child begins to use wordlike utterances, modeling becomes an important component for acquisition (Staats 1968). For example, Hursh and Sherman (1973) demonstrated the effectiveness of modeling and consequent events on the development of specific vocalizations in a study with children from fifteen to twenty-four months of age. Syllables in the children's repertoires received different experimental treatments. Parents were asked to use modeling and praise; the four treatments included repetition of the syllable pro-

duced by the child, modeling alone, praise alone, and praise that included a re-petition of the child's vocalization. The parents of three other children tried to increase their children's productions of a specific vocalization in any manner they chose.

The largest increase in frequency of selected vocalizations occurred when parents used modeling and praise in which the child's utterances were repeated. Modeling alone produced the next largest increase for two of the children; no systematic changes in frequency of untreated child productions occurred during the various treatment phases. In addition, increases in vocalizations were selective; produc-tions not receiving treatment decreased while utterances receiving treatment in-creased. Although all treatment components resulted in some increase in the utterances, modeling and praise with repetition of the utterance resulted in the largest and most systematic increase.

Within the operant paradigm, many studies have demonstrated that imitation and shaping are important principles for language acquisition. Investigators, however, have not explored specific phonological parameters of child productions. Phonetic content of child productions has received little attention thus far, empha-sis having been placed primarily on measures such as frequency of vocalizations and classes of sounds.

LINGUISTIC ASPECTS OF PHONOLOGICAL DEVELOPMENT
Linguistically minded researchers and scholars have pursued their interest in child phonology with renewed vigor in recent years. The activity has generated a con-siderable body of literature in which issues are raised and models are proposed to account for the nature and form in children's acquisition of phonology. The field of child phonology appears to be somewhat unsettled at the present time, at least to those attempting to develop well-defined theoretical models, systematic pro-cesses, and principles that may be useful for understanding and treating com-munication disorders. Theoretically, linguists are not in accord with each other about the way children learn phonology, although there is general agreement about many of the processes involved in development. Ferguson and Garnica (1975) have identified three theoretical positions: the structural position as exemplified by Jakobson's theory, the natural phonology position represented by Stampe (1972), and the prosodic theory proposed by Waterson (1970); but there are other intermediate ones. Although the theories are interesting, they undoubtedly have more intrinsic value for linguists than for clinicians. But some of the issues raised by the theorists may be important and interesting to clinicians, especially those corresponding to issues involved in development of intervention programs. The rest of the paper will be directed toward explicating the issues in child phonology in relation to the degree to which they may contribute directly to clinical matters.

Before proceeding to these issues, it is appropriate to point out that one of the main contributions of linguists to clinical procedures is their method for seeking organization or regularities in phonology or language. Their view of language as a rule-governed system has encouraged clinicians to use similar methods to determine if regularities and organization exist in disordered communication. As a result, processes in phonological development identified by child phonologists have been discovered in some clinical populations when linguistic methodology was used to analyze their production problems.

The five issues that will be discussed are rules and processes in phonological acquisition, analysis of children's productions as forms within their own systems versus adult forms as models, the function of perception and production in the immature forms produced by the child, the relevance of the nature of child productions prior to and during rule formation, and individual variability and environmental influences. Although the issues are listed separately, they cannot be discussed apart from each other.

RULES AND PROCESSES

Support for the notion that a child's productions constitute a system requires that rules and processes functioning to form the system be identified. Child phonologists, through in-depth studies of children's utterances, have discovered the presence of processes and rules in children's early productions that systematically account for their inaccuracies. There is general agreement for some of the proposed processes; investigators present similar examples demonstrating the presence of these processes. Complete agreement is not apparent on all proposed regularities and new ones, untested in some cases, continue to be introduced as additional analyses proceed. In some instances, also, different labels may be applied to processes that appear similar in nature. Perhaps the most important factor influencing the rules and processes proposed and the importance attached to them is the theoretical position held by individual investigators. Processes and rules, if they can be substantiated, could offer important principles to the development of effective treatment programs. Some of the processes are described below.

Some commonly reported processes were presented in the study by Oller and his colleagues (1976) in the infant vocalization section of this paper. They will be listed but not discussed in detail here except when they occur in the context of specific models. Frequent reference in the literature is made to consonant cluster reduction, final consonant deletion, devoicing of final consonants, substitution of stops for initial fricatives and affricates, substitution of glides for liquids, and spirantization (the substitution of fricatives and affricates for final position stops). Two processes not mentioned by Oller et. al. in that particular study but frequently observed in child phonology are reduplication and assimilation. Reduplication refers to repetition of one syllable in words of more than one syllable, such as "dada" for "daddy." Assimilation is discussed by virtually all linguists and refers to the influence of surrounding sounds on the production of a particular sound in context. Oller et al. list deaspiration and fronting as processes found in early child productions, but these are not reported as frequently in the literature as other processes.

The use of substitution rules is widely accepted by child phonologists, particularly those viewing the child's productions as mismatches of adult forms. Smith

(1973) relies heavily on substitution rules to account for the discrepancy between the adult and child forms. According to this view the child's phonetic productions can be described in relation to their correspondence to the adult phonological system by considering three components: The inputs to the child are the adult surface forms; a set of rules map these forms into the forms of the child's system (Moskowitz 1970; Smith 1973). In Smith's view, a child formulates a large number of specific rules, which Smith calls realization rules. The child's output is the result of application of this set of rules functioning to produce vowel and consonant harmony, cluster reduction in order to obtain the general canonical form CVCV, systematic simplification, and grammatical simplification.

Vowel and consonant harmony refer to processes similar to assimilation that have some resemblance to coarticulation. Consonant harmony may operate in terms of place or manner of articulation, from right to left or left to right, in terms of all the features constituting a segment, or in just one feature. For example, a rule requiring that bilabial consonants occur only with back rounded vowels shows an interdependent vowel and consonant harmony. An example of consonant harmony is production of [ga:k] for *dark* in which the /k/ influences production of /g/, a right to left conditioning effect.

Reduction of consonant clusters appears to be universal and takes various forms. For example, if one member of a cluster is a stop and the other is not, the cluster is reduced to a stop alone.

In systematic simplification, the set of realization rules function to simplify the child's inventory of elements. Children master sounds or distinctive features one by one until the adult system is approximated. Acquisition may be in terms of a hierarchy of difficulty; thus the stops are mastered first, sonorants follow (either [w/j] or [r/l]), and fricatives are last. Smith suggests that simplification may not consist merely of a reduction in the number of items in the child's system but may refer to a more economical use of the resources at the child's command. As an example, children at some time may have elements in their system that the adult does not have in addition to missing some adult features.

Realization rules produce grammatical simplification resulting from simplification of the child's phonological system bearing directly on morphological or syntactical events. For example, the morphological complexity of initial unstressed syllables may result in the child's first omitting the unstressed syllable. Later a prefixal form is used in place of the unstressed syllable (for example, [ri:'tæk] for *attack* or [ri'stə:v] for *disturb*.

Motivation for the four functions of the realization rules might be to obtain articulatory simplicity and invoke the principle of least effort. Alternatively, however, the four functions might serve as constraints on the realization rules. That is, only rules that will effect implementation of one of the four functions can be admitted as a realization rule.

Phonotactic rules are important to the identification of processes in that the influence of the phonetic environment is considered during analysis of the child's incorrect productions (Ingram 1974; Menn 1971). Although Ingram emphasizes the role of phonotactic rules, adult forms and substitution rules play a prominent role in his theory. Both the child's forms and adult forms constitute structures for analysis.

An analysis of the child's system requires that the following aspects be considered: the adult pronounced form, the child's perceived form, the child's underlying form, phonotactic rules, substitution rules, and the child's spoken form. Substitution rules are segment and place specific; a particular segment is replaced by another segment in initial, medial, or final word position or a combination of these. They are context free. Phonotactic rules, on the other hand, are derived from larger segments stating that a particular segment does not appear because of the influence of other segments in the context.

The underlying form is derived from comparisons with other words in the child's system. For example, if a child produces *cake, bed,* and *good* with the final consonant intact but omits the final consonant in *bird, spoon,* and *that,* the underlying form will be a CVC syllable. When no instances of inclusion of a sound are found, Ingram designates an X to indicate that the child perceived noise where the adult form has a consonant.

Processes derived by Ingram closely resemble the processes proposed in other substitution analysis systems except they are not entirely segment specific. Thus the child reduplicates or might add an [i] vowle to the end of a word (dot = doti) in a process of diminution. Weak syllable deletion and cluster reduction are other processes described by several authors. In addition, Ingram discusses the processes of assimilation and voic ng in child acquisition. He emphasizes that observing only substitutions may result in missing important aspects of sound development and may be mislead ng. To suggest that a sound may be used correctly only a certain percentage of the time may not show that it is a function of more general processes such as weak syllable deletion and assimilation. The assumption that the child's underlying form and perceived form are different or similar is based on a number of examples from the production repertoire. For example, a child who produces the final consonants in the words *cake, bed,* and *good* but not in the words *bird, spoon* and *that* is assumed to perceive the final consonants in all the words. Thus the child perceives the six words with the final consonants and his or her underlying and perceived forms are similar.

Lise Menn (1971) uses the concept of phonotactic rules in her analysis of phonological acquisition. Three sets of rules are used in her analysis of a child's productions: input rules specifying adult English words are accepted as input to the child's reduction system, reduction rules derive the child's output word from the model form as specified by the input rules, and generative rules describe the child's phonotactic system as an independent entity. The reduction rules transform the model word as generated by the input rules into the child's output word by a succession of assimilations, omissions, losses of contrast, and peculiar distortions. The generative rules consist of context-sensitive rewrite rules.

Several of the processes and rules include subsets specifying forms in specific contexts. Cluster reduction is a general process and includes specific rules for /s/ clusters, /r/ clusters, and so forth. In as much as the function of general processes is similar, they can be found in all children's repertoires, but specific rules tend to be more individualized. Neither are the processes present to an equal degree across children; patterns of processes in children's systems are not identical. One child, for instance, may reduplicate to a greater extent than another.

ADULT MODEL VERSUS CHILD'S SYSTEM: PERCEPTION AND PRODUCTION

An important issue in child phonology concerns the best way to study the process of acquisition (Moskowitz 1970; Smith 1974; Ingram 1974; Kornfeld 1971; Waterson 1971; Ferguson, Peizer, and Weeks 1973). The disagreement centers mainly around the question of the relationship between the child's system and the adult system. A major part of this issue is the difference in views concerning the relationship between a child's perception and production. From this controversy two major positions have emerged, although overlap can be found in specific theoretical positions.

Broadly speaking, according to one view adult phonological distinctions determine the child's system. Those who adhere to this position maintain that children's perception develops in advance of their production; that is, they perceive the adult forms accurately but do not produce what they perceive. Children's productions are analyzed as substitutions of the adult forms; their productions are compared to adult productions and features composing each are noted. From the comparison, rules are derived to account for the child's utterances. In essence, the result of the analysis is a series of substitution rules whose functions are justified according to the investigator's theoretical framework.

The other position contends that children produce what they perceive and their productions are faulty because their perceptions are faulty. Within this view children's productions are seen to be within their own system; therefore the relationship between their productions and the adult forms is not a simple one. Analysis procedure vary among investigators, partially as a function of the theoretical position maintained, but usually entail comparison of the child's productions from time 1 to time 2 and so forth. The referent for comparison is the child's production of a recognizable or unrecognizable item in the context in which the utterance occurs.

A speech pathologist would readily recognize from the above description that the issues are almost identical to issues involved in developing intervention programs, especially concerns regarding the roles of perception and production. The two issues, adult versus child and perception-production, will be discussed together in this paper because they cannot be separated meaningfully.

Smith (1973, 1974) employs adult forms as models for the child's productions. His premise is that the child perceives the correct adult forms but does not produce them. Kornfeld (1971) suggests that in this theory the child's imperfect productions are due to motor problems. Smith agrees that there is a mismatch between perception and production but states that the divergence is not due solely to motor problems. It is true that children's competence reflects the adult form they hear, but their output is the result of application of a set of realization rules, not necessarily tied to motor inability. To support his position he presents several pieces of evidence.

First, children demonstrate an ability to perceive distinctions not produced in their own utterances; that is, passive knowledge is in advance of active knowledge. For example, the child distinguishes between such pairs as *mouth* and *mouse* before beginning to speak. Further evidence for this ability is the child's use of two phonemes in the adult language, /l/ and /r/. The child's productions of [l] and [r] might be in free variation for words beginning with [r] in adult language, but the [l] is produced only in words beginning with [l] in adult language; the [r] is not substituted for the [l]. This suggests that if children stored items in the way they produced them, they would be expected to produce both [l] and [r] bidirectionally.

Another indication that the adult form is available comes from the children's ability to recognize their own deviant productions on a recording during the period when they still use the deviant form. Later, when they have acquired the adult form, they no longer understand their previous production. It appears that children's realization rules allow them to relate their incorrect production to the correct adult form represented internally.

Further evidence is cited. First, a child uses an incorrect form during several stages in acquisition but he will later spontaneously produce the correct form. Therefore, the adult form was stored and perceived correctly even though it was originally produced incorrectly.

Second, children use all the distinctive features of the adult system in their realization rules. They may produce only a limited set of distinctive features, but they employ the remaining adult features in formulating the realization rules. That is, the features they use are the same features used by adults.

Third, children generalize a new sound or combination of sounds almost immediately after they produce it correctly in one context. They do not acquire a sound in piecemeal fashion, one allophone at a time. Instead they begin to produce the sound correctly in the appropriate words and only in that set of words, with little overgeneralization. This is evidence that the words were initially stored in the child's memory in the correct form. Additionally, children go through various phonetic features in their approximations during the acquisition of a correct form. These phonetic changes, however, are not confined to a sound in one context or word. The same process occurs in other words in which the sound is present. Therefore the phonetic changes at one level indicate mastery of a complex articulation that results in the formation of a phonological rule at another level.

Fourth, evidence that phonological difficulty will not account for some forms the child uses comes from the process of restructuring. When a rule is applied to change a form the child is producing, the new form does not change in some items. It is not due to an inability to produce the form since it is produced in other contexts and in imitation. The child simply relexicalizes (renames) a particular word and the rule for changing the sound does not apply. For example, when [t] replaces [g] in words such as [gɔk] for *talk*, it does not replace the [g] in [gheik]—*take*.

The child will name a picture *a take* but continue to use [ɡheik] for the verb form of *take*.

Final evidence that the adult form is the model comes from different plural formations of items that are superficially similar in children's repertoires. The adult forms are different, but children produce the same sound substitution in the different words. However, they use different plural markings in the words, as an adult would.

Smith suggests that puzzles, metathesis, absolute exceptions, and recidivism offer further evidence that children are able to produce sounds or sound sequences identical to adult forms although they do not do so in their utterances in appropriate contexts. In puzzles, children use a form as a substitution that they do not produce correctly in appropriate contexts. For example, they substitute [pʌɡəl] for puddle but produce [pʌdəl] for puzzle. In metathesis, when children transpose two sounds in a word, they may be unable to imitate their own imperfect spontaneous productions; whereas in absolute exceptions a sound is produced in one item correctly although in all other items a substitution is produced for it. Recidivism supports accurate perception in that a child's early productions of an item may be accurate although later they become less so.

At an older age level the primacy of perception in children's acquisition of phonology was shown in a study by Menyuk and Anderson (1969). Children from four to five years of age were tested in identification and reproduction of pairs of words with /r/, /l/, and /w/. Children identified more of the words within the word boundary sets than they reproduced. They produced /w/ more often for all the sets but did not identify the words as /w/ words. Thus their perceptual judgments were in advance of their production ability. Three developmental stages were proposed: the child is unable to identify or produce the difference between a pair of sounds, the child is able to identify but not reproduce the differences, and the child is able to identify and reproduce the differences. The authors concluded that children first establish a perceptual category and then try to match their output to this category.

Further evidence of the relationship between children's perception and production was sought in a study by Edwards (1974), who obtained less conclusive findings. Children from age 1.8 to 3.11 years were studied. The procedure was a modification of the Scvachkin-Garnica technique. At each session the child was presented with two objects consisting of painted wooden blocks varying in shape, color, and size. All blocks were made into faces so they could be identified by the child as personalities. The child was trained to differentiate the blocks according to CVC names differing from each other in the consonants tested. The child was encouraged to say the names after the experimenter.

The basic assumption was that correct phonemic perception of an opposition is acquired before correct production of the opposition. Voiced and voiceless fricatives were tested with corresponding voiced and voiceless stops to see if the stops would be acquired first. Pairs of voiced and voiceless fricatives at different places of articulation were tested for order of acquisition and pairs consisting of a marked and unmarked sound were tested to determine order of acquisition and nature of substitutions. All possible glide pairs were tested also to determine order of acquisition.

In general, perception preceded correct production, but in some cases the performance on both perception and production was too variable to determine which preceded and which followed. It appeared that the two modes were occurring simultaneously in development; in some instances production even appeared to precede perception. The relationship between perception and production appeared to be complex; for example, $/l/ — /r/$ may be acquired earlier than $/w/ — /i/$ in perception but later in production.

Contrary to Smith's results, Edwards found that distinctive features were not acquired in a generalized fashion. A feature acquired in one segment was not rapidly added to other segments that contain that feature in adult forms.

Acquisition tended to be uniform, but details of acquisition varied among the children. Individual strategies used by children and factors not directly related to the content of the features or feature combinations served to influence or interfere with normal acquisition patterns, resulting in less patterning. In other words, individual differences played a strong part in the children's performance.

Although Smith maintains that motor incapacity is not totally responsible for the child's production forms, indirect support for this position comes from a study in coarticulation. Children's inconsistent productions of $/s/$ and $/z/$ in spontaneous speech were found to be context sensitive in a study by Gallagher and Shriner (1975a, 1975b). Approximately two thousand utterances from each of three children between the ages of 3.2 and 3.10 years were collected. The children's productions were divided into correct and incorrect categories for each child based on consonant cluster + vowel (C_nV) syllabic sequences. They observed large individual differences in frequency of error among the three children. More incorrect productions occurred when the $/s/$ or $/z/$ occupied the C_1 position in a syllable; that is, in a $C_3C_2C_1V$ syllable, the consonant immediately preceding the vowel was more likely to be in error. This finding seems somewhat contrary to the cluster reduction rule. However, in their study no omissions or distortions were analyzed. Nevertheless, in a CV syllable the $/s/$ and $/z/$ were produced incorrectly more often than in a context containing several consonants. Specific context appeared to show systematic effects on correct $/s/$ and $/z/$ productions. The cognates $/t$-$d/$ appeared more frequently in correct $/s/$ and $/z/$ samples than in incorrect samples, while the reverse was true for the $/p$-$b/$ and $/k$-$g/$ pairs. The identity of segments following $/s/$ and $/z/$ were found to be more important for correct $/s/$ and $/z/$ productions than the identity of preceding consonants. Right-to-left coarticulation affected production of $/s/$ and $/z/$ more than left-to-right coarticulation. More incorrect productions of $/s/$ and $/z/$ following $/\theta, ð/$ were found. It appeared that place of articulation was probably more important than manner in influencing production. The authors did not study the children's perceptual ability for the $/s/$ and $/z/$ in these contexts but nevertheless interpreted the results in terms of Perkell's physiological model of speech production (Perkell, 1969) in which an anatomical division between the articulation of consonants and vowels is proposed. Vowels are articulated by the larger extrinsic musculature of the tongue; consonant articulation requires additional use of the smaller intrinsic tongue musculature. Thus a transition from consonant to vowel might be a more difficult one than a transition from a consonant to consonant since a transition from consonant to vowel would involve activation of different muscle groups. A transition from consonant to consonant would involve the same anatomical classes of muscles. Thus motor sequencing constraints would affect productions of /s/ and /z/. The authors suggest that the results support the position held by Kornfeld and Smith that children's deviations from adult models may be related to motoric difficulties rather than idiosyncratic lexical representations.

A position somewhat intermediate between the two major views of child phonology reflects a mixture of both. Ingram (1974) maintains that children's perceptions of the adult sound system are incorrect and their underlying system will be a mental representation of the adult model. However, the mental representation is not just the result of faulty perception but also of the organizational principles children use to systematize their perceptions. They organize the adult models into basic syllabic and canonical shapes. In this view another component, organizational principles, has been added to account for the child's incorrect productions. That is to say, perception plays an important part, but it is not totally responsible for the child's forms. It is difficult to determine whether organizational principles bear any resemblance to Smith's realization rules. If so, then the positions have some similarity in that the inaccurate productions are not tied to just one component, either perception or production.

The other major position reflects the assumption that an accurate account of children's acquisition of phonology is possible only if their systems are considered apart from the adult model. In this view substitution rules are insufficient for characterizing the child's productions. Children produce what they perceive and their productions are faulty mainly because their perceptions are faulty. It is recognized that motor constraints and linguistic constraints may be operating but perceptual constraints are the dominant factors determining the form of their productions (Kornfeld 1971). The child perceives some of the adult features and actively selects a subset of them to produce. Moreover, perceptually a child may be marking distinctions not in the adult system and will produce these distinctions. Segmental analysis in which the child's segments are compared to adult segments will result in overlooking constraints operating on the child's productions. Methods for analysis differ somewhat among investigators, but emphasis is on analysis of the child's productions with differing degrees of reference to adult models.

Kornfeld presents spectographic data demonstrating that children produce features that adults do not identify. She analyzed productions of C_1V_1 syllables and $C_2C_1V_1$ syllables in which children simplified the cluster acoustically and found differences in the productions of the two forms although no identifiable C_1 was perceived by adult transcribers. She also found that the [w] substitution for [l] and [r] was different from the [w] produced in words with [w]. Yet to the

adults all the [w]s sounded alike. The author concluded that one-and-a-half- to
two-and-a-half-year-old children do not produce the same distinctions as adults.
Instead they elect to produce features from adult feature sets that they distinguish.

Support for this position is provided by Chaney and Menyuk (1975). In a study
of children's production of /w, r, l, and j/, they made comparisons between
children who had acquired these sounds (control group) and two groups of children
who had not yet acquired them. The developmental group (four-year-olds) produced /w/ substitutions for /r/ and /l/ in initial positions in words and either substituted /w/ or omitted the liquid in consonant clusters. The articulatory-defective
children (six-year-olds) produced similar errors on /r/, although some had acquired
/l/ in some contexts.

A production task and an identification task were administered to the children.
In the production task they were shown four pictures, for example, *light, write,
yite, white*. The items were named and the child repeated a sentence after the experimenter using the carrier phrase, "That's a ———." Following the repetition
the child produced the sentences spontaneously five times. Spectrograms were
made of three spontaneous examples of each sentence from each subject. For the
identification task, examples from productions of an adult and the children's own
productions were presented to the child, who pointed to the pictures named.

In the analysis of the children's productions, the loci of the first three speech
formants, duration of the consonant-vowel transition, and second formant termination point were measured. The control children's productions were similar
to the adult productions. The developmental group did not differentiate among
/w, r, l/ by formant frequencies or rate of transition. However, they did not seem
to produce an exact /w/ for any of the sounds. The articulatory-defective children
also not did differentiate among the consonants in formant patterns or in rate of
second formant transition. The sound they produced was not exactly like /w/,
/r/, or /l/ as produced by control children, but was closer to /w/ than the developmental children.

In the identification task the control children identified the adult and self-
productions correctly 85 to 95 percent of the time. The developmental and
articulatory-defective children scored between 33 and 46 percent correct identification of their own productions; they also performed less accurately than the
control group on adult productions. Furthermore, the parents of developmental
and articulatory-defective children scored low on identification of their children's
productions.

Chaney and Menyuk concluded that their study supports the notion that
children may abstract features from several sounds in production of one segment.
They produced a sound that appeared to be a composite of /w/, /r/, and /l/ rather
than one whose features were common to any one of the target sounds.

Another method for analysis of phonological acquisition within the child's own
system was employed by Waterson (1970, 1971). She applied an articulatory
feature analysis for phonetic description and a prosodic analysis for phonology.
The distinctive features of generative phonology were not used but rather the

features were derived from the child's productions. Analyses of features produced by the child and features composing the corresponding adult words were conducted to determine if relationships between the two exist. For example, the child's features were found to consist of labial structures and continuant, sibilant, stop, and nasal structures. Since the correspondence between child and adult structures was only partial, Waterson concluded that a child produces the most clearly perceived features of the adult form. These are features already in the child's repertoire and the most strongly produced features in adult utterances. Moreover, although children may produce the same segments in items as adults produce, they may reorder them according to their own system. Their productions are influenced by their perceptions in that they perceive some features more clearly than others; these are the features they produce in their utterances, sometimes in reordered sequences. Thus differences between the child and adult forms are explained in terms of children's limited perception of the adult forms and the operation of their own phonological system. Their phonological system is a result of their limited perception and limited ability to produce certain features and combinations of features. To account for the child's use of a sound as a substitution in some words in the case where the sound is not used in appropriate words, Waterson suggests that the sound may not be strongly articulated in the appropriate word and therefore the child does not perceive it. Reduplication and assimilation are explained not in terms of processes the child uses but rather as convenient labels to describe patterning in the child's structure in relation to adult structure. Children may not initially perceive all the features separately; but as they acquire words, they perceive one or some of the basic features in the words. These features are used in the composition of their words. All the specifics of the word are not recognized, but rather a schema of the word, resulting in their producing words with some structures that are similar to adult forms. They may recognize differences in form within a particular structure so that variations in their production of a form are evident. As they progress in perception and articulation, they perceive and produce more and more of the adult features. Essentially, children start with a comparative lack of differentiation; as their skill in differentiation increases, they make progress in approximating adult forms.

Although positions are taken regarding the usefulness of deriving substitution rules with the adult form as a model or analyzing the child's system without reference to adult models, the differences between the two positions are clear only in some respects. Reference at some point in the analysis is made to adult forms in both procedures and the child's productions compared to adult models.

Little can be said about the perception-production controversy at this time. Data for either position are scarce and some of them anecdotal in nature. Perception is sometimes inferred but not tested, as in Ingram's examples of a child's underlying and perceived forms or Gallagher and Shriner's coarticulation study. On the other hand, evidence for faulty perception is sometimes derived from indirect data (spectographic displays of children's productions in which their perception is not measured), as in Kornfeld's study. In such cases alternative explanations are possible since perceptual data are not available for the children.

PHONETIC CONTENT PRIOR TO RULES

It is also possible to analyze a child's system by constructing phone classes and phone trees. Ferguson and Farwell (1975) studied two children from about eleven months of age to when they had uttered their fiftieth word. The children were recorded at home at approximately weekly intervals for half-hour sessions. The phone classes were developed in order to describe how the phones produced by the child related or corresponded to each other during sessions and from one session to another. Words were used as the framework for making this determination. The relationship between perception and production was not discussed; the study was addressed to other issues.

For each session all utterances of a particular word were grouped together and all variants of the initial consonants in the productions were recorded. Then all the words beginning with the same phone or set of variant phones were placed together. The set of variations of each of the groups of words formed a "phone class." For example, the phone class /d ~ tʰ/ consisted of the initial consonants of all those words whose initial consonant sound varied between [d] and [tʰ]. Words placed vertically on the phone trees shared successive phone classes for each succeeding session. Solid vertical lines connected the classes when they contained the same word, whereas dotted lines connected phone classes that did not contain the same word but were related to phone classes that did. For example,

A phone class was similar to a phoneme in that it referred to a class of phonetically similar speech sounds that contrasted with other such classes on the basis of lexical identification.

Children's forms for words varied a great deal from one utterance to another, so the investigators felt unable to make statements regarding underlying forms and systematic rules. They noted that variations in traditional analyses are recognized by investigators but are usually considered minor exceptions to general rules.

As mentioned earlier, an interesting finding was that the children's early productions were more accurate than had been expected and became less accurate as learning progressed. This finding is in common with children's acquisition of morphology, in which a correct form may appear in an item in early stages so that the child appears to have acquired the correct rule. As a new rule is introduced, the rules compete for the old form or item. For a time the two forms appear to alternate while the rule is in the process of becoming established. Likewise in phonology a child may initially have the correct phonetic form of a particular item. When a new rule is added and takes shape, the item changes or alternates, coming under the two rules at different times as the child experiments with new items. When the rule is firmly established, the form no longer alternates.

Furthermore, phonological contrasts may be hard to find if attempts are made to find classes. In some cases contrasts can be found only between individual words. Some words may start with, for example, [m ~ n] or [m] while other words start only with [n]. In such cases one could say a contrast exists. The variations in a form over time and partial contrasts may indicate that a sound change is taking place while a rule is forming. When the change is complete, a rule has been established. Rather than learning an opposition in a Jakobsonian manner, one may actually lose an earlier lexical or phonetic opposition as a result of the gradual sound change. For example, the /p/ word that starts the change may be *papa*, a word that begins with a /p/ in adult language. This /p/ may be used correctly but later becomes variable with /b/ until it finally joins words beginning with /b/. In this change, *papa*, has become less like the adult form.

The variations in forms have been noted by others (Smith 1973; Oller and Warren 1973; Ingram 1972). Menn (1971) discusses children's variable outputs as rules are developed and applied so that a subset of rules is unordered for a time. Rules appear to change slowly, with revisions first appearing in new vocabulary items if the right input is provided at the right time. According to Menn, the revisions later transfer to older forms. Since the rules are strong, a correct form learned earlier may be distorted to conform to the new rule.

Children in the Ferguson and Farwell study showed a great deal of selectivity in the words they produced. They had a limited number of words and they selected ones with features in common. The features influencing selection include semantic, syntactic, and phonological ones (Ferguson, Peizer, and Weeks 1973).

Ferguson and Farwell question Jakobson's assumptions that there is a strict separation between phonetic and phonemic productions in phonological development and that the division between prelanguage and language occurs simultaneously in lexical and phonological parameters. Jakobson's model holds that when true words begin to occur, the child has a much reduced phonological system. Successive division of the initial vowels and consonants results in an adult phonological system. However, as indicated, early words are often more accurate phonetically and the processes in early forms suggest that the phonetic and phonemic aspects are not separated. Not only that, but the order of acquisition may not conform precisely to Jakobson's model since children are selective in the words they chose to produce in early stages.

INDIVIDUAL VARIABILITY AND ENVIRONMENTAL INFLUENCES
In their model, Ferguson and Farwell place importance on both phonetic and phonemic development. Individual variation is emphasized, but the idea of universal phonetic tendencies is recognized in the form of the physiology of the human vocal tract and the central nervous system, as constrained by universal syntactic-semantic processes. Lexical items are considered the most important elements in phonological development, but other elements are included. Phonological rules encompass the sound changes occurring as a function of classes of sounds, lexical

items, and grammatical boundaries. According to the model, children learn words from others in the environment. They construct their own phonologies and gradually become phonologically aware.

The foundation for an individual's phonology, according to the model, is a core of remembered lexical items and the articulation producing them. Lexical items with specific phonetic forms are acquired in the context of appropriate social situations. Changes in this core are effected by lexical, phonetic, and social parameters. Although the lexicon has a primary role in phonological learning, it may be replaced later by other phonological processes. Changes and generalizations that occur are derived from the child's own phonic core and from the input to the child. The child gradually imposes more phonological organization on the stock of lexical representations and articulations. The organization is composed of the many regularities identified by linguists, such as processes of assimilation and allophonic relationships. Children employ various phonological strategies in acquisition. One child may select a pattern of assimilation of second consonant to first or assimilation in reduplication, whereas another child may choose not to employ these. Children may use both assimilatory processes and substitution processes or other combinations. Finally, the model assumes " . . . that phonological development includes the gradual development of phonological awareness; i.e., the child's ability to deal explicitly with phonological elements and relations is seen as a kind of self-discovery of his phonological organization" (Ferguson and Farwell 1975, p. 438). The authors suggest it is important to recognize that children have different inputs and use different strategies, which means that their phonological organization and awareness will develop in different ways and at different rates. Identification of individual variations in all aspects, and especially in strategies, might have implications for diagnosis of phonological and language deviancy.

Ferguson and Farwell stress several factors that deserve consideration from interventionists. The point is made that much information may be lost if an investigator is committed totally to discovery of rules since the productions not fitting into the rules may be ignored or missed. A full understanding of phonological acquisition must account for and explain these productions. Menn's discussion of this point lends support to Ferguson and Farwell's caution, and Smith presents some examples of changes in productions in single items over time.

Children apparently do not follow identical routes during acquisition. Ferguson and Farwell emphasize the individual nature of early utterances. Waterson adds to this emphasis by suggesting that the sequence in which words develop is not determined so much by children's cognitive preferences as by the naming input of adults. The input is determined by the adults; children select words to produce that are important and meaningful to them. For example, some children seem to select largely object-oriented words, whereas others produce a more self-oriented set of words in their first fifty items (Nelson 1973). Mothers appear to have a strong influence on the forms of early utterances. The features composing those forms will determine which features a child will attend to and which will constitute his structures. Thus children have different inputs because each comes from an environment in which different things are said to him. Different structures characterize children's productions in early phonological development. Menn agrees that children produce those words that are important to them. Therefore the nature of their rules (particularly phonotactic rules) is partly determined by the shape of the first few words they attempt and partly by some maturational factors. She indicates that Jakobson's developmental schema may not give direct predictions to what will develop first in a given child. For example, if a child has no use for the syllables /pa/, /ba/, and /ma/, the canonical "labial stage" will not appear.

Not only are children selective in the words they choose to utter, but individual variability is apparent in the strategies and processes they bring to the task of learning phonology. If we hope to gain knowledge about children's acquisition, strategies not only need to be identified and described but patterns in use of these strategies across children should be studied. Variables influencing the kinds of strategies children employ may be important to the understanding of normal acquisition and of communication problems.

Finally, individual variability may occur in the units or segments children select to produce in early stages. Lexical items have been accepted as the initial units by many. However, as Ferguson, Peizer, and Weeks (1973) noted, children may vary; syllables may be more appropriate for some children. Likewise, the unit may shift with time from one segment to another at different stages of acquisition until, as adults, the phoneme may be the most suitable unit.

CLINICAL IMPLICATIONS

The work in child phonology, as in other linguistic disciplines, may relate closely to clinical work in speech and language. Evidence of this relatedness can be found in the successful application of distinctive feature analysis to children's articulation errors (McReynolds and Huston 1971; McReynolds and Bennett 1972; Pollack and Rees 1972; Menyuk 1968). The relationship is even clearer in the phonological analyses applied by Oller (1973), Compton (1970, forthcoming), and Grunwell (1975) to describe children's articulation disorders. Oller and Compton have presented evidence that children's articulation errors are characterized by processes similar to those found in normal acquisition. Distinctive features have also been used to analyze production errors in aphasic populations (Martin and Rigrodsky 1974; Blumstein 1973) with the result that systematic feature errors and patterns have been revealed. Finally, phonological analysis of hard-of-hearing children's productions show that some of the rules and processes present in normal children's phonological repertoires during acquisition are also present in the hard-of-hearing children's systems (Oller and Eilers 1976).

Prospects for application of other regularities proposed by child phonologists are apparent. Fortunately, some of the processes are well defined and allow evaluation. For example, processes such as cluster reduction, final consonant deletion, preservation of CVC forms, assimilation, and weak syllable deletion are all available for careful and systematic testing. The existence of rules and processes needs to be explored in disordered populations before they are introduced into clinical routines. This is especially important in light of the fact that the postulated rules have been derived largely on the basis of diary studies employing very few subjects.

Other less well defined regularities have been proposed. They constitute issues needing further exploration, although they may well have clinical significance in the future. The relationship between the child's perception and production is important for understanding normal acquisition patterns. A similar issue has been explored in the investigation of articulation disorders and language problems. For years, clinicians have been concerned about the role of discrimination in articulation impairments. A causal relationship has sometimes been assumed; discrimination is trained with the assumption that the training will effect a change in defective articulation. At the other extreme are clinicians who discount the role of discrimination entirely, centering their training on the production aspects of target sounds. Resolution of the issue in the clinical sphere is not yet in sight, but the complexity of the relationship between the two modalities is becoming obvious. Linguists cannot be expected to provide clinicians with a solution, but the problems in articulation training and normal acquisition may share common components. If so, information from one may be useful to understanding the nature of the other.

Furthermore, clinicians usually evaluate child articulation within the framework of adult models. That is, adult forms are used as the standards in noting articulation errors and substitution rules are formulated. But is this an appropriate procedure for describing children's articulation errors? What if clinicians were taught to be more flexible in their recording of children's articulation errors? Would we find children producing some features unlike adult features and others identical to them? Perhaps these productions could be related to vocal tract characteristics or perceptual salience. A start in this direction has been made in distinctive feature analysis of articulation errors, but a more appropriate feature system may be one derived directly from characteristics of child productions, perhaps a phonetic feature system. If phonetic features are important for learning correct articulation, that is, production, we might consider introducing synthetic stimuli for perceptual training in clinics. Moreover, an important source for discovering features children will acquire and the order in which they are acquired could be mother's speech. Phonetic analyses of mother's input to children could yield pertinent information. Identification of features they stress, simplify, or somehow make more salient in speech to young children should offer useful data for the clinic.

Another issue in child phonology that may have importance to clinical matters is the relationship between the forms children produce when they are just beginning to acquire words and the forms they produce when their vocabulary has grown considerably, the first fifty words as opposed to two hundred or more words. Ferguson and Farwell (1975) point out that children's very early productions are sometimes phonetically accurate, but these items change over time to inaccurate productions as children's systems impose organization on their utterances. As rules develop, they operate to change single items so that at some point in acquisition these items bear less resemblance to adult forms. Later the items shift back to accurate productions. The shift in accuracy over time may be a function of competing rules. As new rules develop, they compete for the same item until one of the rules stabilizes, and the item is produced incorrectly for a period of time. Later the rules change to conform to adult rules and productions become accurate again.

In the desire to look for organizational principles and generalities researchers frequently treat the early productions as exceptions, worthy of mention but not contributing useful information to the manner in which a child's phonological system develops. But these early productions may tell us something about the child's motoric ability and perception. Equally important, the nature of the changes in items over time may give insight into the development of individual children's strategies.

Children in articulation training may go through similar stages. Do their productions change from better to worse and better again in the course of training? If so, which dimensions in the productions shift and which remain stable? Should clinicians be alert to cues indicating that a rule is forming? If shifting occurs but clinicians are unaware of the expected sequence of changes, they might terminate training at an inappropriate period thinking the problem is tied to subject variables (organic or perceptual problems) with which they are ill equipped to cope. In-depth studies of changes over time in children who are receiving training on error sounds have not yet been completed. More stable data is needed from linguists, but careful clinical studies with attention to details of productions would be useful also. Elbert's (1976) study presents some such detailed information. She phonetically recorded changes in articulation in untrained items over time as children were trained to correct their errors. Children appear to use specific strategies in effecting change in error sounds. These strategies are not identical across children.

Waterson, Menn, Ferguson, Farwell, Garnica, and others emphasize the differences among children's early utterances. Children produce selected features that are salient to them. First lexical items have common properties phonologically, semantically, and syntactically. What items children produce are dependent upon environmental events as well as on motoric and perceptual ability. Input from adults, important objects or events in their lives, functionality of their productions in the environment, and reinforcement they receive for their productions influence the content of early utterances. Children show individual patterns in acquisition because of these variables. As Menn points out, if /ba/ isn't useful to a child, he or she will not arbitrarily produce it in early stages. Although in a general sense all children use the same processes, the degree to which different processes are used differ; strategies appear to be individualized. For example, although all children simplify through cluster reduction, the forms for simplification can vary. One child may commonly insert a schwa between the two consonants; another child may more often delete one of the consonants.

Again, although words may be the initial units in which children begin phonological acquisition, the unit might shift as learning progresses until features compose the relevant units. Likewise, words are not unalterably the only units in acquisition. Some children may prefer syllables as initial units.

Results from Elbert's (1976) study show that misarticulating children use some of the same processes when they learn a target sound in training as children acquiring phonology normally. What is intriguing is that on the generalization probes, which cover a variety of contexts, subgroups of generalization patterns emerge. Some of them appear to be related to the phonetic environment of the target sound (coarticulatory effects) and others appear to be related to subject variables (for example, the form of the original error). Thus, misarticulating children may also show different strategies in their acquisition of errors as well as in correcting them. Subject variables in the form of initial acquisition processes, strategies or content, and past history of error maintenance in all probability contribute to strategies, processes, and content children use in acquisition during training.

Compton (1970; forthcoming) has proposed that articulatory-defective children use the same processes as children acquiring phonology normally but they are arrested in an earlier stage of acquisition and have not progressed as normal children do. Research has not yet enabled identification of stages in a hierarchical arrangement; therefore data to support the proposition still need to be gathered. He may be correct; good clinical studies could reveal whether misarticulating children are arrested in phonological development or if they develop processes or strategies that are somehow different from normally developing children.

Finally, it would be helpful if clinicians had a way to determine which contexts to use for training individual children. Some children may learn better if productions are trained in the context of words; syllables may serve the purpose better for others. Differences among children can be seen in casual observations during training. Some children seem to learn a target sound in syllable contexts while others acquire it only after it is trained in isolation first. This discovery is usually made after a considerable amount of training in one context has proven to be ineffective. For efficiency, it would be useful to make this determination prior to investment of many clinical training hours.

References

Banikiotes, F. G., Montgomery, A. A., and Banikiotes, P. G. 1972. Male and female auditory reinforcement of infant vocalizations. *Developmental Psych.*, 6, 476–481.

Barrett-Goldfarb, M. S., and Whitehurst, G. J., 1973. Infant vocalizations as a function of parental voice selection. *Developmental Psych.*, 8, 273–276.

Berry, M. F., and Eisenson, J. 1956. *Speech Disorders*. New York: Appleton-Century Crofts.

Blumstein, S. 1973. Some phonological implications in aphasic speech. In *Psycholinguistics and Aphasia*, H. Goodglass and S. Blumstein (eds.), Baltimore, Md.: Johns Hopkins University Press, 123–140

Cairns, G. F., Karchmer, M. A., and Butterfield, E. C. 1976. Longitudinal observation of infants' vocalizations. Mimeographed. Kansas City, Ks.: University of Kansas.

Carroll, J. B. 1961. Language development in children. In *Psycholinguistics: A Book of Readings*, S. Saporta (ed.), New York: Holt, Rinehart and Winston, 331–345

Chaney, C. F., and Menyuk, P. 1975. Production and identification of /w, r, l, j/ in normal and articulation impaired children. Paper presented at the American Speech and Hearing Association Convention, Washington, D. C.

Chen, H. P., and Irwin, O. C. 1946. Infant speech vowel and consonant types. *J. Speech and Hearing Dis.*, 11, 27–29.

Compton, A. J. 1970. Generative studies of children's phonological disorders. *J. Speech and Hearing Dis.*, 35, 315–339.

———. Forthcoming. Generative studies of children's phonological disorders: Clinical ramifications. In *Normal and Deficient Child Language*, D. Morehead and A. Morehead (eds.), Baltimore, M.: University Park Press.

Cruttenden, A. 1970. A phonetic study of babbling. *Brit. Journ. of Disorders of Communication*, 5, 110–117.

Delack, J. B. 1974. Prosodic analysis of infant vocalizations and the ontogenesis of sound-meaning correlations. Paper presented at the Sixth Child Language Research Forum, Stanford University, Palo Alto, California, April.

Dodd, B. J. 1972. Effects of social and vocal stimulation on infant babbling. *Developmental Psych.*, 7, 80–83.

Edwards, M. 1974. Perception and production in child phonology: The testing of four hypotheses. *Journ Child Language*, 1, 205–219.

Elbert, M. 1976. An experimental analysis of misarticulating childrens' generalization during articulation training. Ph.D. dissertation, University of Kansas, Kansas City, Ks.

Ferguson, C. A., and Farwell C. B. 1975. Words and sounds in early language acquisition. *Language*, 51, 419–439.

Ferguson, C. A. and Gernica, O. K. 1975. Theories of phonological development. In *Foundations of Language Development*, E. E. Lenneberg and E. H. Lenneberg (eds.), New York: Academic Press.

Ferguson, C. A., Peizer, D. B., and Weeks, T. E. 1973. Model-and-replica phonological grammar of a child's first words. *Lingua*, 31, 35–65.

Fry, D. B. 1966. The development of the phonological system in the normal and the deaf child. In *The Genesis of Language*, F. Smith and G. A. Miller (eds.), Cambridge, Mass.: The MIT Press. 187–206

Gallagher, T. M., and Shriner, T. H. 1975a. Articulatory inconsistencies in the speech of normal children. *J. Speech and Hearing Dis.*, 18, 168–175.

———. T. M. 1975b. Contextual variables related to inconsistent /s/ and /z/ production in the spontaneous speech of children. *J. Speech and Hearing Dis.*, 18, 623–633.

Grunwell, P. 1975. The phonological analysis of articulation disorders. *Brit. Journ. of Disorders of Communication*, 10, 31–42.

Haugan, G. M., and McIntire, R. W. 1972. Comparison of vocal imitation, tactile stimulation, and foods as reinforcers for infant vocalizations. *Developmental Psych.*, 6, 201–209.

Hellmuth, J. (ed.) 1967. *Exceptional Infant. Volume 1, The Normal Infant*. New York: Brunner/Masel.

Hursh, D. E., and Sherman, J. A. 1973. The effects of parent-presented models and praise on the vocal behavior of their children. *Journ. of Experimental Child Psychology*, 15, 328–339.

Ingram, D. 1972. Phonological analysis of a developmental aphasic child. Mimeographed. Institute for Childhood Aphasia, Palo Alto, California: Stanford University.

———. 1974. Phonological rules in young children. *Journ. Child Language*, 1, 49–64.

Irwin, O. C. 1941. Research on speech sounds for the first six months of life. *Psychol. Bulletin*, 38, 277–285.

Jakobson, R. 1941. Kindersprache, Aphasie and Allgemeine Loutgesetze (Child Language, Aphasia and Phonological Universals). Translated by A. R. Keiler, The Hague: Mouton, 1968.

Kagan, J. 1971. *Change and Continuity in Infancy*. New York: John Wiley and Sons, Inc.

Kaplan, E., and Kaplan, G. 1971. The prelinguistic child. In *Human Development and Cognitive Processes*, J. Eliot (ed.), New York: Holt, Rinehart and Winston, 358–381.

Klein, R. 1971. Acoustical analysis of the acceptable /r/ in American English. *Child Development*, 42, 543–550.

Kornfeld, J. 1971. Theoretical issues in child phonology. In *Papers from the Seventh Regional Meeting*, Chicago Linguistic Society.

Lenneberg, E. H. 1964. Speech as a motor skill with special reference to nonaphasic disorders. In The Acquisition of Language. U. Bellugi and R. Brown (eds.), *Monograph of the Society for Research in Child Development*, 92, 115–127.

————. 1967. *Biological Foundations of Language*. New York: Wiley.

Lenneberg, E. H., Rebelsky, F., and Nichols, I. 1965. The vocalizations of infants born to deaf and to hearing parents. *Human Development*, 8, 23–37.

Leopold, W. R. 1939, 1947, 1949a, 1949b. *Speech Development of a Bilingual Child: A Linguist's Record*. Vol. 1. Vocabulary growth in the first two years. Vol. 2. Sound-learning in the first two years. Vol. 3. Grammar and general problems in the first two years. Vol. 4. Diary from age two. Evanston, Ill.: Northwestern University Press.

Lewis, M. M. 1951. *Infant Speech*. London: Routledge.

Lieberman, P. 1967. *Intonation, Perception and Language*. Cambridge, Mass. The MIT Press.

Martin, A. D., and Rigrodsky, S. 1974. An investigation of phonological impairment in aphasia, Part I and Part II. *Cortex*, 10, 317–346.

Mavilja, M. P. 1969. Spontaneous vocalizations and babbling of hearing-impaired infants. Ph.D. dissertation, Columbia University, New York, N. Y.

McCurry, W. H., and Irwin, O. C. 1953. A study of word approximations in the spontaneous speech of infants. *J. Speech and Hearing Dis.*, 18, 133–139.

McReynolds, L. V., and Bennett, S. 1972. Distinctive feature generalization in articulation training. *J. Speech and Hearing Dis.*, 37, 462–470.

McReynolds, L. V., and Huston, K. 1971. A distinctive feature analysis of children's misarticulations. *J. Speech and Hearing Dis.*, 36, 156–166.

Menn, L. 1971. Phonotactic rules in beginning speech. *Lingua*, 26, 225–251.

Menyuk, P. 1968. The role of distinctive features in children's acquisition of phonology. *J. Speech and Hearing Res.*, 11, 138–146.

Menyuk, P., and Anderson, S. 1969. Children's identification and reproduction of /w/, /r/ and /l/. *J. Speech and Hearing Res.*, 12, 39–52.

Moskowitz, A. 1970. The two-year-old stage in the acquisition of English phonology. *Language*, 46, 426–441.

Mowrer, O. H. 1960. *Learning Theory and the Symbolic Processes*. New York: Wiley.

Murai, J. 1963. The sounds of infants: Their phonemicization and symbolization. *Studia Phonologica*, 3, 18–34.

Nakazima, S. 1962. A comparative study of the speech developments of Japanese and American English in childhood (Part One)—A comparison of the speech developments of voices at the prelinguistic period. *Studia Phonologica*, 2, 27–46.

———. 1965/1966. A comparative study of the speech development of Japanese and American English in childhood (Part Two)—The acquisition of speech. *Studia Phonologica*, 4, 38–55.

———. 1970. A comparative study of the speech development of Japanese and American English in childhood (Part Three). *Studia Phonologica*, 20–36.

———. 1972. A comparative study of the speech development of Japanese and American children (Part Four)—The beginning of the phonemicization process. *Studia Phonologica*, 6, 1–37.

Nelson, K. 1973. Structure and strategy in learning to talk. *Monograph of the Society for Research in Child Development*, 38, No. 1–2, Serial No. 149.

Oller, D. K. 1973. Regularities in abnormal child phonology. *J. Speech and Hearing Dis.*, 38, 36–47.

Oller, D. K., and Eilers, R. E. 1976. On phonology in hard-of-hearing children: Learning the linguistic sound system. Mimeographed. Seattle, Wash.: University of Washington.

Oller, D. K., and Warren, I. 1973. Implications of systematic instability in child phonology. Paper presented at Stanford Child Language Forum, Stanford University, Palo Alto, California.

Oller, D. K., Wieman, L. A., Doyle, W. J., and Ross, C. 1976. Infant babbling and speech. *Journ. Child Language*, 3, 1–11.

Osgood, C. E., and Sebeok, T. A., 1965 *Psycholinguistics: A Survey of Theory and Research Problems*. Bloomington, Ind.: Indiana University Press.

Perkell, J. 1969. Physiology of speech production: Results and implications of a quantitative cineradiographic study. *Research Monograph No. 53*. Cambridge, Mass.: The MIT Press.

Peters, A. M. 1974. The beginnings of speech. Paper presented at the Sixth Child Language Research Forum, Stanford University, Palo Alto, California, April.

Pierce, J. E. 1974. A study of 750 Portland Oregon children during the first year. Paper presented at the Sixth Child Language Research Forum, Stanford University, Palo Alto, California, April.

Pollack, E., and Rees, N. 1972. Disorders of articulation: Some clinical application of distinctive feature theory. *J. Speech and Hearing Dis.*, 37, 451–461.

Rees, N. 1972. The role of babbling in the child's acquisition of language. *Brit. Journ. of Disorders of Communication*, 1, 17–23.

Roe, K. V. 1975. Amount of infant vocalization as a function of age: Some cognitive implications. *Child Development*, 46, 936–941.

Routh, D. K. 1969. Conditioning of vocal response differentiation in infants. *Developmental Psych.*, 1, 219–226.

Sheppard, W. C. 1969. Operant control of infant vocal and motor behavior. *Journ. of Experimental Child Psychology*, 7, 36–51.

Siegel, G. M. 1969. Vocal conditioning in infants. *J. Speech and Hearing Dis.*, 34, 3–19.

Simon, C. T. 1957. The development of speech. In *Handbook of Speech Pathology*, L. E. Travis (ed.), New York: Appleton-Century Crofts, 3–43.

Sinclair-de Zwart, H. 1974. On pre-speech. Paper presented at the Sixth Child Language Research Forum, Stanford University, Palo Alto, California, April.

Skinner, B. F. 1953. *Science and Human Behavior*. New York: MacMillan.

———. 1957. *Verbal Behavior*. New York: Appleton-Century-Crofts.

Smith N. V. 1973. *The Acquisition of Phonology*. New York: Cambridge University Press.

———. 1974. The acquisition of phonological skills in children. *Brit. Journ. of Disorders of Communication.*, 9, 17–23.

Staats, A. W. 1968. *Learning, Language and Cognition*. New York: Holt, Rinehart and Winston.

Stampe, D. 1972. A dissertation on natural phonology. Ph.D. dissertation, University of Chicago, Chicago, Ill.

Stark, R. E., Rose, S. N., and McLagen, M. 1975. Features of infant sounds: The first eight weeks of life. *Journ. Child Language*, 2, 205–221.

Studdert-Kennedy, M. 1976. Speech perception. In *Contempory Issues in Experimental Phonetics*, N. J. Lass (ed.), Springfield, III.: C. C. Thomas, 243–293.

Todd, G. A., and Palmer, B. 1968. Social reinforcement of infant babbling. *Child Development*, 39, 591–596.

Van Riper, C. 1963. *Speech Correction: Principles and Methods*. Englewood Cliffs, N.J.: Prentice-Hall.

Waterson, N. 1970. Some speech forms of an English child—A phonology study. In *Transactions of the Phonological Society*, 1–24.

———. 1971. Child phonology: A prosodic view. *Journ. of Linguistics*, 7, 179–211.

Webster, R. L. 1969. Selective suppression of infants' vocal responses by classes of phonemic stimulation. *Developmental Psych*, 1, 410–414.

Webster, R. L., Steinhardt, M. H., and Senter, M. G. 1972. Changes in infants' vocalizations as a function of differential acoustic stimulation. *Developmental Psych*. 7, 39–43.

Weir, R. 1966. Some questions on the child's learning of phonology. In *The Genesis of Language*, F. Smith and G. A. Miller, (eds.), Combridge, Mass.: The MIT Press. 153–168.

Winitz, H. 1966. The development of speech and language in the normal child. In *Speech Pathology*, R. W. Rieber and R. S. Brubaker (eds.), Amsterdam: North-Holland Publishing Co. 42–76.

Winitz, H. and Irwin, O. C. 1958. Syllabic and phonetic structure of infants' early words. *J. Speech and Hearing Res.*, 1, 250–256.

Wood, N. E. 1964. *Delayed Speech and Language Development*. Englewood Cliffs, N.J.: Prentice-Hall.

The Use of Research in the Development of Clinical Services for Individuals with Speech Disorders

A Discussion of McReynolds's Paper

RALPH L. SHELTON

In the preceding paper McReynolds has summarized a great deal of empirico-theoretical work pertaining to infant vocalization and phonological development, and she has avoided the often accepted assumption that remediation need only track normal development. Indeed, she acknowledges that the information she has discussed has little demonstrated value in remedial work. We are in agreement that if scientific information is going to be applied in the rehabilitation and education of persons with language disorders, the applications require empirical testing. For example, use of synthetic speech stimuli for teaching articulation to a suitable group of children seems logical and persuasive. The stimuli should be prepared in terms of what is known about the children to be taught, and the treatment should be tested in well-controlled research before it is adopted in clinical practice. There is no regulatory agency comparable to the Federal Drug Administration to test behavioral treatments, but that does not relieve professionals of the responsibility for carefully testing their services.

However, I must acknowledge that support for such research and development is not universal among clinical workers. Whatever reservations they have about empirical assessment of speech and language treatments probably have multiple bases, including recognition that it is difficult work to accomplish. Simply obtaining subjects and testing and treating them takes great effort. Many early educational services for children should perhaps be evaluated in terms of their impact on various indexes of adult performance, but the investigation of relationships between childhood educational services and adult performance may be impossible to investigate because of the numerous opportunities for confounding in any such long-term study. Some clinicians may mistrust research in fear that comfortable clinical routines will be discredited. Still others may prefer to justify services in terms of clinical rationale and informal assessment. If the latter practice is a fault, a worse error may be made when an occasional scientist relies heavily on hypothetical patients to illustrate the applied significance of a set of data or a theoretical statement.

In a review of the relationship between psychological research and educational practice, Travers (1965) noted that the research of Thorndike and Judd influenced educational practice during the early part of the current century. However, Travers was generally skeptical about the influence of research on educational practice thereafter. He noted that it is difficult for most educators to adopt the doubting, questioning outlook of the investigator. Problems in using research methods in schools are reflected in a newspaper account of a project that called for assessment of certain experimental school services by a set of investigators who would function independently of the school personnel delivering the services (Parsons 1976). The account stated that some school districts tried to impede the work of the independent evaluators. (I have turned to several public and parochial school districts for permission to include their children in research projects involving testing and training that we provided and also for help in locating suitable children. The cooperation has been excellent in every case.)

It is also apparent that experimental and theoretical work in psychology and linguistics has often had great impact on speech and language habilitation and rehabilitation. Indeed, clinicians sometimes seem too willing to incorporate ideas from scientific fields into clinical work. The problem, of course, is to make certain that application of basic knowledge is made skillfully and effectively. Clinical hypotheses and descriptions and applied research based on sound scientific methodology are mutually supportive; and basic research provides concepts, measures, and techniques that deserve testing in clinical research and practice.

Influencing Language and Articulation by Training

LANGUAGE.
McReynolds cited literature indicating that environmental variables can influence infant vocalization and later phonological development. The demonstration of an environmental influence does not account for normal development, but it does lend encouragement to those of us who would facilitate the communication of young children who are not progressing to the satisfaction of their parents or other adults. We recognize that "environmental influence" is not the equivalent of resolution of a clinical problem.

Many clinicians believe that language and articulation disorders should be corrected as early as possible or, similarly, that preschool services are essential if children are to achieve their full cognitive potential. This matter of early training is an important practical issue, for if service is delivered unnecessarily a great deal of money will be wasted. On the other hand, if treatment or service is postponed until a critical period has passed, the potential of many children may be wasted.

McReynolds has stressed the influence of training variables such as shaping and reinforcement. Her comment that stimulation by itself may be ineffective is important, for many speech pathologists consider stimulation a powerful treatment and sometimes provide both language-delayed children and aphasic adults with clinical service that emphasizes bombardment with stimuli and little or no consideration of response, problem solving, or interpersonal relationship. Stimulation as a clinical treatment may be a worthy research topic. Other approaches to language training, of course, are also used. One involves administration of a test and then delivery of training programs based on the client's pattern of test behavior. Some of these tests are professionally prepared and meet high standards of reliability, item analysis, and various kinds of validity. The Illinois Test of Psycholinguistic Abilities is one such test. Others are teacher-prepared criterion-referenced tests (Popham and Husek 1969) wherein teacher-clinicians sample behaviors they think are important. Training will be influenced by test patterns of client strength and weakness.

Hubbell (in press), who would list facilitation among the tools available to the language clinician, points out that a treatment goal for some children is the establishment of spontaneous vocal expression. He cites literature indicating that questions and commands tend to constrain spontaneous speech, whereas spontaneous expression may be facilitated by following the child's lead in a pragmatic interaction and by using declarative sentences to talk about what the child is doing.[1] Hubbell suggests that use of reinforcement and programming may be the treatment of choice for resolving such problems as syntactical errors but not for encouraging spontaneous expression. Indeed, something that reinforces members of one response class may constrain spontaneous utterance.

The matter of training parents to help their children with speech and language is another issue of importance for the application of basic research. Winitz (1975) writes that parent acceptance of articulation errors may contribute to the maintenance of those errors. The work of Hursh and Sherman (1973) cited by McReynolds indicates that parents can be taught to influence their children's language. Hubbell reports that the facilitation procedures noted above can be used effectively by parents. Irwin (1960) reported that children who were read to by their parents during the period from the thirteenth to the thirtieth month of age surpassed control group members in number of sounds produced during recording periods. Levenstein (1970, 1971) taught parents to interact verbally with their children during play and found that the children's IQ scores increased. A committee of British educators (Bullock 1975) has concluded that parents should be taught to help their children with language. The authors recommended including information about language development in antenatal clinics and providing secondary school children with language-centered interactive experiences with young children. If the need for remedial speech and language services can be reduced by training parents to facilitate their children's communication then parent work can be considered a form of disorder prevention.

Bullock and his associates acknowledge that not all parents or educators are amenable to parent work. A criticism of parental involvement in speech remediation was expressed by Goda (1970), who wrote that a teaching role for a parent is incompatible with a loving and supportive role. There are dangers in having parents work with their own children. In our work, parents were instructed to teach their preschool articulation-impaired children to make certain auditory associations and discriminations. Even though the parents were instructed to accept the responses the children produced, some of the parents reported that during the task they had become frustrated and angry with their children's responses. Nevertheless, when parents become concerned about their children's speech, they are likely to attempt to correct it. From interviews with parents of preschool misarticulating children, we found that parents did attempt to help their children talk better (Shelton, Arndt, and Miller 1961), usually by asking the child to imitate sounds or words. The children's imitations were often unsuccessful

---

[1]Questions, commands, and parent influence on children's language are discussed by Bloom (this volume). She commented that mothers frequently present questions and directives to their children.

and both parents and children tended to become frustrated. Hubbell's facilitation procedures may circumvent these dangers in that they may facilitate language usage and parent-child relationship simultaneously.

ARTICULATION
Since the topic of this volume is consideration of the implications of basic speech and language research for the school and clinic, a brief discussion of the methods used by speech pathologists in treating disordered articulation is in order. Articulation treatment is chosen as a focus for several reasons. First, the phonological development literature that McReynolds has reviewed pertains most directly to this topic. Second, large numbers of children who appear to be free of organic or psychological disabilities articulate poorly; the understanding and correction of their articulation deficits is a worthy goal. At the same time, the principles and procedures used may be applicable in articulation training for persons with structural defects such as cleft palate and physiological defects such as dysarthria.[2] Selection of treatment priorities and goals sometimes becomes involved in conflict of an advocacy, sociopolitical nature. For example, there has been some debate about whether articulation disorders have recieved priority that should be given to children with other problems in public school speech correction programs. However, here the concern is with understanding the disorder and with treatment effectiveness rather than with debating priorities.

A final reason for focusing on articulation disorders is that the effectiveness of articulation training can be evaluated in terms of the accomplishment of relatively short-term goals. That is, articulation treatment does not continue throughout childhood, and hence it can be studied from start to finish in a relatively short period of time. The treatment process is also a suitable microcosm for the investigation of training in that we can tell more easily when the problem is solved. If we obtain a representative sample of a child's conversation and the individual makes no articulation errors, we can surmise that no articulation problems exist. This is not true of problems such as poor auditory processing, which are often more difficult to assess directly.

McReynolds has mentioned a number of issues to be considered and procedures speech pathologists might use in serving an individual who misarticulates. The individual's articulation must be sampled and errors produced must be studied to identify any pattern that exists. A decision must be made whether training is warranted, whether the individual is likely to improve without remedial service, or whether training would probably fail. Abiding issues concern whether articulation training should emphasize perception, production, or a combination, and what units should be used to organize training—feature, phone, syllable, word, or a larger unit. Curtis (1970) called for a behavioral unit for use in articulation training, but it is my opinion that several units are needed. Cutting and Pisoni (this volume) discussed the use of multiple units in another context. Correction

[2]Recommendations made by Lahey (this volume) for the treatment of children's language disorders follow a pattern similar to the one that has evolved for articulation remediation.

involves manipulation of some kind, and the current behavioral technology is of demonstrated value. The concept of innate capacity for language development, however, appears to be irrelevant unless it pertains to the selection of training units.

What is it that the speech pathologist does in correcting articulation disorders that we would improve or replace? When dealing with articulation errors in children free from associated pathology (functional articulation errors), the clinician samples the child's articulation and compares errors with norms. This screening function utilizes normative information, but it does not constitute diagnostic evaluation. Given children with articulation problems, clinicians often argue about etiology. Like some of the linguists who have looked at disordered articulation, some speech pathologists think some single variable or class of variables causes all instances of misarticulation except where dysarthria, hearing loss, cleft palate, or other physical conditions exist. However, they disagree among themselves about the cause. Some agree with the linguist that the child's rules are damaged. While this might be useful as a descriptive statement, Pollack and Rees (1972) talk of phonological rules in a way that suggests they have causal properties. Others assume that some physical deficit such as an oral somesthetic deficiency or motor incoordination remains to be found. Still others assume that the child's auditory processing system is at fault even though the child has normal hearing sensitivity or that environmental factors of a reinforcing nature are responsible. It is now recognized that causes often cannot be identified, in which case service is based exclusively on the behavior the client presents (Irwin 1970).

If a child fails the screening procedure or if someone is especially concerned about his or her speech, the speech pathologist will examine the articulation in greater detail. At one time sampling various consonants about three times each as they appeared at the beginning, middle, and end of words was considered sufficient. More recently, sampling of phones from different phonemes sufficiently often to obtain a reliable index to the child's sound production is considered necessary for accurate assessment. Sounds may be sampled systematically in different contexts, and they may be studied as they are obtained under different stimulus conditions: imitation, picture naming, reading, and conversation. Sounds of interest may be observed in different units: syllables, words, phrases, conversation, and out of context (isolation). The resulting data can then be studied to identify an error pattern. For an older child who misarticulates only one or two sounds (probably /s/ or /r/), the clinician has a relatively easy pattern analysis task. In what, if any, contexts or units and under what stimulus conditions are correct responses produced? If the child makes errors in producing many phonemes, then the pattern analysis is more difficult.

McReynolds and Engmann (1975) have devised a technique to analyze articulation errors (not including distortions) using a distinctive features approach. Such an analysis provides a basis for selecting sounds for training so that generalization of correct responses to untaught items may occur more efficiently.[3] Turton (1973)

[3]Use of distinctive feature analysis is based in part on the assumption that phonological

has recommended an error pattern analysis based on a classification scheme that categorizes sounds by place and manner of articulation, and Shankweiler and Harris (1966) used a confusion matrix to display the relationship between target sound and sound produced.

It is not known whether the effects of treatment based on relatively simple pattern analysis such as those presented by Turton (and also by authors of various articulation tests) differ from treatment approaches based on analyses of distinctive features. The McReynolds-Engmann feature analysis system is time consuming because of the extensive amount of testing the authors use. Further research using these types of feature analyses might provide valuable information about the recurrence of key patterns that can be identified without detailed analysis. It seems safe to conclude that information about error patterns will continue to be useful in planning and conducting articulation treatment.[4]

Having identified a child with an articulation problem and having analyzed and described that problem, the speech pathologist must decide what form treatment should take. Consideration should certainly be given to the presence of other communication disorders, including other aspects of language. An abiding issue arises here in that the clinician must decide whether to train articulation directly or to direct treatment to something presumed to be related to the misarticulation. Some clinicians test and perhaps train speech sound discrimination, oral coordination, or even swallowing behavior. Other clinicians attempt to train speech performance more directly.

A large number of tests and measures (such as language, school achievement, auditory processing, and oral structure) have been administered to a group of eight- and nine-year-old children with articulation errors including the misarticulation of /s/ or /r/ (Arndt, W. B., Shelton, R. L., Johnson, A. B., and Furr, M. L., in press). Submission of the data to a clustering analysis procedure indicated that some of the children were characterized by relatively good language and achievement, others by relatively poor language and achievement, and still others by oral structural measures. This suggests that no one treatment plan may be best for all misarticulating children.

The person undertaking direct articulation training must decide what stimuli and practice units to use in training. A procedure used by our students is one that samples the child's articulation of sounds of interest in conversation, reading (if the child is old enough), and in imitation of sentences, words, syllables, and the sounds in isolation. Responses obtained under reading or picture naming may be

---

development involves a rearrangement of rules guiding usage of speech sounds. Bloom (this volume) states that word learning rather than feature learning may be especially important. However, this would not seem to detract from the importance of features in generalization from articulation training.

[4]Some writers seem surprised that articulatory errors follow patterns. I would be more surprised if they did not. McReynolds's citation of Oller's findings of orderly patterns in the vocalizations of infants is welcome. Locke (1968) noted that a speaker may articulate a sound correctly in one production of a given context and misarticulate it in another. Perhaps such errors occur randomly, but I suspect that even here a potentially identifiable pattern exists.

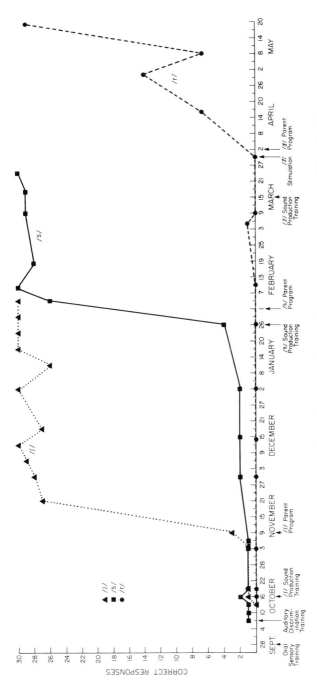

Figure 1. Data plot for a preschool child undergoing articulation training. The ordinate pertains to the child's articulation scores on target sounds in thirty syllables, words, or sentences that are imitated after the examiner but are not used in training. Improved performance on those items during a period of training may reflect generalization from the training provided. The abscissa pertains to time and carries information about the initiation of different clinical services. The child was first taught /ʃ/, then /s/, and finally /r/; and response to training was orderly and satisfactory. The same chart could be used to record counts of the child's use of target sounds in conversation (and reading for an older child). Information about a client's success in articulating a sound in training units might also be clinically useful.

compared with imitative responses. The child who consistently misarticulates a target sound and who does not produce the sound correctly in imitation is then taught to produce the sound in isolation. Auditory stimulation and placement procedures may be used. For the child who can produce the sound in some contexts, training starts with larger units. As the child responds successfully, training is shifted to larger units and to use of stimuli that initially were not successful in eliciting correct responses. Winitz (1975) emphasizes finding stimuli that do not trigger the faulty articulatory responses the clinician is attempting to replace.

When the client can produce target sounds correctly in many units and under different stimulus conditions, we may train a parent to monitor the child's articulation outside the clinic. The parent is to reinforce spontaneous correct responses and to have the child repeat correctly words in which a target sound was misarticulated (Shelton, Johnson, and Arndt 1972; Shelton et al., 1975). One phase of this training is directed to acquisition of new motor speech responses and the other to automatization of available responses (Wright, Shelton, and Arndt 1969). Generalization is a key component of the process.

Having discussed some of the procedures used in the evaluation and treatment of articulation disorders, I should add that speech pathologists must be encouraged to evaluate the child's progress as it occurs (Elbert, Shelton, and Arndt 1967; Shelton, Elbert, and Arndt 1967; Wright, Shelton, and Arndt 1969; Diederich 1973). Tallies may be kept of the child's response to training items and of generalization of correct production to word or sentence lists in which the sound occurs but that are not used for training. (See, for example, figures 1 and 2). Tallies of correct responses in reading and conversation may also be recorded. Charting, which helps one observe change during treatment, is adaptable to different treatment methods but especially to programming, which is described by Gerber (in press) and Costello (in press).

Evaluation of Treatment: Prediction and Tests

Treatment research proves to be difficult to conduct. If one decides to do time-series studies on individual subjects, their baselines are often unstable and it is difficult to determine how representative or applicable the findings are. If group studies are attempted and minimal criteria for membership in a group are established, groups are difficult to fill. In addition, the results of correlational and group comparison studies often fail to account for substantial amounts of the variance as revealed by statistical procedures such as the index of determination (Young 1976; Hays, 1963). However, it is my opinion that a strong effort should be made to predict in precise terms the outcomes of treatment. Ways of predicting an individual's response to treatment from tests and measures that correlate most highly with articulation change must be developed.

A strategy for developing such predictive devices might take the following form. First, predictions about the amount of time required to improve articulation and the form that improvement will take can be tested with one set of subjects. On the basis of the outcome of this initial effort, new predictions can be made with new subjects and the process repeated. Perhaps a program of research of this type can

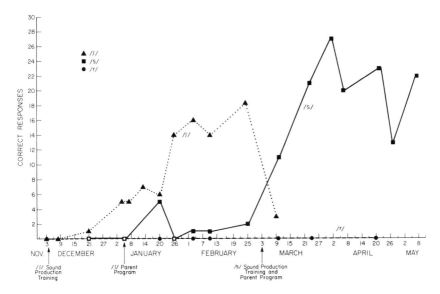

Figure 2. Data plot for a second preschool child undergoing articulation training. The child improved production of /ʃ/ during a period of training but did not achieve asymptote sound production task measure of /ʃ/ generalization. Training was then directed to /s/, which improved, but gains on /ʃ/ were lost. The second child was less responsive to training than many preschool children with articulation problems, but the only thing distinctive about her was that two siblings presented similar problems.

gradually shape a more precise clinical service. Accuracy of prediction might be tested loosely in terms of whether we could anticipate which of a pair of children would perform better on an improvement measure. Tighter predictions would involve specification of the nature of treatment response. I presently advise clinical students to state short-term predictions about the behavior of individual clients and to test those predictions. Correct prediction of spontaneous improvement can be followed by prediction of further improvement. A sequence of testing, predicting, and retesting can both save treatment costs and provide a baseline of sorts against which to evaluate training when it does prove necessary.

Group research using discriminant function analysis might be helpful in identifying measures suitable for use in the predictive studies. Naremore and Dever (1975) wrote that discriminant function analysis can help in the identification of a set of dependent variables that operate together and distinguish between subject groups. These authors indicated that this sort of research can lead to developments that provide the teacher with information about what children are currently doing and what they need to do next. This knowledge is said to be necessary if the teacher is to facilitate children's progress through developmental sequences.

Clinicians spend a great deal of time administering tests that lack sufficient construct validity to allow close prediction of anything. Indeed, society pays great numbers of people to administer tests even though those people cannot say precisely what they are going to do with the test results. The following statement recently appeared in an announcement issued by the University of Arizona:

The National Institute of Neurological and Communicative Disorders and Stroke has announced a program for the evaluation of procedures screening preschool children for signs of impaired language development. The main objectives of this requirement are: (a) to determine the validity of language screening procedures and individual items with instruments which are presently available for detecting children with signs of impaired language and (b) to determine the validity of selected individual items and procedures for detecting preschool children with signs of impaired language when administered by educational or health professionals other than speech and language pathologists and by paraprofessional aides.

It is my hope that the research to be contracted will hold to a narrow definition of construct validity—precise prediction of individual clients' future behavior within a specified theoretical framework. Clinicians are presently reliable in sorting individuals into disorder categories. The research called for seems to be directed to economizing the classification process, but there is a need to go beyond classification to prediction.

Perception and Production in Speech Correction

An issue discussed by McReynolds concerns whether the sounds produced by children that are heard as phonemic substitutions differ phonetically from the sound heard by the adult listener. That is, is the /w/ a child substitutes for the /r/ in *red* different from the /w/ he or she produces in *wed*? Locke and Kutz (1975) reported evidence that children who say *wing* for *ring* point to *wing* rather than *ring* when recordings of their utterances are played back to them. McReynolds reported that some researchers have observed spectrographic differences between the speech of children and that of adults. But can issues of this type be resolved adequately by spectrographic analysis? Curtis (1970) and several authors in this volume have pointed out that perceptual, productive, and acoustic measures of a given speech act often lack simple correspondence with one another. Abbs (1973), in pursuing the study of muscle spindle function in the control of mandibular movements, commented that he wished to study movements directly rather than to infer them from acoustical displays or from perceptual observations. He wrote, "Because measures such as acoustical observation and phonetic transcription are removed from the actual motor output of the system by several transfer functions, they are very likely confounded by several levels of physical and perceptual distortion" (pp. 183–184). Hypernasal speech has some identifiable spectrographic characteristics, but no one has demonstrated that spectrographic analysis has reliability or validity as an index to hypernasality (Moll 1968). Nevertheless, individuals report spectrographic information about hypernasality without bothering to discuss their work operationally or in terms of reliablity.

Another problem that basic scientists might be able to help solve is how to assess one's perception of the correctness of one's own articulation. Speech sound discrimination tests used by speech pathologists often are not sensitive or accurate measures of perception. Indeed, speech pathologists and special educators seem to be targets for the sale of many tests ranging from poor to marginal in quality of development. Confounding this process further are problems in interpreting a child's failure to perform correctly.

For example, children asked to attend to the correctness of /ʃ/ in *ship* may respond in terms of their understanding of the word rather than with reference to articulation of the phone. Also, children may fail discrimination measures because they do not understand the task (Weiner 1972) or do not attend to it (Locke 1971). Too often clinicians fail to differentiate among these sources of error on discrimination tasks. In a listening training study we are currently conducting, observation of some subjects' performance suggests that some auditory perceptual training that appears to be successful does not teach children new perceptions but rather allows them to display perceptions being made all along. A child may recognize the difference between /s/ and /ʃ/ but still take time to catch on to a task intended to test or teach that discrimination.

McReynolds cited the viewpoint that babbling provides some sort of exercise for the speech mechanism. She also cited a statement that as the articulatory organs gain maturity the infant uses them for play. Perhaps maturation of the speech mechanism requires the performance (practice) of coordinated oral utterances. However, the concepts cited are rather vague. The speech mechanism of the newborn is not used to articulate speech, but it does serve airway defense and swallow functions quite skillfully. There is an extensive literature on therapeutic exercise that develops such concepts as strength, endurance, range of motion, and skill. If babbling is to be interpreted as an exercise, one thing we need to know is the explicit purpose it serves.

McReynolds mentions that children may not be able to repeat their prelinguistic utterances once they are associated with meaning. If this is correct, perhaps it suggests that babbling and speech have little in common. The loss of ability to produce utterances used earlier during babbling may be compatible with the viewpoint that different brain centers coordinate speech and nonspeech oral movements (Hixon and Hardy 1964). In this speculation, babbling is considered a nonspeech oral behavior. Interpretation of any loss of oral motor performance might be enhanced by study of other infant behaviors that may be lost in an analogous manner. Bosma (1975) discussed loss and specialization of sensory receptors as part of a process of maturation by diminution. One of the most striking aspects of biological maturation of the speech mechanism is the descent of the mandible, tongue, hyoid, and larynx (Bosma 1975). This process extends beyond the babbling period, but the structural relationships do contribute to articulatory movements. For example, tongue fronting is likely to occur in someone whose tongue fills the oral cavity—and early in life that includes just about everyone.

Those concerned with the correction of articulation errors are involved with movements produced by the speaker. Indeed, McDonald (1964, p. 108) says "Defective articulation consists of movements which are not adequate for producing the sound attempted." Even listening training for persons with speech problems is usually intended to influence speech production movements. Some authors concerned with the analysis of misarticulated speech would use features for their analyses that are more physiological than features associated with Chomsky and Halle (1968) or Jakobson, Fant, and Halle (1952). MacNeilage (1972) concluded a review of speech physiology with the observation that phonetics occupies a rather marginal position within linguistics. He wrote, "The generative phonologists' lack of concern with many aspects of the speech signal is one way in which they indicate their opinion that speech physiology has limited relevance to linguistic theory. The fact that aspects which are of interest are *perceptual* ones further reduces the relevance of speech physiology" (p. 52). A phonological literature little concerned with matters of speech movements will require considerable interpretation and translation if it is to be applied to the correction of articulation disorders. Indeed, in talking about articulation problems, one often finds oneself somewhere between phonetics and phonology and speaking a polyglot language reflecting and abusing the terminology of both groups.

In conclusion, if we wish to influence the work that speech pathologists or educators do with regard to speech and language, we must consider what they are doing now. What are the clinical problems they are trying to solve? It is not appropriate to instruct them to read all the scientific journals and all the advanced texts in speech science and linguistics and to modify their ways accordingly. Some people must try to serve as intermediaries for tying together clinical work and theoretical-empirical developments, and even those individuals must specialize if they are to obtain any depth. What is the process whereby basic knowledge is assimilated into clinical practice? How do we avoid premature assimilation? Surely applied research is involved in the answer to both of these questions.

References

Abbs, J. H. 1973. The influence of the gamma motor system on jaw movements during speech. *J. Speech Hearing Res.*, 16:175–200.

Arndt, W. B., Shelton, R. L., Johnson, A. B., and Furr, M. L., Identification and description of homogeneous subgroups within a sample of misarticulating children. *J. Speech Hearing Res.* in press.

Bloom, L. (This volume). The integration of form, content, and use in language development.

Bosma, J. F. 1975. Anatomic and physiologic development of the speech apparatus. In *The Nervous System*, Donand B. Tower (ed.), *Vol. 3: Human Communication and Its Disorders*. New York: Raven Press, 469–481.

Bullock, A. 1975. *A Language for Life*. London: Her Majesty's Stationery Office.

Chomsky, N., and Halle, M. 1968. *The Sound Pattern of English*. New York: Harper and Row.

Costello, J. In press. Programmed instruction. *J. Speech Hearing Dis.*

Curtis, J. F. 1970. Segmenting the stream of speech. In *The First Lincolnland Conference on Dialectology*, J. Griffith and L. E. Miner (eds.), Tuscaloosa, Ala: University of Alabama Press.

Cutting, J. E., and Pisoni, D. B. (this volume). An information-processing approach to speech perception.

Diedrich, W. M. 1973. *Charting Speech Behavior*. Lawrence, Ks. Extramural Independent Study Center, University of Kansas.

Elbert, M., Shelton, R. L., and Arndt, W. B. 1967. A task for evaluation of articulation change: 1. Development of Methodology. *J. Speech Hearing Res.*, 10: 281–288.

Gerber A. In press. Programming for articulation modification. *J. Speech Hearing Dis.*

Goda, S. 1970. *Articulation Therapy and Consonant Drill Book*. New York: Grune and Stratton.

Hays, W. L. 1963. *Statistics for Psychologists*. New York: Holt, Rinehart, and Winston.

Hixon, T. J., and Hardy, J. C. 1964. Restricted motility of the speech articulators in cerebral palsy. *J. Speech Hearing Dis.*, 29: 293–306.

Hubbell, R. D. In press. On facilitating spontaneous talking in young children. *J. Speech Hearing Dis.*

Hursh, D. E., and Sherman, J. A. 1973. The effects of parent-presented models and praise on the vocal behavior of their children. *J. Exp. Child Psych.*, 15: 328–339.

Irwin, J. V. 1970. Speech pathology and behavior modification. *Acta Symbolica*, 1: 15–23.

Irwin, O. C. 1960. Infant speech: Effect of systematic reading of stories. *J. Speech Hearing Res.*, 3: 187–190.

Jakobson, R., Fant, G., and Halle, M. 1952. *Preliminaries to Speech Analysis*. Cambridge, Mass.: MIT Press.

Lahey, M. This volume. Disruptions in the development and integration of form, content, and use in language development.

Levenstein, P. 1970. Cognitive growth in pre-schoolers through verbal interaction with mothers. *Amer. J. Orthopsychiat.*, 40: 426–432.

———. 1971. Learning through (and from) mothers. *Children Educ.*, 48: 130–134.

Locke, J. L. 1968. Questionable assumptions underlying articulation research. *J. Speech Hearing Dis.*, 33: 112–116.

———. 1971. The child's acquisition of phonetic behavior. *Acta Symbolica*, 2: 28–32.

Locke, J. L., and Kutz, K. J. 1975. Memory for speech and speech for memory. *J. Speech Hearing Res.*, 18: 176–191.

MacNeilage, P. F. 1972. Speech Physiology. In *Speech and Cortical Functioning*, J. H. Gilbert (ed.), New York: Academic Press.

McDonald, E. T. 1964. *Articulation Testing and Treatment: A Sensory-Motor Approach*. Pittsburgh: Stanwix House.

McReynolds, L. V., and Engmann, D. L. 1975. *Distinctive Feature Analysis of Misarticulations*. Baltimore, Md.: University Park Press.

Moll, K. L. 1968. Speech characteristics of individuals with cleft lip and palate. In *Cleft Palate and Communication*, D. C. Spriestersbach and D. Sherman (ed.), New York: Academic Press.

Naremore, R. C., and Dever, R. B. 1975. Language performance of educable mentally retarded and normal children at five age levels. *J. Speech Hearing Res.*, 18: 82–95.

Parsons, C. 1976. "Experimental schools" fail over evaluations. *The Christian Science Monitor*. June 1, p. 29.

Pollock, E., and Rees, N. S. 1972. Disorders of articulation: Some clinical implications of distinctive feature theory. *J. Speech Hearing Dis.*, 37: 451–461.

Popham, W. J., and Husek, T. R. 1969. Implications of criterion-referenced measurement. *J. Educational Measurement*, 6: 1–9.

Shankweiler, D., and Harris, K. S. 1966. An experimental approach to the problem of articulation in aphasia. *Cortex*, 2: 277–292.

Shelton, R. L., Arndt, W. B., and Johnson, A. F. 1975. Multivariate cluster analysis in the search for homogeneous subgroups among children who inarticulate. Paper presented at the annual meeting of the American Speech and Hearing Association. Washington, D.C.

Shelton, R. L., Arndt, W. B., and Miller, J. B. 1961. Learning principles and the teaching of speech and language. *J. Speech Hearing Dis.*, 26: 368–376.

Shelton, R. L. Elbert, M., and Arndt, W. B. 1967. A task for evaluation of articulation change: II. Comparison of task scores during baseline and lesson series testing. *J. Speech Hearing Res.*, 10: 578–588.

Shelton, R. L., Johnson, A. F., and Arndt, W. B. 1972. Monitoring and reinforcement by parents as a means of automating articulatory responses. *Perceptual and Motor Skills*, 35: 759–767.

Shelton, R. L. Johnson, A. F., Willis, V., and Arndt, W. B. 1975. Monitoring and reinforcement by parents as a means of automating articulatory responses: II. Study of preschool children. *Perceptual and Motor Skills*, 40: 599–610.

Travers, R. M. W. 1965. A study of the relationship of psychological research to educational practice. In *Training Research and Education*, R. Glaser (ed.), New York: John Wiley.

Turton, L. J. 1973. Diagnostic Implications of Articulation Testing. In *Articulation and Learning: New Dimensions in Research, Diagnostics, and Therapy*, W. D. Wolfe and D. J. Goulding (Eds.), Springfield, Ill.: C. C. Thomas.

Weiner, P. S. 1972. The perceptual level functioning of dysphasic children: A follow-up study. *J. Speech Hearing Res.*, 15: 423–438.

Winitz, H. 1975. *From Syllable to Conversation*. Baltimore: University Park Press.

Wright, V. A., Shelton, R. L., and Arndt, W. B. 1969. A task for evaluation of articulation change. III: Imitative task scores compared with scores for more spontaneous tasks. *J. Speech Hearing Res.*, 12: 876–884.

Young, M. A. 1976. Application of regression analysis concepts to retrospective research in speech pathology. *J. Speech Hearing Res.*, 19: 5–18.

General Discussion of Papers by McReynolds and Shelton

During the discussion of these papers a general issue arose concerning the processes and problems involved in the application of basic research findings to educational and clinical problems. Questions about effective ways of communicating information to the clinician and educator, the potential problem of premature application, and the need for intermediate clinical research and field testing procedures were broached. Since these issues are not specific to the research presented in the McReynolds and Shelton papers but rather concern the general topic of this volume, a detailed account of the comments made during this session is included in the summary chapter, "Problems and Promise in Applying Basic Research."

Continuity-Discontinuity in Phonological Development

Liberman asserted that the continuity-discontinuity issue as presented by McReynolds was not, in his opinion, a fruitful distinction for understanding and explaining phonological acquisition. He referred to the ethological research on the acquisition of bird song as a related example where the evidence does not fit well into the continuity-discontinuity framework. He summarized some of the facts obtained from studies of the white-crowned sparrow (see Marler 1975).

1. The role of a model. The young male sparrow needs an auditory model to develop normally. Furthermore, the model must be present before the individual is sexually mature (before the time that the young bird will produce the song). The developing bird will not adopt an inappropriate model (the song of a related species). In other words, he is selective in his imitative behavior.

2. The role of practice and reinforcement. The developing sparrow does not have to practice the song at the time the model is present and he does not receive any "reinforcement," in the traditional sense of that concept, while he is learning the song.

3. Sub-song behavior. The young sparrow engages in subsong ("babbling") prior to his acquisition of the full adult song. Auditory feedback is essential during this stage; deafened individuals will not develop normal adult productions.

Liberman suggested that an analogous pattern of development could be described for the acquisition of phonology by a human child. The child needs a model; there may be critical periods for exposure to a model. The child appears never to confuse speech with nonspeech. (No one has ever heard a child trying to imitate a door closing when trying to talk!) The child may be innately preattuned to perceive particular distinctions in speech sounds. The child does "practice" in the form of babbling. However, explicit reinforcement is not necessary for normal acquisition of phonology by normal hearing children. Children must be able to hear themselves when babbling to develop normally.

If this analogy is meaningful, it suggests that the continuity-discontinuity dichotomy fails to capture the interesting facts about the acquisition of human language. Psychologists have not provided the kinds of learning models that account for these data in an appropriate way. The biological models from areas such as the study of birdsong are perhaps more useful for investigating the course of acquisition of language. These models do not distinguish between continuous and discontinuous development but rather describe the interactions of experiential factors and biological maturational factors in determining the complex behavioral patterns of the developing organism.

The Relation between Perception and Production

Labov mentioned that in the research on dialects in which variants are marked in terms of social status, one often finds individuals' perceptions are governed by the prestige norm, even though they do not produce that variant. In other words these people "hear themselves" as producing the prestige variant. In addition, there are cases in which variants that are produced as completely distinct categories in different contexts are not distinguished perceptually.

Systematic Phonological Acquisition in Second-Language Learning

Labov also spoke to the issue of rule-governed behavior in the acquisition of phonology. He reported on some research by the Dickersons at the University of Illinois that studied the articulation of /l/ by Japanese learning English. These researchers have developed rules for describing the production of /l/ in different syllabic contexts. They found there was an orderly production pattern: The articulation of /l/ preceding low vowels (as in "lap") was closest to the correct English target. The same phoneme preceding mid and low vowels (as in "lip" and "leap") was less well articulated. Finally, postconsonantal /l/ (as in "clean") deviated most from the target. They studied the production of /l/ in three conditions: spontaneous speech, reading, and word lists. As has been observed in sociolinguistic variation studies, there was a very regular pattern of articulation; the more carefully the subjects articulated (as in word lists versus spontaneous speech) the closer they came to the target language. Most important with respect to the notion of the systematic nature of phonological development were the results of comparisons of these productions over the course of language learning. In general, the relationships of production accuracy in the different syllabic contexts and the different speaking conditions were preserved over three time periods. The whole system moved closer and closer to the target language.

An interesting question that could be investigated in this context is the effects of training of particular parts of the system on acquisition in general. For instance, one could ask about the effects of training a subject to produce a phoneme in the most difficult or the easiest syllabic environment on the production of that phoneme in other contexts. Labov thought this kind of research with second-language learners could have implications for understanding first-language acquisition in normal children as well as for development of training techniques with articulation-disordered children.

Reference

Marler, P. 1975. On the origin of speech from animal studies. In J. F. Kavanagh and J. E. Cutting (eds.) *The Role of Speech in Language* (Cambridge: The MIT Press), 11–37.

Language through Alternate Modalities

CARL E. SHERRICK

Introduction

Most of us have been raised with the credo that nature will usually compensate us for the losses she imposes, and much of folk legend and personal experience supports this belief. There is in addition medical evidence to show that the loss of one of two symmetrical organs, such as a kidney, will be offset by the hypertrophy of the survivor. Students of the nervous system, remarking on the redundancy and reduplication of some neural structures (for example, some areas of the auditory cortex) have suggested that such lavish oversupply of tissue accounts for the ability of some areas to assume a function that the missing tissue would have provided (Lashley 1938).

The argument for what is sometimes called sensory plasticity has been made by a number of investigators either implicitly or directly. Among these is Bach-y-Rita (1972), who with his colleagues has demonstrated that visually deprived humans can be taught to recognize the shape and disposition in depth of three-dimensional objects when their pictorial representations are projected to the skin of the back as vibrotactile patterns. It is the contention of this group of investigators that the tactile vision substitution system works in part because the user manipulates the TV camera that acts as the substitute for the image-forming system of the eye. The concept of plasticity as applied here describes the reworking of manual sensorimotor systems and the tactile system of the skin, under the pressure of a novel task, in such a manner that the subject can perform at least some of the visual functions with an alternate modality. Moreover, the subject reports that the phenomenal appearance of the stimulus pattern is not at the skin but "out there" in frontal space (White 1970a).

Sensory substitution devices of this kind fall under the general rubric of sensory prostheses, which comprises hearing aids and eyeglasses as well. Whereas hearing aids and spectacles augment or resolve the incoming information for use by the impaired modality, substitution devices process the information to transform it for application to a different modality. The problems of moderately hearing-impaired or vision-impaired adults in adapting to their new gadgets are well known to clinicians. For sensory substitution systems the difficulties are compounded by the need for instructing another sense in the skills for which the lost modality was so well fitted. The hope is, of course, that the nervous system will somehow devote some of its unoccupied tissue to such tasks as translating visual codes to tactile patterns or auditory codes to visual patterns and thus fill the functional work space left by the absent modality.

At the present stage of development of either sensory substitution devices or of neurophysiological techniques it may seem premature to discuss whether profound changes are taking place in the nervous tissues of subjects who have had prolonged exposure to the apparatus. It is more to the point to ask whether such devices are truly adequate for replacing a lost sense or supplementing an impaired one. Of additional interest is the question of whether the improvement in performance with these aids is dependent solely on the learning process. Is it possible that the structure of the patterns generated by these aids might profitably be analyzed and altered to increase both the rate of acquisition and the degree of skill in perform- ance of the task?

It is my intention to argue that the substitution devices and methods thus far developed have leaned heavily upon the learning skills of their subjects in the design and testing of systems and with few exceptions have accepted the patterns generated adventitiously by the electrical or mechanical characteristics of the system. In only a few investigations have there been attempts to analyze the out- put of prosthetic devices to discern the features that the user can or does employ. If, for example, we wish the skin to behave like the eye or the ear, it is not enough to know how the visual and auditory systems behave in order to command the former to do likewise. We must know something of the skin's proclivities before we can command it at all. A propos of this tendency to impose familiar models on unfamiliar phenomena, I am reminded of a colleague's attempts to condition one of the several species of lizard in our laboratory in order to test its hearing. The initial presumption was that reptiles would behave like something between a fish, a bird, and a rat; so an instrumental conditioning strategy that was successful with these animals was attempted, with the result that the experimenter showed all the signs of subzero extinction before a single lizard was conditioned. There has been speculation that operant conditioning would more successfully have been applied to that current object of interest, the Pet Rock. I am told that it can be taught, with a single appropriately administered tactile stimulus, to roll over and play dead—in one trial.

Varieties of Nonauditory Communications Systems

It is neither possible nor desirable to provide an exhaustive listing of the many devices and methods for communicating language that have appeared and reap- peared over the centuries to be hailed as the solution to one or more handicaps. It is instructive, however, to examine the kinds of systems that have developed and to determine why, if they are in use, they have avoided the fate of so many other similar systems.

NATURAL UNAIDED SYSTEMS

Under this category there are two major methods involving sensory substitution. The most commonly taught of these is lipreading or speech reading, in which the visual system replaces the auditory. A secondary method applied more often to instruction of the deaf-blind is the Tadoma, speech-feeling, or vibration method, involving application of the pupil's hand to the speaker's face. These systems are designated natural and unaided because they employ cues available from the normal speaking behavior of the majority of the population and they require no intermediate mechanical or electronic device to process the cues. What is avail- able as a direct cue for the lipreader is a series of visual patterns that appear to have as a major focus the changing shape of the lips but that have in addition minor foci including jaw elevation, tongue movements, general facial expression, and bodily gestures. An overall modulating influence is provided by the situation itself, as well as by the familiarity of the lipreader with the speaker and the subject matter (O'Neill and Oyer 1961).

The Tadoma method, which was named for the first two students successfully taught by Alcorn (1945), involves the application of the "listener's" fingers to the speaker's face. Although positioning of the digits seems to vary among users, it is generally thought that one or more fingers pick up the movements of lips and jaw and perhaps airflow while others monitor vibrations of the throat and perinasal structures. It is difficult to say exactly what cues are extracted by the user, but it would appear that voicing, nasality, breath sounds, and labials are manifestly available. The difficulty in analysis is compounded by the fact that in teaching the method to the sighted deaf the recommended procedure is to combine it with lipreading. Furthermore, contrary to what seem to be the best principles of learning (response with feedback), the child is not encouraged to speak for the first three or four months of training. The argument seems to be that voice quality improves as voice training is delayed in favor of the Tadoma training (Alcorn 1945, p. 118). So far as I know, there has been only one experimental study of the Tadoma method (in the Finnish language; Pesonen 1968), despite the fact that some teachers of the deaf have long asserted that it improves lipreading ability as well as voice quality and language skills (Alcorn 1932). What is a most striking general characteristic of the Tadoma method is that hearing-impaired children whose attention has been focused on lipreading learn that there is a set of dimensions in speech other than visual, that some of them covary with the visual features, and that they can apprehend some of them through their hands when touching the face of the teacher to compare the patterns with those they generate. In the latter case, ideally, both manual and orofacial haptic patterns are available to the child, affording an enrichment of the correlation of sensory input and muscular effort. By this means it is altogether possible, although not yet demonstrated for English speakers, that the constantly available orofacial tactile-kinesthetic cues may be internalized by the subjects to give them better control over the articulation process.

Whereas lipreading has been practiced as a teaching art for the last four centuries (DeLand 1968), experimental work on the subject began only sixty years ago (O'Neill & Oyer 1961, p. 36). Much of the early research was concerned with prediction of achievement levels in lipreading from elementary perceptual skills, but later work (see, for example, Stark 1974) has been concerned with the analysis of the intelligibility of the various classes of articulatory gesture with environmental factors such as visibility of the speaker's face and with the effects of training methods and combinations of lipreading with processed auditory or tactile inputs.

It appears to be a conviction among some segments of the population of teachers of the deaf and the deaf themselves that lipreading cannot be taught. This seems to stem in part from observations that some individuals acquire the skill with very little exposure, whereas others who undergo training for many months exhibit little competence. Another source of the conviction may be traced to the lack of correlation of a variety of standard intelligence, personality, and special skills tests with lipreading ability. The more reasonable conclusion to draw from the results of such educational and psychometric paradoxes is that lipreading skill is not the product of a single aptitude but may be the complex resultant of a number of mental vectors. Furthermore, the poor relationship observed between instructional effort and pupil performance in this case is precisely what would be expected when a standardized method of instruction is imposed on a performance that comprises such a loose aggregation of diffuse aptitudes and skills.

SYNTHETIC UNAIDED SYSTEMS

Included within this classification are the visually oriented systems of sign language and finger spelling and the haptically oriented systems of finger spelling (for the deaf-blind) and the manual dermographic alphabet (block printing on the skin of the palm or other surface). There may be some disagreement among my colleagues in calling these systems synthetic. (It is clear that they are unaided, in the sense used previously for lipreading and the Tadoma method.) In this discussion natural and synthetic are opposed in these categories merely to designate the population base from which the systems spring. This is especially true for American Sign Language (ASL), with whose proponents the disagreement over terminology might originate. To most laymen, however, ASL must seem a secret, arbitrary kind of code. Finger spelling and the manual alphabet are more obviously synthetic.

Before my readers assume that I am ignorant of the depth of feeling of educators of the deaf concerning the issues of oral versus manual teaching methods, let me hasten to say I am not. The controversy between teachers who urge the use of manual and bodily gestures and those who discourage them in favor of lipreading and speech training extends back two or three centuries (O'Neill and Oyer 1961, p. 12). It would appear from some accounts that more than one of the early decisions to adopt one method over the other was based more on pragmatic than ideological grounds, but as time passed the admixture of reason and belief fossilized the structures that compose the two schools of thought. Furth (1964, 1966, 1971) has written at length on the question of language in the deaf, and although he has generally concerned himself with higher mental processes and the role of language or its absence, he has argued pointedly against one dictum of the oral school, that speaking and speech comprehension are in a causal relation to complex conceptual and reasoning behavior in the deaf. There is, on the other hand, research by Meadow (1968) suggesting that early experience with manual language may improve the deaf child's acquisition of speech production and lipreading skills.

With respect to research on the question of efficiency of language transmission, the comparative study of Bellugi and Fischer (1971) is of particular interest. These authors examined the rate at which hearing persons, skilled in ASL and spoken English, transmitted words and propositions. Propositions were defined as "simple underlying sentences . . . all main verbs or predicates which had overt (or covert) subjects" (1971, p. 184). Whereas the number of words transmitted per second for speech was almost twice the number of signs transmitted per second, the rate of propositions for the two modes is about the same. It must be kept in mind that the results are for three subjects. In a study by Ling (Stark 1974, pp. 161–163), the comprehension scores of students trained in the oral method were compared with those trained by the Rochester method, which combines finger spelling with oral methods. Ling found that the comprehension by the Rochester group of arhythmically spoken phrases was not much different whether finger spelling alone or lipreading alone was used (see figure 1). When the two modes were combined in a single communication, there appeared to be a significant but small improvement in comprehension. The latter score was somewhat less than the score of the oral trainees, however. When only syllables or single words were transmitted, the comprehension scores for the Rochester group improved if finger spelling or finger spelling plus lipreading modes were used. When lipreading alone was permitted, the scores of both Rochester and oral groups declined as the message units diminished in size from phrases to words to syllables.

What is striking about these results is that the lipreading mode improves in intelligibility as the message units increase in size and (not shown by figure 1) as the transmission rate increases, whereas the finger spelling mode deteriorates under

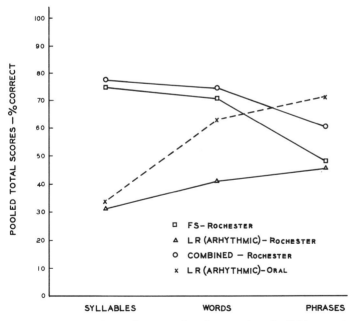

Figure 1. Comparative performance data for reception of syllables, words, and phrases by children trained by the Rochester method, under conditions of lipreading alone, finger spelling alone, or by the combined method. The performance of orally trained children is shown for comparison purposes. After Ling (see Stark 1974, p. 162).

the same conditions. A precise analysis of these data is not possible at present and replication of the experiment should be undertaken, perhaps with ASL modes represented as well. But it may be concluded tentatively that the advantage of lipreading over other codes is, as Liberman has noted, that "the deaf child . . . has access to a reasonably straightforward representation of the phonetic message" (Stark 1974, p. 139). In finger spelling, however, the coding may be letter by letter in a manner equivalent to reading words through a window one letter wide. The burden on visual short-term memory under these conditions must be enormous, as reading studies with normals have shown (Poulton 1962; White 1970b). Moreover, the rivalry between the two visually oriented modes must have caused a great deal of attention-switching behavior, which would tend to disrupt performance.

AIDED (PROSTHETIC) SYSTEMS
The majority of aided communications systems may be classified as natural in the sense that has already been described; they accept as input either the acoustic stream by microphone or the articulatory gestures by means of strategically placed sensors of acceleration on the face or throat of the speaker. Exceptions to these methods will, however, be noted.

A landmark in the history of development of aids for the deaf was established by Pickett (1968) in his conference on speech analyzing aids. Technical papers on the design and testing of a variety of devices and systems, most of which transformed speech sounds into visual patterns by means of electronic circuitry, were presented at this four-day gathering.

VISUAL AIDS
One of the earliest electrical methods for analyzing speech was the oscillograph, which displays variations in mechanical displacement or in voltage as a function of time (see, for example, Fletcher 1929). The common present-day exemplar is the ubiquitous cathode ray oscilloscope. With a suitable microphone one can display the waveform of speech on the face of the cathode ray tube. The intelligibility of such a display for speech sounds, however, is very low, and, as Békésy (1967, p. 113) has remarked, whatever skill may be acquired in translating the visual code can be lost if an apparently irrelevant variable is changed. Liberman and his colleagues (Liberman, 1974; Liberman et al. 1968) have pointed to a major source of difficulty with simple temporal coding of the acoustic stream: The phonetic units of speech are not displayed like a succession of boxcars in a freight train. Instead, a speech sound may be contained in several successive acoustic segments along with other speech sounds sharing those same segments. In other words, the better analogy for the freight train would be between speech sounds and the *contents* of the boxcars.

A more sophisticated analysis of the speech stream is afforded by a variety of derivative visual displays, including the visible speech system of Potter, Kopp, and Green (1947) in which a graphic plot of sound frequency versus time is displayed with intensity represented as darkness of the tracings. A number of such spectrographic displays were exhibited at the Pickett conference already mentioned (for example, Stark, Cullen, and Chase 1968). Even more removed from the acoustic stimulus are displays of selected formants of speech sounds, or the so-called "vowel triangle" graphs derived from plotting the relation between formant frequencies for particular sounds (see, for example, Cohen 1968; Pickett and Constam 1968). An excellent survey and critical analysis of these devices as well as of tactile aids, auditory aids, and evaluation methods is provided by Nickerson (1975).

An important recent development is that of the minicomputer, having a relatively large memory capacity, which can be used to process acoustic stimuli. The construction of elaborate and detailed software programs provide great flexibility in the operation of these devices. With the aid of such a system it is possible to extract several dimensions of the acoustic stimulus or of physical correlates of articulatory gestures and present these as dimensions of visual displays to the system user. With the more powerful memory capability of these aids, a much greater variety of display patterns can be managed and changes in display and controls that are dependent on the trainee's response are permitted. Thus the device assumes to a limited degree the role of tutor as well as providing feedback of articulation efforts to the subject (see, for example, Nickerson and Stevens 1973, 1974).

The visual aids of the type thus far described are not meant to be wearable. They are intended either as bench-top prototypes of aids that may be designed as wearable devices or stationary speech training aids that students visit periodically to improve their skills.

A notable visual aid that is wearable is the Upton eyeglass aid (Upton 1968). This device, invented for his personal use by an individual with a severe hearing loss, consists of a compact speech analyzing system that sorts out five separate phonetic patterns (voiced frication, frication, voicing, stops, and voiced stops). Each of these is displayed on an assigned miniature lamp attached to the user's eyeglass lens (figure 2) at the periphery of the visual field and in such position that a *V* shape is created. When the "listener" regards the speaker's face, the *V* shape frames the cheeks and the throat, so that while lip movements are monitored, the additional cues afforded by the successive illumination of the lamps are perceived

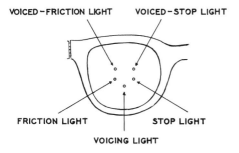

Figure 2. The Upton wearable eyeglass speech reader. After Upton (1968).

at the same time. The "listener's" voice is, of course, similarly displayed when he or she speaks.[1]

HAPTIC AIDS

Attention has been directed for many years to the advantages of tactile or haptic aids for the deaf with a variety of rationales for the use of this modality. The functional similarities of the auditory and tactile systems have been pointed out (Békésy 1960, 1967; Geldard 1970). The advantage of freeing the visual system to permit attention to the lipreading task is obvious. The attractiveness of an aid that may be concealed from the curious has been acclaimed. There is, finally, the feeling that any sense that can be taught to read braille cannot possibly be as primitive and ignorant as it seems to be for the ordinary mortal.

Early attempts to transduce speech sounds for stimulation of the skin were made at the turn of the century (see Breiner 1968), initially by means of electrical stimulation of skin nerves. Owing to the fact that painful stinging or burning sensations could be produced by such means, however, mechanical vibrators were constructed or, more commonly, adapted from telephone receivers or loudspeaker mechanisms (Sherrick 1975). An early investigator in this field was Gault (1927), who first experimented with the mechanical vibrations produced with a speaking tube and later developed a telephone receiver system employing amplified speech waves impressed on a single vibrator. This device was tested with the aid of a sample of deaf persons and proved to be of modest help when lipreading was simultaneously permitted.

In an effort to aid the skin in resolving the various frequencies of speech sounds, Gault, with technical aid from the Bell Laboratories, devised the Teletactor, an apparatus that provided five vibrators, one to each digit of the subject's hand. The speech sounds were filtered and fractionated into five frequency bands so the skin would be confronted with a place code for frequency, as it was thought the ear was. Tests with the Teletactor proved it to have little more advantage than the single vibrator, and although it was employed in teaching at nearby schools for the deaf, it was never very popular.

Displays involving the frequency-place principle have reappeared since Gault's time but the best example of technical development with sophistication of testing methods is that of Pickett and Pickett (1963). These authors employed a device that represented the frequency bands of speech as vibrations of a constant frequency to which the skin is very sensitive (300 Hertz [Hz]), each of ten bands at one of the fingertips. When speech sounds were uttered, the frequencies in a given band were presented to the appropriate finger at a level of vibration proportional to the energy in the band. Thus the frequency spectrum of the speech sound was represented as a set of places on the skin, with intensities in various places varying

[1]The Upton aid has recently been modified to provide a more sophisticated imaging system that removes the distracting lamps from the spectacle lens and provides colored lights as additional cues to the speech sounds. This was reported by Dr. Roy Gengel at the A. G. Bell Association meetings in Boston, June 24–25, 1976.

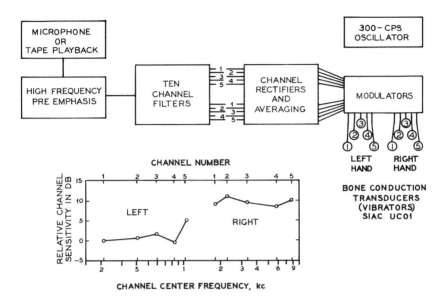

Figure 3. The tactile Vocoder. The graphic plot at the bottom of the figure shows the results of spectrum shaping by the high-frequency preemphasis device to improve the intelligibility of upper formants. After Pickett and Pickett (1963).

with the spectral energy distribution for the speech, as figure 3 shows. By this means Pickett and Pickett avoided a problem that Gault's apparatus had, that of the subject rarely feeling the higher frequencies (above 800 Hz) imposed by his Teletactor. In addition, Pickett and Pickett provided spectrum shaping for the speech sounds in order that the consonants, which contain much less energy than the vowels, be emphasized in relation to vowel sounds.

Besides providing a reliable and informative evaluation of the strengths and limitations of their Tactile Vocoder, Pickett and Pickett suggested a number of modifications for the device that more recent investigators have studied profitably. Aston and Weed (1971) examined the intelligibility of the Tactile Vocoder system for a number of sounds and constructed a computer model of the speech processing capability of the system. With the aid of a measure of the similarities of tactile pattern structures among speech sounds, these authors attempted to predict the effects of changing the parameters of the system, the number of channels, the dynamic range of individual channels, and the effects of spectrum shaping.

Most students of hearing are familiar with the work of Békésy and in particular with his development of a large-scale model of the cochlea (Békésy 1960). By means of his model, Békésy could demonstrate his traveling wave theory of hearing and test a variety of hypotheses concerning the similarity of action of the tactile sense to that of the auditory modality. Although Békésy suggested that complex waveforms were not readily resolved on the model, Keidel (1968) and

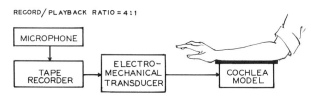

RECORD/PLAYBACK RATIO = 4 : 1

MICROPHONE

TAPE RECORDER — ELECTRO-MECHANICAL TRANSDUCER — COCHLEA MODEL

Figure 4. A simple schematic of the early Keidel speech analyzing aid, using the Békésy mechanical model of the cochlea. After Keidel (1974).

his colleagues were able to show a striking improvement in understanding of speech sounds by subjects who felt the vibrations of the model in association with the name of the sounds (see figure 4). Unfortunately, in order to generate frequencies that the skin could feel (40 to 400 Hz), the speech message (300 to 3000 Hz) was tape-recorded, then played back at one-fourth to one-eighth normal speed. The expansion of time required for single syllables was so great that the subject often forgot the beginning patterns by the time the end appeared. In a more recent version Keidel and his colleague Finkenzeller (Keidel 1974) have devised a computer-aided system that provides the needed frequency transposition of speech in real time, but tests on this device are not completed.

A recent attempt to provide the tactile analog of the visual spectrographic display was reported by Goldstein and Stark (see Sherrick 1975). The display is a matrix of 144 tiny vibrators arrayed in 6 rows and 24 columns. The frequency of speech sounds is represented across columns and intensity level by the number of rows excited. Thus a low-intensity speech sound with only high-frequency components would produce vibrations in pins located near the lower right side of the matrix, whereas a high-intensity, low-frequency speech sound might cause the entire left side of the matrix to vibrate. A stream of speech produces a constant ebbing and flowing of vibration over the matrix surface.

All the tactile displays so far cited have processed only the acoustic correlates of speech. One that accepts vibrations of the throat and nasal region as well as acoustic signals has been reported by Miller, Engebretson, and DeFilippo (1974). The three sources of speech signal are shaped or conditioned electronically to emphasize certain of their dimensions and further processed to display their relative energies at three skin loci as 100-Hz vibrations. Figure 5 shows a schematic diagram of the system. The superficial resemblance of the system to the Tadoma method is obvious, but further analysis would be needed to determine the relationship, if any.

A final vibrotactile display that may be classified as synthetic is the cued speech system of Cornett (1973). Originally designed as an accessory manual signing technique in which the hand signals stood for speech sounds that are ambiguous as lipreading patterns, this system was remodeled to substitute vibrotactile signals on various skin loci for the hand signals. At present the vibrotactile signals are produced by the speaker's operation of a manual keyboard. I am not sure whether

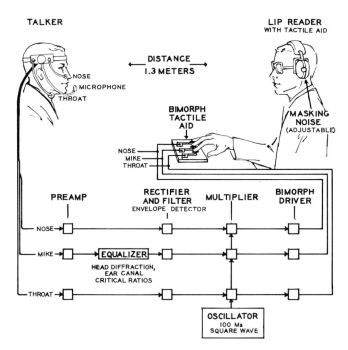

Figure 5. The Central Institute for the Deaf speech training device, employing as signals articulatory features in addition to airborne sounds. After Miller, Engebretson, and DeFilippo (1974).

there are plans to control the tactile input by means of some electrical derivative of the speech signal.[2]

The Constraints on Visual and Tactile Codes

One great advantage of the natural unaided systems such as speechreading over the prosthetic systems is their lack of encumbrance for the teacher and pupil. Lipreading is superior to a synthetic system such as finger spelling in part because it does not require the mediation of a new code, the alphabet. At the same time, however, lipreaders must settle for the visual patterns that are available. They have no choice in the matter and if some patterns are not discriminable, little can be done about it. When synthetic codes are devised, on the other hand, the first

[2]The Cornett system has adapted a speech processing network that channels separate output signals for the various speech sounds that were cued manually in the earlier system. The cues are present visual ones produced by exciting various combinations of the segments of two seven-segment LEDs (light-emitting diodes). The work is still in the experimental phase, as reported by Dr. R. O. Cornett at the A. G. Bell Association meetings in Boston' June 24–25, 1976.

step is usually to ensure that all the elements selected are readily discriminable, although not necessarily equally so. In creating his system of embossed dots for a written language for the blind, Louis Braille (Farrell 1950; Bledsoe 1972) was struggling to replace the tactually ambiguous embossed alphabet that his sighted teachers could easily read with a clearly discriminable set of tactile patterns. (Bledsoe claims that embossed print was used not because it was easy for sighted teachers to read but because it made the blind student use a code that conformed better to the sighted world.) The resulting code set (adapted from one originally devised by an artillery officer for message security in night maneuvers) was much more easily learned by the blind.

The code that Braille developed was modified several times, with accompanying emotional conflicts among protagonists—many of whom could not read the code— but a significant advance was made by a blind teacher of piano tuning, Joel Smith, who applied the principle of frequency of recurrence to recoding the alphabet (Bledsoe 1972, p. 23). The intention to save effort in writing braille was achieved by assigning the characters with the fewest dots (a braille character has six dots in two columns and three rows) to the letters with highest frequency of occurrence in English. In addition, since there are sixty-three possible characters that can be generated, Smith devised a number of word contractions for commonly occurring words in English. In the currently used modified braille system, these two changes have been incorporated along with a number of conventions for cueing the reader to things like capital letters, numbers, and signs.

The evolution of braille illustrates the increasing sophistication of code developers and their interaction with the users. The principles of discriminability and frequency of recurrence seem like obvious steps in code construction today; and if a synthetic code is to be adapted, it should be designed with such principles in mind. There is, however, a third principle of importance to bear in mind when speed of information processing is a consideration, as it is in speech perception. This principle dictates that as far as possible patterns should be selected to permit a smooth transition from one to the next, to afford a fusion into pattern groups (a "chunking" of larger segments from smaller ones). Recent research on braille learning (Nolan and Kederis 1969) concludes that this principle does not pertain to braille. The time required by skilled readers to recognize a word is more than the sum of times required to recognize its individual characters.

An early example of the application of the fusion principle in pattern selection is that of the simplified typewriter keyboard (Dvorak et al. 1936). The problem with the universal keyboard not only was that there was an uneven division of typing labor between the hands and among the strongest and weakest fingers, but that there also was no regard in the design for the commoner two- and three-letter sequences. Thus, one hand must do all the work in typing the sequence E-A-R and must, moreover, hurdle an entire row of keys for sequences such as C-R-A. Such movement patterns are both ponderous and error producing.

The Dvorak or Simplified Keyboard was intended to replace the universal keyboard, and the design process took several years. A lengthy analysis of the sources of error in typing preceded the modification and design phase. During the redesign phase, in addition to rearranging the letter positions to distribute the most-frequently used keys to the strongest fingers (following the frequency of recurrence principle), the most common sequences of two- and three-letter groups were tabulated from analysis of English prose. With these data, the keyboard was again modified to permit successive keystrokes to be executed by alternate hands as often as possible and to limit as much as possible the need for hurdling a row of keys between strokes. The resulting keyboard proved, when tested, to be more quickly learned with fewer errors, higher production rates, and less fatigue when compared to performance on the universal keyboard. The universal keyboard is in use today, although the Dvorak Keyboard can be obtained at extra cost. As the developers say, "the patchwork [universal] keyboard remains. This accords with the usual commercial policy of withholding improvements as long as current sales are satisfactory" (Dvorak et al. 1936, p. 209).

These developments in braille reading and typing can be related to the research on visual and manual codes for the deaf. Aside from the care the developers took in designing the coding systems to speed up information handling while retaining accuracy, some of the observations of the resulting behavior are similar to those made by investigators of lipreading, finger spelling, signing, and in some instances prosthetic devices. These are that in the skilled performance of the task, whether in production or reception, the organizing quanta of perception are not the original code elements but the combinations of these in what might be called suprasegmental groups. In the matter of lipreading, O'Neill and Oyer (1961, p. 47) state "The visibility of the total movement form afforded the best cue for visual identification of a word." In their study of signing, Bellugi and Fischer (1971) noted that the expansion of meaning of an individual sign is achieved by what they called incorporation (changing its spatial position from the normal by changing the direction of movements, signs of one hand made in conjunction with signs made with the other hand, facial gestures, attitudes, or postures). In typing, Dvorak et al. (1936) noted that correction of a keystroke error is best made by correcting the movements that overlap with preceding and following strokes and not simply by focusing on the keystroke itself. There is evidence, therefore, that a hierarchy of pattern structures may emerge in experience and behavior as the individual develops skills of the kind we are discussing. The degree of development of such a hierarchy will probably depend on what elements are selected for coding and the way in which the code elements are assigned to the linguistic system being transformed. This is not to dispute the contentions that the most appropriate channel for speech processing is the auditory system and other modalities lack the apparatus for transforming the speech code to a natural language (see for example, Stark 1974, p. 137). If, on the other hand, the auditory channel is totally lacking, the decision concerning which of several coding systems to adopt should be based on the outcome of careful tests of information processing efficiency and not on decisions of convenience or intuitive appeal.

It is possible to find coding systems that possess what one would regard as an appropriate set of dimensions for use and be entirely wrong in one's prediction. My colleague Professor Geldard and I at one time created a coding system for transforming printed letters to a tactile code (see Geldard 1966), assuming that a primary dimension was the array of places on the body being stimulated. Subjects were able to learn the code reasonably well; and when they had, we jumbled the arrangement so that although all places remained the same, a given letter now excited different places than it had previously. After a trial or two, the subjects did as well as ever. Craig (1974) has recently shown this to happen when vibrating letter shapes are presented to the skin. The subjects can learn to identify the letters when they are presented normally, but spatial rearrangements of such shapes are learned readily as well. This shows that the subject is not extracting the site of the activity, as important information does not require the knowledge of spatial relations (at least as they are perceived visually) to identify code elements. Studies such as these are valuable for directing attention away from coding strategies that are poor or incorrect in conception, but they do not indicate what the optimum strategies are. These will not reveal themselves fully until more is learned about the structural properties of visual, auditory, and tactile stimulus patterns.

The word "structure" has been used in reference to patterns in more than one place with the intention that it be taken in the sense that Garner (1974) has defined it. Garner and his colleagues have performed many studies on the characteristics of visual and auditory patterns and the effects of the interrelations of pattern dimensions on the speed and efficiency of information processing. These investigators have shown that when a large number of patterns is generated by manipulating a relatively small number of dimensions (shape, hue, and area, for example) the ones judged good by subjects are also unique (have fewer closely related alternatives), are more readily discriminated from one another, are processed faster by subjects, and are more readily and accurately retrieved from memory.

If it were only a matter of analyzing coding systems to determine the best patterns, the job of deciding on the proper coding strategies would be greatly simplified. Unfortunately, the goodness of patterns is not internal to them alone but is determined by the characteristics of the set of patterns to which they belong. The same pattern amidst one set of relatives may be good, amidst another set not so good. Moreover, it is not clear that good, unique patterns are all equally capable of fusing with their neighbors in time to permit the emergence of hierarchical pattern structures. Given the example of the work of Garner, however, it should be possible to devise means for examining the structure of a number of coding systems to determine which dimensions to emphasize and which to delete or attenuate in order to arrive at an optimal set of patterns to encode.

Present and Future Applications of Research to Education

It was a little less than a year ago that the National Institute of Neurological and Communicative Disorders and Stroke sponsored a workshop on tactile and visual aids for the deaf in an attempt to summarize the progress in research in this area, exchange ideas and unpublished research results, and formalize to an extent the procedures for training and evaluation of sensory aids. The report of that workshop (Elliott and Sherrick 1976) is intended to inform interested investigators, educators, and clinicians of the expertise of the participants on questions of development, application, and evaluation of current sensory substitution devices for the hearing impaired.

Major emphasis in the report was given to the three problem areas in sensory aid development that have received adequate treatment only rarely in the past. These are the population of subjects on whom the aid is tested and the target population for whom it is intended, the training procedures devised for acquainting subjects with the task and improving their levels of performance skills, and the evaluation procedures available for testing achievement levels or for analyzing the fidelity of transmission of the sensory aid itself. Specific recommendations in any of these problem areas are not easily made without some knowledge of the conditions obtaining in the other areas. For example, it is clearly possible to specify that, whatever the population or the device, training and evaluation procedures should be made in conjunction with whatever other methods are to be available to the subject (such as lipreading or residual hearing). The need to develop the skill with the sensory aid as an integral part of the entire reception process is fairly obvious, since that is the way it will ultimately be used. On the other hand, it is not so clear that the training procedures for use with a population of hearing-impaired adults who have acquired verbal language skills would be the same as those for congenitally deaf children and young adults whose language skills are not as firmly established.

One problem that the workshop did not discuss but that has been considered elsewhere (Sherrick 1974, p. 32) concerns the relationship of the clinic, the class-room, and the laboratory in research enterprises of the sort under discussion. Of the currently employed methods of training in language reception and production, lipreading, Tadoma, signing, and finger spelling are undoubtedly the major systems. These share the common property of requiring no special accessory tools or aids, at least in their simplest forms. They share a second property that is related to the first but that may seem irrelevant to the question of effectiveness (they were developed by teachers with students and underwent the test of repeated use with varying environmental conditions, kinds of student, and types of teachers.) The methods evolved under strict performance demands, with revision upon revision following critical observation by students, teachers, and parents.

This kind of development must be contrasted with that of latter-day systems with which inventors approach the educator or clinician. They offer a partially developed device that promises to aid the student or patient in understanding speech in exchange for the cooperation of one or two teachers and a small group of children, perhaps some space—semipermanent space where they can leave equipment and supplies, maybe a peek at the children's records, some time to train the teachers, and a regular schedule of appointments for the children over the next month. The list grows until the educator begins to feel like the host in the Kaufman and Hart play in which the man who came to dine broke his leg. In the educator's nightmare the person who comes to break a code may stay forever!

It is not usually the researchers' intention to become a permanent part of the classroom or clinic staff. On the contrary, researchers want to use techniques of applied research to compress the period of evolution required by traditional methods in order to ascertain what features of their systems are irrelevant or faulty, and what features are useful. With repeated experiments they may approach the required criterion of utility. In the process one may hope that educators profit by adding a new tool to their bench and learning something new about the ones already there.

If the educator is dissatisfied with current achievements in teaching the hearing-impaired and the clinician is unhappy with the current validity of diagnostic techniques and therapeutic procedures (and from what I have heard, seen, and read, I have no reason to believe they are content with the status quo), then perhaps they should consider providing a place for research in their very midst. Perhaps an experimental classroom in the school building or space in the clinic. On the other side, if the teacher and clinician are willing to modify their environments to provide a hospitable climate for research, surely research workers can modify their behavior to adapt to their new niche. They must learn more thoroughly, through practice if need be, what the current methods of instruction, diagnosis, and treatment are, where the problems lie, and how to go about analyzing and solving them with the least possible disruption of day-to-day routines.

The sincere and dedicated research worker in this context is much more than just a brain searching for hands and feet among teachers, students, and research assistants. The research investigator can provide the analytic, critical attitude, the fresh look, and the information from other problem areas or distant laboratories or classrooms that suggest alternative solutions to practical problems. Many people think of the need for basic research as they do of a cash reserve, a library, or a computer data bank. It is not these things. The real product of basic research is the people who pursue it, who exchange living ideas with their colleagues every day. If basic research is to be applied to the practical problems of the classroom and the clinic, it will more likely be through the active presence of a research worker on the site of the problem than through the hoarse mutterings and dry pen scrapings of writers like me.

References

Alcorn, S. K. (1932) The Tadoma method. *Volta Rev.*, May. Reprinted by Perkins School for the Blind, 3 pp.

———. (1945) Development of the Tadoma method for the deaf-blind. *J. Except. Children*, 11, 117–119.

Aston, R., and Weed, H. R. (1971) A man-machine model for evaluation of the tactile Vocoder. *J. of the Assoc. for Advance. Med. Instr.*, 5, 19–25.

Bach-y-Rita, P. (1972) *Brain mechanisms in sensory substitution.* New York: Academic Press.

Békésy, G. von (1960) *Experiments in hearing.* New York: McGraw-Hill.

———. (1967) *Sensory inhibition.* Princeton, N.J.: Princeton University Press.

Bellugi, U., and Fischer, S. (1971) A comparison of sign language and spoken language. *Cognition*, 1, 173–200.

Bledsoe, W. (1972) Braille: A success story. In N. Guttman (ed.) *Evaluation of sensory aids for the handicapped.* Washington, D.C.: National Academy of Sciences, 3–33.

Breiner, H. L. (1968) Versuch einer elektrokutanen Sprachvermittlung. *Zeit. für Exp. u. Angew. Psychologie,* 15, 1–48.

Cohen, M. L. (1968) The ADL sustained phoneme analyzer. In J. M. Pickett (ed.) Proceedings of the conference on speech-analyzing aids for the deaf. *Amer. Ann. of the Deaf,* 113, 247–252.

Cornett, R. O. (1973) Study of the possibility of developing a speech analyzing hearing aid. Contract NINDS–73–13.

Craig, J. C. (1974) Pictorial and abstract cutaneous displays. In F. A. Geldard (ed.) *Cutaneous communication systems and devices.* Austin, Tex.: The Psychonomic Soc., Inc., 78–83.

DeLand, F. (1968) *The story of lipreading.* Washington, D.C.: The Volta Bureau.

Dvorak, A., Merrick, N. L., Dealey, W. L., and Ford, G. C. (1936) *Typewriting behavior.* New York: American Book Co.

Elliott, L. L., and Sherrick, C. E. (1976) NINCDS workshop on tactile and visual aids for the deaf. *J. Acoust. Soc. Amer.,* 59, 486–489.

Farrell, G. (1950) Avenues of communication. In P. E. Zahl (ed.) *Blindness: Modern approaches to the unseen environment.* Princeton, N.J.: Princeton University Press, 313–345.

Fletcher, H. (1929) *Speech and hearing.* New York: Van Nostrand.

Furth, H. G. (1964) Research with the deaf: Implications for language and cognition. *Psychol. Bull.,* 62, 145–164.

———. (1966) *Thinking without language.* New York: Free Press.

———. (1971) Linguistic deficiency and thinking: Research with deaf subjects, 1964–1969. *Psychol. Bull.,* 76, 58–72.

Garner, W. R. (1974) *The processing of information and structure.* Potomac, Md.: Lawrence Erlbaum.

Gault, R. H. (1927) "Hearing" through the sense organs of touch and vibration. *J. Franklin Inst.* (September), 329–358.

Geldard, F. A. (1966) Cutaneous coding of optical signals: The optohapt. *Percept. Psychophys.,* 1, 377–381.

———. (1970) Vision, audition, and beyond. In W. D. Neff (Ed.) *Contributions to sensory physiology.* New York: Academic Press, 1–17.

Keidel, W. -D. (1968) Electrophysiology of vibratory preception. In W. D. Neff (ed.) *Contributions to sensory physiology.* New York: Academic Press, 1–74.

———. (1974) The cochlear model in skin stimulation. In F. A. Geldard (ed.) *Cutaneous communication systems and devices.* Austin, Tex.: The Psychonomic Soc., 27–32.

Lashley, K. S. (1938) Factors limiting recovery after central nervous lesions. *J. Ment. Nerv. Disease,* 88, 733–755.

Liberman, A. M. (1974) Language processing: State-of-the-art report. In R. E. Stark (ed.) *Sensory capabilities of hearing-impaired children.* Baltimore, Md.: University Park Press, pp. 129–141.

Liberman, A. M., Cooper, F. S., Shankweiler, D. P., and Studdert-Kennedy, M. (1968) Why are speech spectrograms hard to read? In J. M. Pickett (Ed.) Proceedings of the conference on speech-analyzing aids for the deaf. *Amer. Ann. of the Deaf,* 113, 127–133.

Meadow, K. P. (1968) Early manual communication in relation to the deaf child's intellectual, social, and communicative functioning. *Amer. Ann. of the Deaf*, 113, 29–41.

Miller, J. D., Engebretson, A. M., and DeFilippo, C. L. (1974) Preliminary research with a three-channel vibrotactile speech-reception aid for the deaf. Paper presented at the Speech Communication Seminar, Stockholm, Sweden, August 1–3.

Nickerson, R. S. (1975) Speech training and speech reception aids for the deaf. Cambridge, Mass.: Bolt, Beranek, and Newman, Report No. 2980, January.

Nickerson, R. S., and Stevens, K. N. (1973) Teaching speech to the deaf: Can a computer help? *IEEE Trans. Audio and Electroacoust.*, AU-21, 445–455.

———. (1974) Computerized speech-training aids for the deaf. Cambridge, Mass.: Bolt, Beranek, and Newman, Report No. 2914, September.

Nolan, C. Y., and Kederis, C. J. (1969) Perceptual factors in braille word recognition. New York: *Amer. Found. for the Blind Research Series No. 20*.

O'Neill, J. J., and Oyer, H. J. (1961) *Visual communication for the hard of hearing*. Englewood Cliffs, N.J.: Prentice-Hall.

Pesonen, J. (1968) Phoneme communication of the deaf. *Ann. Acad. Scient. Fenn.*, Series B., Vol. 151.2.

Pickett, J. M. (ed.) (1968) Proceedings of the conference on speech-analyzing aids for the deaf. *Amer. Ann. of the Deaf*, 113, 116–330.

Pickett, J. M., and Constam, A. (1968) A visual speech trainer with simplified indication of vowel spectrum. In J. M. Pickett (ed.) Proceedings of the conference on speech-analyzing aids for the deaf. *Amer. Ann. of the Deaf*, 113, 253–258.

Pickett, J. M., and Pickett, B. H. (1963) Communication of speech sounds by a tactual vocoder. *J. Speech Hear. Res.*, 6, 207–222.

Potter, R. K., Kopp, A. G., and Green, H. C. (1947) *Visible speech*. New York: Van Nostrand.

Poulton, E. C. (1962) Peripheral vision refractometers and eye movements in fast oral reading. *Brit. J. Psychiat.*, 53, 409–419.

Sherrick, C. E. (1974) Sensory processes. In J. A. Swets and L. L. Elliott (Eds.) *Psychology and the handicapped child*. Washington, D.C.: U.S.G.P.O., 13–39.

———. (1975) The art of tactile communication. *Amer. Psychologist*, 30, 353–360.

Stark, R. E. (ed.) (1974) *Sensory capabilities of hearing-impaired children*. Baltimore, Md.: University Park Press.

Stark, R. E., Cullen, J. K., and Chase, R. A. (1968) Preliminary work with the new Bell Telephone visible speech translator. In J. M. Pickett (ed.) Proceedings of the conference on speech-analyzing aids for the deaf. *Amer. Ann. of the Deaf*, 113, 205–214.

Upton, H. W. (1968) Wearable eyeglass speechreading aid. In J. M. Pickett (ed.) Proceedings of the conference on speech-analyzing aids for the deaf. *Amer. Ann. of the Deaf*, 113, 222–229.

White, B. W. (1970a) Perceptual findings with the vision substitution system. *IEEE Trans. on Man-Machine Systems*, MMS-11, 54–58.

———. (1970b) Results of effect of window size on visual reading speed. *Amer. Found. for the Blind Research Series No. 20*, 121–123.

Sign Alternates for Learning English

A Discussion of Sherrick's Paper

JAMES M. PICKETT

In the preceding paper, Sherrick presented a good review of the status and problems of visual speech and tactile speech. It is apparent that the work in this field, although promising, does not have extensive implications for current practices in the school and clinic; much research is needed before that will happen. Some of the research problems have been pointed out elsewhere (Pickett 1975). Therefore, instead of discussing possible future research on each of the areas presented by Sherrick, this paper elaborates on the survey of language through alternative modalities by describing the use of systematic gesture systems for the development of English language competence in children. These systems are now being used in schools and homes. They were invented primarily for deaf children but they have also been used with other types of language-retarded children. First, the serious retardation of the language development of the deaf child is discussed briefly. Then the main systems of face-to-face communication that have been used to meet the problem are described.

The schooling of deaf children is intensive, with many dedicated teachers and very small classes. Yet deaf children typically do not acquire a highly useful degree of competence in English. For example, the average deaf graduate from high school reads at about a fourth- or fifth-grade level on standard tests (Gentile and DiFrancesca, 1969). Even in the highly selected group of deaf students admitted to Gallaudet College a satisfactory reading level (about eleventh grade) is found in only 30 percent of the entrants and the remainder must spend a year in our remedial prep program.

What language communication methods are used in the early years to try to improve this situation? Several different methods are used, all based on spoken language and designed for use from infancy. Some are called oral methods; others are called combined methods because they combine the oral methods with manual gesture systems.

Oral Methods

The oral methods eschew the use of any gestures that are coded in any linguistic way. In oral schools every effort is made to prevent the child from using, or even coming into contact with, a gestural language.[1] The purpose is to bring up the deaf pupil to speak, lipread, and hear effectively in the normal-hearing world. It is claimed that only a small proportion of deaf children have too little remaining

---

[1]Actually this does not wholly succeed, particularly in residential schools where the children develop their own gestural patois. These sign patois should be interesting to study, particularly because they may represent "primitive" sign languages. They are probably not closely related to the sign language of the deaf communities because there are no deaf teachers or staff in oral schools and only about 10 percent of deaf children have deaf parents. If this is so, then these children's sign patois might be seen to have characteristics like those of earlier stages in the development of formal sign languages, such as a higher degree of iconicity of sign forms and simpler forms of grammar.

hearing not to be successful with early use of a hearing aid, preferably before age two, and intensive oral training.

There are two different oral approaches to the communication method recommended for the early years: unisensory and multisensory. The unisensory method (Pollack 1970) maintains that all the early communication with children must be purely auditory so that they first become dependent on their residual hearing for communication. Talking to the child should be done from the side or from the front with the mouth and jaw hidden. The rationale is that if the visual speech cues are available, they will become the dominant communication channel because they tend to preempt attention and are clearer than the minimal auditory cues provided by severely damaged hearing, with the result that the auditory residuum will not develop for use. Any residual hearing that is present must be used. It is claimed that because hearing is the normal, natural channel for speech acquisition, it must dominate from the very beginning for the deaf child to learn to speak and to perceive spoken language to optimum capacity. Ling (1976) provides a phonologic instructional system for this purpose. After a certain stage of auditory awareness and response to speech is reached, before school or in a unisensory preschool, then children are allowed to see whatever visual cues they can. Oral schools put great emphasis on the use of hearing, speech, and lipreading, all of which the unisensory advocates believe to be optimized by their method. Oral preschools use some written words but no signing or finger spelling, and the emphasis is on hearing and on speech responses by the children.

The multisensory oral method (Calvert and Silverman 1976) advocates the earliest possible use of lipreading and residual hearing. Here pains are taken to make a speaker's face as visible as possible. When schooling begins, the regular procedures of the oral school are usually multisensory. Some profoundly deaf children seem to have difficulties under the oral methods, but some respond very well; and many deaf children who are not profoundly deaf may be able to transfer to a hearing school. And they do so under programs deliberately set up for this sequence.

The "oral failures" are thought to result mainly from the lack of any discriminative hearing coupled with the high ambiguity of the visible cues to speech. Thus many profoundly deaf children are eventually educated by using a communication system that is much less ambiguous than lipreading and faulty hearing. These systems employ various types of manual communication as a supplement to speaking.

Combined Methods
There are three types of manual or manually supplemented speech communication, two very old ones, finger spelling and sign language, and one new one called Cued Speech. Finger spelling employs a special hand shape for each letter of the alphabet and each numerical digit plus punctuation signs. The sign language of American deaf people (ASL) is a gestural language unrelated to finger spelling in its gestures and having a grammar and lexicon different from that of English. Detailed linguistic descriptions of ASL together with discussion in comparison

with spoken language will be found in the proceedings of the previous NICHD conference in this series (Kavanagh and Cutting 1975).

Finger spelling and signs are used together with speaking in systematic ways called manual combined or simultaneous methods. Schools using these methods are often called manual schools, as distinct from oral schools, where no linguistic gestures are used. Teachers in these schools all use speech together with a manual system. One such method recommends finger spelling together with speaking; this is called the Rochester Method because it was developed at the Rochester (New York) School for the Deaf and disseminated from there (Scouten 1967). The advantages of this method are that it conforms exactly to the written language and it provides unambiguous communication. For a study indicating positive effects on language development, see Quigley (1969). The disadvantages are that finger spelling is slower than speaking and the children is not forced to listen and lipread, thus presumably lessening their chances of functioning well in the hearing-speaking world. The Rochester practice in the 1960s was to emphasize hearing, speech, and lipreading at early ages and then change to finger spelling with speech at about age ten (Alumni Association 1963).

The slowness of finger spelling can be circumvented to a considerable degree by using signs for words instead of spelling them. The signs are taken from ASL. At Gallaudet College, signs and speech are used at the same time; this method is called the simultaneous method. Where there is no reasonably equivalent sign for a word, it is finger spelled. In academic communication quite a bit of finger spelling is seen and sometimes abbreviations are used.

The general philosophy now current in the manual camp of educators is called total communication, which means that good amplification for hearing, good speech, and lipreading must be employed simultaneously with signs and finger spelling; this will provide optimal language function. In the oral camp the belief is that performance in hearing and speaking will be retarded by the use of signs and finger spelling, especially in the early school years.[2]

New Signing Systems
Now let us consider two new systems for communication with deaf children to develop their language competence. From the point of view of the pupils' grammatical development, the signs of ASL, although relatively rapid, lack the systematic syntactical indications of spoken English words. This has led to the development of several new systems of simple signs as syntactic markers. They are chosen to be easy to add to a signed word with a minimum of added time. Markers may indicate such things as plural, past tense, adverbial or adjectival function, comparative, or superlative. At Gallaudet a system called Signed English was designed

[2]I have tried to sketch something about the character of the oral-manual controversy by defining the methods in conjunction with very brief summaries of their rationales. However, my definitions are not the result of extensive discussion and experience in education. I have probably oversimplified too much. Also it now appears that the two camps are trying to accommodate to each other more than they have in the past (Fellendorf 1975).

by Harry Bornstein in the psychology department (Bornstein 1974, forthcoming). He originally designed the system to use with preschool deaf children and selected a standard vocabulary of about twenty-five hundred words. He chose the words that were most frequently used at that level of education. Each English word was equated to an ASL sign. Where necessary, new signs were devised. There are fourteen markers, each of which reflects the meaning of common word endings. Other groups of educators have worked with a system called "Seeing Essential English." This system has a purpose similar to signed English but the gestures represent some combination of spelling, sound, and meaning rather than meaning alone. Since this also obtains for prefixes and suffixes, the system is much more complex (seventy affixes). Similar methods are "Signing Exact English" and "Linguistics of Visual English." Systems of signed English are always used with speaking but actually nothing but the signs is needed for adequate communication. The systems reflect English grammar and are about as fast as a deliberate speech rate.

One would like to have a system where the message would be clear but the pupil is still forced to lipread. Another very different combined visual-manual system has been designed to do that. It was invented by R. O. Cornett at Gallaudet College. He developed a system of gestural cuing used while speaking called cued speech (Cornett 1967, 1975). It is basically a phonetic signing system that uses a consonant-vowel (CV) syllable as the gestural unit but requires lipreading for clarification within sets of CV syllables. The gesturing hand is used in one of four positions and one of eight shapes. The positions indicate classes of vowels and the hand shapes represent classes of consonants; within classes you can discriminate the consonant and vowel by seeing the lip pattern.

For example, one position represents vowels /æ/, /i/, and /u/; the vowel in the CV unit then can be either of those three vowels and the lip pattern, open for /æ/, spread for /i/, or rounded for /u/, determines which one of the three it is. Then there are three consonants indicated by the shape of the hand. So, for example, a given hand shape may mean that the consonant in the CV unit was either /m/, /t/, or /f/ and there is a lip closure, for /m/, no lip closure on the /t/, or dental-labial closure for /f/. So the hand position and shape defines a set of nine syllables. The syllable can be /mi/, /ti/, or /fi/; /mæ/, /tæ/, or /fæ/; /mu/, tu/, or /fu/. And the hand gesture together with what you see in the CV sequence on the lips defines which of those nine syllables it is.

Cornett has succeeded in teaching parents to analyze their speech phonemically as they talk. Apparently, it is not very difficult to do or to use in time with speech, at least well enough to start with a young child, to whom you say only short, uncomplicated utterances.

Several schools have adopted Cued Speech. There are about fifty in the United States and twenty in Australia. In at least five of the Australian schools all levels of children have been taught the system and they use it rather than signs to talk to each other. The children may like it because they can now talk clearly to each other and do not have to depend on lipreading and their faulty hearing alone. In the United States possibly as many as one hundred and fifty additional schools and programs make some use of Cued Speech, such as using it for teaching pronunciation but not as the basic communication method with all children.

At some of the places where these two new systems, Signed English and Cued Speech, are being used, the children's development of vocabulary and syntax is being followed with periodic testing. Preliminary results suggest that the children are almost keeping up with the performance of hearing children of their age level. The Cued Speech group (four children) averaged seventy-two months chronological age in May 1975 and their vocabulary scores were about at fifty-one months on the Peabody Picture Vocabulary Test with cues and fourty-six without cues (lipreading alone). Their syntax scores were about sixty-five months as measured by the Northwestern Syntax Screening Test (receptive), and fifty-six months on the expressive test.

The Signed English group is an unselected group of sixty children from the District of Columbia and nearby Maryland. They average forty-eight months chronological age; their receptive vocabulary level measures thirty-two months in the Peabody Test when Signed English is used. They score at the nine-month level with speech alone. However, they do not seem to be achieving the syntax that was hoped for. They are operating at a thirteen-month receptive level on the Northwestern Syntax Test. Apparently the explicit grammatical structure will take longer to appear than originally hoped.

It seems that systems using manually supplemented communication have a good potential for increasing the language competence of deaf persons. In addition it is believed that the methods ease the psychological relations between the deaf child and his parents (Schlesinger and Meadow 1972).

Cued Speech and Signed English were developed by scientifically trained persons who came into intimate contact with the educational problems of the deaf. The systems might be considered examples of what can happen when scientists work in a school or clinic, as called for by Sherrick at the end of his paper. However, it should also be noted that none of the current studies with these methods is using concurrent control groups receiving equivalent instruction with another mode of communication. This is typical of research in educational settings. It is due to the impracticability of well-matched controls and to ethical feelings against controls, facts of school life that scientists have to learn to tolerate.

References

Alumni Association. 1963. *The Rochester Method of Instructing the Deaf.* Rochester School for the Deaf, Rochester, New York.

Bornstein, H. 1974. Signed English: A manual approach to English language development. *J. Speech and Hearing Research*, 39: 330–343.

————. In press. Sign language in the education of the deaf. In I. Achlesinger and L. Namir (Eds.) *Sign Language of the Deaf: Psychological, Linguistic, and Sociological Perspectives.* New York: Academic Press.

Calvert, D., and R. Silverman. 1976. *Speech and Deafness.* Washington, D.C.: A. G. Bell Association.

Cornett, R. O. 1967. Cued Speech. *Amer. Ann. Deaf*,112: 3–13.

―――. 1975. Cued speech and oralism: An analysis. *Audiology and Hearing Education*, 1: 26–33.

Fellendorf, G. 1975. Should all of us examine definitions? *Volta Review*, 77: 534–535.

Gentile, A., and S. D. Francesa 1969. *Academic Achievement Test Performance of Hearing-Impaired Students of the United States*. Series D, Report 1, Office of Demographic Studies, Washington, D. C.: Gallaudet College.

Kavanagh, J., and J. E. Cutting (eds.). 1975. *The Role of Speech in Language*. Cambridge, Mass. The MIT Press.

Ling, D. 1976. *Speech and the Hearing-Impaired Child: Theory and Practice*. Washington, D.C.: A. G. Bell Association.

O'Rourke, T. (Eds.). 1971. *Psycholinguistics and Total Communication*. Silver Spring, M.d.: National Association of the Deaf (*Amer. Ann. Deaf*, Publisher).

Pickett, J. M. 1975. Speech-processing aids for communication handicaps: Some research problems. In D. B. Tower (ed.) *Human Communication and Its Disorders*, Vol. III of *The Nervous System: 25 Years of Research Progress*. New York: Raven Press, 299–304.

Pollack, D. 1970. *Educational Audiology for the Limited Hearing Infant*. Springfield, Ill.: C. C. Thomas.

Quigley, S. 1969. *The Influence of Fingerspelling on the Development of Language, Communication, and Educational Achievement in Deaf Children*. Urbana, Ill.: University of Illinois Press.

Schlesinger, H., and K. Meadow. 1972. *Sound and Sign: Childhood Deafness and Mental Health* Berkeley, Ca.: University of California Press.

Scouten, E. 1967. The Rochester Method: An oral multisensory approach for instructing prelingual deaf children. *Amer. Ann. Deaf*, 112: 50–55.

General Discussion of Papers by Sherrick and Pickett

Signed English and Cued Speech

A part of the discussion centered around questions about the new signing systems presented by Pickett. Pickett explained that all these methods were used in conjunction with speech. Each child was fitted with a hearing aid and about 25 percent of these children had considerable residual hearing. It is not possible to say precisely how much these children could process by purely aural methods.

The teachers of the deaf involved in these programs have learned to present the Signed English or the Cued Speech simultaneously with speech all the time. Since it is syllabic, the Cued Speech method is easier to coordinate with speech, and rhythm can be indicated by the force of the gestural patterns. Teachers have used these rhythm indications in teaching speech production as well. Pickett did not know of any data on the rates of transmission of propositions in these types of systems. Pickett also explained that in cued speech, consonant clusters and final consonants were cued by a sign in the position for a neutral vowel.

Sherrick mentioned that research on the effects of combining some of these signing systems with the visual displays reported in his paper has just begun. There is no body of sound research findings as yet.

In answer to another question, Pickett reported that the participation of the parents in these programs is very important. Parent participation in the experimental programs he reported in the paper was mixed, but the biggest successes were with children whose parents learned the system and used it in the home as soon as they could. Most parents were able to learn the Signed English system or the Cued Speech system. The discussants expressed amazement that phonetically untrained adults could learn the Cued Speech system easily, since it entails phonemic analysis of their speech. Pickett agreed that it was probably harder than the Signed English system but said it was easier than he had suspected. Since it is based on phonemic structure, Cued Speech would probably not be usable by deaf parents of deaf children. However, only 10 percent of deaf children have deaf parents, and these adults use American Sign Language (ASL) for the most part. Deaf parents do not like Signed English; they consider it a contamination of ASL.

McReynolds asked if there have been any efforts to begin using these or other signing systems with children at very early ages to give them some kind of communication. Are children who start early with signing more advanced when they start their formal education involving aural-oral modes of communication? Pickett reported that there are some programs that attempt to do this, such as the Central Institute for the Deaf program in which parents and children are given instruction in a home life situation. It is now agreed on by special educators that early experience involving the parents' learning and using the system in the home is critically important for success, regardless of the methods used. Knowledge of the importance of early experience stems from the ideas about critical periods that have come out of the basic research on language by Lenneberg (1967) and others. He also noted that deaf children of deaf parents are usually about one-half year ahead of their peers with hearing parents on reading tests.

Another question of interest was whether these new sign systems learned in school settings were used spontaneously by the children or whether they were discarded when the children were out of the classroom. Liberman repeated a comment made by Ursala Bellugi at a previous conference that children who were taught Signed English rejected it as soon as they were out on the playground. Pickett reported that in the Australian schools the Cued Speech system seems to have spread among the pupils in informal situations and replaced the patois signs they had been using. However, these schools were formerly auralist schools, and the spread happened originally with the older pupils who might have had more to talk about than their patois systems could capture.

Reading Problems in the Deaf

A major topic of discussion concerned the problems of deaf children learning to read. Bloom asked if crash reading programs such as those with normal-hearing preschool children had been tried with deaf children. It was agreed that the low reading levels reported by Pickett (fifth grade proficiency in high school graduates) reflected problems in learning English *as a language* as well as learning to comprehend its orthographic representation. In other words, deaf children do not learn to read as normal children do because they do not have the knowledge of the language structures to which the orthographic representations correspond. This is reflected in several phenomena. Liberman reported that teachers of the deaf refer to what deaf children do when they read as "noun-calling." That is, they are able to learn the correspondence between concrete objects (referents) and the orthographic representation of the words that refer to them. But they are not able to learn to read and comprehend sentences containing function words that indicate syntactic structure and other content words for which there are no physical referents. Lahey mentioned some work using a cloze technique (in which subjects are to fill in blanks in sentences) that showed that deaf children filled in function words where they were supposed to be placed, but not the correct function words. That is, they knew something about the correct form of the words to be substituted but did not grasp the content relations. Chapman mentioned some studies by Quigley and his colleagues (Quigley 1976; Wilbur 1975, 1976), who reported severe problems with syntactic construction in the writing of deaf children. These kinds of data on reading and writing suggest that a major difficulty for these children is that they do not have the requisite knowledge of the syntactic structure of the language that is available to the hearing children through the spoken language.

Labov compared these problems of deaf children with those of black children, for whom the black English vernacular dialect that they speak does not correspond to standard English, which they must learn to read. The average reading level for these children is about fifth-grade level also. (See Labov 1972.)

Lahey suggested that the fifth-grade cutoff might be a function of the fact that reading tests change quite drastically from third-grade to fifth-grade levels. The tests for the latter level involve abstract thinking in addition to merely "decoding" the lexical items. Liberman agreed that the difference could very well be that the noun-calling ability provides enough information for the kind of comprehension tested at the lower levels. One can answer questions about the topic of the written material (that it was about boys and girls and dogs); this is enough to obtain fourth-grade level scores but not to carry one through to the more advanced reading skills required to pass the higher level tests.

With respect to the question of the relation between knowledge of spoken language and reading ability, Pickett added that if reading could be done without reference to a spoken language, then the programs in which finger spelling was started very early should produce readers who are performing as well as their hearing peer group. While some of the best readers are from this program, they are still reading at only about the eighth-grade level at high school graduation. Jenkins reported on a Swiss program of education of deaf children. Children are sent to boarding schools at a very young age. They are subjected to written language very intensively. Each child has a slate and a piece of chalk; everything is done in cursive writing. For instance, the teacher will write something on the slate for the children to get from the other end of the room and they practice that. Then the teacher will write something and will not let the child take the slate with him. A child who forgets what was to be retrieved must go back to the slate. Jenkins did not know how this program was being evaluated, but its advocates claim good success in its effectiveness for teaching reading. (Affolter, personal communication).

Chapman brought up the additional consideration that language learning for the deaf differed from the way normal language development takes place in that the input situation is very different. That is, for the deaf child, much of both spoken and written forms of language is taught in formal programs in the classroom. For normal-hearing children, spoken language is learned in the context of interactions with adults and older children in conjunction with other activities and in familiar perceptual environments. She suggested that language learning might be improved for the deaf by incorporating some of the language programming principles presented in Bloom (this volume), which are concerned with language use as well as content and form. These notions reflect the fact that the development of language is now thought of as interrelated with cognitive development in general and that early language acquisition especially is dependent upon the dynamic interaction of linguistic and nonlinguistic aspects of the environment and the child's activities within that environment.

Evaluation of Research and Educational Programs

Shelton brought up the issue of evaluation of programs using alternative modes of language. For instance, what are the criteria of success in reading programs for the deaf? Are the tests given to assess these programs valid? The conferees agreed that in this particular instance school achievement was considered the criterion for success. Pickett suggested that the goal in these programs is to overcome the fifth-grade reading plateau.

Stevens commented that for programs that use tactile or visual aids, the evaluation procedures are often insufficient. Standard tests of word intelligibility are often used; these are not adequate. What is needed is a whole battery of tests that can evaluate ability on segmental (phonemic) variables, prosodic and sentential variables, and other aspects of language. These kinds of tests are not currently available.

Jenkins and Yeni-Komshian both stressed the importance of understanding that with devices such as the tactile vocoder, initial training may take thousands of trials. Many funding agencies and researchers are not aware that it takes an enormous amount of time to learn the first basic distinctions. The question concerning evaluation then is how much training should be given before one decides whether these kinds of techniques will or will not benefit children? If one's expectations are that results can be obtained in a few weeks or months, the effort will be given up before sufficient training has been accomplished to ascertain whether the method has promise.

Psychological/Social Issues in Language Programs for the Deaf

The conferees turned to the very important issues concerning the sociological and psychological problems involved in language programs for the deaf. Labov stressed again that it was analogous to the situation with black children. The language of the subculture (the deaf community or the black community) binds its members to that community but divides them from the larger society. ASL is at the emotional and cultural center of the deaf community. One can imagine a reading system that maps directly onto ASL that would be very efficient and presumably more easily learned by the deaf child who uses ASL. But this would further divide these individuals from the hearing community. In order to integrate these individuals into the larger society, they must somehow learn to communicate in the standard language. But this then causes problems within their own peer group.

It was noted, however (as mentioned before), that only 10 percent of the deaf children have deaf parents; so the majority are not "in the deaf community" at least as children. These individuals, if educated by purely aural methods, usually learn ASL some time in their life; they join the local deaf club and start to learn it. Sherrick stressed again that because of these sociological factors the involvement of deaf people in new research and educational programs is essential. If an idea is thrust upon the deaf community by "outsiders," it will be rejected in a short time. Thus the success of research efforts often depends critically on the participation of deaf individuals. Remember, braille was invented by a blind man.

References

Affolter, F. (Address) Klinik fur Ohren-Nasen-Halskranke und fesichtschirurgie, Kantonsspital St. Gallen, Switzerland-9016, St. Gollen.

Bloom, L. This volume. The integration of form, content, and use in language development.

Labov, W. 1972. *Language in the Inner City: Studies in the Black English Vernacular*. Philadelphia, Pa.: University of Pennsylvania Press.

Lahey, M. This volume. Disruptions in the development and integration of form, content, and use in language development: A discussion of Bloom's paper.

Lenneberg, E. H. 1967. *Biological Foundations* of *Language*. New York: John Wiley and Sons.

Quigley, S., Montanelli, D., and Wilbur, R. 1976. Some aspects of the verb system in the language of deaf students. *J. Speech and Hearing Research, 19*, 536–550.

Quigley S., Wilbur, R., and Montanelli, D. 1976. Complement structures in the language of deaf students. *J. Speech and Hearing Research, 19*, 448–457.

Wilbur, R., Montanelli, D., and Quigley, S. 1976. Pronominalization in the language of deaf students. *J. of Speech and Hearing Research, 19*, 120–140.

Wilbur, R., Quigley, S., and Montanelli, D. 1975. Conjoinal structures in the language of deaf students. *J. Speech and Hearing Research, 18*, 319–335.

The Integration of Form, Content, and Use in Language Development

LOIS BLOOM

It is possible to see language in terms of a very simple trichotomy of three large and general components: form, content, and use. Language form is the mechanism, the code, the actual shapes and configurations of sounds and words and combinations—what children actually say. Language content is the meaning, gist, or semantics of messages—what children talk about, such as objects and relations between objects. Language use consists first of the reasons or functions for language behavior and second of the selection process whereby individuals choose among alternative forms—how children learn to say what to whom and in which circumstances. In order for research in language development to be relevant for educational and clinical needs, it is necessary to recognize that for the child, different aspects of language come together in the integration of form, content, and use in development as schematized in figure 1 (Bloom and Lahey, forthcoming).

However, the study of child language has generally been fragmented in the ways in which attention has been given to one and then another of these three components. In the 1950s and 1960s, linguistic theory (especially the theory of generative grammar by Chomsky 1957) exerted a major influence on child language research and the resulting emphasis was on the form of children's messages, and in syntax in particular. In the 1970s there was a turn toward cognitive theory (especially the works of Jean Piaget), and content or semantics was the focus in studying child language. Most recently there has been influence from philosophy (for example, Austin 1962; Searle 1969) and sociology, and the emphasis has shifted to the use of language. The result has been a fragmentation of the study of language form, content, and use, historically; but it may be possible now to

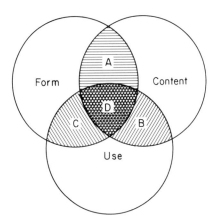

Figure 1. The intersection of the components of form, content, and use in language.

begin to see how the three come together for the child with continuity among behaviors in the course of language development.

Research in language development is restricted to observing behaviors—observing what children do—whether in a naturalistic situation or in a contrived, experimental situation. Unlike other contributions to this volume that describe the speech signal and motor behaviors involved in speaking, there are no instruments for studying language to rely on—no lan uage equivalents of the spectograph or X-ray or myelogram. Nevertheless, persons who study children's language make inferences about what children know, and such research leads to two important questions (see Bloom 1974a). The first: Are the data (from observations) accountable for the conclusions, that is, the descriptions of behavior, that are offered? The second question deals with psychological reality: How close is the description of the child's behavior to what goes in the child's head? (See, for example, discussions of linguistic and mental grammar in Watt 1970; Bloom 1974.) The first question deals with observational adequacy and at that level there is a consensus in the literature about certain aspects of child language. Many studies have converged on a general description of what children do—the behaviors of language and behaviors related to language. The second question deals with explanatory adequacy and at the level of interpretations and inferences about what children know. There is less of a consensus and a number of issues remain. With certain issues it is clear that more research is needed and one or another issue could be resolved. With other issues it is less clear what kinds of evidence would be needed or even if the issue is resolvable.

This chapter has been organized according to consensus and issues relative to several domains of particular interest in the study of form, content, and use in child language and development: the relation of infant behaviors to later language behaviors; the nature of the language-learning environment and input to the child; the relations among form, content, and use in the words that children learn; the grammatical structures that children learn; and how children learn to choose among alternative resources for meeting different needs in different situations.

The Precursors of Form, Content, and Use in Infancy

There is essentially a consensus about the different kinds of behaviors that have been observed in infants. With respect to language form, the discrimination of speech sounds by very young infants has been reported by Eimas et al. (1971); Moffitt (1971), and Morse (1972), among others. The differential production of sounds by infants has been described by Delack (in press), Oller (1976), and others. The use of ordered speech elements has been described by Bloom (1973), Ramer (1976), and others. With respect to language content, children learn about the nature of objects through movement, location, and other object relations. The course of development of sensorimotor intelligence has been well charted in the first two years of life (Piaget, 1954, 1960; Sinclair, 1971). With respect to language use, the systematic dyadic exchanges between mothers and infants that involve gazing and voicing have been described by Bateson (1975), Stern et al. (1975), and others. The influence of the situation on infants' vocalizing has been described by Delack (in press) Lewis and Freedle (1973), and Sander (1975), among others. While such descriptions of infants' behaviors have been generally agreed upon, the issues that remain have to do with how these (and other) behaviors relate to language and language development.

It is not clear how infants' perception of speech sounds at three and four months and vocalizing before twelve months relate to later phonological and lexical development. Much research in the age range from twelve to twenty-four months has indicated that different children use different rules and strategies in learning phonology, apparently influenced by the words they are learning during this period (Ferguson and Farwell 1975; Menn 1971; Waterson 1971; see McReynolds, this volume, for a review of these studies).

There is a question of just how early sensorimotor intelligence relates to later language content. Sensorimotor intelligence results in the achievement of object permanence and the mental representation of information about objects. It is fairly clear that the child needs to have some information about an object or a relation in order to know the meaning of the word for that object or relation. What is not clear is how an individual infant's performance on the scaled tests of object permanence (see, for example, Uzgiris and Hunt 1975; Corman and Escalona 1969) relate to her or his learning words and semantic relations between words. What is the relation between performance on this apparently non-object-specific task and knowing about objects in general and particular object classes (object concepts) and knowing about words (word concepts)? McNeill (1974) has suggested a strong link between the action and location patterns of sensorimotor intelligence and knowing relational concepts and grammatical structure, but there is no consensus on such views as yet.

Finally, how do the dyadic exchanges between infants and their caretakers relate to the later reciprocity of discourse? In the study by Stern et al. (1975) infants and mothers very often vocalized together in unison, which would indicate that the reciprocity of discourse is learned subsequently, apparently depending upon the need to obtain information from a prior utterance in order to produce a contingent reply (see Bloom, Rocissano, and Hood 1976). This is in line with the observations by Delack (in press) and Lewis and Freedle (1973) that infants become progressively sensitive to their environment vocalizing differently in different contexts.

It appears that content, form, and use represent parallel threads of development in the first year of infancy and begin to come together only in the second year as the child learns words, sentences, and discourse (see figure 2). Infants perceive and produce aspects of linguistic form and interact with other persons in the environment at the same time that they perceive, feel, and know about events in their immediate environments. What is the difference then in the interactions of the three components before and after the integration of form, content, and use? The immediate difference between the early and later linguistic behaviors is that the infant begins to become conventionalized, that is, begins to be conditioned by events in the environment, to become aware of the mapping or coding conventions

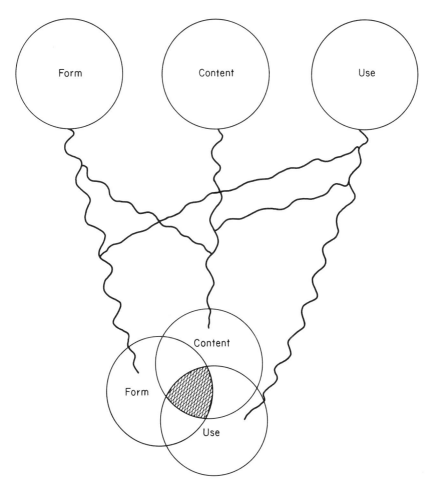

Figure 2. The precursors of form, content, and use in infancy before their intersection in the development of language.

that organize the interaction of the form, content and use components of language. While the infant's behavior is regular and consistent—as indicated, for example, by the intonation patterns described by Halliday (1975) and Delack (in press) in infant vocalization and the patterns of gazing and vocalizing between mother and infant described by Stern, et al. (1975)—the patterns of regularity and consistency do not coincide with conventional systems of reference in language and communication.

There are integral differences between behaviors that are observed before and after the beginning organization of form, content, and use for conventional linguistic coding. The infant behaviors that have been described before they become conventionalized relate to empirical events that are observable, that is, looking and the sounds and intonation contours of vocalization. In contrast, the conventional mapping relation, although it uses observable events, is not itself directly observable; it represents an induction from experience. While the infant is apparently able to perceive and produce segmental and suprasegmental features of phonetic, intonation, and stress events (see, for example Eimas et al. 1971; Kaplan 1970; Morse 1972) and to participate in visual and vocal interactions with others, infants are not able to use these behaviors in conventional ways until after inducing their relationship to elements of experience.

Further, communication in this first year *reflects* feelings and states more than it is intended to *represent* affect and changes in affect or to represent other kinds of information. The messages the infant communicates have to do with feelings and affectual states that come about through experience with persons and objects that move and that change and affect the infant's changing states of well-being, comfort, and discomfort. But such vocalizations are not yet intended to depict or represent such feelings and affectual states so much as they are reactive and reflect such feelings that the child has. Werner and Kaplan (1963) have discussed infants' motor behavior in similar terms. Two things loom large in the transition from vocalization that reflects to vocalization that intends to represent information: One is information about language—the conventional linguistic schemes that societies and cultures have evolved for sharing information among individuals— and the other is information about persons and situations—the conventional pragmatic schemes that societies and cultures have evolved for regulating the exchange of information among persons. The first has to do with language form and the second has to do with language use. Both have to do with language content.

It is not the case that infants learn sound contrasts, intonation and stress contours, and rules for dyadic exchange and put these aspects of form together in connection with meaning and use. Learning language is not an additive process. Rather it seems to be the case that the behaviors of the infant are precursory behaviors or capacities that are slowly and progressively adapted to the conventional requirements of the linguistic and pragmatic schemes of language. Although children can shape their behaviors to coincide with the empirical events that they see and hear, learning language waits upon the conceptual capacities for a linguistic induction of "mapping insight" into the relations between form and content and a psychosocial induction for making inferences about the relations between persons and situations. The integration of form, content, and use and the continuity of behaviors in the transition from infant behaviors to language behaviors result from such conceptual capacities and contact between linguistic and nonlinguistic categories.

The Language-Learning Environment

LINGUISTIC AND NONLINGUISTIC CATEGORIES

Nonlinguistic categories (for example, objects, actions, locations, and relations among objects) form the content of a child's language and are derived from individual topics such as a particular object (a ball), a particular action (throwing), a particular location (on the porch), and a particular relation (mine). Language content, then, can be presented as a taxonomy of categories, with rules for the assimilation of new topics, according to the child's conceptual abilities for classifying and generalizing among events in reality. In addition, there are processes of division and classification of events for learning linguistic categories. Signs and words are concepts. Words have distinguishing physical and acoustic properties as well as distinguishing semantic and syntactic properties. Sounds are concepts. Sounds have distinguishing acoustic and articulatory properties that make meaningful differences between words. And there are grammatical concepts that include information about the ways combinations of words and sounds can represent relational meanings. Learning language content has to do with learning about objects and relations between objects. Learning linguistic form, on the other hand, consists of learning linguistic categories—the lexicon, morphology, and grammar of language—and phonological categories that are basic to lexical, morphological, and grammatical categories. The formation of linguistic and non-linguistic categories and the contact among them have been frequently discussed, for example, by Brown (1958), Collins and Quillian (1969), and Miller (1951).

To what extent do children learn about objects and events in the world through the language they hear and to what extent do children use what they already know about objects and events in the world in order to learn linguistic categories? On the one hand, it has been pointed out by Bloom (1970, 1973, 1974c), Cromer (1974), Leonard (1974), MacNamara (1972), Nelson (1974), Sinclair (1971), and others that children learn their first words and sentence structures after they have acquired relevant conceptual distinctions that are coded by such words and structures. On the other hand, Brown (1958) suggested that the opportunity to see the connection between a linguistic form and the features of the environment to which it refers guides the child in learning the relevant attributes of the environment for forming nonlinguistic categories (see also Church 1961).

It seems safe to conclude that both accounts are somehow correct, despite the apparent contradiction between them. In an ideal world one would like to be able to determine empirically just when a child "has" a concept in relation to precisely when that child can recognize a word and say it. But if one considers that object concepts and word concepts evolve continuously and are not all-or-nothing categorizations, it becomes clear that there is more of a mutual influence between acquiring linguistic categories and acquiring nonlinguistic categories than a simple temporal or causal relation between them. If children know something of an object concept or a relational concept, then hearing a word can direct them to the limits of the concept that define the meaning of the word. Similarly, hearing a word can guide them to discover the relevant aspects of experience that define the limits of the concept. For example, children can have an idea of cookie and an idea of disappearance, but hearing the word "cookie" and hearing the word "gone" and saying the words as well will help to direct them toward new instances and so contribute to the formation of the nonlinguistic categories.

The balance of influence between form and function in language is a shifting one in the course of development, with variation within individual children and differences among children (Bloom 1976; Bloom, Lightbown, and Hood 1975; Bloom, Miller, and Hood 1975). Children must know something about form and content in order to begin to use words and sentence structures, but they also learn more about words and sentence structures as they hear them and use them in new contexts (Bloom 1974c). In studies by R. Clark (1974) and Peters (1976), children have been described who used many stereotype phrases (as described also by Leopold 1939), and many of their phrases and sentences appeared to be unanalyzed, holistically learned units. It has been suggested that such children begin with more globally defined linguistic categories that are only gradually differentiated in relation to nonlinguistic categories of content and use. Regardless of which route a child takes, language development consists of contact between linguistic and nonlinguistic categories; and the dyadic exchange between child and adult is the crux of the process whereby such contact occurs.

Environmental Input for Learning Language
By far most of what has been described about linguistic interactions between children and adults has centered on the linguistic input that children receive from their caretakers. The impetus for the studies that have looked at children's linguistic environment came from the attempt by transformational linguists to minimize the importance of the environment for language learning. Chomsky (1965) pointed to the errors of performance in adult speech—the false starts, circumlocutions, break-offs—and reasoned that language learning would be a superhuman task if the child had to depend only on such deformations of language as are present in the environment. How could children learn the regularities of language if they needed to filter out all of the noisy interference from mistakes in performance?

The answer to the question came rather quickly and it was not a surprise to find out that, indeed, parents' speech to children provides an ideal model to the child for language learning. In its simplicity and redundancy, the speech that is spoken to children is an admirable presentation of form in relation to content. In its flexibility, speech to children is well tuned to the child's needs in different contexts and is progressively modulated to the child's developing capacities.

There is a strong consensus in most of the studies of mothers' speech to children that have described the broad, general characteristics of utterances to children (see, for example Broen 1972; Nelson 1973; Newport 1976; Phillips 1973; Sachs, Brown, and Salerno 1972; Snow 1972). The major result of these studies has been the consensus that the utterances that children hear from their mothers are short, simple, and redundant with many questions and directives and few morphological inflections, syntactic complexities, and nonfluencies. Mothers' speech to young children is generally pitched higher with an exaggerated intonation pattern. However, it is not just mothers who speak this way; young children also modify their speech in similar ways when they speak to younger children (Berko-Gleason 1973; Shatz and Gelman 1973), as do adults who are not parents (Sachs, Brown, and Salerno 1972; Snow 1972). The speech that young children hear from virtually all directions, then, is scaled down, simplified, and repetitive.

Studies of linguistic input have overwhelmingly documented that parents talk to their children about their immediate context i.e., (about what the children are seeing and doing in the "here and now") (Brown, Cazden, and Bellugi 1969; Ling and Ling 1974; Nelson 1973; Phillips 1973; Soderbergh 1974). The fact that parents' comments to children refer to what the child is already attending to or direct the child's attention to something in the context is the *sine qua non* of the language-learning process. Indeed, if speech addressed to children did not make sense relative to events in the immediate context, then it would, quite simply, make no sense at all. Such speech could not be a model for learning. Even if the form of mothers' speech is seriously distorted in other ways, as is the speech of deaf mothers to their hearing children, it can still provide a model for learning the relation between form and content so long as form is presented in a context in which the relevant content exists (Schiff 1976). This mutual attention between parent and child to the pairing of linguistic form and content is preceded by a mutual attention between parent and child to action and event sequences in infancy in which language may play little or no part (Bruner 1975).

These interactions between parents and children have been described as teaching behaviors; for example, Snow (1972 p. 561) described mothers' speech as "a set of 'language lessons' " Such characteristics of mothers' speech as expansions and redundancy, wherein parents repeat and rephrase their messages until some response or recognition occurs, are effective teaching aids. Parents use other prompts and prodding, ask rhetorical questions, and answer their own questions (see, for example, Moerk 1975; Soderbergh 1974; Seitz and Stewart 1975). However, it appears that parents rarely correct their children, except for errors of fact (Brown, Cazden, and Bellugi 1969) and less often for phonological and grammatical errors (Moerk 1975). Thus it appears that parents are most aware of the content of their children's speech and provide the child with a well-formed model of the relations between form and content.

Studies of the input that children receive for language learning have been limited almost exclusively to descriptions of the superficial form of speech. While the obvious fact that parents talk to children in the here and now has been well substantiated, there has been little description of the specific content of such speech. Instead, parents' speech has been described with many of the same measures of children's language that were used in the early "count" studies of the

1930s and 1940s (summarized in McCarthy 1954), for example, mean length, kinds of sentences, completeness of sentences, numbers of words, or numbers of parts of speech.

Snow (1974) recently reported a semantic analysis of Dutch mothers' speech to their children in which she looked for the same semantic relations that have been described in children's early two-word sentences. She found that the same semantic relations provide an adequate description of the mothers' speech content not only with younger children (whose speech was not analyzed but who were presumably using two-word utterances with the same semantic relations) but also later, with more mature children. This result should not be surprising; the content categories or semantic relations in early childhood speech (for example, action, possession, recurrence) would be expected as well in the speech of older preschool children, school-age children, and adults. Even adults talk to adults about action events, locative events, and possession as well as existence, disappearance, and recurrence. Description of semantics alone, like earlier studies of syntax alone, is less informative than description of semantic-syntactic relationship. The meaning or semantic relations in child utterances probably do not change developmentally except that new categories are added. What does change in children's speech is the interaction between content and form, that is, the same kinds of content are presented in more complex forms. One would expect that it is the interaction between form and content in adult speech that is the critical variable for input as well. Further, Shatz and Gelman (1973) and Newport (1976) point out that the communication needs between parent and child in the situation and the functions of their utterances also result in simplification and redundancy of input. The interaction among form, content, and use, then, is the critical factor that makes adults' speech to children the elegant model for learning that it is.

The most potentially important finding in studies of adult input is the flexibility of parents' speech that results in the gradual but consistent modifications that parents make in the model as children learn more about language. Not only do adults talk differently to children than they talk to other adults, but it appears that they talk differently to children of different ages according to how much they have learned about language (Brown 1972; Moerk 1975; Nelson 1973; Phillips 1973). For example, in the study by Phillips (1973), it was reported that mothers used more different words and more different parts of speech per utterance, and more "abstract" vocabulary words with eight-month-old children (who do not understand) and with twenty-four-month-old children than with eighteen-month-old children. The adults in the study by Nelson (1973) produced more expansions and imitations of their children's speech at twenty-four months than at thirteen months (median age).

The general assumption of modulations in the speech to children as a function of linguistic maturity (rather than age alone) was questioned by Newport (1976), who did not observe parents using more complex speech with more linguistically mature children. However, her measures of the children's linguistic maturity were similar to the measures used by Phillips, who found differences. Since these measures of linguistic maturity are superficial and the ranges in each of these measures tended to be quite limited (for example, words per verb ranged from 1.0 to 1.48; noun phrase per utterance ranged from .80 to 1.47; morphemes per noun phrase ranged from 1.0 to 1.46), they may not have provided a sensitive index of the linguistic maturity of the children in Newport's study. The fact that Newport did not find correlations between structural complexity and children's linguistic maturity is not evidence that such correlations did not exist.

In the study of adult-child discourse reported by Bloom, Rocissano, and Hood (1976), there were differences in the adult speech to the children from twenty-four to thirty-six months of age and these differences seemed to reflect the developmental changes that were observed in the children's speech. For example, the adults asked proportionately more questions as the children's linguistically contingent responses to adult questions increased. Adults may be using longer and more complex speech because children are older and are also using longer and more complex speech. But this is less important than the implication that adults are sensitive to many different kinds of signals that children give out—signals about what they already know or are learning and signals about what they are ready to learn.

Form, Content, and Use of the Words Children Learn
Different investigations have described the ways in which children know words according to how they use words at different times in development. Among the many studies that have described children's early referential words are the classic diary studies, including Guillaume (1927) and Leopold (1939), and the more contemporary studies by Bloom (1973), Clark (1973), Greenfield and Smith (forthcoming), and Nelson (1973, 1974). Although the words that children learn can be listed alphabetically or chronologically in the order of their appearance in speech, the consensus is that they are not homogeneous in terms of either the relation between form and use (how they are used) or the relation between form and content (their meaning).

SUBSTANTIVE WORDS AND RELATIONAL WORDS
Certain words that children use in the first two years, before they begin to produce words in combinations, make reference to single objects that are usually persons (for example, "Mommy," "Daddy," "Baby") but may also be such favored items as the child's blanket or bottle. Other words make reference to classes of objects that have been discriminated according to perceptual and functional criteria (for example, "apple," "chair," "truck"). The words that make reference to object concepts are substantive words or nouns in the adult model. A substantive word refers to an object that can be identified according to some constant attribute that is perceptually discriminable and, in addition, the common functions the object may serve. For example, person names or pet names or names of such familiar belongings as the child's blanket or bottle are substantive words that refer to the same repeated perceptual event. Such words are ordinarily among the first words that children learn to say and understand (Bloom 1973; Huttenlocher 1974; Nelson 1974). Other substantive words refer to objects that share perceptually

constant attributes or a class of objects, such as chairs, cookies, and airplanes. Words that refer to classes of objects are acquired with increasing frequency in the second year and ultimately form the major portion of the child's lexicon.

Another class of words, relational words, make reference to relational concepts that share a common element of behavior or experience but that are perceptually different from one another in each instance. For example, many different objects and events can be "this," "more," "no," "up." The verbs that children learn to use are also relational words; there is some constant feature in different events that may be some movement or some state. For example, the verb "put" occurs in situations in which different persons, such as mommy, daddy, or baby, act as agents in relation to different objects, such as a ball, a coat, or a cookie, that are affected by the movement and different locations, such as the floor, a table, or a room. The constant feature has to do with the transfer from one place to another place. Similarly, the verb "run" occurs in situations in which there is the same movement—whether the object performing the movement is mommy, the child, or the dog.

The earliest relational forms that appear in children's presyntax lexicons are those that have to do with the relation of an object to itself (the relations of existence, nonexistence, recurrence, and simple change of location "up," "down," "outside"). Thus the words reported in early lexicons include, for example, "this," "that" (or some stereotype variant, such as "what that"), "there," "gone," "away," "no more," "bye-bye" (in the sense of disappearance), "more," "again," "up," and "down." These words are maximally useful to the child, referring as they can to many different objects and events, and they also refer to important conceptual notions that children acquire about the nature of objects and their own actions. Verbs occur relatively less frequently in the same presyntax period and occur with increasing frequency after the beginning of multiword utterances and the acquisition of syntax (Goldin-Meadow, Seligman, and Gelman 1976).

REFERENTIAL AND SOCIAL WORDS

Another distinction that has been made in early presyntax lexicons by Nelson (1973) has to do with words that do and do not make reference to objects, what Nelson called referential words and expressive words. As defined by Nelson, referential words are general nouns; expressive words are everything else and include forms that are social gestures or learned in social routines. The original distinction was based upon the finding by Nelson that for some children more than 50 percent of their first fifty words consisted of object referencing words, or nouns, whereas for other children, more than 50 percent of their first fifty words consisted of other words that were not nouns, including such social gestures as "hi," "bye-bye," and "thank you." Nelson did not observe the relative frequencies with which the different words were used by the children or how the children used the words but recorded only mothers' reports that the child had said the word at least one time. More first-born children were described by Nelson as referential and more later-born children were described as expressive. Other researchers have reported similar kinds of observations that seem to support differences among children according to whether they use more names of objects or more social routine words (for example, Dore 1975). There are problems for the interpretation of these studies, however, because there is no way of knowing how the different forms were used by the children. Information about which type of speech, referential or expressive, really dominated in terms of relative frequency of the different words is needed to determine which was more important to the child.

There is indeed a distinction among words that are part of a social interaction exclusively and words that refer to ideas about the world. However, words other than nominals also refer to ideas about the world (such as relational words, including verbs). It appears, then, that in addition to the relational/substantive classification, which would subsume referential words, there is a third classification of social routine words such as "hi," "bye-bye" (as a greeting), and "thank you." Such words no doubt facilitate children's interactions with other persons and their consequent social development. These words do not, however, underlie children's later development of grammatical structure. They do not occur as grammatical constituents when children eventually combine words. Although children may or may not differ in the extent to which they use social routine words as single-word utterances, all children combine referential (relational and substantive) words or pronoun forms for such words (for example, "it," "this," "there") when they begin to form sentences.

NARROW AND BROAD REFERENCE: OVEREXTENSION

It is one of the most frequently documented facts of language development that as children begin to say recognizable words, they typically use words in contexts and in reference to objects and events that are inconsistent with adults use of the same words. Children often begin by saying a word in a highly restricted context, the context that corresponds most closely with an original experience of the word (underextension). Examples of underextension reported in Bloom (1973) are a child's use of the word "car" only when she was sitting on the window ledge and saw a moving car on the street below and her use of the word "dog" only when she heard the sound of the identification tags of a neighborhood dog going by outside (see also Anglin 1975; Bowerman 1975). These instances of narrow reference that have been reported anecdotally occur early, when the children first begin to use words, and are the tentative beginning of the child's first word concepts.

Once children make some connection between a linguistic form and some element of experience, they typically begin to test the hypothesis about what the word "means" and will use it in different contexts. Consider, for example, the child who says "water" when he's in the bath, then when he holds a drinking glass filled with water, and when he touches a pane of window glass; the child who calls all four-legged animals "dog"; the child who eats peas from the pod for the first time and then asks for another "book of peas." The child tests hypotheses about the mapping relation between the linguistic form and elements of content when encountering a new situation and guessing that one or another word might "fit." This hypothesis testing continues throughout childhood (Brown 1965) and manifests itself in different ways, particularly in the first three years when the process of matching form with content begins (Bloom 1973; Bowerman 1975; Brown 1965; Clark 1973; Greenfield 1971; Thomson and Chapman (in press). Different kinds of overextension include chained associations (as in the "water" example above), holistic associations (as in the "dog" example), and metaphorical overextensions (such as "book" in the above example). The different patterns of overextension appear to depend upon the relative stability of children's nonlinguistic categories, that is, object concepts and relationship concepts. Such overextensions are errors by the child when compared with the semantic domain within which the adult uses the same word. However, when viewed from the child's perspective, they are reasonable guesses about a relation between form and content in the effort to learn linguistic categories.

The first time a child hears a particular word is the original referent situation (or focusing event, Kates 1974) for that word on the basis of which the child can begin to work out the meaning of the word. When the child hears a word in the original referent situation and attempts to use the word in another situation, she or he will do so on the basis of the similarities or consistencies that are recognized in the two situations. There appear to be at least three ways in which the child can build a chained association based upon similarities between the original referent situation and succeeding situations: through a failure to differentiate among the possible referents for a word when the word is first heard (Brown 1965; Werner 1948); through a shifting chain of associations in which each referent situation in turn provides a new association, a "chain complex" in which there is some consistency between A and B and between B and C, but not necessarily between A and C (Vygotsky 1962); and through an association between some feature of the original referent situation and a similar feature in succeeding events, an "associative complex" (Vygotsky 1962). These three possibilities are not mutually exclusive. These types of extensions have been discussed by Anglin (1975), Bloom (1973), Bowerman (1975), Brown (1965), and Clark (1973), and the literature provides many examples of one or another kind of chained associations characterizing children's early word use.

While there is a strong consensus that overextension is common in children's early use of words, the issues that remain have to do with the occurrence of such different kinds of overextension as above in relation to other aspects of children's linguistic and cognitive development. The main problem has been that virtually all descriptions of overextension have been diary reports, with the exception of Anglin's (1975) experimental study with older children. Attempts to document the occurrence of overextension by recording observation sessions have not been successful because a nearly complete record of the instances in which a word is used would appear to be necessary (Labov and Labov 1973).

Midway through the second year and increasingly in the last half of the second year (after the achievement of object permanence) children's conceptual categories are progressively more stable, and so associations when a word is used are defined more precisely by the criterial features of the original referent situation. A classic example of the child's generalizing the meaning of a word to new instances of the criterial referent is the description by Lewis (1951) of how his son learned the word "fa fa" (flowers) from about sixteen to twenty-three months. The original referent situation was a bowl of yellow jonquils in the living room. The child said "fa fa" the second time in the same situation as the original (in reference to the bowl of yellow jonquils), demonstrating that he had formed an "identity category" for the word "flowers" (Brown 1965, p. 311). However, when he again used the word, he used it to name another kind of flower of another color, although still in a bowl, and had thus formed an "equivalence category" (Brown 1965, p. 311). The child subsequently named pictures of flowers in a book and by the time he was twenty-three months old he was naming embroidered flowers and flowers made of sugar to decorate a biscuit. The child's use of criterial features to distinguish referents for "fa fa" included the same range of phenomena to which the word "flower" can refer in adult use.

Once children begin to represent mentally classes of objects and events, they use increasing numbers of words that have overlapping semantic fields in their adult meanings. For example, the words "dog," "cat," "horse," "cow," "goat," and "tiger" refer to objects that are all animate with four legs, fur, and tails. The words "truck," "car," "fire engine," and "bus" refer to objects that move on the street and have wheels and motors that make noise. When children do not know the different words that refer to such objects, they may use one word to refer to several or all, for example, "dog" to refer to all four-legged animals and "truck" to refer to all vehicles. In such instances, children have clearly discriminated a particular perceptual criterion for reference to objects. When calling a horse a "dog," the child probably has a conceptual representation of an object dog, but it is probably not true that the representation of dog also includes all the perceptual features belonging to horses, cats, and sheep. It is not clear to what extent children know the differences among different quadrupeds, but they do appear to have learned a larger cognitive domain, only part of which has been semantically represented (as "dog"). It seems entirely reasonable for the child to use an available word to represent different but related objects; it is almost as if the child were reasoning, "I know about dogs; that thing is not a dog; I don't know what to call it; but it is like a dog."

Rather than a shifting chain of associations whereby the referent relation is redefined with successive uses of a word, as in earlier overextension, the child's hypotheses about the meanings of a word and these later overextensions come from knowledge of objects that are defined primarily by consistent perceptual criteria (Clark 1973). In a comprehensive review of the diary literature that describes children's early words and the range of referents that have been observed in the overextension of words, Clark (1973) delineated several perceptual criteria such as shape, size, movement, texture, and four legs (but not color). Such perceptual associations provided evidence that children had identified a semantic domain consistent with a superordinate semantic domain in the adult semantic system—a superordinate semantic domain in the sense that the criterial feature is characteristic of each instance and does not differentiate among instances. While children most probably have differentiated among the particular object concepts or relational concepts to which they refer with the same word, the linguistic category or word concept is less differentiated and the word is often used to refer to the "whole" semantic domain.

Structure in Child Language

Linguistic structure concerns the ways that linguistic categories—words and relations between words—are related to nonlinguistic categories—object concepts and relational concepts. While children's knowledge of objects and relations in the world is a major determining factor in their language learning, the ability to say sentences comes about as the result of several linguistic inductions about words and relations between words. Children progress through certain fairly well defined stages in the development of linguistic form: (1) *Successive single-word utterances* occur as children learn the semantic relations among words they hear spoken and use single words in the context of events that they know about in a conceptual sense; (2) certain conceptual relations are coded with specifically relational lexical items that are later mapped onto longer utterances that have *linear syntactic relationship*; and (3) certain other conceptual relations can also be coded with linear syntactic relations but are eventually mapped onto *hierarchical syntactic structures*. Eventually (4) children learn that sentence structures can be combined to express more than one sentential intention with complex syntax in a single sentence.

SUCCESSIVE SINGLE-WORD UTTERANCES

Single-word utterances can most often be interpreted by an adult in relation to particular aspects of the topic and context of the event in which the word is said. In child speech events, factors that identify topics are almost always present in context; children talk about what they see and what they do (in what has been called the "here and now") in a way that would be most strange for an adult. The redundancy between what children say and the context and behavior that go along with what they say allows one to identify what they are talking about more often than not. Events with separate single-word utterances are distinguishable from one another by shifts in the topic and context with which the single words occur. However, when more than one utterance occurs without a shift in topic, there is reason to attribute a relationship between them and, indeed, to perceive them as successive.

When children first begin to say single words, the words occur most often in speech events that include only one utterance that may be repeated many times. For example, trying to climb onto a chair, a child might say either "up" *or* "chair"; or picking up a cookie after having already eaten a cookie, a child might say "cookie" *or* "more." However, children eventually begin to say two different single-word utterances in the same speech event and this later behavior, the use of successive single-word utterances, may come to predominate in children's pre-syntax speech (as happened with the children described by Bloom [1970, 1973]; Dore et al. [1976]; Smith [1970]; Leopold [1939]).

For example,
1. Gia at 19, 1:
(Gia picking up her mother's slipper)   mommy/ mommy/
What is that?

slipper

Slipper.

mommy/

2. Gia at 19, 1:
(Gia looking at a picture of a boy in a
    toy car)   go/

Car.

car/ ride/

3. Eric at 19, 1:
(Eric looking out the window at the street
    below; cars going by/ children and adults
    walking)   car/ see

see.   car/

Car.

boy/

Rather than simply naming objects, it appeared that the children in the examples were talking about the relations in the event among persons and objects, as in "mommy/slipper," and "car/see." Their utterances were successive and related to one another because the children had perceived and understood certain relationships in context and behavior.

In the analysis of videotaped observations reported by Bloom (1973), a careful examination of the sequence of movements in relation to what the child said in each of the successive single-word speech utterances revealed two possible event structures that could occur with such utterances. There appeared to be events with chained successive utterances that occurred with successive movements and events with holistic successive utterances, in which the entire situation appeared to be defined to begin with and utterances were not tied to particular movements or shifts in context. Although both kinds of structures existed in each video sample, there appeared to be a developmental progression from predominantly chained successive single-word utterances to holistic successive single-word utterances in the period form sixteen to twenty-one months. It is possible that when variable word order in children's early sentences has been reported (for example, what Braine [1976] described as a groping pattern), such children might have been producing successive rather than conjoined words, having learned something of the semantic relations between words but not the syntactic rules for encoding semantic relations.

LINEAR SYNTACTIC RELATIONSHIP

When a child says "more" and reaches for another cookie, it is reasonable to expect an eventual connection between the words "more" and "cookie," and indeed such early word combinations as "more cookie" and "more airplane" are among the earliest that children produce. When such two-word utterances as "more cookie" occur, the relational meaning between the words derives from the meaning of the separate words, but, most particularly, from the meaning of the relational, function word, in this case, "more." Thus certain relational meanings in early sentences are *functional* relations, where a constant form with a specific meaning such as "more," "away," or "there" is combined with other words and the meaning of the function word determines the meaning of the two words in each combination.

Brown (1973) pointed out that such relations can be formalized with the formula $f(x)$, a fixed value, f, combined with a variable (x) that can assume many values. That is, the same meaning, f, can combine with many different words (x) and the meaning of the relation $f(x)$ is determined by the meaning of the constant, f. There is no new meaning added to f or to (x). For example, in the phrases "more cookie," "more airplane," and "more cheese" there is the constant f, "more," and the variable (x), "cookie," "airplane," or "cheese" and the same meaning relation between the words, recurrence, which is also the meaning of "more." Such word combinations are additive, that is, there is no new meaning other than the cumulative meaning of the two separate words when they are joined. Because such word combinations are additive and because the relational meaning of the phrase is determined by the meaning of one of the words, the structural relationship between them can be described as linear: The two words in the phrase are joined; the meanings are added; and there is no new meaning as a result of their combination.

Further, the linear word combinations with such function words as "more," "gone," "this," "there," and "no" (among the words that were described as "pivots" by Braine [1963] and McNeill [1966] are each separate relations in that they do not share any meaning in relation to one another or in relation to other phrases that the child uses at the same time. The f words that enter into such functional linear relations do not themselves form a class or category by virtue of some shared meaning with other words; there is no common meaning among all the words "this," "there" (in the sense of existence), "more," "'nother," "no," and "gone" that would be a criterion for assuming that they represent a category. They come together in a linguistic description of children's sentences because they share the same distribution—each as an f constant in relation to the same variable (x) words—but there is no evidence for presuming that the child learns such function words as a category of words. Rather, each such $f(x)$ relation is a separate relation that is unrelated to other word combinations that have different meaning relations. Children learn position rules for such f words and each results in a separate semantic-syntactic formula (Braine 1976).

The verb forms that children learn can be described in similar terms to some extent. Such words as "eat," "throw," "turn," and "push" can each be described as a constant, f, that can be combined with many variable (x) words (for example, "eat meat," "eat raisin," "eat nut" and "throw ball," "throw book," "throw raisin"). There are, however, several important differences between verb forms and the function forms such as "more" and "gone" that have been described. First, verb forms do not have fixed word order distribution (for example, "mommy *eat*" and "*eat* meat" or "baby *turn*" and "*turn* button" occur). Second, when all the phrases with verb forms are compared, it turns out that verbs do share meaning with one another according to how they relate to nouns in sentences and categories of verbs that can be identified on the basis of shared meaning appear to be learned by children sequentially; verbs do have fixed word order position according to their semantic relations with nouns, for example, "mommy eat," "baby eat," "horse eat," "daddy turn," "girl turn"; and there are different relations between nouns and verbs, these different semantic-syntactic relations are the immediate constituents of a higher level of structure, and the structure of children's sentences with verbs is hierarchical rather than linear.

HIERARCHICAL SYNTACTIC RELATIONSHIP

The verbs that children learn are at once the result of their conceptual development—in that children learn those verbs that enable them to talk about what they know—and the major determinant of the development of grammatical structure. Children do not learn verbs and their relations to nouns one at a time. Rather, categories of verbs appear in child speech; several verbs that have the same semantic-syntactic relations to succeeding and preceding nouns appear at about the same time (Bloom, Lightbown, and Hood 1975; Bowerman 1975). The first semantic-syntactic category of verbs is simple action, then locative action, and then state. Within the category of locative action (where one of the noun and verb constituent relations specifies place as the goal of an action), there are three subcategories according to whether the noun before the verb functions as an agent, a patient, or a mover relative to the verb (Bloom, Miller, and Hood 1975). Thus children learn categories of verbs that entail structural relations between a verb and one or more nouns. Within each category of verbs, such as action, the meaning of the relation between verbs and nouns is the same regardless of the individual lexical meaning of the verbs and nouns themselves.

Children's sentences with verbs are not simply additive—that is, the combination of a noun and a verb results in a new (superordinate) meaning that is more than only the meanings of the separate words. In addition to the inherent lexical meaning of such nominal forms as "mommy," "daddy," "baby," "dog," and "Jane," such words assume the relational meaning "agent" in relation to such verbs as "eat," "throw," and "push." Certain other nouns, for example, "toast," "horse," "ball," and "bridge," also assume the relational meaning "affected object" or "patient" in relation to verbs and in addition to their inherent lexical meaning. There are, then, nouns that function similarly in their relation to verbs and form categories such as agent, patient, place, or affected object on the basis of such similar semantic-syntactic function.

Certain nouns relate to verbs as actors or agents of an action; certain other nouns relate to verbs as objects affected by an action; and still other nouns relate

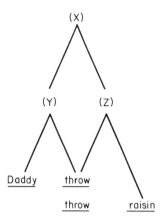

Figure 3. Schematic representation of constituent structure.

to verbs as the place that is the end point of some movement that changes the location of an object. Such semantic-syntactic relations between nouns and verbs are
not separate relations. The relation between a verb and an agent noun such as
"daddy throw" is also related to the relation between that same verb and the
object that is affected by the action, "throw raisin." The relation between the
first relation (y) ("daddy throw") and the second relation (z) ("throw raisin") is
the superordinate relation (x) in figure 3.

Further, categories of verbs such as action, mover-locative action, or agent-
locative action are formed on the basis of the elements of meaning that they share
and the relations that they have with categories of nouns or pronouns. Thus, the
relation between a verb and an agent noun such as "daddy throw" is the same as
the relation between a different verb from the same category and a different agent
noun, such as "mommy push." The relationship, for example, between "mommy
push" and "push swing" is the same superordinate relationship (x) as between
"daddy throw" and "throw raisin." The resulting structure is hierarchical in that
the immediate constituent (y) and the immediate constituent (z) are both related,
in turn, to the higher order relation (x) (see, for example, Lyons 1968, pp. 209–
212).

The constituent structures in hierarchical syntactic relationships can be called
subject and predicate if subject and predicate are defined in these terms or the
constituent structures can be called something else. Children obviously, do not
know what the adult knows about sentence subject and predicate and using the
same terms should not imply that they do. Children do not know the transformational rules that operate on subject and predicate constituents in adult grammar
and they do not know the distinctions between deep structure and surface structure subject/predicate relations in, for example, the following sentences:
1. The girl pulled the wagon.

2. The wagon was pulled by the girl.
3. Pulling the wagon was what the girl did.
4. The girl pulling the wagon is my sister.
where the same deep structure subject/predicate relation is contained in all of the sentences (the relations among girl-pull-wagon), but the surface structure subject/predicate is different in each.

The child's early knowledge of the subject/predicate constituents in hierarchical structure is necessary but not sufficient knowledge about sentences. It is the beginning of the plan or scheme whereby sentences are created with the semantic relations that were formerly represented in successive single-word utterances, and the rest of language development consists of progress toward filling in everything else that one needs to know of the linguistic scheme. Smith (1975, pp. 313–314) suggested "that young children have a general notion of subject and other grammatical relations that corresponds more or less to the traditional notions of subject, etc. . . . [and] may follow general rather than specific principles, especially with respect to word order."

RELATIONS BETWEEN SEMANTICS AND SYNTAX IN CHILDREN'S SENTENCES

Studies that have described children's development of grammar are in agreement in their descriptions of successive single-word utterances appearing prior to word combinations and in the appearance of categories of word combinations having the same semantic relationship. In the 1960s emphasis was placed on the form of such word combinations (for example, pivot grammar). In the 1970s emphasis shifted to the content or meaning of word combinations. There is less of a consensus now about the relation between form and content. The description of the structure of children's sentences in terms of subject and predicate is one of the issues that remains to be resolved within the more general issue of the relation between semantics and syntax in children's language.

While there has been a consensus about the semantics of children's early sentences (Bloom 1970, 1974c; Bloom, Lightbown, and Hood 1975; Bowerman 1973b; Braine 1976; Brown 1973; Lange and Laarsen 1973; Park 1974; Schlesinger 1971; Slobin 1973), these same facts have been described formally in different terms according to different linguistic theories, for example, case grammar (Fillmore 1968), generative transformational grammar (Chomsky 1965), generative semantics (Antinucci and Parisi 1973), or the theory of Chafe (1971). The question of how much of the information of child language could be captured by one or another of these theoretical formulations resulted in a theoretical and empirical emphasis on the semantics of early sentences and generated what may be a false issue in the relation between semantics and syntax in early child sentences.

The emphasis on the semantics of child sentences came about as a result of an interpretation of grammar to consist of rules of syntax rather than both syntax and semantics. Bowerman (1973a, 1973b, 1975), Braine (1976), Schaerlaekens (1973), and Schlesinger (1971) have argued that syntax, rather than being the original force in language acquisition was, instead the result of children's prior semantic development and the development of syntax depended upon the prior development of the semantics of sentences. In order to learn to say sentences, children learn semantic relations between words, and children learn separate rules that enable them to produce combinations of words with semantic relations between them. These two statements characterize the theoretical views put forth by Antinucci and Parisi (1973), Bowerman (1973a), Braine (1976), Schaerlaekens (1973), and Schesinger (1971). Schesinger proposed that the rules children learned were "realization rules" that mapped underlying semantic structures onto the surface structures of sentences. Bowerman described them as "simple rules of word order" and Braine described rules of word position. In the final analysis, then, all such semantic theories have described the surface structure of children's sentences in terms of syntax, with such syntactic learning dependent upon prior semantic learning. As Bowerman (1975, p. 85) states, "Insofar as constraints on word order are by definition treated by that part of linguistic description called syntax, knowledge of word order must be called syntactic knowledge. However, there is more to syntax than word order," as indicated above in the discussion of linear and hierarchical relations in early sentences.

Knowledge of subject and predicate in children's early sentences consists of knowing that semantic-syntactic categories of words are formed by word order, in addition to knowing semantic relations between words and word order relations between words. The sentence subject in early sentences is a category of words that occurs semantically, with different meanings in relation to different categories of verbs, but occurs syntactically before the verb. The predicate in early sentences includes categories of words that occur semantically with entirely different meanings in relation to categories of verbs and occur syntactically after the verb. When subject and predicate are defined in these semantic-syntactic terms, there seems to be little question that children know something about what adults know about grammatical categories.

The requirement that children demonstrate most or all of the adult knowledge should not be necessary in order to describe children's grammatical categories in terms of a subject/predicate distinction. The tests that Bowerman (1973a, 1973b, 1975) suggests for determining the eventual development of syntax are tests of syntactic categorization in adult grammar. Indeed, Bowerman seems to have been saying that children cannot be credited with knowledge of syntax unless that knowledge is equivalent to adult knowledge and moreover that that knowledge can be made explicit by the child. However, as Smith (1975 pp. 313–314) pointed out, it is not clear "that to say children operate with general rules and relations [such as syntactic knowledge of a subject/predicate distinction] means necessarily that they have metalinguistic, abstract syntactic concepts. One might follow a general rule . . . without having an abstract concept of what one is doing."

It is not at present clear what other kinds of evidence will help to illuminate the issue, but it is possible that the issue is a false one and related as much to methods of data collection and analysis as to individual differences among children. With respect to the first point, it may be that the size of a sample of a child's speech that is examined for evidence of regularity is an important factor, as is the point in development at which the child is observed. One needs to observe many sentences in a broad range of situations to observe the regularities in children's use of verbs that have been presented as evidence of superordinate semantic-syntactic structure. The fact of individual differences is the more important point, however.

INDIVIDUAL DIFFERENCES
Bloom (1970) pointed out that of the three subjects whose language behavior was observed, two used sentences that combined subject-verb, verb-complement, and subject-complement when mean length of utterance (MLU) was less than 1.5; the third used only verb-complement structures in the same period. Both this third child and a fourth subject, included in a subsequent study (Bloom, Lightbown, and Hood 1975), eventually began to use sentences with both subject and predicate constituents (subject-verb-complement) when MLU approached 2.0. This finding was replicated in a study by Ramer (1976), who described the development of seven children who divided similarly on this dimension. Four children described by Ramer used subject-verb, verb-complement, and subject-complement among their earliest sentences, when MLU was less than 1.5; three other children in the same study did not use sentences with both subject and predicate constituents until later, when MLU approached 2.0. Mean length of utterance, then, is not a sensitive index of the kinds of knowledge represented in children's early sentences.

The search for regularities in child language in the last decade produced some impressive results. Children are remarkably similar in the kinds of words they use, in the semantics of their early sentences, in their use of word order in early syntax, in acquisition of morphology and complex syntax, and in the ways they use language. On the other hand, there is a growing consensus about the existence of substantial variation among children in parameters dealing with their grammatical development as was just described, their phonological development (Ferguson and Farwell 1975; Farwell 1976), their lexical development (Clark and Garnica 1974), their social use of speech (Dore 1973; Nelson 1973), and the relative extent to which they use nouns and pronouns in relation to verbs in their early sentences (Bloom, Lightbown, and Hood 1975; Huxley 1970; Nelson 1975). Indeed, the variation that has been reported has prompted a tendency to turn away from the pursuit of universals and norms in language development and toward a greater concentration on describing individual capacities. For example, in their study of phonological development, Ferguson and Farwell (1975, p. 438) suggested that

in order to gain a deeper understanding of phonological development and hence of phonology in general, some linguists at the present stage of the art might be well advised to turn away from the fascination of writing rules of maximum generality and conciseness for whole languages, and undertake instead highly detailed analysis of the idiosyncratic paths which particular children follow in learning to pronounce their languages.

But even if some children reach the target language sooner and different children travel different routes to the same goal, all the children for whom data have been reported appear to have converged on the adult model from the beginning. That is, all the variation that has been observed is consistent with variation that is also systematic, in some respect, in the target language.

Communication and the Use of Language

It has become increasingly apparent that children do not learn only linguistic forms, or only the semantics of words and sentences when they learn language. Children also need to learn how to use language, how to recognize and interpret situations and in particular the needs of the listener in different situations for different purposes (see, for example, Ervin-Tripp 1970, 1974; Bates 1976; Garvey, 1975a; Halliday 1975).

There is strong consensus about different aspects of the development of language use. Children learn to do things with speech acts; there are different functions that speech acts serve in meeting the child's needs. Children learn how to use information from the context (for example, the listener) for deciding among alternative forms of reference—such as whether to use a noun or a pronoun, definite or indefinite articles, or different forms of requests. Just as they continually acquire new resources in terms of form and content, children improve in their ability to interpret and make references about persons and situations for language use according to their changing needs.

As with the development of language form and content, the development of language use results from the interaction between the child and the context. In infancy children's needs are basically physiological and emotional, and their resources are biologically determined or fortuitously contrived and adapted only gradually to differences in the context. The same behavior, for example, crying or whimpering, can be used to meet several needs regardless of the situation. Decision making eventually comes to involve conventional means as children's movements and vocalizations become more consistent with those around them and their needs continue to become more social in addition to having to do with physical states and feelings. The child has learned sounds and gestures and the same form can be used in different ways, as when the child uses the same word or word combination to refer to different events (for example, "mommy" or "mommy open" when mommy is opening, is unable to open, or has just opened a door, a box, or a jar) and for the same purpose in different situations (such as to get mommy to open something when she can't or when she doesn't want to).

As children learn more about the code, they also develop conceptually and socially so that they can make inferences about situations to interpret the effects of different forms of messages and use alternative means or forms for achieving the same purpose, according to differences in the situational context. For example, to get water one can issue a command ("Give me a drink"), make a statement ("I want water" or, less directly, "I'm thirsty") or ask a question ("Is there any water?") (see, for example, Ervin-Tripp forthcoming; Garvey 1975a; Shatz 1974). Finally, once children have learned the conventions of language use—that is, the rules for using different forms in different situations to meet the same needs—they can learn how to break the rules. The child needs to have learned the rules in order to learn how to violate the rules for one or another effect, such as humor, emphasis, or metaphor.

FUNCTIONS OF LANGUAGE

The child learns in infancy that vocalizations can serve certain functions. Although these vocalizations do not conform to the sounds and structures of the adult model, they have meaning in the functions they serve for the child. For the period from six to eighteen months, "using his voice is doing something . . . a form of action . . . which soon develops its own patterns and its own significant contexts" (Halliday 1975, p. 10). The first of two functions Halliday identified at age nine months was the "interactional" or "me and you function of language" as the child uses sounds and gestures to interact with others in the environment. The second function at nine months was the "personal function" whereby the infant expresses self-awareness, such personal feelings as interest, pleasure, and disgust. By ten and a half months, three more language functions can be identified, still without children using the forms and structures of conventional language but, rather, the sounds and movements of their own device. The third function Halliday called "heuristic" whereby the child begins to use vocalization and to explore the environment. At the very earliest stage the heuristic use is the demand for a name of something, but it eventually develops into the whole range of child questions. The fourth and fifth functions are the "instrumental functions" whereby children satisfy material needs and obtain objects and help from those around them, and the related "regulatory function" whereby they control the behavior of others, the "do as I tell you" functions of language.

The functions of language are incorporated in the organization of the linguistic system that the child is learning, with rules that change the form of language according to one or another purpose or goal and according to factors in the context of the situation that require one or another alternative form for serving the same purpose or goal. In addition to learning rules for deciding which forms of language to use in order to serve one or another function, such as to ask a question or make a statement, children also learn rules for deciding among alternative forms according to information that is available about the listener and the context (Ervin-Tripp 1972; Hymes 1964, 1974; Gumperz 1972; Halliday 1970).

ALTERNATION IN LANGUAGE USE

The resources of a speaker of a language include rules for alternation—rules for determining which forms of the language are required and appropriate in one or another context—as well as rules for co-occurrence—rules for determining what other behaviors are also required or desirable given the selection of one or another alternative (Ervin-Tripp 1972).

Thus children acquire a linguistic scheme for the relations between form and content and they discover the situational constraints that govern the use of the linguistic scheme and regulate the use of alternative linguistic forms (see for example, Bates 1976; Cazden 1968; Garvey 1975a; Ryan 1973). Language use involves changing needs in changing contexts. Just as there are a fixed number of linguistic items (sounds and words) and rules of grammar that allow for the production and understanding of indefinitely many sentences, apparently there is also a fixed number of language functions or uses of language, but indefinitely many contexts, situations, or environments in which language is used with these functions. The contexts for the use of language change throughout the lifespan— from earliest childhood, through the school years, into adulthood with family and occupational contexts, and eventually into old age with the contexts of loneliness and illness.

ROUTINES AND SPEECH ACTS. There is a difference between messages that state, describe, or report information that is true or false and performative messages that are part of doing an action (Austin 1962). The distinction between statements and performatives was expanded upon by Searle (1969) and has become a focus for the study of children's use of language (for example, by Bates 1976; Dore 1975; Garvey 1975a, 1975b). Most simply, speakers of a language accomplish certain acts with their messages apart from representing the information that is the content of their messages. Some of these speech acts are highly ritualistic, for example, performing a marriage, opening a session in court, and making toasts and introductions. Others are more varied with respect to the contexts in which they occur and with respect to the informational content of the messages in the speech acts, for example, acts of requesting, promising, warning, prohibiting, and apologizing. There are obviously certain specialized speech acts that most individuals never learn because they are particular to an occupation or vocation (such as performing a marriage, opening a session in court, or making a sales pitch). However, acts such as requesting, greeting, promising, warning, apologizing, and prohibiting are far more general and are assumed to be within the competence of most, if not all, adult speakers.

Children appear to learn to use those speech acts first that have the least variation in linguistic form and the fewest degrees of contextual freedom, such as greetings, in which the same or similar forms occur in the same kinds of context. Such speech acts can be learned as routines with the same form, such as a greeting ("hi" and "bye-bye"), an apology ("sorry"), or a prohibition ("no" or "don't") occurring in specific contexts. Words that seem to function as such speech acts have been observed in the early behavior and vocabularies of children (Gruber 1973; Ingram 1971; Bates 1971; Antinucci and Parisi 1973; Dore 1973; Nelson 1974). In contrast, speech acts that entail different message content in different contexts, such as requesting an action, requesting permisison, warning, inviting, prohibiting, or promising, are a later development, usually appearing in the later preschool years (ages three to five years) but continuing to develop and change into adulthood as the invididual encounters new and different contexts.

PRESUPPOSITION AND THE ROLE OF THE LISTENER There is considerable variety in the forms that messages can take as speakers adapt the form and content of their messages according to what they presuppose the listener already knows and what they judge the listener needs to know in order to understand and respond. The egocentrism of children has often been underscored in descriptions of their behavior and in explanations of their thinking, and the assumption that follows is that egocentricity can preclude the child from taking the listener into account in a speaking situation (Piaget 1924; McCarthy 1954; Glucksberg, Krauss, and Higgins 1975).

While the speech of young children is generally conceded to be more creative than adaptive, there has been some evidence that children can and do differ in their ways of speaking to different kinds of listeners. Smith (1933) observed that children from two to five years of age ask significantly more questions when they are interacting with an adult than when they are interacting with children of the same age. Moreover, when children asked questions in situations where they were interacting with a peer, they typically directed their questions to an adult who was also in the room. In a study by Shatz and Gelman (1973), it was demonstrated that four-year-old children talked differently to two-year-old children than to four-year-old children or to adults. In a longitudinal study of the language development of five normal-hearing children born to deaf parents, Schiff (1976) observed that the two-year-old subjects modified their speech according to whether they were talking to their deaf mothers or to a visiting hearing adult. The children used more oral language and longer utterances with the hearing adult than with their deaf mothers and used more manual signing and deaflike distortions in their speech to their deaf mothers than to the hearing adults.

In a study of children's code switching, Berko-Gleason (1973) pointed out that the earliest listener-adapted variation observed in language development is between talking and not talking in infancy, as infants can be observed to vocalize, that is say "bye-bye" to members of the family but become silent in the presence of strangers. Another stylistic variation in children under four years of age is the use of whining only with parents or parent figures and an often abrupt switch to whining when a parent appears. Older children were observed using high pitched "baby talk" intonation and telegraphic speech (without morphological inflections and copulas) when speaking with two-year-olds; and six- and eight-year-old girls were observed using prescriptive and didactically adult formalisms, for example, "now you just carry them home and don't run" and "you share them" (p. 164).

So far, studies of alternation in children's use of speech have primarily described the changes in the form of utterances. There is also evidence that children can vary the content that is represented in alternative messages according to their perceptions of the listener's knowledge (Maratsos 1973; Menig-Peterson 1975). Maratsos asked three- and four-year-old children to talk about toys to a listerner who was presented to them as being blind and to a listener with normal vision. The children were much more explicit in their messages to the "blind" listeners than to the listeners who could see. In the study by Menig-Peterson, three- and four-year-old children were asked to talk about an experience to adults under two conditions, one condition when the adult had also participated in the experience one week earlier and the other condition when the adult was naive about the events. The children made more references to the earlier event and introduced more information about the event to the naive listener than to the knowledgeable listener. Thus children between three and four years old can modify both the form and the content of their speech according to what they presume their listener knows.

DISCOURSE DEVELOPMENT A major result of the child's increasing ability to understand the listener's needs and resources is progress in the development of discourse. Adult discourse has traditionally been described in terms of the occurrence of shared elements in successive messages (Harris 1964), which creates a texting or cohesion in the linguistic exchanges between speakers (Halliday and Hasan 1975). The situation is a controlling variable for determining the amount, the topic, and the form of messages in discourse (see, for example, Bates 1971; Cazden 1968; Shatz 1974). Children have been observed to talk more often and to use longer utterances when they originate the topic of conversation (Cooperman, cited in Cazden 1968; Freedle, Lewis, and Weiner 1974). Differences in the initiation of topics and in the complexity of the linguistic form of utterances of two- to four-year-old children have been observed in situations that differ according to the activity, the participants, and the extent to which the child can control the events that are happening (Bates 1971; Shatz 1974). Initially, according to Corsaro (n.d.), two-year-old children are more concerned with their own intent with respect to the topic than with the listener's intent and participation. Children learn to respond to different ways of initiating the topic of conversation and eventually become competent in using information from the situation to introduce and maintain the topic of discourse (Keenan and Schieffelin 1976).

The rules that speakers and listeners use for initiating and maintaining the topic of conversation result in the maintenance of regularity and reciprocity between speakers. Speakers depend upon feedback from their listeners and "mutual monitoring" for maintaining their part in the reciprocity of conversation; speakers need to know whether the listener is paying attention in the first place. For example, the use of head nods and such indicators as "hm" and "uh huh" were described by Dittman (1972) in the conversational exchanges of school age children. Garvey (1975b) described the quite systematic use of repetition and contingent queries (for example, "What?" and "*Where* did he go?") in the interactions between three- to five-year-old peer dyads, and Keenan (1974) described the use of repetition and utterance completion that regulated the reciprocity of discourse between her twenty-nine-month-old twin sons. Corsaro (n.d.) described several aspects of reciprocity in discourse that children learn to recognize and use.

The exchange of information for varied purposes is at the heart of discourse and depends upon the ability to produce utterances that are semantically related to prior utterances from another speaker. This ability increases substantially from two to three years of age (Bloom, Rocissano, and Hood 1976; Corsaro, n.d.). Children learn to share the information in prior messages in different ways. In certain instances information about a topic is shared because the speakers are both talking about the same event in the context; such successive utterances are semantically related because of contextual contingency.

Adult: I can't get the bolt off.   Child: need a screwdriver.

In other instances semantically related utterances share the same topic and also share some aspect of linguistic form and so are also linguistically contingent on prior adult utterances.

Adult: I see two.   Child: I see two bus come here.

In the longitudinal study of the development of discourse from two to three years of age by Bloom, Rocissano, and Hood (1976), child utterances that were contextually contingent did not change in relative frequency. The important developmental change was a sharp increase in the relative frequency of child utterances that were linguistically contingent on prior adult utterances. The children were learning to share the topic of a previous utterance and add new information relative to the topic by producing utterances that shared the same verb relation as in the adult utterance. Linguistically contingent child utterances occured more often after a question than after a statement from the adults. Regardless of the source of contingency between semantically related messages (whether contextual or linguistic), the children's utterances either expanded the prior adult utterance, for example,

Adult: (getting ready to leave)   Child: home
       I'll put my scarf on first.

or provided an alternative to the adult utterance, for example,

Adult: Shall we sit on the sofa and   Child: (going to orange chair)
       read my book?   orange chair read book

Expansions were more frequent than alternatives and similar kinds of expansions or alternatives have been observed repeatedly in child discourse, for example, by Corsaro (n.d.), Garvey (1975a), Greenfield and Smith (forthcoming), and Keenan (1974).

With both kinds of contingent responses, expansions and alternatives, there was development in the ways in which information given in the prior adult message was marked in the child's utterance as the same information from the child's own perspective. Part of the children's development of discourse, then, consisted of learning the conventions for shifting reference, deixis, and ellipsis in their speech.

SHIFTING REFERENCE, DEIXIS, AND ELLIPSIS One of the difficulties in learning language concerns the fact that there are many words in the language that are not stable in reference because their use depends upon the speaker's perspective, which varies among speakers and within situations. Jespersen (1922) called such words "shifters" and gave as examples such nouns as kinship terms, for example, "daddy," where daddy to one child is not daddy to another child, and "home," where my home is not your home. Other words also differ in their use depending upon the point of view of the speaker and listener in the context of the speech event and in relation to the content of the message—in particular the class of personal pronouns ("I"/"you"), demonstrative pronouns ("this"/"that" and "here"/"there"), certain verbs ("go"/"come" and "bring"/"take"), and the morphological processes on verbs that signal person, time, and aspect. All shifters have a general or lexical meaning, for example, "I" means something like "self" or "ego" and "come" means "to arrive," but in addition they also have an "indexical meaning" (Jakobson 1957) or "deictic function" (Fillmore 1973) in that they point out or indicate the relations between the participants of a speech event and the content of the message.

The appearance of shifting reference in children's speech has been documented in children's use of pronouns (Bloom, Lightbown, and Hood 1975; Huxley 1970; Sharpless 1974), definite and indefinite articles (Brown 1973; Maratsos 1974), recoding in discourses (Bloom, Rocissano, and Hood 1976), deictic verbs ("come"/ "go" and "bring"/"take") (Clark and Garnica 1974), kinship terms (Haviland and Clark 1974; Piaget 1928), and in the use of certain antonymous adjectives ("same"/"different") (Donaldson and Wales 1970; Josephs 1975). With each of these kinds of alternation, acquisition continues often well into the school years and involves the very complex interplay between children's opportunities for using and hearing others use shifting reference and their linguistic, conceptual, and social development. As a result the existing studies have begun to document only the earliest states when children begin to use alternative forms to take account of the shifting relations between the content event that is encoded in messages and the participants and context of the speech event.

ISSUES IN THE STUDY OF LANGUAGE USE

The issues are as yet only generally defined. One question that remains to be answered by future research is the relation between the availability of alternative forms—the fact that children use both nouns and pronouns or both definite and indefinite articles or different forms of request—and the motivation for their use— the regular use of different forms in different contexts. In the study reported by Bloom, Lightbown, and Hood (1975), two-year-old children who used both nouns and pronouns were not motivated in the use of one or another form by the requirements of the speaking situation. Tanz (1976) reported that definite and indefinite reference was still being learned by three-year-old children. In contrast, Nelson (1975) reported that the use of nouns and pronouns by the two-year-old children she studied was motivated by the context.

A second, more general issue is the importance of language use for its influence on the development of language form and content. For Bates (1976), Newport (1976), and Shatz and Gelman (1973), language use or "pragmatics" is the larger part of the story and is seen as the controlling force in the acquisition of the relations between form and content. In contrast, in the study reported by Bloom, Miller, and Hood (1975), factors related to form, content, and use were observed to be mutually influential on the variable length of children's sentences and by extension on the children's language development more generally. Factors related to lexical learning (how well a child knew a word), linguistic complexity (the addition of grammatical morphemes within or between sentence constituents), and discourse (the occurrence of a child utterance in the context of another utterance from the child or an utterance from the listener) were observed to both facilitate and constrain the occurrence of longer sentences. It was observed that words (verbs, nouns, and pronouns) that had been used for a long time and used frequently by a child were more likely to occur in longer sentences and relatively new lexical items were more likely to occur in shorter sentences. Complexity that was added to a constituent (such as morphological inflections on nouns and verbs) did not influence the length of the children's sentences, but complexity that intervened between constituents (such as elaboration of the predicate and negative) occurred more often with shorter sentences than with longer sentences (see also Cazen 1968). A longer utterance such as "mommy eat lunch" was more likely to occur after the child said part of the utterance, such as "eat lunch," and received a prompt from the listener, such as "What?" or "Hm." And finally, according to the results of the study reported in Bloom, Rocissano, and Hood (1976), child speech that was contingent on a prior utterance was apparently more difficult than child speech that originated spontaneously with the semantic intention of the child.

By way of conclusion, it seems reasonable to say that there is no one factor or one component of language that is more or less important than another; learning language involves the intersection of form, content, and use. Although it has been possible to separate the factors related to the substance and process of language for the purposes of research in language development, the three components and the related factors within each component come together for the child who is learning language. By the same token, a disorder in language development may be described as a disruption in one or another of the components of form, content, and use; but the description of the child's behavior and treatment programs directed at changing or improving the child's behavior need to consider the intersection of components of language that are responsible for the child's behavior.

References

Anglin, J. 1975. The extension of the child's first terms of reference. Paper presented at the Society for Research in Child Development.

Antinucci, D., and Parisi, D. 1973. Early language acquisition: A model and some data. In C. A. Ferguson and D. I. Slobin (Eds.), *Studies of child language development*. New York: Holt, Rinehart and Winston, 607–619.

Austin, J. 1962. *How to do things with words*. New York and London: Oxford University Press.

Bates, E. 1971. The development of conversational skill in 2, 3, and 4 year olds. Unpublished masters thesis, University of Chicago, Chicago, Ill.

———. 1976. Pragmatics and sociolinguistics in child language. In D. Morehead and A. Morehead (Eds.), *Directions in normal and deficient child language*. Baltimore, Md.: University Park Press.

Bateson, M. C. 1975. Mother-infant exchanges: The epigenesis of conversational interaction. In D. Aronson and R. Ricker (Eds.), *Developmental psycholonguistics and communication disorders. Annals of the New York Academy of Sciences*, *263*, 101–113.

Berko-Gleason, J. 1973. Code switching in children's language. In T. E. More (ed), *Cognitive development and the acquisition of language*. New York: Academic Press. 159–168.

Bloom, L. 1970. *Language development: Form and function in emerging grammars.* Cambridge, Mass. MIT Press.

———. 1973. *One word at a time: The use of single-word utterances before syntax.* The Hague: Mouton.

———. 1974a. The accountability of evidence in studies of child language. Comment on *Everyday preschool interpersonal speech usage: Methodological, developmental, and sociolinguistic studies.* In F. Schacter, K. Kirshner, B. Klips, and M. Friedricks, *Monographs of the Society for Research in Child Development,* 39 (Serial No. 157).

———. 1974b. Review of J. Hayes (Ed.), *Cognition and the development of language. Language,* 50, 398–412.

———. 1974c. Talking, understanding, and thinking: Developmental relationship between receptive and expressive language. In R. L. Schiefelbusch and L. Lloyd (Eds.), *Language prespectives—acquisition, retardation, and intervention.* Baltimore: University Park Press. 285–311.

———. 1976. An interactive perspective on language development. Keynote address, Child Language Research Forum, Stanford University, April.

Bloom, L., and Lahey, M. Forthcoming. *Language development and language disorders.* New York: John Wiley and Sons, Inc.

Bloom, L., Lightbown, P., and Hood, L. 1975. Structure and variation in child language. *Monographs of the Society for Research in Child Development,* 40 (2, Serial No. 160).

Bloom, L., Miller, P., and Hood, L. 1975. Variation and reduction as aspects of competence in language development. In A. Pick (Ed.), *Minnesota symmposia on child psychology, Volume 9.* Minneapolis, Minn.: The University of Minnesota Press. 3–55.

Bloom, L., Rocissano, L., and Hood L. 1976. Adult-child discourse: Developmental interaction between information processing and lingustic knowledge. *Cognitive Psychology,* 8, 521–552.

Bowerman, M. 1973a. *Early syntactic development: A cross-linguistic study with special reference to Finnish.* Cambridge, England: Cambridge University Press.

———. 1973b. Structural relationships in children's utterances: Syntactic or semantic? In T. Moore (Ed.), *Cognitive development and the acquisition of language.* New York: Academic Press, 197–214.

———. 1975. Comment on structure and variation in child language. L. Bloom, P. Lightbown, and L. Hood, *Monographs of the Society for Research in Child Development,* 40 (2, Serial No. 160).

Braine, M. D. S. 1963. The ontogeny of English phrase structure: The first phase. *Language, 39,* 1–13.

———. 1976. Children's first word combinations. *Monographs of the Society for Research in Child Development, 41,* (1, Serial No. 164), 1–104.

Broen, P. 1972. The verbal environment of the language learning child. *American Speech and Hearing Association Monographs,* No. 17.

Brown, R. 1958. *Words and things.* New York: The Free Press.

———. 1965. *Social psychology.* New York: Free Press.

———. 1973. *A first language, the early stages.* Cambridge, Mass.: Harvard University Press.

Brown, R., Cazden, C., and Bellugi, U. 1969. The child's grammar from I to III. In J. P. Hill (Ed.), *1967 Minnesota Symposia on Child Psychology*. Minneapolis, Minn: University of Minnesota Press, 28–73.

Bruner, J. 1975. The ontogenesis of speech acts. *Journal of Child Language, 2,* 1–19

Cazden, C. 1968. The acquisition of noun and verb inflections. *Child Development, 39,* 433–438.

Chafe, W. 1971. *Meaning and structure of language.* Chicago, Ill.: University of Chicago Press.

Chomsky, N. 1957. *Syntactic structures.* The Hague: Mouton.

————. 1965. *Aspects of the theory of syntax.* Cambridge, Mass.: MIT Press.

Church, J. 1961. *Language and the discovery of reality.* New York: Vintage Books.

Clark, E. 1973. What's in a word? On the child's acquisition of semantics in his first language. In T. Moore (Ed.), *Cognitive development and the acquisition of language.* New York: Academic Press, 65–110.

Clark, E., and Garnica, O. K. 1974. Is he coming or going? On the acquisition of deictic verbs. *Journal of Verbal Learning and Verbal Behavior, 13,* 559–572.

Clark, R. 1974. Performing without competence. *Journal of Child Language, 1,* 1–10.

Collins, A., and Quillian, M. 1969. Retrieval time from semantic memory. *Journal of Verbal Learning and Verbal Behavior, 8,* 240–248.

Corman, H., and Escalona, S. 1969. Stages of sensorimotor development: A replication study. *Merrill-Palmer Quarterly, 15,* 351–361.

Corsaro, W. A. n.d. Sociolinguistic patterns in adult-child interaction. Unpublished manuscript, Indiana University.

Cromer, R. 1974. The development of language and cognition: The cognition hypothesis. In B. Foss (Ed.), *New perspectives in child development.* New York: Penquin Education, 184–252.

Delack, J. B. Aspects of infant speech development in the first year of life. *Canadian Journal of Linguistics,* (in press).

Dittman, A. T. 1972. Development factors in conversational behavior. *The Journal of Communication, 22,* 404–423.

Donaldson, M., and Wales, R. 1970. On the acquisition of some relational terms. In J. Hayes (Ed.), *Cognition and the development of language.* New York: John Wiley and Sons, 235–268.

Dore, J. 1973. The development of speech acts. Unpublished doctoral dissertation. Baruch College, City University of New York.

————. 1975. Holophrases, speech acts, and language universals. *Journal of Child Language, 2,* 21–40.

Dore, J., Franklin, M., Miller, R., and Ramer, A. 1976. Transitional phenomena in early language acquisition. *Journal of Child Language, 3,* 13–28.

Eimas, P. D., Siqueland, E. R., Jusczyk, P., and Vigorito, J. 1971. Speech perception in infants. *Science, 171,* 303–306.

Ervin-Tripp, S. 1970. Discourse agreement: How children answer questions. In J. R. Hayes (Ed.), *New directions in the study of language.* New York: Wiley, 79–108.

————. 1972. On sociolinguistic rules: Alternation and cooccurrence. In J. J. Gumperz and D. Hymes (Eds.), *Directions in sociolinguistics: The ethnography of communication*. New York: Holt, Rinehart and Winston, 213–250.

————. Forthcoming. Wait for me roller skate. *Language and Society*

Farwell, C. 1976. Some ways to learn about fricatives. Paper presented at the Child Language Research Forum, Stanford University, April.

Ferguson, C. A., and Farwell, C. B. 1975. Words and sounds in early language acquistion. *Language, 51*, 419–439

Fillmore, C. 1968. The case for case. In E. Bach and R. Harms (Eds), *Universals in linguistic theory*. New York: Holt, Rinehart and Winston, 1–88.

Fillmore, C., and Deixis, I. 1973. Unpublished lectures delivered at the University of California, Santa Cruz.

Freedle, R., Lewis, M., and Weiner, S. 1974. Language acquisition and situational context. Paper presented at the meeting of the Eastern Psychological Association.

Garvey, C. 1975a. Requests and responses in children's speech. *Journal of Child Language, 2*, 41–63.

————. 1975b. Contingent queries. Unpublished manuscript.

Glucksberg, S., Krauss, R., and Higgins, E. T. 1975. The development of referential communication skills. In F. Horowitz (Ed.), *Review of child development research*, Vol. 4. Chicago, Ill.: University of Chicago Press, 305–346.

Goldin-Meadow, S., Seligman, M., and Gelman, R. 1976. Language in the two-year-old: Receptive and productive stages. *Cognition, 4*, 189–202.

Greenfield, P. 1971. Who is dada? Unpublished manuscript.

Greenfield, P., and Smith, J. Forthcoming. *Communication and the beginnings of language*. New York: Academic Press.

Gruber, J. 1973. Correlations between the syntactic constructions of the child and the adult. In C. A. Ferguson and D. I. Slobin (Eds.), *Studies of child language development*. New York: Holt, Rinehart and Winston, 440–445.

Guillaume, P. 1927. Les debuts de la phrase dans le language de l'enfant. *Journal de Psychologie, 24*, 125.

Gumperz, J. J. 1972. Introduction. In J. J. Gumperz and D. Hymes (Eds.), *Directions in sociolinguistics: The ethnography of communication*. New York: Holt, Rinehart and Winston, 1–25.

Halliday, M. A. K. 1970. Language structure and language function. In J. Lyons (Ed.), *New horizons in linguistics*. Baltimore, Md.: Penquin, 140–165.

————. 1975. *Learning how to mean: Explorations in the functions language*. London: Edward Arnold.

Halliday, M. A. K., and Hasan, R. 1975. *Cohesion in English*. London: Longman (English Language Series).

Harris, Z. 1964. Discourse analysis. In J. Fodor and J. Katz (Eds.), *The structure of language*. Englewood Cliffs, N.J.: Prentice-Hall. 355–383.

Haviland, S. E., and Clark, E. 1974. This man's father is my father's son: A study of the acquisition of English kin terms. *Journal of Child Language,1*, 23–48.

Huttenlocher, J. 1974. The origins of language comprehension. In R. L. Solso (Ed.), *Theories in cognitive psychology*. New York: Halsted, 331–368.

Huxley, R. 1970. The development of the correct use of subject personal pronouns in two children. In G. B. Flores d'Arcais and W. J. M. Levelt (Eds.), *Advances in psycholinguistics*. New York: American Elsevier, 141–165.

Hymes, D. (Ed.), 1964. *Language in culture and society*. New York: Harper and Row.

———. 1974. Ways of speaking. In R. Bauman and J. Scherzer (Eds.), *Explorations in the ethnography of speaking*. London: Cambridge University Press, 433–451.

Ingram, D. 1971. Transitivity in child language. *Language, 47*, 88–91.

Jakobson, R. 1957. Shifters, verbal categories and the Russian verb. Cambridge, Mass.: Harvard University Department of Slavic Languages and Literatures. Russian Language Project.

Jespersen, O. 1922. *Language: Its nature, development, and origin*. London: Allen and Unwin.

Josephs, J. 1975. Children's comprehension of same and different in varying contexts. Unpublished doctoral dissertation, Columbia University, N.Y.

Kaplan, E. 1970. Intonation and language acquisition. *Papers and reports on child language development*. Stanford: Committee on Linguistics, Stanford University.

Kates, C. 1974. A descriptive approach to linguistic meaning. Unpublished manuscript. Department of Philosphy, Ithaca College, New York.

Keenan, E. O. 1974. Conversational competence in children. *Journal of Child Language, 1*, 163–183.

Keenan, E., and Schiffelin, B. 1976. Topic as a discourse notion: A study of topic in the conversations of children and adults. In C. Li. (Ed.), *Subject and topic*. New York: Academic Press, 335–384.

Labov, W., and Labov, T. 1973. The grammar of cat and Mama. Paper presented at the Developmental Psychology Colloquia series, Teachers College, Columbia University, N.Y.

Lange, S. and Larsson, K. 1973. Syntactical development of a Swedish girl Embla between 20 and 42 months of age. Part I. Age 20–25 months. *Project Child Language Syntax*. Report No. 1. Stockholms Universitet: Institutionen for Nordiska Sprak, Stockholm.

Leonard, L. 1974. From reflex to remark. *Acta Symbolica, 5*, 67–99.

Leopold. W. 1939. *Speech development of a bilingual child*. Evanston, Ill.: Northwestern University Press.

Lewis, M. M. 1951. *Infant speech, a study of the beginnings of language*. New York: Humanities Press.

Lewis, M., and Freedle, R. 1973. Mother-infant dyad: The cradle of meaning, In P. Pliner (Ed.), *Communication and affect*. New York: Academic Press. 127–155.

Ling, D., and Ling, A. H. 1974. Communication development in the first three years of life. *Journal of Speech and Hearing Research, 17*, 146–159.

Lyons, J. 1968. *Introduction to Theoretical Linguistics*. London: Cambridge University Press.

MacNamara, J. 1972. Cognitive bases for language learning in infants. *Psychological Review, 79*, 1–13.

Maratsos, M. 1973. Nonegocentric communication abilities in preschool children. *Child Development, 44*, 697–700.

————. 1974. Preschool children's use of definite and indefinite articles. *Child Development*, *45*, 446–455.

McCarthy, D. 1954. Language development in children. In L. Carmichael (Ed.), *Manual of child psychology*. New York: John Wiley and Sons.

McNeill D. Developmental psycholinguistics. In F. Smith and G. A. Miller (Eds.), *The genesis of language*. Cambridge, Mass.: The MIT Press, 15–84.

————. 1974. Semiotic extension. Paper presented at Loyola Symposium on Cognition. Chicago, Ill. April.

McReynolds, L. V., this volume. Behavioral and lingustic considerations in children's speech production.

Menig-Peterson, C. 1975. The modification of communicative behavior in preschool-aged children as a function of the listener's perspective. *Child Development*, *46*, 1015–1018.

Menn, L. 1971. Phonotactic rules in beginning speech. *Lingua*, *26*, 225–251.

Miller, G. 1951. *Language and communication*. New York: McGraw Hill.

Moerk, E. L. 1975. Verbal interactions between children and their mothers during the preschool years. *Developmental Psychology*, *11*, 788–794.

Moffitt A. 1971. Consonant cue perception by twenty- to-twenty-four-week-old infants. *Child Development*, *42*, 717–731.

Morse, P. A. 1972. The discrimination of speech and nonspeech stimuli in early infancy. *Journal of Experimental Child Psychology*, *14*, 477–492.

Nelson, K. 1973. Structure and strategy in learning to talk. *Monographs of the Society for Research in Child Development*, *38*, (1, Serial No. 149).

————. 1974. Concept, word and sentence: Interrelations in acquisition and develop-ment. *Psychological Review*, *81*, 267–285.

————. 1975. Individual differences in early semantic and syntactic development. In D. Aronson and R. Rieber (Eds.), *Developmental psycholinguistics and communication disorders. Annals of the New York Academy of Sciences*, *263*, 132–139.

Newport, E. 1976. Motherese: The speech of mothers to young children. In N. J. Castellan, D. B. Pisoni, and G. R. Potts (Eds.), *Cognitive theory*: Volume 2. Hillsdale, N. J.: Lawrence Earlbaum.

Oller, D. K., Wieman, L. A., Doyle, W. J., and Ross, C. 1976. Infant babbling and speech. *Journal of Child Language*, *3*, 1–11.

Park, T. Z. 1974. A study of German language development. Unpublished manuscript. Psychological Institute, Berne, Switzerland.

Peters, A. M. 1976. Language learning strategies: Does the whole equal the sum of the parts? Paper presented at the Child Language Research Forum Stanford University, April.

Phillips, J. 1973. Syntax and vocabulary of mother's speech to young children: Age and sex comparisons. *Child Development*, *44*, 182–185.

Piaget, J. 1924. *The language and thought of the child*. Cleveland, Ohio: World.

————. 1928. *Judgement and reasoning in the child*. New York: Harcourt, Brace.

————. 1954. *The construction of reality in the child*. New York: Basic Books.

————. 1960. *The psychology of intelligence*. Paterson, N. J.: Littlefield Adams.

Ramer, A. 1976. Syntactic styles in emerging language. *Journal of Child Language*, *3*, 49–62.

Ryan, J. 1973. Interpretation and imitation in early language development. In R. A. Hinde and J. Stevenson-Hinde (Eds.), *Constraints on learning: Limitations predispositions*. New York: Academic Press. 427–444.

Sachs, J., Brown, R., and Salerno, R. 1972. Adult speech to children. Paper given at the International Symposium on First Language Acquisition, Florence, Italy.

Sander, L. 1975. The regulation of exchange in the infant-caretaker system and some aspects of the context-content relationship. Paper presented to the Confreence on the origins of Communication, Educational Testing Service, Princeton, N. J., Fall.

Schaerlaekens, A. 1973. A generative transformational model for child language acquisition: A discussion of L. Bloom, *Language development: Form and function in emerging grammars*. *Cognition*, *2*, 371–376.

Schiff, N. 1976. The development of form and meaning in the language of hearing children of deaf parents. Unpublished Ph.D. dissertation, Columbia University, N.Y.

Schlesinger, I. 1971. Production of utterances and language acquisition. In D. Slobin (Ed.), *The ontogenesis of grammar*. New York: Academic Press, 63–101.

Searle, J. 1969. *Speech acts: An essay in the philosophy of language*. London: Cambridge University Press.

Seitz, S., and Stewart, C. 1975. Imitations and expansions: Some developmental aspects of mother-child communications. *Developmental Psychology*, *11*, 763–768.

Sharpless, E. 1974. Children's acquisition of person pronouns. Doctoral dissertation. Teachers College, Columbia University.

Shatz, M. 1974. The comprehension of indirect directives: Can two year olds shut the door? Paper presented at the summer meeting, Linguistic Society of America, Amherst, Mass.

Shatz, M., and Gelman, R. 1973. The development of communication skills: Modifications in the speech of young children as a function of listener. *Monographs of the Society for Research in Child Development*, *38* (Serial No. 152).

Sinclair, H. 1971. Sensorimotor action patterns as a condition for the acquisition of syntax. In R. Huxley and E. Ingram (Eds.), *Language acquisition: Models and methods*. New York: Academic Press, 121–135.

Slobin, D. 1973. Cognitive prerequisites for the development of grammar. In C. A. Ferguson and D. I. Slobin (Eds.), *Studies of child language development*. New York: Holt, Rinehart, and Winston, 175–208.

Smith, C. 1975. Review of T. Moore (Ed.), Cognitive development and the acquisition of language. *Journal of Child Language*, *2*, 303–335.

Smith, J. 1970. The development and structure of holophrases. Unpublished thesis. Harvard University, Cambridge, Mass.

Smith, M. 1933. The influence of age, sex, and situation of frequency, form and function of questions asked by preschool children. *Child Development*, *4*, 201–213.

Snow, C. 1972. Mother's speech to children learning language. *Child Development*, *43*, 549–565.

————. 1974. Mother's speech research: An overview. Paper presented at the conference of Language Input and Acquisition, Boston, Mass., Sept.

Soderbergh, R. 1974. The fruitful dialogue, the child's acquisition of his first language: Implications for education at all stages. Project Child Language Syntax, Reprint No. 2. Stockholm University, Institutionen for Nordiska Sprak.

Stern, D. Jaffe, J., Beebe, B., and Bennett, S. 1975. Vocalizing in unison and in alternation: Two modes of communication with the mother-infant dyad. In D. Aronson and R. Rieber (Eds.), *Developmental psycholinguistics and communication disorders. Annals of the New York Academy of Sciences*, *263*, 89–100.

Tanz, C. 1976. Learning how *it* works. Paper presented to the Eight Annual Child Language Research Forum, Stanford University.

Thomson, J., and Chapman, R. 1975. Who is "Daddy" revisited: The status of two-year olds' overextended words in use and comprehension. *Journal of Child Language*. Unpublished.

Uzgiris, I. C., and Hunt, J. McV. 1975. *Assessment in infancy*. Urbana, Ill.: University of Illinois Press.

Vygotsky, L. S. 1962. *Thought and language*. Cambridge, Mass.: The MIT Press.

Waterson, N. 1971. Child phonology: A prosodic view. *Journal of Linguistics*, *7*, 179–211.

Watt. W. 1970. On two hypotheses concerning developmental psycholinguistics. In J. Hayes (Ed.), *Cognition and the development of language*. New York: John Wiley and Sons, 137–220.

Werner, H. 1948. *Comparative psychology of mental development*. New York: Science Editions.

Werner, H., and Kaplan, B. 1963. *Symbol formation*. New York: John Wiley and Sons.

Disruptions in the Development and Integration of Form, Content, and Use in Language Development

A Discussion of Bloom's Paper

MARGARET LAHEY

While most children learn their native language in a relatively short period of time and without programmed or preplanned instruction, there are other children who have considerable difficulty—children with a language disorder who learn language only with much help or who never learn language at all. Children with a language disorder can be described and educated from a number of different perspectives. One might, for example, focus on the reasons a child, or group of children similar in certain ways, does not learn language easily. In this case descriptions involve underlying causes and education concentrates on reducing or eliminating causes. Such etiologically oriented approaches have dominated the literature in the field until very recently. Some have attempted to identify syndromes of behaviors associated with disruptions in global factors considered necessary for language learning (such as intelligence, emotional stability, intact peripheral sensory systems, and intact central nervous systems). Others have been based upon information processing models and have attempted to describe and correct processing skills considered necessary for language learning (such as discrimination, memory, and association).

Alternatively, one could focus on the language itself. In this case, assessment focuses on describing what the child knows about language and education is directly related to teaching language. It is this latter approach that has dominated the literature in the past few years and upon which basic research in language development has had the most impact.

Bloom has presented information on normal language development within a paradigm that stresses the integration of language form (the system of linguistic signals), content (the ideas talked about), and use (the functions of language and the influence of differing contexts). She has described how children learn to categorize their linguistic and nonlinguistic environments and gradually induce the relationships among these concepts in order to communicate ideas by a conventional system of linguistic symbols.

The purpose of this paper is to discuss some of the implications of basic research on normal language development (as presented in this volume by Bloom) for the clinician and educator working with children who have not learned language normally. First the language behaviors of various children with a language disorder are described as disruptions in the development and the integration of form, content, and use. Next, applications of information on normal development to goals of language teaching are discussed. Finally, other present and future implications are mentioned.

Describing Language Disorders

There are some children who use the same forms to talk about the same ideas in the same contexts and for the same purposes as does the child with normal development but who begin at a time later than expected or proceed at a rate slower than expected for their chronological age. The language of these children can be represented by the same Venn diagram used to represent the integration of form, content, and use in normal development (see figure 1) because the development within and among components is qualitatively similar to normal. While certain other difficulties in language learning may also be described within the same paradigm, these difficulties are best represented by variations of this diagram since they involve weaknesses within a particular component or problems in the interrelationships among components.

Some children with a language disorder have well developed ideas that they communicate, thus demonstrating the integration of content and use, but have difficulty learning the conventional system of linguistic forms. These children (some of whom are labeled deaf or dysphasic) may be described as exhibiting a dysfunction in the form component of language as represented by figure 2.

There are other children who use linguistic forms to communicate, thus demonstrating an integration of form with use, but whose ideas of the world are less well developed. Such children talk a great deal but say very little as, for example, the hydrocephalic child described by Schwartz (1974, pp. 466–467) who when asked to tell about a button said,

This is a button, it has two holes in it, it's like a lady has. It has a shape. It is round. This is a button. That's big like this. You can roll it and throw it, but you never smash a window, because if you have a button or a shape that goes on the wall or if you take it and hang it on the dress that would be very nice. Would you do that for me? If you have a dress or a coat you can hang it or you can keep it out to take it to the store.

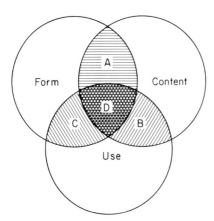

Figure 1. The interaction of form, content, and use in language. From Bloom and Lahey, forthcoming.

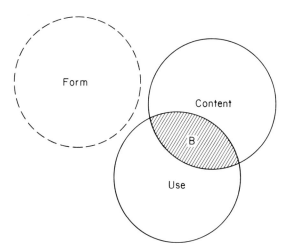

Figure 2. Disruption in the development of the form of language. From Bloom and Lahey, forthcoming.

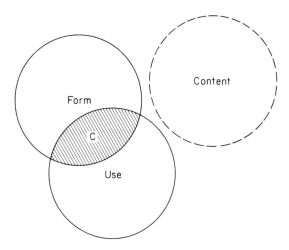

Figure 3. Disruption in the development of the content of language.

Such disruption can be represented by the diagram in figure 3.

In addition, there are children who learn the conventional system of linguistic forms to code well-developed ideas of the world but who rarely use this code to interact with others in their environment. These children, often labeled emotionally disturbed, may talk very little or may talk often but primarily in monologues. Their language disorder can be represented as a weakness in the use component as represented by figure 4. Thus one can describe certain language disorders as weaknesses in one of the three components, form, content, or use.

Other language disorders are better described as disruptions in the integration of these components rather than weaknesses within a particular component. There are some children, for example, who speak only to recite long passages from news reports, weather forecasts, or commercials without apparent understanding of content or apparent communicative intent. This behavior may be described as a separation of components as illustrated in figure 5.

Another disruption in the integration of form, content, and use appears as a distorted interaction where forms are produced to comunicate ideas but in an unusual way. Cunningham (1968) provided an example of this distorted interaction when talking of a boy named Thomas who asked his teacher for ice cream by saying, "Would you like some ice cream, Thomas? Yes, you may?" This distorted interrelationship among form, content, and use is illustrated in figure 6.

One can, in broad terms at least, describe differences among language-disordered children in terms of language itself—differences that relate to the development and integration of language form, content, and use. These broad differences

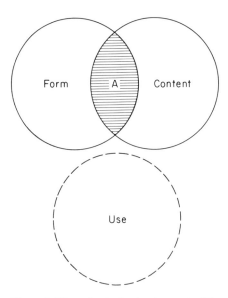

Figure 4. Disruption in the development of the use of language.

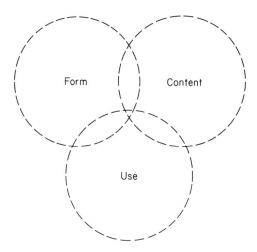

Figure 5. Lack of integration among form, content, and use of language.

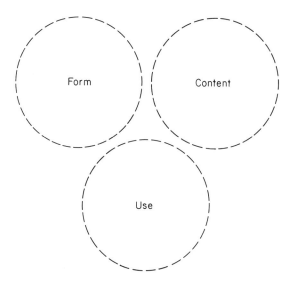

Figure 6. Distorted integration among form, content, and use of language.

can provide a first level of categorization in attempts to understand how various medical, educational, and psychological factors interact with language disorders. Finer taxonomies of each component will be necessary to determine if cause-effect relationships exist among the many correlates of language disorders.

Since little is currently known about etiologies of most language disorders and even less is known about correcting etiological factors, remedial help for these children is primarily in the hands of the educator and clinician responsible for facilitating language learning. Awareness of language learning as an integration of form, content, and use can help in both describing deviations in this development, as illustrated above, and in planning educational programs that focus on developing the interaction of these three components. Basic research in normal language development has had considerable impact on educational programs, particularly in describing the language behaviors to be expected, that is, on specifying the goals of language intervention.

Application of Developmental Information to the Formulation of Goals of Language Intervention

The goals of language intervention are the language behaviors the educator or clinician feels a child must learn in order to be linguistically creative and to use language as a means of representing and exchanging ideas. These objectives are most useful in planning intervention and measuring progress in language learning when they are stated as explicit descriptions of behavior and when they are sequenced in small steps that relate to ease of learning. Research on normal language development has provided both taxonomies for describing behaviors related to language form, content, and use and information about the sequence in which these behaviors appear in the child who learns language without difficulty. The taxonomies and sequence information have influenced (and undoubtedly will continue to influence) speech pathologists and educators as they plan educational objectives for children with a language disorder. This influence has historically paralleled the focus of attention in the study of normal language development. Thus, first applications were related to form and only later did applications include information on content. Information on use has only rarely been applied.

FORM

The taxonomies and sequence of acquisition of linguistic forms derived from the study of normal language development have been increasingly recommended as the goals of language intervention (Miller and Yoder 1972a; Rees 1972). The taxonomies describe intermediary stages of learning adult syntax that often are not a part of the adult model—that is, the intermediary stages do not represent units of the adult model that are gradually added together. Teaching these forms to the language-disordered child is a marked departure from many traditional programs that taught only "correct" forms, either as a total syntactic unit or as parts that were chained together.

Information on the developmental sequence of linguistic forms have been applied to educational objectives at many levels. Some goals have specified the types of single-word utterances to be taught, for example relational words prior to most substantive words (Bloom and Lahey 1972 Miller and Yoder 1974), or have specified criteria for the choice of particular lexical items (Holland 1975; Lahey and Bloom, in press). Forms for two-word utterances have been described as various combinations of adult parts of speech (as nouns and verbs) or as combinations of relational and substantive words. Objectives for two- and three-word combinations have been proposed by Bloom and Lahey (1972, forthcoming), Bricker (1972), Ingram and Eisenson (1972), MacDonald and and Blott (1974), Miller and Yoder (1972b, 1974), Stremel (1972), Stremel and Waryas (1974), and Tyack and Gottsleben (1974). Some grammatical morphemes and questions forms have been included as objectives by Bloom and Lahey (forthcoming), Ingram and Eisenson (1972), Lee and Canter (1971), Lee (1974), Stremel and Waryas (1974), and Tyack and Gottsleben (1974). Because information on the development of complex sentences is less complete, there are no objectives written that approach in completeness the objectives written for the early stages of syntax. A sequence of conjunctions based on developmental data has, however, been proposed by Bloom and Lahey (forthcoming), Lee and Canter (1971), and Lee (1974).

The sources of developmental data vary. For example, Bloom and Lahey (forthcoming) used the sequence found in longitudinal data reported by Bloom (1970, 1973), Brown (1973), and Hood et al. (forthcoming). Tyack and Gottsleben (1974) used the cross-sectional data reported by Morehead and Ingram (1973), which was sequenced by mean length of utterance. Lee (1974) used cross-sectional data sequenced by age and included forms only if they were present in complete sentences (that is, those that included a subject and predicate). In other cases, as Stremel and Waryas (1974), the source of developmental data is not clear. Considering the differences in data base from which the sequences were derived, the similarities in sequence of form suggested by these various programs are striking.

CONTENT

The surge of interest in the semantics of early language has recently begun to influence the formulation of taxonomies and sequences of objectives in language intervention. The meanings to be encoded by the linguistic forms have been specified according to the taxonomies of content that have evolved from basic research in normal language development. Thus while goals of form describe the parts of speech (such as verb plus noun), goals of content include the meaning relations these combinations encode (for example, action-on-object or locative, action, and place). This inclusion of content has been applied to two- and three-word utterances by MacDonald and Blott (1974) and Miller and Yoder (1972b), to both single-word and two- and three-word utterances by Miller and Yoder (1974) and Bloom and Lahey (1972), and to early stages of single-word utterances through later stages including complex sentences by Bloom and Lahey (1972).

In addition to using the taxonomies of content, educational objectives can also take into account the sequence of form/content interactions that has been reported in early child language. For example, the finding that children talk about actions before states (Bloom, Lightbown, and Hood 1975) suggests that goals to code action with two- or three-word utterances (as "throw ball") be sequenced before goals to code internal state with similar forms (as "want ball"). The finding that certain semantic categories of negation, such as nonexistence, occur in children's early syntactic utterances before other semantic categories of negation such as denial (Bloom 1970), suggests that goals for coding nonexistence with two words such as "no ball" to indicate that a ball cannot be found in its usual location precede goals for coding denial such as "no ball" in response to another identifying a balloon as a ball. The sequence of content found in child language is contrary to the emphasis and priority of many language intervention programs, which first stress identity, as "this is a ball," and internal state, as "I want the ball."

These two components, form and content, can be developmentally described and integrated to form a sequence of intervention objectives that are based upon knowledge of normal development. Bloom and Lahey (forthcoming) have, for example, divided the information on language learning into a series of eight phases that represent the behavior sequence observed in normal language learning. The phases were arbitrarily separated according to the mean length of utterance when new behaviors became productive in the longitudinal data on normal development. Descriptions of linguistic form are presented according to the content category they encode. Table 1 illustrates two content categories, action and internal state, as presented in the first four phases. Note that coding of internal state does not become a goal until phase three following the sequence of coding actions before states, which was discussed above. Goals for phase four, which add new complexity to utterances about action, take into account the reduction phenomena discussed in this volume by Bloom and reported by Bloom, Miller, and Hood (1975) by reducing expectations from the full three-constituent structure to two constituents.

USE
Taxonomies and sequences of language learning can include information on how children use the form-content interactions they know. The traditional concen-

Table 1. Examples of Goals of Form-Content Interaction (from Bloom and Lahey, forthcoming).

Phase	Action	Content Category	Internal State
1	single-word utterances		
	verbs		none
2	two constituents*		none
3	three constituents*		two or three constituents*
4	two constituents* plus:	place recurrence attribution nonexistence	same as phase 3

*The constituents referred to are subject-verb-complement.

tration on teaching labeling and demands, using pictorial stimuli and contrived situations that often do not reflect the child's need to communicate, does not mirror normal language use. Young children learning language spend a great deal of time commenting on their own activities, as opposed to labeling static objects or even demanding objects. This implies that goals of language use include commenting as well as labeling and demands. In addition, children slowly learn to exchange ideas with others using language. Hypotheses for the sequence, context, and function of early discourse can also be derived from normal development (as, for example, reported by Bloom, Rocissano, and Hood 1976). The systematic application of developmental information on use has rarely been attempted. In one exception, Bloom and Lahey (forthcoming) have sequenced some information on functions, discourse, and distancing (of a speech event from the object or event talked about) to coordinate with the eight phases they outlined for form-content interactions.

Thus, information on the integration of form, content, and use in normal development can provide a first hypothesis for a systematic, integrated, tripartite approach to language intervention. The term hypothesis is important for two reasons. First, since many gaps exist in any application of developmental information to goals of language intervention (because of the gaps in existing knowledge of normal development), these applications must be flexible to allow for new knowledge as it becomes available. Consequently, no developmentally based objectives can yet be taken as the final word. Second, the effectiveness of using the taxonomies and sequences found in normal development with language-disordered children awaits empirical support. It may be that certain modifications are needed for certain children. It is unlikely that any set of objectives will serve all children without some modification. In this sense, any set of objectives provides a hypothesis for a particular child, a hypothesis that can be tested and changed, if necessary, as intervention proceeds.

Objections to the Use of Developmental Goals
While enthusiasm mounts for the use of developmentally based language intervention goals, particularly in those directly engaged in language intervention, the enthusiasm is not universal. The objections to applying information on normal development to goals of language intervention revolve around three major issues: the need for specific goals; the dearth of empirical support; and the amount of variability found in normal language learners.

NEED FOR GOALS
The statement of specific language behaviors as goals is viewed by some as a constraint that must limit either the linguistic input to the child or the language output of the child. The use of goals to constrain behavior would certainly be deleterious to language learning. In contrast, however, goals can be viewed as guideposts that enrich rather than constrain by focusing on particular behaviors and ensuring that a child is frequently exposed to clear illustrations of both the

linguistic and nonlinguistic contexts necessary for inducing the appropriate relationships. In a program of general language stimulation, an alternative to setting
specific goals, a child may wait for weeks to be exposed to more than one or two
instances of a form that is presented when the content and use are clearly illustrated
in the nonlinguistic context. Goals can be used as reminders to provide multiple
examples of form in connection with illustrations of content and use and to take
into account what the child knows and thus may be ready to learn. They need not
limit what is said to a child or what a child is allowed to say.

WEAK EMPIRICAL EVIDENCE

Perhaps the most common and strongest objection to sequencing language intervention goals according to information on normal development is the absence of
empirical evidence to support the hypothesis that any one sequence is more
effective than another. As stated by Engleman (1970), the sequence in which
normal children learn language is not necessarily the best sequence for teaching a
child who has not learned normally. Opponents to the application of developmental information argue further that the language-disordered child is not normal,
but older and different (Baer as quoted by Bateman 1974) and that the presence
of a developmental sequence does not of necessity mean that one skill must precede
another (Guess, Sailor, and Baer 1974). The answers to these objections can come
only from empirical evidence.

Unfortunately, efficacy studies are as rare in the field of language intervention
as in any field of intervention. However, the few studies that have compared the
use of different sequences in language training have supported the sequences found
in normal development; none have rejected it. Leonard (1975) found children
learned to produce negative utterances about a picture more easily if taught in
a sequence that approximates the sequence found in normal development (for
example, the use of "no" before the negative contraction "don't"). According to
Stremel and Waryas (as reported by Ruder and Smith 1974) children needed
fewer trials to learn "is" as a main verb than to learn "is" as an auxilliary (a
finding that parallels the sequence of normal language learning) and, in general,
training of intermediate structures facilitated the learning of the adult model.
Certainly all would agree that more research is needed, research that compares
the results of programs based on different sequences of language behaviors. Until
such evidence is collected, it would appear that those teaching language to the
language-disordered child should utilize information about normal development
when this is possible and not in conflict with knowledge about learning.

Those critical of using developmental models express the fear that the use of a
developmental orientation will mean waiting for a readiness level rather than analyzing the tasks to be learned and beginning intervention (Engleman 1970;
Gray and Ryan 1973). To test the relevance of a developmental model to the problem of teaching, Englemann (1970) proposed asking whether the model tells what a
child must learn in order to approach some specific criterion of performance.
Current developmental approaches provide a sequence of skills that have led to the

productive use of language in normal children. Whether this is the only sequence or ultimately the best sequence to use in teaching children who have not learned language as their peers awaits further research. The only current alternative to the use of developmental data is for adults to use their intuitions about what is easiest for a child to learn.

Adult intuitions suggest that nouns are easier to learn than relational words (such as "up" or "more") and that attributive relationships (such as "red ball") are easier to learn than action relationships (such as "throw ball"). Following such intuitions, singular noun forms and then plural forms are often taught to children before sentence relations. Also following adult intuitions about ease of learning, the first sentence relations presented in many treatment programs are identity sentences (such as "this is a ball") followed by nonidentity (such as "this is not a ball") or attribution (such as "this ball is red" or "this is a red ball") rather than action statements (such as "throw ball"). It is now apparent that the intuitions that adults may have about the relative simplicity or importance of different words or syntactic structures do not agree with the kinds of words and sentence relations that young normal children first use when they learn how to talk.

Adult intuitions about language learning have similarly resulted in prescriptions for teaching the correct adult model of a sentence rather than approximations of that model for fear of allowing incorrect productions to become established. Thus when teaching sentences like "the boy is chasing the cow," each word is given equal weight. A child might be taught to imitate the entire sentence often by chaining the words in sequence the—the boy—the boy is—etc.) or by selecting the new feature and chaining from that (is—is chasing—boy is chasing—etc.). However, in the normal process of learning language, the basic grammatical relations (such as between "boy" and "chase" and between "chase" and "cow") are expressed long before the articles ("the"), auxilliaries ("is"), or morphological inflections ("-ing") are used. The normal child learning language is most likely to say "chase cow" and then "boy chase cow," before learning "chasing cow" or "is chasing the cow." What children first learn to talk about and the forms they learn to use first are presumably easier and more important for them to learn than are the forms they use later. It would seem reasonable, then, that the more appropriate hypotheses to use in planning the goals of an intervention program ought to come from the information available about sequential development in normal language acquisition. It is certainly conceivable that the use of adult intuitions to prescribe a sequence of language goals may have accounted, in part, for the fact that spontaneous and creative language use often is not reported as a result of intervention programs.

VARIABILITY

Since commonalities among children usually form the basis of developmentally sequenced educational objectives, the recent findings of variability within and among children raise a potential problem. The differences found, however, have not obliterated the striking similarities found among children and thus have not canceled the usefulness of these similarities in determining teaching goals. In fact, the differences themselves are useful in planning intervention, for they can provide alternative means to the same end.

The finding, for example, that certain children tend to use primarily pronouns as subjects and objects in their early syntactic utterances while other children use primarily nouns in similar utterances (reported by Bloom, Lightbown, and Hood 1975; Nelson 1975; and discussed by Bloom, this volume) provides two strategies for teaching early syntax. While some language-disordered children, perhaps those who have difficulty learning names of objects, may learn to code the basic grammatical relations more easily using pronominal reference for subject, object, and place ("put it there"), other children may reach the same point more easily with nominal reference ("put ball box"). Further, the point in normal development when these strategies converge (in this case, at a mean length of utterance at or above 2.0) provides a guideline for when to help a child use both forms of reference in a pattern that is more common in later stages of language development, the use of pronominal subject and nominal object and place. If further research correlates the different strategies different children use in learning language with certain nonlinguistic behaviors, it may be that a child's preferred learning strategies can be predicted early from observations of nonlinguistic behaviors.

Differences found within individual children also provide hypotheses for language intervention. They provide information that, rather than negating the usefulness of developmental information, increases the sophistication with which the information is applied. For example, information on variables that predict the use of three constituents (subject-verb-complement) at some times and the use of only two constituents at other times can be used in writing educational objectives (see table 1, for example). The point was made by Bloom (this volume; forthcoming) and by Bloom, Miller, and Hood (1975) that language learning is not an additive process but involves an interaction of components so that new learning interacts with and influences established behaviors in different ways in different contexts. For instance, certain interactions (such as the use of familiar lexical items) facilitate the use of three constituents while other interactions (such as the addition of grammatical complexity that intervenes between constituents) are more likely to reduce the use of the full three-constituent structure. It would appear, then, that goals of language intervention should not be additive but should include expectations for reduction of full sentence structure when constraining variables are introduced (such as modification of the object or new lexical items) and should take advantage of facilitating factors (such as familiar lexical items) when first teaching the use of three constituents to code a particular content category. Again, as new information is obtained about factors that influence variations within children, these can be incorporated to modify existing goal structures.

Finally, research on variation in language learning may help in the ultimate understanding of childhood language disorders. It has been reported that children with language disorders do not use particular forms as frequently as normal children (Leonard 1972; Morehead and Ingram 1973). Explanations of the variables of content and use that facilitate and constrain the use of these particular forms may aid both in planning goals and procedures of language intervention and in the understanding of factors that interfere with language learning.

Other Implications

This paper has focused on the implications of basic research on language development for determining what to teach the child with a language disorder. In addition, basic research in normal language learning has had some impact upon assessment and intervention procedures.

ASSESSMENT

Assessment aimed at the identification of children with a language disorder—screening—has been influenced only slightly by recent research in normal child language. Screening is by definition a comparison of a child's behavior with the behavior of a large group of children of the same age and thus uses normative data. Recent research on language development has not focused on age norms but rather on the description of particular behaviors and on the developmental sequence in which these behaviors are learned. It has been based largely upon in-depth longitudinal studies of a few children rather than cross-sectional studies of large numbers of children. Thus the influence of this information upon screening has been more in terms of what information is sought—for example, the emphasis on syntax prompted by early psycholinguistic research—and the elicitation tasks used to obtain this information—for example, Lee's (1970, 1971) use of Fraser, Bellugi, and Brown's (1963) tasks.

Recent research in child language has had more influence on assessment procedures that describe the language children use in order to plan what they need to learn (that is, the goals of intervention). To obtain information on what a child knows about language, there has been an increasing reliance on information obtained from observation of children in naturalistic type settings by obtaining a language sample. Analyses of these samples have often used the taxonomies derived from research in normal language development, taxonomies of form (Lee 1966, 1974; Tyack and Gottsleben 1974) or of form, content, and use (Bloom and Lahey, forthcoming).

Objections to using language samples to obtain information about language behavior are related to the time involved in analyzing the sample and the extent to which the language sample can be considered representative of the child's language behavior in general. Critics of using language samples as a method of assessment feel that the length of time needed to obtain, record, and analyze samples of language behavior is impractical for the average clinician. The procedure of analyzing language samples is certainly not brief. However it is also true that the traditional diagnostic procedures, which include the administration and scoring of numerous standardized measures, are not brief. More seriously, while the administration and scoring of standardized tests of language behavior can take as much time as the analysis of language samples, such standardized tests have not been able to provide the rich information potentially available in a representative language sample (information about what kinds of information children can code and how they can use the linguistic code in interpersonal situations).

The second objection of whether the sampled behaviors are truly representative of what the child knows is a less real problem. Information from a sample serves to generate clinical hypotheses that can be checked by other sources and that can undergo continual testing during the intervention period. While representativeness is a problem with any sample of behavior, observing children using language in a naturalistic setting may be more representative of what they actually *do* than is the highly constrained sample of their behavior collected with formal elicitation techniques under artificial and often idealized conditions (Bersoff 1971). Both criticisms—time and representativeness—have, however, limited the use of a language sample as an assessment technique to those clinicians who have been specifically trained in its application or are particularly interested and involved in a linguistic orientation to childhood language disorders.

INTERVENTION

While information on normal development has not provided teaching methods, intervention techniques have certainly been influenced by developmentally based goals. As the goals include emphasis on content and use in addition to linguistic forms, the nonlinguistic contexts in which language learning takes place have increasingly emphasized the demonstration of the concepts that forms encode and the differing situations in which they are used.

Further information on mother-child interaction in normal language may well provide hypotheses that will influence recommended input to the language-disordered child both at home and during formal intervention procedures. Clinical experience with the older language-disordered child suggests the linguistic input to these children may not be the elegant model of simple forms about the here and now to which the normal language learner is exposed. Rather, typical input includes more complex structure about nonpresent events, input that may be more appropriate to the child's chronological age than to the child's linguistic level.

In conclusion, basic research in language development has already been extremely influential in the area of childhood language disorders. There has been a shift in the sequencing of goals in language programs away from sequences determined by adult intuitions of relative simplicity and ways of learning and toward sequences based on what is known about the normal development sequence. There has been a corresponding shift, influenced also by information about normal development, from consideration of linguistic form alone to an increasing emphasis on the ideas coded by linguistic forms. There is an increasingly apparent awareness that the functional use of the language code deserves more attention if the language that is taught to children is not to result in only stereotypic and limited use in specific stimulus situations. Any program directed to teaching language behaviors will probably increase the use of these behaviors to some extent and in some way. It is the efficiency of teaching different behaviors to children that may vary, in addition to the kinds of goals that are eventually achieved. The ultimate goal of any language program is to develop language skills that will enable a child to be linguistically creative and to use language as a means of representing and exchanging ideas. Although most language programs have achieved some success toward reaching this goal, there has been an expanding interest and enthusiasm for more refined use of developmental data to bring even greater success.

References

Bateman, B. 1974. Discussion summary: Language intervention for the mentally retarded. In R. L. Schiefelbusch and L. L. Lloyd (Eds.) *Language perspectives : Acquisition, retardation and intervention.* Baltimore, Maryland: University Park Press, 607–611.

Bersoff, D. 1971. Current functioning myth: An overlooked fallacy in psychological assessment. *Journal of Consulting and Clinical Psychology, 37,* 319–393.

Bloom, L. this volume. The integration of form, content, and use in language development.

———. 1970. *Language development: Form and function in emerging grammars.* Cambridge, Massachusetts: MIT Press.

———. 1973. *One word at a time: The use of single word utterances before syntax.* The Hague: Mouton.

———. Forthcoming. An interactive perspective in language development. Keynote address, Child Language Research Forum, Stanford University, Palo Alto, California, April 1976. Proceedings.

Bloom, L., and Lahey, M. 1972. A proposed program for teaching language to the language disordered child. Unpublished manuscript. Teachers College, Columbia University, New York.

———. Forthcoming. *Language development and language disorders.* New York: John Wiley and Sons.

Bloom, L., Lightbown, P., and Hood, L. 1975. Structure and variation in child language. *Monograph of the Society for Research in Child Development.*

Bloom, L., Miller, P., and Hood, L. 1975. Variation and reduction as aspects of competence in language development. In A. Pick (Ed.) *The 1974 Minnesota Symposium on Child Psychology.* Minneapolis, Minnesota: University of Minnesota Press, 3–55.

Bloom, L., Rocissano, L., and Hood, L. 1976. Adult-child discourse: Developmental interaction between information processing and linguistic knowledge. In *Cognitive Psychology, 8,* 521–552.

Bricker, W. A. 1972. A systematic approach to language training. In R. L. Schiefelbusch (Ed.) *Language of the Mentally Retarded.* Baltimore, Maryland: University Park Press.

Brown, R. 1973. *A first language, the early stages.* Cambridge, Massachusetts: Harvard University Press.

Cunningham, M. 1968. A comparison of the language of psychotic and non-psychotic children who are mentally retarded. *Journal of Child Psychology and Psychiatry, 9,* 229–244.

Engleman, S. 1970. How to construct effective language programs for the poverty child. In F. Williams (Ed.) *Language and poverty.* Chicago, Illinois: Markhan.

Fraser, C., Bellugi, U., and Brown, R. 1963. Control of grammar in imitation, comprehension and production. *Journal of Verbal Learning and Verbal Behavior, 2,* 121–135.

Gray, B. B., and Ryan, B. 1973. *A language training program for the non-language child*, Champaign, Illinois: Research Press.

Guess, D., Sailor, W., and Baer, D. 1974. To teach language to retarded children. In R. Schiefelbusch and L. Lloyd (Eds.) *Language perspectives: Acquisition, retardation and intervention*. Baltimore, Maryland: University Park Press, 529–563.

Holland, A. 1975. Language therapy for children: Some thoughts on context and content. *Journal of Speech and Hearing Disorders, 40*, 514–523.

Hood, L., Lahey, M., Lifter, K., and Bloom, L. Forthcoming. The development of syntactic connectives and the meaning relations they code. Paper prepared for the Conference on the Application of Observational/Ethological Methods to the Study of Mental Retardation, Lake Wilderness, Washington, June 1976. Proceedings.

Ingram, D., and Eisenson, J. 1972. Therapeutic approaches in congenitally aphasic children. In J. Eisensen, *Aphasia in children*. New York: Harper and Row.

Lahey, M., and Bloom, L. In press. Planning a first lexicon: Which words to teach first. *Journal of Speech and Hearing Disorders*.

Lee, L. 1966. Developmental sentence types: A method for comparing normal and deviant syntactic development. *Journal of Speech and Hearing Disorders, 31,* 311–330.

———. 1970. A screening test for syntax development. *Journal of Speech and Hearing Disorders, 35,* 103–112.

———. 1971. The Northwest Syntax Screening Test. Evanston, Illinois: Northwestern University Press.

———. 1974. *Developmental sentence analysis*. Evanston, Illinois: Northwestern University Press.

Lee, L., and Canter, S. 1971. Developmental sentence scoring: A clinical procedure for estimating syntactic development in children's spontaneous speech. *Journal of Speech and Hearing Disorders, 36,* 315–341.

Leonard. L. 1972. What is deviant language? *Journal of Speech and Hearing Disorders, 37,* 427–447.

———. 1975. Developmental considerations in the management of language disabled children, *Journal of Learning Disabilities, 8,* 232–237.

MacDonald, J., and Blott, J. 1974. Environmental language intervention: The rationale for a diagnostic and training strategy through rules, context, and generalization. *Journal of Speech and Hearing Disorders, 39,* 244–257.

Miller, J., and Yoder, D. 1972a. On developing the content for a language teaching program. *Mental Retardation*, April, 9–11.

———. 1972b. A syntax teaching program. In J. E. McLean, D. E. Yoder, and R. L. Schiefelbusch (Eds.) *Language intervention with the retarded: Developing strategies*. Baltimore, Maryland: University Park Press, 191–211.

———. 1974. An ontogenetic language teaching strategy for retarded children. In R. Schiefelbusch and L. L. Lloyd (Eds.) *Language perspectives: Acquisition, retardation and intervention*. Baltimore, Maryland: University Park Press, 505–528.

Morehead, D., and Ingram, D. 1973. The development of base syntax in normal and linguistically deviant children. *Journal of Speech and Hearing Research, 16,* 330–352.

Nelson, K. 1975. Individual differences in early semantic and syntactic development.

In D. Aronson and R. Rieber (Eds.) *Developmental psycholinguistics and communication disorders*. New York: New York Academy of Sciences, 132–139.

Rees, N. 1972. Bases of decision in language training. *Journal of Speech and Hearing Disorders*, *37*, 283–305.

Ruder, K., and Smith, M. 1974. Issues in language training. In R. Schiefelbusch and L. L. Lloyd (Eds.) *Language perspectives: Acquisition, retardation and intervention*. Baltimore, Maryland: University Park Press, 565–605.

Schwartz, E. 1974. Characteristics of speech and language development in the child with myelomeningocele and hydrocephalus. *Journal of Speech and Hearing Disorders, 39*, 465–468.

Stremel, K. 1972. Language training: A program for retarded children. *Mental Retardation*, April, 47–49.

Stremel, K., and Waryas, C. 1974. A behavioral approach to language training. In L. McReynolds (Ed.) Developing systematic procedures for training children's language. *American Speech and Hearing Association Monograph ♯ 18*.

Tyack D., and Gottsleben, R. 1974. *Language sampling, analysis and training*. Palo Alto, California: Consulting Psychologists.

General Discussion of Papers by Bloom and Lahey

Bloom-Lahey Intervention Program

Much of the discussion centered on the approach to intervention presented by Lahey. Zurif took issue with the disregard for precipitating factors (etiology) of the disorder in planning the intervention program. He remarked that the type of language disorder involved would surely influence the application of the developmental approach in remediation. Lahey responded that according to their approach, the goals of the intervention program do not vary as a function of etiology; however, the procedures for carrying out those goals differ depending on the particular disorder. The neurologically impaired child, the deaf child, and the retarded child all have the same language to learn and they may well learn it best in the same sequence as for normal children. Zurif and Lahey agreed that the limits of language development might differ as a function of the precipitating factors, but Bloom and Lahey asserted that those limits often cannot be predicted on the basis of etiology. The program uses an approach in which the teacher starts at a place appropriate for the child's current level of knowledge and proceeds as far as possible, given the child's capacities. Lahey agreed, however, that there was a need for research that explores the relationship between precipitating factors and effective intervention procedures. She referred to the research described by Tallal, Sherrick, and Pickett as good instances of this kind of investigation.

Tallal asked Lahey about how their intervention approach differed from those used by others, for example, Laura Lee and her associates. (See references in Lahey, this volume). Lahey answered that the goals differ primarily in the fact that Lee's program uses form goals (syntactic structure) that are not coordinated with goals of language content and use. Lee uses both elicitation and language sampling techniques but the data are described only in terms of language form. The form sequences described by Lee are very similar to those that Bloom and Lahey describe. However, in the Bloom-Lahey approach, the content (what the forms talk about) and the use are included in the sequencing description.

McReynolds suggested that most language intervention programs assume that language comprehension is intact and work primarily on production. She asked how comprehension was considered in the Bloom-Lahey program. Did they give any special training in comprehension? Lahey responded that comprehension and production are considered simultaneously in their program. Given the approach that language learning is an inductive process that includes learning relations between external (nonlinguistic) contexts, including social contexts, and linguistic form and content, comprehension cannot be separated from language production. Bloom added that the relationship between comprehension and production has been an issue in language development for a long time. It has been assumed that comprehension necessarily preceded production, but this idea has been challenged very seriously in the last few years (see Bloom 1974).

Chapman stressed that an important implication of the approach taken by

Bloom and Lahey is the idea that in intervention one attempts to change a single aspect of the behavior expected from the child at a time. For example, one does not work on a new lexical item (a new verb, for example) in the context of the top level of form the child is currently controlling. Instead one should expect the return to a simpler formal level (one-word utterances) and then perhaps two-word utterances in a familiar external context, and so on. One does not expect the generalization of a new form or content to a new functional use until after they are controlled in an old function. By specifying an individual child's current command of form, content, and function, one can specify the next steps the child should take in each of these components. This provides for a very powerful program that in principle could be completely individualized to the child. This rests on knowing in detail about normal language acquisition of form, content, and use. Bloom agreed that a great deal of the program's power rests on the realization that language acquisition is not merely an additive process.

Physiological Factors in Language Development and its Disorders
Stevens suggested that the developmental sequence from one-word to two-word to multiword utterances involves among other things the maturation of anatomical and physiological mechanisms that control the production of longer utterances. In the case of the language-disordered child, the physiological capability to produce these longer utterances may not be present. For instance, a deaf child with a very breathy voice cannot produce more than two words in one breath. Stevens wondered whether there was experimental evidence on the number of words uttered within a single breath for children of different ages and developmental stages. Bloom mentioned the research by Branigan at Boston University (1976), who has compared the intonation contours of single words, successive single-word utterances, and multiword utterances by children. She added that John Delack (in press) was also studying the prosodics of utterances by children, but at a much younger age.

The "Observer Effect" and Assessment Procedures
Labov commented on the effects of different language-behavior measurest standardized tests, elicitation techniques, or observational techniques such as language sampling, on the outcome of the assessment. He repeated Rogor Brown's statement that in general behavior on formal tests always lags behind spontaneous performance. For example, Labov knew of some research with retarded children that tested the use of plural endings using the elicitation procedure developed by Berko (1958) (for example "Here is a wug. Here are two———.") In case after case children did not use the plural at all on the tests but in spontaneous speech showed perfect use of the same constructions. There appears to be a fundamental paradox here if the researcher's goal is to understand how people use language when they are not being observed. However, Labov went on to say that this seeming paradox is perhaps not the deep philosophical issue that it appears to be because this observer effect is primarily evident when a member of the "dominant class" is testing a member of a "subordinate class" (in terms of age

or social status). This has implications for the interpretation of assessments of language behavior of social or racial minority groups as well as children.

Labov asked Lahey if she had any thoughts on how informal observational techniques might be combined with more systematic testing procedures to overcome the observer effect. Lahey reported that they have conducted pilot studies comparing data from language samples obtained in informal observation with very carefully structured parent questionnaires. For instance, they ask questions such as, "Does your child talk about a particular subject with particular kinds of grammatical forms?" "In what contexts does your child talk about this?" These studies yielded very high correlations, but the questionnaire that has been used is very long and complicated. Few parents are willing to complete it.

Lahey added that other research groups have been developing elicitation procedures that can be used in an informal context. For example, the experimenter plays with children and tries to elicit language about the toys they are playing with and the activities in which they are engaged. Lahey has found it more efficient to assess language through a sampling procedure first and then attempt to elicit behaviors that were not found in the language sample. The amount of time spent in their procedures is not much greater than that needed to do thorough testing and scoring.

Lahey also mentioned that a group in Chicago using the Bloom-Lahey model with nursery school children do all their assessment in the classroom. The aids and teachers always have a paper and pencil and they collect a great deal of data over the course of several weeks. Lahey thought that drawbacks due to transcription errors and omissions were probably outweighed by the amount of data they collect.

Evaluation of Intervention Programs

Jenkins again stressed the critical need for good evaluation of these intervention programs at every step in the process. It is not adequate to leave the evaluation of success to the end and then use some standardized test that may not be a valid indicator of progress. Lahey agreed and emphasized that this was one of the advantages of a program such as the Bloom-Lahey approach. The criteria are indicated at each level; thus the evaluation procedure is built into the program if one keeps records of a child's progress through the levels.

References

Berko, J. 1958. The child's learning of English morphology. *Word*, 14, 150–177.

Bloom, L. 1974. Talking, understanding, and thinking: Development relationship between receptive and expressive language. In R. L. Schiefelbusch and L. Lloyd (Eds.), *Language Perspective: Acquisition, Retardation, and Intervention*. Baltimore: University Park Press, 285–311.

Branigan, G. 1976. Sequence of single words as structured units. Paper presented to the Stanford Child Language Research Forum, to appear in *Papers and Reports in Child Language*, Stanford University.

Delack, J. B. In press. Aspects of infant speech development in the first year of life. *Canadian Journal of Linguistics*.

Coming to Understand Things We Could Not Previously Understand

JOHN D. BRANSFORD AND KATHLEEN E. NITSCH

The purpose of this chapter is to discuss aspects of the comprehension problem that seem relevant to educational and clinical issues. The most pertinent problem seems to be how people come to understand things they could not previously understand or how they come to understand things in new ways. We therefore focus on how one moves beyond a particular state of knowing and understanding (the growth problem) and how particular changes permit subsequent understanding (the transfer problem). In short, we ask how people learn to know and comprehend better.

Questions about learning to comprehend seem directly relevant to educational and clinical settings. For example, effective clinicians and educators use a variety of (intuitively based) techniques for promoting growth and transfer. They may ask questions, provide examples, relate new inputs to already familiar domains by way of analogy and, encourage particular types of drill and practice. As psychologists begin to clarify how people come to understand things in new ways and to clarify what the nature of the changes are that permit such transfer, we should become better able to evaluate techniques for intervention. Furthermore, we might begin to improve upon techniques currently in use.

Exploring the Development of Expertise

The basic problem under consideration can be viewed as an attempt to understand better the processes involved in the development of expertise in particular domains of knowing (see Bransford, Nitsch, and Franks, forthcoming, for further discussion). Some simple examples can be used to clarify the types of problems to which this chapter is addressed.

The first example involves the domain of reading comprehension. Marks, Doctorow, and Wittrock (1974) varied the relative familiarity of 20 percent of the words in a story in order to create two versions that could be read by elementary school children. Story comprehension and retention were nearly doubled when the selected words in the story were changed from less familiar terms (such as lad) to more familiar terms (such as boy). This experiment provides a vivid illustration of the importance of mapping into the current state of a comprehender's knowledge in order to ensure adequate comprehension. From the present perspective, the important question involves the processes by which terms such as "boy" became meaningful and the processes by which terms such as "lad" can become as meaningful. Through what procedures can students be helped to comprehend inputs in more accurate, efficient, and automatic ways?

Similar questions can be asked about other aspects of comprehension, for example, the ability of adult speakers of English to know that the sentence *John hit Mary* is more closely related to *Mary was hit by John* than is *Mary hit John*. Beilin and Spontak (1969) and Olson (1972) report that elementary school children have considerable difficulty making such intersentential judgments. However, they are quite good at selecting a picture that is an accurate description of each of the above-mentioned sentence types. What do they know that permits accurate sentence-picture but not sentence-sentence judgments and how do they develop the linguistic expertise characteristic of a normal adult?

The final example derives from an informal study we conducted. Freshmen in an introductory psychology seminar were provided with excerpts from a passage by Karl Buhler that discussed certain aspects of language comprehension (the passage was taken from Blumenthal 1970, pp. 50–57). The students were asked to read and attempt to understand the passage so that they could answer essay questions to be provided later on. Examination of these essays revealed that most of the students were able to understand what the passage said, but they were unable to do much with the information. For example, most were generally unable to generate novel examples relevant to Buhler's discussion or to state the relevance of Buhler's ideas for clarifying experiences in everyday life. What is involved in helping such students come to understand a domain in a manner that permits transfer, that permits a clarification of subsequent experiences they may have?

The preceding examples raise questions regarding the problem of coming to understand things one did not previously understand or of coming to understand things in new ways. Our purpose is to sketch an abstract framework that might be fruitful for conceptualizing such problems of growth and transfer. We shall argue that appeals to variables such as frequency of exposure and practice, especially when they refer to the formation of stronger and more durable "memory traces," seem less than adequate for characterizing processes leading to growth and transfer. Similarly, appeals to the induction of "rules" or "higher order units" also seem less than adequate because such accounts provide little discussion of the conditions necessary for their acquisition.

Our discussion of the growth problem will focus on learner-environment relationships that seem necessary in order to learn effectively from exposure and practice and on the "remodeling" of the system (Bransford, Nitsch, and Franks, forthcoming) necessary in order to "know with" information (Broudy, forthcoming) rather than merely "know about" information. The acquisition of higher order cognitive information that one knows with will also be shown to affect what some consider to be lower order processes, for example, to affect the perception of speech in white noise.

The remainder of the chapter is organized as follows. First, the minimal unit for analyzing comprehension is considered and defined as a situation-input relationship rather than a mere input (a sentence); one wishes to understand his momentary situation, not simply the input. Second, situational prerequisites to understanding are discussed. What types of cognitive and perceptual support are necessary in order for someone to understand an input? The development of language comprehension is viewed as a process of moving away from the need for explicit-cognitive-perceptual support. The next section attempts to tie the above two points together. It focuses on the reciprocal influences of one's current knowledge on comprehension of subsequent inputs, as well as the effect of inputs on one's knowledge. Here an "abductive" (cf. Peirce 1932) framework is proposed for conceptualizing the problems of helping someone come to understand things in new ways.

The final section discusses implications of the proposed framework for programs of evaluation and intervention.

Discovery and the Minimal Unit for Analyzing Comprehension

This section begins by discussing experiences of insight and discovery as paradigmatic exemplars of the process of coming to know something in a new way. It is argued that insight is not a matter of comprehending new (for the organism) as opposed to old input information. Indeed, it is not the input information per se that is the primary target of one's comprehension activities; it is the relevant aspects of one's momentary cognitive-perceptual situation that one wishes to understand. The minimal unit of analysis is therefore defined as a situation plus input; never a mere input. The latter assumption has implications for clarifying the relationship between meaning and understanding. In addition, it leads to questions about what is being studied when the comprehension of individual sentences in the linguistic or experimental laboratory is investigated.

AN EXAMPLE OF DISCOVERY

Recently, one of the authors played a simple game of discovery with two elementary school students.[1] The game consisted of drawing a pattern (a schematic face) with a stick. The task was to discover the critical aspects of the "teacher's" movements and to copy them exactly. Following each unsuccessful attempt the children were told that their imperfect performances were wrong but no specific corrective feedback was provided. Through repeated juxtapositions of observations and attempt to mimic, the children gradually articulated all the necessary movements. The last and most difficult discovery was that the teacher was drawing with his left hand. (The children were right handed and naturally drew this way.)

During the game, the children were excited as they struggled to master the task. With each subsequent demonstration by the teacher, they expressed excitement that they had now discovered the "crucial" detail. They would jump up with a "Now I've got it," only to find that additional details still remained to be discovered. There was excitement when the game was finally mastered, but this excitement was short-lived. It was no fun to continue correctly drawing the pattern over and over. The children might have done so if rewarded each time with some appropriate token, but the excitement of discovery still would have vanished as quickly. Indeed, once the children had mastered the game, they expressed a very simple but urgent request: "Change the rules so we can try again."

To understand the excitement of mastery, one must focus on the growth of understanding. The excitement is in the discovery of something new, not the mere repetition of something old. The discovery of something new can be breathtaking. Consider Helen Keller's discovery that entities have names, Archimedes' shout of "Eureka" when he noticed that his body displaced the water in his bath and that the same principle could be used to measure the mass of objects, the excitement generated in students by a fresh idea or perspective, the excitement of a child who

[1]We thank Todd and Tommy Boehm for sharing their enthusiasm with us in this game.

grasps a new word or concept and tries it out in a number of instances, the excitement of a scientist who discovers something new. An analysis of such phenomena places constraints on what understanding entails.

THE RELATIONSHIP BETWEEN INSIGHT AND OLD VERSUS NEW FACTS

How might one characterize comprehension that leads to discovery and insight? Does it simply involve understanding new (to the comprehender) rather than old facts? Archimedes shouted "Eureka" upon seeing water rise in the tub when he entered it. Note that people see essentially the same thing every day, yet seeing the water rise rarely fosters an insight. Similarly, imagine understanding a sentence like *A pliers can be used as a weight*. To most of us this information is also less than breathtaking. Yet imagine that someone attempting to solve Maier's (1930) two-string problem either generates or hears this information. This information will allow this person to restructure and clarify the perceived situation and an insight occurs.

A distinction between old and new facts does not illuminate the factors involved in insightful comprehension. Information may be old (and even quite familiar), yet it can lend clarification and insight to one's immediate situation. It is the situation one seeks to understand, not simply the input. For example, the reader undoubtedly knows the word *parachute*. It is old and its occurrence on the page probably suggests little more than the recognition of familiarity (or perhaps an image). But imagine a different situation: You have been trying to understand the utterance *The haystack was important because the cloth ripped* (Bransford and McCarrell 1974). The clue *parachute* now permits a restructuring of the situation; an "aha" experience occurs. (Buhler, reprinted in Blumenthal 1970). Similarly, the punch line of a joke can restructure one's knowledge and produce laughter, but it is not the punch line in isolation that is funny. The humor stems from the restructuring of the cognitive situation that had been specified by the telling of the first part of the joke.

Consider a more general illustration of the relationship between situations and old information. We have all undoubtedly experienced conversations where the nature of a problem under discussion was ill defined and fuzzy. A discussant may suggest something that clarifies the issue, yet the suggestion frequently consists of information that everyone already knows. A typical example for an academic discussion might be "Look, we seem to be assuming that correlation implies causation." In such instances it is not uncommon to think, "Of course, why didn't I think of that?"

How can one feel that a comment is clarifying and insightful when that comment consists of already known information like "correlation does not imply causation"? The preceding question appears paradoxical only when the more general problem of comprehension is tacitly equated with the special case of understanding an isolated input. For example, imagine that you are stranded in the desert and need water. You know some is near, but where? A few desert animals go by and you notice tracks of others; but you need water, not food.

Besides, you are too weak to catch them. You could know that desert animals need water, but the potential meaning of this fact for your present situation may never occur to you. If it does, it transforms your understanding of the present situation. Following the animal tracks is a better bet than blindly searching on your own.

To understand comprehension, we must focus on the relationship between an input and one's immediate cognitive-perceptual situation. It is the situation one seeks to understand. The minimal unit of analysis must therefore be a situation plus an input. Lashley (1951, p. 112) emphasizes the importance of this type of analysis:

My principal thesis today will be that the input is never into a quiescent or static system, but always into a system which is already actively excited and organized. In the intact organism, behavior is the result of interaction of this background of excitation with input from any designated stimulus. Only when we can state the general characteristics of this background of excitation, can we understand the effects of a given input.

RELATIONSHIPS BETWEEN UNDERSTANDING AND CONCEPTS OF MEANING

Lashley's orientation has implications for characterizing the problem of meaning as well as for clarifying what is being studied when comprehension is investigated in the laboratory. Since comprehension is usually assumed to involve meaning, the two concepts appear intimately related. However, by focusing on the relationship between situations and inputs, some ambiguities in concepts of meaning are revealed.

Assume that you are in an experiment. Your task is to state whether or not you understand the inputs presented when the inputs include words like *gex*, *zebra*, and *bagpipe*. You will probably state that you understand the latter two words but not the first. Now assume a different situation. Your task is to understand the utterance *The notes were sour because the seam split* (Bransford and McCarrell 1974). You will hear various cues and should mark whether you now understand. In this situation, neither *gex* nor *zebra* is likely to facilitate understanding. The cue *bagpipes*, however, will help. Of course, you will know the meaning of *zebra*, but your task is not to indicate whether you understand the input. Your task is to indicate whether the input helps you understand.

The latter task appears to be quite representative of everyday comprehension situations. For example, our previously mentioned discussant in a meeting may claim "We're assuming that correlation implies causation." The statement may be readily comprehended, but does it help you understand? What counts is whether the input helps you clarify the immediate problem. If it doesn't, you will say something like "I don't understand your point" or "I don't see what you mean."

What does the preceding discussion suggest about the relationship between meaning and understanding? It is easy to accept the assertion that comprehension involves "grasping meaning." However, there are important differences between knowing the meaning of a word or sentence and using information to understand a particular situation. Understanding involves grasping the significance of an input for the situation at hand (Bransford, McCarrell, and Nitsch 1976; Nitsch 1975). The problem of significance extends to nonverbal as well as verbal inputs (for further discussion see Bransford and McCarrell 1974; Brewer 1974; Franks 1974), yet there clearly seems to be something called "linguistic meaning." Fillmore's (1971, p. 274) approach to linguistic meaning seems fruitful:

The difficulties I have mentioned exist, it seems to me, because linguistic semanticists, like the philosophers and psychologists whose work they were echoing, have found it relevant to ask, not *What do I need to know in order to use this form appropriately and to understand other people when they use it?*, but rather, *What is the meaning of this form?* And having asked that, linguists have sought to discover the external signs of meanings, the reflexes of meanings in the speech situation, and the inner structure of meanings. It is apparent that the wrong question has been asked.

This discussion focuses on the concept of significance or understood meaning rather than on linguistic meaning. This does not deny the crucial importance of linguistic meaning for understanding. It will be argued later that some level of understood meaning is a prerequisite for acquiring linguistic meaning in the first place.

SITUATION-INPUT RELATIONSHIPS IN EXPERIMENTAL RESEARCH

The minimal unit of analysis has been defined as a situation plus input. All experimental research on comprehension occurs in some situation, yet this aspect is seldom analyzed. If understanding depends on situation-input relations, the nature of the experimental situation will have important effects on the results obtained in the experiment.

Consider a typical experiment where subjects hear individual sentences like *The boy hit the ball* or *John hit Mary*. It is extremely easy for adults to understand such sentences. It is tempting to assume that this type of task taps the simplest, most basic level of linguistic understanding. Note, however, that an experimenter does not simply walk into the room and begin uttering *The boy hit the ball*. If he or she did, the subjects would be extremely confused. The most important type of understanding that takes place in an experiment involves understanding the instructions so that one can define one's immediate situation. This affects how the experimental inputs are understood.

In most experiments the stimulus sentences are understood to have a very special significance; they are objects to be comprehended, rated, or remembered. They are viewed as examples of sentences that might be uttered by someone for some reason at some time and place. Treating a sentential input as an example of a potential utterance is very different from using an input to clarify a particular situation. For example, one can understand the isolated sentence *Desert animals need water*. This is quite different from understanding the potential meaning or significance of this fact for surviving in a desert. Note further that subjects frequently seek clarification after an experiment. Some ask all kinds of questions in an attempt to understand. These subjects are not trying to understand the sentences previously presented as stimuli; they are trying to understand the experiment.

An experimenter's words of explanation will now be understood to the degree that they clarify the subject's previous experiences in the experiment.

There are important differences between comprehension in experimental situations and many everyday communication situations. The most striking contrast is between the experimental situation and the conditions under which language is originally acquired. One does not sit down with a two-year-old child and say "O.K. Billy, *The boy hit the ball, John hit Mary.*" A child would never acquire language in this manner. Children learn by understanding the significance of utterances relative to their cognitive-perceptual situation at the time (see MacNamara 1972; Nelson 1974; Bloom, this volume). Even older children have a strong tendency to understand information in terms of their immediate situation. For example, an adult will respond "true" to the proposition "Either it is raining outside or it is not." In contrast, children seek empirical support for the truth value of the statement: They will look to see whether it is actually raining or not (Osherson and Markman 1975). Similarly, consider Scribner's (1975) studies comparing schooled and unschooled Kpelle villagers in their ability to understand classical syllogisms (see also Brown, forthcoming). Unschooled villagers refused to consider a problem such as "All Kpelle men are rice farmers. Mr. Smith [Western name] is not a rice farmer. Is he a Kpelle man?" They had to know Mr. Smith in order for the task to make sense to them.

Schooled adults also normally attempt to understand the significance of inputs in terms of their immediate situation. They can treat inputs as examples of possible utterances and as objects of logical analysis, but it is easy to forget that this involves a special mode of understanding. For example, *Bill has a red car* is readily understood in an experimental context, but try walking into someone's office and simply uttering that statement. In such cases, people are extremely confused by the utterance. They know what was said but not what was meant (Bransford, McCarrell, and Nitsch 1976).

What, then, is being studied in experiments that investigate the comprehension of individual, isolated sentences (or diagnose people on this basis)? Surely it is not the most basic and simplest level of language comprehension. Instead, the experimenters are relying on people's abilities to specify or invent particular situations in which an input could make sense. A number of studies suggest that sophisticated comprehenders do indeed spontaneously invent situations in which sentences might be meaningful (Bransford, Barclay and Franks 1972; Brewer 1974; Johnson, Bransford and Solomon, 1973; Schweller, Brewer and Dahl, in press). Furthermore the ability to do so appears to be a prerequisite for effective comprehension (Bransford and Johnson 1972, 1973; Bransford and McCarrell 1974; Dooling and Lachman 1971). The ability to specify or invent situations in which inputs can be meaningfully interpreted is clearly important. However, these studies do not necessarily specify how people got to the point where they are able to do this or how they understand given that they are immersed in a particular cognitive-perceptual situation. The effects of one's situation on comprehension of inputs is discussed in the next section.

The focus of this discussion has been on a general characterization of the problem of understanding. A basic question has been "What is it that one wants to understand?" Generally one seeks to understand one's experience or momentary cognitive-perceptual situation. It is the situation that is the primary focus of one's comprehension activities, not merely the input. Identical inputs (such as *A pliers can be used as a weight; We're assuming that correlation implies causation*) can therefore be insightful, mundane, or anomolous depending on one's situation. Already known information can be just as insightful as novel information. It is in coming to understand something in a new way that the inherent excitement of understanding occurs. Of course, the use of the term cognitive-perceptual situation presupposes considerable understanding on the part of the listener. Indeed, new understanding is built on previous understanding. It is those general processes that permit the growth of understanding that we eventually want to understand.

There are important differences between everyday comprehension situations and those that frequently occur in the experimental (and linguistic) laboratory. In the experimental situation, individual sentences are treated as objects of analysis, as examples of something that might be said. The ability to understand under such circumstances is clearly important, but it is surely not the most basic mode of understanding. This ability is the result of basic processes that we seek to understand. Children would never acquire language under experimentlike conditions. Such situations rarely permit adults to understand something in a new way. It is therefore important to focus on situational prerequisites for understanding. What types of situational support are necessary for understanding certain types of syntactic structures, statements, or lexical items? Furthermore, what types of support must be provided in order to move one beyond one's particular level of knowing and understanding? Some of these questions are examined in the next section.

Before proceeding it may be helpful to clarify the differences between this and the following section. Here the question of how the comprehension of inputs can clarify and restructure one's understanding of one's immediate situation was emphasized. The next section will emphasize the opposite side of the coin: How one's immediate situation affects comprehension of a subsequent input. Following this, we will attempt to put the coin back together by emphasizing the reciprocal nature of the influence of input on situation and situation on input. That is, an input may both clarify one's situation yet be clarified by the situation.

Cognitive and Perceptual Support Necessary for Understanding
In this section the emphasis is on the situational support necessary to understand subsequent inputs rather than on the effects of the input toward clarifying one's situation. As will be argued in a later section, this division between situation and input influences is actually artificial, but it seems descriptively useful nonetheless. Some relations between situations and linguistic inputs for the adult comprehender are discussed first, followed by a consideration of some of the additional situational support often necessary for younger children to comprehend effectively. In general, early comprehension skills seem to be context specific or situation specific. That is, young comprehenders seem to require considerable situational support in order to

understand utterances. More sophisticated comprehenders appear better able to supply such information on their own.

SYNTACTIC DIFFICULTY AS SITUATIONALLY DEFINED

In the 1960s linguistic theories emphasized the primacy of the sentence (Chomsky 1965, 1972). Linguistic theories of this decade dealt with intersentential relationships, but these were relationships of transformational relatedness for individual sentence types. For example, *John hit Mary* and *Mary was hit by John* were assumed to differ in terms of surface structure but to be similar in deep structure (Katz and Postal 1964). In contrast, sentences like *John is eager to please* and *John is easy to please* were assumed to share a similarity in surface structure while their deep structural descriptions were markedly different (Chomsky 1965). For example, one can say *It is easy to please John* but not *It is eager to please John*.

Chomsky's theories clearly revolutionized thinking about the nature of both language and understanding (see Dixon and Horton 1968). Yet in subsequent years many linguists' analyses of deep structure led them to make it "deeper and deeper" (McCawley 1974; Ross 1974). For example, on the basis of linguistic analysis, Ross (1970) argued that the deep structural representation of declarative sentences contain the information "I say to you that. . . . " Such analyses begin to converge on what has been termed here the situation underlying linguistic communication (for example, that it always presupposes a speaker or a writer). There are, of course, numerous additional situational aspects as well. For example, the notions of sentence relatedness considered in Chomsky's theories are different from the intuitive coherence or relatedness of sentences in a normal flow of conversation ("I bought a new bike. The tires are bright red."). Interest in the constraints differentiating coherent and noncoherent flows of conversation is reflected in current attempts to construct text grammars rather than sentence grammars (Frederikson 1972, 1975; Kintsch 1974; Schank 1972; van Dijk 1973; see Lakoff 1971 on constraints on conjoining sentences). Text grammars reflect a concern with the relationship of a sentence to the more global macrostructure of a text.

Like the linguistic theory from which it took its impetus early psycholinguistic research focused on the individual sentence. For example, active sentences were found to be easier to comprehend and remember than passives, affirmatives easier than negatives (Gough 1965, 1966). Psychological complexity was almost universally assumed to have a direct correspondence to the derivational complexity of the sentences (as computed according to then-current versions of linguistic theory). However, subsequent investigators questioned the validity of such indices of psychological complexity (see Fodor, Bever, and Garrett 1974 for an overview). In addition, more attention was focused on the function of certain types of grammatical constructions. The same grammatical structure may be more or less appropriate depending on the context or situation in which it appears.

A number of studies explored contextual or situational constraints on ease of comprehension. For example, Wason (1961) investigated contexts of plausible denial. Slobin (1966) and Olson and Filby (1972) investigated situations that were conducive to the processing of passive sentences, and Huttenlocher, Eisenberg, and Strauss (1968) showed that the same sentence may differ in ease of comprehension depending on the contextual situations to which it refers. Clark and Haviland (forthcoming; see also Clark 1973) recently discussed a number of these results in terms of a "given-new contract." Following Halliday's (1967) linguistic analysis, they assume that sentences contain both given and new (for the comprehender) information. Thus, a sentence like *It was John who saw Mary* presupposes that *someone saw Mary* is already known as given and that *it was John* is new. If the sentence that precedes *It was John who saw Mary* in a conversation happens to be *Someone saw Mary*, the second sentence in the conversation seems appropriate and is readily comprehended (assuming that the prosodic stress was on John). The given information in this sentence is congruent with the information that the listener in fact already knew. In contrast, assume that a comprehender has just heard the utterance *John saw someone*. Under these conditions the sentence *It was John who saw Mary* seems inappropriate and is less quickly comprehended. A more acceptable and more easily understood sentence would be *It was Mary who was seen by John*. In this latter sentence, *John saw someone* is given and *Mary* is new.

The basic point of these studies is that syntactic structure has semantic implications and that syntactic appropriateness is determined relative to the situation in which a sentence is uttered. Even the appropriateness of using "the" versus "a" and the ease of comprehending the resulting utterances depends on the preexisting communicative situation (Chafe 1972; Clark 1973; Osgood 1971). As Glucksberg and Danks (1975) argue, the results of most studies of comprehension difficulty that involve sentence-sentence and picture-sentence verifications indicate differential difficulties in decision times rather than differential difficulty in processing certain types of linguistic constructions. Furthermore, decision difficulty varies as a function of the situation in which an input occurs (Olson and Filby 1972).

Assumptions about "inherent" syntactic difficulty have also been questioned from a somewhat different perspective. Some investigators have argued for the communicative efficiency of moderately complex, embedded sentences as compared to sets of grammatically simple sentences (Bransford and Franks 1973; Pearson 1969). Such communicative efficiency is obscured if one simply compares comprehension and memory for simple as opposed to more complex sentences. However, assume that one establishes a goal of communicating a particular constellation of semantic information, that is, the goal is to get someone to understand that there is a tall boy who hit a red ball. It seems obvious that use of a set of syntactically simple sentences is not necessarily the most efficient form for communicating such information. Compare, for example, *The tall boy hit the red ball* with *The boy was tall, The boy hit the ball, The ball was red*. Pearson (1969) reports data on children's comprehension indicating greater efficiency of certain types of embedded sentences relative to sets of grammatically simpler forms.

FURTHER INVESTIGATIONS OF SITUATIONAL SUPPORT

Most of the previously mentioned research took place in an experimental context. Studying the ease of comprehending a sentence in the context of a previous input is one step toward more natural communication conditions, but the subjects may still regard inputs as examples of sentences that might be uttered by someone at some time for some purpose. In settings other than the experimental laboratory, knowledge of who is speaking, when they are speaking, and why they are speaking is frequently necessary in order to understand adequately. This knowledge forms part of one's situation that may affect how the inputs are understood.

Brewer and Harris (1974) present data illustrating that sentences heard under conditions approximating those of ordinary conversation are understood differently from the same sentences heard in an experimental context. They approximated conversational situations by having the person uttering the sentence actually present and by having him converse as if he were presenting his own views at that particular time and place. In the experimental condition, subjects simply listened to sentences as in a normal experiment (where they are understood as possible sentences that someone might say). Free recall was used as an index of what was understood. Subjects in the experimental condition made many errors during recall. For example, the sentence *Marijuana grows wild in this county* was frequently recalled as *Marijuana grows wild in* the *or* that *county*. Such results are not surprising given that the sentences were viewed simply as examples of potential utterances. Without a well-specified temporal-spatial framework, words like *this* (and even *county*) may be understood at a linguistic level, but this does not ensure that the significance of these inputs for a particular domain is understood (Bransford, McCarrell and Nitsch 1976; Nitsch 1975). In the conversational condition, subjects did have a well-defined temporal-spatial framework and their recall results differed radically. For example, subjects rarely miscalled *that* or *the* for *this*.

The importance of situational support for understanding can also be illustrated with verb tenses. Consider a newspaper headline like *War Breaks Out in Europe*. The headline is in a quasi-present tense, but the significance of this information depends on the cognitive-temporal framework from which it is viewed. If one realizes one is reading an old newspaper, the significance of this headline is historical. If it is today's paper, the significance of the present tense is very different indeed.

Many experimentally presented sentences fail to suggest a well-defined cognitive-temporal framework. Therefore whether a subject mentioned in a sentence already has, is, or will be doing something has very little meaning; and all kinds of tense confusions occur in recall (see Clark and Stafford 1969). If cues are added to make the tenses more meaningful, recall errors diminish greatly. For example, Harris and Brewer (1973) compared subjects' recall of sentences like *The astronauts will see a UFO* with recall of sentences like *Tomorrow, the astronauts will see a UFO*. In the first condition results were similar to those of Clark and Stafford (1969). In the latter situation tense shifting during recall was markedly reduced. Of course, in a normal conversation tense is usually meaningful even without using words like *yesterday and tomorrow*. If used in normal conversation, these words have a more well defined significance as well.

DEVELOPMENT AND COMPREHENSION SKILLS

The preceding examples illustrate how one's situation can affect linguistic comprehension. Identical syntactic structures may be easy or difficult to understand depending on the situation, and linguistic elements may vary in understood meaning as a function of the situation in which they occur. (See also Anderson and Ortony 1975; Barclay et al. 1974 on the flexibility of understood meanings). Of course, no one doubts the fundamental influence of context on comprehension. However, it is still easy to believe that comprehension of context-free words and sentences is a prerequisite for any deeper level of understanding. From this perspective one must first comprehend the individual word or sentence and then elaborate it as a function of context. There are strong reasons for questioning this assumption, particularly as it applies to the development of linguistic expertise.

Consider the fact that adult speaker-listeners can recognize deep structural equivalences among different surface structures (for example that *John hit Mary* is similar to *Mary was hit by John*). Is this ability purely a function of linguistic knowledge or is it somehow more cognitively based? Experiments by Olson (1972, 1974) mentioned previously are very important in this context. Olson (1972) presented young school children with sentences like *John hit Mary* and asked them to verify whether these were like other statements (for example *Mary hit John* and *Mary was hit by John*). Children's performance in this task was very poor. They were much better at deciding whether a picture was congruent with a sentence they had heard. In subsequent studies Olson (1974) explored the conditions under which children of the same age could make accurate sentence-sentence verifications. When he systematically increased the richness of the children's situation or knowledge context, performance consistently improved. Performance was lowest when arbitrary names (John and Mary, for example) were used; it was improved by simply including known characters, even though the events remained arbitrary. The addition of a story context in which both characters and their relations were nonarbitrary further facilitated the children's performances. In short, the nature of the cognitive situation in which the sentences were embedded affected the children's ability to deal with so-called syntactic (active-passive) relationships among the sentences. These results support the notion that as one moves to younger subjects language comprehension becomes even more situation bound.

Predictably, the most extreme dependence on the situation occurs during the early stages of language acquisition. As MacNamara (1972, p. 1) suggests, "The infant uses meaning as a clue to language, rather than language as a clue to meaning" (see also De Villiers and De Villiers 1974; Dore et al. 1976; Nelson 1974; Wells 1974). In general, the infant must have some clue to the intended significance of a speaker's utterance in order to determine what the words mean (or even that they are used to mean; note, for example, Keller 1903). This dependence on nonlinguistic situational support exists at many levels of language acquisition. For example, Bloom (1974) notes that her daughter first recognized the word "birds" in the context of a mobile above her dressing table and the word "music" in the context of the record player in her room. Bloom states, "She did not recognize the words 'birds' and 'music' in any situations other than her mobile and her record player for many months" (p. 289).

Reich (1976) discusses a related situation. He played a game called "Where?" with his eight-month-old child, Adam. He would say "Where is mommy?" and

Adam would crawl to his mother, "Where's the bed?" and Adam would crawl to the bed. Reich's discussion focused on Adam's understanding of "shoes." When asked "Where's the shoes?", Adam would crawl to his mother's closet and play with the shoes that were lined up on the rack (the game was played in the bedroom). When Adam was placed by the open door of his father's closet and asked "Where's the shoes?", he would not play with those shoes but instead would proceed to his mother's closet and play with hers. Indeed, when a pair of his mother's shoes was placed near him in the middle of the bedroom and he was asked "Where's the shoes?", Adam would still go to the shoes in his mother's closet. Adam's understanding of shoes involved a whole action sequence that was strongly linked with his mother's closet. Only gradually did Adam begin to understand that shoes could include those in daddy's closet, those in the middle of the floor, and those that someone was wearing at the time.

Situation-specific linguistic abilities can be illustrated in the domain of speech production as well as comprehension. For example, Bloom, Hood and Lightbown (1974; cited in Bloom 1974) played a "Simple Simon" game of imitation with Peter (age thirty-two months, two weeks) in which they presented sentences such as the following: *This is broken, I'm trying to get this cow in here, I'm gonna get the cow to drink milk, you make him stand up over there.* Peter's imitations were (respectively) as follows: *What's broken, Cow in here, Get the cow to drink milk, Stand up there.* As Bloom (1974) notes, such imitation data suggest that Peter had not yet developed certain levels of linguistic competence (he apparently lacked a consistent use of the copula *is* and lacked causal connectives like *trying, gonna,* and *make*). However, each of the sentences that the experimenter had presented for imitation were examples of utterances that Peter himself had spontaneously produced at a previous time. For example, Peter had said "I'm gonna get the cow to drink milk" while returning to a toy cow with some toy barrels fetched from a sack. Similarly, Peter said, "You make him stand up over there" while trying to get the experimenter to spread an animal's legs so that it could stand in a spot Peter had cleared. These data provide a striking illustration of the importance of external and internalized situational knowledge on linguistic performance (see Slobin and Welsh 1973). Labov (1970) has supplied similar illustrations of the critical importance of situational considerations in his criticism of research purporting to show a linguistic deficit in the language abilities of many black Americans (see also Cole and Bruner 1971).

In general, initial comprehension abilities seem closely tied to particular situational settings and domains of knowledge. Chapman (this volume) provides an excellent discussion of situation-dependent comprehension. It seems doubtful that the ability to understand adequately sentences out of context is a prerequisite to deeper levels of understanding. Instead, the ability to understand isolated sentences seems to result from processes underlying the development of linguistic expertise. Factors influencing one's abilities to comprehend without the need for explicit situational support will be discussed in the next section.

To summarize, initial abilities to understand through the medium of language appear to be situationally dependent. The ability to understand isolated words and sentences seems to develop from more primary, conceptually dependent ways of knowing (see Bever 1970; Bloom 1974; Chapman 1974; MacNamara 1972; Nelson 1974; Sinclair-de Zwart 1969 for further discussion). Comprehension is therefore not a unitary phenomenon. For example, children may be able to understand and communicate in some circumstances (in situations with rich social-perceptual support) yet have great difficulty in others. Assessments of comprehension difficulties may actually reveal problems of understanding and communicating in certain types of situations rather than reveal intrinsic linguistic deficits (Bloom 1974; Labov 1970).

The studies cited in this section suggest that externally and internally defined situations can affect comprehension of inputs. They can affect one's ability to recognize a word (Bloom 1974), produce utterances (Bloom, Hood, and Lightbown 1974), judge intersentential relationships (Olson 1974), or affect the speed with which one can comprehend (Clark 1973). This section therefore focused on situational prerequisites to comprehension, while the previous section focused on the influence of inputs on one's comprehension of the immediate situation. One's momentary situation can both clarify and be clarified by inputs. The next section sketches a framework for growth that integrates these two influences. Through this assimilative-accommodatory process (in Piagetian terms) one can move to a point where one can understand things in new ways.

Toward a Framework for Conceptualizing Growth
The framework sketched in this section for schematizing the growth problem, the problem of how one comes to understand things that one did not previously understand or how one comes to understand things in new ways, focuses on the reciprocal influences of situation on input and input on situation. Emphasis is placed on those situation-input relations that take one beyond one's current state of knowing and allow better comprehension of subsequent events. Our views of the types of changes or growth that permit such transfer will be contrasted with views assuming that learning simply involves amassing a storehouse of more and more knowledge or facts (see also Bransford, Nitsch, and Franks, forthcoming).

SCHEMATIZING THE GROWTH PROBLEM
It seems intuitively reasonable to assume that one needs appropriate knowledge in order to understand inputs. For example, Einstein's knowledge of relativistic physics permitted him to understand events in ways different from someone who lacks that knowledge. Someone else who acquires this knowledge should also be able to understand. It is tempting to conceptualize growth as the accumulation of more and more knowledge, but there are problems with such descriptions. When it is said that someone has come to understand something because he or she was given the knowledge to understand it, it is presupposed that the person can and does understand the new knowledge that was given. Entailed in this presupposition is the problem that needs to be explained. Similarly, the statement that some knowledge is easier to acquire than other knowledge because the former is more meaningful also presupposes that which needs explanation. As Jenkins (1974)

warned, meaningfulness is not a property of stimuli. How might the growth process be conceptualized in order to make these issues clearer?

In a previous section it was argued that the minimal unit for analyzing comprehension must involve the relationship between one's current cognitive-perceptual situation (or perspective) and subsequent inputs. The proposed growth schema is organized around an analysis of situation-input relations in order to emphasize that one not only learns *from* experience, one also learns *to* experience. One's momentary situation or perspective affects how inputs are experienced, which determines what is learned from the experience. The reciprocal influences of situation on input (assimilation) and input on situation (accommodation) are assumed to lead to a remodeling or redefinition of one's current perspective so that subsequent inputs can now be understood (and learned from) in new ways. This schematization is therefore neither solely empiricistic nor rationalistic. It is neither solely deductive nor inductive, but perhaps more equivalent to Peirce's (1932) notion of abduction. The schema highlights the relatively gradual "bootstrapping" nature of the growth process and focuses attention on the situational support necessary to learn effectively from exposure and practice. It also directs attention to questions about the nature of the changes in the system that permit transfer to occur.

EXEMPLIFICATION AS AN ILLUSTRATION OF ABDUCTION

The abduction schema is best illustrated by considering one of the most intuitively powerful means for helping someone come to understand something, the use of examples.[2] Listeners frequently know what speakers said yet need one or more examples in order to grasp adequately the intended message. Recent research by Pollchik (1975) documents the powerful effects that examples can have for helping people come to understand textual material in a manner that permits transfer, that permits them to understand subsequent statements and examples in new ways.

As an illustration of the process of exemplification, assume that one wished to use examples to communicate the concept of abduction (sketched above) to college sophomores. Initially, they hear the description of the concept stating that the minimal unit of analysis is a situation-input relation, that situations clarify inputs and inputs further clarify situations, and that this approach to learning is an abductive characterization of the growth process. Given this information, they might understand what was said. However, if someone simply stopped with this description, the students would be likely to ask, "So what?" They would need to know something more in order to understand what the concept could mean. Similarly, the students could memorize the description and hence be able to talk and think about it at some level. However, what significance would this knowledge have?

[2]Exemplification is not to be equated with abduction because the latter concept has a broader range of application. One can make an abductive analysis of other communicative techniques in addition to those that explicitly utilize examples. One can analyze the nature of analogy, well-structured discourse that is relevant to a particular audience, or well-written texts. Nevertheless, most of this discussion will center around exemplification. This discussion will set the stage for clarifying the relation between abduction and analogies or texts.

How could it become something they use to think "in terms of" (Bransford, Nitsch, and Franks, forthcoming) or "know with" rather than something they merely "know about"?

A basic process involved in communicating the abduction concept (or any new concept) is essentially to point to certain phenomena and say, "There, that's an example of what I mean. There's another, and another." This process of pointing to phenomena looks like nothing more than simple ostensive definition. It is easy to interpret the resulting learning processes as one of forming associations between a concept label (such as abduction) and various referents. However, assumptions about the formation and storage of word-referent associations are insufficient for understanding the growth processes by which information can become useful for clarifying subsequent events.

Consider what is involved in utilizing exemplification to help communicate the abduction concept. The descriptive information about the concept is assumed to become part of an individual's situation or perspective. This initial information affects how the individual understands the inputs or examples that are pointed to, while the examples in turn further clarify the concept. It is through the reciprocal influences of concept on examples and examples on concept (or situation on input and input on situation) that one gradually becomes able to use the concept (in this case abduction) and hence understand subsequent inputs in new ways.

The effects of initial knowledge of a concept on examples is analogous to the effects of labels on droodles. Assume that one tells a comprehender to notice the umbrella in the drawing presented in figure 1. A listener is likely to say, "I don't see what you mean." However, if the drawing is presented as an example of a bear climbing up the opposite side of a tree, one perceives the drawing differently—a restructuring occurs.

The abduction schema can be viewed as a potential alternative to other basic paradigms for conceptualizing acquisition, for example, paired-associate learning or the establishment of word-referent associations. From the present perspective, assumptions that people learn the meaning of a word like "dog" (or a word like "abduction") by associating the label with concrete referents ignore two important points. First, learners' momentary perspective affects how they understand the referents (or examples) and hence what they learn from them. Second, what is learned is not simply a list of examples that are attached to a concept label. One also learns what the examples are examples of. Thus, knowledge of the concept becomes refined (made more precise and more useful) in the process of comprehending the examples.

Consider the first point. Imagine that a speaker says, "Notice the sepia," while pointing to a complex painting (Hester, 1977). A listener who does not know that sepia refers to a color (and more specifically, to a brownish color), will have difficulty understanding the significance of the pointing act and hence fail to see what the speaker intends. As Wittgenstein (1953) argued, even ostensive definition (saying "This is red" while pointing to something colored red) presupposes that one has some knowledge of what the ostensibly defined thing is supposed to be an example of (in this case, color). Knowledge of the category color affects one's

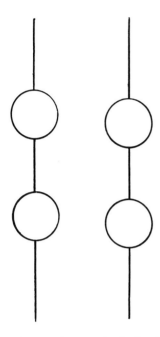

Figure 1. An example of a droodle.

understanding of the object of the pointing gesture, which in turn clarifies one's understanding of the color red.

This emphasis on the perspective from which one views examples becomes especially important when attempting to understand initial language acquisition. One must focus on those nonlinguistic actions and events that children understand in their social-perceptual environment in order to clarify the perspective from which they grasp the significance of linguistic utterances. For example, Hoffman (1968; cited in MacNamara 1972) discusses some of the errors that frequently occur during the language acquisition period. A seventeen-month-old child used the word *hot* as the name for *stove*. Perhaps as the child was about to touch the stove an adult had said "hot." To this child, the significance of the utterance could easily have been understood as the name for *stove*. Of course, if the adult had instead said "no, no, hot" and displayed considerable affect, the child might well have understood that the significance of the word *hot* was not as a name for an object. Social-perceptual information (from the external environment) is an integral part of a child's momentary perspective. This in turn affects the child's understanding of linguistic utterances (Bates 1976; Bloom, this volume; Chapman, this volume; Nelson, 1974, forthcoming).

The abduction schema stresses that one's momentary situation or perspective not only affects comprehension of subsequent inputs (examples), but that the inputs further clarify one's perspective. It is through this reciprocal, assimilative-accommodatory process (cf. Piaget's notion of equilibration) that one becomes able to use a concept and hence better understand subsequent events. This latter assumption reflects the second previously noted contrast between abduction and association paradigms, that one learns more than a mere list of examples attached to a concept label. As Bransford and Franks (1976) note, it is easy to assume that examples are beneficial simply because they are usually concrete and hence more easily learned and remembered. However, such explanations of the process of exemplification focus only on the acquisition and storage of facts or inputs. The abduction schema stresses that what is learned is not simply a list of facts or examples but rather a concept that transcends any enumeration of its exemplars (see Cassirer 1923). Through practice at thinking in terms of or knowing with a concept, one gradually develops usable knowledge in the form of an abstract framework or perspective to guide articulation of subsequent events. It is this acquired framework or perspective that indicates such things as what counts as distinctive features and what aspects of events are momentarily important or nonimportant (see Bransford and Franks 1976 for further discussion). In short, by coming to know with this abstract framework, one is able to understand subsequent events in new and more adequate ways

AN EXPERIMENTAL INVESTIGATION OF EXEMPLIFICATION

Mary Lessick Hannigan (1976) recently completed a dissertation that explores some problems involved in becoming able to use a concept or schema. Her studies can be viewed as an analog of the previous discussion concerning the use of examples to help students understand the abduction concept. There it was suggested that initial knowledge of the concept affects understanding of the examples, which in turn further clarifies the concept. Furthermore, the resulting changes were assumed to affect transfer, and transfer was assumed to involve something more than storage of the list of examples that was heard. Hannigan's measures of learning and transfer also explore the degree to which certain experiences can result in more direct apprehension of subsequent inputs. Her primary dependent measure was the ability to detect sentences embedded in white noise.

Group one in Hannigan's study (the no-framework group) heard a list of seventy sentences and were asked to rate them on ease of comprehension. Examples of her acquisition sentences are as follows: The man set up housekeeping in the airplane, The man threw the curtain over the metal bar. The man propped the door against the rock wall. The man thrashed the leaves with his cane. The man put the chair at the base of the tree. The man piled the bricks under the tree. The man opened his briefcase. The man turned the bell upside down. The man made a sack out of the sheet. All of these sentences are understandable in isolation. Indeed, Hannigan's subjects rated them as very easy to comprehend.

The subjects in group two (the framework group) heard the identical set of seventy acquisition sentences. However they were asked to understand each sentence as a description of survival on a deserted island and also as an illustration of one of seven particular aspects (subcategories) of survival (such as making shelter). The subjects were instructed to imagine that anything mentioned in a sentence was actually on the island, so ratings of comprehensibility should simply indicate their ability to see how a certain activity could be related to a particular subtopic. The examples and particular subtopics are as follows: *Making a shelter*. The man set up housekeeping in the airplane. The man threw the curtain over the metal bar. The man propped the door against the rock wall. *Reaching for food on a branch above your head*. The man thrashed the leaves with his cane. The man put the chair at the base of the tree. The man piled the bricks under the tree. *A container for carrying food*. The man opened his briefcase. The man turned the bell upside down. The man made a sack out of the sheet.

Understanding the preceding sentences from the perspective of survival clearly influences one's comprehension of them. This illustrates the effects of situations on the comprehension of subsequent inputs, yet inputs further clarify initial perspectives as well. In order to investigate the degree to which examples can further clarify initial concepts or schemas, Hannigan included a third group in her study, the framework-after group. These subjects heard all seventy sentences without any topic or subtopics (their task was equivalent to the no-framework subjects'). They were told about the survival topic and subtopics immediately after sentence acquisition (prior to testing). If comprehending the examples provided further clarification for the initial concept, the framework-after procedure should not provide sufficient opportunity for subjects to move beyond their normative knowledge of survival (and its seven subcategories). These subjects should therefore perform less adequately than the framework group.

Following acquisition, Hannigan compared the performance of subjects in the no-framework, framework, and framework-after conditions. As a test, she took advantage of the finding that meaningful sentences are better identified under conditions of white noise than are less meaningful sentences (Miller, Heise, and Lichten 1951). She reasoned that subjects in the framework group should now be able to understand novel but appropriate sentences that deal with aspects of survival (for example, *The man got up on the box*). If these sentences were, in fact, more meaningful for the framework group, they should be better detected in white noise.

During the test all subjects heard the same sentences embedded in white noise. Their performance was compared to a baseline group that received no initial experimental inputs prior to the detection test. Test sentences included olds (those heard by all groups except baseline), novel appropriates (appropriate in that they could be seen as related to the previous survival theme), and novel inappropriates (inappropriate in that they could not readily be seen as related to the survival theme). For example, *The man put the eraser under the table* was a novel inappropriate. The subjects' task was to listen to each sentence embedded in white noise and attempt to repeat it aloud as best they could.

For old sentences, accuracy of repetition in the no-framework, framework, and framework-after groups was superior to the baseline group. In addition the framework group was better on olds than were the other two groups. All three groups were equivalent to the baseline subjects on the novel inappropriate sentences. However, the most important data involved performance on the novel appropriate test sentences. On these, the no-framework and framework-after groups were no better than the baseline group. In contrast, the framework group performed much more accurately at repeating the novel appropriate sentences. The subjects in this group were slightly less accurate on these than on olds. Nevertheless, the framework group was as accurate on novel appropriates as the no-framework group was on olds.

Subsequent experiments revealed that subjects in the no-framework and framework-after groups exhibited excellent recognition memory for the old sentences (tested without white noise). They had not simply failed to learn the inputs. However, the mere accumulation of inputs does not necessarily allow one a degree of clarity sufficient to understand something in a new way at a later point in time.

Hannigan also explored the degree to which the framework group's ability to transfer to novel appropriate sentences in white noise depended on making contact with related stored acquisition sentences. For example, the subjects may have originally heard *The man propped the door against the wall* as an example of *Making shelter* during acquisition. The novel appropriate sentence *The man leaned the car hood against the tree* is more similar to this acquisition sentence than any other. Other *Making shelter* acquisition sentences involved different types of relations (throwing a curtain over a metal box, setting up housekeeping in an airplane) that were in turn similar to other novel appropriates.

Hannigan reasoned that if transfer to a novel appropriate depended on making contact with a similar acquisition sentence, there should be strong dependencies between subjects' abilities to detect a particular acquisition sentence (an old) and its novel appropriate counterpart. Her analyses revealed no such dependencies, suggesting that memory mediation was not the basis for transfer. This is not particularly surprising, since one must interpret the novel appropriate sentences in a specific manner in order to perceive adequately their similarity to the acquisition sentences. The no-framework group subjects showed no transfer yet received identical acquisition sentence-novel appropriate counterparts. The ability to comprehend novel appropriate sentences in a particular manner is presumably what was learned by the framework subjects. This apparently provided the basis for transfer, not contact with stored acquisition sentences.

CONTEXTUAL CONSTRAINTS ON KNOWING

Hannigan's experimental paradigm raises interesting possibilities for investigating further the processes involved in acquiring knowledge in a form useful for clarifying subsequent experiences. Her framework group illustrates processes of exemplification, but the general principles of abduction apply to other communicative techniques as well. Consider the use of metaphor and analogy. Here a speaker utilizes already known information about some domain X in order to clarify some subsequent domain Y. Learners' understanding of the Y domain is thus influenced by their momentary perspective (which includes X). At the same time, information about Y may further clarify and articulate previous information about X (Hesse 1966; Verbrugge, 1977).

Similar analyses can be made of well-structured discourse and text. The understood significance of any sentence is influenced by the text or discourse structure in which it is embedded, yet each sentence may further clarify this overall structure. The basic purpose of effective communicative techniques is to marshal a listeners' momentary assets so that these can be used to understand subsequent inputs, which can in turn clarify and restructure their initial knowledge. Hannigan's results suggest that such clarifications are not simply a function of having stored particular propositions in memory. Her framework subjects appeared to acquire a more abstract framework or perspective that guided their comprehension of subsequent inputs. Similar analyses of what is learned may be necessary in order to characterize how people can learn from discourse and texts in a manner that permits them to transfer to subsequent events.

Hannigan's experiments also provide a reference point for identifying additional factors that must be considered in order to understand better the growth of comprehension abilities. At least two additional factors appear relevant to this discussion. The first involves a fine grained analysis of the process by which people develop usable knowledge of a concept. The second involves the contextual constraints under which particular acts of knowing can occur.

Hypotheses regarding the first factor have been discussed elsewhere (Bransford and Franks 1976; Bransford, Nitsch, and Franks, forthcoming). During early stages of acquisition, knowledge of a concept seems to be closely tied to the original situation in which it was exemplified. For example, Bransford and Franks (1976) discuss students' early knowledge of a concept like operant shaping. They note that an instructor's initial requests for a definition frequently elicited statements like the following: "It's like when you want a rat to press a bar and you give him food for first orienting to the bar, then gradually approaching it. . . ." The ability to apprehend the meaning of the concept seemed to depend on mediating steps involving retrieval of context-specific conditions under which the concept was originally learned (Bransford and Franks 1976; Bransford, Nitsch, and Franks, forthcoming).

The question of the contextual constraints under which concepts can be used is closely related to the preceding discussion. This question involves contextual constraints on the range of possible conditions under which one can spontaneously carry out certain acts of knowing. For example, Hannigan's framework and framework-after subjects were explicitly informed that many of their test sentences would be related to the concept of survival on a deserted island. It is interesting to consider the limited extent to which their laboratory-gained knowledge might spontaneously affect their comprehension of subsequent, real-world experiences. Pushing this question even further, could certain contextual conditions be necessary in order even to recognize the meaning of a previously learned concept?

The following example suggests that the identification of a concept can be context dependent. One of the authors supplied members of an introductory freshman seminar with a list of concepts that had been discussed during the semester. An example was *ablation*. No one in the class knew its meaning until the instructor said, "Of course you do, think of when we discussed ways to study how various parts of the brain affect behavior." Given this contextual support, over half the class "lit up" and said "oh yea" (or some reasonable paraphrase). They could then discuss the concept. This observation seems analogous to studies of early language acquisition discussed above where the ability to perform certain acts of comprehension (recognition or production) seems context dependent. Additional observations suggest that many concepts employed by adults may be context or domain specific as well. For example, concepts or principles used to describe wartime activities may become ambiguous or anomalous when applied to everyday activities (*We had to destroy the city in order to save it*), and psychological concepts that seem perfectly clear in the context of laboratory experiments may become ambiguous when applied to everyday life. On the positive side, one may import a concept used in one domain (such as physics) to another domain (such as psychology) and thereby clarify a number of inadequately understood phenomena. The processes by which people expand ("decontextualize") their comprehension abilities seems to be an extremely important area to understand.

Why should people contextualize their knowledge in the first place? We suggest two possible reasons. The first is that people must learn information in some context and may have difficulty resisting contextual influence (see Tulving and Thomson 1973 on "encoding specificity"). This seems especially true for younger children. The second reason stems from some informal pilot studies on vocabulary acquisition. If one must learn a number of new concepts, interference among them is minimized when the concepts are dissimilar. Presenting each concept in a distinct domain of application seems to facilitate the acquisition process. However, the ability to generate a definition or example of a newly acquired concept does not necessarily indicate the degree to which one can sufficiently use it in order to clarify a new domain or situation. For example, our informal data indicates that if people acquire the meaning of "lem" (a verb) in the context of antique dealers, they have great difficulty in initially using it to understand sentences about cowboys or sailors, despite the fact that the basic concept is readily applicable.

Further study of the processes by which people expand or decontextualize their ability to know with concepts and principles might have important educational implications. Note, for example, that traditional flash card drills may not be the most beneficial method for promoting the growth of flexibly usable knowledge. Our pilot studies indicate that subjects can become quite adept at recognizing new words (for instance *lem*) and at stating their definitions and providing examples. However, each act of recognition can involve the recreation of a particular domain of application (such as the subject always thinking of the verb *lem* in terms of antique dealers). This appears to inhibit the ability to apply the concept to some new domain (such as sailors). Such limits on flexibility become important when one considers skilled acts of comprehension, for example, reading. Skilled readers do not simply recognize words; instead they understand the significance of inputs for clarifying the topic of concern. Readers must also be able to read about numerous topics and so need a flexible ability to use the words they know.

Although further research is clearly needed, it is possible that traditional flash card techniques might be more useful if inputs were presented in some meaningful context and students were asked to judge whether the inputs were appropriate in that context (for example, Could these items be used on a picnic?). Such a procedure could make one's apprehension of inputs an activity that is related to the purpose of an overall theme or topic, as in reading and comprehending. By varying the contextual settings in the exercises, students might be helped to develop a flexible ability to use what they know.

KNOWING WHAT TO DO IN ORDER TO UNDERSTAND

Previous discussion focused on abduction as an abstract characterization of the processes by which one can come to understand things differently (and more adequately). However, questions about those processes that may provide the major contributions to the development and maintenance of expertise have not been discussed. These questions involve the problem of learning how to structure situations actively in order to bring oneself to a point where adequate understanding is possible. For example, the development of comprehension skills seems to be more closely related to the ability to ask relevant questions (of oneself and others) than to the ability to state factual content. What are the prerequisities for actively doing something (for example, asking questions) in order to understand better?

One prerequisite would seem to be realizing that a particular domain is indeed comprehensible. In his book *How Children Fail*, Holt (1964) argues that many children do not even realize that certain domains (such as mathematics) could be comprehensible. Such children exhibit different patterns of problem-solving activities from those who have some grasp of the notion that these domains should make sense (see also Bransford, Nitsch, and Franks, forthcoming, for discussion).

A second prerequisite appears to be the possession of criteria for evaluating the adequacy of one's present understanding. For the case of linguistic comprehension, such criteria must involve much more than the ability to distinguish between acceptable and anomalous statements. One can understand a statement at some level yet inadequately grasp a speaker or writer's intended meaning. Theoretically there is a need to differentiate the problem of the correctness or veridicality of comprehension from the problem of the feeling of understanding. Comprehenders who feel they understand will not perform any additional activities that might be necessary in order to grasp the point that the speaker actually intends.

Consider the following passage generated by Bransford, Johnson, and McCarrell (cf. Bransford and McCarrell 1974, p. 214):

The man was worried. His car came to a halt and he was all alone. It was extremely dark and cold. The man took off his overcoat, rolled down the window, and got out of the car as quickly as possible. Then he used all his strength to move as fast as he could. He was relieved when he finally saw the lights of the city, even though they were far away.

College subjects heard this passage and were asked if they felt they adequately understood it. All said "Yes." However, their confident feelings of understanding could be easily dispelled. When the subjects were asked questions such as "Why did the man take off his overcoat?" and "Why did he roll down the window?", they suddenly realized they did not adequately understand the passage. For example, some subjects noted that taking off the coat seemed strange since the passage stated that the weather was cold. Given the above mentioned questions, some subjects (but a very few in this study) suddenly realized that the man's car must have fallen into the water. This reinterpretation of the story permitted the coat and window questions to be easily answered. Without these questions, however, all subjects seemed content with their initial feelings that they had indeed understood.

The criteria utilized in assessing feelings of understanding seem flexible. They vary as a function of the cognitive-perceptual situation in which inputs occur as well as with the nature of the input itself. For example, subjects in Hannigan's no-framework group rated the acquisition sentences as more comprehensible than did subjects in the framework group, despite the fact that subjects in the latter group were far superior in the transfer test. We have conducted a study indicating that college subjects in an experimental context rate the sentence *Bill has a red car* as very easy to understand. Are particular criteria for understanding employed when one is in an experimental task?

Contrast the comprehension of sentences in an experimental context with one in which the situation is a social context. As mentioned above, Bransford, McCarrell, and Nitsch (1976) carried out such experiments. One involved the sentence *Bill has a red car*. In the experiment, a colleague (hereafter C) was sitting in his office. A friend (hereafter E) walked in and uttered *Bill has a red car*. C's reactions were interesting:

He looked very surprised, paused for about three seconds, and finally exclaimed "What the hell are you talking about?" After a hasty debriefing session C laughed and told the E what had gone on in his head. First, C thought that E was talking about a person named Bill that C knew. Then C realized that E could not in all probability know that person; and besides, Bill would never buy a red car. Then C thought that E may have mixed up the name and really meant to say J (a mutual friend of C and E). The C knew that J had ordered a new car, but he was surprised that it was red and that it had arrived so soon. The C also entertained a few additional hypotheses—all within about three seconds of time. After that he gave up, thereupon uttering "What the hell are you talking about?" (p. 340).[3]

It is instructive to consider the differences in comprehending *Bill has a red car* in the experimental as opposed to the social situation. In the first instance the subjects comprehended; in the second the subject did not. Do we simply classify the second instance as an error or failure and the first as a success? Is it better to understand than to fail to understand?

Note the subject's activities in the social situation. He had some well-specified criteria about what he needed to know in order to feel that he understood the speaker. For example, he was not willing to accept that Bill was someone unknown to him; he wanted to know which particular Bill. He even realized the possibility that the speaker had not said what he meant. In short, the colleague tacitly entertained questions of clarification like "Wait a minute, I don't understand who

---

[3]The page number cited for this quotation refers to the published version of this manuscript in French translation. Copies of the article are available in English from the authors.

Bill is. Did you mean to say another name rather than Bill?" In contrast, subjects in the experimental situation seemed perfectly comfortable with their shallow understanding of the *Bill* sentence. The information they received was sufficient given their cognitive-perceptual situation at the time.

It seems clear that the sophistication of one's comprehension activities does not necessarily correlate with success versus failure to understand at any particular moment. There is a need to explore what sophisticated comprehenders do in order to generate interesting questions regarding particular (and perhaps previously accepted) domains of knowledge. It is possible that such styles of knowing might then be facilitated by effective teaching.

We have taken some very modest and simple steps in this direction. We asked how college freshmen might be helped to learn to learn from and evaluate written material. Blumenthal's (1970) translation of Buhler's theory of comprehension was selected as the textual material. We asked whether certain personal experiences might provide a framework for understanding the significance of Buhler's theory as well as evaluating its adequacy. Our assumption was that more accomplished comprehenders might spontaneously relate what they read to other domains of knowledge (such as personal experiences) and hence understand more adequately. Before presenting Buhler's text, the students were provided with one of two different experiences. They were then instructed to attempt to understand the Buhler text in relation to their particular experience and the differences in what they learned were assessed.

Prior to reading the text, all students heard a potentially incomprehensible passage (Brasnford and Johnson's 1972; 1973, *washing clothes* passage) and were asked to recall it. However, students in group one heard the passage with the topic and hence did not realize it might be incomprehensible. Students in group two heard the passage first without the topic and then a second time with it. They therefore experienced a failure of comprehension followed by the ability to comprehend. Students from group one were told to notice the paraphrasing that occurred in their recall. Those in group two were told to notice the feeling of not understanding followed by the ability to understand.

All students were told to attempt to relate what they would read from the Buhler passage to their prior experiences with the *washing clothes* passage. Buhler's discussion dealt with paraphrase (consonant with group one experiences) but mainly with prerequisities to comprehension (consonant with group two experiences). Hence the passage was superficially applicable to both sets of experiences, but more directly relevant to group two. Students read the passage at their own rate (overall reading times did not differ) and were then given essay questions related to what they had read.

Blind scoring of the essays revealed that students in group two were superior to group one. Group two students were better able to generate novel examples and to relate the passage to their general life experiences. Furthermore, these students spontaneously generated more questions about the degree to which Buhler's theory explained other phenomena of comprehension. The act of understanding the text in terms of real life experiences had a positive impact on their ability to go beyond the text. One of the essay questions asked subjects to state their feelings about the experiment plus passage experience. The following is a spontaneous comment from one of the group two students:

The idea of the shared field [a concept from the Buhler passage] especially struck me after the description [the washing clothes passage] we listened to earlier. The paragraph [the washing clothes passage] did not make sense to me but once I was given a context—sharing the same field as the person that wrote the description— it made sense. This idea of a shared field or experience seems obvious, but was one I had never really thought about.
I also knew what was meant by the separation of word perception and sentence comprehension because the same thing happened to me while listening to the clothes-washing passage. I understood every word yet was confused.
Also going through that "experience" helped me to understand the article. It was a very abstract article and if I hadn't had a concrete example to identify with, most of it would have been meaningless to me. As it was, when something was described that happened to me, the whole thing had more meaning.

The above mentioned investigation suggests that one aspect of skilled compre-hension involves acts of relating inputs to other domains and experiences. Effective comprehenders may do this spontaneously. Questions about ways to help people learn what to do in order to further their understanding seem important to pursue.

In this section, an abduction framework for conceptualizing problems of growth and transfer was proposed. It was argued that one not only learns *from* experience, one learns *to* experience. One's momentary situation or perspective affects the ways in which one experiences subsequent inputs, which in turn further clarify one's perspective. Through this reciprocal, assimilative-accommodatory process, one's perspective may be redefined or remodeled, thereby allowing one to understand subsequent inputs in new ways.

Acts of exemplification were analyzed in terms of the abduction framework. An example is both clarified by one's perspective and further clarifies that perspective. Similar analyses can be made for the communicative efficiency of analogies, well-structured discourse, and well-written texts. The abduction schema was contrasted with other traditional paradigms for conceptualizing acquisition, for example, paired-associate learning and the acquisition of word-referent associations. The latter seem inadequate for conceptualizing preconditions for meaningful acquisi-tion (see MacNamara 1972) as well as for characterizing what is learned (one does not simply learn a list of concept-example associations). Hannigan's (1976) studies were cited as experimental investigations of the processes by which subjects can come to understand things differently. Her analyses suggested that transfer (for the framework group) was not mediated by contact with stored examples that the subjects had previously learned.

Two additional problems involved in the growth of understanding were con-sidered. The first involved contextual constraints on people's abilities to perform certain acts of knowing. Contrary to many models (Collins and Loftus 1975; Smith, Shoben, and Rips 1974), knowledge may not exist in one unified (and completely interrelated) semantic or conceptual memory. Both children and adults sometimes appear to need explicit contextual or situational support in order to utilize effectively aspects of their knowing abilities. The processes by which people expand (decontextualize) their abilities to use certain types of information was cited as an important problem to pursue.

The second problem considered involved the processes by which comprehenders learn to structure situations actively in order to facilitate their own understanding. It was suggested that the development of comprehension skills seems more related to the ability to ask appropriate questions than the ability to state factual content. The criteria utilized to modulate feelings of understanding seem to be flexible and depend on one's current perspective or situation. Research is needed in order to assess what accomplished comprehenders do in order to understand inputs effectively. Appropriate educational techniques that facilitate acquisition of such activities might then be devised.

Toward a Framework for Understanding Assessment and Intervention
We have discussed problems of comprehension from a global perspective. The guiding question has been how one can come to understand things that one could not previously understand or how one can come to understand things in new ways. It has been emphasized that the minimal unit of analysis must always be in terms of the relationship between one's cognitive-perceptual situation and inputs. One implication of this orientation is that meaning is not something possessed by stimuli or inputs or something stored solely within the organism. Meaning resides in organism-environment relations. From this perspective, growth does not result from the mere accumulation of inputs and their meanings. To help persons change or grow, one must focus on those relationships between their current cognitive-perceptual situation and inputs that permit them to acquire information in a form useful for understanding subsequent inputs in new ways.

In the introduction to this chapter it was noted that effective teachers use a variety of intuitively based techniques for helping students come to understand things. Theoretical psychology should ideally provide a framework that helps clarify those intuitions about effective and ineffective modes of facilitation and intervention. Some reasons why theoretical psychology (at least the adult, cognitive literature) fails to provide a coherent framework suitable for this purpose has been discussed elsewhere (Bransford, Nitsch, and Franks, forthcoming). In general, the failure revolves around the lack of explicit concern with problems of growth. This chapter represents an attempt to focus more directly on growth problems. In this section some potential implications for the school and clinic are presented. Like the discussion of comprehension, these implications will be at a macrolevel.

AN EXAMPLE OF INTERVENTION
Anita Willis, an undergraduate student at Vanderbilt, recently completed a project aimed at teaching new vocabulary items to a boy diagnosed as developmentally delayed. Although we were not involved in the project, we were struck with Willis's observations and tentative conclusions. She warns that her study was

informal and that she lacks hard data to back up her observations, but her experiences provide valuable hints about what someone might look for in order to understand intervention processes in more detail.

Willis worked with a male who was three years, nine months of age and had been diagnosed as developmentally delayed. At the beginning of the intervention project the boy's behavior was very erratic. He engaged in considerable self-stimulation behavior and exhibited an extremely short attention span, although this varied depending on the task and mood. The boy was easily excited and often difficult to calm down. He did have some receptive vocabulary; Willis's goal was to help him learn some new words.

Willis utilized the training technology generally referred to as behavior modification. She was aware that, as powerful a technique as this is, its success depends on the sophistication of its user. She therefore began by observing the thirteen children in her toddler group and noted their reactions in and out of behavioral modification sessions. She felt that the children did not really understand what their teachers wanted them to learn. For example, she noted that the children frequently performed an activity inappropriately yet clapped their hands mimicking the social praise they had received in training sessions. Furthermore she observed that children frequently performed a task correctly yet remained uncertain (as evidenced by a blank face or a questioning look) until the teacher clapped or in some way praised the child. At this point the child would realize that he or she had responded correctly and his or her facial expression would change. How might one bring children to a point where they have their own criteria for knowing whether their actions are appropriate? How might one make events more meaningful for children?

Willis decided to teach the child to understand words like *comb*, *brush*, and *mirror*. One might do this by placing objects on a table and teaching the child to respond correctly to requests like "Hand me the comb," but Willis did not proceed in this way. Instead she fashioned a minienvironment consisting of a small room equipped with such items as a comb and brush and a mirror on the wall in which the boy could see himself. She wanted to help the boy come to understand this environment and to teach him more about language in this context.

Willis noted that in the beginning of the sessions the boy exhibited extremely erratic behavior and was very inattentive. The objects seemed to have no meaning to him and he kept them in his mouth more often than not. However with each session the boy became more attentive. He kept the objects out of his mouth more and more and was observant when Willis used the comb and brush. Soon he was combing Willis's hair as well as his own. She notes that he became increasingly conscious of his image in the mirror and watched himself using the comb and brush. Throughout these sessions Willis would say things that were meaningful in the context of the child's actions (such as "You're using the comb very well") and would reinforce the child when he could respond to requests (such as "Where's the brush?"). All this training was done in an environment that was becoming increasingly meaningful to the child.

In the final session Willis tested the child's ability to understand the words and requests she had taught him. For example, she made requests like "Please hand me the brush." The child carried out the correct actions without hesitation. Willis was more impressed by the look on the child's face when he performed the actions than the mere correctness of these actions. These facial expressions demonstrated to Willis that the boy knew he was performing correctly. He still enjoyed and responded to the social praise from Willis, but the look of understanding occurred before Willis provided social praise.

INTERVENTION AND SIMPLE TASKS

At a global level, Willis's procedure can be viewed as an attempt to simulate some of those conditions under which language acquisition occurs naturally. She first helped the child come to understand a particular nonlinguistic situation. Given this cognitive-perceptual situation, the significance of linguistic utterances could be better understood and could further clarify the boy's situation as well (including the nature of his relationship with Willis). Note, however, that she created an extremely simple environment for the child. The child was able to come to understand this environment and his place in it, but it may have been very difficult for him to come to understand an environment that was more complex. The notion of beginning with a simplified situation and building on it seems intuitively obvious, and it follows from the present emphasis on situation-input relations. However, this usage of simplicity differs in important ways from many other uses of the term.

McCarrell and Brooks (1975) provide an insightful analysis of prevalent theoretical conceptions of simple versus complex processes. They note that many theories view development as hierarchical in nature. Development is characterized as progressing from simple to more complex ways of processing information, and the simpler processes are assumed to be prerequisites for the more complex. The important point is that these simpler processes are viewed as involving something like copying. For example, McCarrell and Brooks cite Gagne (1970), who identifies the representational copying of stimulus-response connections as a prerequisite for higher learning; Berlyne (1965), who claims that basic associations provide the building blocks for subsequent thought and actions; and Jensen (1970; 1972), who distinguishes between level one and level two abilities. Level one abilities are assumed to involve only minimal processing of data and establish simple and direct stimulus-response correspondences. Level two abilities involve more sophisticated elaborations of inputs.

McCarrell and Brooks's analysis highlights some basic assumptions underlying many theories of development. From their perspective as well as our present orientation, such assumptions are highly questionable. The argument is not against intuitive assumptions about building blocks or prerequisites for further understanding. Instead, the argument is against equating these building blocks with basic processes of copying or forming simple stimulus-response connections. It is not at all clear that these are the basic processes that are prerequisites to higher order understanding and thought.

Note, for example, that Willis's project involved an attempt to eliminate the painstaking procedure of acquiring meaningless associations. She did not experimentally contrast the effectiveness of her procedure with other possible approaches, but there is sufficient literature to suggest that meaningful entities are learned much more readily. For example, Johnson et al. (1974) show that repetitions produce greater recall increments over trials if one is exposed to meaningful as opposed to less meaningful materials. Similarly, recent research in animal learning (see Garcia and Koelling 1966; Seligman and Hager 1972) suggests that the speed of learning can vary tremendously depending on the degree to which stimulus-response pairings are ecologically significant or meaningful to the organism. This ecological significance is frequently due to the genetic preattunement of the organism (which forms part of its situation), yet it can depend on previous experiences as well (Birch 1945). Finally, the data from Bloom, Hood, and Lightbown (1974) showed that their subject, Peter, was quite poor at simply copying or repeating a set of target sentences, even though these sentences were ones that he had spontaneously produced at a previous time. He had produced these in a meaningful context, but in the copying task this contextual information was not supplied.

One can understand why notions like nonelaborative copying might be mistakenly viewed as a prerequisite for higher order thinking and understanding. For example, if unsophisticated college sophomores are presented with a statement like *The Tao that can be spoken is not the great Tao*, the best they might be expected to be able to do is repeat the sentence or perhaps paraphrase it at a linguistic level. In contrast, a more sophisticated student of Eastern philosophy could elaborate on the statement and better explain what it means. It therefore looks as if copying occurs before more elaborative and meaningful understanding. However, this latter analysis ignores the fact that understanding also affects copying and memorizing. For example, considerable development must take place in order to know how to memorize explicitly (Brown 1975; Flavell and Wellman, forthcoming), and it is easier to remember things that one understands. The fact that there are prerequisites for effective copying suggests that copying per se cannot be the most basic process upon which everything else is dependent.

From this perspective, one's ability to deal with information depends on the relationship between the inputs and one's momentary cognitive-perceptual situation. If one's situation includes knowledge of Eastern philosophy, one will be able to expand on a statement about the Tao. Yet even the less sophisticated student's ability to copy these sentences presupposes knowledge of language as well as an understanding of the nature of memory tasks. Surely one would not want to claim that the student who could only repeat the sentence had some deficiency in more elaborative thought processes. What one can do depends on the relationship between an input and one's current cognitive-perceptual situation.

PROBLEMS IN ASESSING "WHERE PEOPLE ARE"

In the context of the above mentioned college students, it seems absurd to talk about cognitive deficits. No one would consider using such data as evidence that one student could think better than the other. However, assumptions about cognitive deficits are frequently made in situations that seem directly analogous to the *Tao* example noted above.

Assume that one is attempting to assess children's abilities to think (solve problems) at various age levels. Younger children will usually perform more poorly than older children. It is therefore easy to believe that they must develop more complex thought processes before they can perform adequately in these tasks. Similarly, it is easy to assume that children who perform below their normal age group are deficient in certain cognitive skills (see Cole and Bruner 1971 for a criticism of similar assumptions affecting cross-cultural research). According to the present orientation, such conclusions require serious reconsideration. Are current inabilities to perform a result of inherent deficits in thought processes or of differences in the relationships between inputs and a person's current cognitive-perceptual situation? Until the latter can be carefully analyzed, we have no idea of what deficit means.

Research by Odom and his colleagues (Odom and Mumbauer 1971; Odom, Astor, and Cunningham 1975) is very important in this context. In essence, their position is that one must carefully analyze a child's current situation in order to understand what he or she can do. Their method is to determine those aspects of the environment that are perceptually salient to individual children. Salience does not refer simply to what children can discriminate perceptually; it refers to those dimensions of stimulation that an individual child automatically notices and to which he or she attends. By first independently assessing saliency preferences for each child, Odom and his colleagues have been able to measure children's abilities to perform tasks (for example, a Piagetian matrix problem) that contain critical information that is either congruent or incongruent with children's saliency preferences. Their data strongly suggest that children as young as four years can perform in highly effective and sophisticated manners when task solutions require attention to dimensions that are highly salient for the individual child.

It is intriguing to compare Odom's results with the conclusion reached by de Groot (1966) in his studies comparing expert or master chess players with lesser skilled players. Why were experts so much better than lesser experts at determining the best move? His original hypothesis was they "thought more elaborately or deeply," but he found no evidence to support this conclusion. Instead he concluded that experts actually perceived the total chess board in a much more adequate manner. Their superiority in problem solving was due to the fact that they began at a much "higher place."

We know that increasing experience and knowledge in a specific field (chess, for instance) has the effect that things (properties, etc.) which, at earlier stages, had to be abstracted, or even inferred are apt to be immediately perceived at later stages. To a rather large extent, *abstraction is replaced by perception*, but we do not know much about how this works, nor where the borderline lies. . . . As an effect of this replacement, a so called 'given' problem situation is not really given since *it is seen differently* by an expert than it is perceived by an unexperienced person, but we do not know much about these differences (de Groot 1966, pp. 33–34).

The preceding discussion in conjunction with arguments by Cole and Bruner

(1971) as well as Labov (1970) suggests the need for serious clarification and reconsideration of deficit hypotheses and the normatively based tests by which people's abilities are assessed. Of course, people *do* differ in their current abilities to perform particular acts of knowing in certain situations and in their current abilities to learn from certain types of instruction. However, it is not clear that this is due to some inherent deficit in their ability to think and learn. The boy Willis worked with was unable to learn language as effectively as normal children. But this does not mean that he could not learn under appropriate conditions. By beginning where he was, he could be helped to come to understand a simplified environment and further understanding could be built on that understanding. If Willis had not begun where the boy was, he might easily have remained helplessly lost.

Many have observed that experienced teachers become intuitively sensitive to assessing where students are and teach on this basis. For example, questions asked by students can reveal what they must be assuming in order to ask these questions at all. Frequently, however, education and intervention takes the form of boring, meaningless drill that fails to take the student beyond his current state of knowing. An additional problem is that students may become lost because instructional materials do not allow children to use what they already know in order to understand effectively. Imagine, for example, a paragraph describing various activities of six people. If adults hear such a passage, they find it almost impossible to keep who did what straight. However, when time is taken to learn about the people and their names first, the story is readily understood. One's current knowledge must provide a basis for learning something new. Bloom (this volume) presents data indicating that children's language acquisition proceeds in such a manner. She notes that new linguistic constructions appear to be learned and applied initially in the context of linguistic and conceptual knowledge that is already well known to the child. Rather than employ intervention strategies based on normative tests and procedures, it might be more fruitful to identify those domains in which an individual performs adequately and work from there.

Summary and Conclusions

The major purpose of this chapter has been to sketch a general framework for conceptualizing problems of understanding. Since one's understanding of events changes, it seemed important to consider the problem from a perspective that is sensitive to this dynamic aspect (the problem of growth). Therefore our guiding question has been "How can we come to understand things that we did not previously understand?" or "How can we come to understand things in new ways?" The reasons for choosing to discuss understanding at this macrolevel are congruent with the types of arguments expressed in this paper. A global framework seems necessary in order to understand the meaning or significance of particular events (more specifically, the significance of various experimental results). One's framework frequently remains tacit. By attempting to make frameworks explicit, one can hope to evaluate more effectively the assumptions they entail. (See the physicist Bohm 1969 on the assumptive nature of knowing and understanding.)

The basic theme has been that understanding is a function of the reciprocal relationships between inputs and one's current cognitive-perceptual situation. The minimal unit of analysis must therefore be a situation plus an input, never the mere input. At many levels the importance of situation-input relations is obvious: What we say to young children and what we deem appropriate to teach at various age levels reflect our appreciation of the importance of these relations. As long as these assumptions remain tacit however it is easy to ignore many factors that may be crucial to understanding understanding. For example, it is easy to overlook the importance of the instructions in a sentence comprehension experiment. These instructions help define the subjects' situation so that sentences can be understood as examples of utterances that might be stated by someone, at some time, for some purpose. If one overlooks the specialized nature of the process involved in understanding sentences in this manner, it would then be easy to assume that such activities constitute the simplest and most basic form of comprehension. Higher order comprehension would then follow from this basic mode of understanding via processes of deductive inference. Someone incapable of higher order comprehension might therefore be assumed to have cognitive deficits of some kind.

Assumptions about the basic level of comprehension involved in understanding an isolated sentence like *The boy hit the ball* ignore the influence of situations on inputs. For example, a young child requires explicit social-perceptual situational support in order to understand linguistic utterances. The college freshmen presented with the term *ablation* needed certain support (such as the teacher's statement "Recall when we were discussing ways to study brain functions . . . .") in order to identify its meaning. Available situational support is necessary to realize that one needs to know something further in order to understand a speaker adequately (as in the *Bill has a red car* example). Similarly, Hannigan's subjects needed situational support (such as the survival framework) in order to understand better the significance of sentences. Situational support is also necessary in order to realize that the sentence *I had a book stolen* (cf. Chomsky 1965) is syntactically ambiguous in many ways.

As one becomes acquainted with various domains, one's need for explicit situational support decreases. For example, adults can understand numerous sentences in relative isolation. Aspects of their linguistic knowledge have become decontextualized. Similarly, the above mentioned college freshmen may eventually grasp the meaning of *ablation* without the need for such explicit situational support. Essentially, more sophisticated comprehenders (experts in a particular field) are able to supply this support on their own. The processes by which one develops expertise were discussed in terms of the concept of abduction. Acts of exemplification were analyzed in terms of this abductive schema. Hannigan's (1976) studies were used to illustrate factors involved in acquiring knowledge in a form useful for clarifying subsequent events.

One's current situation or perspective is a function of relatively invariant, partially decontextualized information plus momentary, context-specific assumptions and expectations. Many theories attempt to characterize the relatively stable or normative aspects of one's knowledge that affect how one understands. For example, theories of semantic or lexical memory attempt to describe the relatively stable structure of lexical knowledge. Such theories are characterizations of the results of previous processes of growth and decontexturalization. For example, Bolinger (1965, p. 567) refers to lexical memory as a "frozen pantomime" whose entries are "nosegays of faded metaphors." Indeed, aspects of the growth process seem analogous to progressions from "live" to "dead" metaphor. One may first need to view explicitly domain Y from the perspective of an already known X. Gradually, the need to recall X in order to use concept Y may be eliminated. The live metaphor through which one initially understood a situation gradually becomes dead (Hanson 1970; Hesse 1966; Verbrugge, 1977).

Normative theories of knowledge (such as semantic memory theories) are extremely important. They provide reference points for what knowledgeable people know. For example, normative theories of lexical memory can be used to assess what "normal" children know at various age levels (Anglin 1970, 1976). They can identify basic concepts and suggest reasons for their basic nature (Rosch et al. 1976). They can suggest shifts in modes of organization, for example from functional or paradigmatic modes of organization in young children to syntagmatic modes of organization (Nelson, forthcoming). In short, normative theories can provide information that places important constraints on theories of growth and development. The most salient example of the importance of such constraints is illustrated by Chomsky's theories (1972) of an "ideal, adult speaker-hearer." Based on Chomsky's analysis of language, large classes of potential theories were seen as inadequate because they could not possibly account for the types of information available to adult speaker-hearers (see Dixon and Horton 1968; Fodor, Bever, and Garrett 1974).

The value of normative theories is enhanced by considering what they do not tell us as well as what they do tell us. For example, they do not necessarily tell us how people arrived at a particular level of knowing or how they can move beyond that level (Bransford, Nitsch, and Franks, forthcoming). Indeed, linguists have frequently been plagued by disagreements about basic data. These data involve speaker-hearer's intuitions about such things as grammaticality, acceptability, and intersentential relations. Yet intuitions about these questions frequently differ. If experienced linguists move to a point where they become more sensitive to linguistic subtleties than "normal" speaker-hearers, it seems reasonable to assume that their judgments about intuitive acceptability may differ as well.

Probably the most difficult problem in learning from normative theories involves understanding their relationships to the actual form of people's knowing and understanding abilities. It is easy to slip into the mode of assuming that a lexical structure or set of grammatical rules is actually embodied in a person's head. One is then tempted to ask how someone can contact a particular structure or move through it (see Bransford and Franks 1976; Bransford et al., 1977, for further discussion). Normative theories are invaluable for representing information. However, representations are used by comprehenders to understand something. A representation of what someone knows is not necessarily equivalent to the form of that person's knowledge, which is assumed to be stored somewhere. Yet it is frequently assumed that representations are "in the head" and that the ability to know the meaning of something involves contacting some stored "meaning representation."

There are a number of reasons for questioning the assumption that the assessment of meaning involves contact with some stored meaning representation. The most basic reason is that one can come to understand things in new ways. How could one understand something new if meaning simply involved contact with old, stored representations? Assumptions about novel concatenations of old meaning elements are not sufficient because the elements themselves change in meaning. Indeed, how could children ever acquire linguistic meanings if meaning involved making contact with representations of meanings that were stored?

It has been suggested here that meaning resides neither in the input nor in the organism. Instead, meaning resides in the situation-input (organism-environment) relation. Both the environment and one's knowledge can be said to provide support for meaning or set the stage for meaning (Bransford and Franks 1976), but meaning does not necessarily result from contacting a meaning representation stored in the head (see also Gibson, 1977; Mace, 1977; Shaw and McIntyre 1974; Shaw and Pittenger, 1977, on Gibson's concept of affordances and its congruence with the position adopted here).

Problems in assuming that meaning involves contact with a stored trace can be clarified by noting that the meaning of an input can affect the speed with which it can be recognized. This frequently seems paradoxical because meaning somehow seems to affect recognition, yet one must recognize an input in order to find its meaning (see Turvey 1974). However, it is only paradoxical if one assumes that comprehending the meaning of something involves finding a stored meaning trace. An input has meaning only by virtue of its relationship to the organism's current situation. A normatively meaningful input is therefore one that maps into the organism's current cognitive-perceptual situation. The latter exists prior to the input and will affect its recognition, just as a relatively decontextualized knowing system allows an adult to recognize an isolated sentence like *The boy hit the ball*. However, if a person's knowledge is not in a relatively decontextualized state, the input will not be normatively meaningful (the *ablation* example). One will therefore need additional contextual support in order to recognize the input readily.

The most important aspect of viewing meaning as residing the organism-environment relationship is the effect it has on thinking about growth processes. As perspectives change, understood meanings change. However, if meaning is a function of situation-input relations, effective change will take place only by beginning with a person's momentary situation and working from there.

References

Anderson, R. C., and Ortony, A. 1975. On putting apples into bottles—a problem of polysemy. *Cognitive Psychology*, 7, 167–180.

Anglin, J. M. 1970. *The growth of word meaning*. Cambridge, Mass: The MIT Press.

———. 1976. *Word, object, and conceptual development*. New York: Norton.

Barclay, J. R., Bransford, J. D., Franks, J. J., McCarrell, N. S., and Nitsch, K. 1974.

Comprehension and semantic flexibility. *Journal of Verbal Learning and Verbal Behavior*, *13*, 471–481.

Bates, E. 1976. *Language and context: The acquisition of pragmatics*. New York: Academic Press.

Beilin, H., and Spontak, G. 1969. Active-passive transformations and operational reversibility. Paper presented at the biennial meeting of the Society for Research in Child Development, Santa Monica, Ca., March.

Berlyne, D. E. 1965. *Structure and direction in thinking*. New York: John Wiley and Sons.

Bever, T. G. 1970. The influence of speech performance on linguistic structures. In G. B. Flores d'Arcais and W. J. M. Levelt (Eds.), *Advances in psycholinguistics*. Amsterdam: North-Holland Publishing, 4–30.

Birch, H. G. 1945. The relation of previous experience to insightful problem solving. *Journal of Comparative Psychology*, *38*, 367–383.

Bloom, L. 1974. Talking, understanding, and thinking. In R. L. Schiefelbusch and L. L. Lloyd (Eds.), *Language perspectives: Acquisition, retardation, and intervention*. Baltimore, Md.: University Park Press, 285–311.

———. This volume. The integration of form, content, and use in language development.

Bloom, L., Hood, L., and Lightbown, P. 1974. Imitation in language development: If, when and why. *Cognitive Psychology*, *6*, 380–420.

Blumenthal, A. L. 1970. *Language and psychology*. New York: John Wiley and Sons.

Bohm, D. 1969. Further remarks on order. In C. H. Waddington (Ed.), *Towards a theoretical biology*. Vol. 2. Chicago: Aldine, 41–60.

Bolinger, D. 1965. The atomization of meaning. *Language*, *41*, 553–573.

Bransford, J. D., and Franks, J. J. 1973. The abstraction of linguistic ideas: A review. *Cognition: International Journal of Cognitive Psychology*, *1*, 211–249.

———. 1976. Toward of framework for understanding learning. In G. Bower (Ed.), *The psychology of learning and motivation*. Vol. 10. New York: Academic Press, 93–127.

Bransford, J. D., and Johnson, M. K. 1972. Contextual prerequisites for understanding: Some investigations of comprehension and recall. *Journal of Verbal Learning and Verbal Behavior*, *11*, 717–726.

———. 1973. Considerations of some problems of comprehension. In W. Chase (Ed.), *Visual information processings*. New York: Academic Press, 383–438.

Bransford, J. D., and McCarrell, N. S. 1974. A sketch of a cognitive approach to comprehension. In W. Weimer and D. Palermo (Eds.), *Cognition and the symbolic processes*. Hillsdale, N. J.: Lawrence Erlbaum Associates, 189–229.

Bransford, J. D., Barclay, J. R., and Franks, J. J. 1972. Sentence memory: A constructive versus interpretive approach. *Cognitive Psychology*, *3*, 193–209.

Bransford, J. D., McCarrell, N. S., and Nitsch, K. E. 1976. Contexte, comprehension et flexibilite semantique: quelques implications theoriques et methodologiques. In S. Ehrlich et E. Tulving (Eds.), *La memoire semantique*. Paris: Bulletin de Psychologie, 335–345.

Bransford, J. D., Nitsch, K. E., and Franks, J. J. Forthcoming. Schooling and the facilitation of knowing. In R. C. Anderson, R. J. Spiro, and W. E. Montague (Eds.), *Schooling and the acquisition of knowledge*. Hillsdale, N. J.: Lawrence Erlbaum Associates.

Bransford, J. D., McCarrell, N. S., Franks, J. J., and Nitsch, K. E. 1977. Toward unexplaining memory. In R. E. Shaw and J. D. Bransford (Eds.). *Perceiving, acting and knowing: Toward an ecological psychology*. Hillsdale, N. J.: Lawrence Erlbaum Associates, 431–466.

Brewer, W. F. 1974. The problem of meaning and the interrelations of the higher mental processes. In W. Weimer and D. Palermo (Eds.), *Cognition and the symbolic processes*. Hillsdale, N. J.: Lawrence Erlbaum Associates, 263–298.

Brewer, W. F., and Harris, R. J. 1974. Memory for deictic elements in sentences. *Journal of Verbal Learning and Verbal Behavior, 13,* 321–327.

Broudy, H. Forthcoming. Kinds of knowledge and the purposes of schooling. In R. C. Anderson, R. J. Spiro, and W. E. Montague (Eds.), *Schooling and the acquisition of knowledge*. Hillsdale, N. J.: Lawrence Erlbaum Associates.

Brown, A. L. 1975. The development of memory: Knowing, knowing about knowing, and knowing how to know. In H. W. Reese (Ed.), *Advances in child development and behavior*, Vol. 10. New York: Academic Press, 103–152.

———. Forthcoming. Development, schooling and the acquisition of knowledge about knowledge. In R. C. Anderson, R. J. Spiro, and W. E. Montague (Eds.), *Schooling and the acquisition of knowledge*. Hillsdale, N. J.: Lawrence Erlbaum Associates.

Cassirer, E. 1923. *Substance and function*. Chicago, Ill.: The Open Court Publishing Co.

Chafe, W. L. 1972. Discourse structure and human knowledge. In J. B. Carroll and R. O. Freedle (Eds.), *Language comprehension and the acquisition of knowledge*. Washington, D. C.: Winston, 41–70.

Chapman, R. S. 1974. Developmental relationship between receptive and expressive language. In R. L. Schiefelbusch and L. L. Lloyd (Eds.), *Language perspectives: Acquisition, retardation, and intervention*. Baltimore, Md.: University Park Press, 335–344.

———. This volume. Comprehension strategies in children.

Chomsky, N. 1965. *Aspects of a theory of syntax*. Cambridge, Mass.: The MIT Press.

———. 1972. *Language and mind*. New York: Harcourt, Brace, and Jovanovich.

Clark, H. H. 1973. Comprehension and the given-new contract. Paper presented at the conference on the role of grammar in interdisciplinary linguistic research, University of Bielefeld, Bielefeld, Germany, December.

Clark, H. H., and Haviland, S. E. Forthcoming. Comprehension and the given-new contract. In R. Freedle (Ed.), *Discourse production and comprehension*. Hillsdale, N. J.: Lawrence Erlbaum Associates.

Clark, H. H., and Stafford, R. A. 1969. Memory for semantic features in the verb. *Journal of Experimental Psychology, 80,* 326–334.

Cole, M., and Bruner, J. S. 1971. Cultural differences and inferences about psychological processes. *American Psychologist, 26,* 867–876.

Collins, A. M., and Loftus, E. F. 1975. A spreading activation theory of semantic processing. *Psychological Review, 82,* 407–428.

de Groot, A. B. 1966. Perception and memory versus thought. In B. Kleimutz (Ed.), *Problem solving: Research, method, and theory*. New York: John Wiley and Sons, 19–50.

De Villiers, J. G., and De Villiers, P. A. 1974. Competence and performance in child language: Are children really competent to judge? *Journal of Child Language, 1,* 11–22.

Dixon, T. R., and Horton, D. L. (Eds.) 1968. *Verbal behavior and general behavior theory.* Englewood Cliffs, N. J.: Prentice-Hall.

Dooling, D. J., and Lachman, R. 1971. Effects of comprehension on retention of prose. *Journal of Experimental Psychology, 88,* 216–222.

Dore, J., Franklin, M. B., Miller, R. T., and Ramer, A. L. H. 1976. Transitional phenomena in early language acquisition. *Journal of Child Language, 3,* 13–28.

Fillmore, C. J. 1971. Verbs of judging: An exercise in semantic description. In C. J. Fillmore and D. T. Langendoen (Eds.), *Studies in linguistic semantics.* New York: Holt, Rinehart and Winston, 273–290.

Flavell, J. H., and Wellman, H. M. Forthcoming. Metamemory. In R. V. Kail, Jr. and J. W. Hagen (Eds.), *Perspectives on the development of memory and cognition.* Hillsdale, N. J.: Lawrence Erlbaum Associates.

Fodor, J. A., Bever, T. G., and Garrett, M. F. 1974. *The psychology of language: An introduction to psycholinguistics and generative grammar.* New York: McGraw-Hill.

Franks, J. J. 1974. Toward understanding understanding. In W. Weimer and D. Palermo (Eds.), *Cognition and the symbolic processes.* Hillsdale, N. J.: Lawrence Erlbaum Associates, 231–261.

Frederickson C. H. 1972. Effects of task-induced cognitive operations on comprehension and memory processes. In J. B. Carroll and R. O. Freedle (Eds.), *Language comprehension and the acquisition of knowledge.* Washington, D.C.: V. H. Winston, 211–245.

———. 1975. Acquisition of semantic information from discourse: Effects of repeated exposures. *Journal of Verbal Learning and Verbal Behavior, 14,* 158–169.

Gagne, R. M. 1970. *The conditions of learning* (Rev. ed.). New York: Holt, Rinehart and Winston.

Garcia, J., and Koelling, R. A. 1966. Relation of cue to consequence in avoidance learning. *Psychonomic Science, 4,* 123–124.

Gibson, J. J. Forthcoming. The theory of affordances. In R. E. Shaw and J. D. Bransford (Eds.), *Perceiving, acting and knowing: Toward an ecological psychology.* Hillsdale, N. J.: Lawrence Erlbaum Associates, 67–82.

Glucksberg, S., and Danks, J. H. 1975. *Experimental psycholinguistics: An introduction.* Hillsdale, N. J.: Lawrence Erlbaum Associates.

Gough, P. B. 1965. Grammatical transformations and speed of understanding. *Journal of Verbal Learning and Verbal Behavior, 4,* 107–111.

———. 1966. The verification of sentences: The effects of delay of evidence and sentence length. *Journal of Verbal Learning and Verbal Behavior, 5,* 492–496.

Halliday, M. A. K. 1967. Notes on transitivity and theme in English: II. *Journal of Linguistics, 3,* 199–244.

Hannigan, M. L. 1976. The effects of frameworks on sentence perception and memory. Unpublished Ph.D. dissertation, Vanderbilt University, Nashville, Tenn.

Hanson, N. R. 1970. A picture theory of theory meaning. In R. G. Colodny (Ed.), *The nature and function of scientific theories.* Pittsburgh, Pa.: University of Pittsburgh Press, 233–274.

Harris, R. J. and Brewer, W. F. 1973. Deixis in memory for verb tense. *Journal of Verbal Learning and Verbal Behavior, 12,* 590–597.

Hesse, M. B. 1966. *Models and analogies in science.* South Bend, Ind.: University of Notre Dame Press.

Hester, M. 1977. Visual attention and sensibility. In R. E. Shaw and J. D. Bransford (Eds.), *Perceiving, acting and knowing: Toward an ecological psychology.* Hillsdale, N. J.: Lawrence Erlbaum Associates, 135–169.

Hoffman, M. 1968. Child language. Unpublished Master's thesis, McGill University, Department of Psychology, Montreal, Canada.

Holt, J. 1964. *How children fail.* New York: Dell Publishing Co.

Huttenlocher, J., Eisenberg, K., and Strauss, S. 1968. Comprehension: Relation between perceived actor and logical subject. *Journal of Verbal Learning and Verbal Behavior, 7,* 527–530.

Jenkins, J. J. 1974. Can we have a theory of meaningful memory? In R. L. Solso (Ed.), *Theories of cognitive psychology: The Loyola Symposium.* Hillsdale, N. J.: Lawrence Erlbaum Associates, 1–20.

Jensen, A. R. 1970. A theory of primary and secondary familiar mental retardation. In N. R. Ellis (Ed.), *International review of research in mental retardation.* Vol. 4. New York: Academic Press, 51–66.

———. 1972. *Genetics and education.* New York: Harper and Row.

Johnson, M. K., Bransford, J. D., and Solomon, S. 1973. Memory for tacit implications of sentences. *Journal of Experimental Psychology, 98,* 203–205.

Johnson, M. K., Doll, T. J., Bransford, J. D., and Lapinski, R. H. 1974. Context effects in sentence memory. *Journal of Experimental Psychology, 103,* 358–360.

Katz, J. J., and Postal, P. M. 1964. *An integrated theory of linguistic descriptions,* Cambridge, Mass.: MIT Press.

Keller, H. 1903. *The story of my life.* New York: Doubleday, Page.

Kintsch, W. 1974. *The representation of meaning in memory.* Hillsdale, N. J.: Lawrence Erlbaum Associates.

Labov, W. 1970. The logical non-standard English. In F. Williams (Ed.), *Language and poverty.* Chicago: Markham Press, 153–189.

Lakoff, R. 1971. If's, and's, and but's about conjunction. In C. J. Fillmore and D. T. Langendoen (Eds.), *Studies in linguistic semantics,* New York: Holt, Rinehart and Winston, 63–72.

Lashley, K. S. 1951. The problem of serial order in behavior. In L. A. Jeffress (Ed.), *Cerebral mechanisms in behavior.* New York: John Wiley and Sons, 112–136.

Mace, W. M. 1977. James Gibson's strategy for perceiving: Ask not what's inside your head, but what your head's inside of. In R. E. Shaw and J. D. Bransford (Eds.), *Perceiving, acting and knowing: Toward an ecological psychology.* Hillsdale, N. J.: Lawrence Erlbaum Associates, 43–65.

MacNamara, J. 1972. Cognitive basis of language learning in infants. *Psychological Review, 79,* 1–13.

Maier, N. R. F. 1930. Reasoning in humans. I. On direction. *Journal of Comparative Psychology, 10,* 115–143.

Marks, C. B., Doctorow, M. J., and Wittrock, M. C. 1974. Word frequency and reading comprehension. *Journal of Educational Research, 67,* 259–262.

McCarrell, N. S., and Brooks, P. H. 1975. Mental retardation: Comprehension gone awry. Research colloquium sponsored by the John F. Kennedy Center for Research on Education and Human Development, Nashville, Tenn., September.

McCawley, J. D. 1974. On what is deep about deep structures. In W. Weimer and D. Palermo (Eds.), *Cognition and the symbolic processes*. Hillsdale, N. J.: Lawrence Erlbaum Associates, 125–128.

Miller, G. A., Heise, G. A., and Lichten, W. 1951. The intelligibility of speech as a function of the context of the text materials. *Journal of Experimental Psychology, 41,* 329–335.

Nelson, K. 1974. Concept, word, and sentence. Interrelations in acquisition and development. *Psychological Review, 81,* 267–285.

———. Forthcoming. Cognitive development and the acquisition of concepts. In R. C. Anderson, R. J. Spiro, and W. E. Montague (Eds.), *Schooling and the acquisition of knowledge*. Hillsdale, N. J.: Lawrence Erlbaum Associates.

Nitsch, K. E. 1975. Toward a conceptualization of the problem of meaning. Major area paper, Vanderbilt University, Nashville, Tenn.

Odom, R. D., and Mumbauer, C. C. 1971. Dimensional salience and identification of the relevant dimension in problem solving. *Developmental Psychology, 4,* 135–140.

Odom, R. D., Astor, E. C., and Cunningham, J. G. 1975. Effects of perceptual salience on the matrix task performance of four- and six-year-old children. *Child Development, 46,* 758–762.

Olson, D. R. 1972. Language use for communicating, instructing and thinking. In J. B. Carroll and R. O. Freedle (Eds.), *Language comprehension and the acquisition of knowledge*. Washington, D.C.: V. H. Winston, 139–168.

———. 1974. Towards a theory of instructional means. Invited address presented to the American Educational Research Association, Chicago, April.

Olson, D. R., and Filby, N. 1972. On the comprehension of active and passive sentences. *Cognitive Psychology, 3,* 361–381.

Osgood, C. E. 1971. Where do sentences come from? In D. D. Steinberg and L. A. Jakobovitz (Eds.), *Semantics: An interdisciplinary reader in philosophy, linguistics, and psychology*. London: Cambridge University Press, 497–529.

Osherson, D. N., and Markman, E. 1975. Language and the ability to evaluate contradictions and tautologies. *Cognition, 3,* 213–226.

Pearson, P. D. 1969. The effects of grammatical complexity on children's comprehension, recall, and conception of semantic relations. Unpublished Ph.D. thesis, University of Minnesota, Minneapolis, Minn.

Peirce, C. S. 1932. In C. Hartshorne and P. Weiss (Eds.), *Collected papers of C. S. Peirce.* Vol. II. *Elements of Logic.* Cambridge, Mass.: Harvard University Press.

Pollchik, A. 1975. The use of embedded questions in the facilitation of productive learning. Unpublished Ph.D. dissertation, Vanderbilt University, Nashville, Tenn.

Reich, P. A. 1976. The early acquisition of word meaning. *Journal of Child Language, 3,* 117–123.

Rosch, E., Mervis, C. B., Gray, W., Johnson, D., and Boyes-Braem, P. 1976. Basic objects in natural categories. *Cognitive Psychology, 8,* 382–439.

Ross, J. R. 1970. On declarative sentences. In R. A. Jacobs and P. S. Rosenbaum (Eds.), *Readings in English transformational grammar*. Waltham, Mass.: Ginn, 222–272.

————. 1974. Three batons for cognitive psychology. In W. Weimer and D. Palermo (Eds.), *Cognition and the symbolic processes*. Hillsdale, N. J.: Lawrence Erlbaum Associates, 63–124.

Schank, R. C. 1972. Conceptual dependency: A theory of natural language understanding. *Cognitive Psychology*, *3*, 552–631.

Schweller, K. G., Brewer, W. F., and Dahl, D. A. In press. Memory for illocutionary forces and perlocutionary effects of utterances. *Journal of Verbal Learning and Verbal Behavior*.

Scribner, S. 1975. Recall of classical syllogisms: A cross-cultural investigation of error on logical problems. In R. Falmange (Ed.), *Reasoning: Representation and Process in Children and Adults*, Hillsdale, N. J.: Lawrence Erlbaum Associates, 153–174.

Seligman, M. E. P., and Hager, J. L. (Eds.). 1972. *Biological Boundaries of Learning*. New York: Appleton-Century-Crofts.

Shaw, R. E., and McIntyre, M. 1974. Algoristic foundations to cognitive psychology. In W. Weimer and D. Palermo (Eds.). 1974. *Cognition and the symbolic processes*. Hillsdale, N. J.: Lawrence Erlbaum Associates, 305–362.

Shaw, R. E., and Pittenger, J. 1977. Perceiving the face of change in changing faces: Implications for a theory of object perception. In R. E. Shaw and J. D. Bransford (Eds.), *Perceiving, acting and knowing: Toward an ecological psychology*. Hillsdale, N. J.: Lawrence Erlbaum Associates, 103–132.

Sinclair-de Zwart, H. 1969. Developmental psycholinguistics. In D. Elkind and J. H. Flavell (Eds.). 1969. *Studies in cognitive development: Essays in honor of Jean Piaget*. New York: Oxford University Press, 315–336.

Slobin. D. I. 1966. Grammatical transformations and sentence comprehension in childhood and adulthood. *Journal of Verbal Learning and Verbal Behavior*, *5*, 219–227.

Slobin, D. I. and Welsch, C. A. 1973. Elicited imitation as a research tool in developmental psycholinguistics. In C. A. Ferguson and D. I. Slobin (Eds.) *Readings in child language acquisition*. New York: Holt, Rinehart and Winston, 485–497.

Smith, E. E., Shoben, E. J., and Rips, L. J. 1974. Structure and process in semantic memory: A feature model for semantic decisions. *Psychological Review*, *81*, 214–241.

Tulving, E., and Thomson, D. M. 1973. Encoding specificity and retrieval processes in episodic memory. *Psychological Review*, *80*, 352–372.

Turvey, M. T. 1974. Constructive theory, perceptual systems, and tacit knowledge. In W. Weimer and D. Palermo (Eds.), *Cognition and the symbolic processes*. Hillsdale, N. J.: Lawrence Erlbaum Associates, 165–180.

van Dijk, T. A. 1973. Models for text grammars. *Linguistics*, *105*, 35–68.

Verbrugge, R. R. Resemblances in language and perception. In R. E. Shaw and J. D. Bransford (Eds.), *Perceiving, action and knowing: Toward an ecological psychology*. Hillsdale, N. J.: Lawrence Erlbaum Associates, 365–389.

Wason, P. C. 1961. The contexts of plausible denial. *Journal of Verbal Learning and Verbal Behavior*, *4*, 7–11.

Wells, G. 1974. Learning to code experience through language. *Journal of Child Language*, *1*, 243–269.

Wittgenstein, L. 1953. *Philosophical investigations*. Oxford: B. Blackwell.

Comprehension Strategies in Children
A Discussion of Bransford and Nitsch's Paper
ROBIN S. CHAPMAN

Bransford and Nitsch (this volume) have argued that skilled language comprehension requires one to grasp the significance of the language input for the situation at hand. It is the relation between sentence and situation rather than the sentence alone that determines what one understands and how easily understanding takes place. There is more to understanding than the derivation of a semantic reading of the sentence, and there are more cues to a speaker's purpose and meaning than those contained in the utterance.

Bransford's view focuses on understanding as it takes place in actual communicative interaction in the world. He has reminded researchers that the communication event (see Gumperz and Hymes 1972; Searle 1969) is always the framework within which understanding takes place, even in experimental tasks. Knowledge about the world (see Winograd 1972), about pragmatic aspects of communication (see Dore 1974; Bates 1974, 1976; Grice 1975), and about the immediate setting (see Cazden 1970) play important roles in determining what is understood and how easily.

There are a number of issues that arise in applying Bransford's framework to the interpretation and generation of experimental studies of skilled adult comprehension. Among them are questions of level and order of processing in the skilled listener's performance. Most current methods of study present problems in parceling out effects as a result of comprehension, memorial, or retrieval processes. Sentence repetition and recall tasks in particular are slender reeds upon which to base inferences about comprehension.

These problems in working out a model of adult language comprehension are raised here only to be set aside, however. The more immediate problem in considering language development is that of establishing the critical nature of young listeners' situations and knowledge of the world in their understanding of what is heard or read. Because the adult is so good at interpreting isolated sentences, it is tempting to assign only a minor role to the relation of sentence and situation in a model of the child's language comprehension. Such an assignment would create a very misleading picture of language comprehension in the language learning child. The purpose of this chapter is to instantiate Bransford's framework developmentally by describing a number of examples in which comprehension requires situational cues to be successful.

An Apparent Paradox

There exists an apparent paradox in current generalizations about children's comprehension skills. Parents of one-year-old children just beginning to talk typically report that children understand everything said to them. Observations of children's performance in natural language settings support this belief. For instance, children at the level of putting two words together in production respond appropriately to parental commands (Shipley, Smith, and Gleitman 1969; Shatz 1975). Longitudinal studies of children's sentences (see Bloom, this volume) conclude that acquisition of most basic language structures occurs rapidly—by three or four years of age. And comprehension, say the introductory textbooks, precedes production.

Experimental tests of children's language comprehension provide evidence that contrasts with the foregoing conclusions. For example, children can be asked to select pictures illustrating sentences that differ only in word order, such as "Mommy kisses daddy" and "Daddy kisses mommy" (Miller and Yoder 1973). Many children may fail to use word order as a cue to agent and object-of-action for such sentences on both picture pointing and object manipulation tasks until five years of age, despite use of appropriate word order in their own sentences at two years (Fraser, Bellugi, and Brown 1963; Lovell and Dixon 1965; Slobin 1966; Carrow 1968; Owings 1972; Baird 1972; Fernald 1972; de Villiers and de Villiers 1973; Strohner and Nelson 1974; Chapman and Miller 1975; Horgan 1975; Chapman and Kohn 1977). Use of word order as a cue to agent and object status occurs even later for passive sentences (Fraser, Bellugi, and Brown 1963; Bever 1970; Owings 1972; Maratsos 1974; Maratsos and Abramovitch 1975; Horgan 1975).

Comprehension mastery assessed experimentally is reported later than one would expect on the basis of production data and informal observation for a wide variety of other structures as well (Palermo and Molfese 1972; Lahey 1974). These include grammatical cues to object number (Keeney and Wolfe 1972; Vygotsky 1962; Piaget 1969); possessor and object possessed (Owings 1972); cause and effect (Katz and Brent 1968; Corrigan 1975; Kuhn and Phelps 1976; Epstein 1972; temporal order of event (Lovell and Slater 1960; Olds 1968; Katz and Brent 1968; Weil 1970; Clark 1971; Hatch 1971; Montroy, McManis, and Bell 1971; Amidon and Carey 1972; Barrie-Blackley 1973; Beilin 1975; Johnson 1975; Keller-Cohen 1975); contingent events, for example, "If you smile you get a cookie" (Matalon 1962; Peel 1967; Olds 1968; Roberge 1970; O'Brien and Shapiro 1968; Shapiro and O'Brien 1970; Shine and Walsh 1971; Paris 1973); and contrastive events, for example, "We jumped but he hopped" (Vygotsky 1962; Olds 1968; Katz and Brent 1968; Hutson and Shub 1975).

What is a Comprehension Strategy?

Children, unlike adults, frequently show actual failures in processing a linguistic construction rather than just longer decision times. These failures vary as a function of sentence content and the situation in which the input occurs. Through variation of sentences and situations, the cues the child is using to understand the sentences presented can be identified.

Some of the children's systematic response patterns can be categorized as *comprehension strategies*. It is important to distinguish comprehension strategy from the more general *response bias* or *response preference*. Response preference denotes systematic responding on the part of the subject that is not based on the experimenter's criterion for correctness but rather on some other aspect of the stimulus situation (for example, position, size, color, novelty) or a preference for a particular response regardless of stimulus characteristics (for example, vocalizing to speech).

When the basis of the response bias includes no aspect of that test sentence's content or structure, one may speak of the bias as a *nonlinguistic response strategy* (Clark 1973, 1975). When the basis of the systematic (but not always correct) response can be shown to depend on some aspect of the sentence content in a comprehension task, one may call the response bias a comprehension strategy (Bever 1970; Ervin-Tripp 1973; Clark 1975). Unlike comprehension, which denotes the complete process of understanding a sentence, a comprehension strategy is a short-cut, heuristic, or algorithm for arriving at sentence meaning without full marshaling of the information in the sentence and one's linguistic knowledge. In the case of a child, it can serve as a device for understanding in the absence of full linguistic knowledge. Thus it will sometimes yield the incorrect answer, although it may more usually give the appearance of understanding. (See Carroll and Freedle 1972; Bloom 1974; Ingram 1974; Huttenlocher 1974; Chapman 1974, on theories of comprehension.)

Finally, there is an intermediate category of response bias that incorporates some aspect of sentence content or structure but also some aspect of the test situation, failing to generalize to other testing or response modes. These behaviors will be referred to as *task-specific response strategies*. We may wish to view them as task-specific comprehension strategies when the task is one encountered in ordinary communication.

The central puzzle of our paradox is this: How do children who cannot yet use grammatical cues to meaning appear to understand so much of what is said to them? Here I argue that the answer lies largely in the child's use of comprehension strategies, which are frequently successful in the situation. The resolution of the inconsistencies in children's understanding of sentences lies in the fact that children depend not on sentence structure but on the situation and their previous experience for understanding the relations among words. In the following section I will suggest some specific ways in which children of different developmental levels can appear to understand the speech they hear.

Comprehension Strategies in Language Acquisition
Even the infant is responsive to speech in very limited ways. Six-week-olds can discriminate phonetic differences. Mothers and their three-month-old children may coo back and forth to each other in turn-taking "conversations" (Lewis and Freedle 1973). Greenfield's (1972) four-and-a-half-month-old son Matthew smiled in response to "peek-aboo" and the sight of his mother's face when the game was played in a familiar location. But the behaviors that lead to the first frequent reports that children understand speech do not emerge until the child begins to show communicative intent and intentional action in the last third of the first year (Piaget's sensorimotor stage IV, approximately eight to twelve months).

NONLINGUISTIC RESPONSE STRATEGIES IN
SENSORIMOTOR STAGE IV

In this stage the child neither understands nor uses words (Lézine 1973). One apparent counter-example is the frequent report that an infant understands "no" when it is said sharply. In stage IV "no" spoken sharply can have the effect of startling infants, interrupting their activity, and possibly causing them to cry; but so can "yes" spoken in a similar fashion (Spitz 1957). There are a number of other ways in which the appearance of language comprehension can arise when children are playing with their parents who know their repertoire of actions well. Three such ways are discussed. These are really contextually bound response preferences with no dependence on the lexical content of the parent's utterances.

1. *Look at objects that mother looks at.* Bruner (1975a, 1975b) discusses evidence that mother and child learn early to focus their attention jointly on objects. If the child is looking at something, the mother looks at it, too. If the mother looks at an object, and particularly if she makes it salient by pointing to it or shaking and banging it, the child looks at the object, too. If the mother has said "Look!" at the same time, the child may appear to be complying with her command.

2. *Act on objects that you notice.* In stage IV the child has a very limited repertoire of activities: Objects are explored only briefly, most often through looking, mouthing, banging, or grasping and releasing (Lézine 1973). If the mother is knowledgeable about the child's usual actions and judicious in her choice of commands while the child plays, she can achieve a semblance of comprehension: "Pick up the block" as the child's hand moves toward the block; "Throw the ball" as the child picks up and releases the ball; "Give me the cup" as she moves an outstretched hand toward the cup the child is holding. The child does what he or she was going to do already.

3. *Imitate ongoing action.* The child in stage IV has begun syllabic babbling (ma-ma-ma; da-da-da) that hopeful mothers and fathers may take as evidence of first words. Observation usually reveals that these vocalizations have no consistent meaningful use; they may be addressed to the child's toes, dog, and night light as often as to mother. When parents repeat the child's babbling, the child repeats again, imitating ongoing action just for those actions that can be produced spontaneously.

The child in stage IV will play a number of communication games with the parents that lead to reports of sentence comprehension. Bruner (1975b) has discussed the relation of these games to later acquisition in detail. For example, the mother will say "Give me a kiss!" and smack her lips several times; and the child supplies a loud smack. "Give me a hug!" says the father, holding out his arms; the child does likewise. "Hi, Joshua," shouts the older brother, waving his hand; Joshua waves back. John shakes his head, stops; his mother says "Shake your head," shaking hers, and John shakes his head again, grinning at her. "Clap your hands," say the family, clapping theirs; the baby complies.

The situations in which these three "response rules" might be invoked differ in terms of the child's attention. In all three cases mother and child are playing together. But in the first instance the mother introduces an object as a focus for further interaction. In the second the child's attention is already directed to an object; actions follow. And in the third the mother's action is the focus of the child's attention.

COMPREHENSION STRATEGIES IN SENSORIMOTOR STAGE V
The first evidence of true language comprehension usually emerges in sensorimotor stage V, when the child is able to search successfully for an object seen hidden in several successive locations (Lézine 1973). This cognitive growth is, of course, not always a sufficient condition for the emergence of language comprehension (Cromer 1974; Beilin 1975; Corrigan 1976); but Lézine's (1973) observations suggest it may be necessary. The following rules apply to this stage of development:

1. *Attend to object mentioned.* Huttenlocher (1974) reports an experimental study of four children's language comprehension in the age range typical of sensorimotor stage V. She was able to obtain clear, unambiguous evidence of word comprehension in the child's looking, reaching, or grasping behavior when several objects were arrayed in front of the child. She tested comprehension by first securing the child's attention (calling his name in the exaggerated sing-song fashion) and then asking the question "Where's the ball?" or whatever object name the mother had reported that the child comprehended. Each word was tested against several other familiar objects several times in a session, with play intervening. A child did not go and get a requested object if it was absent from the room, however, even if it had a permanent and familiar location.

Shipley, Smith, and Gleitman (1969) reported that fifteen-month-old children in a one-word stage (most of whom would typically be in sensorimotor stage V) would most frequently attend to a mentioned object when its name was spoken (*ball!*) rather than when the name was embedded in a longer well-formed command, "Go get the ball" or a nonsense command.

2. *Give evidence of notice,* and 3. *Do what you usually do in the situation.* The preceding studies suggest that the child in sensorimotor stage V is able to attend to those objects present in the situation that are mentioned in a sentence. Thus there is evidence of word, if not sentence comprehension. Usually the object mentioned is the last word in the sentence (Limber 1973). The child's subsequent behavior is either to give evidence of noticing the object or to act on the object in the usual fashion rather than to carry out the action specifically mentioned in the sentence.

For example, Lewis and Freedle (1973) tell the story of a thirteen-month-old child said by her parents to understand sentences. When handed an apple in the high chair and told "Eat the apple," she bit into it. When handed an apple in her playpen and told "Throw the apple," she threw it. The skeptical researchers intervened by handing the child an apple in her highchair and requesting "Throw the apple." The child bit into it. Later, as she played in her playpen, she was handed an apple and told "Eat the apple"; she threw it. The basis for her apparent comprehension might be summarized as the strategy, "Do what you usually do in the situation."

My own son Joshua at stage V understood the name of his dog Heidi. When asked "Where's Heidi?" he would look around the room, see her, say "unh", and point. A stage earlier, prior to any evidence that he understood the word "Heidi," he would frequently look left over his shoulder when asked "Where's Heidi?" Sometimes she was there, and sometimes not.

A typical mother-child interchange giving rise to the mother's belief that the child understands everything he or she hears is the following interchange recorded in my older son John's diary at thirteen months, one week. John is walking around; his shirt is the only loose object on the rug. Mother points to it and says "Get your shirt" three times. John then begins to walk toward his shirt. Mother says "Good!" John picks up the shirt and turns to mother, who says "Good for you" and extends her hand palm up. John places the shirt in her hand; mother says "Thank you."

During stage V children begin to learn the conventional uses of objects. They begin to act on objects not only through mouthing, shaking, throwing, and banging, but also, and increasingly, to use the object in the way that they have seen it used (Lézine 1973). Brushes are used for brushing—self, dolls, elbows, telephone. Brooms are used for sweeping—floor, teddy bear, table. Telephones are answered—again and again. And so as the mother plays with the child there is a marked increase in the child's apparent compliance with her commands: "Brush your hair" as the child reaches for the brush; "Sweep the floor" as the child reaches for the broom. Many of the requested actions are carried out, although the object of action is selected in a rough and ready manner. It is through knowledge of the child's limited comprehension vocabulary and judicious choice of time, instruction, encouragement, and gesture that mothers make themselves "understood" to their one-year-old children.

COMPREHENSION STRATEGIES IN SENSORIMOTOR STAGE VI

1. *Locate the objects mentioned* and 2. *Do what you usually do.* Huttenlocher's (1974) study showed that as the children got older, sometime late in sensorimotor stage V or the beginning of stage VI, they became able to look for absent objects successfully if the locations were familiar. Cognitively, children in stage VI are able to search for an object successfully even if it has been concealed during successive displacements.

Examples of word comprehension in the absence of the mentioned object are provided by entries in John's diary shortly after he began to show a number of stage VI behaviors: John is standing in the living room. His father asks "Do you need a dry diaper?" John feels his diapers and hurries into his bedroom where the diapers are kept, returning with a diaper. There is much laughter from mother and father. His father changes him, stands him up, pats him on the seat and says "There! Now you have a dry diaper." John feels his diapers and hurries into his bedroom, returning with two diapers. John only understood *diaper*, but initially he gave the appearance of understanding the whole question.

In stage VI when asked "Do you want some lunch (or dinner, or yumyum)?" John hurries to his high chair; when asked "Do you wanna play runrunrun?" (a hands-and-knees chase game), he hurries over to the armchair (the game's customary starting place) and gets ready to crawl. If asked "Do you want a bath?" he goes directly to the bathroom and tries to climb in the tub. Thus he is no longer dependent on the situation or the presence of the object in order to evoke the meaning of a word. Now the comprehended word evokes its meaning despite the absence of diapers, food, chasing, or bathing in the immediate surroundings.

At the same time John is dependent on the situation to understand the speaker's communicative intent and the semantic relations among the actions and objects mentioned. John and other stage VI children still do not understand relations among words on the basis of the sentence's structure alone. During stage VI they can process at least one (or two or even three) words of the sentence, bringing those actions or objects to mind (and to mother) given only the word as a cue, without situational support. Thus we have evidence for lexical but not syntactic comprehension.

The child's play with familiar objects has become increasingly conventionalized. Beginning in stage VI objects of action as well as action are appropriately selected. The brush is used to brush hair, the broom to sweep the floor, the cup to drink out of, a container to put things in. Clark (1974), for example, found that the twenty-one-month-old children she tested for comprehension of *in*, *on*, and *under* appeared to understand *in* until responses on the other items were examined. It became apparent that children were simply putting objects into containers whenever that was possible; otherwise they put them on surfaces. Wilcox and Palermo (1975) and Hodun (1975) have shown in somewhat older children that the particular preferred arrangement will vary as a function of the usual uses of the toys: Conventional use determines response, given the child's cognitive level (Parisi and Antinucci 1970; Johnston 1973). Here we have evidence for lexical comprehension coupled with the strategy of "Do what you usually do."

3. *Act on objects in way mentioned.* A striking example of the child's comprehension of lexically, but not syntactically, cued meaning is offered by the *child-as-agent* strategy exhibited by children who are beginning to put two words together in appropriate English word order (Sinclair and Bronckart 1972; de Villiers and de Villiers 1973). When handed the alligator and cow and told "Make the alligator kiss the cow," the child performs the indicated action on the objects, kissing alligator, cow, or both.

When children are trained not to give child-as-agent responses but to act out the sentence using both objects, we still find failure to understand who is *kisser* and who *kissee*. Now, however, children may comply by systematically choosing as the *kisser* (or hitter or pusher or other agent) the object nearer their right hand or the object most appropriately sized for picking up (*choose handier object*); or they may simply demonstrate one object kissing or hitting or pushing the other randomly, without regard to the test sentence or object positions or sizes (Chapman and Miller 1975; Chapman and Kohn, 1977).

It is not surprising to discover that children in sensorimotor stage VI do not use word order as a cue to agent and object of action. First, studies of children's play with toys (Lowe 1975) show that use of dolls as agents in imaginary play (for example, doll feeding self) rather than recipients occurs later than stage VI. It does not occur until twenty-four to thirty months, although children have recognized since stage V that other people can carry out actual actions that they desire. Second, there has been no prior evidence of comprehension of syntactic cues. And third, Bloom's recent work (Bloom, Miller, and Hood 1975) has shown that children are learning to make sentences longer verb by verb. There is no evidence until much later that children have a rule underlying production of the general form *agent-action-object*, which would lead them to discover the correspondence between word order and meaning in comprehension.

If children are really processing only a few words of the sentence—those with obvious referents in the situation—how can we account for the appearance of more sophisticated processing? How do stage VI children use the utterance and the situation as cues to speaker intent? How do they decide when to do something, when to repeat something, or when to say something in response to the other's utterances? Shatz (1975) has shown that even children in the eighteen- to twenty-four-month age range (just putting two words together) give the appearance of understanding sophisticated indirect requests such as "Why don't you put the ball in the truck?" or "Can the ball fit in the truck?" by complying rather than answering. When such sentences are presented in a neutral context, with the toys present, the children almost always act on the toys rather than answer the question forms. In fact, they act on them even if the sentence is a declarative that carries no obligation either to act or to answer. Shatz argues this evidence suggests that children use an action strategy in responding to speech unless there is some specific cue not to act.

This strategy, *act on the objects in the way mentioned*, is the one the children in the experimental tasks testing word order were using as well (see the description in the first section of this paper). What situational or lexical cues might the child learn as prompts to talk or repeat or just attend rather than to act? Folger and Chapman (in press) have shown that children's early imitations are contingent on the mother's imitations. Children just putting two words together repeat part of a mother's prior utterance most frequently when the mother's utterance was itself an explicit lexically marked request to imitate ("say moo!"), a repetition, or an expansion of the child's previous utterance. We could hypothesize that ongoing action in the situation would serve as a prompt to talk (for example, the mother pointing to or drawing attention to objects as she said "What's that?") and that mother's speech without the presence of the mentioned activity or objects would serve as a prompt to act), but there is no evidence to support these points. The situational cues to meaning that children use at different developmental levels are only just beginning to be studied systematically (but see Wetstone and Friedlander 1973; Huttenlocher, Eisenberg, and Strauss 1968; Huttenlocher and Strauss 1968; Huttenlocher and Weiner 1971; Huttenlocher 1974; Bloom 1974; Goldin-Meadow, Seligmen, and Gelman 1976).

COMPREHENSION STRATEGIES IN THE EARLY
PREOPERATIONAL PERIOD (TWO TO FOUR YEARS)

1. *Do what is usually done.* Children in the two- to four-year-old period resemble the

stage VI children in many of the comprehension strategies that have been identified. Their knowledge of conventional object uses and relations is much greater, allowing them to show a greater variety of toy-specific responses when their comprehension of locative prepositions indicating spatial relations is tested: Do what is usually done. (Clark 1974; Wilcox and Palermo 1975; Hodun 1975).

Understanding of prepositions indicating spatial relations is still limited, however, by the child's conceptualization of space. Children do not yet have a metric or measuring rod for comparing distances or a way of visualizing how the same space might look from another person's perspective (Piaget and Inhelder 1967). Thus their understanding of *deictic* words indicating motion to or from the speaker (*come, go, bring, take*) or proximity to the speaker (*here, there*) is bound to their own perspective as listener rather than the speaker's perspective (Clark and Garnica 1974). It is only simple topological relations that they come to master in this period (see Parisi and Antinucci 1970; Johnston, 1973).

In "doing what is usually done" children show their growing awareness of the usual relations between object pairs rather than the few generalized response preferences that characterized their stage IV interactions with objects. They put blocks into ovens and trucks over bridges (as cars) or under them (as boats). They select the *probable location* for their spatial placement (Wilcox and Palermo 1975).

Another facet of the "doing what is usually done" strategy is found in the word order comprehension studies. Two-year-olds at the end of stage VI and beginning of preoperations did not show consistent interpretations of sentences like "Mommy kisses daddy" in which one individual was always the agent. Nor did they represent objects as agents in their own play. Dolls were fed by the children; the dolls were not arranged to feed themselves. Between two and two-and-a-half, however, the child's play (Lowe 1975) and the child's demonstrations of the test sentences (de Villiers and de Villiers 1973; Chapman and Kohn, 1977) show the ability to use the toys as agents. The doll can now feed itself; the child-as-agent strategy disappears.

What replaces the child-as-agent or choose-handier-object or do-what-you-usually-do strategies for a given sentence is a *probable event* strategy. Children still do not use word order as a cue to sentence meaning. But now, in the absence of context, they supply the meaning that their own past experience makes most probable (Bever 1970; Strohner and Nelson 1974; Chapman and Miller 1975; Chapman and Kohn 1977. In some children's experience boys may hit girls, in others girls may hit boys. When a sentence contains an animate and an inanimate noun, past experience frequently dictates that the particular animate noun mentioned is the agent: Kitties push doors, girls bump swings (Chapman and Kohn 1977). But the same children will also show preferred interpretations in which inanimate nouns are agents or instruments; for example, the boat usually carries the horse (Chapman and Kohn 1977). We see that the children are using their knowledge of the usual relations between the particular objects tested rather than a general semantic rule such as "animate nouns are agents" as a cue to the sentence's meaning.

Most parental speech to children in this period, as in the earlier ones, is about the here and now: what is currently happening or has just happened. In the natural setting, language comprehension may be simplified for the child because the relations among the mentioned objects and events are obvious from the situation. A speaker's meaning could often be successfully understood through the comprehension strategies previously outlined, especially if the child can correctly identify—or appear to identify—the communicative intent of the speaker. For example, remember Shatz's (1975) suggestion that children in this period might learn that specific cues, situational or lexical, signified that something other than an action response was appropriate. Shatz showed that children in the preoperational period can switch from an action strategy in response to indirect directives to an information-giving strategy when the preceding sequence of questions made one interpretation more probable than the other.

For example (Shatz 1975), "Can you talk on the telephone?" was interpreted as a request for action when preceded by the directive contextual sequence "Come get the telephone; push the button; find the one; ring the bell." The same question was answered *yes* or *no* when preceded by the information-seeking sequence "Who talks on the telephone in your house? Can mommy talk on the telephone? Can daddy talk on the telephone?" Thus the children chose the functional interpretation that preceding context made more probable.

2. *Supply missing information.* One situation in which questions are clearly requests for answers rather than requests for actions is that of reading a book together. Studies of children's comprehension of questions in this context show that two- to four-year-old children will frequently supply answers even when they do not understand the meaning of the interrogative words (Ervin-Tripp 1970; Chapman 1973). Their incorrect answers can be summarized by the *supply-missing-information* strategy where the children's past experience must dictate the most probable missing element. For example, two- to three-year-olds may answer all of the following questions with "cereal": "How do you eat? Why do you eat? When do you eat?" In each case, the missing object of action has been supplied. Or they may give locational answers such as "in chair" to "How does he sit? Why does he sit? When does he sit?" At approximately three years of age, when children typically begin to demand and offer causal explanations ("Why Mom?" and "Cause I wanna"), they also begin to supply explanations when they don't understand the interrogative word: Adult: "When did the deer eat?" Child: "Cause he was hungry." (Ervin-Tripp 1970).

COMPREHENSION STRATEGIES IN LATE PREOPERATIONS (FOUR TO SEVEN YEARS) AND CONCRETE OPERATIONS (SEVEN TO ELEVEN YEARS)

1. *Word-order strategy.* Between three-and-a-half and five English-speaking children typically learn to use word order as a cue to agent and object of action in simple active sentences (Owings 1972; de Villiers and de Villiers 1973; Chapman and Miller 1975; Chapman and Kohn 1977). Children now correctly act out both "The swing bumps the kitty" and "The kitty bumps the swing." At the same time, children's performance on reversible passive sentences goes from bad to

worse (Bever 1970; Owings 1972; de Villiers and de Villiers 1973; Maratsos 1974; Beilin 1975; Maratsos and Abramovitch 1975). "The mother is patted by the dog" is acted out as mother pats dog; "The dog is patted by the mother" is acted out as dog pats mother! Here, then, is evidence of the child's overgeneralization of a grammatical rule for sentence comprehension.

2. *Order-of-mention strategy.* Children's comprehension of sentences containing the conjunctions *before* and *after* shows the use of a similar strategy based on order of mention in the sentence (Ferreiro and Sinclair 1971; Clark 1971). When asked to demonstrate, for example, "The girl jumped before the boy hopped" the child will demonstrate jumping and then hopping. But when asked to demonstrate "Before the girl jumped the boy hopped," the child again demonstrates jumping and then hopping.

3. *Probable-relation-of-events strategy.* Children in the late preoperational period and elementary school age may rely on the probable relation between events to interpret complex sentences containing conjunctions that are understood late, such as *because, if, although,* and *but.* For example, the child may understand "I broke my balloon because I cried" as having happened in the reverse order (Epstein 1972).

SUMMARY OF DEVELOPMENTAL CHANGES IN STRATEGIES

The comprehension strategies and nonlinguistic response strategies I have described are summarized in table 1. It can be seen that there is developmental change in the strategies available to the child. The earliest response biases allow children to give some appearance of language comprehension although they are actually unable to understand any of the words (stage IV). Later comprehension strategies allow the child to give the appearance of understanding entire sentences on the basis of lexical processing only—one or two words—first for objects that are present (stage V), then for objects that are absent (stage VI and afterward). Still later lexical comprehension is coupled with probable-event strategies that, allow children to understand relations among the words of a sentence on the basis of what they know about the usual relations of such things in the world; they now have sufficient past experience to know what is most probable for a specific set of objects and events. Finally, they link structural cues in the sentence—word order or clause order—to meaning.

Thus the child begins (stage IV, approximately eight to twelve months) by being entirely dependent on the context of the interaction for obtaining the speaker's meaning. In stage V, approximately twelve to eighteen months, words begin to determine meaning jointly with the context. Later still, in stage VI (approximately eighteen to twenty-four months), lexical comprehension takes place in the absence of context. Finally, in the preoperational period and later, children have sufficient experience and can free themselves sufficiently from the immediate situation to construct probable event interpretations. Simple sentence meaning during early preoperations (two to four years), however, is still derived from knowledge of the world rather than from knowledge of syntactic structure. It is not until five years that most children are able to use the syntactic cue to word order to under-

Table 1. Summary of Nonlinguistic Response Strategies and Comprehension Strategies

Piagetian State (Approximate Age Range)	Strategy
Sensorimotor Stage IV (8–12 months) Context-determined responses	1. Look at objects that mother looks at 2. Act on objects that you notice 3. Imitate ongoing action
Sensorimotor Stage V (12–18 months) Lexical guides to context-determined responses	1. Attend to object mentioned and . . . 2. Give evidence of notice 3. Do what you usually do in the situation
Sensorimotor Stage VI (18–24 months) Lexical comprehension but context determines sentence meaning	1. Locate the objects mentioned and give evidence of notice or 2. Do what you usually do a. Objects into containers b. Conventional use 3. Act on the objects in the way mentioned a. Child as agent b. Choose handier object as instrument
Early Preoperations (2–4 years) Lexical comprehension but context or past experience determines sentence meaning	1. Do what is usually done a. Probable location strategy b. Probable event strategy 2. Supply missing information
Late Preoperations and Concrete (4–11 years) Lexical and syntactic comprehension for simple structures Context and overgeneralized syntactic strategies Past experience determine complex sentence meaning	1. Word order strategy 2. Order of mention strategy 3. Probable relation of events

stand agent and object in a simple sentence. For later learned structures probable event strategies can be identified in elementary school children.

Implications for Further Research

Although there is good evidence for developmental change in the comprehension strategies that children use, there is less evidence about the detail of their use within each period. For example, there is evidence that several different strategies are available to the child at any one time. How does the child determine which to use? The reasons children choose one or another strategy are an important focus for future research. Whether individual differences exist in comprehension strategies is a topic for future work. The extent to which comprehension strategies play important roles in the comprehension of later acquired structures, especially embedded and conjoined sentences, needs further research. The reported difficulty of fourth graders in understanding subordinate sentence structures in tests of reading comprehension, for example (Watts 1944; Bormuth et al. 1970), may arise from children's difficulty in understanding these same structures in oral language as well rather than from reading skill deficiencies (Robertson 1968; Stoodt 1970).

Relation of Comprehension to Production

To return to the original paradox introduced at the beginning of this chapter, knowledge of syntactic structure as indexed by comprehension experiments comes late indeed in relation to use and understanding of the same sentence in context (see Bloom 1973; Lahey 1974). Figure 1 shows a hypothetical developmental line for a given grammatical construction. Testing should reveal comprehension in context, when situational cues to meaning are present, earlier than comprehension out of context, when the linguistic cues to meaning are the only ones available. Through comprehension strategies using the situation and knowledge of probable meanings, the child gives the appearance of comprehending a sentence long before it can be done on the basis of its structural cues alone.

Figure 1 also suggests that apparent mastery of a form on the basis of use in context will emerge earlier than apparent mastery on the basis of use out of con-

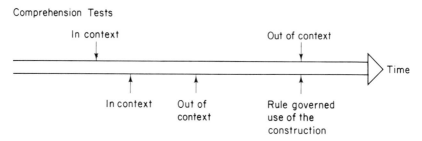

Figure 1. Hypothetical development of apparent mastery of a grammatical construction.

text. This suggestion is based on Bloom's (1974, this volume) report of instances in which children are unable to repeat sentences out of context that they had spontaneously produced in context the day before. The situational context may have served as a sort of external short-term memory, allowing children to construct longer utterances in context than they could remember without mnemonic support.

Finally, figure 1 summarizes the speculative conclusion that rule-governed production of a given syntactic form will coincide in time with the comprehension of a sentence on the basis of that form as linguistic cue. For example, comprehension of simple semantically reversible sentences on the basis of word order cues may emerge just at the time that the child has developed general rather than verb-specific three-term ordering rules, such as the ordered rule *agent action object-of-action*. Bloom, Miller, and Hood's (1975) finding that children produce longer sentences with old verbs than with new verbs suggests that children's early rules for sentence production are verb specific. We might expect to find the emergence of a general grammatical rule for word ordering in production. (agent action object) just when the child is able to use word order as a cue in comprehension. One test for the emergence of the more general rule would be its productivity: New verbs learned after this time should immediately appear in three-term utterances and novel overgeneralizations of words in the action slot should appear. For example, my son, John, produced sentences such as "Who deaded my kitty?", "Who greyed it?", and "You sad me" after his average utterance length passed 3.0 morphemes. Bowerman (1976) has reported a number of such overgeneralizations of causative verbs at ages and stages of language development that are compatible with this prediction.

The de Villiers (1974) and Brown (1973) have suggested that every performance measure of language competence introduces apparent variation in the age when a form is mastered. Some of that performance variation, I have suggested in figure 1, is systematically accounted for by the comprehension strategies that context (and later, knowledge of the world) makes possible. Another portion of that variation I have suggested is accounted for by changes in the sentence rules underlying produced sentences and by contextual support for production.

Implications for Clinical Work and Classroom Instruction
To the extent that children rely on word comprehension, the situation, and their knowledge of the world to obtain sentence meaning, sensitive teachers will provide multiple avenues to meaning rather than verbal instruction alone. Language is no royal road to meaning for the child. Contextual support geared to the child's current level of comprehension skill is necessary. Tasks requiring the child to rely solely on the teacher's (or the book's) language may pose very severe comprehension problems for the language-learning child, despite apparent understanding when context is present. Paraphrase, example, demonstration, and illustration are all helpful devices for the teacher to use. Checking to see what the children have understood and giving them the skills to check on their own understanding through paraphrase, question asking, request of examples, or demonstrations are important.

Assessment of a child's comprehension of a word or grammatical cue is clearly a complex task that will require the clinician to take current cognitive level and possible comprehension strategies into account. If the clinician wishes to identify the comprehension strategies that the child is using and can use, assessment must be planned to test these strategies in appropriate ways. Current remedial programming for language-delayed children is often based on normal developmental sequences (for example, Miller and Yoder 1974; Lahey, this volume). Application of the introductory text axiom that "comprehension precedes production," however, could produce serious dislocations in the appropriate sequence if the clinician understands comprehension to mean comprehension based on the grammatical cue. Comprehension strategies appropriate to the child's developmental level should be incorporated into the goals of remedial programming. For example, hearing-impaired children should not be deprived of visual and contextual support for a speaker's meaning until the later stages of the language-learning process.

In conclusion, learning to understand language cannot take place in the absence of shared social and situational context. Meaning for the child arises from experience. Only gradually, through successful use of comprehension strategies based on lexical understanding, do children see the way in which language structures systematically reflect the sentence meanings they independently construct. In Bransford's words (Bransford and Nitsch, this volume), it is the immediate situation that first determines the significance of the input for the language-learning child. MacNamara (1972, p. 1) has summarized this argument: "To put it another way, the infant uses meaning as a clue to language, rather than language as a clue to meaning."

References

Amidon, A., and Carey, P. 1972. Why 5-year-olds cannot understand before and after. *Journal of Verbal Learning and Verbal Behavior, 11*, 417–423.

Baird, R. 1972. On the role of chance in imitation, comprehension, and production test results. *Journal of Verbal Learning and Verbal Behavior, 11*, 474–477.

Barrie-Blackley, S. 1973. Six-year-old children's understanding of sentences adjoined with time adverbs. *Journal of Psycholinguistic Research, 2*, 153–167.

Bates, E. 1974. Acquisition of pragmatic competence. *Journal of Child Language, 1*, 277–281.

———. 1976. Pragmatics and sociolinguistics in child language. In D. Morehead and A. Morehead (Eds.), *Normal and deficient child language*. Baltimore, Md.: University Park Press, 411–463.

Beilin, H. 1975. *Studies in the cognitive basis of language development*. N. Y.: Academic Press.

Bever, T. G. 1970. The cognitive basis for linguistic structures. In J. Hayes (Ed.), *Cognition and the development of language*. New York: Wiley, 279–352.

Bloom, L. 1973. *One word at a time: The use of single word utterances before syntax*. The Hague: Mouton, 285–311.

———. 1974. Talking, understanding, and thinking. In R. L. Schiefelbusch, and L. L. Lloyd (Eds.), *Language perspectives: Acquisition, retardation, and intervention*. Baltimore, Md.: University Park Press, 285–311.

————. This volume. The integration of form, content, and use in language development.

Bloom, L., Miller, P., and Hood, L. 1975. Variation and reduction as aspects of competence in language development. In A. Pick (Ed.), *Minnesota Symposia in Child Psychology*. Minneapolis, Minn.: University of Minnesota Press, pp. 3–55.

Bormuth, J., Carr, J., Manning, J., and Pearson, D. 1970. Children's comprehension of between- and within-sentence syntactic structures. *Journal of Educational Psychology*, *61*, 349–357.

Bowerman, M. 1976. Semantic factors in the acquisition of rules for word use and sentence construction. In D. Morehead and A. Morehead, *Normal and deficient child language*. Baltimore, Md.: University Park Press, 99–179.

Bransford, J. D., and Nitsch, K. E. This volume. Coming to understand things we could not previously understand.

Brown, R. 1973. *A first language*. Cambridge, Mass.: Harvard University Press.

Bruner, J. S. 1975a. The ontogenesis of speech acts. *Journal of Child Language*, *2*, 1–19.

————. 1975b. From communication to language—A psychological perspective. *Cognition*, *3*, 255–287.

Carroll, J. B., and Freedle, R. O. 1972. *Language comprehension and the acquisition of knowledge*. Washington, D.C.: V. H. Winston.

Carrow, M. 1968. The development of auditory comprehension of language structure in children. *Journal of Speech and Hearing Disorders*, *33*, 105–108.

Cazden, C. 1970. The neglected situation in child language research and education. In F. Williams (Ed.), *Language and Poverty*. Chicago, Ill.: Markham Publishing Co. 81–101.

Chapman, R. S. 1973. The development of question comprehension in preschool children. Paper presented to American Speech and Hearing Association, San Francisco, November.

————. 1974. Discussion Summary: The developmental relationship between receptive and expressive language. In R. L. Schiefelbusch and L. L. Lloyd (Eds.), *Language perspectives: Acquisition, retardation, and intervention*. Baltimore, Md.: University Park Press, 335–344.

Chapman, R. S., and Kohn, L. L. 1977. Comprehension strategies in preschoolers: Animate agents or probable events? Paper presented to Stanford Child Language Research Forum, Stanford University California, March.

Chapman, R. S., and Miller, J. F. 1975. Word order in early two and three word utterances: Does production precede comprehension? *Journal of Speech and Hearing Research*, *18*, 355–371.

Clark, E. V. 1971. On the acquisition of the meaning of "before" and "after." *Journal of Verbal Learning and Verbal Behavior*, *10*, 266–275.

————. 1973. Non-linguistic strategies and the acquisition of word meaning. *Cognition*, *2*, 161–182.

————. 1974. Normal states and evaluative viewpoints. *Language*, *50*, 316–332.

————. 1975. Knowledge, context, and strategy in the acquisition of meaning. Paper presented at the 26th Annual Georgetown University Round Table: *Developmental Psycholinguistics: Theory and Applications*, Georgetown University, Washington, D.C., March.

Clark, E. V., and Garnica, O. 1974. Is he coming or going? On the acquisition of deictic verbs. *Journal of Verbal Learning and Verbal Behavior, 13,* 559–572.

Corrigan, R. 1975. A scalogram analysis of the development of the use and comprehension of "because" in children. *Child Development, 46,* 195–201.

———. 1976. The relationship between object permanence and language development: How much and how strong? Paper presented at Stanford Child Language Research Forum, Stanford University, April.

Cromer, R. 1974. The development of language and cognition: The cognition hypothesis. In B. Foss (Ed.), *New perspectives in child development.* Baltimore, Md.: Penguin, 184–252.

de Villiers, J., and de Villiers, P. 1973. Development of the use of word order in comprehension. *Journal of Psycholinguistic Research, 2,* 331–342.

———. 1974. Competence and performance in child language: Are children really competent to judge? *Journal of Child Language, 1,* 11–22.

Dore, J. 1974. A pragmatic description of early language development. *Journal of Psycholinguistic Research, 4,* 343–350.

Epstein, H. L. 1972. The child's understanding of causal connectives. Unpublished doctoral dissertation. University of Wisconsin, Madison, Wisconsin.

Ervin-Trips, S. 1970. Discourse agreement: How children answer questions. In J. Hayes (Ed.), *Cognition and the development of language.* New York: Wiley, 79–108.

———. Some strategies for the first two years. In T. Moore (Ed.), *Cognitive development and the acquisition of language.* New York: Academic Press, 261–286.

Fernald, C. 1972. Control of grammar in imitation, comprehension and production: Problems of replication. *Journal of Verbal Learning and Verbal Behavior, 11,* 606–613.

Ferreiro, E., and Sinclair, H. 1971. Temporal relationships in language. *International Journal of Psychology, 6,* 39–47.

Folger, J. P., and Chapman, R. S. In press. A pragmatic analysis of spontaneous imitations. *Journal of Child Language.*

Fraser, C., Bellugi, U., and Brown, R. 1963. Control of grammar in imitation, production, and comprehension. *Journal of Verbal Learning and Verbal Behavior, 2,* 121–135.

Goldin-Meadow, S., Seligman, M., and Gelman, R. 1976. Language in the two-year-old. *Cognition, 4,* 189–202.

Greenfield, P. M. 1972. Playing peekaboo with a four-month-old: A study of the role of speech and nonspeech sounds in the formation of a visual schema. *Journal of Psychology, 82,* 287–298.

Grice, H. 1975. Logic and conversation. In P. Cole and J. Morgan (Eds.), *Syntax and semantics,* Vol. III. New York: Academic Press, 41–58.

Gumperz, J. J., and Hymes, D. 1972. *Directions in sociolinguistics.* New York: Holt. Rinehart and Winston.

Hatch, E. 1971. The young child's comprehension of time connectives. *Child Development, 42,* 2111–2113.

Hodun, A. 1975. Comprehension and the development of spatial and temporal sequence terms. Unpublished Ph.D. dissertation, University of Wisconsin, Madison, Wisc.

Horgan, D. 1975. Language development: A cross-methodological approach. Unpublished Ph.D. dissertation, University of Michigan, Ann Arbor, Mich.

Hutson, B. A., and Shub, J. 1975. Developmental study of factors involved in choice of conjunction. *Child Development, 46,* 46–53.

Huttenlocher, J. 1974. The origins of language comprehension. In R. L. Solso (Ed.), *Theories of cognitive psychology.* Potomac, Md.: Lawrence Erlbaum Associates, 331–368.

Huttenlocher, J., and Strauss, S. 1968. Comprehension and a statement's relation to the situation it describes. *Journal of Verbal Learning and Verbal Behavior, 7,* 300–304.

Huttenlocher, J., and Weiner, S. 1971. Comprehension of instructions in varying contexts. *Cognitive Psychology, 2,* 369–385.

Huttenlocher, J., Eisenberg, K., and Strauss, S. 1968. Comprehension: Relation between perceived actor and logical subject. *Journal of Verbal Learning and Verbal Behavior, 7,* 527–530.

Ingram, D. 1974. The relationship between comprehension and production. In R. L. Schiefelbusch and L. L. Lloyd (Eds.), *Language perspectives—Acquisition, retardation and intervention.* Baltimore, Md.: University Park Press, 313–334.

Johnson, H. L. 1975. The meaning of *before* and *after* for preschool children. *Journal of Experimental Child Psychology, 19,* 88–99.

Johnston J. 1973. Spatial notions and the child's use of locatives in an elicitation task. Paper presented at the Fifth Child Language Research Forum, Stanford University, April.

Katz, E., and Brent, S. 1968. Understanding connectives. *Journal of Verbal Learning and Verbal Behavior, 7,* 501–509.

Keeney, T., and Wolfe, J. 1972. The acquisition of agreement in English. *Journal of Verbal Learning and Verbal Behavior, 11,* 698–705.

Keller-Cohen, D. 1975. Children's verbal imitation, comprehension and production of temporal structures. Paper presented at the biennial meeting of the Society for Research in Child Development, Denver, April 10–13.

Kuhn, D., and Phelps, H. 1976. The development of children's comprehension of causal direction. *Child Development, 47,* 248–251.

Lahey, M. 1974. Use of prosody and syntactic markers in children's comprehension of spoken sentences. *Journal of Speech and Hearing Research, 17,* 656–668.

―――. This volume. Disruptions in the development and integration of form, content, and use in language development.

Lewis, M., and Freedle, R. 1973. Mother-infant dyad: The cradle of meaning. In P. Pliner, L. Krames, and T. Alloway (Eds.), *Communication and affect.* New York: Academic Press, 127–156.

Lézine, I. 1973. The transition from sensorimotor to earliest symbolic function in early development. Research Publication of the Association for Research in Nervous and Mental Disease Vol. 51, 221–228.

Limber, J. 1973. The genesis of complex sentences. In T. Moore (Ed.), *Cognitive development and the acquisition of language.* New York: Academic Press, 169–185.

Lovell, K., and Dixon, E. 1965. The growth and control of grammar in imitation, comprehension, and production. *Journal of Child Psychology and Psychiatry, 5,* 1–9.

Lovell, K., and Slater, A. 1960. The growth of the concept of time: A comparative study. *Journal of Child Psychology and Psychiatry*, *1*, 179–190.

Lowe, M. 1975. Trends in the development of representational play in infants from one to three years—An observational study. *Journal of Child Psychology and Psychiatry*, *16*, 33–47.

MacNamara, J. 1972. Cognitive basis of language learning in infants. *Psychological Review*, *79*, 1–13.

Maratsos, M. 1974. Children who get worse at understanding the passive: A replication of Bever. *Journal of Psycholinguistic Research*, *3*, 65–74.

Maratsos, M., and Abramovitch, P. 1975. How children understand full, truncated, and anomalous passives. *Journal of Verbal Learning and Verbal Behavior*, *14*, 145–157.

Matalon, B. 1962. Étude génétique de l'implication. *Études d'éspistemologie génétique* XVI, *Implication, formalisation et logique naturelle*, 69–93.

Miller, J. F., and Yoder, D. E. 1973 *Miller-Yoder Test of Grammatical Comprehension*. Madison, Wisconsin: University Bookstore.

————. 1974. An ontogenetic language teaching strategy for retarded children. In R. Schiefelbusch and L. Lloyd (Eds.), *Language perspectives—Acquisition, retardation, and intervention*. Baltimore, Md.: University Park Press, 505–528.

Montroy, P., McManis, D., and Bell, D. 1971. Development of time concepts in normal and retarded children. *Psychological Reports*, *28*, 895–902.

O'Brien, T. C., and Shapiro, B. J. 1968. The development of logical thinking in children. *American Educational Research Journal*, *5*, 531–542.

Olds, H. F., Jr. 1968. An experimental study of syntactical factors influencing children's comprehension of certain complex relationships. Report No. 4, Harvard University Center for Research and Development on Educational Differences, Cambridge, Mass.

Owings, N. 1972. Internal reliability and item analysis of the Miller-Yoder Test of Grammatical Comprehension. Unpublished master's thesis, University of Wisconsin, Madison, Wisc.

Palermo, D. S., and Molfese, D. L. 1972. Language acquisition from age five onward. *Psychological Bulletin*, *78*, 409–428.

Paris, S. G. 1973. Comprehension of language connectives and propositional logical relations. *Journal of Experimental Child Psychology*, *16*, 278–291.

Parisi, D., and Antinucci, F. 1970. Lexical competence. In G. B. Flores d'Arcais and W. J. M. Levelt (Eds.), *Advances in psycholinguistics*. Amsterdam: North Holland, 197–210.

Peel, E. 1967. A method for investigating children's understanding of certain logical connectives used in binary propositional thinking. *British Journal of Mathematical and Statistical Psychology*, *20*, 81–92.

Piaget, J. 1969. *Judgment and reasoning in the child*. Totowa, N.J.: Littlefield, Adams.

Piaget, J., and Inhelder, B. 1967. *The child's conception of space*. New York: Norton.

Roberge, J. J. 1970. A study of children's abilities to reason with basic principles of deductive reasoning. *American Educational Research Journal*, *7*, 583–596.

Robertson, J. E. 1968. Pupil understanding of connectives in reading. *Reading Research Quarterly*, *3*, 387–417.

Searle, J., 1969. *Speech acts: An essay in philosophy of language.* Cambridge, Mass.: Cambridge University Press.

Shapiro, B., and O'Brien, T. 1970. Logical thinking in children ages six through thirteen. *Child Development 41,* 823–829.

Shatz, M. 1975. On understanding messages: A study in the comprehension of indirect directives. Unpublished Ph.D. dissertation, University of Pennsylvania, Philadelphia, Pa.

Shine, D., and Walsh, J. F. 1971. Developmental trends in the use of logical connectives. *Psychonomic Science, 23,* 171–172.

Shipley, E., Smith, C. S., and Gleitman, L. 1968. A study in the acquisition of syntax: Free responses to verbal commands. *Language, 45,* 322–342.

Sinclair, H., and Bronckart, J. 1972. SVO—A linguistic universal. *Journal of Experimental Child Psychology, 14,* 329–348.

Slobin, D. I. 1966. Grammatical transformations and sentence comprehension in childhood. *Journal of Verbal Learning and Verbal Behavior, 5,* 219–227.

Spitz, R. A. 1957. *No and yes: On the genesis of human communication.* New York: International University Press.

Stoodt, B. L. D. 1970. The relationship between understanding grammatical conjunctions and reading comprehension. Unpublished Ph.D. dissertation, Ohio State University, Columbus, Ohio.

Strohner, H., and Nelson, K. 1974. The young child's development of sentence comprehension: Influence of event probability, nonverbal context, syntactic form, and strategies *Child Development, 45,* 567–576.

Vygotsky, L. S. 1962. *Thought and language.* Cambridge, Mass.: MIT Press.

Watts, A. F. 1944. *The language and mental development of children.* London: George G. Harrap.

Weil, J. 1970. The relationship between time conceptualization and time language in young children. Unpublished Ph.D. dissertation, City University of New York.

Wetstone, K. S., and Friedlander, B. Z. 1973. The effect of word order on young children's responses to simple questions and commands. *Child Development, 44,* 734–740.

Wilcox, S., and Palermo, D. 1975. "In," "On" and "Under" revisited. *Cognition, 3,* 245–254.

Winograd. T. 1972. Understanding natural language. *Cognitive Psychology, 3,* 1–191.

General Discussion of Papers by Bransford and Nitsch and Chapman

Functional versus "Decontextualized" Comprehension

A general topic of discussion arose from Tallal's question about what kind of comprehension the clinician or educator is (or should be) interested in. Is it *functional* comprehension, that is, comprehension within a situational context, or *decontextualized* comprehension, that is, comprehension of linguistic materials as evaluated out of natural situational contexts? For example, an adult aphasic patient can often get along in everyday life even when tests of linguistic comprehension show severe deficits. What are the clinical and educational implications of distinguishing between these definitions of comprehension? What kind of comprehension should tests measure? What kind of comprehension *do* current tests measure?

Chapman cited one important implication for language education and remediation programs. The textbooks of the 1970s advise that comprehension (of syntactic structure, for example) should be taught prior to production. If comprehension is interpreted as decontextualized comprehension (and that is the kind of comprehension most assessment tools currently measure), then the teacher following this advice would wait far too long to begin to teach the production of these structures in context. The advice should read, "Work on comprehension in context before working on production in context."

The conferees agreed that most current tests that assess comprehension, and indeed most assessment methods used in school settings, require decontextualized comprehension. Kavanagh cited the familiar experience of trying to help one's high school child with a homework assignment. Upon first reading the questions (with no prior context such as having read the textbook or being given the instructions) the parent often cannot answer any of the question even though the subject matter is one in which he or she is knowledgeable. After having read the entire test, which provides some contextual support for what the assignment is about, one is often able to answer the questions easily.

Miller and Chapman both emphasized that success in formal educational programs requires decontextualized comprehension skills. Most instruction, especially instruction via textbooks, depends on mastery of linguistic comprehension out of context. Miller asserted that this was a skill for which the school instills a "support system" (to use Bransford's term) in the successful student. Those students who do not learn this skill from this kind of support system fail academically.

Jenkins commented that with respect to adult aphasia, comprehension in context appears to be very good because these patients are highly skilled at using the situational support, especially the social situation, to infer the meaning of the linguistic message. But when one tests decontextualized linguistic comprehension, the aphasic's receptive functions are seen to be as impaired as his or her productive capacities. If one is interested in aphasic's *linguistic* processing deficits, one must test those abilities out of the normal situational contexts.

In general the conferees agreed that tests that measure both kinds of comprehension were needed and that the users of those tests must understand what it is that the tests are measuring. Tests that assessed comprehension at several levels from situation-specific to decontextualized comprehension mastery would be most desirable. These kinds of graded tests do not exist currently.

Social and Educational Implications of Comprehension Testing

On a related topic, Labov commented that tests (specifically language comprehension tests) are often used as discriminative instruments as well as diagnostic instruments. For example, children are placed in reading groups according to their scores on tests that measure decontextualized comprehension. As was reported in the *Harvard Education Review* a child who is labeled a poor reader (as early as in kindergarten) rarely advances out of the lowest reading group. These tests can therefore become barriers to full social advancement through an education.

Labov added that the kinds of tests that assess decontextualized comprehension often become teaching devices in themselves. For instance, drills of word meaning out of context become part of the teaching process. Children are actually taught how to pass tests. Those children who are not motivated to work in this manner or who do not yet have the particular skills necessary to bridge between comprehension in situational contexts and decontextualized comprehension fall further behind.

Miller agreed with Labov's statements and added that many anthropologists have made this same kind of mistake. They ask questions out of context and find that the people they are studying are "childish" or "primitive." In the same manner, children who have a great capacity to deal with meanings in context are assessed as "inferior" on the basis of tests that measure the wrong thing.

Gradation of Contextual Support in Children's Reading Materials

Liberman asked how one might investigate what kinds of supporting contexts were necessary at various stages of development and how children learn to deal with decreasing contextual support. He related his own experience with reading materials given his children in the elementary grades. From his point of view, the content of the stories (episodes about the mailman and the milkman) were exceedingly dull. When he inquired of the teachers why the children were not given more interesting stories (such as fairy tales), he was told that the children were familiar with the "community helpers." That is, the stories provided a familiar context in terms of the content.

Liberman's experience with his own children, however, was that they responded very well to all kinds of stories in which a tremendous amount of the material was totally unfamiliar and even bizarre or impossible. He wondered how children are able to comprehend these materials. How do they learn to cope with materials in which comprehension is only marginally supported by the situational context? Indeed, should reading materials or children challenge them to extend their power to comprehend in minimally supported contexts—to make inferences, to adopt hypotheses, and so on? How does one gauge how much contextual support the child needs? If full contextual support is always given, could it be stultifying for the development of comprehension?

Bransford responded that one of the most important skills a child must acquire is to know how to obtain the information needed to make something understandable. That is, children must learn how to assess their state of understanding and seek further information by asking questions. Bransford had no firm ideas on how this capacity develops; he knew of no research that spoke directly to these issues. In his interactions with his own children he sometimes plays games in which he says something that is not quite true. But he added that explicit training of this sort was probably not a part of many children's upbringing.

Bransford and Liberman agreed that ideally materials and experiences should be graded such that they keep children working at the limits of their capabilities so that they progress steadily toward decontextualized comprehension. Chapman stressed, however, that children must have full contextual support at early stages of the development of comprehension. With respect to learning to read, normal children have mastered the comprehension of most linguistic structures in spoken language (except for subordinate clausal constructions) by the time they start school. She wondered whether the reading comprehension problems with subordinate structures reported by Bormuth et al. (1970) were due to a lack of prior comprehension mastery of these forms in spoken language. She is currently conducting some studies of comprehension of spoken sentences that investigate this possibility.

Reference

Bormuth, J., Carr, J., Manning, J., and Pearson, D. 1970. Children's comprehension of between- and within-sentence syntactic structure. *Journal of Educational* Psychology, *61*, 349–357.

Language and Memory

ROBERT G. CROWDER

There may be manifestations of memory that are totally independent of language, for example, the olfactory-gustatory episode that qualifies Marcel Proust for citation in psychology books. There may also be areas of linguistic study that can safely remain innocent of memory, perhaps comparative semantics. But these examples are difficult to find and the burden of this paper will be the extraordinary and deep interpenetration that otherwise marks these two subjects. There are three major sections in the chapter: First the role of memory in the perception and comprehension of language is considered. Second the learning and retention of linguistic events is discussed with respect to the issues of levels of language representation and the message-medium relationship. Finally the role of language in the service of memory is taken up. Within each of these headings, cases are considered at the level of speech processing and of syntactic-semantic processing. In addition, because the act of reading provides such a vivid natural setting for the interplay of language and memory, research on the reading process is considered.

Memory in the Service of Language

The basic point to be made in this section is that linguistic category states correspond generally to events that cover an appreciable span of time. This makes memory an integral part of the perception process because the processor must have available information about energy from several different points in the past (see Norman 1972 for a similar discussion). Especially in auditory perception, the association of category states with instantaneous patterns of stimulation is simply preposterous. The formant transitions that are sufficient cues for the perception of stop consonants (Delattre, Liberman and Cooper 1955) occur within time periods of about 40 milliseconds (msec). During this period no category decisions can be reached because the evidence is not yet all in, but after the formant transition has been completed, unless there was memory, the information about the early part of the signal would be lost. The format for memory subserving this function must be at a logical stage of coding inferior to that demanded by the ultimate categorical decision. If Gibson (1950) is right about the dynamics of visual perception, this argument applies in an equally profound way to visual perception, although the easiest examples come from auditory perception.

MEMORY IN SPEECH PERCEPTION

At the phonological (or phonetic) level there is little direct evidence about percept-forming memories, but the concept is consistent with many known facts. We may tentatively separate the segmental features from the prosodic features for this discussion without in the least meaning to imply the participation of different memory systems in the two.

SEGMENTAL FEATURES As Massaro (1974, p. 199) has commented, "small portions of the acoustic input are not unique . . . [and therefore] larger chunks of the acoustic input are necessary for recognition." In Massaro's experiments with linguistic (1974) and nonliguistic (1970) stimulus events, the technique of backward recognition masking is employed to estimate the auditory memory system (echoic memory) underlying the use of "larger chunks." He finds that performance on a two-choice recognition measure (in which the subject must decide which of two prearranged stimulus categories occurred prior to some third, masking stimulus) reaches asymptote when the mask is delayed by intervals on the order of 100 or 200 msec. Although Massaro would like to use this figure as an estimate of decay time for auditory memory (1974, p. 200), it is more likely an estimate of how long people need to process the information within the echoic trace (see Crowder 1976, chapter 3; Studdert-Kennedy 1974, pp. 22-23). In all events, the memory trace produced from the target must last at *least* this long.

Huggins (1975) has offered evidence related to the memory substrate of speech perception in his studies of temporally segmented speech. This is produced by inserting silent periods into a continuous speech stream. Huggins found that 63 msec segments of running speech could be shadowed at about 55 percent accuracy when the segments were separated by silent intervals of from 125 to 500 msec, independent of the duration of silence within this range. The percept-forming work of auditory memory was shown in performance with intervals of less than 125 msec separating the 63 msec speech segments: Performance improved sharply as the silent gaps were reduced from 125 to about 60 msec, at which point scores were too good to permit detection of any possible further changes in intelligibility. Huggins calls this improvement in performance as the gap between speech segments is reduced the phenomenon of "gap bridging" and he assigns the process to auditory memory in exactly the way the introduction to this section anticipated. If two segments, individually only 55 percent intelligible, can reside together in auditory memory, then some higher order process can draw information from both segments pertinent to some category state. However, if the first segment has departed before the second arrives, the system has to depend on isolated snatches.

Studdert-Kennedy (1976) has expressed the view that the phenomenon of coarticulation or parallel transmission is necessarily indicative of auditory memory for syllabic duration. The basic empirical result is that in a consonant-vowel (CV) syllable starting with a stop consonant, information about each of the two phonemes is distributed over the entire duration of the syllable. Thus what information cues a stop is different depending on the vowel following. For instance, Liberman, Delattre, and Cooper (1952) showed that the categorization of a stop burst depended on the following vowel. Since this implies postponement of the categorization of the stop until arrival of vowel information, there must have been an auditory memory operating at some prephonetic level.

Shankweiler, Strange, and Verbrugge (1975) have now demonstrated that such parallel processing—the dependence on a temporal context for classification of momentary auditory stimulation—is a quite general characteristic of speech perception, not restricted to the class of stop consonants. It had been widely believed, though with scant evidence (Gerstman 1968; Ladefoged and Broadbent 1957), that vowel perception could be accommodated by a model that included normalization for the speaker's vowel space prior to an analysis of the first two or three formant frequencies (considered to be the major cues for vowel identity). Shankweiler, Strange, and Verbrugge (1977) comment that whereas isolated vowels as often presented in laboratory experiments can indeed be specified by steady-state formant frequencies, vowels in continuous natural speech cannot; the latter are very often characterized by "articulatory undershoot," the tendency of vowels in running speech not to reach their official destinations before falling under the coarticulatory influence of the following segment. In their experiments Shankweiler, Strange, and Verbrugge found only weak evidence for the use of same speaker precursor stimuli in the identification of rapidly articulated vowels in syllables. However, these authors found excellent evidence that information within the syllable played a large role. They conclude that "it is futile to seek a solution to the [vowel] constancy problem by analysis of any acoustic cross-section taken at a single instant in time, and we must conclude that the vowel in natural speech is inescapably a dynamic entity" (p. 338). If the perception of vowels is inescapably a dynamic process, it is also inescapably dependent on auditory memory.

A CAVEAT: FEATURE DETECTORS Although the strong position has been taken here that the time dependence of most segmental features is almost logical proof of a memory-dependent mode of processing, recent work on adaptation to speech sounds (Eimas and Corbit 1973) may force reconsideration of the argument. Eimas and Corbit showed that if subjects listened to massed presentations (over two per second for two munutes) of tokens from one extreme of such a continuum as that separating /b/ and /p/, they later placed their discrimination boundary closer toward the adapting stimulus than it otherwise would have been. That is, listening to repeated presentations of a /b/ leads the subject to identify ambiguous cases as /p/ more often than before adaptation. (See Cutting and Pisoni, this volume, for a further discussion.) Eimas and Corbit (1973) believed that the adapting stimulus produced fatigue in a feature detector specialized for that phonetic feature and thus temporarily impaired its processing. This finding raises an important empirical question and several important theoretical questions.

The empirical question is whether the adaptation effect is properly considered a performance decrement. Having just heard a flood of /b/ tokens, subjects might not be fatigued at detecting its features; they might instead have a stricter criterion of what they are willing to call a /b/. A recent analysis by Cooper, Ebert, and Cole (1976, experiment III) tackles this issue from the viewpoint of signal detection analysis and shows that at least some of the boundary shift is a matter of true sensitivity rather than criterion shifting.

The theoretical issues raised by the adaptation procedure concern the level of processing at which the putative feature detectors operate, especially whether the level is auditory or phonetic. These matters are the subjects of recent reviews by Cooper (1975), Darwin (1975), and Studdert-Kennedy (1974). While the level of feature detection is an urgent matter for models of speech perception, it makes less difference for the point being made in this section: Any kind of feature detector may be considered greatly to reduce the burden of perception on the memory system. If there is a feature detector for isolated formant transitions (Darwin 1975, p. 77), the necessity for storage of early values during the subsequent glide is reduced; the transition somehow resonates as a unit with its waiting detector. It is as if the cues for pitch were interpreted not by a memory-dependent wave-counting process but by a bank of tuning forks set to different frequencies (an analogy suggested by Ulric Neisser): The tuning forks carry, in some abstract sense, a memory process, but not the type of sensory memory that was promoted earlier.

It was previously noted that dynamic cues for segmental features operate on several levels, including not only the formant transitions for individual segments but also influences spanning the duration of a syllable. It remains to be seen whether processes interpretable as feature detection can be assigned likewise to each of these various levels.

PROSODIC FEATURES The segmental features are treated as digital signals carried as passengers on a speech stream whose prosodic features are analog. Rhythm stress, and intonation stand in what Garner (1974, pp. 136–137) calls a relation of of asymmetric integrality with the segmental features. It is possible to present messages containing the prosodic features without segmental features, for example, by humming sentences (Darwin 1975, p. 72) or by putting the message into an unknown language. However, it is not possible to present speech messages containing the segmental features without prosody. (More will be said about asymmetric integrality later.)

The use of prosodic information demands a prelinguistic auditory memory system or *echoic memory*. To know that cues of intonation, stress, and so on have changed during an utterance, some system must be able to compare current with past values of these parameters. It is unthinkable that these memories are carried in some verbal or categorical form. Such a digitization of the prosody would predict conflict or interference between segmental and prosodic channels when the opposite, facilitation, is the case. For this reason the prosodic features need a relatively raw form of memory.

Crowder and Morton (1969) proposed such a system of echoic memory on the basis of experiments on immediate memory for lists of verbal characters. The two main performance manifestations of echoic memory according to Crowder and Morton are the *modality effect* and the *suffix effect*. In the modality effect the comparison is between ordered memory for lists of items that have been presented either visually or auditorily. These presentation modes result in equal performance except for the last item or the last few items in the list, where auditory presentation produces superior recall. The supposition was that this auditory advantage resulted from a lingering echoic trace that was set up by auditory but not by visual presentation. The echoic system was assumed to be of such limited capacity that each successive auditory input would mask previous ones, leaving only the last item or items relatively unmasked.

The suffix effect is observed in a comparison of normal auditory presentation of a memory list with an identical condition containing an extra word, called the stimulus suffix, occurring after the last memory item in rhythm with the presentation rate. Performance in the two conditions does not differ except for the last part of the list, where the condition with the added suffix yields less accurate recall. Crowder and Morton assumed that the suffix exerted the same masking effect on the last part of the list as is exerted by each auditory list item on its predecessor. The suffix thus acts to mask echoic information about the end of the list before the subject can use this information.

Extensive consideration of the modality and suffix effects and of other manifestations of echoic memory are found in Crowder (1976, chapter 3; forthcoming). There are two reasons for believing that the memory system revealed by these phenomena is especially appropriate for the integration of prosodic cues. First, the time dimensions of these effects are such as to make them compatible with the timing of prosodic information. The fact is, unfortunately, that there are no experimentally sound decay estimates for echoic information in the modality and suffix effects, previous claims (Crowder 1972; Massaro 1974) notwithstanding. However, Crowder and Morton (1969) surmised that the system must be capable of holding information over periods of about two seconds. With a different technique, Darwin, Turvey, and Crowder (1972) showed evidence for echoic storage surviving on the order of seconds and their demonstration may be related to the modality and suffix effects. Thus there is reason to believe without hard estimates that the echoic memory system responsible for these two phenomena is capable of mediating periods appropriate to the interpretation of prosodic information.

The second reason for associating the Crowder and Morton hypothesis of echoic memory to prosodic information is that the experimental demonstrations of it are curiously selective according to the category of speech sound being remembered. Crowder (1971, 1973) found that when subjects had to remember distinctions among the stop consonants (as with the list, BAH, BAH, GAH, BAH, DAH, DAH, GAH), neither the pronounced recency effect usually obtained with auditory but not visual presentation (modality effect) occurred nor did the suffix effect. On the other hand, an identical experimental task where distinctions among vowel sounds were critical (as with the list, GAH, GEE, GEE, GOO, GAH, GOO, GAH) led to the return of the modality and suffix effects in their familiar forms. This dependence of the echoic memory demonstrations on the phonetic class of the memory items has important implications for several issues (see Crowder 1976, chapter 3), but the issue of immediate interest here is how this selectivity is related to formulations about the role of memory in language comprehension. That the echoic store is useful for holding vowel sounds but not consonant sounds suggests it would not assist in mediating delayed decisions about segmental features. But it would be ideal for mediating delayed decisions about prosodic features since the prosodic features are carried by the vowel sounds and not by the consonant sounds. It is possible, even likely (Darwin and Baddeley 1974; Pisoni and Tash 1974), that echoic information even about stop consonants lasts for a short period—perhaps long enough to mediate syllabic or subsyllabic perceptual units—but only the vowel information lasts long enough to show up in the suffix and modality paradigms. Thus it is convenient to preserve the functional distinction between echoic memory for stops and for vowels even though it may turn out to be the same format.

PROSODIC FEATURES IN READING "Schoolgirl punctuation" allows digitization of the prosodic features in written language through multiple underlines, ellipses, and so on. Even normal punctuation can serve to "disambiguate" otherwise equivalent surface representations: That dog bit the man. That dog *bit* the man? That *dog* bit the man? *That* dog bit the man? and so on.

The issue of how prosody and punctuation function in fluent reading leads us rapidly to the recurrent basic issue of what the relation is between reading and speech. One view is that it is partly because of the need for clarity of statements on a prosodic basis that readers employ recoding through speech as a strategy (Liberman et al.; forthcoming). These researchers remark that syntactic parsing is almost certainly aided significantly by prosodic features in speech and that it is therefore likely that one uses punctuation and word order cues to recover the prosodic features in the writer's original spoken intention. Another view would be that prosodic cues in the orthography contact their "meaning" directly, without mediation of inner speech. A third possibility would be that prosodic information is never recovered, with the possible exception of the question mark. Punctuation in this case would be a message from the writer to the reader that for the moment the reader should engage a phonological mediation mechanism because the particular passage would otherwise be ambiguous.

Knowing of no evidence on the role of punctuation in reading and related matters, I conducted a modest pilot experiment on what may be called optional punctuation, punctuation not necessary for distinguishing between two or more possible underlying meanings. The purpose was to see whether punctuation cues to pausing would slow down either silent or overt reading. Pairs of sentences differing only in the presence or absence of four punctuational cues to pausing were developed. For example:

1(a). The children—aged six through ten—were, generally, in trouble.
1(b). The children aged six through ten were generally in trouble.
2(a). He thought, secretly, that, of the six ducks, only two would live.
2(b). He thought secretly that of the six ducks only two would live.

There were pairs of sentences of lengths nine, ten, eleven, twelve, and thirteen words. In counterbalanced order, each of the ten sentences (five pairs) was read four times, twice aloud and twice silently, by a single subject. Reading times were recorded by hand with a stopwatch. Since the duration of silent reading would not otherwise be detectable, before each reading in all conditions the subject was instructed to say "go" and at the end to say "period."

Figure 1 shows the reading times at each length separately for the silent and aloud conditions.[1] Despite the use of a single subject and a single sentence at each length, there was a regular lengthening of reading times as a function of the number of

[1]Since every condition was tested twice and since these two replications were taken at different times, a rough measure of the reliability of the experiment is given by the correlation coefficient across the twenty conditions (five sentences by two punctuation conditions by two vocalization conditions). This correlation coefficient was .83, which is significantly different from zero, $z = 4.9$, $p < .0001$. Thus, what differences there were among conditions were not mainly caused by error variance.

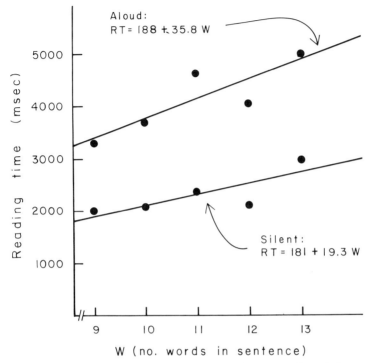

Figure 1. The relation between reading times and number of words in a sentence for silent and overt pronunciation. Lines are fitted to points by linear regression.

words. The overall correlation between these variables was .88, z = 1.95, p = .026. However, the regression of reading times upon sentence length was much sharper for the spoken task than for the silent task, as is indicated by the different slope values. A further measure of the validity of the experiment is that the intercept values were almost identical in the two conditions. The slope values for silent reading are in good correspondence with the three hundred word per minute estimate of normal reading speed. The difference in times for the silent and aloud conditions was, of course, highly significant: t (4 df) = 13.88, p = .0016.

The main result of the experiment was that it made absolutely no difference whether the optional punctuation was present or not (t = 0.04) nor was there any hint of an interaction involving punctuation. This null finding astonished both the subject and the experimenter; it apparently *felt* like the punctuated versions took longer. This result suggests that the presence of optional punctuation does not produce differential reconstruction of pauses in silent and overt reading. It could be that the insertion of pauses was syntactically necessary in both conditions. Alternatively, it could be that with syntactically unambiguous sentences the subject can simply do without timing information; on this second hypothesis the subject backtracks to reconstruct prosody only when an ambiguity has been detected.

In any case, it may be concluded (if a proper experiment sustains the conclusions from figure 1) that punctuation marks are not automatic cues to the application of prosodic features in reading.

THE SYNTACTIC LEVEL

The same points that were made about the dynamic nature of auditory signals and the consequent memory requirements apply on a higher level for structures that are defined syntactically. A sentence whose major constituents may be widely separated can be parsed syntactically only if the earlier elements are held in memory while the later ones arrive. The burden that can be placed on memory by these structures can be especially conspicuous in left-branching structures such as the sentence *The mouse that the cat that the dog chased ate squeaked* compared with the corresponding right-branching *The dog chased the cat that ate the mouse that squeaked.* Particular attention to the association of memory with left-branching constructions has been given by Yngve (1960) in a model quantifying at least one aspect of the process. Yngve proposed that each word in an immediate constituent phrase marker such as that shown in figure 2 could be characterized by a number giving its depth; these numbers are shown below each word in the example. Notice that the depth of each word corresponds to the number of left branches leading to it from the top of the structure.

One psychological interpretation of the depth numbers is a word-by-word count of the expectations shared by the speaker and the receiver. The first word, *The,* minimally implies two things, a subject and a predicate, but not more, for the sentence could have read, *The ambassador scintillated.* The next word, *greatly,* not

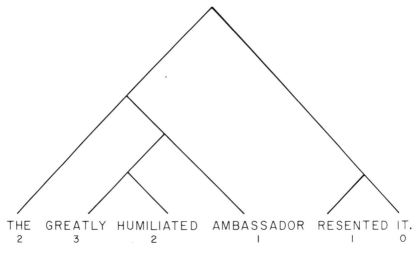

Figure 2. Phrase structure diagram of a sentence and the Yngve numbers (depth) associated with each word.

only does not resolve either of these two expectations; it adds another, that the subject will be modified by an adjective. This last expectation is resolved by the following word, *humiliated*; but there still remains the necessity for a subject and a predicate. In like manner the rest of the words in the sentence can be analyzed. Here these depth numbers are considered to count expectations on the part of the listener, but they also represent obligations undertaken by the speaker for what must be done to resolve the implications of what is being said at each point in the utterance. For both the speaker and receiver, they amount to an index of memory load incurred by the syntactic structure of the message.

Martin and Roberts (1966) found that sentences whose mean depth (averaged across the sentence) was low were processed more efficiently than sentences whose mean depth was high (see also Wearing and Crowder 1971). Although Yngve's analysis does therefore offer some degree of psychological reality to the demands of syntactic processing upon memory, it is by no means a perfect index of that. There is imperfect agreement even among specialists as to how some sentences should be parsed into constituents (represented by hierarchical tree structures such as the one shown in figure 2), to say nothing of the disagreement of ordinary subjects with specialists (Martin 1970). Furthermore, some words do not clearly imply further constituents. The following sentence could end at any point after the third word: "The judge resigned yesterday morning angrily."

Johnson's (1968) model of sentence storage and retrieval begins from a rather similar analysis of how a sentence is represented in memory and from a similar hierarchical performance model to that used by Yngve. The subject supposedly retrieves a sentence from the top down, following a number of rules: (1) The subdivision of a sentence into structural codes is a more reliable process that the retention of the information contained in those codes. Thus, for example, the subject may remember that a series is divided by one binary branching and then by two subordinate branchings with four and three nodes, respectively; but at the same time the subject may not recall the contents of those nodes. (Prosody, for example, could serve to maintain the structure of syntactic divisions without comparable retention of the verbal information.) (2) Subunits are recalled as units and this recall is initiated only if each of the codes within the unit leads to an available memory trace. (3) The probability of initiating recall of a subunit is (therefore) inversely proportional to the number of nodes it subsumes. It follows from these assumptions that transition error probabilities (the conditional probability that an error will follow a correct recall in the sequence) should be high at major syntactic breaks but low within syntactic units. Johnson is also able to predict the incidence and locations of omission errors from his model. It is notable that Johnson's model of sentence retrieval works equally well for digit strings where syntactic breaks are simulated by pauses. Johnson (1970) has therefore been testing the model with the latter materials since they are simpler to work with than sentences.

Yngve's and Johnson's models of ongoing processing demands reveal a common attitude toward the role of memory in serial hierarchical representations (see Crowder 1976, chapter 12, for a further discussion of such representations). Basically, the point is that information about the current, past, and future portions of the message is carried in parallel, just as parallel transmission of information was observed in CV syllables. As Liberman (1970) has argued, the property of grammaticality is thus similar at both the speech level and the sentence level.

Memory, Levels of Language, and the Message-Medium Problem

In the first section memory in the service of language was considered; the final section will consider language in the service of memory. In this section the focus is on how people remember linguistic events. Emphasis is placed on questions of how memory processes relate to levels of language representation and to the dual characterization of language in terms of both message (content) and medium (form).

ASYMMETRIC INTEGRALITY AND LEVELS OF LANGUAGE

In characterizing language, at least the following levels of analysis can be distinguished: auditory, phonetic, phonological, morphemic, lexical, syntactic, semantic, and pragmatic. In visual language the levels of type font, graphemic features, and graphemes can be substituted for the first three levels, after which written and spoken language converge. While there may be some argument about the choice and ordering to these levels, they will serve as a point from which three further issues can be discussed: a logical issue, an empirical issue, and some generalizations about memory of lingustic materials.

LOGICAL RELATIONS AMONG LEVELS Garner (1974) has observed that when a stimulus set is defined by two dimensions, there are three logical relations that can exist between those dimensions. In *separable* dimensions there is nothing about the presence of one dimension that implies the presence of the other. For example, consider the set of four stimuli defined by a binary choice of numeric character and the presence or absence of surrounding parentheses: (1), (2), 1, 2. With these two dimensions there is no necessary rule that, having one, the other must also be present. However this is not the case for *integral* dimensions. For instance, the brightness and hue of a single color patch have this relation to each other: One cannot have brightness represented without hue and vice versa. The pitch and amplitude of tones are related integrally also.

It is the intermediate case, *asymmetric integrality*, that is of interest here (recall the earlier mention of this concept in connection with the prosodic and segmental features). In dimensions related by asymmetric integrality it is possible to realize variation in one dimension without having a second, but not the other way around. Garner (1974, p. 137) cites color and form as an example: Form cannot be achieved without some color but through the use of some device, such as a ganzfeld, one can have color without form. Prosodic features in speech can be achieved through humming, with no segmental message, but it is not possible to present the segmental features through speech without also having prosody.

Each of the levels of language has the relation of asymmetric integrality with the other levels. It is possible to realize the auditory features of speech through backward speech without at the same time realizing phonetic or phonological features (except through accident). But one cannot produce the phonetic features without also having auditory ones. The phonetic features can be combined to yield sounds that are phonologically meaningless, at least for a particular language; but the phonological categories cannot be produced without necessarily producing the associated phonetic ones.

At higher levels the same relations hold: With inflected nonsense words such as used in the "Jabberwocky," syntactically rich messages that contain no semantic message are possible, but the reverse is not possible. Anomalous sentences such as *Colorless green ideas sleep furiously* (Miller and Isard 1963) may exemplify the same thing except for people who take pride in devising a content for even the most anomalous of these. The difference between anomalous sentences and permutations of the same words (such as *Ideas green furiously sleep colorless*) distinguishes the lexical and syntactic levels. It is probably possible to devise messages that are pragmatically vacant but show absolutely perfect form up to that level; however, a pragmatically effective communication must carry information on at least one of the lower levels.

The levels of language all possess a message-medium relation to one another with the higher level defined as some type of modulation in the lower level. The medium can occur without the message but not the other way around. It may tentatively be proposed that if this relation of asymmetric integrality does not distinguish two proposed levels of language processing, then they are not really at different levels.[2]

DISCRIMINATION OF ASYMMETRICALLY INTEGRAL DIMENSIONS
Work of Garner and his associates (Garner and Felfoldy 1970; Garner 1974) has established quite general empirical results corresponding to the logical relations of integrality, separability, and asymmetric integrality. The result of interest here is that, for the latter, performance on the lower level dimension (the medium) is not impaired by irrelevant variation in the higher level dimension (the message); but the converse is not true. The first evidence for this generalization came from Day and Wood (1972) and Wood (1974) with auditory and phonetic discrimination. Specifically, Wood found that when subjects were making a pitch discrimination on CV syllables it made no difference if the initial phoneme of these syllables varied as well. When the subject was judging pitch, performance was the same when there was only one pitch-varying syllable, say /bae/, as when there were two syllables, /bae/ and /dae/, whose pitch varied. However, when the task was to distinguish between /bae/ and /dae/, irrelevant variation in pitch slowed down responding. This suggested to Wood that there was a serial extraction process, with pitch processed earlier than the phonetic feature. If the decision can be based on the earlier level it should make no difference what is going on at the later stage.[3]

[2]Garner (1974) has questioned whether asymmetric integrality implies a difference in level of language processing. He cites nonlinguistic dimensions in support of this point, particularly color and form; and the point has to be conceded. However, I would argue that color and form are representative of fundamentally different (physiological) levels of information processing. That is, color distinctions occur at the individual retinal photoreceptors whereas form comes from a higher level of visual processing.

[3]It is interesting that by the proposed criterion for distinguishing levels of language, the

THE ISSUE FOR MEMORY What consequences for memory does this analysis of language levels have? Is there a correlate within memory to the generalization from Wood (1974) that lower level dimensions are handled without interference from higher level dimensions but not vice versa?

Conventional wisdom in recent years among memory specialists (for example, Craik and Lockhart 1972) suggests that there is indeed such a correlate. The process of committing linguistic messages to memory entails progressively deeper analysis, each stage of which results in a form of coding. The codes resulting from early, preliminary analyses are more transitory than those resulting from deeper analysis, with the result that the earlier codes appear to be discarded. This fits well with evidence that sensory attributes survive at most for tenths of a second, that speech-related short-term storage lasts only seconds, and that an underlying abstract representation lasts minutes, hours, or longer. The abstraction of meaning is in this view the Holy Grail of linguistic processing and its attainment is rewarded by virtually permanent memory storage. There is now enough evidence clashing with this characterization that it can be called seriously into question. Before reviewing this new evidence and the general question of memory persistence at different levels of language, a more systematic introduction to the problem of coding for linguistic information is in order.

MODALITY-SPECIFIC CODING IN SPOKEN LANGUAGE

To begin, echoic memory, phonological coding in memory, and auditory memory imagery are distinguished briefly. Some new evidence on memory for a speaker's voice is then reviewed.

DISTINCTION BETWEEN ECHOIC MEMORY AND PHONOLOGICAL CODING In an earlier section, the topic of echoic memory was treated in some detail.[4] With respect to phonological coding, Conrad (1964) was the first to present a comprehensive demonstration that errors in visual immediate memory tend to be phonologically similar to the correct letters. He showed that confusions among letters missed in a visual memory experiment were, letter by letter, the same confusions that occurred in an experiment on listening to individual letter names presented for identification against noise.[5] This was interpreted as evidence that

---

phoneme and the syllable do not qualify as separate levels. They seem, rather, to be integral; one cannot define a spoken syllable without realizing phonetic features and one cannot have a phonological segment without putting it into a syllable. This fits with the observation of Liberman (1970) that the transmission of phonemic information is parallel during the course of some CVC syllables. It also fits with the result of Healy and Cutting (1976) showing no difference in the detection speeds for phonemes and syllables in the search paradigm first introduced by Savin and Bever (1970).

[4]In particular the proposal by Crowder and Morton (1969) that the suffix and modality effects could be ascribed to the operation of a limited-capacity sensory store within the auditory system was presented. So far, the only other sustained program of research on echoic memory has been led by Massaro (1975), although there are numerous other demonstration techniques for echoic memory (Crowder, forthcoming).

[5]Full discussion of this form of coding, which Conrad chose to call "acoustic" but which Morton and Crowder assigned to the articulatory system, will be deferred until the last section of this review.

the subject in the visual experiment recoded the input into a phonological representation at some level of analysis.

For the moment it will suffice to draw a careful distinction between these two memory systems. The formal distinction between them is quite circular with respect to their defining operations: Phonological coding is a consequence of either visual or auditory presentation, whereas echoic memory can occur only when information has arrived through the ears.

Why is it incorrect to envision a single auditory speech-related code with direct access from auditory input and indirect access from visual input? There are several lines of support for retaining the distinction. Crowder and Cheng (1973) reasoned that if there were but a single auditory speech code in memory, then the suffix effect would have to be assigned to the same system responsible for Conrad's confusion errors. If this were true, the suffix effect should be larger the greater the phonological similarity between the suffix item and the memory items. To test this, they had subjects remembering strings of seven vowel sounds from the vocabulary /gi, gɪ, gu/. The suffix was the syllable /ba/ in one condition and in the other condition it was the syllable /bɪ/. The former was chosen to be as remote as possible from the vowel sounds being remembered in terms of vowel space, and the latter was chosen to be maximally similar.

Crowder and Cheng (1973) found that both suffix items were sufficient to remove completely the recency effect obtained in the control condition but they were not different in the extent to which this was true. The phonologically-similar suffix did impair performance slightly more across all list positions, but by a constant amount. Thus it was concluded that the effect of the suffix in removing the normal recency effect was a functionally distinct phenomenon from the phonological similarity effect.

The same conclusion may be drawn from an experiment by Cheng (1974) that used a different procedure. In his study the same list of seven consonant letters was simultaneously presented in two different modalities. The first was a visual-articulatory mode in which written-out syllables appeared on the screen and the subject had to pronounce each covertly as it occurred. The second mode was auditory, in which the syllables were presented through a loudspeaker. On each trial a different permutation of the letters FRGKMVY was presented over both channels. These letters all have a distinctive vowel sound when given their conventional names: /ef/, /ar/, /dʒi/, and so on. However, when presented in the initial position of CV syllables ending in /a/ (/fa, ra, ga/ and so on), they are much less distinctive. Thus Cheng had two input modes, visual-articulatory and auditory, and two phonological forms, distinctive and similar. The similarity was varied orthogonally within each mode to produce four conditions: similar forms in both modes, similar forms in the visual-articulatory mode but distinctive forms in the auditory mode, distinctive forms in the visual-articulatory mode but similar forms in the auditory mode, and distinctive forms in both modes. The question was whether distinctiveness in form, which was expected generally to facilitate memory, would have the same effect in the visual-articulatory mode as in the auditory mode. Cheng found that the similarity effect was uniform across all list positions when varied in the visual-articulatory mode but that it was located exclusively on the last one or two positions when varied in the auditory mode. This experiment shows that the very same manipulation of phonological similarity leads to different consequences in the phonological code and in the (auditory) echoic code.

Levy (1975) showed much the same thing in a study on sentence memory. (It is significant that these generalizations about phonological and auditory coding hold true whether the memory stimuli are as impoverished of meaning as Cheng's syllables or as rich in meaning as the sentences used by Levy.) She found a modality effect favoring auditory presentation of three sentences over visual presentation of the same material. She also found that articulatory suppression, counting softly from one to ten during presentation of the sentences, affected performance adversely. The observation of interest here is that these two effects were functionally distinct: The modality contrast was evident only on the last sentence in the series of three but the manipulation of articulatory suppression impaired performance equally across the three sentence items. Thus again the phonological code shows itself across all items whereas the auditory code is selective to the last information received.

The final argument for distinguishing the phonological from the auditory code is that the effects attributed to echoic memory (the suffix and modality effects) are consistently absent in experiments that present stop consonants, as reported earlier. Yet it is precisely with these particular letters that the evidence of phonological confusions in memory is the strongest.

AUDITORY MEMORY IMAGERY (MEMORY OF A SPEAKER'S VOICE)
One can easily recognize hundreds, perhaps thousands, of human voices whose distinct timbres are a subtle consequence of different vocal tract configurations. One can likewise classify sounds and recognize melodies through systems that almost surely are not mediated by verbal coding. But these can be considered semantic memories rather than episodic memories, to borrow the distinction proposed by Tulving (1972). That is, these auditory memories form part of one's store of knowledge that exists quite independently of the particular circumstances and content of individual events. It is not the sound of a friend's voice saying anything in particular that is retained but rather it is the sound of the voice in the abstract. These memories are instances of auditory imagery in memory. The test is that they can be initiated from within: One can summon at will the sound of a bassoon or of Churchill's voice. In distinction, the coding of linguistic episodes, such is now under consideration, requires storage of the content "in" the medium.

The story of episodic auditory memory systems would now be complete were it not for experiments on the facilitation of word recognition by presentation of test items in the same voice as had originally been used in presentation. There are also experiments showing that people can recall with some success which of two voices had presented a particular word on a list (Light et al. 1973). This modality recall is an interesting result but it is not an indication that a true episodic record of the word's presentation has been kept in memory. Instead, the subject could have stored a proposition of some kind to the effect that a particular word occurred in a particular voice. Having such a modality tag—word x occurred in modality *b*—would not be useful in deciding whether a particular word occurred at all, although it would help, in retrospect, to decide what the presentation modality had been. Nor would recognizing the voice in which a test word is presented assist in deciding whether the word being spoken in that voice had occurred. Thus, memory for modality and recognition facilitation mean quite different things; the former implies at least a tagging process whereas the latter implies a record of the episode including the modality information.

Coltheart and Allard (1970) and Cole, Coltheart, and Allard (1974) presented an experimental procedure measuring reaction time to same-different judgments based closely on the technique devised by Posner and Keele (1967) to study visual memory. The subjects heard two English letter names pronounced in succession with delays of .5, 2, or 8 seconds (sec) between. The letters in each pair either had the same or different names and were either both presented in the same voice (male or females) or were presented in different voices. The judgment of same or different was always on the basis of the names of the two letters and not on the basis of voice information. The results showed an advantage for same-voice conditions. This advantage was around 50 msec in magnitude and it did not diminish as a function of the retention interval separating the two events. As Cole, Coltheart, and Allard (1974) observed, the interpretation would pose no problems if this effect had been present only on trials where the two letters indeed had the same name; in this case the advantage could be ascribed to a persistent episodic echoic trace of the first test event assisting the decision about the second event. However there was a same-voice advantage for the "different" responses also. According to their preferred model of the entire pattern of results, the subject first reaches a decision on whether the two voices were the same. If so, the subject matches the two events on the basis of a physical auditory code; if not, he or she generates encoded representations of each to be compared. This alternative of course includes the assumption that the physical code persists until the second stimulus occurs. A final possibility, which does not include this assumption, is that the same-voice effect here results from a speaker normalization operation that must precede identification of phonetic features.

Same-voice recognition facilitation was also found in a set of experiments by Craik and Kirsner (1974) and their studies are not open to the ambiguity of interpretation present in the Cole, Coltheart, and Allard (1974) data. Craik and Kirsner presented strings of 436 words, one every 4 sec, with repeated words in the series. The task was simply to detect whether each presented word had yet appeared in the series. The words were presented in two voices, male and female. They varied both the lag separating the first and second occurrences of repeated words (up to 128 items, or 128 sec) and whether or not the voices presenting a particular word were the same on the two occasions.

In three experiments, the result was a small accuracy advantage (about 3 percent) in recognizing old words when they were repeated in the same voice as the first occurrence. There was also a modest latency advantage (about 22 msec). Both effects were statistically reliable and showed no signs of disappearing as a function of lag. The authors concluded that their subjects had had access to episodic voice information for at least two minutes. In the second and third experiments, Craik and Kirsner found that recall of the voice in which a word had been presented was excellent. Furthermore, the added task of making voice judgments did not result in a "cost" to accuracy of word recognition. This makes it likely that in their experiment, but not necessarily in others, the voice recall task was mediated by the literal episodic record rather than by a tagging process. The general expectation would be that tagging, as a deliberate and perhaps even verbal process, would depend on the same limited-capacity memory system as does verbal recognition and therefore reduce the latter when the task requires it as opposed to a pure recognition task. When there is no cost, on the other hand, one would expect to find recognition facilitation (see Light et al 1973; Light and Berger 1974 for more on these matters).

MODALITY-SPECIFIC CODING IN WRITTEN LANGUAGE

In this section, as in the last, some preliminary remarks about sensory memory are presented before considering the survival in memory of modality-specific information from written language.

ICONIC MEMORY Despite the passing of over fifteen years, the seminal work of Sperling (1960) and of Averbach and Coriell (1961) on iconic memory stands largely intact both empirically and conceptually. (Recent reviews by Coltheart [1975] and Crowder [forthcoming] may be consulted for a further discussion of this research.) The only sharp conceptual reorientation appears to be a new report by Sakitt (1975) showing evidence that strongly suggests a locus of iconic storage at the level of the rod photoreceptors. However, as others have commented, the peripheral locus for the icon itself does not prejudice the question of where, in terms of central or peripheral stations, visual masking occurs (Turvey 1973).

POSTICONIC REPRESENTATION OF TYPOGRAPHY Posner and Keele (1967) demonstrated that subjects responding "same" or "different" on the basis of the letter names of two successive stimuli were faster if these stimuli on "same" trials were either both upper case (AA) or both lower case (aa) than if they were of different type cases (Aa). Later work (Posner et al. 1969) has established this to be a case of visual memory imagery lasting on the order of a few seconds, that is subject to deliberate rehearsal, temporal decay, and capable of generation from auditory input. This work was important in denying the growing belief that the only processing stations for written material were iconic memory and verbal-phonological short-term storage. There are now data on more varieties of visual memory clearly separable from the system examined by Posner and his associates.

Light, Berger, and Bardales (1975) and Light and Berger (1974) showed that subjects could recall the case and color of words that had been presented in a memory experiment. They concluded that such retention was not automatic but was rather due to deliberate encoding strategies of attribute tags. This conclusion follows properly from their evidence that incidental memory for such features was not as good as intentional memory and that there was a trade-off for memory of such features and memory of the words themselves (that is, a "cost"). Rothkopf (1971) found excellent incidental memory for the location on a page in which substantive information had occurred and for where in a sequence of pages of test it had occurred. For Rothkopf's studies, however, it is impossible to analyze for either the recognition-facilitation effect or for the cost effect; therefore it cannot be determined whether this memory is an incidental byproduct, an intentional byproduct, or part of a true episodic record.

In two experiments, however, Kirsner (1973) obtained a diagnostic pattern of results. A long list of single words was studied for recognition; those presented twice occurred in all possible combinations of upper and lower case letters which allows one to examine whether recognition of the repeated words was better when the typographical cues matched than when they did not. In two different experiments, Kirsner obtained recognition facilitation with matching typographies. This effect extended out to the longest intervals tested, about 1.5 minutes. Furthermore, in accord with expectations, the requirement to report what form old words had appeared in (instructions to study for memory of modality as well as memory for words) was accomplished at no cost in terms of the primary task.

Kolers and his associates (Kolers 1973, 1975a, 1975b; Kolers and Ostry 1974) have presented the most systematic program of research on this topic, conclusively demonstrating a very longlasting memory for encoding operations performed on the typographic representation. In these studies Kolers has examined the consequences for memory of reading coherent sentences in normal or in inverted (upside down) typography. In the study by Kolers and Ostry (1974) subjects read a deck of sixty sentences, half in each of the two typographic orientations, and later were tested for recognition of these same sentences among sixty sentences they had never seen before. All combinations of normal and inverted type were represented in the repeated items (inverted-inverted, inverted-normal, and so on) and the new sentences were equally often in each orientation. Analyses based on recognition of sentences according to several different criteria revealed the following results: First, the content of a sentence was remembered better if it occurred in the original typography than if it did not (Kolers and Ostry 1974; but see Kolers 1973 for a qualification on this finding). The recognition facilitation persisted when a full month intervened between the original study session and testing. This result is consistent with the interpretation that orientation is a part of the episodic visual information. Some measures of memory for typography actually showed higher performance than some measures of memory for content. Second, there was an advantage to sentences appearing originally in the unfamiliar typography over those appearing in normal typography. It was shown that this advantage in retention of the originally invested sentences was not caused by the greater study time accorded them. Third, the correlation across subjects, between measures of the semantic components and measures of the typographic components of the materials, was low, indicating some degree of independence between them.

Kolers and Ostry concluded that their results falsify theories that propose a serial analysis always in the direction of more abstract encodings in which surface features are discarded along the way. Nor do they accept a naive pictorial-encoding interpretation of their results as a general model for linguistic analysis (in part because pictorial encoding would be useless in incorporating contextual features of the learning episode). Rather, they say, the analytic operations themselves constitute the memory trace:

The analytic operations the reader performs on the graphemes do not merely extract from its shell the semantic nugget that is delivered to mind; they constitute a crucial aspect of the representation. What is meant by this is that the operations directed at the analysis of graphemes at the time of reading are reinstituted in significant measure at the later time, and this reinstatement of operations accounts for recognition (Kolers and Ostry 1974, p. 609).

If the subject's attention is directed away from surface features and toward semantic features, as in the experiments of Bransford and Franks (1971), it is these semantic operations that will form the memory trace. It is not, thus, the depth of processing that determines what will be recognized but rather the complexity of processing. There is nothing more or less memorable about abstract meaning per se than about the most mundane surface features; what makes a difference is how complex the operations were at that particular level.

In further experiments on inverted typography, Kolers (1975a) showed that transfer between two readings of the same sentence could be related to memory for superficial aspects of the sentences. A series of experiments on this problem led to the conclusion that there were both isolable semantic and typographic components to such transfer. The latter, it should be noted, refers to a visual memory of a particular sentence as it appeared in a particular typography. Kolers found that such memory persisted to the longest interval between readings, in which the processing of ten other sentences intervened. In another study Kolers (1975b) showed that over comparable periods the influence of typography depended on the skill of subjects in dealing with inverted text. Those who had had extensive practice at it showed much less evidence in their memory performance for the retention of episodic information about typography. This is as it should be if it is the complexity of encoding operations that determines their durability. But Koler's studies cannot be dismissed as dependent on grotesque stimulus materials; these materials only demonstrate the point that it is the complexity of codes and not their closeness to deeply abstract linguistic codes that determines memorability. Subjects are not inherently good at remembering what linguistic messages mean. They are good at remembering what they had trouble with when trouble is defined by complexity rather than sheer effort. Highly automatized encoding operations, such as occur with different colored type or with different cases, may leave no such processing residue and thus need to be retained by a costly, deliberate encoding operation (Light et al, 1975; Light and Berger 1974).

This interpretation can be extended to account for the memory for the voice in which the words were spoken. It can be speculated that vocal tract normalization is perhaps almost always a complex operation and thus does leave an automatic residue.

MEMORY FOR HIGHER LINGUISTIC LEVELS
Let us turn now to a consideration of how memory relates to higher linguistic levels. Two sources of data are relevant here: studies of memory for language form

in bilinguals and comparisons of memory for form and gist (medium and message) in sentence memory experiments.

LANGUAGE OF INPUT IN BILINGUALS The main thrust of recent experiments on bilingual memory is the opposition between one-store and two-store notions.[6] According to the former hypothesis, information is stored in memory through an abstract format connected with, but separate from, both languages of a bilingual. For instance, the encoding and retention of the words *shame* and *verguenza* would both depend centrally on some single representational format that contains some deep abstraction of their meaning. If the encoding were automatic to the extent that attaining this format were not a complex process for bilinguals, they might need a language tag, as a separate proposition in order to recall what the language of input was. According to the two-store hypothesis (Tulving and Colatla 1970) there are separate episodic word stores for the two languages; if subjects remember the word, they automatically remember the language in which it occurs.

Recent experiments seem to favor the one-store-with-tags position. Liepmann and Saegert (1974) used a list discrimination paradigm in which successive lists had high overlap in words. In one condition the language in which the words were presented varied randomly between presentations on successive lists; in the other condition the list was consistently monolingual. If the one-store hypothesis were true, subjects ought to have more difficulty with the bilingually varying lists because they would have to keep track not only of which "concepts" occurred on lists but also of the language in which these had to be recalled. The two-store hypothesis makes the opposite prediction; since the words from two languages are placed in different storage locations, there would be essentially less overlap in the bilingually varying list and therefore it should be easier than the monolingual list. The first result was obtained, favoring the one-store notion. Saegert, Hamayan, and Abmar (1975) found that the ability to remember which of two languages had been used to present an item (tested by a third language) was reduced when meanings of items within a list were related than when the meanings were isolated. This suggested that memory for languages required use of a limited capacity tagging system rather than being an automatic consequence of two storage systems. Rose et al. (1975) obtained a similar result and applied the same interpretation to it.

This rapid survey of recent studies on memory for input languages has offered little to deny the proposition that subjects can, if not distracted by other features of

[6]Studies of memory in bilinguals have usually included very careful selection of subjects with impeccable bilingual credentials. From the point of view of Kolers's complexity hypothesis, this is rather a pity because traces of language decoding should occur primarily when this operation has been difficult. In terms of the analytic logic that was examined in the last section, only Kintsch (1970) seems to have looked for and found the phenomenon of recognition facilitation in a task whose main object was discriminating old from new word concepts. This technique may be inherently dubious, however, when the influence of language of input (rather than voice or typography or some other such formal feature) on recognition is to be evaluated. Word translations between languages may not be exact and if the concepts do not match across the two languages, the medium is not formally independent of the message, as it needs to be for the present purposes.

the text, record input language as a deliberate tag when the experimental contingencies favor this type of information. Thus nothing may be adduced about levels of information processing and memory from these studies.

FORM VERSUS GIST IN SENTENCE MEMORY Most of the research on memory for sentences has been generated to answer questions about psychological representations of grammar rather than about memory per se and there will be no effect to cover this vast area here. Instead, those studies that are continuous with the issues already raised in this section—the relative persistence of memory at different levels of language—will be reviewed.

It is generally agreed that the representation of sentences in memory potentially includes at least two separable levels: one that records surface form and the other that records the abstract propositional core of the sentence. The disagreement beyond this point as to whether and where the abstract syntactic structure is represented need not be discussed here (see Wanner 1968). The interplay of form and substance in sentence memory has been examined in three experimental techniques—the false recognition, word probe, and verification latency methods (see also the review of some of this literature in Anderson and Bower 1973, pp. 222–234). These three methods have been exploited to yield a list of factors that lawfully influence the balance between verbatim and proposition representation; these factors include instructional emphasis, decay time, memory load, and coherence of the material.

The false recognition method was first used by Sachs (1967) to show differential memory for form and gist of sentences that had been read within the context of a meaningful paragraph (see also Sachs 1974). Following exposure to a critical sentence within the text, subjects were tested at various delays by presentation of a test sentence. This latter could be related to the critical sentence in several ways: It could be identical; it could represent a change in form but not meaning (such as active to passive form of the sentence); or it could contain a change in both form and meaning. The question of interest was how much subjects were "fooled" into accepting the changed sentences as having occurred in the paragraph they had heard. Results indicated that immediately after hearing the critical sentence, subjects were very good at detecting all changes; however, after some delay, subfects were able to detect only changes that affected the meaning of the sentence and not those that merely affected the form. Performance was not quite at chance for form alterations, but it was low. Sachs (1974, p. 99) concludes, "the material in a sentence is encoded in an abstract representation, and the exact words are rapidly forgotten."

Wanner (1968, chapter 3) has shown that retention of surface characteristics may have been overestimated by the Sachs technique in which the subject was aware that retention of surface form would be tested, once into the experimental session. Wanner accomplished a complete surprise test of memory for form versus gist by using a sentence from the experimental instructions as the critical target sentence. When tested on a sentence that altered the meaning of the critical sentence, subjects (who were excused after this single test) were uniformly perfect at rejecting it, whether or not they had been warned that sentences even from the instructions could be tested. But when the alteration that transformed the critical sentence in the instructions to the test sentence was only a formal one (inversion of two clauses), the subjects that were forewarned about a test on instruction sentences did a bit better than those not forewarned; the latter showed no appreciable difference from chance. From a further study, which used the same manipulation but also varied delay before testing, Wanner concluded that unless surface features are tested within about ten syllables of the time they occur, they are lost with unwarned subjects. In order to guarantee the special condition of a completely unanticipated test, Wanner had to sacrifice the broad sampling of stimulus material usually demanded of proper experiments. However, this probably does not affect the validity of his conclusion that implicit instructions to encode surface features can enhance performance on such features.

In a related experiment, Tzeng (1975) varied the instructional set at testing. Following texts containing interrelated sentences, one group was told to respond to questions on the basis of their propositional truth value (rather than verbatim accuracy) and the second group was told to respond on the basis of exact wording. Performance on test sentences that had not appeared in the stimulus text but that were consistent with its meaning was of special interest. One finding was that judgments of validity for the group responding on that basis were little affected by the familiarity of surface form; that is, they did only slightly more poorly on valid (true) sentences that were superficially unfamiliar than on valid sentences appearing in the exact form as originally presented. However, judgments of verbatim memory for the other group were powerfully affected by the (ostensibly irrelevant) truth value of the test statement; thus distractor sentences were more easily rejected if they were inconsistent with the meaning of the text than if not. Tzeng's result is perplexing in light of the contention presented above that levels of language show the property of asymmetric integrality with neighboring levels. Form and gist, of course, have just this relation but the interference of the higher level (gist) with the lower level (form) obtained by Tzeng is opposite to the outcome reported by Wood (1974), who found that phonetic judgments were slowed down by variation in pitch but that pitch judgments were not affected by phonetic variation. The organizing concept of asymmetric integrality helps to provoke uniform theoretical analysis of different regions in the language chain, but in this particular case it provides no empirical generalization that organizes these different areas of study.

In word probe experiments subjects receive a stimulus sentence and then a test word; they must make as fast a decision as possible about some relation between that test word and the sentence they read. An experiment reported by Walter (1973) showed that the memory organization of a sentence differed from that of an incoherent word string. A given critical word was embedded either in a normal sentence or in a word series made up by scrambling that sentence. The subject was instructed to respond to test words on one of three criteria (in different conditions of the experiment): Is the test word identical, synonymous, or homonymous with any of the words that just occurred? Walter found that correct responding was consistently best under the identical instructional condition but performance on the other two tasks was s function of the stimulus condition. With scrambled word strings, subjects were more accurate and faster when they responded on the basis of a word's phonological similarity than on the basis of its meaning; however, when the stimuli were coherent sentences the reverse was true. This shows that the coherence of the material affects even the short-term memory representation. A somewhat similar study by Green (1975) extends this conclusion from the word probe method to an instructional manipulation. He found that inhibitory effects of semantic similarity depend on whether the subjects had been set to memorize the material at input or to invent a plausible continuation of the stimulus text.

It is well established that if a stimulus sentence has to be evaluated according to its truth value relative to a previous input, it can be verified faster if it has the same surface form as well as the same meaning as the previous input than if only its meaning is the same (Anderson 1974; Garrod and Trabasso 1973; Olson and Filby 1972). This research has mainly been concerned with the surface feature of active-passive voice. This result has the same form, logically, as Posner and Keele's (1967) demonstration that the typographic medium of case facilitated the nominal message of letter identity, the demonstrations that the medium of a speaker's voice facilitated decisions on the word message, and the facilitation of the medium of typographic inversion for the message of sentence identity. The extent of the same-surface form facilitation effect, when testing is for meaning, can be used as another converging measure of which factors influence the balance of the two kinds of memory.

The influence of stimulus coherence and of testing delay on the active-passive form effect were examined in a pair of studies by Anderson (1974). When the sentences later to be tested were embedded in coherent stories, there was a strong facilitation of form on judgments of meaning so long as testing occurred immediately after occurrence but there was only a weak and unreliable facilitation effect when a minute or so intervened. This is just what Sachs (1967) and Wanner (1968) found. However, Anderson suspected that the coherent nature of the stimulus stories he had used in this first experiment was causing subjects to forget surface features and thereby limiting whatever facilitation these features could exert on judgments of validity. This reasoning was tested in a second study containing the same materials but with the sentences scrambled so they no longer formed a coherent story. In this second study the facilitating influence of form on gist was evident on both the immediate and delayed tests. The results of both studies were well accommodated by a model assuming both a propositional and verbatim representation under both the high and low coherence conditions, the subjects' decisions to adopt one or another strategy being the main difference.

Layton and Simpson (1975) showed that the matching of voice facilitated recognition latency and accuracy, but only when the memory load was relatively light. The accuracy effect was present when the subjects had only a single sentence in storage; however, when they had to remember two, four, or eight sentences at the time of testing, there was no facilitation.

Kintsch (1975) has addressed this problem from a slightly different perspective. His subjects heard multisentence texts generated from a single explicit propositional base. Comprehension of the stimulus text depended on the incorporation of a critical proposition into the total structure. The main contrast was between conditions in which this proposition was stated explicitly in the text and conditions in which it was left out and therefore had to be inferred by the subject. For example, two such texts are as follows: A carelessly discarded burning cigarette started a fire. The fire destroyed many acres of virgin forest (explicit version). A burning cigarette was carelessly discarded. The fire destroyed many acres of virgin forest (implicit version). The question Kintsch posed was how long it would take subjects in each of these conditions to verify the truth of the proposition—that the fire was caused by the cigarette—that occurred always in the putative representation in propositional form but that had appeared in the explicit surface form of only one of the conditions.

Kintsch found that immediately after presentation and up to a delay of 30 sec, there was faster verification of the crucial proposition by subjects in the explicit condition than by subjects in the implicit condition, indicating some memory for surface form. However, at delays of 20 minutes (min) and 48 hours (hr) between acquisition and testing there was no such advantage. Like the other studies reviewed here, this study showed a highly transient memory for surface form.

A CONCLUDING PARADOX Memory for surface form has always been the loser in this section when pitted against memory for gist. However, Kolers and Ostry (1974), who were interested in a vastly more superficial aspect of surface form than reviewed in this section, found memory for typography was comparable to memory for meaning. This continued to be the case at retention intervals as long as one month. This poses a severe problem for a levels-of-analysis approach (presented briefly in a previous section) that insists on an orderly progression in decay rates as one moves away from superficial and toward deeper, more abstract, representations. Perhaps Kolers is right that persistence is a function of complexity, not of the level at which this complexity occurs. If so, the choice of the active-passive transformation is a very poor one to use in experiments on form and gist because it is not clear that either is a particularly difficult structure to process or that the two are differentially difficult. More challenging surface forms might change the strength of the conclusion from these studies that it is mainly meaning that gets stored. More challenging surface forms as experimental materials would not move the research further from the outside world either; it would draw it closer.

Language in the Service of Memory

Just as language is the main carrier for communications with the past and future at the level of oral and written chronicles, it is an important medium within the memory system of the individual. In this section a few of the ways language mediates the storage and retention of information will be reviewed. (See Crowder 1976, chapters 4 and 5, for a full discussion of when language is the carrier of memory.) The discussion here will emphasize the phonological level at the expense of the semantic and syntactic levels.

PHONOLOGICAL RECODING IN MEMORY
As mentioned earlier, Conrad (1964) showed that when people are recalling letters from a visually presented test of immediate memory, they tend to make the same pairwise confusions as when they are listening to single letters (names) spoken in noise. Just why and when this is so are still unresolved issues, but this does not detract from the fact that Conrad's association of visual memory with the speech system was probably the single most important influence on information-processing models of short-term memory. Several of the reliable empirical generalizations about aspects of phonological coding are examined here before turning to developmental evidence and to the possible role of phonology in reading.

PHONOLOGICAL CODING IN ADULTS There are actually two related phenomena offered by Conrad: the *confusion effect* reported in Conrad (1964) showing similar substitutions in listening and in visual memory and the finding of Conrad and Hull (1964) that correct performance suffers in short-term retention when lists contain a high density of phonologically similar items as opposed to phonologically diverse items. The second of these effects will be referred to as the *similarity decrement*. The confusion effect occurs with phonologically heterogeneous materials; it is defined as the conditional probability that an error will reflect phonological similarity. The similarity decrement can be defined as the unconditional probability of an error as a function of the phonological homogeneity of the list. Although it is prudent to keep these two effects separate, it is hoped that they will co-vary as a function of many experimental variables.

The effect of a delay period on phonological coding is a case in point. With respect to the confusion effect, there is ample evidence that phonology plays a decreasing role as the time spent performing some demanding distractor task is increased. Conrad (1967) first showed this in an experimental situation that has since been used by other investigators. A list of letters is presented serially in some display unit followed at once by a series of numbers that must be shadowed at a rapid rate. Recall of the letters is tested after varying periods of digit shadowing. The occurrence of phonological confusions depended on the amount of time spent shadowing: With a period of 3 sec the confusions were highly correlated with the letters' sounds, but with a period of 7.2 sec confusions were unrelated to sound. A similar pattern of data was observed in the same situation by Estes (1973), who found a monotonic decline in phonological confusions across retention intervals of .4, 1.2, 2.4, 4.8, and 9.6 sec, the level reaching chance only at 9.6 sec. In the same situation, Healy (1975) found the confusion effect at 1.2 and 3.2 sec, but not at 7.2.

In the Conrad, Estes, and Healy studies, the overall probability of correct response also declined with longer shadowing time. However, the latter two sets of data show that performance was above chance at intervals for which no phonological confusions appeared. In other words, the subjects showed above chance performance even when their errors did not give any evidence for phonological coding. This fact belies a simple equation of short-term storage with phonological coding.

Experiments on the similarity decrement have not yielded the same outcome as far as the disappearance of phonological coding with time. Baddeley (1966) presented series of several words to be retained and then stream of digits to be copied prior to a test of written recall. In cases where he was able either to measure or eliminate the initial performance advantage for phonologically heterogeneous lists (FEW, PIT, COW, SUP, and so on) over phonologically homogeneous lists (MAN, CAB, MAX, CAT, and so on), there was no difference at all in the rate of forgetting for the two types of material. Thus in these cases the similarity effect neither increased nor disappeared for intervals comparable to those described above (0 through 10 sec). Posner and Konick (1966) compared performance on items uniformly high or low in phonological similarity after intervals filled with tasks whose cognitive complexity was varied. They found that the size of the similarity decrement depended critically on how long the retention interval was but not at all on how difficult the task was that occupied that interval. Finally, Liberman et al. (forthcoming) tested five-letter strings high or low in phonological similarity at either an immediate test or an unfilled interval of 15 sec. The subjects were first-graders separated according to their reading ability. Like Posner and Konick, Liberman et al. found an increase in the similarity decrement over the 15-sec interval for the good readers but no change for the intermediate and poor readers.

The inconsistency between confusion and similarity decrement effects as indexes of phonological coding across lengthening delay intervals might be rationalized in terms of a rehearsal mechanism. The two studies showing an increase in similarity decrement at longer delays are also those with the most opportunity for rehearsal during those delays. The good readers in the Liberman et al. study are probably the best rehearsers. In the Posner and Konick study the intervening task was numerical rather than verbal. The rapid shadowing task (over two per second) used by Conrad, Estes, and Healy, which effectively prevents rehearsal, produced a decline in the confusion effect over delays. The studies by Baddeley that observed no change in the size of the similarity decrement over time used shadowing also, but the rate was much slower (only one response per second). Thus the inconsistencies can be resolved on the basis of differences in opportunity for rehearsal. Rehearsal, as an inherently phonological activity, would restore any otherwise fading phonological code. (The concept of rehearsal will be discussed further in another section.)

A number of studies have shown that inhibition of the articulatory machinery during encoding of memory stimuli is sufficient to remove the confusion effect. Conrad (1972) and Estes (1973) showed that requiring a vocal response simultaneous with the occurrence of the to-be-retained letter eliminated the phonologically based errors. In Conrad's experiment the subject pronounced the word *the* in unison with the presentation cadence and in Estes's experiment subjects were required to make an overt classification of each letter as being high or low in the alphabet. In these studies it was also the case that the concurrent response requirement reduced performance overall. In a second experiment Estes (1973, experiment II) tried to suppress phonological coding at input by speeding up the presentation rate of four memory letters to 200 msec rather than the 400 msec presentation time previously used. This experiment also included a 1.6 sec re-hearsal period inserted early, intermediate, or late in the total shadowing interval separating presentation from test. The result was that the confusion effect occurred only if the subjects were allowed to rehearse the items within 2 sec of their presenta-tion (the early condition). Otherwise phonological confusion errors were no more prevalent than would be expected on a chance basis. These studies of suppression tie the phonological effects to the opportunity for speech responses to occur.[7]

The case for speech coding was advanced by work of Locke and Fehr (1970) in monitoring the electromyographic (EMG) signals during encoding and rehearsal of verbal materials. The special feature of Locke's method was using stimuli rich in labial phonemes (BUFFALO, WAFFLE, BOMBER, and so on) or lacking such phonemes. Large EMG deflections were associated with chin and lip site record-ings when adults both encoded and rehearsed the libial loaded lists, but not with control lists.

Together these experiments all support the view that the opportunity for covert speech during or immediately following the occurrence of verbal stimuli affects the nature of memory errors and can, when artificial materials are heavily weighed with similar sounds, actually reduce performance. But what good is such phono-logical coding? Is it a basic medium for memory of verbal information or is it a supplemental code employed strategically?

Several experiments suggest a special relation between phonological coding and memory for the order in which events have occurred, as opposed to memory for the fact that they occurred. Watkins, Watkins, and Crowder (1974) compared lists that were phonologically homogeneous (KEY, BEE, PEET, DEEP, and so on) to lists that were phonologically heterogeneous (TUB, CAB, PAY, GOD, and so on). Subjects were tested for free recall in one experiment and serial recall in another. The similarity decrement was observed in serial recall but in free recall similarity caused a substantial improvement in performance rather than a decre-ment. The enhancement of free recall by phonological similarity would be quite uninteresting if it were due to guessing. That is, the subjects could note during presentation that all words on the homogeneous lists have the same vowel in association with a collection of stop consonants; then at recall they could simply generate recall candidates on the basis of this rule. Watkins, Watkins, and Crowder (1974) took the precaution of leaving out of lists at least two words that could have met any such criterion for guessing. Since these critical items almost never occurred in free recall, the possibility is discounted that homogeneous lists are better than heterogeneous lists because they permit a simple guessing strategy more easily.

[7]There are two studies employing a suppression method based on voluntary suppression assisted by biofeedback techniques. Glassman (1972) and Cole and Young (1975) trained subjects to inhibit articulatory responses, especially covert articulatory responses, by giv-ing them auditory feedback concerning their own momentary EMG activity in speech-related sites. Internal checks indicated that training had been effective. The outcomes of these studies were contradictory in important respects and it is almost impossible to de-termine the facts of the matter from the information given. In one of the studies suppres-sion caused no change in overall errors but eliminated the confusion effect whereas the opposite was true in the other.

(Alice Healy has pointed out in a personal communication that a sophisticated guessing strategy could, however, be responsible.)

Watkins, Watkins, and Crowder also found evidence that within the serial recall task, similarity simultaneously improves memory for items and impairs memory for order. When the task was serial recall, they scored either on a strict order criterion (where misplaced responses were thrown out) or on a free-recall criterion (where any item was accepted if it had indeed occurred on the list). This application of two scoring criteria revealed that the order and item components of serial recall were oppositely affected by similarity even within the same performance sample. This relation between similarity and the contrast of item information and order information is not at all restricted to similarity defined by phonological features. Horowitz (1961) showed the same pattern with structural similarity (common graphemes in syllables) and I have examined the same interactions with semantic similarity. It appears that any kind of similarity within a list assists memory for the items on the list while at the same time inhibiting retention of their order.

Healy (1975) has recently shown that phonological coding in short-term memory is not just restricted to memory for order, as opposed to memory for items, but that it is temporal order and not spatial order that seems to be involved. She devised two tasks in which the subjects always saw the same four letters on a trial throughout the session. In the temporal order task the spatial positions of these four letters were permanently fixed in four windows of a horizontal visual display (B always left, K always next to left, P always next to right, and M always right, for example). What changed was the temporal order in which these four letters were presented on each new trial, and it was this that the subject had to remember. In the spatial order task, Healy always exposed the four letters in the same temporal order (B first, K second, P third, and M last, for example); what changed from trial to trial was in which of the four windows these letters appeared. It was this latter aspect that the subject had to remember. The main findings were that digit shadowing had little effect on spatial memory but the usual strong effects on temporal memory; there was a strong confusion effect owing to phonological similarity at early retention intervals with the temporal task but not with the spatial task, and articulatory suppression had a strong adverse effect on the level of temporal order memory but no clear effect on spatial order memory. These and other aspects of her data led Healy to conclude that phonological coding is employed for the retention of temporal order but not for spatial position. It is impossible to resist the comment that speech, which likely modulates the phonological coding system, is inherently set up for temporal representations, as opposed to visual coding, where spatial layout predominates (see O'Conner and Hermelin 1973). Further evidence consistent with this point is that phonological coding effects are not specific across the serial positions within a memory list (Baddeley 1966; Watkins, Watkins, and Crowder 1974) unlike echoic memory effects (Crowder and Morton 1969).

From all of this, it can be surmised that phonological coding is a strategy employed by subjects in order to enhance their performance on tests of temporal order. The code achieved for this purpose may consist of phonetically distinctive features (see Cole and Young 1975) and such information is subject to complete displacement by a few seconds of some distractor task that itself involves phonetic content.

NONPHONOLOGICAL CODING IN SHORT-TERM RETENTION Some of my recent research indicates that even temporal order may assume a nonphonological coding in short-term retention. In one previously unpublished experiment, subjects saw lists of seven words that were either phonologically identical (PAIR PAIR PARE PEAR PEAR PAIR PARE) or phonologically distinct (PAIR PAIR PORE POOR POOR PAIR PORE). Some subjects pronounced the words aloud as they appeared for 5 sec on the screen and others pronounced them silently under instructions to mouth them vigorously. Thus the experiment was a two-by-two opposition of phonological identity and overt vocalization. The results are given in figure 3, which shows the error probability at each position as a function of the experimental conditions. In the phonologically distinct condition, a conventional modality advantage of auditory stimulation is observed in the overt vocalization case (Crowder and Morton 1969). However, the modality effect is reversed in the condition with phonologically identical items.

The main point about the phonologically identical items, however, is that subjects do, after all, retain them. The possibility that they were constructing a

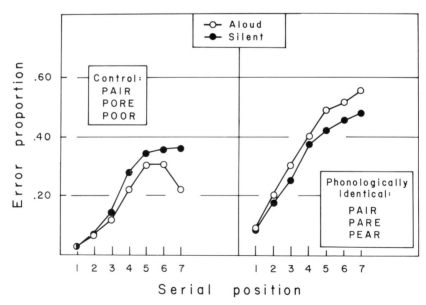

Figure 3. The relation between error probability and serial position for phonologically distinctive lists (panel a) and phonologically identical lists (panel b). Visual presentation was either vocalized aloud (open circles) or covertly read (closed circles).

subversive, articulatory distinctive code for these items can be discounted for two reasons: They had to pronounce the items aloud in one of the conditions, and they were not better on the second of two successive trials with the same vocabulary. Of course, subjects reported that their learning strategy had been to detect patterns of repetition of the three words across the seven positions and to organize their memory around these patterns. This strategy does not in the least sidestep the issue of coding, however, for they needed something with which to label the entries into their patterned memory.

These experimental materials are admittedly contrived, but the message of the study corresponds well to other evidence that the phonological code is a supplementary, rather than a primary agent for retention in ordered recall tasks. Thus, Estes found that his subjects performed far above chance even when deprived of a phonological code. Healy was able to tie performance in her temporal order task to spatial patterning when subjects were similarly deprived by the suppression method. In the experiment reported above, subjects were hurt by having to give up the phonological modality; but this produced only about a 20 percent decrement in performance, not a total collapse of memory.

DEVELOPMENT OF PHONOLOGICAL CODING Although there have been studies showing a growing sensitivity to phonological features across childhood, that is then superceded by sensitivity to semantic features (Hasher and Clifton 1974), there are not many experiments tracing the manifestations of phonological coding in memory through childhood. The notable exception is a study by Conrad (1971) on memory for pictures of objects whose names are either phonologically similar (CAT, RAT, HAT, and so on) or phonologically distinctive (FISH, GIRL, BUS, and so on). Children between the ages of three and eleven were tested by exposure to cards containing pictures from one or the other of these sets. The cards were then placed face down and the subject had to point to pictures that were identical to those exposed from among an array showing all possible stimulus pictures. The task was calibrated so that all subjects performed at about 50 percent accuracy on the phonologically distinctive items (thus the younger children received shorter lists than the older children—three items versus six items). The measure of interest was the similarity decrement, that is, whether performance was less than 50 percent for the phonologically homogeneous items. Conrad (1971) found that there was a similarity decrement that increased steadily as a function of the age of the subjects, with no detectable effect at three to five years and a very substantial one at eight to eleven years. (At the younger age, performance on the homogeneous items was 52.4 percent errors and at the latter age it was 75.3 percent errors.) Conrad reported having observed informally that the prevalence of mouthing and whispering among the subjects was similarly dependent on age and that the older subjects expressed distress when they learned that some trials contained only phonologically similar items. It is important to stipulate, further, that children even at the youngest age were fully capable of correctly naming the stimulus items pictured in the materials.

These data are interpreted as showing that, although capable of naming the items, the younger subjects had not yet developed the strategy of using those names in rehearsal to enhance memory. Even though the older, rehearsing subjects were shown to suffer on the lists of similar-sounding items, still the net effect of their developmental change was positive since they were handling lists twice as long as the younger subjects. The "penalty" of which Conrad (1972) speaks is extracted mainly in psychologist's laboratories; the phonological rehearsal strategy is probably a fantastically beneficial device overall. It is odd that Conrad's experimental task seems to rely heavily on memory for spatial position, which, we learned from Healy's experiment, seems not to receive phonological mediation. However, with correlated temporal and spatial order one cannot tell which is being used primarily, a circumstance that Healy's special tasks were devised to correct. Although there are no further experiments that bear directly on this hypothesis as does Conrad's, the following brief review of developmental phenomena in memory is perfectly consistent with it.

GENERAL MEMORY TRENDS IN DEVELOPMENT The first point to be made is the surprising one that in some respects there seems to be absolutely no development of memory capacity with increasing age. On tasks of certain kinds, particularly those that are strategy free and that do not depend upon memory for temporal order, children perform just as well as adults.

Fajnszejn-Pollack (1973) showed series of two hundred and eighty colored pictures taken from magazines to children of three age groups and to adults, half of the pictures presented once and the other half presented twice. At intervals of two, five, ten, twenty, and forty weeks later, the subjects were asked to recognize items that they had seen earlier from among new distractor items. Although overall performance was related to age in this task, the decline in performance with the passage of time was completely parallel up to a year. The rate of forgetting for such material was thus independent of age.

Brown (1973) presented a series of eighty-four colored pictures to four age groups (grades one, two, four, and college). Each item was presented only once and in a later test session the subjects had to pick old items from pairs including one old item and one new distractor. Brow argued, with some support from the earlier literature on adults, that with such long lists strategies of rehearsing order information simply do not occur. The absolute level of performance in this study was completely independent of age but constrained by neither ceiling nor floor effects. It is significant, as Brown states, that age-dependent effects have been found with the same task and much shorter lists of around ten items (Mathews and Fozard 1970); such shorter lists would make rehearsal a viable strategy. If we accept Brown's comment about the usefulness of rehearsal with short lists and its futility with long lists, these studies support her contention that children will give poorer performance than adults mainly when rehearsal is a useful device.

Studies on semantic organization by Rosenberg, Jarvella, and Cross (1971) and by Steinberg and Anderson (1975) show that the use of other types of linguistic mediation does not depend on age. The former experiment showed that while there were age effects in memory for sentences, the amount of facilitation caused by a coherent, unifying theme relating the sentences was constant across age.

Steinberg and Anderson found that first-graders are capable of using the same class-inclusion hierarchies to improve their recall as are employed by adults.

Brown (1975) showed within a single experiment the differential patterns of item and order information in development. In a cumulative paired-associate learning task that used the same stimulus term repeatedly for new responses, she found that kindergarten, second-, and fourth-graders were not different in their ability to remember which responses went with which stimuli; but there were large and consistent differences across age in the ability to reconstruct the order in which the successive responses occurred. However, Brown showed in a follow-up experiment that if kindergarteners were carefully instructed in the use of mnemonic techniques for retaining order information, they could perform as well in this aspect of the task as the older children. Thus Brown concluded that the deficit of younger children in retaining order information is not a matter of conceptual immaturity but rather is caused by a generally passive approach to problem solving. That is, the "machinery" is there but it is not used appropriately (see also Belmont and Butterfield 1971).

Flavell (1970) has introduced the terms *production deficiency* and *mediation deficiency* to describe what it is that younger children lack in some memory tasks. The former refers to the case in which the child is fully capable of using some linguistic mediator to enhance memory performance but for some reason fails to do so. The latter term refers to cases in which the putative mnemonic is spontaneously produced but does not work to improve performance. The five experiments reviewed by Flavell (1970) all tend to support the notion of a production deficiency, according to his interpretation. When means exist for measuring the mediation activity indirectly or even directly (for example, by lipreading with rehearsal), subjects who use the mediation device perform better than those who do not. However, the crucial observation is that when the nonmediators are instructed to mediate and are shown how, their performance improves so as to be indistinguishable from that of the original mediators. This latter result is taken to mean that the deficiency was in failing to produce the mediator in the first place rather than in using it.

Other evidence suggests that there may be an intermediate difficulty when the mediator (such as naming items during presentation) is demonstrably present but is not applied to the task. One might wish to call this an application deficiency and it seems especially useful in the area of phonological coding and rehearsal. For example, the child may readily name the stimuli that are presented, but only when they first occur (Conrad 1972, p. 529). It is only later that the naming process continues and thus consitutes rehearsal in the absence of the stimulus. This developmental process has been charted experimentally by Kellas, McCauley, and McFarland (1975) in a free recall procedure employing overt rehearsal during presentation. While the studies of Rosenberg, Jarvella, and Cross (1971) and Steinberg and Anderson (1975) suggest that young children are not inherently deficient in semantic mediation, other studies show that the application of this semantic knowledge to free recall does grow with age (Lange 1973; Scribner and

Cole 1973). Other, even more task-oriented strategies have also been shown to develop with age, such as the selective study of items that are difficult to learn (Masur, McIntyre, and Flavell 1973).

Thus there is ample documentation for the growth of strategic behavior in memory performance across childhood. Can we connect this trend directly with phonological coding? The Conrad (1971) experiment reviewed above was surely consistent with the application deficiency hypothesis but also with the hypothesis of a straight production deficiency, according to which the youngest group simply did not produce the names of the objects pictured at all (even though they could have done so). That some failures for speech mediation are not simply such failures of visual-to-verbal translation is shown in the study by Liberman et al. (forthcoming) testing immediate recall as a function of phonological similarity among good, intermediate, and poor readers in the first grade. They found that the similarity decrement was larger for the good readers than for the other groups and two factors suggest that the difference was a function of rehearsal strategies. First, the test occurred either immediately or following an unfilled 15-sec delay. The main difference in the size of the similarity decrement was at the 15-sec delay rather than immediately after presentation. Thus the rehearsal period potentiated the difference. Secondly, the same pattern of results was obtained with auditory presentation as with visual presentation, suggesting that difficulty with encoding visual stimuli into a speech-related format was not the cause of the decrement.

Research by Locke and his associates (Locke and Fehr 1970; Locke and Kutz 1975) has made the case even more convincingly that the main developmental trend is in the use of speech for rehearsal and not in its availability as a mediator. As noted earlier, Locke and Fehr showed that chin-lip EMG monitoring was sensitive to whether subjects were encoding and rehearsing words with a high frequency of labial phonemes or whether they were encoding and rehearsing word without such phonemes. The finding of interest here compares patterns of performance for children and adults on basically the same task. Both children and adults showed distinctive EMG activity for labial phonemes when the words were presented initially for study. However, during the 5-sec pause between input and testing, the children did not show differential EMG patterns for the two types of stimulus lists while adults continued to show the distinctive response to the labials. That is, for the adults the naming process continued into the rehearsal period whereas for children it did not. This fits the definition of an application deficiency quite well.

The same conclusion is permitted by a recent study of Locke and Kutz (1975), which relied on a clever application of a common articulatory disorder in children, the /w/-/r/ substitution (both *ring* and *wing* pronounced "wing"). They showed first that their subjects could distinguish quite well two such words when they were spoken by a normal adult speaker. Second, they showed that the children suffering from this articulatory disorder could not distinguish previous recordings of their own voice when on some occasions they had named a picture of a ring and on other occasions they had named a picture of a wing. Locke and Kutz were interested, finally, in the occurrence of confusion errors assignable to the articulatory defect—when the child saw a picture of a ring but remembered the series later as having included a wing. They found that such confusions occurred for the experimental children under exactly those circumstances that would have promoted rehearsal as a strategy, even though the items were perfectly distinguishable on presentation and even though the output mode was pointing to pictures.

PHONOLOGICAL CODING IN READING

The closing section of this survey will deal with the issue of phonological coding in the process of perceiving written language. In one way or another this central issue pervades almost every significant theoretical question about reading, including, for example, what the proper beginning instruction in reading should be, the significance of the evolution of different orthographies and writing systems, and the possible effects of dialect differences upon learning to read. Further it is a convenient topic to treat now because it integrates several of the major themes that have been covered in this chapter.

WHAT GETS RECODED INTO WHAT? Previous debate on the role of speech in reading has been too concerned with the question *whether* phonological coding occurs in fluent reading and too little concerned with the issues of *when* and *under what circumstances* recoding occurs and with the further issue of what levels of the written language connect with what levels of the spoken language. The question of exactly when spoken language is used in the perception of written language will be taken up in the next subsection but first it is important to deal with the issue of levels of information in recoding. There are two aspects to this matter of processing levels: the form of representation that enters the recoding operation and the form of representation that emerges. The latter is dealt with first.

Figure 4 shows an extremely simplified layout of some of the possibilities. Along the left are a few of the many landmarks generally accepted for the speech communication chain. The figure emphasizes the transformation, through use of phonological rules, between an underlying, abstract, phonological code (corresponding to the level of systematic phonemes proposed by Chomsky and Halle 1968) and the surface phonology. The level of systematic phonemes is closer to the meaning, of course, than is the surface form. This has led several commentators (Chomsky 1970; Klima 1972; Weir and Venezky 1968) to observe that English orthography has a potential advantage since it corresponds roughly to the systematic phonemic level, as opposed to orthographies that correspond more closely to the surface sounds. In the former case, a reader who knows the set of phonological rules well is presented with a representation that corresponds more closely to the meaning than would be the case with an orthography that better reflected the surface representation (sound). Thus, for example, a phonological rule dictates how to pronounce the vowel in the second syllables of the pair of words, *extreme* and *extremity*: the fact that the letter is *e* in both cases can then help us appreciate that the two meanings are related. The spellings, *extrehmity* and *extreem*, might be easier to connect with speech but their visual appearance might distract the com-

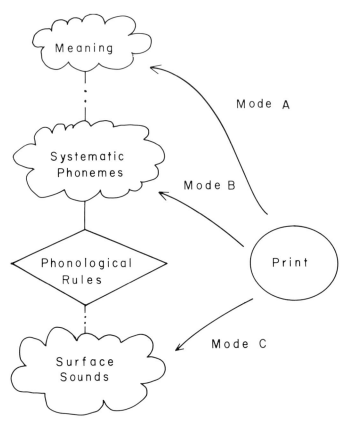

Figure 4. Three levels at which there could be contact between written and spoken language during silent reading.

prehender from the similarity in meaning. According to this argument, since the vowel alteration rule is known by the speaker-hearer, there is no need to represent it redundantly in the spelling. (See also Liberman et al., forthcoming.) The correlation of spoken and written language could occur at any of the three points indicated on the diagram or at any combination of them. The previous controversy has gone on as if it were only possibilities A and C that could occur (respectively, transformation of the written symbol directly to meaning or transformation to any internalized form of complete speech). But consider the economy of a recoding process occurring at point B. One would have access to the already existing pathways to meaning from a lifetime of processing spoken language rather than having to lay down a completely new set of symbol-to-meaning pathways, as in plan A. At the same time, however, the reader would not be obliged to perform complex internal surrogates to articulation. A recoding operation at point B in the figure is certainly in keeping with what Huey (1908, p. 117) meant when he described the inner speech of reading as "a foreshortened and incomplete speech in most of us." Evidence that speech recoding may be switched on or off depending on the task will be presented below. Rather than an alternation between modes A and C, the possibility that there is switching between B and C can also be considered. EMG recordings might, for another example, pick up activity at level C but not at B.

In connection with the earlier treatment of prosody as a memory-dependent process in comprehension it can now be speculated that mode B evades any expression of prosodic features in the reading process, as opposed to mode C, which would certainly contain them. Perhaps it is when ambiguous constructions come along in the text that a reader engages the phonological machinery and switches from mode B to mode C.

A second issue illuminated by the consideration of mode B as the normal one is the problem of dialect differences in early reading. If speakers of different dialects share common representations at the level of systematic phonemes, then speakers of one dialect should not be penalized by an instructional system based on another dialect, as indeed seems to be the case with speakers of Black English in Standard English school systems (Labov 1970).

The opposition of modes B and C also illuminates the expectations for the relative ease of reading aloud and reading silently. With "easy" reading perhaps there would not be detectable differences, but when the system is burdened the extra mediational stages involved in mode C should impair performance, as is indeed the case with a high memory load (Crowder 1970; Tell and Ferguson 1974). Speakers of a nonstandard dialect would, furthermore, be selectively handicapped in reading aloud unless their teacher had the wisdom to accept their phonological rules and their consequent surface mismatch as appropriate.

The next question is which forms of the written language are the ones that enter the speech transformation operation. Here again Liberman et al. (forthcoming) have identified some logical boundaries on this issue. It could be the entire word as a unit that gets related to the speech system. They consider this possibility unlikely on the grounds that the beginning reader would then have to learn each new word as a distinctive shape and would sacrifice the analytic benefits of an alphabetic language. Of course, there is no reason that the fluent reader in dealing with highly frequent words like *the, and,* and so on could not use word shape for direct transformation. Indeed, new evidence on mixed typography (for example tYpo-GrApHY) suggests that, quite against the earlier conclusion of Smith (1971),[8] people do indeed store at least some words as typographical units (see Brooks, forthcoming and Coltheart and Freeman 1974).

On the other hand, Liberman et al. (forthcoming) argue that the letter is also an unlikely unit for the speech transformation. Certainly the letter is a preposterous candidate for the transformation in fluent reading. But children do sound out new words letter by letter. Since the names of the letters are often uninformative about

[8]Smith had claimed that mixed typography was no more difficult to process than unmixed, as it should have been if word shapes are treated as units. Brooks and Coltheart and Freeman showed that this conclusion was a result of an insensitive set of experimental comparisons.

their role in particular orthographic settings, children are taught to pair the spoken letter sounds with the schwa /ə/ sound.

All these considerations force the conclusion that there is an intermediate level of transformation between writing and speech at least some of the time. Spoehr and Smith (1975) have maintained that a unit corresponding roughly to the syllable is the appropriate entity for this role. Theirs is the most detailed model of exactly when and how the recoding step occurs. They claim that purely visual processes are carried out to the level at which individual letters are identified. A parsing operation then subdivides words on the basis of rules respecting the vowel-consonant distinction. The resulting syllablelike units are then matched against a register of phonological conversions whose activation places the printed information along the same route that handles speech processing also.

There are thus arguments favoring at least three candidates for the phonological recoding units. Children undeniably sound out new words letter by letter. Adults undeniably use word shape cues at least some of the time. What remains is a syllablelike unit serving in perhaps many of the more usual cases.

EVIDENCE FOR PHONOLOGICAL RECODING IN READING To return to the question posed above, how good is the evidence that the transformation from visual representation to phonological code occurs? There are five main lines of research that favor the conclusion that recoding does occur at least some of the time. Excellent reviews of this literature are available elsewhere (Meyer, Schvaneveldt, and Ruddy 1974; Kleiman 1975) so it is presented here only briefly. In addition, some new research is examined that serves to tie together the themes of phonological recoding, rehearsal, and the role of memory in facilitating language comprehension.

Conrad's (1964) demonstration of phonological coding in immediate memory has been covered above. It stands as one basis for the claim that processing written language entails a speech conversion. But it could be claimed that the immediate memory task is unsuitable for generalization to reading because it includes an unrealistically large burden on memory and an unrealistically small burden on comprehension. It has been argued that rehearsal might be responsible for the speech mediation and not those aspects of the memory task that are part of reading, although Levy (1975) shows that the results of speech-related variables are about the same whether or not meaning is present.

Corcoran (1966) showed that in letter cancellation, a silent visual task involving coherent text, there was nonetheless a phonological component. His subjects were to cross out all the letter e's they could find in a page as fast as possible. They missed targets more often when the letter was silent in a particular word (for example, the e in RAKE) than when it was pronounced (for example, as in RENT). In letter cancellation, there is absolutely no premium on remembering the text to be processed and therefore this demonstration overcomes some of the problems in the immediate memory task. However, letter cancellation shares little with the process of genuine reading and so whatever the results were they would hardly change many minds about how reading works.

Eriksen, Pollack, and Montague (1970) showed that the time taken to initiate vocalization of a displayed word or number was a function of the number of syllables in that item so long as there was uncertainty as to which words or number would occur. Thus it took longer to start naming 47 than 14, even though the initial sounds are just the same and the visual lengths are the same. One may object that in this paradigm the subject does eventually pronounce the entire item and that response preparation is where the differential result occurs (see, for example Klapp 1971). However, a recent extension of the syllable effect by Pynte (1974) largely evades this criticism and is promising of further important findings. Pynte timed the interval between eye movements across a display of several two-digit numbers. These numbers were separated so that subjects had to shift fixations for each number. Since the number of items and the original point of fixation was known, one can reconstruct from the schedule of saccadic movements just how many msec were spent looking at each number. In the critical third position, Pynte put two-digit numbers with varying number of syllables. The subject was told to read the numbers silently and he did not have to report them directly. The main finding was that the fixation time on the critical number was a direct function of the number of syllables of the item even though the subject was neither required to pronounce it during his fixation time nor to prepare such a pronunciation. It would be simple to extend this method to the silent reading of connected text. In fact there is reason to believe that numbers may be processed differently than ordinary words (Ellison 1975), so such an extension is a matter of some theoretical urgency. With the reservation that such further research has not been done, the Pynte extension of·Eriksen, Pollack, and Montague's syllable method appears to be one of the most realistic and valuable methods for investigating phonological mediation in reading.

Another approach has been to train subjects through biofeedback to inhibit their EMG activity in speech regions. Hardyck and Petrinovich (1970) employed a number of suitable controls to determine what effect on reading such voluntary inhibition might have. The upshot of their study was that the reading of light, easy fiction was unimpaired by concurrent suppression of articulatory EMG activity but that the reading of harder material was impaired. Direct monitoring of speech EMG by Edfelt (1960) indicated much the same thing; evidence of phonological involvement in silent reading occurred both when the material being read was difficult rather than easy and for poor readers rather than good readers. These two studies are useful in establishing beyond doubt that some phonological mediation occurs sometimes. The measurement is not completely unobtrusive but the actual reading behavior observed is quite natural. However, since the performance measure with regard to the text has to be a gross comprehension score, the EMG method is not discriminative among the various detailed hypotheses about the nature of the mediation process.

In one form or another, measuring the speed with which subjects can make acceptability decisions has been the most popular method for determining the extent and nature of phonological recoding. In the single-word lexical decision task first used for this purpose by Rubenstein, Lewis, and Rubenstein (1971), the task is simply to decide as rapidly as possible whether a test letter string is a word or not.

The initial finding was that such decisions were especially slow for nonwords that share a phonological rendering with a real word (such as BRUME) and also for words that are homophones (such as YOKE). Both effects are very hard to accommodate without reference to some phonological participation in lexical decision. Meyer, Schvaneveldt, and Ruddy (1974) have reviewed the work in this area with particular care and have established through their own experiments that graphemic properties of letter strings affect their decision times as well as purely phonological ones.

Acceptability decisions on strings of words, as to whether they were grammatical, have been used by Baron (1973) for determining the phonological role in reading longer stimuli. Baron asked subjects to determine the acceptability of such strings as MY KNEW CAR as opposed to MY NO CAR, the first possessing a phonologically acceptable but graphemically unacceptable reading but the second acceptable on neither criterion. The reaction times were comparable in the two cases, but errors were more prevalent in the first.

Ellison (1975) employed a decision task in which the subject was asked to respond only on the basis of a semantic property of a word rather than on its lexicality. He observed that when subjects were to decide whether a letter string was the name of an animal or not, responses were slower to the homophone BARE than to neutral or visually similar words such as BEAT. However, this effect was not apparent with words that were number names (FOUR-FORE). Ellison's experiment is an important step in refining experimental techniques because it requires no covert or overt pronunciation, has no memory requirement for the target string, and bases performance on a realistic semantic feature of words. All the more attention should be paid it because it conflicts somewhat with the final experiment in this survey.

Kleiman (1975) has suggested three necessary stages in fluent reading: visual encoding, lexical access, and short-term memory. The latter is included because of the inherent distribution across time of syntactic structures that are necessary for comprehension, as was discussed earlier. Given that some phonological coding occurs in reading, Kleiman states, the real question is whether it occurs before lexical access or after lexical access but before short-term memory. In the former case, the identity of words is obtained through phonological properties but in the latter case the meaning of words is determined without a phonological stage. In this latter case, phonology becomes important when committing information to short-term memory, perhaps through rehearsal.

Kleiman's main task included three instructional conditions concerning the relation between two simultaneously exposed words: Were they graphemically similar (HEARD, BEARD)? Were they phonologically similar (FLAME, BLAME)? Were they semantically similar (MOURN, GRIEVE)? Subjects made timed decisions on these criteria under two conditions. In a shadowing condition subjects were shadowing digits at the same time they were making decisions on the primary verbal stimuli; in the control condition there was no concurrent shadowing task. It was expected that the shadowing would not greatly affect graphemic decisions but that it would strongly affect phonological decisions (by interfering with internal speech). The crucial question was whether shadowing would interfere with the semantic task. If so, it would imply that to gain access to meaning the subject needed to consult phonology. If not, it would indirectly suggest that only after lexical access does the speech process enter the picture, perhaps in the service of short-term memory. Since short-term memory was not necessary in this simultaneous semantic comparison condition, the phonological effect would not be anticipated.

The finding was that shadowing slowed down all three tasks. However, the effect on the graphemic task was much smaller (125 msec) than the effect on the phonological task (372 msec). The semantic task was very much like the graphemic task, showing comparable inhibition from shadowing (120 msec). Kleiman concluded that semantic processing can go on without phonological mediation just as readily as superficial visual processing. That there was some inhibition in all three tasks can be attributed to some peripheral response competition.

Kleiman replicated this finding in a task where the correspondance between a target word and a previously exposed sentence had to be judged, The criterion was either graphemic (BURY judged against the sentence YESTERDAY THE GRAND JURY ADJOURNED), phonemic (CREAM after HE AWAKENED AFTER THE DREAM), or semantic (GAMES after EVERYONE AT HOME PLAYED MONOPOLY). The result among these three conditions was just the same as before: Only the phonological task produced a large effect of shadowing. There was an even smaller effect of shadowing on the semantic task than on the graphemic task. In a fourth condition Kleiman directly evaluated the hypothesis that phonological recoding occurs through intervention of short-term memory in the service of syntactic analysis. In this condition the subjects had to judge the overall semantic acceptability of a sentence (NOISY PARTIES DISTURB SLEEPING NEIGHBORS). The assumption was that to judge the semantic acceptability of a word string (as opposed to seeing whether a target word matched the meaning of any of its constituents) the full system of syntactic parsing and analysis would need to be enlisted, placing demands on short-term memory. The result confirmed this hypothesis in that there was a large decrement in the semantic acceptability task caused by shadowing (394 msec), larger even than that caused by shadowing during the phonological task (312 msec). Kleiman concluded from this, that phonological mediation occurs not in order to gain access to meaning but when the task places a heavy load on short-term memory. This conclusion does not rule out the possibility that some abstract phonological system is involved even in lexical access (mode B in figure 4); it means only that concurrent shadowing, sufficient to disrupt deliberate phonological processing, did not disrupt access to meaning any more than access to visual appearance.

This separation of speech mediation into that employed for encoding per se as opposed to that employed for rehearsal is the same distinction made earlier in considering the evidence with children. Children seem quite capable of using speech to name objects before they can enlist speech for the purpose of memorization. Likewise, Kleiman's conclusion fits the generalization that phonological recoding occurs when reading is difficult—it is partly the complexity of syntactic structures that is responsible for such difficulty. And finally, these conclusions fit nicely with the suggestions made above about the role of prosody. A consistent finding is that grouping and stress greatly enhance short-term memory for unrelated items, thus phonological recoding to a sufficiently peripheral level to allow surrogates for prosodic features would be one means of coping with the memorial demands of processing difficult written materials.

References

Aaronson, D. 1974. Stimulus factors and listening strategies in auditory memory: A theoretical analysis. *Cognitive Psychology*, 6, 108–132.

Anderson, J. R. 1974. Verbatim and propositional representation of sentences in immediate and long-term memory. *Journal of Verbal Learning and Verbal Behavior*, 13, 149–162.

Anderson, J. R., and Bower, G. R. 1973. *Human associative memory*. Washington, D. C.: Winston.

Averbach, E., and Coriell, A. S. 1961. Short-term memory in vision. *Bell System Technical Journal*, 40, 309–328.

Baddeley, A. D. 1966. How does acoustic similarity influence short-term memory? *Quarterly Journal of Experimental Psychology*, 20, 249–264.

Baron, J. 1973. Phonemic stage not necessary for reading. *Quarterly Journal of Experimental Psychology*, 25, 241–246.

Belmont, J. M., and Butterfield, E. C. 1971. Learning strategies as determinants of memory deficiencies. *Cognitive Psychology*, 2, 411–420.

Bransford, J. D., and Franks, J. J. 1971. The abstraction of linguistic ideas. *Cognitive Psychology*, 2, 331–350.

Brooks, L. Forthcoming. Visual pattern in fluent word identification. In A. S. Reber and D. Scarborough (Eds.) *Towards a Psychology of Reading*: The Proceedings of the CUNY Conference, Hillsdale, N.J.: Lawrence Erlbaum.

Brown, A. L. 1973. Judgments of recency for long sequences of pictures: The absence of a developmental trend. *Journal of Experimental Child Psychology*, 15, 473–480.

————. 1975. Progressive elaboration and memory for order in children. *Journal of Experimental Child Psychology*, 19, 383–400.

Cheng, C. -M. 1974. Different roles of acoustic and articulatory information in short-term memory. *Journal of Experimental Psychology*, 103, 614–618.

Chomsky, C. 1970. Reading, writing, and phonology. *Harvard Educational Review*, 40, 287–309.

Chomsky, N., and Halle, M. 1968. *The sound pattern of English*. New York: Harper and Row.

Cole, R. A., and Young, M. 1975. Effect of subvocalization on memory for speech sounds. *Journal of Experimental Psychology: Human Learning and Memory*, 1, 772–779.

Cole, R. A., Coltheart, M., and Allard, F. 1974. Memory of a speaker's voice: Reaction times to same- and different-voiced letters. *Quarterly Journal of Experimental Psychology*, 26, 1–7.

Coltheart, M. 1975. Iconic memory: A reply to Professor Holding. *Memory and Cognition*, 3, 42–48.

Coltheart, M., and Allard, F. 1970. Variations on a theme by Posner: Physical and name codes for spoken letters. Paper presented to Psychonomic Society, San Antonio, Texas, November.

Coltheart, M., and Freeman, R. 1974. Case alternation impairs word recognition. *Bulletin of the Psychonomic Society*, 3, 102–104.

Conrad, R. 1964, Acoustic confusions in immediate memory. *British Journal of Psychology*, 55, 75–84.

———. 1967. Interference or decay over short retention intervals? *Journal of Verbal Learning and Verbal Behavior*, 6, 49–54.

———. 1971. The chronology of the development of covert speech in children. *Developmental Psychology*, 5, 398–405.

———. 1972. Speech and reading. In J. F. Kavanagh and I. Mattingly (Eds.) *Language by ear and by eye*. Cambridge: The MIT Press, 204–240.

Conrad, R., and Hull, A. J. 1964. Information, acoustic confusion, and memory span. *British Journal of Psychology*, 55, 429–432.

Cooper, W. E. 1975. Selective adaptation to speech. In F. Restle, R. M. Shiffrin, N. J. Castellan, H. Lindman, and D. B. Pisoni (Eds.) *Cognitive theory: Volume I*. Hillsdale, N. J.: Laurence Erlbaum, 23–54.

Cooper, W. E., Ebert, R. R., and Cole, R. A. 1976. Perceptual analysis of stop consonants and glides. *Journal of Experimental Psychology: Human Perception and Performance*, 2, 92–104.

Corcoran, D. W. J. 1966. An acoustic factor in letter cancellation. *Nature*, 210, 658.

Craik, F. I. M., and Kirsner, K. 1974. The effect of a speaker's voice on word recognition. *Quarterly Journal of Experimental Psychology*, 26, 274–284.

Craik, F. I. M., and Lockhart, R. S. 1972. Levels of processing: A framework for memory research. *Journal of Verbal Learning and Verbal Behavior*, 11, 671–684.

Crowder, R. G. 1970. The role of one's own voice in immediate memory. *Cognitive Psychology*, 1, 157–178.

———. 1971. The sound of vowels and consonants in immediate memory. *Journal of Verbal Learning and Verbal Behavior*, 10, 587–596.

———. 1972. Visual and auditory memory. In J. F. Kavanagh and I. G. Mattingly (Eds.) *Language by ear and by eye*. Cambridge: The MIT Press, 251–275.

———. 1973. Precategorical acoustic storage for vowels of short and long duration. *Perception and Psychophysics*, 13, 502–506.

———. 1976. *Principles of learning and memory*. Hillsdale, N. J.: Laurence Erlbaum.

———. Forthcoming. Sensory memory systems. In E. C. Carterette and M. Freidman (Eds.) *Handbook of perception, volume 9*. New York: Academic Press.

Crowder, R. G., and Cheng, C. -M. 1973. Phonemic confusability, precategorical acoustic storage, and the suffix effect. *Perception and Psychophysics*, 15, 145–148.

Crowder, R. G., and Morton, J. 1969. Precategorical acoustic storage (PAS). *Perception and Psychophysics*, 5, 365–371.

Cutting, J. E., and Pisoni, D. B. This volume. An information-processing approach to speech perception.

Darwin, C. J. 1975. The perception of speech. In E. C. Carterette and M. P. Freidman (Eds.) *Handbook of perception, volume* 7, New York: Academic Press.

Darwin, C. J., and Baddeley, A. D. 1974. Acoustic memory and the perception of speech. *Cognitive Psychology*, 6, 41–60.

Darwin, C. J., Turvey, M. T., and Crowder, R. G. 1972. An auditory analogue of the Sperling partial report procedure: Evidence for brief auditory atorage. *Cognitive Psychology*, 3, 255–267.

Day, R. S., and Wood, C. C. 1972. Interactions between linguistic and nonlinguistic processing. *Journal of the Acoustical Society of America*, 51, 79 (A).

Delattre, P. C., Liberman, A. M., and Cooper, F. S. 1955. Acoustic loci and transitional cues for consonants. *Journal of the Acoustical Society of America*, 27, 769–773.

Edfeldt, A. W. 1960. *Silent speech and reading*. Chicago, Ill.: University of Chicago Press.

Eimas, P. D., and Corbit, J. D. 1973. Selective adaptation of linguistic feature detectors. *Cognitive Psychology*, 4, 99–109.

Ellison, G. C. 1975. Phonetic coding of words in a taxonomic classification task. *Haskins Laboratories: Status Report on Speech Research*, SR-41, 95–104.

Eriksen, C. W., Pollack, M. D., and Montague, W. E. 1970. Implicit speech: A mechanism in perceptual encoding? *Journal of Experimental Psychology*, 84, 501–507.

Estes, W. K. 1973. Phonemic encoding and rehearsal in short-term memory for letter strings. *Journal of Verbal Learning and Verbal Behavior*, 12, 360–372.

Fajnszejn-Pollack, G. 1973. A developmental study of decay rate in long-term memory. *Journal of Experimental Child Psychology*, 16, 225–235.

Flavell, J. H. 1970. Developmental studies in mediated memory. In H. W. Reese and L. P. Lipsitt (Eds.) *Advances in child development and behavior*, volume 5. New York: Academic Press, 181–211.

Garner, W. R. 1974. *The processing of information and structure*. Potomac, Md.: Erlbaum.

Garner, W. R., and Felfoldy, G. L. 1970. Integrality of stimulus dimensions in various types of information processing. *Cognitive Psychology*, 1, 225–241.

Garrod, S., and Trabasso, T. A. 1973. A dual-memory information processing interpretation of sentence comprehension. *Journal of Verbal Learning and Verbal Behavior*, 12, 155–167.

Gerstman, L. J. 1968. Classification of self-normalized vowels. *IEEE Transactions Audio Electroacoustic*, AU-16, 78–80.

Gibson, J. J. 1950. *The perception of the visual world*. Boston: Houghton Mifflin.

Glassman, W. E. 1972. Subvocal activity and acoustic confusions in short-term memory. *Journal of Experimental Psychology*, 96, 164–169.

Green, D. W. 1975. The effects of task on the representation of sentences. *Journal of Verbal Learning and Verbal Behavior*, 14, 275–283.

Hardyck, C. D., and Petrinovich, L. F. 1970. Subvocal speech and comprehension level as a function of the difficulty level of the reading material. *Journal of Verbal Learning and Verbal Behavior*, 9, 647–652.

Hasher, L., and Clifton, D. 1974. A developmental study of attribute encoding in free recall. *Journal of Experimental Child Psychology*, 17, 332–346.

Healy, A. F. 1975. Temporal-spatial patterns in short-term memory. *Journal of Verbal Learning and Verbal Behavior*, 14, 481–495.

Healy, A. F., and Cutting, J. E. 1976. Units of speech perception: Phoneme and syllable. *Journal of Verbal Learning and Verbal Behavior*, 15, 73–83.

Horowitz, L. M. 1961. Free recall and ordering of trigrams. *Journal of Experimental Psychology*, 62, 51–57.

Huey, E. B. 1908. *The psychology and pedagogy of reading*. New York: MacMillan. Reprinted Cambridge: MIT Press, 1968.

Huggins, A. W. F. 1975. Temporally segmented speech. *Perception and Psychophysics*, 18, 149–157.

Johnson, N. F. 1968. Sequential behavior. In T. R. Dixon and D. L. Horton (Eds.) *Verbal behavior and general behavior theory*. Englewood Cliffs, N. J.: Prentice-Hall, 421–450.

―――. 1970. The role of chunking and organization in the process of recall. In G. H. Bower and J. T. Spence (Eds.) *The psychology of learning and motivation*, volume 4, New York: Academic Press, 171–247.

Kellas, G., McCauley, C., and McFarland, C. E. 1975. Developmental aspects of storage and retrieval. *Journal of Experimental Child Psychology*, 19, 51–62.

Kintsch, W. 1970. Recognition memory in bilingual subjects. *Journal of Verbal Learning and Verbal Behavior*, 9, 405–409.

―――. 1975. Memory representations of text. In R. L. Solso (Ed.) *Information processing and cognition: The Loyola symposium*. Hillsdale, N. J.: Laurence Erlbaum, 269–294.

Kirsner, K. 1973. An analysis of the visual component in recognition memory for verbal stimuli. *Memory and Cognition*, 1, 449–453.

Klapp, S. T. 1971. Implicit speech inferred from response latencies in same-different decisions. *Journal of Experimental Child Psychology*, 91, 262–267.

Klapp, S. T., Anderson, W. G., and Berrian, R. W. 1973. Implicit speech in reading reconsidered. *Journal of Experimental Psychology*, 100, 368–374.

Kleiman, G. M. 1975. Speech recoding in reading. *Journal of Verbal Learning and Verbal Behavior*, 14, 323–339.

Klima, E. S. 1972. How alphabets might reflects speech. In J. F. Kavanagh and I. G. Mattingly (Eds.) *Language by ear and by eye*. Cambridge: MIT Press.

Kolers, P. A. 1973. Remembering operations. *Memory and Cognition*, 1, 347–355.

―――. 1975a. Specificity of operations in sentence recognition. *Cognitive Psychology*, 7, 289–306.

―――. 1975b. Memorial consequences of automatized encoding. *Journal of Experimental Psychology: Human Learning and Memory*, 1, 689–701.

Kolers, P. A., and Ostry, D. 1974. Time course of loss of information regarding pattern-analyzing operations. *Journal of Verbal Learning and Verbal Behavior*, 13, 599–612.

Labov, W. 1970. The reading of the -*ed* suffix. In H. Levin and J. P. Williams (Eds.) *Basic studies in reading*. New York: Basic Books, 222–245.

Ladefoged, P., and Broadbent, D. E. 1957. Information conveyed by vowels. *Journal of the Acoustical Society of America*, 29, 98–105.

Lange, G. 1973. The development of conceptual and rote recall skills among school age children. *Journal of Experimental Child Psychology*, 15, 394–406.

Layton, P., and Simpson, A. J. 1975. Surface and deep structure in sentence comprehension. *Journal of Verbal Learning and Verbal Behavior*, 14, 658–664.

Levy, B. A. 1975. Vocalization and suppression effects in sentence memory. *Journal of Verbal Learning and Verbal Behavior*, 14, 304–316.

Liberman, A. M. 1970. The grammars of speech and language. *Cognitive Psychology*, 1, 301–323.

Liberman, A. M., Delattre, P., and Cooper, F. S. 1952. The role of selected stimulus variables in the perception of the unvoiced-stop consonants. *American Journal of Psychology*, 65, 497–516.

Liberman, I. Y., Shankweiler, D., Liberman, A. M., Fowler, C., and Fisher, F. W. Forthcoming. Phonetic segmentation and recoding in the beginning reader. In A. S. Reber and D. Scarbarough (Eds.) *Towards a Psychology of Reading:* Proceedings of the CUNY Conference. Hillsdale, N. J.: Laurence Erlbaum.

Liepmann, D., and Saegert, J. 1974. Language tagging in bilingual free recall. *Journal of Experimental Psychology*, 103, 1137–1141.

Light, L. L., and Berger, D. E. 1974. Memory for modality: Within-modality discrimination is not automatic. *Journal of Experimental Psychology*, 103, 854–860.

Light, L. L., Berger, D. E., and Bardales, M. 1975. Trade-off between memory for verbal items and their visual attributes. *Journal of Experimental Psychology: Human Learning and Memory*, 1, 188–193.

Light, L. L., Stansbury, C., Rubin, C., and Linde, S. 1973. Memory for modality of presentation: Within-modality discrimination. *Memory and Cognition*, 1, 395–400.

Locke, J. L., and Fehr, F. S. 1970. Subvocal rehearsal as a form of speech. *Journal of Verbal Learning and Verbal Behavior*, 9, 495–498.

———. 1971. Young children's use of the speech code in learning. *Journal of Experimental Child Psychology*, 10, 367–373.

Locke, J. L., and Kutz, K. J. 1975. Memory for speech and speech for memory. *Journal of Speech and Hearing Research*, 18, 176–191.

Martin, E. E. 1970. Subjective phrase structures. *Psychological Review*, 45, 651–678.

Martin, E. E., and Robert, K. H. 1966. Grammatical factors in sentence retention. *Journal of Verbal Learning and Verbal Behavior*, 5, 211–218.

Massaro, D. W. 1970. Preperceptual auditory images. *Journal of Experimental Psychology*, 85, 411–417.

———. 1974. Perceptual units in speech perception. *Journal of Experimental Psychology*, 102, 199–208.

———. 1975. *Experimental psychology and information processing*. Chicago, Ill.: Rand McNally College Publishing Co.

Masur, E. F., McIntyre, C. W., and Flavell, J. H. 1973. Developmental changes in apportionment of study time among items in a multitrial free recall task. *Journal of Experimental Child Psychology*, 15, 237–246.

Mathews, M. E., and Fozard, J. L. 1970. Age differences in judgments of recency for short sequences of pictures. *Developmental Psychology*, 3, 208–217.

Meyer, D. E., Schvaneveldt, R. W., and Ruddy, M. G. 1974. Functions of graphemic and phonemic codes in visual word recognition. *Memory and Cognition*, 2, 309–321.

Miller, G. A., and Isard S. 1963. Some perceptual consequences of linguistic rules. *Journal of Verbal Learning and Verbal Behavior*, 2, 217–228.

Norman, D. A. 1972. The role of memory in the understanding of language. In J. F. Kavanagh and I. G. Mattingly (Eds.) *Language by ear and by eye*. Cambridge, Mass.: The MIT Press, 277–288.

O'Conner, N., and Hermelin. B. 1973. The spatial or temporal organization of short-term memory. *Quarterly Journal of Experimental Psychology*, 25, 335–343.

Olson, D. R., and Filby, N. 1972. On the comprehension of active and passive sentences. *Cognitive Psychology*, 3, 361–381.

Pisoni, D. B., and Tash, J. 1974. Reaction times to comparisons within and across phonetic categories. *Perception and Psychophysics*, 15, 285–290.

Posner, M. I., and Keele, S. W. 1967. Decay of visual information from a single letter. *Science*, 158, 137–139.

Posner, M. I., and Konick, A. W. 1966. On the role of interference in short-term retention. *Journal of Experimental Psychology*, 72, 221–231.

Posner, M. I., Boies, S. J., Eichelman, E. H., and Taylor, R. L. 1969. Retention of visual and name codes of single letters. *Journal of Experimental Psychology Monographs*, 79, 1–17.

Pynte, J. 1974. Readiness for pronunciation during the reading process. *Perception and Psychophysics*, 16, 110–112.

Rose, R. G., Rose, P. R., King, N., and Perez, A. 1975. Bilingual memory for related and unrelated sentences. *Journal of Experimental Psychology: Human Learning and Memory*, 1, 599–614.

Rosenberg, S., Jarvella, R. J., and Cross, M. 1971. Semantic integration, age, and the recall of sentences. *Child Development*, 42, 1959–1966.

Rothkopf, E. Z. 1971. Incidental memory for location of information in text. *Journal of Verbal Learning and Verbal Behaivor* 6, 608–613.

Rubenstein, H., Lewis, S. S., and Rubenstein, M. A. 1971. Evidence for phonemic recoding in visual word recognition. *Journal of Verbal Learning and Verbal Behavior*, 10, 647–657.

Sachs, J. S. 1967. Recognition memory for syntactic and semantic aspects of connected discourse. *Perception and Psychophysics*, 2, 437–442.

———. 1974. Memory in reading and listening to discourse. *Memory and Cognition*, 2, 95–100.

Saegert, J., Hamayan, E., and Ahmar, H. 1975. Memory for language of input in polyglots. *Journal of Experimental Psychology: Human Learning and Memory*. 1, 607–613.

Sakitt, B. 1975. Locus of short-term visual storage. *Science*, 190, 1318–1319.

Savin, H. B., and Bever, T. G. 1970. The nonperceptual reality of the phoneme. *Journal of Verbal Learning and Verbal Behavior*. 9, 295–302.

Scribner, S., and Cole, M. 1973. Cognitive consequences of formal and informal education. *Science*, 182, 553–559.

Shankweiler, D., Strange, W., and Verbrugge, R. 1977. Speech and the problem of perceptual constancy. In R. Shaw and J. D. Bransford (Eds.) *Perceiving, acting, and knowing.* Hillsdale, N. J.: Laurence Erlbaum, 315–345.

Smith, F. 1971. *Understanding reading.* New York: Holt, Rinehart, and Winston.

Sperling, G. 1960. The information available in brief visual presentations. *Psychological Monographs,* 74, No. 498, 1–29.

Spoehr, K. T., and Smith, E. E. 1975. The role of orthographic and phonotactic rules in perceiving letter patterns. *Journal of Experimental Psychology: Human Perception and Performance,* 1, 21–34.

Steinberg, E. R., and Anderson, R. C. 1975. Hierarchical semantic organization in 6-year olds. *Journal of Experimental Child Psychology,* 19, 544–553.

Studdert-Kennedy, M. 1976. Speech perception. In N. J. Lass (Ed.) *Contemporary issues in experimental phonetics.* Springfield, Ill.: Thomas. 243–293.

Tell P. M. and Ferguson A. M. 1974. Influence of active and passive vocalization on short-term recall. *Journal of Experimental Psychology,* 102, 347–349.

Tulving, E. 1972. Episodic and semantic memory. In E. Tulving and W. Donaldson (Eds.) *Organization of memory.* New York: Academic Press, 381–403.

Tulving, E., and Colatla, V. 1970. Free recall of trilingual lists. *Cognitive Psychology,* 1, 86–98.

Turvey, M. T. 1973. On peripheral and central processes in vision. *Psychological Review,* 80, 1–52.

Tzeng O. J. L. 1975. Sentence Memory: Recognition and inferences. *Journal of Experimental Psychology: Human Learning and Memory* 1, 720–726.

Walter, D. 1973. The effect of sentence context on the stability of the phonemic and semantic memory dimensions. *Journal of Verbal Learning and Verbal Behavior,* 12, 185–192.

Wanner, E. 1968. *On remembering, forgetting, and understanding sentences.* The Hague: Mouton.

Watkins, M. J., Watkins, O. C., and Crowder, R. A. 1974. The modality effect in free and serial recall as a function of phonological similarity. *Journal of Verbal Learning and Verbal Behavior,* 13, 430–447.

Wearing, A. R., and Crowder, R. G. 1971. Dividing attention to study sentence acquisition. *Journal of Verbal Learning and Verbal Behavior,* 10, 254–261.

Weir, R. H., and Venezky, R. L. 1968. Spelling-to-sound patterns. In K. S. Goodman (Ed.) *The psycholinguistic nature of the reading process.* Detroit, Mich.: Wayne State University Press.

Wood, C. C. 1974. Auditory and phonetic levels of processing in speech perception: Neurophysiological and information-processing analyses. *Journal of Experimental Psychology: Human Perception and Performance,* 1, 3–20.

Yngve, V. H. 1960. A model and a hypothesis for language structure. *Proceedings of the American Philosophical Society,* 104, 444–466.

Comprehension, Memory, and Levels of Representation: A Perspective from Aphasia

A Discussion of Crowder's Paper

EDGAR B. ZURIF AND ALFONSO CARAMAZZA

The clinical population considered here consists of adult patients with language deficits consequent to acquired brain damage. This paper will chart what is spared and what is disrupted of such patients' tacit language knowledge and of their ability to process language in real time. By doing so, it is hoped that many matters of interest to those concerned with basic research in normal language will be included; the authors particularly hope to provide a different perspective on the nature of the representations listeners assign to sentences. In addition, this discussion will establish some context for thinking about the practical issue of reasonable forms of remediation in aphasia.

In carrying out this task, the details in Crowder's chapter will be examined only obliquely from the clinical vantage point. However, there will be some continuity between this chapter and Crowder's. Occasionally the tie will be substantive; more often it will derive from a similarity in the form of our respective inquiries. Like Crowder, and also like Cutting and Pisoni (this volume), the framework adopted here is one in which the input is conceived of being processed and stored at different levels of representation—a phonological level, as one example, and as another, a level at which the semantic structure of a sentence is recovered. Most importantly, and as stressed by Crowder, each representation will be assumed to unfold over time and required memory.

This approach is particularly apt for an analysis of aphasic language. Nothing in the literature or in the authors' experience has demonstrated convincingly that the type of aphasics to be described here have a generalized memory deficit. Rather, to the extent they are unable to cope with and remember the form and meaning of utterances, the problem can be traced to an imperfect representation of the linguistic input at one or another level (Strub and Gardner 1974). The details intended to support this claim on information processing follow.

Speech Perception

A distinction much discussed in this volume is that between a level of auditory feature processing whereby, for example, the presence or absence of rapid spectral change is registered and a more abstract level at which the phonetic feature composition of a syllable is recovered (Crowder, this volume; Cutting and Pisoni, this volume; Tallal, this volume). Given the aforementioned intention to describe aphasic deficits at different levels of representation, an obvious question to ask is whether the effects of brain damage in the adult even honor such a distinction between an auditory feature level and more abstract levels.

Some data that bear on this question stem from a recently completed examination of the ability of aphasics and of neurologically intact control patients to identify and discriminate among synthetically constructed speech sounds differing on voice onset time (VOT) (Blumstein et al., in press). VOT is realized articulatorily by the temporal relation between glottal pulsing and consonant release; it is manifested acoustically as the temporal onset of the lowest speech formant relative to the higher formants (Lisker and Abramson 1964).[1] A continuum of synthetic stimuli can be generated by varying this acoustic parameter in small equal interval steps.

As mentioned elsewhere in this volume (Cutting and Pisoni; Tallal) and as observed for our control group, when normal listeners are asked to identify the dozen or so sounds along the continuum, they typically divide them into two distinct categories: one voiced, the other voiceless (Liberman, Delattre, and Cooper 1958). Thus there is a point along the VOT continuum (actually a narrow region) such that a listener will consistently and confidently identify stimuli with VOT values less than that point as voiced and stimuli with greater VOT values as voiceless. In fact, normal users of the language do not even appear to hear acoustic differences within categories. Discrimination of the same physical difference is reliably better across the category boundary than within a phonetic category. That is, corresponding to the categorical crossover point for the identification or labeling of stimuli forming the continuum, there is a peak of discrimination such that successive stimuli along the continuum are perceived as different only in this restricted crossover region (Liberman et al. 1957).

Some aphasic patients also show these characteristic patterns of speech identification and discrimination. But the performance of other patients violates both. They do not generate a normal discrimination peak for stimuli belonging to two different phonetic categories and they do not categorically identify the sounds of the continuum in terms of these discrete phonetic classes.

There is, however, a third type of outcome shown by aphasic patients at this level of performance, one that seems to distinguish between auditory and phonetic codes. Specifically, there are patients who show a peak of discrimination at the appropriate region of the VOT continuum yet fail to show a corresponding ability to identify the speech sounds categorically. They may consistently identify good exemplars of /d/ and /t/, but their identification functions are not characterized by the normally sharp demarcation between voiced and voiceless responses. There is, rather, a large range of uncertainty in their identifications. Equally noteworthy, the reverse of this pattern has never been observed, that is, categorical identification never occurs without a corresponding discrimination peak between phonetic categories.

This asymmetry has interesting implications for theories of speech perception. It runs counter to the notion that the ability to discriminate between speech sounds is limited by the categorical fashion in which listeners label or identify such sounds. Instead, given that discrimination peaks appear to have an independent status but that categorical identification functions do not, the former would appear to represent a prior, presumably more primitive stage of processing that may or may not eventuate in a stable phonetic configuration. Stated more generally, the phonetic

---

[1]Actually, in addition to the timing relation between glottal pulsing and consonant release, VOT represents a constellation of acoustic attributes including the presence or absence of frication noise upon consonantal release (cf. Lisker and Abramson 1964; Stevens and Klatt 1974).

configuration of a syllable appears to be constructed on the basis of detectors sensitive to a limited range of acoustic properties (Stevens 1975; Eimas and Corbit 1973; Cutting and Pisoni, this volume).

Interactions among Levels of Representation

This dependency of one level of speech representation upon another should not be taken as evidence for a corresponding temporal dependency. Obviously, some minimum quantity of auditory information has to be available for structure to emerge at any level of speech and language. But that does not amount to the claim that processing at one level must await a complete recovery of information at another. Nor, for that matter, should one extrapolate from the findings presented above the notion that there exists a strict dependency on the operation of acoustic property detectors once the comprehender is beyond the phonetic level. While a proper phonetic representation might crucially entail fully operative acoustic property detectors, the level at which a meaning representation is recovered will accept as input different types of converging information and therefore will be less dependent on this early stage of auditory recoding. A relevant finding in this respect is that the aphasic patients' ability to understand spoken sentences could not be predicted with any significant degree from their patterns of VOT identification and discrimination (Blumstein et al., in press). Of the eight patients tested who generated normal perceptual functions, six showed relatively good understanding at the sentence level. But more important, three of the seven patients who failed to identify the stimuli consistently or to discriminate them categorically also appeared to have good comprehension for spoken sentences.[2]

This latter finding is especially damaging to any notion of language processing that conceives of the direction of information flow as fully serial. Given that an imperfect representation of the sound structure does not necessarily block further processing, it would seem that comprehension is more plausibly modeled as a partially parallel and interactive process (cf. Marslen-Wilson 1975). Stated differently, there is likely to be some degree of overlap of processing at the different levels such that initial doubt and imperfect resolution at the phonetic level (and presumably also at the stage of phonological organization) can be resolved by lexical and semantic data.

This notion obviously carries an obligation to specify what the sufficient input is to these higher levels. One possibility suggests itself: In the absence of a fully available phonetic configuration upon which to organize the input phonologically, information is likely to filter into the lexical and semantic levels in a relatively unencoded form (see Crowder, this volume). Once patients have applied this information (as well as other, contextual information) to decide upon a candidate

[2]A word about the validity of the tasks employed in the VOT experiment, that is, about their ability to reveal interesting properties of the perceptual system. There is, of course, the possibility that identifying and discriminating among synthetic speech sounds may not tap those processes involved in the perception of natural speech. But while this possibility remains, there is no obvious reason at present to suggest that it be considered as a reasonable alternative to the interpretations advanced here.

lexical item, they can then use this decision to further sharpen the item's phonological shape. That is, an initially imperfect phonological representation based on imprecise acoustic and phonetic coding may be more fully elaborated in a "top-down" fashion.[3]

Sentence Comprehension

To be sure, the argument advanced to this point—that aphasics are capable of gaining meaning without first constructing a normal phonetic representation—glosses over an ostensibly disagreeable fact. Namely, comprehension for spoken sentences in aphasia is usually less than normal (Goodglass and Geschwind, 1970b). The question arises, therefore, whether the claim made here is wrong or whether this limitation on comprehension can be better related to other levels of language. To pursue this issue, the performance of those patients who were most likely to "understand" sentences whether or not they performed normally on the VOT task must be examined in more detail. These patients are termed Broca's aphasics or expressive, motor, or nonfluent aphasics.

The most widely disseminated description of Broca's aphasics is that they appear to have good comprehension and seem to know what they want to say yet they talk effortfully and in a telegrammatic manner. This telegrammatic or agrammatic output is characterized by the use of simple syntactic forms, a relative omission of the grammatical morphemes—often called functors—whether bound or free, and a concomitant dependence upon nouns and to a lesser extent upon verbs in their uninflected form (Goodglass and Kaplan 1972).

Having accepted these powerful clinical impressions at face value, a number of investigators claim that Broca's area is not importantly involved in the representation of language knowledge (Lenneberg 1973; Locke, Caplan, and Kellar 1973; Weigl and Bierwisch 1970). They argue that the problem is one of motor implementation of speech and that, given this problem, the agrammatic output reflects nothing other than an economizing measure.

Closer examination, however, shows that the clinical neurologist's practical and intuitive approach to language assessment provides a rather shaky foundation for psycholinguistic theory construction. Recall the earlier statement that comprehension was usually limited in aphasia. Broca's aphasia, unfortunately, does not prove an exception to this claim (Goodglass 1968). As a number of recent studies make clear, comprehension by Broca's patients is limited to a number of probabilistic strategies or "competence-independent" routines. These routines operate upon regularities of lexical ordering and on plausibility constraints, by which is meant sampling from the sentence in terms of what makes sense and applying a probable event strategy (Scholes, forthcoming; Caramazza and Zurif, in 1976; see also Chapman, this volume).

[3]In our discussion of the interactive process we have failed to elaborate on a second type of data that invariably plays an important part in assigning a structural description to an utterance: These are hypotheses about the intended message available from the context in which the utterance occurs. The direction of flow of this type of information is from top to bottom and it serves to constrain hypotheses generated at lower levels.

Consider, for example, the following study in which Broca's patients were orally presented with single sentences of either a center-embedded or simple active declarative nature and were required to point to that picture in a two-choice alternative that correctly represented the sentence (Caramazza and Zurif, in press). On some trials the center-embedded sentences were such that both the relativized and matrix nouns were capable of performing the action specified by the verb: for example, *The girl that the boy chases is tall* (both boys and girls can chase and both can be tall). In these instances the patients were as likely to point to a picture incorporating a subject/object reversal (a picture of a girl chasing a boy) as they were to the correct depiction. In contrast, the patients performed at an exceptionally high level of accuracy when presented orally with either center-embedded sentences that had only one plausible reading—for example, *The worm that the bird eats is brown* (birds eat worms; worms do not eat birds)—or with simple declarative sentences in which a noun-verb adjacency could be mapped as actor and action at a level of meaning representation—for example, *The boy chases a tall girl*. In sum, comprehension by Broca's patients failed when they were unable to use heuristic strategies to gain sentence meaning but rather had to decode the structural relations among the words in the sentence on an autonomous, brute-force basis.

Given this limitation on the Broca's ability to assign meaning to spoken sentences, the question of interest is whether it is valid to maintain that a normally elaborated phonetic representation is less than critical for the extraction of an utterance's meaning. In other words, can the notion of information flow from sound to meaning as being primarily and importantly serial continue to be dismissed? After all, given the data to this point, one could argue that Broca's area has a very limited commitment to language processing. Namely, one could argue that damage to this area disrupts only the operation of acoustic property detectors. If so, the problem would have to do with an increase in the burden of storing the relatively unencoded sound structure of the utterance, such that when strategies to shortcut the comprehension process cannot be applied, the input fades before a meaning representation can be computed. The alternatives, therefore, are these: The phonological shapes of words are insufficiently specified for lexical look-up and subsequent syntactic organization, or the input does filter into higher levels but the linguistic facts at these levels are no longer available to the patient.

Linguistic Intuitions

In order to judge the relative merits of these alternative possibilities, other data are needed. For the past several years, we and others have been observing the linguistic intuitions of Broca's aphasics in situations—usually involving written material —that presumably avoid real-time demands and consequences such as "trace fading" (Andreewsky and Seron 1975; Gardner, Denes, and Zurif 1975; Ulatowska and Baker 1975; von Stockert 1972; Zurif, Caramazza, and Myerson 1972; Zurif et al. in press).

In one set of studies (Zurif, Caramazza, and Myerson 1972), the specific intuitions sought were in the form of judgments of the relatedness of words within a sentence. The patients were given three words at a time from an always present written sentence and for each triad were required to point to the two words they felt "went best together" in the sentence from which the words were taken. Though the approach was simple and quite structured, the screening and training procedures incorporated in the study were highly elaborate. For one thing, reading was always carefully assessed. Only those Broca patients who could read each word in the sentence were selected. (They invariably could, if their attention was focused on each word.) Second, through the use of nonverbal as well as verbal material, the patients were trained extensively on the triadic comparison task, including its subjective nature and the need to consider each possible grouping. The details of these procedures are presented elsewhere (Zurif, Caramazza, and Myerson 1972); all that need be emphasized here is that Broca's aphasics, as well as neurologically intact control subjects, appeared by all subjective criteria to master the triadic comparison procedure and to understand its subjective basis.

The judgments obtained via these triadic comparisons permitted the application of a hierarchical clustering scheme (Johnson 1967) that in turn provided graphic descriptions of the within-sentence relatedness judgments in the form of subjective phrase structure trees (cf. Levelt 1970; Martin 1970).

Inspection of these trees strongly suggests that both Broca's and the control patients carried out their judgments on the basis of implicit hierarchical organizations. What is especially instructive, however, are the very striking differences in the subjective hierarchies of the two groups. The control patients appropriately incorporated all of the surface elements of each sentence when carrying out their relatedness judgments. Notably, they used articles to mark noun phrases and they consistently linked auxiliary and main verbs. Broca's aphasics, in contrast, reliably coupled only the content words together. They did not ignore the functors; rather, they did not seem to know what to do with them, clustering them inappropriately such as grouping an article with a verb or with another article. As a consequence, the judgments of the agrammatic patients violated the linguistic integrity of the noun phrases and verb phrases. To state this outcome more generally, the patients seemed relatively incapable of using the grammatical morphemes as syntactic place holders to mark the boundaries of sentence constituents—*even though the input was not likely to fade*. In this respect, then their tacit knowledge of language seems limited in the same manner as their spontaneous speech. The problem, in other words, does not seem to be entirely one of initial perceptual representation of the sentence in real time.

Memory for Sentences

The fact that Broca's patients more often than not grouped the function words inappropriately provides only one sort of evidence for the claim that their problem lies with an inability to process these words at syntactic and semantic levels. Other, possibly more direct evidence on this point is also available, evidence obtained through the use of a memory paradigm. We undertook a study motivated by the basic contention that grammatical morphemes are processed at some level of auditory representation but not beyond (not to a level of meaning representation) and also by the necessary assumption that memory for sentential items is a function of the degree of processing or elaboration at different levels that the items receive at the time of input (Cermak 1972; Cermak and Moreines 1976; Craik and Lockhart 1972). It was hypothesized that the relatively shallow processing of functions would result in less stable memory traces for these items relative to content words that would likely receive more elaborate processing.

The actual experimental paradigm made use of a memory probe technique. The patients were orally presented with a sentence and immediately afterward were given a word from that sentence. The patients' task was to produce the word in that sentence that followed this probe item. Patients who failed to make a response or produced a sound that could not readily be identified as one of the words in the target sentence was given a multiple-choice alternative. Patients were therefore not penalized for any difficulties they may have had in the implementation of speech. A response was scored as incorrect if it was any item other than the one immediately following the probe word.

The transition errors probabilites for two of the sentence types used in this experiment are presented in table 1. The most striking result to be observed in this table is the clear difference between how effectively a functor serves as a probe for a content word and how ineffectively a functor is retrieved when probed for by a content word. In sentence type 1, this general effect could admittedly be attributed to the presence of a constituent boundary (although not if, as was proposed, the facts about functors are not recovered at this level). But this problem does not arise in the type 2 sentence. Here it can be seen that *cat* serves as effectively as a probe for *ate* as *a* does for *cookie*. Further, both are dramatically more effective than *ate* probing for *a*.

This representative example suggests that functors do get perceptually represented but memory traces for functors are less stable than those for content words. The functors seem to be processed only to a certain level—too superficially for the words themselves to be retrieved but sufficiently for their traces to be reinstated.

Some Components of a Sentence Processor

Some instructive patterns emerge from the probe and triadic comparison studies. There is first of all the finding that grammatical morphemes are as poorly controlled at a metalinguistic level as they are in spontaneous speech. Second, the inability of Broca's patients to process these small words does not seem critically due to the fact that brain damage may also cause disruption at the level of phonological organization. As the probe study indicates, these, patients process such words at least to some level of sound representation; otherwise the patients would

Table 1. Transitional error probabilities for two sentence types.

1. The	books	were	delivered	by	Jane.
.33	.83	.40	.70	.44	

2. The	cat	ate	a	cookie.
.58	.40	.80	.38	

not have been able to use the functors as cues, which they did. These two findings strongly suggest that agrammatism in Broca's aphasia is more importantly rooted to a deficit at the level of syntactic representation than to a deficit at the phonological level.

An inability to make use of the structure-marking function of grammatical morphemes excludes the ability to assign content words to their grammatical category and correspondingly forecloses a representation of the input in terms of logical subject, logical object, and so on—a representation that is critical when sentences do not directly correspond to extralinguistic context. Indeed, it may well be that a minimum requirement of a syntactic processor, and one that Broca's patients fail to meet, is just this: to assign form class designations to content words as a function of sequencing constraints on grammatical morphemes (Garrett 1976; Zurif and Blumstein, forthcoming). Given this interpretation of the data reported here, it is not surprising that the Broca aphasic is unable to disentangle the logical relations expressed in a center-embedded sentence.

The question arises, of course, as to why anterior brain damage should have such a different effect upon content words and functors. The explanation that it is based on differences in auditory representation (and, by implication, on differences in the perceptual salience of the two classes) has been shown here to be insufficient. Rather, the reason appears to have more to do with differences at higher levels. But if so, are the linguistic and referential facts associated with these two classes stored in different ways? As yet there has been no research that speaks to this question properly. All that is known from the work to date is that Broca's aphasics are unable to access the subtle modulations of meanings expressed by functors (Goodenough, Zurif, and Weintraub, in press). But then, even information about content words in the Broca's "internal dictionary" seems to be less than normal. There appear to be restrictions on the sorts of conceptual relations that such aphasics can trace within semantic domains (Zurif et. al. 1974). To use Miller's (this volume) distinction, the entries in their lexicons seem elaborated more in terms of practical knowledge (likely functions and perceptual features associated with the referents of words) than in terms of their lexically defining or sense features. In fact, the more salience a referent has for different information channels (the more easily an object can be interacted with via multiple sensorimotor modalities), the more easily that object can be named by Broca's aphasics (Gardner 1973; Gardner and Zurif 1975).

Considerations for Therapy

Bridging research and the healing arts is a notoriously difficult task. The literature on aphasia therapy is not easily assimilated into the framework often used by basic researchers. Technique is often stressed without any discernible theoretical foundation (Agranowitz and McKeown 1964; Griffiths 1970); and where theory does appear, there is a certain understandable arbitrariness to the manner in which it is tied to a specific therapeutic practice. (For a review of these problems see Martin 1975.) Further, whatever the technique used, its success is difficult to gauge

(Darley 1972; Holland 1975a). There is often no control for the type of syndrome treated, follow-up is sporadic, spontaneous recovery is an intrusive factor, and ethical considerations disallow a strict control over incidental therapeutic activity.

What, then, can be said on the basis of the research described in this paper? We have attempted to analyze the character of the representations Broca's aphasics can construct from sentences. At every level examined there appears to be imprecision in the representation. Obviously, then, there are too many deficits to hope for a panacea. But if sentence comprehension is modeled as at least a partially interactive process, there is a simple lesson to be gained for aphasia therapy: The therapist should engage as many different levels in the sound-to-meaning chain as possible. Translated into the practice of therapy, it suggests that the therapist speak slowly; make use of structurally simple sentences; use prosodic variation for semantic contrast; and most important, use the extralinguistic environment as supportively as possible. By doing so the therapist will provide the patient with data at many different interactive levels, including, most importantly, information about context and intention—pragmatic information that can interact with and help the patient resolve the sound structure and propositional content of an utterance. In fact, approaches of this nature have already been consciously employed with some success (Flowers 1973; Whitney 1975; Holland 1975b).

Admittedly, the lessons advanced here are vague and intuitively obvious to many. But despite their intuitive appeal and despite the published record of therapy failures involving techniques that strip language of its communicative purpose (Brookshire 1973; Holland and Sonderman 1974), the habit of disembodied naming and imitation drills continues. Given this context, the research findings described here may have some positive implications for therapy.

References

Agranowitz, A., and McKeown, M. 1964. *Aphasia Handbook*. Springfield, Ill.: Charles C. Thomas.

Andreewsky, E., and Seron, X. 1975. Implicit processing of grammatical rules in a classical case of agrammatism. *Cortex, 11*, 379–390.

Blumstein, S. E., Cooper, W. E., Zurif, E., and Caramazza, A. In press. The perception and production of voice-onset time in aphasia. *Neuropsychologia*.

Brookshire, R. 1973. *An Introduction to Aphasia*. Minneapolis, Minn.: BRK Publishers.

Caramazza, A., and Zurif, E. B. 1976. Dissociation of algorithmic and heuristic processes in language comprehension: Evidence from aphasia. *Brain and Language*. 3, 572–582.

Cermak, L. S. 1972. *Human Memory: Research and Theory*. New York: Ronald Press.

Cermak, L. S., and Moreines, J. 1976. Verbal retention deficits in aphasic and amnesic patients. *Brain and Language, 3*, 16–27.

Chapman, R. S. This volume. Comprehension strategies in children.

Craik, F. I. M., and Lockhart, R. S. 1972. Levels of processing: A framework for memory research. *Journal of Verbal Learning and Verbal Behavior, 11*, 671–684.

Crowder, R. G. This volume. Language and Memory.

Cutting J. E., and Pisoni, D. B. This volume. An information-processing approach to speech perception.

Darley F. L. 1972. The efficacy of language rehabilitation in aphasia. *Journal of Speech and Hearing Disorders, 37,* 3–21.

Eimas, P. D., and Corbit, J. D. 1973. Selective adaptation of linguistic feature detectors. *Cognitive Psychology, 4,* 99–109.

Flowers, C. R. 1973. How to talk effectively to adult aphasic patients. *Journal of the Minnesota Speech and Hearing Association, 12,* 26–30.

Gardner, H. 1973. The contribution of operativity to naming in aphasic patients. *Neuropsychologia, 11,* 200–213.

Gardner, H., and Zurif, E. 1975. Oral reading of single words in aphasia and alexia. *Neuropsychologia, 13,* 170–181.

Gardner, H., Denes, G., and Zurif, E. B. 1975. Critical reading at the sentence level in aphasics. *Cortex, 11,* 60–72.

Garrett, M. F. 1976. Word perception in sentences. Paper presented at MIT-AT&T Convocation on Communications, Cambridge, Mass.

Goodenough, C., Zurif, E. B., and Weintraub, S. In press. Aphasias' attentions to grammatical morphemes. *Language and Speech.*

Goodglass, H. 1968. Studies on the grammar of aphasics. In *Developments in Applied Psychologuistics Research.* S. Rosenberg and J. Koplin (Eds.), New York: MacMillan. 177–208.

Goodglass, H., and Geschwind, N. 1976. Language disorders (aphasia). In *Handbook of Perception, Volume 7.* E. Carterette and M. Friedman (Eds.), New York: Academic Press. 389–428.

Goodglass, H., and Kaplan, E. 1972. *The Assessment of Aphasia and Related Disorders.* Philadelphia, Pa.: Lea and Febiger.

Griffiths, V. 1970. *A Stroke in the Family.* New York: Delacorte Press.

Holland, A. 1975a. The effectiveness of treatment in aphasia. In *Clinical Aphasiology.* R. Brookshire (Ed.), Minneapolis, Minn.: BRK Publishers, 1–16.

————. 1975b. Aphasics as communicators: A model and its implications. Paper presented at American Speech and Hearing Association. Washington, D.C.

Holland, A., and Sonderman, J. C. 1974. Effects of a program based on the token test for teaching comprehension skills to aphasics. *Journal of Speech and Hearing Research, 17,* 589–598.

Johnson, S. C. 1967. Hierarchical clustering schemes. *Psychometrika, 32,* 241–254.

Lenneberg, E. H. 1973. The neurology of language. *Daedalus, 102,* 115–133.

Levelt, W. J. M. 1970. Introduction—Hierarchical clustering algorithms in the psychology of grammar. In *Advances in Psycholinguistics.* G. B. Flores d'Arcais and W. J. M. Levelt (Eds.), Amsterdam: North Holland Publishing Co, 109–121

Liberman, A. M., Delattre, P. C., and Cooper, F. S. 1958. Some cues for the distinction between voiced and voiceless stops in initial position. *Language and Speech, 1,* 153–167.

Liberman, A. M., Harris, K. S., Hoffman, H. S., and Griffith, B. C. 1957. The discrimination of speech sounds within and across phoneme boundaries. *Journal of Experimental Psychology*, *54*, 358–368.

Lisker, L., and Abramson, A. 1964. A cross-language study of voicing in initial stops: Acoustical measurements. *Word*, *20*, 384–422.

Locke, S., Caplan, D., and Kellar, L. 1973. *A Study in Neurolinguistics*. Springfield, Ill.: Charles C. Thomas.

Marslen-Wilson, W. D. 1975. Sentence perception as an interactive parallel process. *Science* *189*, 226–227.

Martin, A. D. 1975. A critical evaluation of therapeutic approaches to aphasia In *Clinical Aphasiology*. R. Brookshire (Ed.), Minneapolis, Minn.: BRK Publishers, 67–78.

Martin, E. 1970. Toward an analysis of subjective phrase structure. *Psychological Bulletin*, *74*, 153–166.

Miller, G. This volume. Lexical meaning.

Scholes, R. J. Forthcoming. Syntactic and lexical components of sentence comprehension. In *The Acquisition and Breakdown of Language: Parallels and Divergencies*. A. Caramazza and E. Zurif (Eds.), Baltimore, Md.: The Johns Hopkins Press.

Stevens, K. N. 1975. The potential role of property detectors in the perception of consonants. In *Auditory Analysis and Perception of Speech*. G. Fant and M. A. A. Tatham (Eds.), New York: Academic Press.

Stevens, K. N., and Klatt, D. H. 1974. Role of formant transitions in the voiced-voiceless distinction for stops. *Journal of the Acoustical Society of America*, *55*, 653–659.

Strub, R. L., and Gardner, H. 1974. The repetition deficit in conduction aphasia: Mnestic or linguistic? *Brain and Language*, *1*, 241–256.

Tallal, P. This volume. Implications of speech perceptual research for clinical populations.

Ulatowska. H., and Baker, W. 1975. Linguistic study of processing strategies in right—and left—brain damaged patients. Unpublished manuscript. Austin, Texas: University of Texas Press.

von Stockert, T. 1972. Recognition of syntactic structure in aphasia. *Cortex*, *8*, 323–334.

Weigel, E., and Bierwisch, M. 1970. Neuropsychology and linguistics: Topics of common research. *Foundations of Language*, *6*, 1–18.

Whitney, J. L. 1975. Developing aphasics' use of compensatory strategies. Paper presented at American Speech and Hearing Association. Washington, D. C.

Zurif, E. B., and Blumstein, S. E. Forthcoming. Language and the Brain. In M. Halle, J. Bresnan, and G. A. Miller (Eds.) *Linguistic Theory and Psychological Reality*. Cambridge, Mass.: The MIT Press.

Zurif, E. B., Caramazza, A., and Myerson, R. 1972. Grammatical judgments of agrammatic aphasics. *Neuropsychologia*, *10*, 405–417.

Zurif, E. B., Caramazza, A., Myerson, R., and Galvin, J. 1974. Semantic feature representations in normal and aphasic language. *Brain and Language*, *1*, 167–187.

Zurif, E. B., Green E., Caramazza, A., and Goodenough, C. In press Grammatical intuitions of aphasic patients: Sensitivity to functors. *Cortex*.

General Discussion of Papers by Crowder and Zurif and Caramazza

Specificity of Feature Detectors in Vision and Audition

There was some discussion regarding the specificity of auditory feature detectors inferred from the results of selective adaptation experiments. (See Cutting and Pisoni, this volume, for a description of this experimental paradigm.) It has been reported that the adaptation effect for speech stimuli is specific to voice, that is, the repeated presentation of an adapting stimulus produced by voice 1 does not produce a shift in the identification boundary on an appropriate test series produced by voice 2 (Ades in press). Tallal suggested that this might be analogous to the specificity found in visual property detector systems. Studies that record from single cells in the visual cortex of subhuman species (Hubel and Wiesel 1962, 1968) have found cells that respond only to lines of a particular orientation with respect to the animal's retina. Tallal asked whether this research has revealed any orientation-specific cells that are also selective with respect to the color of the lines or the width of the lines. She thought this would be analogous to auditory feature detectors that were voice specific.

Crowder and Jenkins responded that the research on the McCollough effect with humans (that uses the selective adaptation procedure) does show orientation-specific color adaptation effects (McCollough 1965). Furthermore, the effect does not hold up if the widths of the lines during testing are different from those presented during adaptation. However, no one has done single-cell recording in conjunction with the McCollough experiment, so these results cannot be interpreted as direct evidence for the existence of physiological (single-cell) detectors with this kind of selectivity.

Shelton commented that the implication that feature detectors as postulated in speech perception models involved distinct pieces of tissue (single cells) is not necessary for the concept to be meaningful. Cutting agreed and added some comments on the interpretation of the contingent adaptation experiments. He asserted that in any one condition adaptation may be distributed throughout the (speech perceptual) system; detector mechanisms that function at early (acoustic) levels of analysis as well as at more abstract levels are fatigued. Thus the adaptation procedure may affect processing at a number of levels simultaneously. If one conceived of speech perception as involving a dynamic pathway of the flow of information, this pathway could be modified in complex ways during adaptation. Contingent adaptation effects might be a function of interactions among the several levels. Thus one does not have to postulate the existence of different feature detectors for every different contingent effect obtained in an adaptation experiment. (See also the general discussion of the paper by Cutting and Pisoni for comments on the specificity of feature detectors.)

Perception and Memory of Different Voices

Another topic of discussion concerned the facilitation effects of voice identity on memory reported by Crowder. Bransford asked if the study had been performed only with a male and female voice or if two male voices (which are presumably more similar) had been tested also. Crowder knew of no study that had used two male voices.

Liberman commented (and Crowder agreed) that memory for voice identity could probably not be accounted for by the "complexity of processing" explanation forwarded by Kolers for memory of other characteristics of the "medium." (See section 2 of Crowder's paper.) Liberman asserted that voice identification or differentiation was a very fundamental ability that may be accomplished by right hemisphere mechanisms (Doehring, and Bartholomeus 1971). This ability is functionally very important both for speaker recognition and for separating sources of messages in situations where several people are talking. Furthermore, it appears that voice differentiation is an automatic and obligatory process. Research by Summerfield and Haggard (1975) has shown that subjects "normalize" for different voices even when the task in which they are engaged does not require such adjustment for the speaker. Liberman and Crowder agreed that this ability probably did not involve echoic memory processes in the same way as do other perceptual processing of medium characteristics as described by Crowder.

The Role of Memory in Perception

Jenkins again expressed concern about auditory/speech perception models that postulate memory processes to account for the perception of information that is distributed over time. (See also the general discussion of the paper by Cutting and Pisoni.) Taken to the extreme, one would postulate that information about energy present at each instant must be stored and later put back together via memory processes. This is analogous to the "snapshot" theory of visual perception, in which the perception of depth or motion is mediated by "unconscious inferences" that put together static two-dimensional information from each instant. The snapshot metaphor is particularly bad for acoustic events because there is no signal at any one instant; acoustic information is inherently temporal information. One must talk about intervals or "windows" within which (change in) energy is detected. The question is, then, how large an interval does one allow as the basic unit of analysis? For instance, one would probably not want to describe the perception of a thousand-cycle tone as putting together stored information (memories) of the occurrence of peaks of the cycle (peak counting, in Crowder's terms). That is, no one seriously asserts that the perception of pure tones involves memory. Rather, tones are considered as basic units that can be perceived directly even though the information occurs over time. Why not then consider glides as basic units or semisyllables or whole words? The problem of specifying the appropriate temporal intervals over which information is perceived directly without having to reconstruct or encode or integrate from stored "memories" is present at all levels of perceptual processing. This is the problem that Gibson addresses in visual perception when he talks about direct perception of information that is distributed over time.

Postulation of Specialized Memories

Jenkins remarked that the proliferation of different memories and memory processes (echoic memory, phonological coding, memory imaging, episodic memory, semantic memory, acoustic feature analysis, and phonetic feature analysis) was, in his opinion, distressing. Each time the experimental paradigm is changed, it seems the phenomena change and a new memory is postulated with different decay characteristics and capacity limitations. People in Jenkin's laboratory have been investigating the interaction of stimulus materials, orienting tasks (what the subject does with the materials during presentation), and criterion measures (such as recognition and recall) in studies of remembering. He asserted that how much and what is remembered is a function of the interaction of all three of these aspects of the experimental situation. For instance, subjects can be given a list of words to remember and required to rate the words for pleasantness or to count the number of letters (orienting tasks). Subjects who rate the words for pleasantness recall twice as many words as those who count the letters (Jenkins 1974). If pictures are used instead of words (materials), subjects recall more of them and orienting task differences have smaller effects (McCabe and Jenkins 1975). If a recognition test is used instead of a recall test (criterion measure), differences between orienting tasks will be decreased for words and obliterated entirely for pictures. If the pictures used are drawn from the same category (such as snowflakes or faces) (Goldstein and Chance 1970) or fit together to tell a story (Jenkins, Wald, and Pittenger, forthcoming), subjects will falsely recognize pictures they have never seen before if they fit the category or the story. Jenkins asserted that these differences reflect the experimental constraints and conditions and probably should not be accounted for by postulating different memories or memory processes for each new outcome.

Crowder responded that he now thinks that "memory is just a property of persistence of various kinds of analytic operations performed" on inputs. He is convinced by his research that memory and perception are completely bound up in each other. There are different kinds of perceptual analyses that are performed on inputs. They all have "memory," that is, they all persist awhile.

Meaningfulness, Memory, and Learning

Bransford commented on the postulation of memories from a somewhat different perspective. He traced a train of thought that he believed led to many current theoretical characterizations of memory. In cognitive psychology, the concept of learning has been replaced by the concept of memory. In other words, the problem of what is learned has become the problem of what is stored. Specifically, the problem of memory for linguistic materials takes the following form: First, stimulus materials are thought of as meaningful or nonmeaningful independent of the comprehender. Then it is assumed that meaningful materials are "stored" better than nonmeaningful materials. Models are postulated to describe the representations of those stored entities and how those stored entities are contacted, retrieved, and so on.

Bransford asserted that this approach has several difficulties. First, inputs are not meaningful in and of themselves. Meaning is a function of the relationship between comprehender and inputs. This notion is inherent in Gibson's characterization of "affordances" (Gibson 1977; Shaw, McIntyre, and Mace 1974). If one takes this approach, the question becomes, "how does the present situation 'remodel' the organism so that it can subsequently 're-create' (remember) some previous event?" Everyone agrees that past experience has an effect. The question to be asked is why learning is not equivalent to the formation of memories. What is learned determines what the organism is able to re-create or remember later on. What is learned is a function of the meaning of the interaction between the comprehender and the materials. In experiments one must select the appropriate criterion task to discover what the subject has learned. So-called meaningless tasks often produce good memory if one tests the right thing, and meaningful tasks or materials can be remembered poorly if the wrong measure is used.

Jenkins cited an example of this. If words are presented with different type faces and subjects are required to make up rhymes, they don't even notice that there are different type faces; memory for this aspect of the stimuli is very poor. But if subjects are required to count the number of straight and curved lines when the words are presented, they can recognize which words were presented in which type face. That is, memory for the type faces is good. However, recall of the words is very poor.

Perception of Phonetically Relevant Acoustic Dimensions by Aphasics
Liberman commented on the data reported by Zurif that aphasics produced peaked discrimination functions or differences in voice onset time but poor identification. This is not different in principle from what Eimas and others have shown for two-month-old infants (Eimas et al. 1971), that is, infants show discontinuous discrimination of the acoustic dimensions but the experimental paradigms used do not allow one to ask about the infants' ability to identify these stimuli in linguistically relevant ways. There is also some preliminary unpublished research by Bruno Repp that suggests a disjunction of discrimination and identification with normal adult listeners similar to that reported by Zurif. In a dichotic listening situation, subjects produce discrimination peaks at the phoneme boundaries, but they do not produce good identification functions. Liberman asserted that detecting whether two stimuli are the same or different is a good deal easier than telling what they are (identifying them). He added that this disjunction of discrimination and identification found with aphasics and normals (under demanding circumstances) is interesting in light of the claim that categorical perception is a superficial phenomenon. That is, the categorical result in discrimination does not depend merely on the fact that the subject can attach a phonetic label to the stimuli. In fact, these data support the notion that (categorical) discrimination is in some sense prior to identification.

Tallal also commented on Zurif's report of aphasics' perception of acoustic dimensions. While he reports no positive correlation between their performance on the acoustic task and comprehension ability, Tallal has found high correlations between auditory perceptual ability and comprehension. She and Zurif agreed that this could be due to differences in how comprehension had been measured. (See the general discussion of papers by Bransford and Nitsch and by Chapman on problems of measuring comprehension skills.)

Language Development versus Language Maintenance

Tallal wished to stress the point that the functions necessary for the development of language may not be the same as those necessary for the maintenance of language in normal adults or even in adults where there is a breakdown in language, such as with the aphasic patient. For instance, the effect of a phonological or acoustic deficit on the adult who already has an established knowledge of language may be quite different from the effect of such a deficit on a child trying to learn a language. This is one reason why research on normal language development is necessary for an understanding of disabilities in children. It is not sufficient to use as a model the adult language speaker/hearer.

References

Ades, A. E. In press. Source assignment and feature extraction in speech. *Journal of Experimental Psychology: Human Perception and Performance*

Cutting, J. E. and Pisoni, D. B. This volume. An information-processing approach to speech perception.

Doehring, D. A., and Bartholomeus, B. W. 1971. Laterality effects in voice recognition. *Neuropsychologia*, 9, 425–430.

Eimas, P. D., Siqueland, E. R., Jusczyk, P., and Vigorito, J. 1971. Speech perception in infants. *Science*, 171, 303–306.

Gibson, J. J. 1966. *The Senses Considered As Perceptual Systems*. Boston: Houghton Mifflin.

———. 1977. The theory of affordances. In R. Shaw and J. D. Bransford, *Perceiving, Acting and Knowing: Toward an Ecological Psychology*. Hillsdale, N. J.: Lawrence Erlbaum Assoc., 67–82.

Goldstein, A. G., and Chance, J. E. 1970. Visual recognition memory for complex configurations. *Perception and Psychophysics*, 9, 237–240.

Hubel, D. H., and Wiesel, T. N. 1962. Receptive fields, binocular interaction and functional architecture in the cat's visual cortex. *Journal of Physiology*, 160, 106–154.

———. 1968. Receptive fields and functional architecture of monkey striate cortex. *Journal of Physiology*, 195, 215–243.

Jenkins, J. J. 1974. Remember that old theory of memory: Well forget it! *American Psychologist*, 29, 785–795.

Jenkins, J. J., Wald, J., and Pittenger, J. Forthcoming. Apprehending pictorial events: An instance of psychological cohesion. In C. W. Savage (Ed.), *Minnesota Studies in the Philosophy of Science*, Vol. 9. Minneapolis, Minn.: University of Minnesota Press.

McCabe, L., and Jenkins, J. J. 1975. Orienting tasks that yield poor recall have more effect on words than on pictures. Paper presented to the Midwestern Psychological Association, May.

McCollough, C. 1965. Color adaptation of edge-detectors in the human visual system. *Science*, 149, 1115–1116.

Shaw, R. E., McIntyre, M., and Mace, W. 1974. The role of symmetry in event perception. In R. B. MacLeud and H. L. Pick, Jr. (Eds.) *Perception: Essays in Honor of James J. Gibson*. Ithaca, N. Y.: Cornell University Press, 276–310.

Summerfield, A. Q., and Haggard, M· P. 1975. Vocal tract-normalizations as demonstrated by reaction times. In G. Fant and M. A. A. Tatham (Eds.), *Auditory Analysis and Perception of Speech*. New York: Academic Press, 115–141.

Lexical Meaning

GEORGE A. MILLER

If you know what a chair is, what more is involved in knowing the meaning of *chair*? One answer is that the phonological shape *chair* must be associated with what you know about chairs. There is nothing necessary about this association; persons who know what a chair is might associate *Stuhl* or *silla* or *chaise* with what they know. But speakers of English have agreed to observe a convention that *chair* is associated with what they know about chairs. Similarly, *table* is associated with what they know about tables, *couch* with what they know about couches, *bed* with what they know about beds, *furniture* with what they know about chairs, tables, couches, beds, and certain other things, and so on.

The set of phonological shapes that people know is the vocabulary of their language or, in more technical terminology, the lexicon. When one learns a vocabulary, therefore, one acquires a second kind of knowledge. For expository purposes, let us refer to what one knows about the world and the things in it as one's practical knowledge and to what one knows about what these things are called as one's lexical knowledge. Brain scientists have not yet discovered how all this knowledge is represented in the nervous system, but it must be represented somehow. Let us refer to that reperesentation, whatever it may be, as memory, and to the part of memory that represents lexical knowledge as lexical memory. This terminology should not suggest that lexical memory and practical memory are separate cognitive organs; lexical memory disconnected from practical memory would be an engine without fuel. The major value of lexical knowledge is that it provides access to practical knowledge.

Although the mechanisms of memory are poorly understood, there can be no doubt that lexical memory is large. No one knows all the words of English, of course, but there are thousands of common words that all speakers do know. Several psychologists have tried to count them. For example, Seashore and Eckerson (1940) estimate that an average college undergraduate can recognize more than one hundred and fifty thousand words. (The number of words persons can recognize correctly is, of course, much larger than the number they will actually use in their own speech.) Estimates of vocabulary growth in children have been of special interest, in part because such information is so valuable in designing methods for the teaching of reading and writing. Templin (1957) reports that six-year-old children of average intelligence can recognize thirteen thousand words. Since this estimate increases to twenty-eight thousand and three hundred by age eight, one assumes that the average seven-year-old must become familiar with new words at a rate of $15,300/730 = 21$ words per day (13.4 root words + 7.6 compound and derivative words). If it took, say, thirty days to learn each new word, the child would be learning about six hundred and thirty words at any given time. Vocabulary grows even faster in children of superior intelligence; scores on vocabulary tests have long been recognized as closely related to general mental ability. Although a child's rapid acquisition of grammatical constructions has been frequently noted in recent years, the rapid acquisition of vocabulary is no less remarkable.

Numbers of this magnitude imply that young children face a formidable task in mastering the lexical knowledge they will require as adults. It is difficult to imagine how they could accomplish it if every word they learned was unrelated to every other word. It is obvious, however, that words are related to one another in addition to being associated with practical knowledge that gives them meaning. These relations are due in large measure, but not entirely, to the fact that practical knowledge is itself highly structured and this practical structure is reflected in lexical structure. It is a matter of practical knowledge that tables and chairs are frequently used together; it is not surprising to find that the words *table* and *chair* are associated in lexical memory. There are, however, other sources of association that are independent of practical knowledge. For example, words are categorized by their grammatical privileges of occurrence in sentences: Nouns tend to be associated with other nouns, adjectives with other adjectives, and so on. Hence children encountering a new word can usually bring to bear on it information already acquired about other words—that it is associated with knowledge in a field of practical knowledge they have already begun to learn other words for, that its use in sentences is similar to other words they know, and so on. In short, a particular word is easier to learn if other words related to it in various ways are already known. Learning the generic word *furniture* is surely easier if one already knows such more specific words as *chair, table, couch,* and *bed.* Consequently, a child's vocabulary grows along reasonably predictable lines: Words for concrete things and perceptible events are learned before words for generic classes of things or abstract events (Brown 1958). In such ways a child can transfer previous lexical learning to new lexical learning, and one is encouraged to believe that the rapid acquisition of a vocabulary might someday be explicable.

In any case, the lexical knowledge that a child gathers must have a structure of its own. Since some of this structure arises from sources other than the structure of practical knowledge that gives most words their meanings, the description of lexical knowledge becomes something different from a description of practical knowledge plus associated phonological shapes. In addition to meaning and pronunciation, a person who knows a word well enough to use it appropriately in ordinary speech or written language must also know implicitly or explicitly such things as spelling, variant pronunciations, morphology, syntactic category, syntactic contexts of use, alternative meanings, truth conditions, semantic contexts of use, semantic decomposition, presuppositions, implicatures, situational contexts of use, discourse contexts of use, affective tone, and technical uses. Although explication of all these aspects of lexical knowledge lies beyond the scope of this chapter (but see Miller and Johnson-Laird 1976), the list suggests the variety of problems involved.

Because words are enmeshed in this complex matrix of properties and relations, it is often convenient to speak of lexical meaning as something different from referential meaning. The referential meaning of a word—the objects or events with which a word is associated—is only part of what will here be called the lexical meaning of the word, which must also include lexical knowledge relating this word to others. Analysis of this complex system of lexical relations is a critical problem for anyone who hopes to understand human speech and language.

Different psychologists have developed different ways to describe the system of lexical relations in which individual words and their meanings are embedded. A somewhat arbitrary classification will be imposed on these alternatives for the purposes of this survey: associative networks, multidimensional spaces, semantic features, prototypes, and conceptual relations. It will become clear in the course of this chapter that the boundaries between these different approaches are vague; it is sometimes difficult to know whether a notational difference or a basic disagreement is at issue. By proceeding more or less historically, however, the spectrum of theoretical options can be presented as one of growing complexity—as more methods of research have developed, as psychological theory in general has matured, and as more attention has been paid to the relation of lexical memory to other components of language use.

The work to be reviewed is related at various points to matters of educational and clinical concern. It would be an exaggeration to say that the results had been "applied" to practical problems, but the ideas and methods of observation employed have been shared by psychologists in laboratories, schools, and clinics. Rather than collect educational and clinical contributions in a special section at the end, therefore, passing reference will be made to them where they seem most appropriate. I am not competent to review all of the applied work relevant to lexical meaning; I hope this method of exposition will at least suggest some of the points at which practical implications have been explored.

Word Associations
Francis Galton is generally credited with having published the first experimental investigation of word associations in 1879. Subsequent research inspired by Galton's method has been reviewed many times (references can be found in Cramer 1968 or Esper 1973) and that history need not be repeated here. For the present purposes it is sufficient to note that the first word you think of when I say W can be taken as evidence relevant to the structure of your lexical memory for W. The age and bulk of work with word associations justify taking them as a starting point, but attention will be limited to those findings most revealing for questions of lexical memory.

In this discussion the word presented by the experimenter will be referred to as the "probe" and the word produced by the subject will be called the "reply." Results known to be reliable that seem relevant to lexical memory can then be summarized as follows (where only some of the earliest reports are cited):

1. Many people give the same reply (Cattell and Bryant 1889). This result suggests that in spite of different personal histories of language use, normal people who speak the same language develop similar organizations of practical and lexical memory. Words that are most frequently used in the language are among the most frequent replies (Dauber 1911).

2. Common replies have the shortest latencies (Thumb and Marbe 1901). Median latencies range from about 1 second (sec) for the commonest replies to about 2 sec for infrequent replies. Since the values are an order of magnitude longer than simple reaction times to lights or tones, they suggest that lexical meanings are involved in generating the reply. Long latencies may allow time for intermediate associations and thus infrequent replies; frequent cooccurrence in thought or speech may strengthen lexical associations and thus explain short latencies.

A reply that is seldom given by other people, coupled with a longer than average latency, may indicate that the probe word has aroused some affective reactions that interfere with the associative process. The probe may suggest, for example, ideas that the person is reluctant or unwilling to voice; the long latency is required to repress the first reply and find another that is more acceptable. Jung (1918) used the word association technique to explore emotional complexes in his patients, and the first extensive tabulation of association norms (Kent and Rosanoff 1910) was collected for psychiatric use in order to provide a more objective basis for judging a reply to be idiosyncratic. Such norms have also proved useful in the study of effects of brain damage on language. Patients having Broca's aphasia will show a near normal occurrence of common replies, although it takes them much longer to find the word; patients having Wernicke's aphasia, if they can carry out the experiment at all, will give a great preponderance of rare, idiosyncratic replies and their latencies will not conform to Marbe's law (Howes 1967).

3. Many common replies are from the same field of knowledge as the probe. These meaning relations are most obvious in the high frequencies of replies that are logically superordinate, coordinate, or subordinate to the probe or that bear part-whole relations to it (Trautscholdt 1882). The effect of practical knowledge on the structure of lexical knowledge is clearly demonstrated.

4. Replies to common probes tend to be in the same syntactic category as the probe word (Kraepelin 1883). Noun probes elicit predominantly noun replies; adjective probes elicit many antonymous adjective replies; verbs elicit verb replies (though noun replies to verb probes are not infrequent). Effects of syntactic relations on the structure of lexical memory are also shown by replies that frequently follow the probe word in grammatical sentences.

It may be of some educational significance that preschool children tend more frequently to give replies that are thematically related to the probe word (Woodrow and Lowell 1916; see review in Entwisle 1966). For example, whereas an adult will usually give *chair* as his reply to *table*, young children may say *eat*; the probe *hot* will elicit *cold* from most adults, whereas a child may say *fire*; and so on. Thus young children tend to give fewer replies in the same syntactic category as the probe and consequently fewer superordinate, coordinate, or subordinate replies. Although logical and syntactic sources of association are less apparent, the influence of practical knowledge is even more clearly revealed by such thematic replies.

5. Replies are influenced by the context of the probe (Wreschner 1907–1909).

If preceding words combine with the probe to determine the response, it suggests mechanisms of interaction in retrieval from lexical memory (Howes and Osgood 1954).

6. Subjects can reply with words bearing predetermined relations to the probe (Trautscholdt 1882; Cattell 1887). These so-called controlled associations (for example, to reply with its country when given the name of a city) take no longer than free associations. Indeed, self-instruction probably limits the freedom of so-called free associations (Koffka 1912). Different people adopt different but consistent strategies for replying: functional, relying on practical knowledge; synonym-superordinate, relying on logical relations among words; or contrast-coordinate, emphasizing speed of reply (Moran, Mefferd, and Kimble 1964). Individual differences therefore need not reflect different organizations of lexical memory but only different ways of using lexical memory to satisfy the demands of a word association task.

Of particular importance for studies of lexical memory are the controlled associations that have been tabulated as "category norms" (Cohen, Bousfield and Whitmarsh 1957; Battig and Montague 1969). Respondents are given a generic category as the probe and allowed a limited period of time to write all of the instances of that category they can think of. For example, Battig and Montague gave 442 college students 30 sec to reply to the probe, *a bird*. The reply *robin* was included among the responses of 85 percent of the students; *sparrow* was included by 54 percent; *cardinal* 47 percent; *blue jay* 41 percent; *eagle* 36 percent; *crow* 34 percent; *bluebird* 31 percent; *canary* 30 percent; *parakeet* 26 percent; *hawk* 25 percent; *blackbird* 20 percent; *wren* 19 percent; *oriole* 17 percent; *parrot* 16 percent; *pigeon* 13 percent; *hummingbird* and *starling* 11 percent; *woodpecker* and *vulture* 10 percent; *swallow* and *chicken* 9 percent. The first response written by 43 percent of the students was *robin*; *cardinal* was the first response of 9 percent; *sparrow* 6 percent Batting and Montague obtained similar distributions of replies for fifty-six different categories, some of which were: *a precious stone, a unit of time, a relative, a unit of distance, a metal, a type of reading material, a military title, and a four-footed animal.* Not only do adults have their lexical memory organized into categories, but there is considerable agreement as to which instances in a category they think of first.

Most of the basic facts about word association were known for many years before attempts were made to account for them in terms of formal models. Early workers generally assumed that a probe generates an idea related to other ideas expressed by the replies. How ideas come to be associated with each other was considered a central problem of psychology; principles of contiguity, frequency, similarity, contrast, attention, and emotion were discussed at length (Warren 1921). The subsequent rejection of mentalism by American psychologists led to a translation of these principles into the language of behaviorism (Watson 1913), but the assumption that an association is a two-termed relation was retained. For behaviorists the terms in associative relation became stimulus and response rather than ideas, thus making the direction of association explicit; and the process of conditioning was substituted for the process of introspection as the source of psychological data (Holt 1931), thus making the strength of association an important variable. For example, a chair might be the discriminative stimulus and the word *chair* would be the conditioned response; the frequency, latency, or amplitude of this response could provide an index of the strength of the association. However, since people often see chairs without reflexly uttering *chair*, some mechanism to disconnect the vocal response from the discriminative stimulus was required.

Razran (1939) and others demonstrated that a response conditioned to a stimulus word will generalize to other phonologically and semantically related words. Cofer and Foley (1942) explained such observations in terms of mediated generalization. For example, a person conditioned to salivate to the word *vane* will also salivate (with lesser magnitude) to *vein* and *vain*. Cofer and Foley regarded this as an example of direct generalization on the basis of stimulus similarity. A person conditioned to *vane* will also respond to *weathercock*, however, where the response is assumed to be mediated by previously conditioned language behavior. This previous conditioning was supposed to establish an implicit, fractional, kinesthetic response r_x to both *vane* and *weathercock* so that when a person is experimentally conditioned to salivate to *vane*, r_x becomes conditioned to salivation and when *weathercock* is subsequently presented and also leads to r_x, the salivation response again occurs. Cofer and Foley postulated a variety of generalization gradients (homophony, synonymy, causal relations, egocentrism, subordination) borrowed from the work on word association (Wells 1911). The central idea, however, was that two words have the same meaning if both elicit the same implicit mediating response r_x. In this way unobservable responses were substituted for unobservable ideas, and gradients of generalization were substituted for mentalistic associations.

Lexical memory, therefore, came to be viewed as a network based on shared mediating responses; word associations provided only one of many behavioral manifestations of these connections. This line of argument, based on the behavior theory of Hull (1939), was subsequently extended (Mowrer 1954; Osgood 1963; Staats 1969) to account for grammatical relations between words in sentences. Less was done to analyze mediating responses (however, see discussion below of the semantic differential). That they must be sufficiently complex to admit analysis is obvious from the fact that if two words have different meanings, they must have different mediating responses (Fodor 1965); and therefore any r_x that they may share can be only part of the implicit, fractional, kinesthetic responses that are assumed to constitute their distinct meanings. The semantic decomposition that seems to be called for, however, is difficult to carry out by conditioning techniques; and American behaviorism was more concerned with the possibility of influencing behavior (in schools or clinics, for example) than with questions of cognitive structure.

One class of word-word associations of great practical importance are those between languages. Since the problems of bilingualism and second-language learning are too extensive to be reviewed here, however, the following will be limited to monolingual (usually English) phenomena.

Associative Networks

With the introduction of computers, psychologists began to consider more complex theories of learning and memory; the objectivity of the new theories was guaranteed, not by reduction to conditioned reflexes but by their instantiation in programs of instructions that enabled a computer to simulate important aspects of human performance (Newell and Simon 1972). In particular, it became possible to represent lexical memory as a network of nodes in a computer's memory, nodes that can be reached by one-way associative links starting from any input word. The relation of this approach to the historical doctrines of association psychology has been reviewed by Anderson and Bower (1973).

A problem that every theory must face is that words can have several senses. The word *line*, for example, can be either a noun or a verb. As a noun it has different senses in *line of poetry, line of rope, line of sight, line of kings, toe the line*, and so on, and as a verb it has different senses in *He lined up the men* and *He lined the coat* (MacNamara 1971; Caramazza, Grober, and Zurif 1976). This illustrates the problem of polysemy. It raises two questions for any theorist: First, how are different senses of a word represented in lexical memory? Second, how does a listener know which sense the speaker intended? These questions are important because the most frequently used words are also the most polysemous (Zipf 1945). Experimental evidence indicates that the more senses a word has, the more quickly it can be recognized as a word (Rubenstein, Garfield, and Millikan 1970; Jastrzembski and Stanners 1975), even when frequency of use is equated.

When presented in isolation, a polysemous word cannot be disambiguated, but in context it usually can be (Kelly and Stone 1975). The lexical representation of a polysemous word must therefore be organized in such a way that other words in the same phrase or sentence can combine with it to determine the most appropriate sense. (Maher 1973 finds schizophrenic patients are usually deficient in using context to determine the meaning of ambiguous words.) One approach is to assume that the lexical meaning is very general and that context is used to infer or construct a specific interpretation (Anderson and Ortony 1975). An easier approach to implement for computers is to assume that all the different senses are included as separate entries and that context is used to select the appropriate interpretation. One way to implement this latter approach in an associative network was proposed by Quillian (1968) in one of the first explicit theories of lexical memory.

A person given two words and asked to compare their meanings can produce a sentence stating how the two concepts are (or could be) related. For example, given the words *cry* and *comfort*, one might say that a person who is crying is sad and needs to be comforted. That is to say, one converges on a particular sense of *cry* and a particular sense of *comfort* that will go together naturally in the same context. Quillian simulated this performance with a computer program, the important component of which was the "semantic memory" provided to the computer. He selected a group of words whose definitions provided the information in the memory, looked those words up in a dictionary, encoded all of their definitions in a predetermined format, and loaded them into a computer along with a program to combine them into a single network of semantic components. Then he asked the computer to take two words and search their meanings for any semantic components they had in common. In the case of *cry* and *comfort*, the computer found *sad* (*makes sad sounds* and *makes less sad*) and thereby selected the appropriate senses of the two words.

The format in which Quillian coded definitions for storage in semantic memory associated a word with other words. As in conditioning theories, associations were assumed to be directed but unlike most versions of conditioning theory different kinds of directed associations were used. One kind of link pointed from a word to its superordinate word (or "superset"); another pointed to a modifier; two others represented conjunctive (*and*) and disjunctive (*or*) associations; and still another pointed from any relational term to the arguments it related. In Quillian's system, therefore, each labeled link represented a particular associative relation (essentially, a proposition) between the semantic components of the definition; the total pattern of links for all the words that were defined formed an associative network. Because Quillian made no attempt to build up the memory structure from a limited set of primitive, elementary concepts, Anderson and Bower (1973, p. 81) call this a configurational theory of lexical meaning—"every unit in the network is defined in terms of other units in the network." In particular, different senses of one word are represented by different configurations and disambiguation is achieved by finding the intersection of a particular configuration with another configuration representing another word in the same context.

The representation of lexical information in the form of propositions was a considerable advance in theoretical sophistication over the undifferentiated stimulus-response bonds of conditioning theories. Moreover, a system that is able to represent lexical meanings in propositional form is also well adapted to express sentential meanings. Norman and Rumelhart (1975) have developed and applied these ideas further; they also introduce associative links based on grammatical case (like agent, object, and recipient) (Fillmore 1968) where the link no longer represents a proposition (Woods 1975). Anderson and Bower (1973) proposed a theory for how such structures might be learned by analyzing sentences and storing the results. Moore and Newell (1974) have added a simple but powerful operation to determine whether one concept in a network can be "viewed as" another (whether a *canary* can be viewed as a *bird* or a *beehive* as a *home*). Schank (1973) proposed an analysis of all lexical and sentential concepts into networks of primitive concepts (a reductionistic theory of lexical meaning). Fiskel and Bower (1976) assume that a finite automaton is embedded at every node in the network, thus endowing semantic memory with autonomous computational powers. Reviewing recent work in this rapidly developing branch of artificial intelligence research lies beyond the scope of this chapter, but the works cited provide extensive references for an interested reader.

The superset (superordinate) relation plays a particularly important role in most theories based on associative networks. If there is information that is part of the meaning of all instances of, say, *machine*, that information should be stored once with the superset word *machine* and not repeated for every instance—for *typewriter, drill press, computer,* and so on. Quillian used this superset relation to increase the efficiency of information storage and defined a word's full concept to include all the information that could be reached by tracing the paths from it to other nodes in the network. The entry for *typewriter* would, therefore, include not only the information stored immediately at that node (*has keys, prints,* and so on), but also any information stored under the superset *machine.* This aspect of Quillian's theory was tested by Collins and Quillian (1969). They found, for example, that it takes longer to decide *A canary is an animal* than to decide *A canary is a bird* which in turn took longer than *A canary is a canary.* These results supported the model of semantic memory, since the time required to find the intersection of two words separated by one level in the superset hierarchy was longer than the no-search case (identity) but shorter than for words separated by two levels. However, the time required to reject a false sentence (*A canary is a fish*) was significantly longer and no clear picture of the apparently complex process emerged.

The use of reaction times in this experiment is worth noting. Most psychological experiments on verbal memory have been concerned with learning and forgetting new associations between words or nonsense syllables. As Tulving (1972) pointed out, the results of such studies are usually limited to memory for the experimental episode in which training occurred and so can shed little light on the kind of permanent memory that supports intelligent behavior and that schooling is presumably intended to instill. Studies of new associations typically rely on errors as the major source of information about the stage of learning that has been achieved, but errors are so infrequent in the use of old and well-established associations that the traditional methods of investigation have been of little value. Meyer and Schvaneveldt (1976, p. 27), who review the use of reaction times to investigate lexical memory, comment that, "Unlike other procedures, the reaction time method provides a powerful tool for assessing mental processes even when memory failures are very rare." Although mental chronometry is not the only technique available to study lexical memory, much of the current interest in such studies has been stimulated by the new data that this method has provided.

Insofar as the superset relation defines a hierarchical structure in lexical memory, it shares certain formal characteristics of a semantic theory developed independently by Katz and Fodor (1963), who proposed that the meanings of words can be represented by semantic markers. For example, the word *wife* might be semantically marked in the lexicon as +MARRIED, +WOMAN, +FEMALE, +PERSON, +ANIMATE, whereas the word *husband* might be marked as +MARRIED, −WOMAN, −FEMALE, +PERSON, +ANIMATE. According to this model, different senses of a word are represented by different sets of semantic markers and disambiguation is achieved by "projection rules" for combining the markers of two or more words to obtain a semantic reading for the combination. In configurational network theories, the superset is usually another word, whereas in the theory of semantic markers it is thought of as a generic concept that may or may not happen to be expressed by some word in the language. Inasmuch as the semantic marker theory seems to decompose a word into the concepts that it expresses, it is potentially a reductionistic theory, although Katz and Fodor did not propose any finite set of primitive concepts.

Psychologically this formulation would seem to explain why the words *wife* and *husband* are so closely related in meaning—because they share so many semantic markers. Formally, however, attaching all these markers to every word is highly redundant. To say that *wife* denotes a married woman should be enough; it is not necessary to say also that a wife is an animate female person. Any word whose meaning is marked either + or − for WOMAN will necessarily be marked as +PERSON; any word whose meaning is marked + or − for PERSON will necessarily be marked +ANIMATE. These relations between semantic markers are therefore stated by Katz and Fodor as redundancy rules; they summarize information that is part of a person's general knowledge available for using the lexicon and do not have to be included redundantly in every lexical entry. Moreover, many redundancy rules can be expressed together as a hierarchy (Miller 1967), in which form they closely resemble (parts of) associative networks.

In logical terms, however, the cognitive structure represented by redundancy rules is not a part of the lexicon but part of an inferential system that uses the lexicon (Fodor, Fodor, and Garrett 1975). That is to say, when one hears the sentence *My wife has a pet canary* and retrieves the words *wife* and *canary* from lexical memory as part of the work of comprehending the sentence, one understands these words in some immediate way without reconstructing, even unconsciously, the fact that a wife is an animate person or that a canary is an animal. If necessary, however, inferences involving these semantic relations can be rapidly performed by the part of the system that uses the output of lexical memory. What associative networks represent according to this view is not concepts that words express, but inferential relations among those concepts.

In psychological terms, redundancy rules (or superset relations) can be thought of as characterizing those parts of the meanings of words that are learned over and over for different words—learning that presumably becomes easier with repetition. Potential implications for the optimal order of learning words have been explored (Clark 1973), but further elaboration and testing are needed.

Multidimensional Spaces

Some words are related to one another by differences of degree. For example, *baby*, *child*, *adolescent*, and *adult* differ in degree of aging; each represents a different range of ages along a continuum extending from birth to old age. Similarly, *grayish*, *moderate*, *strong*, and *vivid* represent different degrees of color saturation; *none*, *few*, *some*, *many*, *most*, and *all* represent different proportions. It seems to be part of the meanings of many adjectives (*heavy*, *tall*, *hot*) that they vary in degree—it makes possible the comparative and superlative forms.

In order to determine how such degree words are used, people can be presented various values along the continuum and asked to select the appropriate term or alternatively they may be given a term and asked to indicate an appropriate value. For example, Mosier (1941; see also Jones and Thurstone 1955) asked people to rate such adjectives as *poor, fair, good,* and *excellent* on an eleven-point scale in terms of their favorableness. Subsequently Cliff (1959) obtained similar subjective ratings for adverb-adjective pairs: *decidedly bad, rather contemptible, quite ordinary, pretty good, extremely nice.* He then separated the contribution of the adverb to the rating assigned a pair from the contribution of the adjective by the method of factor analysis, on the assumption that the role of the adverb is to multiply the rating of the unmodified adjective. For example, *extremely* multiplied the adjective it modified by 1.5, that is, if the adjective denoted a positive (or negative) value, it became 1.5 times more positive (or negative) when it was modified by *extremely.* The adverb *somewhat,* on the other hand, multiplied the rating of its adjectives by 0.7, thus reducing their strength. Since many psychological studies of preferences elicit such phrases from people, a precise calibration of their meaning can contribute to the interpretation of the results. The semantic implications of these studies were initially of secondary interest.

It was Osgood (1952; Osgood, Suci, and Tannenbaum 1957) who first used this method (rating scales plus factor analysis, which he called the semantic differential) to explore lexical meaning systematically. It was assumed that lexical concepts are located in a semantic space whose coordinates can be determined from subjective ratings. The rating scales used were defined by pairs of bipolar adjectives: *angular-rounded, weak-strong, rough-smooth, active-passive, small-large, good-bad,* and so on. In one early study a total of fifty such pairs was used to obtain ratings (on a seven-point scale) by one hundred college students for twenty different concepts. The fifty scales were then intercorrelated and the resulting 50 × 50 matrix was factor analyzed to determine the number of dimensions required to represent the correlations. In this study (and in many subsequent replications) it was found that three factors were most important. Osgood called them evaluation (representing such scales as *good-bad, clean-dirty, nice-awful*), potency (*strong-weak, brave-cowardly*), and activity (*active-passive, fast-slow*), with the evaluative factor accounting for more of the variance. The hope was to represent lexical meanings by their positions in this three-dimensional space; two words having similar locations would have similar meanings.

Because the concepts expressed by adjectives do not exhaust all the concepts that words can express, it is clear that the semantic differential cannot provide a complete definitional account of lexical meanings. For example, the concepts *sleep* and *gentleness* lie nearly together in this space, yet any dictionary that treated these two words as synonyms would be harshly criticized. However, the method does provide a three-dimensional measure of the attitudinal or affective component of word meanings, which is an aspect that is psychologically important and impossible to capture in purely cognitive terms. Consequently, the semantic differential has been used extensively by social and clinical psychologists (references can be found in Snider and Osgood 1969; Osgood, May, and Miron 1975). Progressive changes in attitude, for example, can be measured by repeated scaling of a diagnostic set of words as a patient continues in psychotherapy.

Stated in the most general terms, multidimensional theories presuppose the existence of a metric that can be applied to the similarity of any two lexical meanings. That is to say, behind any spatial representation of lexical memory is a matrix of numbers that can be interpreted as subjective distances between lexical entries. If a study of N words yields distances from every word to every other word, those results can be represented in a symmetric matrix having N rows and N columns, where each cell in the matrix contains a number representing the distance between two words. Scaling methods provide one way to obtain such a matrix of distances between words, but many other techniques have also been used. For example, Deese (1965) collected associations to nineteen related words from one hundred college students and then for every pair of words calculated an "intersection coefficient" that reflected the relative number of common replies. Since the closer two probe words are associatively, the more replies they should elicit in common and the higher their intersection coefficient should be, these coefficients can be regarded as measures of proximity (inversely related to measures of distance). Deese subjected this matrix to factor analysis in order to explore the spatial representation of "associative meaning." Other techniques that can be used to obtain matrices of interword distances (or proximities) for a list of words include direct ratings or rankings of synonymy (Rubenstein and Goodenough 1965; Henley 1969; Fillenbaum and Rapoport 1971, sorting words into groups on the basis of similarity of meaning (Miller 1967, 1969; Herrmann et al. 1975), intersubstitutability in sentential contexts (D'Andrade et al. 1972), forming all possible triads from a list of words and asking people to judge which member of each triad is most different from the other two (Romney and D'Andrade 1964), and scoring adjacency of words (clustering) in free recall of a list (Henley 1969; Caramazza, Hersh, and Torgerson 1976). Comparisons of different methods can be found in Henley; Fillenbaum and Rapoport; and Caramazza, Hersh, and Torgerson. All of these methods, however, are sensitive to context. That is to say, different distances will be estimated between any particular pair of words depending on the other words that are included in the list. Since it is difficult to study more than about fifty words at a time, context sensitivity places an important constraint on the use and interpretation of these methods.

Factor analysis is not the only technique available to analyze such matrices of interword distances. Recent developments in the theory of multidimensional scaling (Shepard, Romney, and Nerlove 1972) have provided a variety of analytic techniques among which a research worker can choose, and new variants are currently appearing rapidly enough to confuse all but the experts. For the present purpose, however, it is sufficient to understand that these techniques make it possible to represent data structures spatially and that they can be applied to appropriate data on relations among lexical meanings.

For example, Henley (1969) used a multidimensional technique to represent lexical memory for the names of thirty mammals. She used ratings of dissimilarity (on an eleven-point scale) to obtain a matrix of interword distances and found that the data could be reasonably represented in a space of three dimensions, two of which she was able to identify as size and ferocity. This representation was used by Rumelhart and Abrahamson (1973) to generate analogy problems. For example, people were given the analogy *rat*:*pig*: :*goat*:—— and asked to rank order *chimpanzee, cow, rabbit,* and *sheep* from most to least appropriate. According to Henley's results, the vector distance from *rat* to *pig* was the same as the vector distance from *goat* to *cow*; the most divergent alternative was *chimpanzee*. The rank orderings that people gave agreed closely with predictions based on Henley's spatial semantics, which not only confirms the multidimensional representation but also indicates that people can use it in analogical reasoning.

The method can be used to compare different groups of people. Zurif et al. (1974) asked groups of normal and brain-damaged people to sort twelve words that included six denoting people and six denoting animals. Patients with anterior damage (Broca's aphasia) sorted the words in much the same way normal people did, although their clusters were not as well integrated; patients with posterior damage (Wernicke's aphasia), on the other hand, put together words that could be used together easily in a sentence and showed no evidence of an underlying semantic organization. Anglin (1970) asked groups of third to fourth grade, seventh to eighth grade, eleventh to twelfth grade, and college students to sort twenty words that included six nouns, six verbs, four adjectives, and four adverbs. The youngest group showed the greatest tendency to put together words on a thematic basis; with increase in age there was a steady progression toward clusters that respected the syntactic categories.

The method can also be used to compare different groups of words. Fillenbaum and Rapoport (1971) applied sorting and scaling techniques to color terms, kin terms, pronouns, names of emotions, prepositions, conjunctions, verbs of possession, verbs of judgment, and evaluative adjectives. A spatial representation was clearly needed for color terms, but other domains seemed to require a hierarchical structure, or hierarchies with cross-classification. Names of emotions produced the largest individual differences among the judges and consequently showed no clear structure; evaluative adjectives also showed little structure beyond the basic *good-bad* opposition, perhaps because any subtler meanings of these words must be inferred from the nouns they modify. Fillenbaum and Rapoport conclude that "the general lesson of this is that different domains may be organized in terms of different structural principles" (p. 245). The conceptual heterogeneity of lexical meanings is a challenge for psychologists who want to describe them, but a comfort to anyone who is more concerned to use words to express the infinite shades and varieties of human experience.

Multidimensional models illuminate a different aspect of lexical memory from that which is the central concern of network models. In both cases the focus is on pairs of lexical meanings, but network models are basically theories in search of empirical data, whereas multidimensional models are basically data structures in search of theoretical explication. Even in those cases where a spatial representation of the data is required, no one has seriously proposed that, say, meanings are stored at places in the brain separated by distances proportional to the subjective distances measured in the psychological experiments. However, the reproducibility of results obtained by widely different methods of data collection and their obvious relation to one's intuitions about lexical meaning lend strong support to the claim that lexical memory is not only highly structured, but structured in much the same way for different people. There is, in short, something to be explained.

Semantic Features
Current network models tend to emphasize the number and kind of associative links between words, whereas multidimensional models emphasize the distances (strengths of association) between words. Other approaches can be viewed as attempts to bring these two aspects of lexical associations together in a single theory.

A network theorist has various ways to explain different subjective distances between words. One is to attribute them to differences in the number of intervening nodes in the network. Another is to assign the link from A to B a criteriality value depending on how essential B is to the meaning of A (Quillian 1968) or an accessibility value depending on how often a person thinks of B in connection with A. Collins and Quillian (1969) assume both structural (number of intervening nodes) and quantitative (differential accessibility) mechanisms, and Collins and Loftus (1975) add to those the idea that excitation spreads with diminishing intensity as it travels out from any activated node. Still another device is to assign each of the links leaving a node an order in which they are to be explored; close associates would be those explored first.

Such additional mechanisms are needed if network theories are to account for data on reaction times. For example, it takes longer to reply "true" to sentences like *A stork is a bird* than to sentences like *A robin is a bird* (Wilkins 1971); according to category norms, *robin* is a frequently given reply to the probe *bird*, whereas *stork* is not. If all the links in an associative network were equally accessible, this difference could not be explained. The initial test of the network theory (Collins and Quillian 1969) emphasized its structural aspects and subsequent critics largely ignored the possibility that criteriality or accessibility, as well as kind of link, could be included in an associative network. In considering alternative theories, therefore, we should concentrate on their positive aspects and discount claims about what network theories can or cannot explain.

Schaeffer and Wallace (1970) presented pairs of words and asked people to judge whether they were both instances of the same superordinate term, where the words could be names of trees, flowers, mammals, or birds. These superordinates, in turn, are instances of the higher superordinates, plants and animals. They found that it took longer to respond "different" when the words were both plants or both animals (*cedar-daisy* or *robin-camel*) than when they were not (*cedar-robin* or *daisy-camel*). Schaeffer and Wallace argued that this result should be explained in terms of the process of comparing lexical entries, not the process of retrieving them from memory. Concepts, they say, can be decomposed into elements; comparing concepts involves comparing their elements; reaction times will depend on the number of elements that must be compared. Thus, a comparison of *cedar* and *daisy* takes longer than a comparison of *cedar* and *robin* because *cedar* and *daisy* share all those elements that are common to plants, whereas *cedar* and *robin* do not. If two concepts have some elements in common, more elements must be compared on the average before a difference is found.

Schaeffer and Wallace suggest that it takes longer to respond "true" to *A canary is an animal* than to *A canary is a bird* because the more generic term *animal* contains fewer elements than the more specific term *bird*. The overlap in elements between *canary* and *bird* is therefore greater than between *canary* and *animal*, and this overlap facilitates the comparison process. Meyer (1970), however, draws the opposite conclusion: The fewer the elements, the faster the comparison should be. Hence Meyer rejected any simple version of this theory and argued instead for a two-stage process of comparison: First, are the words related at all? If so, second, is the relation appropriate? He argued that since unrelated (disjointed) concepts can have elements in common, a system of the type proposed by Schaeffer and Wallace would yield too many positive decisions at stage one; Meyer does accept their characterization, however, as a plausible account of stage two. Meyer's stage one is similar to the network of Collins and Quillian, but without labeled links to indicate the superordinate relation. However, some of the complexity of the experimental observations may be attributable to the weight of meaning elements that are unique to the two words, in which case the results could not be predicted solely from those elements they have in common.

The "elements" into which lexical concepts might be analyzed require further specification. Smith, Shoben, and Rips (1974) propose that they are semantic features, similar to the semantic markers of Katz and Fodor (1963) but without deletion of repetitive features by redundancy rules. That is to say, each word's lexical entry includes a list of all of its features rather than just those features required to differentiate it from other instances of its superordinate concept. Moreover, features vary in the extent to which they define the word. For example, being a biped and having feathers are considered more defining for the word *bird* than are perching in trees and being undomesticated. This variation in the definingness of semantic features makes it possible to divide features into those they call defining versus those they call merely characteristic but nondefining. Defining features are required to explain the obvious logical relations between words; characteristic features are required to explain the nonequivalence of instances. If people are asked to rate instances for typicality (Rips, Shoben, and Smith 1973; Caramazza, Hersh, and Torgerson 1976), they will agree that *robin* is a more typical bird than *stork* or *chicken* and that *horse* is a more typical mammal than *mouse* or *rhinoceros*, and these ratings of typicality can be used to predict reaction times to such sentences as *A robin is a bird* or *A mouse is a mammal* (correlation coefficients ranged from 0.42 to 0.73). According to Smith, Shoben, and Rips, the most typical instances have all of the defining and characteristic features of the superordinate, whereas the least typical instances have only the defining features. Herrmann et al. (1975) showed, by a method of multidimensional scaling, that interword distances among superordinate terms are very similar to those among highly typical instances, as the theory would predict.

Although the formal simplicity of the semantic feature theory is attractive and accounts for many experimental observations, it is not entirely clear that it differs formally from the theory of associative networks. That is to say, any feature model can be represented as a network (Hollan 1975) if links are drawn from every word to all of its features, particularly to all of its superordinates (Glass and Holyoak 1974/75). Thus the substantive difference (if there is one) seems to be whether the measured reaction times should be explained as the time required to search through an associative network or as the time required to compare two concepts that have been retrieved from lexical memory (regardless of how the concepts are stored).

The distinction between defining and merely characteristic features relates to the distinction between lexical and practical knowledge. The claim is that of all a person knows about chairs, some facts are necessary and sufficient for the definition of the word *chair*, whereas other facts may be of practical importance (for example, chairs are usually found indoors, they are frequently used with tables, their seats can be upholstered) but are not essential to the meaning of *chair*. Smith, Shoben, and Rips focus on the need to include characteristic as well as defining features, but there are weaknesses in the dogma of necessary and sufficient criteria (defining features) that all such theories must face.

Consider, for example, words like *iron* or *cancer*. Only experts are able to state the true defining features of these words, yet they are the most frequent replies in the category norms for *a metal* and *a disease*. Laypersons can use these words in conversation without being able to define them and would have no difficulty evaluating such sentences as *Iron is a metal* or *Cancer is a disease*. If in order to use and understand *iron, cancer*, and many other words it is not necessary to know their defining features, why assume that it is necessary to know the defining features of *chair, machine, wife, canary*, or *cedar* in order to use and understand them? Does a person know that *A whale is a fish* is false because he knows the defining features of *whale* and *fish* or because he has learned explicitly: *Whales are mammals, not fish*? If one plucks all the features off a chicken, does it stop being a bird? In short, the most important question of all is how can one be sure that there really is a necessary and sufficient defining feature for every lexical concept?

Object Naming
The various approaches to lexical meaning discussed so far have concentrated on interword associations. But the words used in these studies are not only related to one another; most of them can refer to concrete objects. Since many people would say that what such a word refers to *is* its meaning, it is curious that less experimental attention has been paid to word-object associations than to word-word associations.

One simple technique for investigating word-object relations is the reaction time experiment. The first observations on how long it takes to see and name objects were collected by Cattell (1886), but thereafter the question was ignored for almost eighty years. In 1965 Oldfield and Wingfield established that the time it takes to name a picture of an object increases as a function of the frequency with which its name is used in the language. For example, a picture of a chair was named in 0.55 sec on the average, a typewriter in 0.82 sec, a microscope in 0.96

sec, and a gyroscope in 1.68 sec (as the names get less probable, the reaction times get longer). (Howes and Solomon 1951 found a similar relation between reaction time and frequency of use for simply reading the words aloud.) Lexical memory is clearly organized in such a way that the more frequently required entries are the most quickly and easily accessible.

This finding is of some practical significance. For example, a variety of brain lesions have as one of their symptoms that finding names for objects is difficult (slower, with more mistakes). It is frequently observed that a patient's errors will not be random but will bear some associative relation to the correct name. Moreover, when a set of objects is arranged in order of difficulty for dysphasic patients, this same ordering applies to the age at which children can name them (Rochford and Williams 1962), and children make very similar mistakes. Carroll and White (1973) show that there is a significant correlation (0.70 and 0.75) between frequency of use and age of acquisition and an even higher correlation (0.77) between age of acquisition and picture-naming latency; they suggest that many of the effects in psychological experiments that have been attributed to frequency of use might better be attributed to age of acquisition.

Although subcultural factors have not been adequately controlled, it is generally agreed that vocabulary size is related to general mental ability; one of the standard intelligence tests for young children (Peabody Picture Vocabulary Test) asks them to match pictures to their names. When Blount (1970) compared normal and mentally retarded children on a concept usage task (select three of five pictures of familiar objects that go together and give a name to the concept), there was no difference in their ability to recognize a concept, but the handicapped children were inferior in labeling it. Apparently retarded children are just that—their linguistic development seems to unfold in the same order as normal children's but much more slowly until maturity, at which point it comes to a standstill (Lenneberg, Nichols, and Rosenberger 1964).

It is obvious, therefore, that both theoretical and practical justification can be found for studying word-object associations. Let us begin with the obvious fact that the ability to name a concrete object presupposes an ability to recognize it. Persons who know the word *chair* know how to recognize a chair when they see one. They also know what they are used for. If it were possible to characterize that knowledge theoretically, it might be possible to use the characterization to explain certain relations (superordinate, subordinate, part-whole) between the word *chair* and other words. As a starting point, therefore, it is assumed that the knowledge a person has available to identify objects such as chairs can be characterized by a proposition of the form: Something x is a chair if $P(x)$ is true and $F(x)$ is possible, where P represents the perceptual properties that chairs are expected to have and F represents the functions that chairs are expected to serve. Then the task is to characterize P and F in some reasonable manner that might account for the semantic features of the word *chair*.

Consider first the perceptual properties P of concrete objects. If persons can recognize a chair when they see one, all the objects that people categorize as chairs may have some perceptual attribute in common (their shape, perhaps). Psychologists who study perception have had much to say about shape and programs have even been written to enable computers to recognize particular shapes, but it is not a simple process and review of this work would not be appropriate here (see Miller and Johnson-Laird 1976). It is simply assumed, therefore, that people can learn to recognize complex shapes by applying some set of perceptual tests, such as if it has a single horizontal seat supported by one or more vertical legs and has a vertical back, it can be called *chair*. The elements into which *chair* is analyzed on this approach are not semantic features, but perceptual features.

Several important questions are left unanswered by this perceptual definition, however. Some objects are more typical chairs than others, yet all objects passing the tests specified in the perceptual definition are equally entitled to be called *chair* (Rosch 1973). Perhaps some weighting of perceptual features for criteriality could be invoked here, as in the theory of semantic features, to explain why some chairs look more typical than others. Or perhaps there is a prototype chair stored in memory and instances are judged in terms of their perceptual deviations from the prototype. Rosch points out that this formulation is particularly appropriate for words like *red*, where there are neurophysiological grounds for distinguishing a focal red from which other tints and shades of red deviate.

Variation along some dimensions can lead to objects that have different names. For example, how wide can a chair be before we stop calling it *chair* and start calling it *bench, couch, divan,* or *sofa*? If such a dimension is systematically varied, people will show some uncertainty about the exact boundary between the two categories; they may know that something is either a wide chair or a short bench but not be confident which disjunct is correct. Since many of the different perceptual cues used to recognize chairs can vary more or less continuously, *chair* is vague in several dimensions. One assumes that in the actual world chair cues are correlated (an object that is marginal on a few criteria will generally fail on most of them and therefore when all the criteria are taken together an object can usually be definitely accepted or definitely rejected). But it is always possible to create deliberate exceptions to these natural categories in order to reveal the underlying vagueness. Moreover, the point of maximum uncertainty about the chair-bench boundary can be shifted by context (Labov 1973), for example, by having two or three children or a single fat person sit in it, by putting two pillows side by side on the seat, or by putting rockers on it. The perceptual definition suggested above makes no provision for shifts in category boundaries as a function of what an object is used for.

This last difficulty might be met if a functional criterion F were also included in the identification process. A chair must not only meet certain perceptual criteria but must serve a definite purpose (for example, it must be possible for one person to sit in it and recline against its back). Little is known about how a person decides whether a particular object can be used to perform a particular function, but presumably it depends on one's previous experience in performing that function with a variety of similar objects.

Several sources of evidence suggest the need to include function in many lexical meanings. It has frequently been observed that children's first definitions are functional (*A hole is to dig*: Krauss 1952) and Blank (1973) has suggested that teachers should exploit this functional predisposition, especially in teaching the meanings of abstract words where showing multiple instances may not lead a child to induce the intended concept. Moreover, certain types of brain damage seem to dissociate words from perceptual or functional criteria selectively. In discussing patients with damage resulting in what he calls modality-specific anomias, Brown (1972, pp. 24–25) writes, "Usually such patients can name to functional description what cannot be named perceptually. Thus, failing to name a razor on visual or tactile presentation, they will succeed with a description of its use, i.e., 'What you shave with in the morning.'" Conversely, Goodglass and Baker (1976) have found that patients with Wernicke's aphasia have special difficulty in associating an appropriate function or context of use with pictured objects. For example, when shown a picture of an orange and told to press a bulb whenever they heard a word that was related to the object in the picture, they were abnormally slow to respond to *eat* or *breakfast*, although with words related to oranges in other ways they responded more normally. Such observations support common sense in calling for functional as well as perceptual criteria for object naming.

There are also linguistic arguments for a functional component. Consider the apparent polysemy of *good*, which means *sharp* in *a good knife*, *comfortable* in *a good bed*, *competent* or *skillful* in *a good driver*, and so on. Katz (1964) argues that the word *good* in such expressions must be understood as assigning an evaluation to the function that objects are normally expected to serve. *A good chair*, for example, is good for sitting in. If the function of chairs were not included in the meaning of *chair*, it would be necessary to append some descriptive phrase to explain what was good about it (as, for example, in *good electricity*), whereas in fact everyone who knows what a chair is understands immediately that *a good chair* is one that serves well the function that chairs are reasonably expected to serve. Thus, a rock formation might be called *a good chair* if it served well the function that chairs are expected to serve. In order to account for these interpretations of *good*, therefore, all words denoting objects that have a standard function must include that function as part of the meaning of the word.

Since a picture of a chair can be called *chair* even though it does not serve the function of a chair, and a rock formation can be called *chair* even though it does not provide the perceptual cues characteristic of chairs, both perceptual and functional components of meaning are required. (An intentional component may also be needed; a poorly constructed chair that looks odd and is nonfunctional may still be called *chair* if the carpenter's intention was to construct a chair.) In short, category boundaries must be labile enough to include all the referential uses of *chair* that can plausibly occur. The point is that the set of objects to which *chair* can refer (the "extension" of *chair*) is not something fixed once and for all, like the standard meter bar in Paris, but can vary according to the needs of the moment. For the purposes of communication, *chair* can successfully identify a great variety of objects as long as there is nothing more chairlike in the current domain of discourse. Thus the category boundaries, the lines between what is a chair and what is not, will vary according to the particular context of use. But this variation cannot be unlimited. Some objects will always be included in the category, however much context narrows or broadens the category boundaries—in the actual world most chairs are of this type, though some (beanbag chairs, for example) are not.

Since function is an important component of the meanings of many words, we should consider how F might be formulated. How does a person evaluate whether F is possible with particular objects? It might be assumed that the modal notion *possible* would be represented as a program to search through memory for any organized body of knowledge (k) such that under appropriate circumstances (c), k, and c together lead to F. If the functional component of lexical meanings were formulated in this way, there would be a slot, k, for the insertion of practical knowledge; but the particular body of knowledge that occupies that slot would not be specified uniquely in advance. This formulation thus amounts to a hypothesis about the interface of practical and lexical knowledge.

Consider how people understand such tentative identifications as *That should be a chair* or such emphatic identifications as *That must be a chair*. The modal auxiliary verbs *should* and *must* are generally considered to be ambiguous. *That should be a chair*, for example, might mean either the factual (epistemic) claim *I believe that that object is a chair* or the moral (deontic) claim *It is improper for the object in that location not to be a chair*. The former reading amounts to a tentative identification of an object as a chair; the latter reading suggests that it is not a chair. The two readings are clearly different meanings and the ambiguity is attributed to *should*, which is said to have either an epistemic or a deontic interpretation. However, Wertheimer (1972) argues that the real source of ambiguity is not *should*, but the body of knowledge k that is used to interpret the *should*. If *x should F* is defined to mean that there is a body of knowledge k and a set of circumstances c such that k and c entail F, then the first reading is obtained if the body of knowledge inserted for k is factual and the second reading is obtained if it is moral, ethical, or socially prescribed knowledge. Which body of knowledge is invoked is important, of course, since violations of an epistemic k are usually understood to mean that k is wrong and violations of a deontic k are usually understood to mean that F is wrong. But the modal auxiliary verb *should* plays the same role in both readings; it simply provides a slot into which different values of k can be substituted. (The modal verb *must* is stronger than *should*. It means that *x should F* under circumstances c and those circumstances actually do obtain.)

Although it is a detour from the discussion of object naming, it should be pointed out that this formulation of the functional component of meaning in terms of a modal notion *possible* or *should* has broad implications. For example, psychotherapists know to pay close attention when patients talk about what should or must be the case (Bandler and Grinder 1975). Such statements are open invitations to a therapist to explore the unspoken assumptions they contain about the circumstances that are thought to prevail and the knowledge, epistemic or deontic, that is considered relevant, with potential implications for the patient's reeducation.

Prototypes

Prototype theory has its origins in the image theory of ideas. If one holds, as many empiricist philosophers in the seventeenth and eighteenth centuries did, that one's idea of a chair is an image of a chair, one must face the criticism that the image must be an image of a particular chair, whereas the idea of chairs must include all chairs, many of which will look nothing like whatever image one happens to hold. A plausible reply to this criticism is that the image is merely a prototype, not an image of all chairs. The general category can be defined to include all those objects that are closer in appearance to the prototype chair than to any other prototype image. This general line of argument has recently been revived in modern guise and used to explain a variety of perceptual and linguistic facts.

A prototypical chair will, of course, satisfy all of the perceptual and functional (and intentional) criteria for the category. Even within the set of objects that meet these criteria, however, some can be judged more prototypical than others (Rosch 1973). The most prototypical instances are presumably those with the highest cue validity—those whose features serve most efficiently and univocally to identify instances of the category. The notion of prototypical instances of a category, however, raises difficult questions about how knowledge is represented in a person's memory. Does a person store a memory image of a prototype chair along with some way to estimate deviations of any candidate instance from that image? Or is the prototype represented by a list of perceptual and functional features that any candidate instance must satisfy?

Minsky (1975) has proposed a theory of "frames" to explain the representation of knowledge in computer memories, and the proposal is suggestive of a comparable theory for human memory. A frame is a structure that represents knowledge about some limited domain of objects or events. A frame for chairs, for example, would provide an elaborate structure for describing any instance, including perceptual, functional, and any other features characteristic of chairs. An object is recognized as a chair if the perceived values for these features can be successfully inserted into the frame; features whose values have not been determined are represented by "default values." If the observed values do not fit the frame, the system can analyze the anomaly and propose an alternative frame. If the observed values do fit the frame, any unobserved features can be used to predict what will be observed on further inspection of the object.

Kuipers (1975) illustrates how a frame system might work in terms of a simple scenario. As you are walking through an unfamiliar house you come to an interior-type door, open it, and walk through. Since your normal expectations have already brought a *room* frame to mind, you expect four walls, floor, and ceiling; there is no delay in inserting observed features into this frame. A window on the opposite wall is quickly recognized in terms of a *window* frame, and this value is inserted into the room description that you are building with the help of the *room* frame; it will be treated as a stereotype window unless your attention is directed to it. A bed in the room causes the general *room* frame to be replaced by a more specific *bedroom* frame, in which a dishwasher is no longer a serious possibility. In constructing your description of the room, you verify in passing a number of easily observable facts and leave most details unobserved—the component frames are filled with default values. You may, for example, quickly observe a clock and allow the *clock* frame to substitute stereotyped values for all of its details; then later you may think that the clock had hands, even though it was a modern clock without hands, because the *clock* frame provided those values by prediction.

Although the details of frame theory are difficult to make precise, some such approach seems necessary in order to explain how practical knowledge can support and organize perception and perceptual recognition. In terms of the theory of prototypes, a prototype instance would be one whose actual feature values corresponded very closely to the values that would be predicted from the frame by default. Indeed, a good description of a prototype can be obtained by asking people to list from memory the features that an instance has, where the response must come from default values that the frame would predict. These are the values, presumably, that persons would use to construct an image of a chair in their imaginations.

As described above, a frame theory of perceptual recognition must include an elaborate system of connections between frames. The *room* frame, for example, was replaced by a *bedroom* frame when a bed was recognized in it; in terms of lexical relations, a superordinate was replaced by a subordinate concept. Moreover, if a frame does not provide a correct description of the perceptual data, the system must select some alternative frame that will provide a better description. Each frame, therefore, must be related to all the other frames with which it shares feature values. If this system of frame relations were fully worked out, it would provide the kind of structure of practical memory that must underlie the structure of lexical memory. Unfortunately, however, frame theory is still in a programmatic state.

Some evidence about relations between categories in such a system has been gathered by Rosch et al. These workers argue that in the categorization of concrete objects there is a clear and determinable level of abstraction at which the most basic category cuts are made. For example, they asked people to list attributes of object categories from memory, then had other people judge whether those attributes were true of actual instances. For the superordinate category called *furniture* they found no attributes common to all instances. For the categories called *table*, *lamp*, and *chair* they found an average of 7.0 attributes common to all instances; for the subordinate categories called *kitchen table, dining room table, floor lamp, desk lamp, kitchen chair*, and *living room chair* they found an average of 7.8 attributes common to all instances. The categories *table*, *lamp*, and *chair* were distinguished as the most generic categories that have many attributes in common and so are "basic categories"; their instances are "basic objects."

Rosch et al. also asked people to describe in detail the motor patterns that would be involved in using these various objects and found a similar pattern of results for common motor movements. Thus the basic categories are also distinguished as being the most generic level of categorization at which people behave the same way toward all instances. They also found that these category names were the ones people used almost exclusively when asked to identify pictures of objects.

These results were obtained for *musical instrument, fruit, tool, clothing,* and *vehicle,* as well as for *furniture*. They also tested the biological categories *tree*, *fish*, and *bird* and discovered, contrary to anthropological predictions, that these superordinate categories are basic (*cardinal* and *eagle*, for example, added few attributes or motor movements not common to all birds). The appropriate superordinates, therefore, would be *plant* and *animal*.

There apparently is a basic level of entry into lexical hierarchies of this type. Since prototypes are instances that share the most attributes with other members of the category, prototypes presumably are formed by the same principles that govern the formation of basic categories. Basic objects are the most general categories for which a prototype can be reasonably representative of the category as a whole. More general, superordinate categories are probably represented by their most typical basic instances (Anderson and McGaw 1973; Herrmann et al. 1975).

It is not surprising, therefore, that labels for basic categories are the words that children learn first. Rosch et al (1976) report that these are the categories for which children are earliest able to sort instances and to provide names. Anglin (1976) reaches a similar conclusion and adds that these are the words that parents spontaneously use in naming objects for their children. Anglin argues that common motor movements are probably more important to a young child than are common perceptual attributes, but there are so few cases where the two kinds of definition might diverge that the course of lexical development would be much the same in any case. These observations settle a venerable argument as to whether children begin learning words by acquiring very generic concepts that are later differentiated or by learning specific instances that are later gathered into more general categories. Both alternatives are right. Children start in the middle—with names of basic objects—and develop both more generic and more specific vocabulary from there.

Where in a theory of this type would one draw a line between lexical and practical knowledge? The advantage of drawing such a distinction is that it limits the range of phenomena that a theory of linguistic communication can be expected to treat. If the theory must include a general representation of all knowledge, it is likely to become unmanageable. Moreover, one feels that the relation of *His children are here* to *He has children* is somehow different from its relation to *He is married*. The former seems to be required by the lexical meaning of *his children*, whereas the latter can be justified as probable by practical knowledge but is not required. Students of language are therefore strongly motivated to draw the distinction.

Such a distinction could be included in a frame theory of categories by marking certain features as criterial, although this solution has an ad hoc character that is theoretically unsatisfying. A more perspicuous formulation might be to formulate lexical knowledge, as suggested previously, in terms of stipulations that P is true and F is possible. Then the evaluation of "is true" and "is possible" could be represented in such a way that any relevant practical knowledge could be used to evaluate them, but without prejudging what practical knowledge will be relevant to any particular evaluation. If practical knowledge is organized in frames, the same frame might be used on different occasions to evaluate different labels or different frames might be used on different occasions to evaluate the same label. In that case the association of frames to words would be more complex and flexible than the illustrations given above would suggest. It will be difficult to evaluate such proposals, however, until much more experience has been gained with alternative ways of organizing memories for large bodies of knowledge.

Conceptual Relations

Most of the theory and research reviewed so far has been rather singlemindedly concerned with nouns denoting concrete objects. This approach not only neglects other parts of speech, but even leaves such puzzling nouns as *behalf*, *dint*, and *sake* totally unexplained. Although it is obvious that lexical meanings are the building blocks from which phrases and sentences are constructed, little use has been made of that fact.

The various approaches reviewed here have each in their separate ways left open the possibility of incorporation of word meanings into grammatical constructions. It is probably not unfair to say, however, that their lexical components can be understood in isolation from any grammatical system that might exploit them. It is difficult to present a conceptual theory of lexical meaning, however, without beginning at the level of sentences. A brief digression is presented, therefore, to establish some necessary background.

Assume that a well-formed sentence used in an appropriate context expresses a sentential concept. Since the number of different sentences is unlimited, the set Σ of sentential concepts must also be unlimited. Sentential concepts should be analyzed into concepts resembling functions and their arguments. We will, therefore, introduce a set Π of predicative concepts and a set A of assignable pointers. Then we can propose such rules of (sentential) concept formation as: If $x \in$ A and $p \in \Pi$, then $P(x) \in \Sigma$. For example, if x is a pointer assigned to some particular boy and P is a predicate for singing, then $P(x)$ might be the sentential concept expressed by the sentence *The boy sings*. For concepts expressed by sentences with transitive verbs a more complex rule of concept formation is required: If $x, y \in$ A and $P_r \in \Pi_r$, then $(P_r(y))(x) \in \Sigma$. Here Π_r is the set of relational predicates (taking two arguments). For example, if x is a pointer assigned to a particular boy, y is a pointer assigned to a particular girl, and P_r is the relation of hitting, then $P_r(y)$ might be the predicative concept expressed by *hit the girl* and when this is applied to x, $(P_r(y))(x)$ might be the sentential concept expressed by *The boy hit the girl*. (Note that another rule of concept formation has been assumed implicitly: If $y \in$ A and $P_r \in \Pi_r$, then $P_r(y) \in \Pi$.)

To work out how all the different possible forms of sentential concepts might be represented in such a notation would be a formidable task, and different theorists have approached it in rather different ways (compare, for example, Katz 1972 with Montague 1974). Fortunately for the present purposes it is unnecessary to do more than indicate the general nature of the task, which is to represent the concepts associated with each of the syntactic constituents of any grammatical sentence. Some way to represent sentential concepts is essential to any theory of lexical meaning, not only because lexical concepts must combine to form sentential concepts but also for the simple reason that the definitions of words always come round, one way or another, to sentences—sentences that paraphrase a word, sentences into which a definition can be substituted for the word defined, sentences illustrating how a word is used, sentences comparing or contrasting a word with other words. According to this approach, therefore, lexical concepts must be defined in terms of sentential concepts.

An example may be helpful. Suppose someone asks about the verb *sprint* and is told that it means *move rapidly*. This definition would not satisfy a lexicographer, but let us take it for what it is worth—after all, sentences like *He was sprinting* and *He was moving rapidly* seem interchangeable in some contexts. This observation might lead to such relations between sentential concepts as $SPRINT(x)$ entails $(RAPID(MOVE))$ (x), where the predicative concept $(RAPID(MOVE))$ is taken as a (partial) conceptual analysis of the predicative concept $SPRINT$. This entailment relations is essentially what Katz and Fodor (1963) call a redundancy rule.

This example can be used to make several comments about a conceptual approach to lexical meanings. For one thing, no claim is made that when one hears the word *sprint* one must first analyze it into $(RAPID\ (MOVE))$ before understanding it. It would be claimed, however, that (if the analysis is correct) the process of understanding and evaluating sentences like *He is sprinting* would involve all of the information processing (and more) that would be required to understand *He is moving rapidly*. But someone who has determined that *He is sprinting* is true will not necessarily have determined that *He is moving rapidly* is also true, even though one will have performed all the mental computations that such a determination would require.

Second, the relation of entailment between $SPRINT(x)$ and $(RAPID(MOVE))$ (x) is a hypothesis about how people who know English are able to determine that the sentence *He is sprinting* entails the sentence *He is moving rapidly*. The former sentence would be represented conceptually as $SPRINT(x)$ and the latter sentence as $(RAPID(MOVE))$ (x), where x is a pointer assigned to *he*; the appropriate entailment relation would then be sought in lexical memory. That is to say, judgments of entailment relations between sentences can provide empirical data to test hypotheses about entailment relations between sentential concepts, and entailment relations between sentential concepts can provide constraints on representations of the lexical concepts they contain and the redundancy rules relating them.

Third, similar formulations can be given for nominal concepts. For example, if x is a pointer to some small furry animal and $(ISA(CAT))$ is the predicative concept expressed by *is a cat*, then $(ISA(CAT))$ (x) might represent the concept expressed by the sentence *That is a cat*. A redundancy rule of the form $(ISA(CAT))$ (x) entails $(ISA(MAMMAL))$ (x) would presumably be available in lexical memory, which could support the judgment that *That is a cat* entails *That is a mammal*. To evaluate the sentence *A cat is a mammal*, it would first be represented conceptually as $(ISA(MAMMAL))$ (CAT); if this sentential concept is stored somewhere in memory as (part of) the person's knowledge of cats, that information can simply be retrieved and the sentence confirmed. If, as is likely the case, this sentential concept is not stored in memory, an inferential process must ensue. *ISA* can be replaced by a computational definition leading to some such formulation as: For all x, $(ISA(CAT))$ (x) entails $(ISA(MAMMAL))$ (x). If this entailment is stored in memory as a redundancy rule, that information can be used to confirm the sentence. In the unlikely case that the redundancy rule is not stored, one may actually examine the definitions of *cat* and *mammal* in search of information to support one's decision (for example all and only mammals have hair and cats have hair, therefore. . . .). Nothing new is added here to the earlier discussions of such cognitive processes in terms of networks or features or prototypes except the stipulation that entailment is the basic relation involved and since entailment is a relation defined for sentential concepts, that sentential concepts must be used to evaluate relations between lexical concepts.

How would referential aspects of meaning be treated in a conceptual theory of lexical meanings? It must be assumed that associated with each nominal concept that can be used to refer to a concrete object there is some perceptual/functional procedure that can be used to identify instances of the concept. Exactly how these procedures are performed is not the critical problem; the discussion of object recognition in connection with prototype theory will serve as well as any. It is essential to a conceptual theory, however, that the procedure for identifying instances of a concept should not be regarded as equivalent to the concept itself. Much psychological research on concept formation has proceeded as if this equivalence were valid (see, for example, Hunt 1962).

The procedure used to identify an object as a chair is not the same thing as the concept of chairs. A venerable counterexample is *featherless biped*. It may indeed be true that if you use *featherless biped* as an identification procedure, it will correctly select all and only those organisms in the extension of the word *man*, but no one would care to argue that *featherless biped* is an adequate characterization of the concept expressed by *man*. The problem is that identification procedures can be formulated in indefinitely many ways. In general—taxonomists have provided many examples—when one is given two or more equivalent but different identification devices (or "keys") for categorizing the same collection of objects, it is extremely difficult, if not impossible, to decide which one is true. Indeed, if both keys give correct results, it is not even clear what is to be decided; and therefore it is equally unclear how any constraints on identification devices could lead to a unique solution.

The procedure for identifying chairs, whatever it may be, may be part of the concept that *chair* expresses; but it cannot be the whole of it. According to conceptual theory, lexical concepts must be characterized by locating them in some body of organized knowledge, lay or technical, in which they are related to other concepts. In the case of *chair*, it is assumed that a person who knows the meaning of the word has some organized knowledge and belief (the lay equivalent of a scientist's theory) about furniture, about where it is found and what it is used for, about its economics and esthetics and so on, all of which is part of a more general body of organized knowledge about concrete objects. *Chair* takes its meaning from the place that its concept occupies in this general conceptual system. The word *chair* and the percept of a chair provide two routes for gaining access to this conceptual location.

On this view, entailment relations between lexical meanings represent some of the structure of the system of conceptual knowledge. Indeed, at the present time lexical analysis seems to be the most promising approach to an analysis of this conceptual system. Because the variety of concepts is so great, these structures come in an amazing variety of forms, as Fillenbaum and Rapoport (1971) discovered when they explored a variety of lexical domains. Some broad outlines can be sketched, however, and perhaps the best way into the topic is through a discussion of semantic fields.

The claim that languages are organized around semantic fields has been developed differently by different writers (see Miller 1968). It is usually assumed that a semantic field has two parts, a conceptual field and a lexical field. The meaning of any word depends on how it works together with other words in the same lexical field in order to cover or represent the conceptual field. This formulation is vague, but it might be made less vague if it were possible to decide whether two words (or two meanings of words) were in the same semantic field. There are two approaches toward the making of such decisions. The analytic hypothesis (exploited by the theory of semantic features) is that any two words that can be analyzed into common conceptual components are to that extent in the same semantic field and that the more component concepts two words have in common the smaller is the smallest semantic field that contains them both. The intuitive hypothesis (exploited by the theory of multidimensional semantic spaces) is that people can judge the similarity of meanings and that the greater the judged similarity the smaller is the smallest semantic field that contains them both.

One might hope to find that both hypotheses are correct. Indeed, one might argue that the analytic hypothesis should explain people's intuitive judgments of semantic similarity. It seems, however, that this hope must be disappointed. Consider some examples of the facts that must be accounted for in describing semantic fields of English verbs.

The verb *move* expresses a concept that might be paraphrased as *x* moves *y* entails that *x* does something *s* and *s* causes *y* to travel. One of the component concepts here is traveling. Miller (1972) identified a well-behaved semantic field of about two hundred verbs of traveling, all of which have *TRAVEL* as a component concept: *move, come, go, bring, take, walk, run, rise, raise, drop, fall*, and so on. If attention is confined to examples like this, there is a congruence of analysis and intuition; it is apparently possible to account for people's subjective judgments of similarity of meaning in terms of shared concepts that can be identified by lexical analysis.

But now consider a negative example. Another of the component concepts in *move* is causation. Although *CAUSE* must be at least as important a concept as *TRAVEL*, it is not possible to isolate a well-behaved semantic field of causative verbs, all of which have *CAUSE* as a component concept. It would have to include, for example, *raise* (cause to rise), *give* (cause to have), and *kill* (cause to die); yet these verbs are obviously dissimilar in meaning. Moreover, it would have to exclude *rise, receive*, and *die*, which are semantically similar to *raise, give*, and *kill*, respectively, but which do not express the concept *CAUSE*. The causative verbs clearly do not work together to cover an underlying conceptual field of causal relations; they cannot qualify as a semantic field. Miller and Johnson-Laird (1976) identify causal relations, temporal relations, spatial relations, quantitative relations, and personal relations as counterexamples to the hope that judgments of similarity in meaning will always be correlated with shared conceptual components. It is interesting to note that these are concepts that can be expressed by morphological rules in the grammar. Moreover they are concepts that aphasics seem to retain at a nonlingustic level even when extensive brain lesions have destroyed any usable lexical memory. Miller and Johnson-Laird suggest that these concepts are too important to be confined to any single semantic field; they are concepts that are used to elaborate and ramify the senses of verbs that do form well-behaved semantic fields, just as the important relations of class inclusion and part/whole are used to elaborate and ramify nominal concepts.

Jackendoff (1976), however, building on Gruber (1965), has formulated these lexical relations somewhat differently. Note that there are verbs like *go* that have a positional sense in *The man went to his son* and a possessional sense in *The inheritance went to his son*. There are verbs like *turn* that have a positional sense in *The coach turned into the driveway* and an identificational sense in *The coach turned into a pumpkin*. There are verbs like *keep* that have a positional sense in *He kept it in the drawer*, a possessional sense in *He kept all his money*, and an identificational sense in *He kept the coach a coach*. Beginning from the polysemy of the most common verbs rather than from the concepts to be expressed, Jackendoff arrives at a different (though not unrelated) analysis into the conceptual functions *GO, BE, STAY, CAUSE(GO)*, *CAUSE(STAY), LET(GO)*, and *LET(BE)* that can define verbs having positional, possessional, or identificational senses. This system reduces a large number of verbs to a relatively small set of primitive concepts. It is still a cross-classification, however; if one thinks of position, possession, and identification as semantic fields and the functions as ways of elaborating different senses within each field, the analysis is roughly compatible with that proposed by Miller and Johnson-Laird. Although details differ, judgments of semantic similarity cannot be predicted by either approach simply from shared components of meaning. In both theories there is a distinction drawn between two types of concepts that are required for the representation of lexical meanings.

The analysis of verbs is central to a conceptual theory of lexical meaning, since such a theory is designed to explain sentential concepts and verbs are the basic functions that organize such concepts. Relatively little psychological research has focused on verbs, however, so the empirical (and practical) consequences of this type of theory are presently unexplored.

Appraisal

Much valuable theory and research relevant to the psychology of lexical meaning has not been reviewed here because of space limitations. An attempt was made to represent all the major approaches, however, along with illustrative work and references that should lead to fuller discussions elsewhere.

Comments evaluative of the various approaches have been made as those approaches were reviewed; they need not be repeated here. One general comment that may help to put the whole enterprise in perspective can be made, however.

Using language for the human purposes of thought and communication is one of the most complicated things we do. The lexical knowledge that supports this activity is correspondingly complicated. No single, simple formula will suffice to account for all of the twists and turns in this conceptual leviathan. Each approach that has been summarized has its own range of plausible application but viewed in the light of the total range of phenomena to be accounted for each can be made to seem incomplete or superficial. At present there is no psychological theory adequate to all of the word-word, word-object, and word-concept relations that must be explained. There is not even a compelling argument (other than theoretical convenience) for distinguishing between practical and lexical memory or between information that is stored in lexical memory and information that must be available to the system that consults lexical memory.

Perhaps a limited range of applicability is all that should be expected. It is, after all, the only way we could hope to begin. The story, viewed over almost a century of active research by psychologists, reveals that the present inadequate formulations have evolved from even more inadequate formulations in the past. A critic might claim that a delusion of progress has been achieved simply by changing the theory, but a defender can plausibly reply that many of the changes have been obvious improvements. And where there is progress, there is hope.

The range of practical concerns that are related to the problems of lexical meaning—teaching vocabulary, spelling, reading, and writing to children; teaching second languages, diagnosing aphasic and schizophrenic language; facilitating psychotherapy—suggests that as long as there is hope, continued research is justified. But greater relevance to practical problems can only be achieved by greater theoretical integration, since the language users who are the central object of the practical concerns use whatever language skills they command as an integrated, organic system. In the current state of the art, we still have far to go before we will have achieved a theory or set of related theories adequate to explain the lexical practices that can be observed every day in the school and clinic.

References

Anderson, J. R., and G. H. Bower. 1973. *Human Associative Memory*. New York: Wiley.

Anderson, R. C., and B. McGaw. 1973. On the representation of meanings of general terms. *Journal of Experimental Psychology, 101,* 301–306.

Anderson, R. C., and A. Ortony. 1975. On putting apples into bottles—A problem in polysemy. *Cognitive Psychology, 7,* 167–180.

Anglin, J. M. 1970. *The Growth of Word Meaning*. Cambridge, Mass.: The MIT Press.

———. 1976. *Word, Object, and Conceptual Development*. New York: Norton.

Bandler, R., and J. Grinder. 1975. *The Structure of Magic. I. A Book About Language and Therapy*. Palo Alto, Calif: Science and Behavior Books.

Battig, W. F., and W. E. Montague. 1969. Category norms for verbal items in 56 categories: A replication and extension of the Connecticut category norms. *Journal of Experimental Psychology Monograph, 80* (No. 3, Pt. 2), 1–46.

Blank, M. 1973. *Teaching Learning in the Preschool: A Dialogue Approach.* Columbus, Ohio: Merrill.

Blount, W. R. 1970. *Retardate and Non-retardate Concept Usage Performance: Abstraction Ability, Number of Referents and Item Familiarity,* Vol. 1. Tampa, Florida: University of South Florida, Institute III, Exceptional Children and Adults.

Brown, J. W. 1972. *Aphasia, Apraxia, and Agnosia: Clinical and Theoretical Aspects.* Springfield, Ill.: C. C. Thomas.

Brown, R. 1958. How shall a thing be called? *Psychological Review, 65,* 14–21.

Caramazza, A., E. H. Grober, and E. B. Zurif. 1976. A psycholinguistic investigation of polysemy: The meanings of *line.* Unpublished manuscript, Dept. of Psychology, Johns Hopkins University, Baltimore, Md.

Caramazza, A., H. Hersh, and W. S. Torgerson. 1976. Subjective structures and operations in semantic memory. *Journal of Verbal Learning and Verbal Behavior, 15,* 103–117.

Caramazza et al. Unpublished manuscript. Department of Psychology, the Johns Hopkins University, Baltimore, Maryland.

Carroll, J. B., and M. N. White. 1973. Word frequency and age of acquisition as determiners of picture-naming latency. *Quarterly Journal of Experimental Psychology, 25,* 85–95.

Cattell, J. McK. 1886. The time it takes to see and name objects. *Mind, 11,* 63–65.

———. 1887. Experiments on the association of ideas. *Mind. 12,* 68–74.

Cattell, J. McK., and S. Bryant. 1889. Mental association investigated by experiment. *Mind, 14,* 230–250.

Clark, E. V. 1973. What's in a word? On the child's acquisition of semantics in his first language. In T. E. Moore (ed.), *Cognitive Development and the Acquisiton of Language.* New York: Academic Press, 65–110.

Cliff, N. 1959. Adverbs as multipliers. *Psychological Review, 66,* 27–44.

Cofer, C. N., and J. P. Foley, Jr. 1942. Mediated generalization and the interpretation of verbal behavior. I. Prolegomena. *Psychological Review, 49,* 513–540.

Cohen, B. H., W. A. Bousfield, and G. A. Whitmarsh. 1957. Cultural norms for verbal items in 43 categories. Office of Naval Research Technical Report 22, Nonr 631 (00) Storrs, Conn.: University of Connecticut.

Collins, A. M., and E. F. Loftus. 1975. A spreading-activation theory of semantic processing. *Psychological Review, 82,* 407, 428.

Collins, A. M., and M. R. Quillian. 1969. Retrieval time from semantic memory. *Journal of Verbal Learning and Verbal Behavior, 8,* 240–247.

Cramer, P. 1968. *Word Association.* New York: Academic Press.

D'Andrade, R. G., N. R. Quinn. S. B. Nerlove, and A. K. Romney. 1972. Categories of disease in American-English and Mexican-Spanish. In A. K. Romney, R. N. Shepard, and S. B. Nerlove (eds.), *Multidimensional Scaling: Applications. Volume 2.* New York: Seminar Press. 9–54.

Dauber, J. 1911. Über bevorzugte Assoziationen und verwandte Phänomene. *Zeitschrift für Psychologie, 59,* 176–222.

Deese, J. 1965. *The Structure of Associations in Language and Thought.* Baltimore, Md.: Johns Hopkins Press.

Entwisle, D. R. 1966. *Word Associations of Young Children.* Baltimore, Md.: Johns Hopkins Press.

Esper, E. A. 1973. *Analogy and Association in Linguistics and Psychology.* Athens, Ga.: University Georgia Press.

Fillenbaum, S., and A. Rapoport. 1971. *Structures in the Subjective Lexicon.* New York: Academic Press.

Fillmore, C. J. 1968. The case for case. In E. Bach and R. T. Harms (eds.), *Universals in Linguistic Theory.* New York: Holt, Rinehart, and Winston, 1–88.

Fiskel, J. R., and G. H. Bower. 1976. Question-answering by a semantic network of parallel automata. *Journal of Mathematical Psychology, 13,* 1–45.

Fodor, J. A. 1965. Could meaning be an r_m? *Journal of Verbal Learning and Verbal Behavior, 4,* 75–81.

Fodor, J. D., J. A. Fodor, and M. F. Garrett. 1975. The psychological unreality of semantic representations. *Linguistic Inquiry, 6,* 515–532.

Galton, F. 1879–1880. Psychometric experiments. *Brain, 2,* 149–162.

Glass, A. L., and K. J. Holyoak. 1974/75. Alternative conceptions of semantic theory. *Cognition, 3,* 313–339.

Goodglass, H., and E. Baker. 1976. Semantic field, naming, and auditory comprehension in aphasia. Mimeo.

Gruber, J. 1965. Studies in Lexical Relations. Ph.D. dissertation, Massachusetts Institute of Technology.

Henley, N. M. 1969. A psychological study of the semantics of animal terms. *Journal of Verbal Learning and Verbal Behavior, 8,* 176–184.

Herrmann, D. J., E. J. Shoben, J. R. Klun, and E. E. Smith. 1975. Cross-category structure in semantic memory. *Memory and Cognition, 3,* 591–594.

Hollan, J. D. 1975. Features and semantic memory: Set-theoretic or network model? *Psychological Review, 82,* 154–155.

Holt, E. B. 1931. *Animal Drive and the Learning Process.* New York: Holt.

Howes, D. 1967. Some experimental investigations of language in aphasia. In K. Salzinger and S. Salzinger (eds.), *Research in Verbal Behavior and Some Neurophysiological Implications.* New York: Academic Press. 181–199.

Howes, D., and C. E. Osgood. 1954. On the combination of associative probabilities in lingustic contexts. *American Journal of Psychology, 67,* 241–258.

Howes, D., and R. L. Solomon. 1951. Visual duration threshold as a function of word probability. *Journal of Experimental Psychology, 41,* 401–410.

Hull, C. L. 1939. The problem of stimulus equivalence in behavior theory. *Psychological Review, 46,* 9–30.

Hunt, E. B. 1962. *Concept Learning: An Information Processing Problem.* New York: Wiley.

Jackendoff, R. 1976. Toward an explanatory semantic representation. *Linguistic Inquiry, 7,* 89–150.

Jastrzembski, J. E., and R. F. Stanners. 1975. Multiple word meanings and lexical search speed. *Journal of Verbal Learning and Verbal Behavior, 14,* 534–537.

Jones, L. V., and L. L. Thurstone. 1955. The psychophysics of semantics: An experimental investigation. *Journal of Applied Psychology, 39,* 31–36.

Jung, C. G. 1918. *Studies in Word-Association.* London: Heinemann.

Katz, J. J. 1964. Semantic theory and the meaning of "good." *Journal of Philosophy, 61,* 739–766.

————. 1972. *Semantic Theory.* New York: Harper and Row.

Katz, J. J., and J. A. Fodor. 1963. The structrue of a semantic theory. *Language, 39,* 170–210.

Kelly, E. F., and P. J. Stone. 1975. *Computer Recognition of English Word Senses.* Amsterdam: North-Holland.

Kent, G. H., and A. J. Rosanoff. 1910. A study of association in insanity. *American Journal of Insanity, 67,* 37–96, 317–390.

Koffka, K. 1912. *Zur Analyse der Vorstellungen und inherer Gesetze.* Leipzig. Quelle and Meyer.

Kraepelin, E. 1883. Experimentelle Studien über Associationen. *Versammlung deutscher Naturforscher und Aertzte.* Breisgau: Freiburg.

Krauss, R. 1952. *A Hole is to Dig.* New York: Harper and Row.

Kuipers, B. J. 1975. A frame for frames: Representing knowledge for recognition. In D. G. Bobrow and A. Collins (eds.), *Representation and Understanding: Studies in Cognitive Science.* New York: Academic Press, 151–184.

Labov, W. 1973. The boundaries of words and their meanings. In C-J. N. Bailey and R. W. Shuy (eds.), *New Ways of Analyzing Variation in English,* Vol. 1. Washington, D.C.: Georgetown University Press. 340–373.

Lenneberg, E. H., I. A. Nichols, and E. F. Rosenberger. 1964. In *Disorders of Communication,* Vol. 24. Research Publication of the Association for Research in Nervous and Mental Disease. Balimore, Md.: Williams and Wilkins.

MacNamara, J. 1971. Parsimony and the lexicon. *Language, 47,* 359–374.

Maher, B. 1973. Language and psychopathology. In G. A. Miller (ed.), *Communication, Language, and Meaning: Psychological Perspectives.* New York: Basic Books, 256–267

Meyer, D. E. 1970. On the representation and retrieval of stored semantic information. *Cognitive Psychology, 1,* 242–300.

Meyer, D. E., and R. W. Schvaneveldt. 1976. Meaning, memory structure, and mental processes. *Science, 192,* 27–33.

Miller, G. A. 1967. Psycholinguistic approaches to the study of communication. In D. L. Arm (ed.), *Journeys in Science.* Albuquerque, N.M.: University of New Mexico Press, 22–73.

————. 1969. A psychological method to investigate verbal concepts. *Journal of Mathematical Psychology, 6,* 169–191.

————. 1972. English verbs of motion: A case study in semantics and lexical memory. In A. W. Melton and E. Martin (eds.), *Coding Processes in Human Memory.* Washington: Winston, 335–372

Miller, G. A., and P. N. Johnson-Laird. 1976. *Language and Perception.* Cambridge, Ma.: Harvard University Press.

Miller, R. L. 1968. *The Linguistic Relativity Principle and Humboltian Ethnolinguistics.* The Hague: Mouton.

Minsky, M. 1975. A framework for representing knowledge. In P. Winston (ed.), *The Psychology of Computer Vision.* New York: McGraw-Hill. 211–277

Montague, R. 1974. *Formal Philosophy: Selected Papers.* New Haven, Conn.: Yale University Press.

Moore, J., and A. Newell. 1974. How can Merlin understand? In L. W. Gregg (ed.), *Knowledge and Cognition.* Hillsdale, N. J.: Erlbaum, 201–252.

Moran, L. J., R. B. Mefferd, and J. P. Kimble. 1964. Idiodynamic sets in word association. *Psychological Monographs, 78* (2, No. 579).

Mosier, C. I. 1941. A psychometric study of meaning. *Journal of Social Psychology, 13,* 123–140.

Mowrer, O. H. 1954. The psychologist looks at language. *American Psychologist, 9,* 660–694.

Newell, A., and H. A. Simon. 1972. *Human Problem Solving.* Englewood Cliffs, N.J.: Prentice-Hall.

Norman, D. A., and D. E. Rumelhart. 1975. *Explorations in Cognition.* San Francisco, Ca.: Freeman.

Oldfield· R. C., and A. Wingfield. 1965. Response latencies in naming objects. *Quarterly Journal of Experimental Psychology, 17,* 273–281.

Osgood, C. E. 1952. The nature and measurement of meaning. *Psychological Bulletin, 49,* 197–237.

———. 1963. On understanding and creating sentences. *American Psychologist, 18,* 735–751.

Osgood, C. E., W. H. May, and M. S. Miron. 1975. *Cross-cultural Universals of Affective Meaning.* Urban: University of Illinois Press.

Osgood, C. E., G. J. Suci, and P. H. Tannenbaum. 1957. *The Measurement of Meaning.* Urban: University of Illinois Press.

Quillian, M. R. 1968. Semantic memory. In M. Minsky (ed.), *Semantic Information Processing.* Cambridge, Mass.: The MIT Press, 216–270.

Razran, G. H. S. 1939. A quantitative study of meaning by a conditioned salivary technique (semantic conditioning). *Science, 90,* 89–90.

Rips, L. J., E. J. Shoben, and E. E. Smith. 1973. Semantic distance and verification of semantic relations. *Journal of Verbal Learning and Verbal Behavior, 12,* 1–20.

Rochford, J., and M. Williams. 1962. Studies in the development and breakdown of the use of names. *Journal of Neurology, Neurosurgery, and Psychiatry, 25,* 222–233.

Romney, A. K., and R. G. D'Andrade (eds.). 1964. Cognitive aspects of English kin terms. *Transcultural Studies in Cognition. American Anthropologist Special Issue, 66* (3, Pt. 2), 146–170.

Rosch, E. 1973. On the internal structure of perceptual and semantic categories. In T. E. Moore (ed.), *Cognitive Development and Acquisition of Language.* New York: Academic Press.

Rosch, E., C. B. Mervis, W. Gray, D. Johnson, and P. Boyes-Braem. 1976. Basic objects, in natural categories. *Cognitive Psychology.* Psychology *8,*382–439.

Rubenstein, H., and J. B. Goodenough. 1965. Contextual correlates of synonymy. *Communications of the ACM, 8*, 627–633.

Rubenstein, H., L. Garfield, and J. A. Millikan. 1970. Homographic entries in the internal lexicon. *Journal of Verbal Learning and Verbal Behavior, 9*, 487–494.

Rumelhart, D. E., and A. A. Abrahamson. 1973. A model for analogical reasoning. *Cognitive Psychology, 5*, 1–28.

Schaeffer, B., and R. Wallace. 1970. The comparison of word meanings. *Journal of Experimental Psychology, 86*, 144–152.

Schank, R. C. 1973. Identification of conceptualizations underlying natural language. In R. C. Schank and K. M. Colby (eds.), *Computer Models of Thought and Language*. San Francisco, Ca.: Freeman, 187–247.

Seashore, R. H., and L. D. Eckerson. 1940. The measurement of individual differences in general English vocabularies. *Journal of Educational Psychology, 31*, 235–247.

Shepard, R. N., A. K. Romney, and S. B. Nerlove. 1972. *Multidimensional Scaling: Theory*. New York: Seminar Press.

Smith, E. E., E. J. Shoben, and L. J. Rips. 1974. Structure and process in semantic memory: A feature model for semantic decisions. *Psychological Review, 81*, 214–241.

Snider, J. G., and C. E. Osgood (eds.), 1969. *Semantic Differential Technique: A Source Book*: Chicago, Ill.: Aldine.

Staats, A. W. 1969. *Learning, Language, and Cognition*. New York: Holt, Rinehart, and Winston.

Templin, M. C. 1957. *Certain Language Skills in Children: Their Development and Interrelationships*. Minneapolis, Minn.: University of Minnesota Press.

Thumb, A., and K. Marbe. 1901. *Experimentelle Untersuchungen über die psychologischen Grundlagen der sprachlichen Analogiebildung*. Leipzig: Engelmann.

Trautscholdt, M. 1882. Experimentelle Untersuchungen über die Assoziation der Vorstellungen. *Philosophische Studien, 1*, 213–250.

Tulving, E. 1972. Episodic and semantic memory. In E. Tulving and W. Donaldson (eds.), *Organization of Memory*. New York: Academic Press, 381–403.

Warren, H. C. 1921. *A History of the Association Psychology*. New York: Scribners.

Watson, J. B. 1913. Psychology as the behaviorist views it. *Psychological Review, 20*, 158–177.

Wells, F. L. 1911. A preliminary note on the categories of association reactions. *Psychological Review, 18*, 229–233.

Wertheimer, R. 1972. *The Significance of Sense: Meaning, Modality, and Morality*. Ithaca, N.Y.: Cornell University Press.

Wilkins, A. J. 1971. Conjoint frequency, category size, and categorization time. *Journal of Verbal Learning and Verbal Behavior, 10*, 382–385.

Woodrow, H., and F. Lowell. 1916. Children's association frequency tables. *Psychological Monographs, 22*, No. 97.

Woods, W. A. 1975. What's in a link: Foundations for semantic networks. In D. B. Bobrow and A. Collins (eds.), *Representation and Understanding*. New York: Academic Press. 35–82.

Wreschner, A. 1907–1909. Die Reproduktion und Assoziation von Vorstellungen. *Zeitschrift für Psychologie*, Ergänzungsbang 3.

Zipf, G. K. 1945. The meaning-frequency relationship of words. *Journal of General Psychology*, *33*, 251–256.

Zurif, E. B., A. Caramazza, R. Myerson, and J. Galvin. 1974. Semantic feature representations for normal and aphasic language. *Brain and Language*, *1*, 167–187.

Addendum to "Lexical Meaning"

GEORGE A. MILLER

I have three issues I would like to raise, but I will not have time to discuss them all. They are the growth of vocabulary, the problem of polysemy (the fact that words have multiple meanings), and the problem of semantic decomposition. These are three clusters of problems about which people disagree violently.

I will not say much about vocabulary growth. There is not much in my previous paper about it, either, because I assumed that Lois Bloom would treat it—and she did. It should be noted, however, that there is an aspect of vocabulary growth related to intelligence testing that from a practical point of view is enormously important. An adequate treatment of the controversial issues involved in the verbal component of general intelligence would take far more time than would be appropriate to devote to it at this conference. But there are many other hotly debated issues about semantic development, only some of which Bloom discussed.

Polysemy

Polysemy is an old problem. Psychologists have long been aware of it: Homonyms and homophones have been used in many experiments to provide various kinds of control conditions. But although the phenomenon has been recognized in psychology for a long time, most psychologists have not realized how important it is. In 1945 George Kingsley Zipf published one of his well-known straight lines on log-log coordinates relating the frequency of use of a word to the number of different senses that were found in the Lorge-Thorndike semantic count. It is a well-established fact that the more frequently a word is used the more senses it has.

Consider the problem that this poses. If we studied Chinese, where they have only a few hundred syllables to express thousands of concepts, there would be no question about it. We would have to face the fact that the problem of homonomy in that language is extremely severe. But even in English, where we have many more different phonological shapes to use as words, homonomy is a severe problem. The real fascination of it is that it does not bother anybody in either language. How do people disambiguate words so easily? If you try to think how a computer

Editors' note: Miller's previous chapter on lexical meaning is organized around three themes: classification of psychological theories about lexical meaning, historical development of the field, and types of relations about which the researchers were concerned. However, at the conference Miller organized his oral presentation around an alternative scheme: some issues of current concern in the field of lexical meaning. As Miller's previous paper indicates, although research on lexical meaning has had a long history, current theories are nevertheless in a formative stage at present. The several approaches by which researchers attempt to frame general statements about the nature of understanding and using one's lexical knowledge are currently hotly debated. The editors thought, therefore, that it would benefit the reader to have available this issue-oriented way of viewing the "state-of-the-art" of research in lexical meaning that Miller so ably presented. Upon our request, he kindly agreed to render his oral presentation into the written form that is presented here.

might deal with language, you will recognize that a major problem is telling the computer how to select the correct meanings in each context. Nobody has a very clear idea what kind of support system to give a computer for disambiguating words, but nearly every word has to be disambiguated.

The fact that the most frequent words are the most polysemous is related to vocabulary development. John B. Carroll and M. N. White's (1973) work establishes that the most frequent words are the words that children learn first. Carroll and White actually suggest that many of the effects in experiments testing perception or memory for words—effects that have usually been attributed to frequency of use—would probably be better explained in terms of age of acquisition of the word. In any case, the words learned first and used most frequently in adult speech are also the most ambiguous words in the language.

How should we deal with that? One approach that psychologists have taken revolves around the question of what you retrieve when you retrieve a word. Take the word *line*, for example. (Various people have used this example and I am well prepared with examples of the polysemy of *line*.) Suppose the word *line* is flashed on a screen and you retrieve something; you think of something. What is it?

Experiments by Herbert Rubinstein and others (1965, 1970) presented various sequences of letters and asked the subject to say whether each sequence of letters spelled an English word. It is a simple experiment that has been replicated many times. The discovery of interest here was that polysemous words, words with more senses, were recognized as words more rapidly than were monosemous words. The obvious hypothesis that suggests itself is that if there are many senses around when you reach for one, the more there are the faster you will find one. On this hypothesis, however, senses are relatively independent; you can find one without finding others.

The other side of this argument has more evidence to support it. It comes from work with sentences that contain polysemous words in context; there is a variety of ways to do the experiment. When all the proper controls are carefully executed, it does seem to cost something to have a polysemous word. The results suggest that it is as if you were retrieving all of the senses of a word at the same time and then having to decide somehow which sense is appropriate in the given context. Under these circumstances, retrieval seems to have two stages. One stage has to do with consulting the lexicon and finding the list of senses; another stage involves a system that uses what has been retrieved in order to decide which sense is appropriate in the context in which the word occurred. Thus we have an argument about lexical retrieval. Can you retrieve one meaning without thinking of any others or must you retrieve them all and then very quickly suppress all but one?

For the purpose of discussion, let us suppose that you do retrieve something like a list or set of meanings. There are still two possible ways to describe what is going on. One way would be to say a lexical entry really consists of a list. For example, there are all these different senses of *line*: line of sight, line of talk, line of poetry, line of rope, line of battle, line of whatever. Suppose each sense is listed separately in your mental dictionary. Then you have some device that looks at the context around this word and applies simple rules (for example, if word *A* occurs before it and word Q occurs after it, then you should select meaning seven; but if something else occurs, select meaning three, and so on). That is essentially the way Kelly and Stone (1975) tried to implement the process in their general inquirer in order to perform disambiguation automatically. It is a brute force method; Kelly and Stone complained about having to do it that way.

A more sophisticated way to do it is the one Ross Quillian (1968) suggested. He represents words by associative nets of some sort; you take two words and the computer looks for an intersection between their nets. When it finds two senses that have something in common, it picks out those two as the senses that are appropriate for those two words in that context. It is more sophisticated than Kelly and Stone's approach in the sense that it is more complicated to put a dictionary into a computer in that particular way.

Neither of these models is a very good representation of the psychological processes involved in disambiguation. I prefer a second way of describing what is going on. (Nearly all the psychologists who have written on this question prefer the second view until they try to write a computer program.) The second idea is that people have a very general concept associated with a word plus some kind of machinery that sharpens that general concept in the light of the specific context. (Perhaps there are two or three general concepts, but as few as possible.) The assumption is that disambiguation is primarily an inferential process, not a selectional process. It is a form of problem solving. Of course, it may be the case that after you have disambiguated a word in the same way thousands of times, certain patterns of inference become automatic.

How to formulate this inferential process is a fascinating and difficult psychological problem. Let me take an example. (Mark Aaronoff gave me this example, it is not mine.) You are sick. You have a friend John who is a stockbroker. While you have a bad cold, John takes care of you; he brings you orange juice and tea, makes sure you are warm, and gives you aspirin. When you recover from your cold you tell a friend about it. You say, "John is a good nurse." This is an interesting sentence because it is true. In fact, however, John is a stockbroker; so there is a sense in which the sentence "John is a nurse" is false. It is a little puzzle. How can it be that "John is a nurse" is false and "John is a good nurse" is true? What is the word *good* doing in this situation? Think back to Jerry Katz's (1964) argument that *good* selects the function of a noun, that is, a good knife is a knife that cuts well, a good chair is a chair that seats well, and so on. (I do not agree entirely with Katz's explanation, but I will accept it for the present purpose.) Let us say that *good* is an adjective that selects the function of the head noun and assigns a positive evaluation to it.

Now suppose that we have (at least) two senses of the word *nurse*. One sense of *nurse* is a person who has been trained to take care of the sick and who earns a living this way. Let us say that that is the "standard" definition. Then we also have an extended definition that could be anyone who performs the functions of a nurse. And *good* tells you that it is not that first sense you want, but the second sense. Now that would be a list way of doing it. You come to the word *nurse*. You look to see if it is modified by *good*. If so, you take sense two. That means that every noun that can be modified by *good* in this way is going to have to have two senses. The alternative would be to say that there is just the standard sense of *nurse* plus something that you might call a construal rule that says whenever a noun is modified by *good* you construe that noun to be "something that performs the function of." That was essentially Katz's suggestion. And it would be an inferential solution.

This is a trivial example because we do not have time to work through a complicated example. But how to deal with extended senses of words is not a trivial issue. If we take the construal rule approach, we are going to have to look for lots of these rules. As I go through the literature I can find maybe a dozen; they are usually offered as I offered this one, as examples. I have never seen anyone really try to list all of them or propose any general description of what a complete calculus of construal rules would look like or how a child might learn such a system. But it is at least a theoretical possibility.

If we try to push the construal rule approach, we will soon realize that we are going to have to account not only for minor extensions like this but also for the use of words in analogies and even in the complex phrases and sentences that express metaphors. Psychologically, analogies and metaphors do not seem very different from simple semantic extensions. But if we demand a psychosemantic theory that will account for all of those generalization phenomena, I am inclined to agree with John Bransford that we are going to need something even more powerful than sets of isolated rules. Perhaps certain rules like the example I gave become crystallizations of frequently used parts of the "support system."

Metaphor is a whole cluster of problems in itself. It is obviously important and everyone seems to have an opinion about it. Within the last couple of months several people have told me they are launching research programs on metaphor. I wish them luck. I do not know how to approach it. I can see how to work with extensions of meaning and that sort of thing, but the larger problem looks very difficult. I expect to see some heated disagreements about metaphor in the years ahead.

Semantic Decomposition

The next cluster of issues centers around semantic decomposition. There seem to be even more problems associated with decomposition than with polysemy.

First of all, what is meant by semantic decomposition? The simplest way to answer is to give an example. In the previous paper I took *sprint* and decomposed it into *move* and *rapidly*. You take a word and define or replace it by other words, other concepts, other semantic markers, or something that you believe will decompose the original word's meaning into its component parts.

One way to do this is the way Quillian adopted; the meaning is decomposed into lexical associations. You enter a large associative net; everything that gets activated is the meaning. This is a configurational approach where one word is defined in terms of all the other words it makes you think of. The alternative to a configurational theory is a reductionistic theory. (For example, we might use basic English and think of it as providing eight hundred and fifty primitive lexical concepts.) A reductionistic approach assumes irreducible semantic atoms of the system; we try to decompose the meaning of any word into some functional configuration (or list or whatever) made up of these atoms. When we come to an atom, we stop the decomposition. Roger Schank (1973) is the only person I know who has been bold enough to propose an explicit list of semantic atoms or primitive concepts for natural language. But reduction is implicit in the Katz and Fodor (1963) theory of semantic analysis. Katz and Fodor did not try to propose what the atoms are, but they would presumably include concepts like "animate," "human," and "male."

So, configurational versus reductionistic is one of the arguments. Another kind of argument concerns whether these decompositions should be conjunctive or disjunctive. Without thinking much about it most people assume they are going to be conjunctive: In order for something to be an X, it must be Y *and* Z *and* so on *and* so forth. Only something that has all of these features satisfies all the criteria for membership. But then you run into concepts like *furniture*. (Remember Wittgenstein and his claim that the concept *game* cannot be defined in terms of a property common to all games.) The concept of *furniture* has no component feature or concept common to all articles of furniture. You begin to realize you must also have disjunctive concepts. A simple disjunctive concept for furniture might be: something is an article of furniture if it is a chair *or* a bed *or* a lamp *or* a table *or*. . . . You have to know this list to know what *furniture* means. It is characteristic of disjunctive concepts that they have vague boundaries; we are not sure whether some things are furniture or not. Are the books on your shelves furniture? It depends on your attitude toward books. Is a piano furniture? Is a piano a musical instrument, an article of furniture, or both? The boundary problems of disjunctive concepts contrast with those of a concept like *body*. If we were as uncertain about what the various parts of the human body are as we are about what the various articles of furniture are, we would never have survived as long as we have. Lexical concepts can be either conjunctive or disjunctive. Recent work by Eleanor Rosch and her colleagues (1976) provides an interesting psychological approach to this distinction.

Another kind of argument that arises in the context of decomposition is whether you should decompose into concepts that are in some peculiar sense lexical or linguistic or whether any kind of concepts are possible atoms. Are your lexical concepts separable from all the other concepts you have? Take your concept of the permanency of objects, for instance. You would probably not regard object permanency as a lexical concept even though in some sense or other a concrete object that has a lexical label must also exhibit object permanency. Should object permanency be included as one of the concepts into which the meaning of that label is to be decomposed?

Should we draw a distinction between lexical and practical or general concepts, between the dictionary in your head and the encyclopedia in your head, as some people put it? And if so how do we draw the distinction? Some theorists seem to assume that when you hear a word you consult your memory and retrieve anything you know; what you know does not come labeled "L" or "G" for "lexical" or "general." Other theorists say that if we have to have a general theory of all knowledge before we can have a theory of lexical knowledge, if we must explain everything before we can explain anything, the task is impossible. Strong opinions have been expressed on both sides of this issue, too.

There are still other questions that arise as soon as you have played this game long enough to get some feeling for the great variety of lexical concepts. Let me take the narrowly lexical side for the purpose of discussion. If you admit all knowledge into the lexicon, then clearly the variety is not going to surprise you. But if you try to work with purely lexical concepts, you will be impressed when you begin to look at different semantic fields and discover their heterogeneity. The principles of conceptual organization behind the color terms are very different from the principles of organization behind the kin terms, which are both very different from the principles of organization behind botanical terms, which are all very different from the principles of organization behind verbs of motion, and on and on. You begin to say that lexical domains can take all sorts of shapes and sizes.

Some psychologists who work in this field seem to think all lexical concepts are alike. I do not know whether they do so explicitly or whether they just have not thought about it. The assumption may come from an optimistic faith that some favorite method can be used to unravel everything. If you are ever tempted to make such a mistake, please read Fillenbaum and Rappaport's (1971) monograph in which they look at ten different lexical fields and use exactly the same method to study all of them, then limp out in the last chapter complaining that people must think differently about all these different things because every structure seems different from every other. I should confess that when I first got into this field I had some silly notion (I should have known better, but enthusiasm overpowered wisdom) that there is a superordinate concept like *entity* that is differentiated into a huge, exhaustive, lexical taxonomy. Men as distinguished as Roget seemed able to work on that principle and it looked good to me. But when I got into the lexicon in first-hand detail, I discovered that it is not quite so simple.

What should we do about the conceptual heterogeneity of the lexicon? This is not really a controversy, but it is an issue that arises. Should we take seriously someone who works only with a small hierarchy of nouns and then claims to be studying the structure of the subjective lexicon? Someone who studies a small suburb in West Peoria and claims to be studying American geography is right in a sense, and Peorian geography may be very interesting. But the perspective is misleading.

Another kind of issue comes up frequently in computer work with language. What is the relation of a semantic decomposition to a sentence meaning? Linguists and logicians have worked intensively on how to decompose the meaning of a sentence into the meanings of its constituent clauses and phrases. The question is how to assign meanings to those constituents so that we can put them all together into the meaning of the sentence. It is "sentential semantic decomposition," if you like. The temptation is great to play that same game, which we can now do with great formal elegance, at the level of the lexicon. That is to say, if we can somehow represent the meanings of words by sentences, then we can play the sentence decomposition game on the definitions of the words.

One innovation that moved Quillian ahead of everybody else at the time he first worked on semantic memory was that he wrote his definitions in the form of propositions. This is a much more sophisticated representation than using just S's and R's connected by arrows, which was the way most people had been thinking about associative nets before. But more recently, Norman and Rummelhart (1975) have begun to relate words in networks in terms of case relations. In *The boy hit the ball*, for example, *boy* is related to *hit* by being the agent, in the agent case, whereas *ball* is the patient, in the object case. A case relation is not a proposition; Norman and Rummelhart use a mixture of associations, case relations, and propositions in their model of semantic memory. Other people insist on a purely propositional decomposition; I tend to feel more comfortable on the propositional side myself. In a very thoughtful article, Bill Woods (1975) looks at the various network theories and raises many important issues concerning the relation between associative nets and propositional or sentential types of semantic theory.

A final issue I want to raise is whether decomposition is a process, particularly whether decomposition is a process that occurs in the course of comprehension. It may not be; decomposition could be just a form of lexical classification. You can classify people as Republicans or Democrats; that does not mean that you decompose them into a republican atom or a democratic atom. Perhaps we are, for example, just taking a set of verbs and saying these are the causative and those are the noncausative verbs, these are the stative and those are the nonstative verbs, or whatever. If decomposition is simply a way that theorists have of classifying lexical meanings, it might not represent any psychological process that people must perform in order to understand what a word means in a particular sentential context.

Various workers with very little substantive evidence have been arguing rather strongly that you do not decompose when you understand a word. When I want to persuade myself of this point of view I think of sentences like *John is thirty years old; The temperature outside is thirty; It has been thirty years since I was back there.* I feel I can understand these sentences just as quickly and easily as I can understand *John is twenty-nine years old; The temperature is twenty-nine; It hs been twenty-nine years since I was back there.* But thirty, of course, is the product of two, three, and five, whereas twenty-nine is a prime. If I understood primes more quickly and easily than I understood things that can be decomposed into primes, there should be a difference. Should it take me longer to understand kill than to understand die just because kill can be analyzed as cause to die? You could probably find situations that require reasoning about the relation between kill and die, just as you could find arithmetic problems in which I would have to factor thirty into two, three, and five; the information is available, but it is not part of the immediate "gestalt" meaning of thirty or of kill.

Those who object to decomposition as a psychological process are probably on the right track. But if understanding a word does not mean reducing it to its atomic structure, what could it mean? Prototype theories offer one possibility, at least for certain lexical domains. Something like the computer theorists's frame theory (Minsky), which seems rather different from decomposition and yet enables you to decompose things, may be the kind of theory we will have to go to.

At the present time in philosophy (to venture for a moment outside my mandate) an interesting semantic argument, first presented by Saul Kripke and more recently by Hillary Putnam, is underway. I can illustrate it with the word *gold*. Many philosophers talk about meaning in terms of extension and intension. The extension of the word *gold* is all the gold in the world; the extension of the word *chair* is all the chairs in the world; and so on. (Some behaviorists have talked as if the meanings of words were their extensions.) These philosophers also talk about intensions, which are essentially what you have to know in order to determine the extension. Thus, if you know the meaning of *gold*, you must know the intension of the term; presumably you have learned some intentional device or procedure whereby you can recognize objects that are in the extension of the word *gold*.

I cannot. Most people cannot. There are experts to whom you take things; they know how to determine whether they are gold. Putnam talks about this as the "division of linguistic labor." In every culture, he claims, there are terms that require experts to determine the true extension. Does the fact that I cannot personally determine the extension of *gold* imply that I do not know what *gold* means?

Without becoming involved in all of their arguments, let us simply focus on the fact that there do seem to be technical terms of this sort in our language, and many of them are very important to us. There are occasions when we do have to know whether a particular tumor is in the extension of the word *cancer* or not or whether a particular piece of metal is in the extension of the word *gold* or not and we are personally unable to decide the matter for ourselves. Yet we think we know what these words mean. If that is true, then how could anyone say that in order to know the meaning of words like *gold, cancer, iron*, or the like you must be able to determine whether something is an instance or not? We use the words perfectly well in conversation and are seldom embarrassed by lack of expert knowledge. Perhaps we have them labeled in our mental lexicon as words for which experts must be consulted on important occasions.

When I think of technical words like this and try to fit them into theories that say a person who knows the meaning of a word must know the criterial attributes of all instances, I begin to remember all the philosophical arguments against this ancient Aristotelian notion. But that is the state of the art at the moment: We have many reasons to be dissatisfied with the things that have been worked on and only foggy notions as to where we should look for more sophisticated answers.

References

Carroll, J. B., and M. N. White. 1973. Word frequency and age of acquisition as determiners of picture-naming latency. *Quarterly Journal of Experimental Psychology, 25*, 85–95.

Other references cited in the text of this chapter may be found in the reference section of "Lexical Meaning."

Gaining Access to the Dictionary

A Discussion of Miller's Paper

WILLIAM LABOV

George Miller's paper on lexical meaning deals with the most difficult type of linguistic material that has been considered in this volume. Not even the most ambitious student of semantics would pretend that as much progress or agreement has been achieved in this area as in the study of articulation and acoustic phonetics. The chances of applying the results of research to educational or clinical problems are correspondingly remote. Miller's paper holds out no false hopes on this score. He presents a number of theoretical approaches that are plainly in competition with each other and makes it clear that some or all may be inadequate without achieving the merit of being right or wrong. Nonetheless it would be helpful to see what kind of problems could be attacked if our knowledge of lexical meaning should make substantial advances in the near future.

It is clearly an important matter for educators to know more about the lexical knowledge of young children when they first come to school. For instance, experienced educational researchers have often reported to me that black children come to kindergarten without knowing the words for knife, fork, and spoon. From my research in Newark and South Harlem, I have reason to doubt these statements (Labov 1970). Given the techniques at their disposal, teachers have been unable to gain access to the lexical knowledge of the child. Conversely, one might say that the children fail to gain access to their own knowledge when faced with the Peabody Picture Vocabulary Test. None of the tests developed so far gives a complete view of the underlying mental dictionary the child brings to school and so these tests do not answer the needs of an educational program that would utilize the child's resources for further learning. (See Bloom, this volume; Lahey, this volume; Bransford and Nitsch, this volume; Chapman, this volume.)

An even more dramatic problem of gaining access to lexical meanings has arisen in the test programs carried out in New York City in response to the *Lau* v. *Nichols* decision of the Supreme Court, which argues that children must not be denied the opportunity to be educated in their "dominant" language. Two hundred thousand children were tested for their knowledge of English words of ordinary subjects and one hundred and five thousand failed the test. Of these, thirty-five thousand failed a comparable test in Spanish. The inference drawn by the school authorities was that these children were not competent in English or in Spanish.[1] One might draw the converse conclusion: that the educators do not yet have the competence to determine the children's dominant language.

Are the methods for gaining access to the lexical meanings of adults that much better? Apparently not. In 1962, Uriel Weinreich performed a simple experiment with the words *gloomy, sullen, morose, sad, unhappy, melancholy, dismal,* and *glum.* He

[1]This information was drawn from a working paper of the Center for Puerto Rican Studies, New York City.

printed a randomized list of these words next to a randomized list of their definitions from *Webster's Second International Dictionary* and obtained random results when he asked adult subjects to match them.[2]

It would seem then that the problem of gaining access to the data for the study of lexical meaning is a difficult one; and in the absence of reliable data, it does not seem likely that much progress will be made on a theory of feature analysis or combinatory processes.

Miller's view of the field makes it clear that one of the major tasks is to obtain a means of representing lexical meaning that is linguistically plausible and psychologically realistic. This representation is often referred to as the "mental dictionary." But a dictionary is material organized for the problems of speech perception that have been discussed in other papers at this conference: Words are arranged in alphabetical (that is, phonological) order so that they can be located through a knowledge of their sounds and the corresponding meanings assigned. Most of the problems discussed by Miller pertain to the reverse kind of organization, that is, a thesaurus that will allow us to locate a given meaning and find lexical items suitable to convey it. It is thus the problem of speech production that raises the most challenging semantic problems: How does one locate a word to convey a given meaning?

Some psychologists believe that words are simply associated with images or other stimuli, but the problems of combination and limitation and disambiguation have convinced most linguists that some more complex organization is required. They certainly do not agree what that organization is. In 1967 the publishers of Roget's *Theasurus* contacted me while trying to locate research assistants who could help in revising the organization of that thesaurus for a second edition. In spite of the desperate need for financial support at the time, none of the students at our university felt he or she had the knowledge or training to make a contribution to this problem. It was probably a realistic assessment on their part.

If more were known about such organization, it might be possible to attack directly a number of theoretical and practical problems closely related to educational and clinical issues. Are there bilingual speakers who carry two distinct semantic systems in their heads ("coordinate" as opposed to "compound" bilinguals)? How do fast readers extract semantic information with only a fraction of the phonological information deciphered? Is there any method of reeducation that will help anomic aphasics regain lexical knowledge they have lost? It is clear that many of these problems revolve about the same issue of access that forms the principal theoretical and methodological problem posed here.

[2]The task of distinguishing these near-synonyms might seem too difficult; surely we could pass a similar test with the meanings of *house, chair, table, man, dog, star, gold,* and *camera.* But an illuminating contrast with the taxonomic definitions developed in botany can be made. As an amateur, I have been able to use the keys provided without pictures by Gleason (1935) to identify accurately a large range of closely related species of local plants. Yet given the clear advantage of botany over linguistics in this respect, it is instructive to note that there is no agreement on a "natural" hierarchy of features for the classification of plants, especially in the light of the strong position of numerical taxonomists who deny the existence of any such hierarchy (Sneath and Sokal 1973).

One way of finding out whether persons "know a word" is to ask them. This is the strategy followed by many linguists who base their work on introspection (that is, asking themselves questions) or on the formal elicitation of meanings from others. The techniques that most linguists use for obtaining semantic information are not much more sophisticated than the Peabody Picture Vocabulary Test. Miller's review cites many examples of experimental ingenuity in the psychologist's study of the processing of words, but there is no corresponding tradition of experimental methods in descriptive semantics. In fact the realistic descriptive semantics called for by Weinreich in 1965 (oral communication; no reference available) has not yet come into being; instead the field is primarily concerned with the manipulation of data obtained by introspection. But as Chomsky (1964) pointed out at the very outset of the generative tradition, there is no reason to think that one has immediate access to one's intuitions.

In this discussion, a number of research strategies will be reported briefly that have shown promise as ways of gaining access to the lexical entries. They involve both experiment and the observation of spontaneous speech. While introspection serves as a handy guide in forming hypotheses and designing experiments, it is not taken as evidence for any given theory of lexical structure.

"Knowledge" of a Word: The Case of Positive *anymore*

It will first be helpful to review the range of evidence that would show that someone "knows" a word or any other feature of language. In our investigation of the boundaries of syntactic dialects (Labov 1972; Rickford 1975) six aspects of such knowledge are distinguished including the ability to

1. recognize a given word or form as a grammatical element of the language (recognition);
2. identify the speakers who use it and its social status (evaluation);
3. paraphrase its meaning in a given context (interpretation);
4. provide a general gloss out of context (labeling);
5. predict its appropriate use in a variety of other contexts (prediction); and
6. use it productively in a variety of appropriate contexts (use).

To illustrate this range of skills, the word *anymore* can be cited in a sentence such as (1) John is smoking a lot anymore. This lexical entry (and its associated grammatical constructions) is regularly present in dialects spoken in about half of the geographic United States (those within or influenced by the "midland" area as identified by Kurath [1949]).

Many Americans do not recognize (1) as English at all. Others recognize it but wrongly evaluate it as a mistake or slang.[3] Some who are closer to the east midland area will attribute it to Pennsylvania Dutch. Outsiders who have lived in the midland area for several years (for example, a New Yorker who has moved to Salt

---

[3]See the responses of the usage panel of Morris and Morris (1975), p. 41: "The overwhelming rejection of *anymore* in this new or semi-dialect sense [of nowadays] reflects two factors: (1) a profound belief on the part of most panelists that the formulation makes no sense at all, and (2) a refusal on the part of some panelists, since they themselves have never heard the expression, to believe that it even exists."

Lake City) will recognize it accurately as a local form but usually mistranslate (1) as "John is still smoking a lot." Those with a better feeling for the use of *anymore* will guess more accurately that (1) means "John is smoking more than he used to" but be unable to give the general gloss provided by native speakers, that in positive sentences *anymore* means "nowadays" (Labov 1972; Hindle 1975).

The fact that someone can label the term does not show that it is firmly in place within one's linguistic system. One would also have to predict whether *anymore* could be used in this sense in

2. Anymore, I don't go there.
3. Where is he anymore?
4. When would you rather live, in 1920 or anymore?
5. Secretaries write most of the letters anymore anyhow.

Even if the speakers gave the correct answers (yes, yes, no, yes), it remains to be determined that they are capable of using *anymore* productively and accurately. In the study of the Philadelphia speech community, some speakers were encountered who showed no overt knowledge of positive *anymore* and did not seem to use it even though they were observed closely for many months. One of the major conditioning factors is that positive *anymore* is used in the context of a complaint. One man, a jeweler, was noted for not complaining very much and his daughter reported that he had never used *anymore*. But one day she reported a complaint. "He said, *Gold—you could sell it for the price of scrap anymore*."

From a series of such observations it was concluded that positive *anymore* is firmly established in the mental dictionary of the vast majority of Philadelphians. This result and others led to the conclusion that the observation of spontaneous speech in everyday social contexts is the most accurate and powerful route for gaining access to a speaker's mental dictionary. It is equally obvious that spontaneous speech cannot be relied on exclusively; a vast number of rare and unusual forms must be observed through experimental elicitation, and careful comparison of subgroups of the population can only be done through more structured approaches. But the experimental devices that are developed will be gauged by the extent to which they approximate the use of language in spontaneous speech.

Vocabulary Size

One of the most challenging tasks for educators is to determine the size of the productive vocabulary of any given speaker and to determine the factors in the person's early environment that lead to larger or smaller vocabularies. Many educational programs are based on the notion that lower-class children suffer verbal deprivation as a result of the verbally impoverished environment of lower-class homes (Bereiter and Engelmann 1966). The most accurate analysis of this situation is provided by Sankoff and Lessard (1975, p. 689), who studied a stratified random sample of French speakers in Montreal (Sankoff and Sankoff 1973). They derived a regression equation that relates D, the total number of different words used, to T, the total number of words:

$$D = 24.7 + .912\ T^{0.7} + 2.775\ A^{0.7}\ E$$

where A is measured in years and E in coding categories 1 to 5, each representing an increment of about four years' schooling. This result indicates that "each person incorporates new words into his/her productive vocabulary at a slowly decreasing rate over time, but this rate can be magnified up to five times through extensive education." The most notable fact that emerges from this analysis is that other factors usually associated with socioeconomic class (such as the occupation or educational achievement of the parents or their area of residence) contribute nothing additional to the prediction of vocabulary size. There is no support for the idea that lower-class children come to school with a serious disadvantage due to a verbal impoverishment of their home environment.

Conditions for Denotation: The Interdependence of Form and Function
Let us now consider the problem of determining in more detail the competence of a speaker to use an ordinary word of the language. First the general strategy is presented that was used in a series of investigations of the conditions for denotation (how a speaker decides whether a word is appropriate to use for a given object). It is a primary axiom of semantics that any given referent of a term is distinct from the meaning of the term. Referential meaning is a more general concept; it is a statement of the general conditions that enable the speaker to decide whether a given object is an appropriate referent or if a word can be applied appropriately to an object so that others will know what one is talking about.

In most semantic discussions, the conditions for denotation are conceived as a conjunctive series of independent conditions; whether or not each one is met has nothing to do with any of the other conditions. This is the model of componential analysis in which the use of semantic features was developed by anthropologists (Goodenough 1956) prior to the use of features by the psychologists discussed in Miller's review. (See also Tyler 1969.)

Componential analysis was typically applied to kinship terms and provides us with orthogonal sets of features such as sex, generation, or colinearity. At the same time, anthropologists have been interested in the important capacity of speakers to name ordinary objects and in particular to apply terms to the continuum of possible shapes and uses that they find in the course of everyday life. The question raised by Miller (this volume)—what is involved in knowing the meaning of *chair*—is best approached by looking at the conditions of denotation of everyday objects.

My own investigations began with a very abstract term—common sense—but switched to a more workable series of picturable objects: containers in the shape of *cups, glasses, bowls, mugs,* and *pitchers* (Labov 1973). This work began with an approach to the delineation of vague boundaries influenced by Black (1949), who has inspired many other investigations of denotation. Subjects are asked to name a random series of line drawings that vary systematically along several physical dimensions and are then asked to rename the series in a different functional context or considering them made of different materials.[4] For example, the sub-

---

[4]The full series is shown in Labov (1973) and a partial view in Miller and Johnson-Laird (1976).

jects are asked to imagine the container sitting on a dining room table filled with mashed potatoes or they are asked to picture someone drinking coffee out of it or stirring in sugar with a spoon.

For any given context and term, an area of complete consistency is found and a declining profile across the area of "vagueness," where it is difficult to say if the term denotes or not. The observation of greatest importance for a theory of dictionary representation is that these consistency profiles are regularly shifted by the context: For example, with containers of increasing width, the area of 100 percent use of *cup* expands in the "coffee" context but shrinks for the "food" context and the crossover point with *bowl* shifts left or right accordingly. (See figure 1.)

Similar results have been reported by Boertien (1975) and Andersen (1975) has reported on the acquisition of such patterns by young children. Leech (1976) has explored the use of purely linguistic methods to track the same patterns so that more abstract items can be investigated.

At a conference organized by Eleanor Rosch on the nature and formation of categories, it appeared that these results intersected with the work of a number of psychologists who were investigating learning and naming patterns and who found that the model of orthogonal sets of features was inadequate to account for their experimental data (Reed 1974). Miller's review (this volume) organizes much of this research. He also notes precisely the problem raised by the interrelation of form and function in the experimental results (see also Miller and Johnson-Laird 1976). However, the formal representations he finds most workable still rely upon orthogonal features. In the effort to segregate lexical from practical knowledge, he suggests two major predicates: "is true" and "is possible." Formal criteria are assigned to the first and functional criteria to the second (Miller and Johnson-Laird 1976). Thus a speaker might judge that it is true that a container has a certain ratio of width to depth and that it is therefore possible to drink hot liquids from it without spilling. But this formulation does not easily provide for the symmetrical interaction between the two sets of criteria: One needs a formal representation

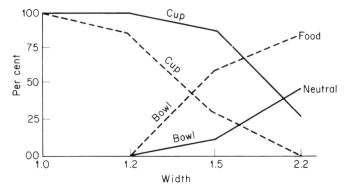

Figure 1. Consistency profiles for *cup* and *bowl* in neutral and food contexts, group A, N = 11.

that encompasses the finding that given a prototypical shape, almost any function allows a term to denote; given a prototypical function, almost any shape permits the use of the term.

One cannot criticize Miller's decision to work within a set-theoretical algebra to represent lexical meanings, since the best first approximation to linguistic structure is a categorical one. However, one can question his endorsement of the Aristotelian approach to definition: that "function—at least for artifacts—is more basic to the definition than form" (Miller and Johnson-Laird 1976, p. 229). Neither the experimental evidence nor the practical experience of lexicographers supports this view. While Miller is critical of the dictionary definition of *table*, I find the the definition of *cup* in *Webster's New International Dictionary* (second edition) represents all of the features found to be important, with a reasonable balance among them:

cup, n. 1. A small open bowl-shaped vessel used chiefly to drink from, with or without a handle or handles, a stem and foot, or a lid; as a wine cup, a Communion cup; specif., a handled vessel of china, earthenware, or the like commonly set on a saucer and used for hot liquid foods such as tea, coffee, or soup.

It is simply missing the quantitative functions that would implement the interaction of function and form.

Two aspects of this work suggest some interesting applications to the classroom. In one variant of our procedure the subjects were asked whether or not the object was a *cup* rather than being asked for a name in general. The same general pattern appeared as in figure 1. However, a considerable difference in the internal consistency of responses was found. In the normal procedure the names for these randomized series were always ordered in a monotonic series: If a person has named an object of width W a *cup*, then no object with width less than W will be named a *bowl*. This did not hold true for the answers to the questions that encouraged the subject to form the category *cup* and then judge if it applied. There were many cases of internal inconsistency in this series. This can be related to the observation in other investigations that the more subjects focus on language, the more confused they become. That is, more regular behavior was obtained when the subjects did not reflect on their language than when they did. In the latter case the subjects presumably formed the difinition of *cup* by some fairly rigid but inadequate set of criteria and then applied it in an inconsistent manner. Speakers have far more experience in using words than in defining them; it follows that any test designed to gain access to dictionary representations should avoid instructing speakers to search their own intuitions for that representation.

When the container experiment was conducted with bilingual speakers of Spanish and English, one result of particular interest was obtained. A series of eight subjects in Buenos Aires used the term *bol* quite often for containers that were wider than they were deep. But native Spanish speakers studying in the United States, even those who had come from Buenos Aires in the last six months, avoided the term *bol* completely. It appears that they had no means of knowing that it was not a recent *English* loan word that had entered their speech from English within the last few months. Further explorations along these lines may help to distinguish the criteria by which people separate lexical items belonging to two different systems.

The issue is particularly urgent if we are to understand what is happening to young children from Spanish-speaking homes who are tested for Spanish- or English-dominance at the age of five. Surveys I have conducted on the streets of New York and Philadelphia show that anyone over the age of five who is speaking Spanish was in all probability born in Puerto Rico. Children growing up in the United States regularly make the shift from Spanish-dominance to English as their dominant language at the age of five or six. It is important to know how that shift interacts with test response; it seems likely that it would throw considerable light on the problem of the thirty-five thousand children who failed both the Spanish and English tests, as reported earlier in this chapter.

The Status of the -ed Suffix as an Underlying Form

Let us turn now to a consideration of a different series of techniques that have been used to study whether the past tense suffix -ed exists in the underlying dictionary of black children learning to read standard English. The direct observation of speech shows that this suffix is sometimes present, sometimes absent. This could be due to a rule that variably inserts the -ed as a separate morpheme or to a rule that variably deletes an -ed that is always present in the underlying representation.

A long series of sociolinguistic studies points conclusively to the second alternative. Several studies have found that for every speaker and for every group, the following relations hold:

1. final -t, d is deleted more often when the next word begins with a consonant than with a vowel;
2. final -t, d is deleted more often when it is a part of the stem than when it is a separate past tense signal.

These relations are confirmed in all studies of -t, d deletion (Labov et al. 1968; Wolfram 1969, 1974; Fasold 1972; Guy 1975; Biondi 1975). Thus, a regular series of four relations may be symbolized from maximum deletion to minimum deletion as follows:

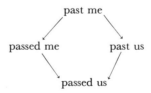

This pattern is produced by two independent constraints on the process of -t, d deletion, (a) and (b). Constraint (b) argues that the speaker must have some knowledge of the past tense morpheme. But this could be a case of dialect mixture: The -ed might be inserted as a "formal" element from another dialect with a label that limits the application of the deletion rule to such formal elements. It is constraint (a) that argues strongly for the presence of an underlying -ed that is variably deleted; for if the following phonological environment is to have an effect, it must have something to operate on.

These constraints are not constant. While black speakers show constraints (a) and (b) just as white speakers do, their overall level of deletion is higher and the effect of the past tense constraint is much less. It is also observed that the effect of the past tense constraints becomes stronger with age. This implies that knowledge of the past -ed role of the -ed suffix grows, a conclusion that coincides with studies of other grammatical morphemes (Labov et al. 1968; Labov 1972).

A practical question of great interest to teachers of reading can be raised here. Given the existence of an -ed morpheme in the underlying representation and the implied knowledge of its past tense role, is this knowledge available for the task of reading the -ed suffix, that is, deciphering the printed -ed as a carrier of past tense information?

To investigate this problem, the unique homograph *read* was used in sentences such as the following:

6. Last month I read the book.
7. When I passed by, I read every word.

In both sentences, past tense information at the beginning can be used to decide

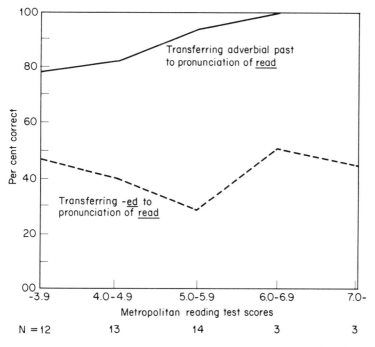

Figure 2. Correlation between Metropolitan Reading Test scores and reading of the past tense for forty-six BEV speakers in South Harlem. From Labov et al. 1968, vol. I., figure 3–6.

Table 1. Reading of the Past Tense versus Articulation of the -*ed* Suffix by Southern High School Students [from Summerlin 1972, table 7, appendix D].

	Black		White	
	Male	Female	Male	Female
% correct reading of				
read as [rɛd] after				
past adverbials	71	81	100	100
-*ed* suffix	42	47	58	77
% retention of -*ed* suffix	44	60	84	91
in spontaneous speech				

whether the appropriate pronunciation of *read* is present tense [rid] or past tense [rɛd]. In (6) the information is contained in an adverbial phrase, in (7) by the -*ed* suffix on *passed* before a word beginning with a consonant. Figure 2 shows a correlation of this task with overall reading test scores for forty-six speakers of the black English vernacular (BEV) in Harlem. Skill in interpreting the adverbial past is correlated with overall reading scores at a high level for all speakers. Results for the use of the -*ed* suffix are not so correlated and remain at a lower, chance level throughout.

This result suggests that there may be a relation between low-level phonological deletion rules and the status of the dictionary entry—or least its accessibility to the speaker engaged in the task of deciphering the printed page. Further application of this research strategy by Summerlin (1972) gives greater weight to this possibility. Summerlin studied -*t*, *d* deletion of black and white Florida children in grade school and high school. She found the same general pattern of consonant cluster simplification. For all groups, there was much less deletion for past tense clusters than for monomorphemic clusters. But black speakers showed much more deletion than whites at all levels, males more than females.

Summerlin also applied the test for the reading of the -*ed* suffix. Table 1 shows the results for the reading of the homograph *read* compared to the overall retention of the -*ed* suffix in spontaneous speech. The same pattern appears as with the Harlem studies. For the past tense adverbials, there is a high level of success for everyone. The reading of the -*ed* suffix is again at a much lower level. In each case blacks score lower than whites and males lower than females. The overall retention of the -*ed* suffix in speech production is highly correlated with reading of the -*ed* suffix.

It is of course possible that the retention of -*ed* in speech and the reading of -*ed* are both the product of a third factor of general assimilation to school styles of speech and school values. But these results strongly suggest that the variable rule for deletion affects access to the underlying forms.[5] Despite the fact that past tense

[5]Further evidence in this direction is provided by the discrimination test for /ð/ versus /d/ used by Biondi (1975) in his study of the speech of Italian-American children in Boston. Here there was a close correlation between the use of stops for *th*- words and low discri-

information is preserved more often than monomorphemic clusters, there is still a 50 percent likelihood that the suffix will be deleted.[6] One possible mechanism that might be responsible for this is an analysis by synthesis procedure. If the subjects pose the question to themselves, *pass* does have something on the end of it when we are talking about yesterday, they may come back with the observation that there is nothing there. In other words, it is possible that the past tense category can only be inspected by producing instances of it and this production gives no reliable information about the underlying suffix.

Gaining Access to the Phonological Structure of the Dictionary: The Case of Short *a*

The last area of investigation that will be reported here concerns the phonological composition of dictionary entries. This topic is somewhat removed from the main focus of Miller's review, but the technical developments in this area are of strong enough interest to warrant this further step.

For some time, I have been studying an extremely complex distribution of words spelled with "short *a*" in English. In New York, Philadelphia, and other Middle Atlantic cities, these words are sharply divided into "tense" and "lax" forms that may be located phonetically at two extreme points of the vowel triangle: *mad* [mi · əd] versus *mat* [mæt]. Though a "tensing rule" has been proposed that divides the short *a* words into two classes, there are good reasons to argue that this is not a rule at all but rather a distribution of the words in the dictionary with two separate entries, m-ā-d versus m-a-t.

In the first place, there is grammatical conditioning: Philadelphia *tin can* (tense) versus *I can* (lax); *fan, van, tan* (tense) versus the irregular verbs *ran, swam, began* (lax). There is lexical irregularity: tense *mad, bad, glad* versus lax *sad, dad, brad*. There are perhaps a dozen other conditions that complicate the rule. But on the other hand, the basic conditioning factors are plainly phonetic. In New York City words ending in front nasals, voiceless fricatives, and voiced stops are tense; all others are basically lax. In Philadelphia words ending with front nasals and front voiceless fricatives are tense; all others are basically lax. It is hard to believe that speakers do not avail themselves of such strong regularities in their learning of the language.

There was an opportunity to investigate this question in a study of the Philadelphia speech community. Arvilla Payne (1975) undertook to study the acquisition of the Philadelphia dialect by children who moved into the area speaking other dialects. The new suburb of King of Prussia was chosen because it contained 50 per cent immigrant families with large numbers of children and 50 per cent local

---

mination, which could not have been due to general test-taking ability, since fourth graders had a higher use of stops and lower discrimination than first or eighth graders.

[6]It is interesting to note that the black senior high school students showed no phonological distinction in past tense cases, though they showed the normal phonological effect for monomorphemic forms. This suggests the possibility that for them the *-ed* form may be inserted as a variable grammatical element, unlike the Harlem youth who showed a very strong phonological effect on past tense forms.

families with parents raised in the Philadelphia area. The predominantly middle-class character of the community ensured that the dialects of the immigrant speakers were not stigmatized, and there was ample opportunity for the children to follow either the dialect patterns of their parents or the dialects of the Philadelphia area.[7]

Payne's first results followed the pattern of earlier observations. Almost all the children raised in the area acquired the phonetic features of the Philadelphia dialect after a year or two of exposure, even when they lived on blocks dominated by out-of-state families. Their parents did not. These phonetic features are all low-level rules that operate without changing underlying forms (for example, /uw/ and /ow/ are fronted in all words except those ending in /l/; /ay/ is raised in all words ending with a voiceless consonant; /aw/ is fronted in all environments).

On the other hand, phonological features of the Philadelphia dialect, which concerned differences in the inventory of underlying forms, were not easily acquired by the immigrant children. The merger of /e/ and /ʌ/ before /r/ in *merry* and *Murray*, for example, was shown by only a small minority of the out-of-state children. The most extreme example is the short /a/ distribution. With one near-exception, none of the children born in other areas learned the Philadelphia pattern. Furthermore, none of the children born in Philadelphia of out-of-state parents learned it.

The interpretation of this result is that the Philadelphia short *a* distribution is not produced by a rule but for native children is the result of an original distribution of two different categories in the dictionary distribution (*mad* is first learned with a tense vowel and *sad* with a lax one). There is some evidence that out-of-state children do attempt to form rules when they are learning these forms, but the limited nature of their success contrasts sharply with their success in learning the simple phonetic rules of the Philadelphia dialect. It would appear that the only information that must be obtained from one's parents and not from any other source is the original distribution of underlying forms.

In pursuing further the question of "one phoneme versus two," the techniques for measuring categorical discrimination developed at Haskins Laboratories have been applied (Liberman et al. 1957, Pisoni 1971). Using the facilities at Bell Telephone Laboratory at Murray Hill, we analyzed the formant structure of a natural pronunciation of *mad*, altered the formants systematically along the dimension of low front to upper midnuclei, and then resynthesized a series of ten vowels ranging from (mæ·d) to [me·əd].[8] In a categorization task, subjects were asked to label each token as type 1 or type 2, where the two types were the two extremes of the series. In an ABX discrimination task, subjects were asked to decide whether

---

[7]This was an important consideration, since previous studies of immigrant families often involved southern rural or foreign-speaking parents whose English dialect was stigmatized by the local peer groups. Parents in the King of Prussia area typically worked in computing, chemical, and electronic industries.

[8]Each step upward differed from that below by a decrease of 25 Hertz (Hz) in the first formant (F1) and an increase of 50 Hz in the second formant (F2). This diagonal series matches the progression of the sound change in natural vowel systems.

X was similar to A or B. All one-step and two-step combinations in the series were used on the ABX test.

The first results of this work are shown in figures 3 and 4. Each figure shows the categorization curve and correct responses in ABX discrimination for one-step or two-step contrasts. Figure 3 shows average values for New Yorkers and Philadelphians: The ABX discrimination curve peaks over the crossover point for categorization, the same kind of effect found for vowel contrasts /i/ and /ɪ/ (Pisoni 1975). The contrast with figure 4 is clear: Speakers from the Midwest and New England show a crossover point in categorization two steps to the right (higher vowels) and fail to show any clear categorical discrimination.

Figure 5 shows the distribution of individual responses to these tests: The horizontal axis shows the crossover point on categorization and the vertical axis the relation of the discrimination pattern to degree of categorical discrimination. The top line shows an ABX peak that coincides with the crossover point for both one-step and two-step tasks, next, only a two-step effect. The third line shows a broad ABX peak on the two-step task and also a one-step peak the fourth, only a broad two-step ABX peak. The next two lines are informants who show two peaks on the two-step task the next two those whose two-step peaks fail to coincide with the crossover in categorization and the last line, those who show no categorization.

The differences in dialect distribution are clear. At the top only New Yorkers and Philadelphians are found; all those from New England and New York are concentrated in the region of broad discrimination; a few individuals fail to discriminate; and three midwesterners fail to categorize. The only speakers who clearly show categorical discrimination are those from the Middle Atlantic states whose linguistic patterns follow the irregular and complex distributions outlined above. The midwestern speakers (from Chicago and other northern cities) have a single short *a* phoneme, which is tensed throughout. Those from New England follow the "nasal pattern" in which all vowels before nasal consonants are tensed and all others are lax. Thus speakers who have two distinct allophones show no greater tendency toward categorical discrimination than those with one continuous range.[9]

These results are encouraging signs that it is possible to use phonetic and sociolinguistic techniques to gain access to the phonological structure of dictionary entries. I hope to continue the investigation of categorical discrimination and dialect acquisition for other major differences in the structure of American English (for example, the merger of short open *o* and long open *o* in eastern New England, western Pennsylvania, and the West). The value of such information for the teaching of reading is clear. Even more urgent will be an examination of the underlying structures available to bilingual speakers of Spanish and English, who have many sharp contrasts between the inventories of their two languages. For example, Spanish lacks the contrast of tense and lax /i/ and /u/ that is so important for English; it also lacks a contrast between /ʃ/ and /tʃ/ as in *ship* and *chip*. By mapping

---

[9]For the raising of short *a* in the northern cities and in Middle Atlantic states, see Labov, Yaeger, and Steiner (1972).

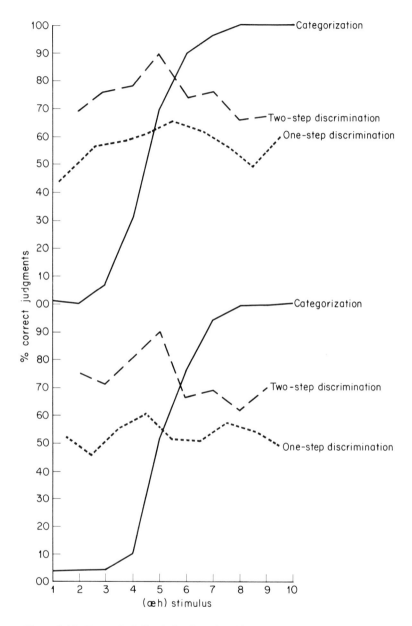

Figure 3 (a). Categorical discrimination of [æ h] by seven New York City subjects. (b). Categorical discrimination of [æ h] by seven Philadelphia subjects.

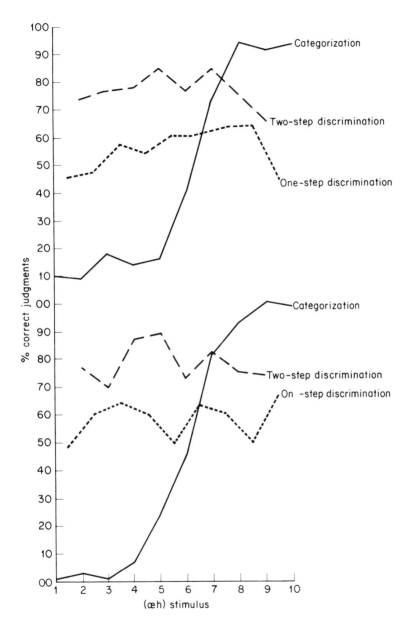

Figure 4 (a). Categorical discrimination of [æ h] by seven subjects from New England and New York State. (b). Categorical discrimination of [æ h] by seven subjects from the Midwest and Pacific Coast.

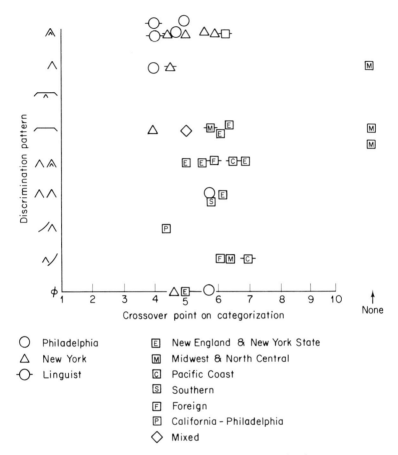

Figure 5. Individual patterns on categorization and discrimination.

the state of the underlying contrasts, it will be possible to probe more deeply into children's progress in acquiring English and to predict more precisely the problems they will have in mastering the English alphabet.

In the first approach to this discussion, it seemed realistic to adopt a pessimistic tone about our capacity to apply semantic theory to problems of educational and clinical practice. The various approaches reviewed here are all developments of empirical techniques on the linguistic side of the psycholinguistic frontier. Until recently psychology and phonetics have provided the experimental ingenuity in our field, while linguists have provided intuitive and formal analysis. But only better linguistic techniques will solve the fundamental problem of gaining access to the underlying forms that are actually used as well as the rules that operate upon them. These techniques must necessarily involve methods of observation and experimentation that are closely related to the language used in everyday life.

References

Andersen, E. S. 1975. Cups and glasses: Learning that boundaries are vague. *Journal of Child Language*, 2: 79–103.

Bereiter, C., and Engelmann S., 1966. *Teaching Disadvantaged children in the pre-school.* Englewood Cliffs, N.J.: Prentice-Hall.

Biondi, L. 1975. *The Italian-American child: His sociolinguistic acculturation.* Washington, D.C.: Georgetown University Press.

Black, M. 1949. *Language and philosophy.* Ithaca, N.Y.: Cornell University Press.

Bloom, This volume. The integration of form, content, and use in language development.

Boertien, H. S. 1975. Vagueness of container nouns and cognate verbs. Unpublished University of Texas dissertation.

Bransford, J. D., and Nitsch, K. E. This volume. Coming to understand things we could not previously understand.

Chapman, R. S. This volume. Comprehension strategies in children.

Chomsky, N. 1964. The logical basis of linguistic theory. In H. Lunt (Ed.), *Proceedings of the ninth international congress of linguists.* The Hague: Mouton, p. 914–1008.

Fasold, R. 1972. *Tense marking in black English.* Washington, D.C.: Center for Applied Linguistics.

Gleason, H. A. 1935. *Plants of the vicinity of New York.* New York: New York Botanical Garden.

Goodenough, W. H. 1956. Componential analysis and the study of meaning. *Language*, 32: 195–216.

Guy, G. 1975. Variation in the group and the individual: The case of final stop deletion. *Pennsylvania Working Papers on Linguistic Change and Variation* I, No. 4.

Hindle, D. 1975. Syntactic variation in Philadelphia: Positive *anymore. Pennsylvania Working Papers on Linguistic Change and Variation* I, No. 5.

Kurath, H. 1949. *Word geography of the eastern United States.* Ann Arbor, Mich.: University of Michigan Press.

Labov, W. 1970. Finding out about children's language. Paper given at the Hawaii Council of Teachers of English, Honolulu.

———. 1972. Where do grammars stop? In R. Shuy (Ed.), *Georgetown monograph on languages and linguistics* No. 25, 43–88.

———. 1973. The boundaries of words and their meanings. In R. Shuy and C.-J. Bailey (Eds.), *New ways of analyzing variation in English*. Washington, D.C.: Georgetown University Press, pp. 340–373.

Labov, W., Yaeger, M. and Steiner, R. 1972. *A quantitative study of sound change in progress*. Report on National Science Foundation Contract GS-3287. Phliadelphia, Pa.: U. S. Regional Survey.

Labov, W., Cohen, P., Robins, C., and Lewis, J. 1968. A study of the non-standard English of Negro and Puerto Rican speakers in New York City, U.S. Regional Survey, 204 N. 35th Street, Philadelphia, Pa.

Lahey, M. This volume. Disruptions in the development and integration of form, content and use in language development.

Leech, G. 1976. Being precise about lexical vagueness. In *New York papers in linguistics*.

Liberman, A. M., Harris, K. S., Hoffman, H. S., and Griffith, B. C. 1957. The discrimination of speech sounds within and across speech boundaries. *Journal of Experimental Psychology*, 54: 358.

Miller, G. A. This volume. Lexical meaning.

Miller, G. A., and Johnson-Laird, P. N. 1976. *Language and perception*. Cambridge, Mass.: Harvard University Press.

Morris, W. and Morris, M. 1975. *Harper dictionary of contemporary usage*. New York: Harper and Row.

Payne, A. 1975. The re-organization of linguistic rules: A preliminary report. *Pennsylvania Working Papers on Linguistic Change and Variation* I, No. 6.

———. 1977. The acquisition of the phonological structure of a second dialect. Dissertation, University of Pennsylvania.

Pisoni, D. B. 1971. On the nature of categorical perception of speech sounds. *Status report on speech research* (SR-27). New Haven, Conn.: Haskins Laboratories.

———. 1975. Auditory short-term memory and vowel perception. *Memory and Cognition*, 3: 7–18.

Reed, S. K. 1974. Categorization models. Paper presented at the Workshop on the Nature and Structure of Categories, May.

Rickford, J. R. 1975. Carrying the new wave into syntax: The case of Black English *been*. In R. Fasold and R. Shuy (Eds.), *Analyzing variation in language*. Washington, D.C.: Georgetown University Press, 162–183.

Sankoff, D. and Lessard, R. 1975 Vocabulary richness: A sociolinguistic analysis. *Science*, 190: 689–690.

Sankoff, D, and Sankoff, G. 1973. Sample survey methods and computer assisted analysis in the study of grammatical variation. In R. Darnell (Ed.), *Canadian languages in their social context*. Edmonton, Albert.: Linguistic Research, 7–63.

Sneath, P. H. A., and Sokal R. A., 1973. *Numerical taxonomy: The principles and practice of numerical classification*. San Francisco, Ca.: Freeman.

Summerlin, N. C. 1972. A dialect study: Affective parameters in the deletion and substitution of consonants in the deep South. Unpublished Florida State University dissertation.

Tyler, S. A. 1969. *Cognitive anthropology*. New York: Holt, Rinehart and Winston.

Winreich, U. 1962. Lexicographic definition in descriptive semantics. *International Journal of American Linguistics*, 28: 2, 25–43.

Wolfram, W. 1969. *A sociolinguistic description of Detroit Negro speech*. Arlington, Va.: Center for Applied Linguistics.

———. 1974. *Sociolinguistic aspects of assimilation: Puerto Rican English in New York City*. Arlington, Va.: Center for Applied Linguistics.

General Discussion of Papers by Miller and Labov

Semantic Decomposition as an Inferential Process

In answer to a question by Zurif, Miller spoke to the issue of whether semantic decomposition is an automatic part of comprehension or whether it is an additional, inferential act required in tasks such as sentence verification. For example, when a listener is asked to verify the sentence *A canary is an animal*, does the act of comprehending the sentence necessarily involve "retrieving" the information that a canary is a bird, birds are animals, and so on or does the verification task require the subject to do something more than would normally be done in order to understand the word canary? Miller thought that the latter was probably the case, that is, decomposing words into their semantic constituents when the task required it is a special, additional inferential act over and above retrieving the "static" knowledge about the meaning of the words in the sentence that is sufficient for comprehension. Semantic decomposition is not something comprehenders dos automatically when they understand a sentence in a reasonable context. Miller added that this is an issue about which researchers in comprehension are not in agreement. It is related to the question of how polysemous words are understood and how sentences like *This stump is a good table* are comprehended. Generally, one can ask whether the comprehension of these kinds of materials involves an inferential process or a selection process.

Miller and Zurif agreed that in the case of a person whose language functions have been disrupted, as in the case of an aphasic, the role of the inferential system might be different than in normal comprehenders. It may be that these people can use inferential processes that are not damaged to recover semantic information not otherwise available.

Organization and Growth of Vocabularies

Liberman posed the question of whether certain observations about vocabulary growth and organization such as the following have implications for the issues presented by Miller. First, all natural languages have large vocabularies; the number of words tends to increase. This is not logically necessary. If vocabularies were organized in terms of a hierarchically ordered set of features, any thought could presumably be expressed with very few words. Second, semantic features or class membership are in no way reflected in the phonology of any language (that is, it is possible all words referring to animals could begin with stop consonants, but this does not occur). Miller agreed that these facts about languages provide relevant evidence with respect to the notion of semantic decomposition and feature organization of lexical knowledge.

Labov commented that a study of gender systems is interesting in this regard. There are languages that classify the entire lexicon into a system of from eight to thirty gender classes. Some of these categories reflect the physical form of the object referents, for instance, round objects, ropelike objects, flat objects. He did not know of any functional categories captured by gender systems. These facts about gender systems do give insights into how people categorize the world.

Labov also mentioned that the study of the development of Pidgin languages into Creoles was interesting. It appears that the evolution is not driven by the need for logical elaboration. For instance, tense systems are logically redundant in these languages. Pidgins have a very efficient system that uses an adverb of time. When there is a need to change the time referred to, the adverb changes. So the development of tense systems does not seem to be motivated by logical necessity.

In answer to a question, Labov added that the development of Pidgins into Creoles was very rapid. Many syntactic constructions seem to develop within one or two generations. Labov is doubtful that language change of this kind can be motivated by logical necessity.

The Problem of Polysemy in Chinese

With respect to polysemy in Chinese, Miller commented that there are about four hundred syllables in the language and each is a morpheme. The amount of polysemy is therefore enormous. There are also many compound words in which each syllable is also a free form (as in *bull dog* in English). This extreme potential for ambiguity does not seem to bother the language user or learner. This is a phenomenon that psychologists must take into account in their thinking about lexical meaning.

Labov commented that in looking at a dictionary of Chinese characters, one notices that beyond the first ten thousand characters that one might acquire there are few basic logical distinctions. One realizes that words are differentiated by fine degrees of cultural affect and social status.

Word Associations and Word Frequency Effects

On a somewhat different topic, Jenkins commented that the effects of word associations and frequency of usage are powerful phenomena that psychologists still cannot explain satisfactorily. Aphasics show associative errors all the time, but we do not know the sources of the associations. Perceptual effects of word frequency can be demonstrated readily in both the auditory mode (listening to words in noise) and the visual mode (tachitoscopic presentation). (See Cutting and Pisoni, this volume, for a discussion of frequency effects.) It is a most useful fact to know in the treatment of aphasics. When one begins to work with an aphasic, one starts with high-frequency words, including words that are highly familar to the patient (such as words related to the patient's profession). As patients recover, they are able to comprehend and use words of lower and lower frequency. Patients can be graded along the frequency function when they come in for therapy. As they respond to therapy, they move up the frequency function gradually, in the same way as children do. (See Carroll and White 1973, also reported in Miller, this volume.) Thus the progression in the aphasic's object-naming skill is very similar to the development of object naming in children, and they make the same kinds of errors. This is highly correlated with frequency of usage and age of acquisition.

Labov commented that in the development of readability indices word frequency is also very important. The percentage of common words used is the best measure of difficulty, regardless of which measure of syntactic complexity is utilized.

References

Carroll, J. B., and M. N. White. 1973. Word frequency and age of acquisition as determiners of picture-naming latency. *Quarterly Journal of Experimental Psychology*, 25, 85–95.

Cutting J. E. and Pisoni, D. B. This volume. An information-processing approach to speech perception.

Miller, G. A. This volume. Lexical Meaning.

Problems and Promise in Applying Basic Research

JAMES J. JENKINS, ALVIN M. LIBERMAN, AND JAMES F. CURTIS

The final session of the conference was organized around a set of questions formulated by Curtis, Jenkins, Kavanagh, Liberman, and Strange. The questions
elicited observations, discussions, and comments on five general topics:
1. The important research issues and new directions for work apparent in the
   conference papers from both basic and applied researchers.
2. Instances of applications of the findings of basic research, including applications
   that had been overlooked in the papers.
3. The differences between basic researchers and clinicians and the implications
   of these differences for the accomplishment of the mission of the conference.
4. Observations on the processes of transmitting the findings of basic research to
   the applied domain.
5. Evaluating the product of the conference.
   Discussion of all of these topics was lively and far-reaching and in the usual manner
of such things, incomplete, suggestive, and often hortotory. Now, several months
later, we have taken the liberty of recasting these remarks, along with our own
thoughts and afterthoughts, into the five categories above. We have deleted and
added freely, making no attempt to preserve the credit (or blame) for the particular observations. The conference participants will undoubtedly forgive us; we
trust that the reader will be equally generous and will find something of interest
and value in these remarks.

Research Issues and Directions
One very impressive aspect of the conference was the extent to which the issues
currently looming in basic research are closely related to the problems one encounters in the application of basic research to clinical and educational problems.
We do not think that this convergence is accidental and we do not believe that it is
merely in the eye of the biased observer; we think it is genuine, a common outcome
of many separate causes that seem to be working in the same direction. Here we
will consider only two examples: the invariance problem in speech perception and
production and the role of context in meaning and comprehension.

THE INVARIANCE PROBLEM
Early in the conference it became apparent that the identification of invariants
in speech perception and speech production is a key problem for researchers in
those areas. Stevens's and Cutting and Pisoni's papers are both concerned with the
identification of invariants in the acoustic stream that serve to identify phonemes.
Liberman pointed out in the discussion that the "distortions" of simple cues for
phonemes carry in themselves further information about the structure of the linguistic message (that is, dynamic information of a higher sort influences and transforms the already dynamic information concerning lower units). The paradox that
arises here is a challenge to all research workers: How does the listener recognize

the phonemic structure of an utterance without knowing in advance what higher level prosodic transformations have been applied to the acoustic stream? And how can the listener identify the higher level transformations without prior knowledge of the units at the phonological level that are being transformed? (See Klatt 1976 for a similar paradox concerning duration of vowels.) Work on the dynamic information for prosodics clearly must be pursued hand in hand with the continuing work on phoneme identification.

But this is exactly the problem that Stevens and Harris point to when they consider the speech of the deaf. Hearing-impaired children, they tell us, characteristically have extraordinary trouble with the prosodic features of production. At present it is not obvious to us what such patients should be taught. No one understands prosody well enough to know what to teach or how to teach it, except on an intuitive level. Thus the same research need arises both in the laboratory and in the clinic; fundamental information on prosodics is needed.

In this instance it is apparent that there is concern at both poles of the hypothetical dimension from basic research to application for the same issue. The basic researcher sees it as the next frontier of the speech perception problem that must be approached and the clinician sees it as a pressing need in improving the therapy for or training of deaf children. The fact that this common need is seen so clearly in this conference is surely not unrelated to the fact that Stevens does both basic research on speech perception and applied research on the development of devices to help in training vocal production of deaf children and that Harris, although she pursues fundamental research in speech production, has done articulation research with aphasic and hearing-impaired clinical populations.

THE ROLE OF CONTEXT

In parallel fashion there has been convergence on the importance of the examination of the role of linguistic and nonlinguistic contexts in language comprehension. Bloom and Lahey have presented both fundamental research on language development and a schema for research and remediation with children whose language is not developing normally. The schema makes considerable use of the notion of nonlinguistic determinants of what and how the child communicates. Bransford has devoted his paper to considering the importance of both linguistic and nonlinguistic contexts for message comprehension. Chapman gives us examples of children's comprehension based on strategies of treating with a linguistic communication in particular nonlinguistic settings. Finally, Crowder shows us that memorial tasks are influenced by both linguistic and nonlinguistic contextual variables.

Here it appears that the *Zeitgeist*, or spirit of the times, is moving strongly in the direction of this neglected aspect of verbal behavior. The papers at this conference are just one set of examples of the concern for contextual variables that is now making itself felt in psychology, philosophy, linguistics, and communication. Both basic and applied researchers are turning their attention to an exploration of the role of context at approximately the same time. Perhaps these instances reflect the observation reported in the introduction to the conference that there is little lag between basic research and application in a field where there are many investigators advancing along a broad front.

Throughout the course of the conference we observed little surprise on the part of the participants. Clinical researchers were well informed as to the state of basic research and in general did not find anything dramatically new in the papers. A more general source of surprise was probably found in the results of particular applications, that is, basic researchers were less likely to have known Tallal's research with dysphasic children than clinical researchers were to know the fruits of basic research. This observation again suggests that the gap between the basic and applied researchers is not wide in speech and language areas; applied researchers are likely to know the basic areas related to their work, even though basic researchers may not know what applications are being made.

Application of the Findings of Basic Research

Neither the state-of-the-art papers nor their discussions were particularly rich in examples of knowledge that could be exported immediately to the applied fields. There appear to be two reasons for this: First, as is apparent from a study of the papers, the authors tended to concentrate on the problems most on their minds, namely the current, vexing issues in speech and language research. They were more likely to point to problems, controversies, and unsettled issues than to describe what is known in an even-handed, textbooklike manner. This was probably inevitable, although we thought we had taken care to minimize current issues in designing the conference. When researchers get together, they tend to talk about what they are doing, regardless of their assignments. Second, there seemed to be no great urgency in moving basic findings out into the field because they are already there. In some cases the transfers have been so successful that the writers overlooked them entirely or believed they could be omitted as something that everybody knows. Thus it was nowhere explicitly pointed out that we can readily synthesize intelligible speech under computer control and that we can now build a reading machine for the blind, tasks that were impossible just a few decades ago.

Let us consider for a moment what this means. It means that research workers have patiently discovered an impressive body of information about the necessary and sufficient acoustic patterns for speech perception. It means that they have also discovered how to manipulate and combine those fragments of knowledge into rule structures that are sufficient to create an intelligible acoustic stream; it is possible to write and implement a set of rules that will synthesize speech. Many systems can now produce synthetic speech from an input of discrete phonetic symbols. The speech is far from perfect, but it is intelligible and reasonably satisfactory. And it is getting better all the time. This means that basic research has made it possible to build a reading machine for the blind. Indeed, such devices are being field tested at the present time.

It is also worth noting that the basic research referred to here emerged from an unsuccessful effort to build a reading machine in the mid-1940s. The failure of that applied effort made clear how little was known about the speech signal and how wrong were the theories of speech perception. The failure forced investigators into fundamental research on the speech signal, necessitated the invention of speech synthesizers as research tools, and eventually culminated in rule-governed speech synthesis. Now, thirty years later, the applied problem has a working solution.

The story is not over, however. The demands of such an applied device show us the inadequacies of the current state of our science. An ideal reading machine would have three major components: an optical scanner that converts ordinary print into appropriate computer signals, a program that converts those signals from an English orthography to a phonetic code, and a program that translates the phonetic string into an acoustic stream.[1] The first component (which has nothing to do with speech and language) already exists. The third component is the one we have talked about in the state-of-the-art papers, a rule-driven speech synthesizer. But the second component again requires more research. If it is correct to suppose that English orthography in part reflects the level of systematic phonemes underlying phonology (Chomsky and Halle 1968), then the rules we need to go from the orthography to a phonetic transcription will include many of the more interesting rules of phonology.

Still further, when we study the acceptability of the end product of such a machine, we encounter the issue of supersegmentals and the problem of prosody that was already discussed above. Even speech that is intelligible at the level of the syllable and the word can be difficult to listen to for extended periods and hard to comprehend even in short stretches because of incorrect prosody. The prosody problem cannot be solved without more research on acoustics and without a procedure that will parse sentences automatically. The former is obviously needed and the second is almost certainly going to be needed as a condition for applying the former.

It should be obvious, although again it was not made explicit, that we have gained an enormous amount of knowledge about how to manipulate the acoustic signal and that we have a highly flexible technology that enables us to create a variety of signals tailored to special needs. It should be emphasized that this technology, developed by basic researchers, is now being applied to clinical research with very good effect. Tallal's work is a most dramatic instance of the application of this knowledge and technology, but the same techniques can be applied to the task of altering or tailoring the speech signal to transmit it more effectively to hearing-impaired populations or to prepare training materials and feedback information for deaf children.

It may be less obvious initially that the work on biological foundations of language may be useful clinically. We have at present only scratched the surface in the examination of the predispositions to language that the human infant brings to the speech and language acquisition task. When we understand more fully these

---

[1]The reading machine we know best circumvents the second stage by incorporating a large "dictionary" component in the memory banks of the computer. The dictionary gives the phonetic spelling that corresponds to English orthography (bug→/bʌg/; bugle →/bugɔl/; the→/ðə/; theater→/θiətə). This is costly in both search time and required computer size.

predispositions, we will be in a better position to discuss the pathologies of acquisition and perhaps to diagnose, to plan therapies, and to locate infants at risk.

Finally, although it has not been treated in detail at this conference, it is clear that basic research on speech and language can contribute in many ways to the study of reading (see Kavanagh and Mattingly 1972). Reading is by no means the simple mapping of visual forms onto discrete entities at each level of language. It seems reasonable to suppose, however, that reading at some stage must make contact with the phonological level of language. It may be that explicit awareness of phonology is essential to mastering the alphabetical system. When fledgling readers try to read a three-letter combination like b-a-g, it is not helpful for them to know that the word on the page has three segments, one for each symbol, unless they realize that the word already in their lexicon, "bag", also consists of three segments. Studies of the nature of speech perception and speech production tell us why it is hard for them to know that fact. We now know that the acoustic stream and the articulatory system do not recognize the "threeness" of the syllable in any simple way. Instead they blur the discreteness of these elements with the result that the awareness of the segmentation is a sophisticated, abstract achievement. In identifying the origin of this problem, we may see ways to work toward its solution.

Basic Researchers and Practitioners

Throughout the course of the conference several discussions of the nature of basic researchers and practitioners revealed that there was some disagreement in our stereotypes of these groups. In general, however, the disagreements were matters of emphasis as to which aspects of each stereotype were most salient.

Let us preface further remarks here with the admission that we are talking about archetypes, archetypes that may well not exist. As was observed in the introduction, a reasoned view is that there is a hypothetical dimension from basic research to application along which investigators and practitioners may be distributed. Virtually all positions along that dimension are filled, that is, there is every shade of combination of basic researcher and practitioner that we can imagine. Further, real investigators and practitioners are flexible; at one time they may work in one mode in one setting and at another time they may work in the other mode in a different setting. Most of the participants at the conference have held (or do hold) several positions along the hypothetical dimension. Our remarks, then, are not about real people but about perceived tendencies that may hold for the mythical average person occupying a polar position. Such simplifications may be helpful even though they stretch the truth.

One view endorsed by many of the participants was that the differences between the poles are exaggerated and the similarities ignored. Practitioners and basic researchers are said to be concerned with the same subject matter and to operate on the subject matter in much the same fashion. The problems of diagnosis and prognosis and the selection and evaluation of therapy are in principle just special applications of the scientific method. Whether one is scientist or practitioner, one has some hypotheses and one collects data that bear on the hypotheses and verifies or refutes them. If one is wrong, one collects more data, examines different hypotheses, and so on. The use of basic science information is essential; the use of the scientific method is common; the respect for data is crucial. Both scientists and practitioners should see that they are engaged in the same kind of task; it is merely the scope of the hypotheses and the level of generality that are different.

Adherents to this view hold that it is important to make it explicit to both basic researchers and practitioners so that they will foster and develop their common and shared viewpoints and come to see that their work is closely interrelated. The popular picture of differences between researchers and practitioners should be overcome with educational efforts and joint experiences.

A second view was voiced by those who have had a good deal of experience with the education of both basic researchers and clinicians. Since it has serious consequences if it is true, it is developed here in some detail.

This view holds that there is a real gap between basic researchers and practitioners and that the gap results in a serious communication problem. It argues that basic researchers and practitioners are appreciably different with respect to their backgrounds in scientific knowledge, the tools they command, the habits of thinking with which they approach their daily work, and the kinds of things that interest and challenge them.

Basic researchers are said to be excited about ideas. Their fundamental motivations are related to understanding abstract relationships in the subject matter, finding better ways of describing and explaining events, and testing descriptive and explanatory models for various phenomena. Practitioners, on the other hand, are believed to be excited about people. Their interests often center on one person in a face-to-face clinical setting. Their primary motivation is to be helpful to people or to a particular person in an immediate and concrete way. (Students of interest measurement have long observed such independent or even negatively correlated interest clusters in "scientific" and "helping" professions. See Strong 1943 and Holland 1973.) Thus, abstract ideas, hypothetical models of behavior, explanatory hypotheses, and the like may fascinate the first group but be of little interest to the second group unless they can be translated into methods or procedures that have substantial promise for the immediate solution of a problem that the practitioner has encountered in the clinic or the classroom.

Implicit in this description is a difference between the basic researcher and practitioner that, though obvious, may nevertheless be worth emphasizing. This is a difference in respect to time. For practitioners, the urgent need is for immediate solutions for problems. Their interest is in solving this immediate problem for this particular person now. They cannot afford to be interested in a hypothesis that still must be verified by a long process of experiment and the slow accumulation of data. They are not intrigued by a new explanatory model for some phenomenon that may suggest numerous interesting hypotheses, each of which needs to be tested by critical experiment, even though such hypotheses may eventually have important practical implications. They want suggestions that have a sufficient degree of certainty to justify replacing established practices and procedures with something new.

If this view is correct, the basic researcher and the practitioner are neither very well prepared to talk to one another nor to listen to one another. They not only speak from very different backgrounds, they listen with very different sets of attitudes and motivations. If the resulting communication gap is to be bridged, it will probably require considerably more than persuading the practitioners and the investigators that they are really engaged in the same enterprise at an abstract level. Even if everyone shared that conviction, it would not in itself solve the communication problem.

Perhaps the most useful thing that the basic researcher can do for the practitioner is *not* to explicate specific implications for clinical or classroom practice but rather provide the best possible foundation of knowledge and understanding concerning speech, hearing, language, and other relevant human behavior, on the basis of which the clinician can hope to develop better clinical insights, make better clinical evaluations of the problems presented by a particular individual at a particular time, and make better judgments concerning what set of procedures may work for a given individual. What practitioners notice in the clinic, what they can have hypotheses about, depends in part on what they already know. If they are sensitive to many kinds of relations of speech and language phenomena, they have the implicit distinctions that will permit them to see interesting constellations when they occur in patients.

An interesting example of just this sort of thing is found in McReynolds's paper. The idea that speech behavior of children with articulation or perception problems could be fruitfully studied by analyzing their production and perceptions in terms of distinctive features instead of in terms of phones could only arise in a prepared mind that knew something of the work that had been done in linguistics. Once this idea appeared, however, clinical researchers picked it up rapidly, studies were undertaken in many clinics, and a great deal of interest was demonstrated in the approach. Perhaps this case is an important model for us to consider when we are concerned about the relation between basic research and applied implications. It is not necessary for basic researchers to know or even to conjecture that such a relationship might hold. It appears more crucial that practitioners have a sufficiently wide background in the related sciences to be able to see the phenomena that were, so to speak, available for them to see once they knew what to look for.

On the Transmission of the Findings of Basic Research

If the second view in the preceeding section is correct, it suggests that effective communication between the basic researcher and the practitioner will require several different kinds of intermediaries to do the very important and difficult job of interpreting.

One set of interpreters ought to be the faculties of our training institutions who are charged with preparing professional workers in the clinical and teaching professions. The first responsibility of such faculties is to keep abreast of the results of basic research, to integrate those results into their teaching, and to see that their students become well informed concerning the current state of basic knowledge. If the teachers are to succeed in this, they must present the information in a form and at the level that is optimal for assimilation by the practitioner-in-training. This is not an easy task. A second and equally important obligation of such faculties is to prepare their students to assimilate new information as it is developed by the persons engaged in basic research.

Many of our training institutions seem to have failed in meeting these obligations. Too much of the curricula of these institutions consist of how-to-do-it courses based on tradition rather than on rational analysis of the best existing scientific information. Furthermore, in too many of these institutions students are not provided with an adquate foundation in the relevant sciences. Thus they are ill prepared to assimilate new information as it is generated by basic research.

A second group of interpreters consists of those persons engaged in clinical research and carrying out demonstration projects. Often the implications of basic research are themselves only hypotheses that still must be tested in the classroom and the clinic. This is difficult research to perform because it is often virtually impossible to design experiments or demonstrations in which all the relevant conditions are controlled in such a way that it is possible to obtain a straightforward, uncontaminated, and clearly interpretable set of observations from which to draw conclusions. Nevertheless this research occupies a critical role both in the transmission of information and in the transformation of hypotheses arising in basic research into practices and procedures useful to practitioners. There is no shortcut around this stage. Evaluation of applications is crucial. Findings of basic research may no more be applied directly in the clinic without evaluation and careful study than the hunches of the practitioner or the precepts of folk wisdom. All of these may be right or all of them may be wrong; only careful evaluation can reveal which are which.

The Product of the Conference
The original purpose of the conference, as viewed by the planners, was to summarize the current status of knowledge resulting from basic research in speech and language in a form that would be intelligible to clinical practitioners and classroom teachers (the people who are on the firing line where such information may be applied to the modification of behavior and the solution of human problems). It was hoped that a suitable group of state-of-the-art papers, followed by appropriate commentary, would give relatively explicit expression to practical implications of the results of basic research for practitioners in the clinic and in the classroom.

Looking at the conference from our present perspective, it seems clear that we did not achieve that goal. As we pointed out above, the state-of-the-art papers are still concerned with current problems and with frontiers of research rather than with catalogs of principles waiting to be applied to problems just a short distance away. The discussants, too, tackled harder problems than we had imagined for them, often talking about clinical research that interfaced between the basic worker and the still-to-be developed practices for direct application. The result, then, is no handbook of practical applications.

During the course of the conference, however, our perspective changed and we now see the product that has arisen as perhaps the only one that could have developed with the kinds of people that we assembled and the kinds of assignments that we gave them. The participants felt that the conference was extremely valuable for them, but wondered whether it had achieved its objective. Toward the end of the conference, however, we began to see the objective differently. If our observations concerning the relations of basic research and application, as given immediately above, are correct, the kind of product we should have been aiming for was a collection that could be given to clinical researchers and to the teachers of practitioners. The researchers should find both information and inspiration herein. The teachers should find a basis for instruction, that is, a framework that could be used as a text to support well-informed instructors as they try to broaden the knowledge base and deepen the understanding of students who are training to be practitioners and applied researchers.

When we look at the conference in the light of revised objectives, we are more optimistic about the achievement of these goals. That is to say, the conference should be a halfway step along the hypothetical dimension we have talked about in this book. It should reach from basic research toward applied research, and we think that it does. It now remains, as always, that the transmission from here on rests in the hands of the clinical researchers and the teachers who must perform the difficult tasks of interpretation that constitute the second step.

We know the book is rich in information. Its pages furnish many examples of applications, some explicit and some implicit. We believe the book is capable of performing the support task that we now think is its appropriate aim in reaching out to clinical researchers and in providing materials for use in the basic training of practitioners. We hope that experience will confirm our opinion. The only appropriate evaluation, of course, lies, in the future behavior of the readers.

References

Chomsky, N., and Halle, M. 1968. *The sound pattern of English*. New York: Harper and Row.

Holland, J. L. 1973. *Making vocational choices: A theory of careers*. Edgewood Cliffs, New Jersey: Prentice-Hall.

Kavanagh, J. F., and Mattingly I. G. 1972. *Language by ear and by eye: The relationship between speech and reading*. Cambridge, Massachusetts: MIT Press.

Klatt, D. H. 1976. Linguistic uses of segmental duration in English: Acoustic and perceptual evidence. *Journal of the Acoustical Society of America*, 59, 1208–1221.

Strong, E. K. 1943. *Locational interests of men and women*, Stanford, California: Stanford University Press.

Glossary

KATHERINE MCGOVERN

Abduction A comprehension process in which the reciprocal influences of situation on input and input on situation lead to a modification of one's current perspective so that subsequent inputs are understood in new ways. Similar to equilibration. Also a muscular action that draws a limb or body part away from the medial axis of the body or a neutral position.

Accelerometer An instrument for measuring acceleration or for detecting and measuring vibrations.

Accommodation In Piagetian theory, the tendency to change in response to environmental demands, particularly the effect of new experience in modifying a preexisting cognitive structure; complementary to assimilation. Cf. assimilation, equilibration.

Acoustic Referring to sound.

Acoustic feature analysis In information-processing models, an early stage in the speech perception process during which acoustic features such as rapid frequency transitions and noise are detected in the input signal.

Adequacy A criterion for the evaluation of grammars and theories. Observational adequacy is the weak requirement that the theory generate all and only the observed data (grammatical sentences). Explanatory adequacy is the strong requirement that the grammar assign structural descriptions in accordance with a theory of linguistic universals, based on the assumption that children develop one universal type of grammar.

Affricate The class of consonants produced by blending a stop consonant and a fricative consonant; for example, /tʃ/ as in *church*, (dʒ) as in *judge*. Cf. Stop consonant, fricatives consonant.

Agent A semantic case referring to the instigator of action (often animate) that is perceived to have its own motivating force. Cf. Case grammar.

Allophone A variant of a class of speech sounds that differ phonetically but are identified by the speaker of a particular language as the same phoneme; for example, in English, the initial /k/ in *keep* and *cool* differ in aspiration and place of articulation, although both are identified as the same phoneme. Cf. Phoneme.

Alveolar Referring to the ridge of the roof of the mouth immediately behind the teeth; also, those consonants produced by making contact between the apex of the tongue and the alveolar ridge, for example, /d/, /t/, /s/, /z/, /n/.

American Sign Language (ASL) A system of manual communication used by the American deaf community that has a syntax and lexicon different from spoken English. Contrast with finger spelling or signed English. Cf. Signed English.

Analysis-by-synthesis A theory of perception that operates by hypothesis testing. The perceiver generates a first approximation of the to-be-identified signal and then compares the synthesis with the stored input signal. If they match, the synthesis is accepted as an accurate interpretation of the signal; if not, a new synthesis is generated and the process continues until a match it obtained.

Anomia A form of aphasia in which the names of objects cannot be recalled.

Apraxia A speech disorder involving the inability to execute simple voluntary motor acts; a deficit in motor planning. Contrast with dysarthria.

Articulation index Calibrated index that predicts speech intelligibility for restricted and nonrestricted vocabularies; a weighted mean of intensity differences between speech and noise measured in five frequency regions for normal hearing.

Artificial intelligence A branch of computer science concerned with developing computational devices whose output (not intermediate processing) is similar to human behavior that is called intelligent (for example, natural language understanding, problem solving, machine vision).

Arytenoid cartilages Small cartilaginous bodies at the back of the larynx to which the vocal folds are attached; the glottal opening is controlled by moving the arytenoids apart.

Assimilation In Piagetian theory, the process by which new experience is interpreted and integrated in terms of preexisting cognitive structures; complementary to accommodation. Cf. Accommodation, equilibration.

Association norms A compilation of common responses (associates) to a set of words tabulated by frequency of response; generally, free associations. Cf. Free association.

Associative network A model of lexical memory consisting of a network of nodes connected by one-way associative links. The links may be labeled according to the associative relation that holds between two lexical items.

Associative principles Rules governing the formation of associations, such as contiguity, similarity, contrast, frequency.

Asymmetric integrality A relationship between stimulus dimensions where variation in one dimension can be realized without the second dimension being represented but where the reverse does not hold. Cf. dimension.

Audiogram A curve representing the sound pressure level at which tones at different frequencies must be presented in order to be perceived; equal sensitivity curve.

Auditory Referring to hearing.

Auditory undershoot The failure of vowels in running speech to reach their characteristic formant frequencies due to the influences of coarticulation.

Backward masking A phenomenon in which the detection or identification of a brief sound signal is prevented by the presentation of a second signal within 100 msec *after* the first signal.

Bilingual An individual who is fluent in two languages. A coordinate bilingual is one who has acquired the two languages in separate and distinct environments; a compound bilingual has acquired the two languages in the same environment.

Biofeedback A method in which an individual monitors internal bodily processes and modifies or conditions physiological responses on the basis of information feedback.

Bootstrapping Improving a theory or method by trial and error. The process of applying a method and making successive refinements based on the analysis of results.

Broca's aphasia Expressive aphasia; a disorder in which the individual gives evidence of being able to formulate communications but is unable to produce utterances. Cf. Wernicke's aphasia.

Buffer A term taken from computer science used to designate a temporary memory or holding store between stages of processing.

Case grammar A grammar that focuses on semantic-conceptual relations within sentences rather than syntactic relations. The verb is commonly taken as the central organizing unit; nouns are related to the verb by case relations such as agentive, instrumental, and locative. Cf. Agent, locative, patient.

Categorical perception The perceptual phenomenon where discrimination of accoustic differences within phonemic categories is poor compared to discrimination across category boundaries. A strong criterion requires that individuals discriminate only those stimulus pairs whose members have been identified as belonging to different categories.

Category norms Association norms produced by tabulating responses to category labels when subjects are instructed to produce members of the category named; controlled association.

Cathode ray tube (CRT) A vacuum tube in which a beam of cathode rays is projected on a fluorescent screen to produce an image; a television screen.

Chromatic afterimage In vision, when viewers have stared at a colored stimulus for some seconds, they will perceive an image in the shape of the original stimulus but in the complementary color if they direct their gaze to a neutral surface or close their eyes.

Cinefluorography X-ray motion pictures used to examine movement of the articulatory organs during speech.

Clustering analysis A statistical procedure similar to factor analysis used to classify or group variables for developing taxonomies. Cf. Factor analysis.

Coarticulation In the production of sequences of phonetic segments, movements toward the articulatory target for one segment are initiated well before the time when the target is to be achieved (anticipatory effect) and may extend into the succeeding segment (carry-over effect); results in context-sensitive modification of the output at neural, muscular, and acoustic levels.

Cochlea The fluid-filled, snail-shell-shaped cavity of the inner ear to which sound is transmitted; at the basilar membrane within the cochlea, sound signals are converted to neural signals.

Concatenation A series of things that are adjoined or that depend on each other; a chain.

Componential analysis Decomposing the denotative meanings of words into three or more dimensions; for example, describing kinship systems in terms of sex, generation, and linearity of relationship.

Comprehension strategy A kind of response bias used by children to produce systematic responses to sentence comprehension tasks by using only part of the linguistic information or context. Contrast with nonlinguistic response bias. Cf. Response bias.

Concrete operation stage In Piagetian theory, the period between seven and eleven years of age characterized by increasing abstractness of thought, a developing concept of hierarchical structures, and conservation.

Conditioned response Generally, a response that occurs in the presence of a particular stimulus situation because of prior pairings with that stimulus and reinforcement.

Conjunctive association One kind of labeled link between nodes in an associative network representing an "and" relation between the elements. Cf. associative network, disjunctive association.

Constituent structure The pattern of syntactic relationships or derivational history among subunits of a sentence, often represented by a tree diagram.

Construct validity The extent to which the measurements obtained on a test conform to the theories of the particular construct (hypothetical entity) that the test is designed to assess; one of several means of establishing test validity.

Continuant A distinctive feature shared by a class of sounds produced with incomplete vocal tract closure and continuous sound generation during construction (for example, vowels, /r/).

Continuity theory A position with regard to language acquisition that holds there is developmental continuity from the infant's earliest vocalizations to later language learning; early vocal productions are considered to be differentiated progressively until they match those of the adult community. Cf. Discontinuity theory.

Controlled association A method of obtaining responses (associates) to stimulus materials in which subjects are instructed to produce responses of a particular class (categorial associations). Cf. Free association.

Coronal A distinctive feature shared by the sound class produced with the tongue blade raised with contact between the edges of the tongue blade and the hard palate (for example, /l/ and /d/).

Creole A stabilized Pidgin language which becomes the native language acquired by children of a linguistic community. Cf. Pidgin.

Cricothyroid muscle Two muscle bundles connecting the cricoid cartilage and thyroid cartilage in the larynx; contraction of either bundle modifies the length or tension of the vocal folds resulting in a change in fundamental frequency.

Cued speech A manual cuing system for use with speech; based on a phonetic signal system that uses the consonant-vowel syllable as the gestural unit and requires lipreading for disambiguation within sets of CV syllables.

Deep structure In Chomskian theory, the output of base rules, which specify basic syntactic relations and semantic features, from which the meaning of a sentence is derived. Cf. Surface structure.

Deixis The function of lexical items in pointing out or indicating relations between the participants in a speech event and the content of the message; for example, the personal pronouns "I" and "you" serve the deictic function.

Denotation The generic idea or concept represented by a word that remains relatively constant across sentences and contexts. Contrast with referential meaning, which is the particular object, event, or relationship specified by a word, or with connotation, which is affective meaning.

Deontic Referring to the obligatory or moral; contrast with epistemic, which refers to the information-bearing character of a sentence. For example, the obligatory sense of *should* or *must* in sentences like "You should be working now."

Derivational complexity The number of rules or transformations involved in the derivational history of a sentence; often taken as a factor in the difficulty of understanding or acquiring a particular construction.

Dichotic fusion A phenomenon sometimes observed in dichotic listening tasks where the perceived signal is a combination of the features of the two signals that have actually been presented. For example, the perception of /da/, which combines the voicing of /ba/ and the place of articulation of /ta/.

Dichotic listening task In general, a task in which the subject is instructed to monitor auditory inputs when different signals are presented simultaneously at equal intensity to each ear; the subject may be required to report the input to one or both ears.

Dichotic split-formant presentation A method of presenting synthetic speech signals in which the first formant is delivered to one ear and the remaining formants to the other ear; a possible means of eliminating first formant masking of other formants.

Dimension An aspect of a stimulus that can vary over a range of values (for example, brightness). Integral dimensions are those that cannot be instantiated separately (color and brightness). Separable dimensions can appear separately (color and shape).

Discontinuity theory A position with regard to language acquisition that holds there is no essential relationship from one stage of infant vocalization to the next; any relationship is considered superficial since early infant productions are randomly produced, not under voluntary control. Cf. Continuity theory.

Discriminant function analysis A statistical procedure that yields predictions of class membership, derived from a weighted linear composite of predictor variables.

Discriminative stimulus In operant conditioning, a stimulus that marks the occasion for an operant response and signals that reinforcement is available.

Disjunctive association One kind of labeled link between nodes in an associative network representing an "or" relation between the elements. Cf. Conjunctive association.

Dysarthria A general term denoting difficulty in articulating speech due to a central nervous system disorder of motor coordination; muscle weakness. Contrast with apraxia.

Dysphonia An impairment of the larynx that affects voice production; disorder of phonation.

Echoic memory In information-processing models, an initial auditory store in which acoustic information may be held in a unprocessed state for up to 200 msec. All information is lost if not processed further within that period. Cf. Sensory information store.

Ellipsis The omission of words that can be understood from context (for example, "You shouldn't have! " for "You shouldn't have brought these flowers!").

Entailment With regard to lexical items, a relation that holds where the meaning of one word is a logically necessary consequence of another, the meaning of one term is implicitly available when the meaning of the other is understood ("married" is entailed by "husband").

Episodic memory Memory that is specific to the time and place in which information is acquired; retains perceptual properties and autobiographical reference; susceptible to transformation and information loss. Contrast with semantic memory.

Equilibration In Piagetian theory, the child's cognitive self-regulatory process that leads to progressively more effective states of equilibrium or balance between accommodation and assimilation. Cf. Accommodation, assimilation.

Evoked potential Electrical change recorded from the surface of the skull in response to stimulation of the sense organs; occurs in definite time relations to the evoking stimuli and may be used to map the central representation of the sensory systems.

Factor analysis A statistical procedure used to isolate underlying factors that account for observed covariation in a set of dependent variables.

False recognition method A method of studying sentence memory using a recognition task in which false identifications of "new" items (*not* previously presented) as "old" items (previously presented) are taken as an indication of the structure or content of sentence memory. Cf. Recognition task.

Faucial pillars The palatoglossus and palatopharyngeus muscles of the soft palate; function in opening and constricting the velopharyngeal port. Cf. Palatoglossus, palatopharyngeus.

Formant A concentration of sound energy corresponding to a resonant frequency of the vocal tract in a particular configuration. In spectrographic displays formants are represented as dark bands.

Frame theory A theory about the representation of knowledge from the field of artificial intelligence in which a frame is a structure that represents knowledge about some limited domain of objects or events. Recognition of an object is achieved when perceived values of features of the object can be matched with features in the frame representing that class of objects.

Free association A method of obtaining responses (associates) to stimulus materials in which the subjects' responses are not constrained by the experimenter. Cf. Controlled association.

Frequency weighting A procedure for emphasizing various frequency bands in the acoustic spectrum; intensifying particular frequencies to counteract poor response of an amplifying device.

Fricative consonant The class of consonants produced by a partial closure of the vocal tract causing turbulence in the airstream. Cf. International Phonetic Alphabet at end of the glossary.

Fronting The tendency to articulate speech sounds toward the front of the mouth (for example, production of /b/ for /d/ or /g/).

Functor Something that performs a function or operation; an operator.

Fundamental frequency (F_0) The frequency of vocal fold vibration; the lowest frequency component of the speech spectrum corresponding to the pitch of the speaker's voice.

Gain The ratio or relationship of output to input in an amplifier.

Ganzfeld A visual field devoid of visible contours or texture; a real-world example is the homogeneous whiteness of a blizzard.

Generalization gradient A function representing gradations in the degree of response to stimuli varying in similarity to the stimulus to which an organism has previously been conditioned to respond. For example, the gradual decline in number of bar presses produced by a rat as the stimulus changes from a green conditioning light to successively bluer lights.

Generative semantics A theory of grammar in which the base component generates strings of semantic clusters, specifying semantic relations between them; the syntactic component then interprets the output of the base semantic component. Contrast with Chomskian transformational grammar, in which the semantic component interprets output of a base syntactic component.

Generative transformational grammar A grammar such as Chomsky's in which phrase structure (or base) rules generate deep structure, from which meaning is derived, and in which transformational rules map deep structure onto surface structure, from which the phonological shape of a sentence is derived.

Glottis The space between the vocal folds in the larynx; voiced speech sounds are produced by the rapid opening and constricting of the glottis as air is exhaled; voiceless sounds are produced with an open glottis.

Haptic Referring to the active sense of touch; tactile.

Harmonic A component of a periodic wave whose frequency is a whole-number multiple of the lowest frequency component or fundamental frequency. Cf. Fundamental frequency.

High-risk infant An infant is said to be "at risk" (high risk) for a particular disorder, for example, deafness or schizophrenia, when biological (familial) or environmental factors are present that increase the probability of his/her developing the disorder above the base rate in the general population.

Homograph One of two or more words that are spelled alike but differ in derivation, meaning, or pronounciation (*lead* pencil and *lead* time).

Homophony Characteristic of two or more words that are pronounced alike but differ in spelling, derivation, or meaning (*night* versus *knight*).

Hyoid A bone in the neck to which numerous tongue muscles are attached and from which the larynx is suspended.

Hypernasality The presence of nasal resonances in production of speech sounds; nasal voice quality resulting from insufficient palatal closure.

Hypertonia Excessive muscular tension produced by involuntary overcontraction of antagonistic muscles; rigidity.

Iconic memory In information-processing models, the persistence of a visual impression for about one second after the stimulus is terminated; a sensory store analogous to echoic memory in which information is available in an unprocessed form. Cf. Echoic memory.

Implicature A relation between lexical items where the meaning of one follows from or is logically deducible from the other; logical implication. Cf. Entailment.

Incidental learning (memory) Learning that occurs while subjects perform an orienting task, directing their attention to some aspect of the stimulus materials that is not being directly tested; learning in the absence of specific instructions to learn. Cf. Intentional learning.

Index of determination The statistic R^2 taken between variable x and variable y; the proportion of the total variability in y due to correlation with x.

Information processing A model of perception and memory based on a computer analogy that represents the analysis of sensory information in terms of a sequence of stages (often hierarchically organized) and limited capacity memory stores.

Intentional learning (memory) Learning that occurs when the subject is specifically instructed to attend to and remember particular aspects of stimulus materials. Cf. Incidential learning.

Isometric contraction The tension developed when the ends of a muscle or its tendons are fixed so that the muscle as a whole cannot shorten.

Labial Referring to the lips; also those consonants produced by closing the airway at the lips, for example. /b and /p/.

Lax vowels A term used when dividing vowels into classes on phonological grounds in English; those vowels that can occur in monosyllables closed by /ŋ/. Cf. Tense vowels.

Levator palatini muscle The muscle that forms the bulk of the soft palate; its contraction lifts the soft palate upward and backward; participates in velopharyngeal closure.

Lexical memory Functionally defined permanent memory for words including phonological, syntactic, and semantic features and word uses.

Lexicon A component of grammars that contains the syntactic, phonological, and semantic features (selection restrictions) of individual words; the mental dictionary.

Locative A semantic case referring to the place (or, in some theories, time) in which an action takes place. Cf. Case grammar.

Long-term memory (LTM) Permanent memory; a general term that encompasses semantic, episodic, and lexical memory. Contrast with short-term memory.

Maier two-string problem A problem-solving situation in which two strings are suspended from the ceiling, hanging down too far apart to be grasped at the same time. The subject's task is to tie the two strings together using miscellaneous equipment in the room; for example, a small object (pliers) can be tied to one of the strings and set swinging as a pendulum that the subject can then grasp while holding the other string.

Marbe's law The tendency for more frequent responses on association tests to occur with lower response latencies; taken as an indication of strength of association between stimulus and response.

Maxillary branch (of trigeminal nerve) One of three branches of the fifth cranial nerve that serves a sensory function for the teeth, mucous membranes of the nose and mouth, and skin of the face.

Mean length of utterance (MLU) The average length of a child's utterances measured by number of morphemes; used in place of chronological age as an index of linguistic development.

Mediating response A hypothetical, internal response that serves as a connection between the observable stimulus and response.

Metathesis A transposition of two phonemes in a word, such as "aks" (æks) for "ask" (æsk).

Modality effect Superior recall of the last items on an auditorally presented list of items as compared with a visually presented list; presumed to result from availability of an echoic trace. Cf. Suffix effect.

Morphology The component of a grammar that specifies the minimal meaningful linguistic units in a language (root words, affixes, and inflections).

Multidimensional theory A class of theories that presupposes a metric for scaling similarity or distance relationships among elements along two or more spatially represented dimensions; often supported by factor analytic or related statistical techniques.

Muscle spindle A sheath of connective tissue containing intrafusal muscle fibers that are sensitive to muscle stretch.

Myelogram An X-ray of the spinal cord after injection of opaque dye.

Nasal A distinctive feature shared by the class of sounds produced with an open velopharyngeal port whose acoustic spectrum is characterized by additional (nasal) resonances. In English, /m/, /n/, and /ŋ/.

Neuraxis The central nervous system; brain and spinal cord.

Object permanence A major achievement of the sensorimotor stage of development; the child's realization that objects have an existence independent of his or her perception of them. Cf. Sensorimotor intelligence.

Obstruent (nonsonorant) A distinctive feature shared by a class of sounds produced by pressure buildup behind a vocal tract constriction; noise is present in the acoustic spectrum; characterizes stops, fricatives, and affricates.

Orbicularis oris A sphincter muscle that encircles the mouth slit and closes the mouth and puckers the lips when it contracts.

Orosensory feedback Proprioceptive information returned to the central nervous system from the oral cavity; for example, information concerning position of articulators.

Oscillograph An instrument that displays electrical or mechanical fluctuations as a visible waveform. Used for displaying the irregular variations in amplitude over time in speech signals.

<u>Overextension</u> The use of a linguistic form by a child in contexts that are broader than the semantic domain in which adults use the form; overgeneralization. Cf. Underextension.

<u>Paired associate learning paradigm (PAL)</u> Learning pairs of terms in a task that requires the subject to produce the second (response) term whenever the first (stimulus) term is presented.

<u>Palate</u> The roof of the mouth consisting of two regions: 1) the hard palate is an immovable plate dividing the nasal and oral cavities, and 2) the soft palate or velum is a movable fold suspended from the posterior border of the hard palate which can be raised to block the nasopharynx during articulation. Cf. Pharynx.

<u>Palatoglossus</u> A muscle connecting the soft palate and tongue that raises the back of the tongue or lowers the soft palate when it contracts. Cf. Faucial pillars.

<u>Palatopharyngeus</u> A muscle connecting the soft palate and pharynx walls that functions in swallowing; its contraction raises the larynx or lowers the soft palate. Cf. Faucial pillars.

<u>Parallel processing</u> A property of information-processing systems in which information is operated on simultaneously by several channels or stages. Contrast with serial processing, in which operations at one stage must be completed before processing at the next stage can begin.

<u>Parallel transmission</u> Information specifying several phonetic segments is carried simultaneously on the same stretch of the acoustic signal; a result of coarticulation. Cf. Coarticulation.

<u>Patient</u> A semantic case referring to someone or something either undergoing a change in state or receiving the force of an action; object. Cf. Case grammar.

<u>Performatives</u> Acts that are accomplished with communications apart from representing the information that is the content of the message, (promising, apologizing); speech acts.

<u>Pharynx</u> The muscular tube that connects the mouth and nose with the larynx and esophagus; the oropharynx is that portion between the soft palate and the hyoid bone; the nasopharynx extends from the nasal cavities to the soft palate.

<u>Phasic contraction</u> Recurring or periodic contraction.

<u>Phonemic</u> Referring to speech sound distinctions that make a meaningful difference within a particular language; determined by a minimal pairs procedure. The phonemic distinctions made within a language are a subset of all possible (phonetic) speech sound distinctions made in the languages of the world.

<u>Phonetic transcription (IPA)</u> *See* International Phoenetic Alphabet.

<u>Phonotactic rules</u> Rules in a grammar specifying the environments in which phonemes can occur and phonetic adjustments of sounds in different contexts (for example, the nasalization of vowels before final nasal consonants in English).

<u>Pidgin</u> An amalgam of two languages, one's native language and a new one, in which lexical items are borrowed from the new language, but much of the phonological and syntactic structure is retained from the native language. Cf. Creole.

<u>Pivot</u> In early language acquisition, one of two word classes in a pivot grammar that has limited class membership and that occurs in the same position in a child's two-word utterances.

<u>Polysemy</u> Literally "many meanings"; a characteristic of lexical items that have more than one meaning or sense.

Posterior cricoarytenoid muscle The abductor muscle of the larynx that opens the glottis; laryngeal dilator.

Pragmatics The rules governing the occurrence of linguistic forms in various social contexts.

Precategorical store A temporary memory store that holds auditory input prior to phonological coding; functionally equivalent to echoic memory. Cf. Sensory information store, echoic memory.

Preliminary auditory analysis In information-processing models, a stage during which acoustic energy is transformed into neural energy. The result of preliminary auditory analysis may be characterized as a "neural spectrogram."

Preoperational stage In Piagetian theory, the period between two and seven years of age characterized by the increasing use of language and symbolic thought.

Presupposition A syntactic condition on the contexts in which a class of lexical items can occur, based on sense relationships among the items. In general, a restriction or condition on the linguistic or social context in which a construction may be used.

Probe A test word in memory experiments to which the subject responds by producing some remembered material or by judging its relationship to the remembered material.

Prosodic features Rhythm, stress, and intonation; nonsegmental or suprasegmental aspects of the speech signal.

Prosody The rhythmic aspect of spoken language; stress and intonation.

Reaction time The interval between the onset of a stimulus and the beginning of the subject's response; a dependent measure in memory research; latency.

Real-time spectrum analyzer (RTA) A device that displays the frequency and intensity characteristics of an acoustic signal as it is produced; a concurrent spectral display.

Realization rules Rules that translate the abstract or formal entities of a grammar into actually producible forms; in semantic theories, rules that map underlying semantic structures onto surface structures.

Recall task An experimental paradigm in which the subject is asked to retrieve and reproduce stimulus materials from memory. In serial recall the items must be recalled in the original presentation order; in free recall items may be retrieved in any order.

Recency effect The tendency to recall last-learned items best when recall is tested immediately; attributed to presence of end items in short-term memory.

Recognition task An experimental procedure in which subjects are required to select previously experienced (old) items from a list or group of stimuli containing both old items and new, unfamiliar items (foils). Cf. False recognition method.

Recurrence A semantic relation (or operation of reference) found in children's early two-word utterances meaning the reappearance of a referent or a request for an additional quantity of some object; for example, "more + _____."

Reductionistic Descriptive of a theory or method that seeks to explain phenomena in terms of irreducible basic elements or "atoms."

Redundancy Words or elements in a communication that can be eliminated without loss of meaning or essential information; multiple or overspecification.

Reduplication In child language, repetition of one syllable in words of more than one syllable ("dada" for "daddy").

Rehearsal Repeating or operating on information in order to keep it in awareness or to organize it for long-term memory; an operation occurring in short-term memory. Cf. Short-term memory.

Response bias Systematic responding not based on the experimenter's criterion for correctness but rather on some aspect of the stimulus situation or on a preference for a particular response regardless of stimulus characteristics.

Right ear advantage (REA) In a dichotic listening task, the greater accuracy in reporting verbal stimuli presented to right ear as compared to the left ear. Cf. Dichotic listening task.

Rochester method A method of communication for the deaf developed at the Rochester School for the Deaf that combines finger spelling with speaking and lipreading.

Saccade A conjugate eye movement in which both eyes make a rapid parallel shift in fixation, often to correct for drift or errors in fixation. Contrast with tracking movement, a slower continuous shift made while fixating a moving object.

Seeing essential English A system of manual communication for the deaf in which each gesture represents a combination of the spelling, sound, and meaning of an English word.

Selective adaptation An experimental procedure in which the subject is presented with numerous tokens of the same stimulus and then asked to identify members of a stimulus array. This results in identification of more items as members of the stimulus category complementary to the one experienced during adaptation. For example, adaptation with numerous tokens of /ba/ will result in identification of more tokens in a VOT-varying array as /pa/.

Semantic decomposition Breaking down a word's meaning into its component parts, either a configuration of related words or a list of atomic features.

Semantic differential Osgood's method of decomposing lexical meaning into semantic dimensions (for example, evaluation, activity, and potency) by means of rating scales and factor analysis. Cf. Multidimensional theory.

Semantic marker Elementary bipolar semantic units into which a lexical item can be decomposed, each word being viewed as a combination of units. For example, "wife" might be represented as + MARRIED, + HUMAN, + FEMALE.

Semantic memory Permanent memory for rules, concepts, and referents in which information is independent of the time and place where it is acquired. Contrast with episodic memory. Cf. Episodic memory.

Sensorimotor intelligence The mental capabilities of a child between birth and two years of age; preverbal intelligence characterized by development of object constancy and mental representations of objects in the environment.

Sensorineural deafness Loss of sensitivity to sound because of damage to the auditory nervous system.

Sensory information store In speech perception, functionally equivalent to echoic memory. Cf. Echoic memory, Precategorical store.

Sensory plasticity The ability of a sensory system to take over the functions of an alternate modality that is damaged or lost. For example, the ability of visually deprived persons to recognize spatial characteristics of objects represented via a vibrotactile display projected on their backs.

Shadowing Following and repeating aloud verbal stimuli as they are heard, staying as close behind the speaker as possible.

Short-term memory (STM) Time- and capacity-limited memory of information held in awareness by rehearsal; for example, the kind of memory used to remember a phone number between looking it up and dialing. Contrast with long-term memory. Cf. Rehearsal.

Signal detection theory A theory of signal detectability that distinguishes between the receiver's response bias and actual sensitivity or ability to discriminate.

Signal-to-noise ratio The difference between intensity levels of the designated signal and background noise expressed in decibel units (or the ratio when expressed in linear intensity units).

Signed English A manual system of communication for the deaf in which American Sign Language signs have been equated with English words and supplemented by new signs designating syntactic affixes and function words. Cf. American Sign Language.

Sociolinguistics The study of the social organization of language use and behavior toward language across social groups or within a single group on different occasions.

Spectrogram A visual display of an acoustic signal in which frequency is represented on the vertical axis, time on the horizontal axis, and intensity in the darkness of the patterns.

Speech acts Acts that are accomplished by linguistic communications, apart from transmitting the information content of the message (for example apologizing, commanding, making a toast); performatives.

Speech babble An acoustic signal produced by splicing together short segments of speech from numerous speakers; recognizable as speech but not comprehensible.

Speech lateralization Localization of speech perception and production functions primarily in the dominant (usually left) cerebral hemisphere of the brain.

Spirantization Substitution of fricatives and affricates (spirants) for stop consonants in final position.

Spondaic Referring to a spondee, a metrical foot containing two stressed syllables. Cf. trochaic.

Spoonerism A transposition between phonemic segments of two or more words; for example, "darn bore" in place of "barn door."

Stoma noise In laryngectomized patients, the noise produced at the artificial respiratory aperature in the neck (the stoma) when the patient breathes or speaks.

Stop consonant The class of consonants produced by complete closure of the vocal tract. Cf. International Phonetic Alphabet.

Suffix effect Poor recall of the last items on an auditorally presented list when an additional stimulus word is added after the last memory item; presumed to result from a masking effect exerted on the last part of the list by the additional (suffix) word. Cf. Modality effect.

Superior pharyngeal constrictor A muscle in the upper pharynx that participates in closure of the velopharyngeal port.

Supraglottal cavities Vocal tract cavities above the vocal folds whose resonant characteristics determine the acoustic structure of speech; the buccal, oral, pharyngeal, and nasal cavities.

Suprasegmental Prosodic (nonsegmental) aspects of speech such as stress, duration, and tone.

Surface structure In Chomskian theory, the output of transformational rules from which the phonological shape of a sentence is derived. Cf. Deep structure.

Syntagmatic organization The organization of lexical items often seen in the word associations of children when they produce, in response to the stimulus word, a word that would follow it in normal speech; for example, run-fast or red-ball. Contrast with paradigmatic organization, which is responding with a word of the same from class (table-chair, red-yellow).

Tactile vocoder A sensory substitution device that represents the frequency bands of speech as vibrations of a constant frequency on the skin, each of ten bands on one of the fingertips; spectral energy is reflected in the amplitude of vibration. All spectral bands are presented at one vibration frequency to which the skin is very sensitive. Cf. Teletactor.

Tadoma method A method of deaf communication in which the listener positions his or her fingers on a speaker's face to pick up movements of the articulators and airflow; often combined with lipreading.

Telegraphic speech Children's early speech composed largely of nouns and verbs in which morphological inflections, copulas, articles, and prepositions are omitted.

Teletactor A sensory substitution device for representing speech tactually consisting of five fingertip vibrators vibrating at different frequencies. Cf. Tactile vocoder.

Template matching A perceptual theory in which recognition of a stimulus is accomplished by matching the input with a stored representation of the item to be recognized.

Temporal fusion threshold That frequency at which temporally repeating events cease to be distinguishable as separate events and become perceptually fused into one continuous signal.

Tense vowels A term used when dividing vowels into classes on phonological grounds; in English, those vowels that can occur in stressed open syllables, such as "bee, bay, bah, saw, low, boo, buy, bough, boy, cue." Cf. Lax vowels.

Text grammars Grammars that focus on underlying propositions and their logical structure in connected prose rather than on sentences; an attempt to describe the information structures that readers abstract from text.

Thermal noise See White noise.

Timbre The resonant characteristics of a voice determined by vocal tract configuration.

Tip-of-the-tongue phenomenon (TOT) The inability to recall or say a particular, well-known word that is "on the tip of one's tongue" and yet be able to describe the meaning, phonological shape, or other aspects of the desired word.

Token Test of Language Comprehension A series of subtests of increasing difficulty that assess the patient's comprehension of various requests to manipulate a set of colored geometric forms.

Tonic contraction Sustained muscular tension.

Transfer The effect of learning one thing on the learning of another; the ability to use information or skills acquired in one environment in a different environment.

Transitional error probability (TEP) The probability that an error in recall will occur given that the immediately prior item in a sequence has been remembered correctly.

Trochaic Referring to a trochee, a metrical foot consisting of a stressed syllable followed by an unstressed syllable (for example, apple). Cf. Spondaic.

Underextension A child's use of a word in a highly restricted context, corresponding closely with the context in which the word was first experienced; undergeneralization. Cf. Overextension.

Velopharyngeal port The opening between the oropharynx and the nasopharynx when the soft palate is lowered.

Velum The soft palate. Cf. Palate.

Vibrotactile transducer A general term for sensory substitution devices that convert acoustic energy into mechanical vibrations that can be felt on the skin.

Vocal tract normalization Calibrating the speech perception system to the vocal tract frequencies of a particular speaker in order to identify vowels in natural speech.

Voice onset time (VOT) The interval between the release of closure and the onset of periodic pulsing of the vocal folds in production of stop consonants; reflected acoustically in the interval between onset of the first formant and higher formants. In English, VOT variation cues the voiced-voiceless distinction.

Volume velocity waveform The modulation of airflow through the glottis over time; the sequence of air puffs emitted by the larynx.

Vowel alternation rule Shifting from one vowel to another in different forms of a morpheme (for example, the /i/ in *serene* becomes /ɛ/ in *serenity*).

Vowel neutralization The tendency for lax vowels to be pronounced as a schwa /ə/ in unstressed syllables; collapsing of contrasting vowels toward a neutral sound.

Vowel nucleus The most vocalic or sonorous portion of a diphthong or vowel-glide cluster; syllable nucleus.

Wernicke's aphasia Receptive aphasia; a disorder in which the individual is unable to understand speech. Cf. Broca's aphasia.

White noise Noise in which all spectral frequencies are presented at equal sound pressure level.

Zipf's law The positive relationship between the number of meanings of a word and its frequency of occurrence.

Name Index

Subject Index

Abduction growth schema, 280–284, 292–293
Accelerometers, 23
Achievement tests, 30
Acoustic properties
  articulatory movement with, 99
  laryngeal pathology and, 98
  of sentences, 13–21
  sound generation sources and, 5–6
  vocal tract shape estimates with, 98–99
Acoustic signal. *See also* Speech signal
  lack of invariance in, 56–58
  perceptual analysis of, 75
  sensory registration of, 74–75
  speech perception stages and, 40–41
  speech production and, 98
  in young infants, 54
Action relationships, 258
Active sentences, 275
Adaptation
  auditory feature analysis and, 90
  feature detectors and, 333–334
  phonetic process research with, 62
  specificity of, 388
  speech perception and, 51, 53
Adjectives, 395
Afferent mechanisms, 116–117, 118–119, 124–125
Affirmative sentences, 275
Affricatives, 144
Afterimage, 51–52
Age
  alternative articulation patterns and, 124
  memory capacity related to, 360–361
  mother-child dyadic patterns related to, 218
  neural controls in speech and, 120
Airflow, 3–4
Alphabetic writing, 62
American Sign Language (ASL), 184
  combined method with, 200–201
  deaf parents and, 205
  efficiency of transmission of, 184–185
  linguistic analysis of, 59
Amplitude
  cerebral hemisphere processing of, 56
  word associations and, 399
Analogy, 286, 342
Anastomoses, 116
Animal studies
  speech perception experiments with, 55
  vision studies in, 388
Anomias, 412

Anticipatory coarticulation, 105
Antonymous adjectives, 238
Aphasia
  Broca's (*see* Broca's aphasia)
  comprehension in, 328
  hemisphere processing studies in, 82–83
  memory, comprehension, and levels of representation in, 377–387
  phonological disorders in, 157
  semantic fields used by, 421
  sequencing abilities in, 75–76, 77
  speech perception and, 60–61, 377–379, 391
  temporal processing in, 92–94
  therapy for, 384–385
  Wernicke's (*see* Wernicke's aphasia)
  word associations in, 457–458
Aphasoid children, 76
Articles, 237–238
Articulation
  acoustic analysis of movement in, 99
  afferent feedback in, 124–125
  alternatives in, 124
  animal experiments with, 55
  babbling stage and, 129
  biofeedback control of, during reading, 367
  cinefluorography in studies of, 99–100
  deaf child's, 21
  diagnostic value of disorders of, 95
  electromyographic studies of, 100–102
  goals of organization in, 103–107
  plasticity in, 124
  second-language learning and, 180
  somesthetic monitoring of, 37
  speech production and, 7–13
  speech training and, 168–172
  timing strategies for segmental cues in, 12–13
  tremor and, 122
Articulation disorders
  analyses of, 169–170
  diagnostic value of, 95
  form of treatment for, 170–172
  phonological analysis of, 157
  speech production and, 175–176
  /w/-/r/ substitution in, 362–363
Articulation index, 32
Arytenoid cartilages, 4
Aspirated consonants, 12
Assimilation, in infant vocalizations, 144, 153, 156, 157
Associative complex, 222
Asymmetric integrality, 340, 341

language acquisition related to, 128–
142
modeling in, 142–143
mother-child exchanges in, 212
phototactic rules in, 145–146
Piagetian framework for, 138–139,
310–313
recent studies of, 131–142
rules and processes in, 144–147
shifts in accuracy and rules in, 158–
159
stages of, 128
substitution rules in, 144–145
vowel and consonant harmony in, 145
Vocal tract
acoustic output and, 104
acoustic techniques for size estimation
of, 98–99
articulatory-acoustic relations and,
9–10
filter function of, 98
sound generation by, 3–6
speech perception research with, 59
speech production and, 97
Voice disorders, 95
Voice onset time (VOT), 53
animal experiments with, 55
aphasia and, 377–378, 379, 391
Vowels
acoustic targets production of, 103–
104
auditory memory and, 333
babbling and, 134, 136
consonant patterns with (*see* Consonant-vowel (CV) patterns)
continuity theory of vocalizations
and, 130
deaf child's speech production and,
21
dialect differences and, 91
different processes in perception of, 6
discrimination studies of, 78–79
echoic memory and, 50, 92, 335
infant vocalizations and, 145
neutralization of, 99
reading errors and, 36–37
steady-state (*see* Steady-state vowels)
as test signals, 34
timing strategies with, 12
Vowel triangle group, 187

Wernicke's aphasia
function in meaning and, 412
scaling methods for, 406
word associations in, 397

Western dialects, 91
Word associations, 396–399
Word boundaries, 104
Word identification, 48
Word intelligibility, 29